Advance Praise for *Fundamentals of Entrepreneurial Finance*

"Da Rin and Hellmann masterfully combine academic and case studies to analyze how entrepreneurs with ideas and financiers with capital can strike mutually advantageous deals that power society's future innovations. The result is a lucid and comprehensive book that will be an invaluable resource for anyone with an interest in this topic."

—Oliver Hart, Department of Economics, Harvard University,
2016 Nobel laureate in economics

"While getting to scale fastest in a global economy can take significant capital, money has always been just one part of venture financing. Using clear frameworks that show how venture financing really works, Da Rin and Hellmann point out how the networks of talent and expertise that investors can help entrepreneurs access are critical to a start-up's success. This is especially true for big, ambitious, and even contrarian ventures. So if you're an entrepreneur ready to pursue a truly bold idea, be sure to read this book."

—Reid Hoffman, Co-founder of LinkedIn and co-author of *Blitzscaling*

"This textbook achieves a wonderful balance in providing students with a broad and insightful introduction to entrepreneurial finance; but at the same time opens up many avenues for interested students to pursue the material more deeply. The authors draw from a wealth of intriguing examples to make the material come to life and their in-depth knowledge of the subject matter shines through at every turn. A great resource for any student of entrepreneurial finance as well as a lay audience that wants to understand this fast growing part of finance better."

—Antoinette Schoar, Michael M. Koerner (1949) Professor of Finance and
Entrepreneurship at the MIT Sloan School of Management.

"This book provides the foundational knowledge MBAs need to master entrepreneurial finance. The authors are leading academics, trained at Stanford, who taught and researched in many countries. They understand not only how Silicon Valley works, but also how venture financing is a global phenomenon."

—Ilya A. Strebulaev, Professor of Finance,
Stanford Graduate School of Business

"The financing of start-ups is crucial for their very survival and development, yet it is often thought of as a narrow technical issue. It is not! Da Rin and Hellmann build a comprehensive framework that helps the reader understand the entire entrepreneurial financing process, and how entrepreneurs and investors navigate through it. I highly recommend this book to anyone who wants to understand the fuel that fires the modern innovation economy, and especially to those venturing into it."

—Eugene Kandel, CEO of Start-Up Nation Central, and Professor of Economics and Finance at the Hebrew University of Jerusalem

"This book will help students from different backgrounds understand how venture financing works. The authors masterfully combine insights from finance, economics, strategic management, organizational behavior, legal studies and other academic fields. They introduce many new practical tools and present materials in a direct and engaging style."

—David Hsu, Professor of Management, Wharton Business School

"Da Rin and Hellmann have crafted a seminal contribution to the teaching of Entrepreneurial Finance. The issues addressed in their book are critical for any entrepreneur who is considering starting a company and raising capital. The material is applicable to any industry or country context making the book a "must read". Furthermore, the lessons are rigorous yet practical and allow an entrepreneur to put the recommendations into action. The book will become a staple not only in the classroom, but on the shelf of every aspiring entrepreneur."

—Paul Gompers, Eugene Holman Professor of Business Administration, Harvard Business School

"The financing of start-ups has become a global phenomenon with ambitious start-ups being funded by venture investors across many countries, including China. This is the first book to provide a truly global perspective on entrepreneurial finance. Da Rin and Hellmann build their framework step-by-step from core academic concepts, making the material accessible and engaging to the students at all levels around the world."

—Yingyi Qian, Distinguished Professor and former Dean, School of Economics and Management, Tsinghua University

"Having taught entrepreneurial finance for many years, one of the problems has been to find an appropriate textbook, which both provides practical skills and at the same time is grounded in modern research. I am happy to see that this problem has now been solved. Da Rin and Hellmann are two of the most well-known and accomplished researchers in this area. They have managed to write a comprehensible, accessible, and up-to-date textbook, which I predict will become the standard reference for courses in entrepreneurial finance and venture capital for years to come."

—Per Strömberg, SSE Centennial Professor of Finance and Private Equity, Swedish House of Finance

Fundamentals
of Entrepreneurial Finance

MARCO DA RIN AND THOMAS HELLMANN

OXFORD

UNIVERSITY PRESS

OXFORD
UNIVERSITY PRESS

Oxford University Press is a department of the University of Oxford. It furthers
the University's objective of excellence in research, scholarship, and education
by publishing worldwide. Oxford is a registered trade mark of Oxford University
Press in the UK and certain other countries.

Published in the United States of America by Oxford University Press
198 Madison Avenue, New York, NY 10016, United States of America.

CIP data is on file at the Library of Congress
ISBN 978-0-19-974475-6

Printed by Sheridan, United States of America

About the Authors

Dr. Marco Da Rin is an Associate Professor of Finance at Tilburg University, and previously held positions at the London School of Economics, Bocconi University (Milano, Italy), at the University of Torino, and the Universitat Autónoma de Barcelona. His research focuses on entrepreneurial finance, venture capital, private equity, and public policy for entrepreneurship. His academic articles have been published in leading scholarly journals and have been covered by the business press, including *The Economist*, Forbes.com, venture capital and private equity online magazines, and national business papers. He has been a consultant to several international organizations including the European Commission, the OECD, and the United Nations, as well as regional governments and private companies. He has advised and contributed to several start-ups.

Dr. Thomas Hellmann is the DP World Professor of Entrepreneurship and Innovation at the Saïd School of Business, University of Oxford. He previously was faculty at the Stanford Graduate School of Business and the University of British Columbia (Vancouver, Canada), as well as holding visiting positions at Harvard Business School and Wharton. He is a pioneer of the academic literature on entrepreneurial finance, with numerous scholarly contributions to venture capital, entrepreneurship, innovation, and public policy. His consulting clients include the World Economic Forum, Barclays Bank, and countless start-up companies. He is the founder of the NBER Entrepreneurship Research Boot Camp. He serves as the Academic Advisor of the Oxford Foundry, and the Academic Director of SBS Entrepreneurship Centre. Most recently he led the launch of the Creative Destruction Lab at Oxford.

Marco and Thomas met in 1989 at Stanford University during their PhD in Economics. Studying in the heart of Silicon Valley they discovered a passion for entrepreneurial finance, starting a scientific collaboration that resulted in several high-impact academic studies. Throughout their careers they designed and taught numerous entrepreneurial finance courses in many countries at the undergraduate, graduate, MBA, and executive levels. This is how they recognized the need for a modern entrepreneurial finance book that would explain the subject in a rigorous and accessible way.

To Sofia, for her loving patience, and to Cristiana, for her joyful laughter.

To Anne and Sophie, whose love and support made all the difference.

Acknowledgments

We are indebted to numerous people for the support and feedback we received in writing this book. We are particularly grateful for the insightful feedback we received from Alex Brabers, Wendy Bradley, Jim Brander, Brian Broughman, Geraldo Cerqueiro, Paul Cubbon, Carolina Dams, Qianqian Du, Gilles Duruflé, Gary Dushnitsky, Frank Ecker, Chuck Eesley, Ed Egan, Shai Erel, Michael Ewens, Andrea Fosfuri, Rik Frehen, Tim Galpin, John Gilligan, Martí Guash, Deepak Hegde, David Hsu, Anne Lafarre, Kelvin Law, José Liberti, Laura Lindsey, Richard MacKellar, Sophie Manigart, Gordon Murray, Ramana Nanda, Oliver Hart, María Fabiana Penas, Ludovic Phalippou, David Robinson, Christoph Schneider, Paul Schure, Merih Sevilir, Veikko Thiele, and Justin Tumlinson.

We are particularly thankful for the excellent research assistance provided by Neroli Austin, Vin Dogre, Carolyn Hicks, Dunhong Jin, Adrian Johnson, Anantha Krishna, Che Mitchell, Alexander Montag, and Joanna Stachowska.

We are thankful to the many investors and entrepreneurs with whom we had the privilege of interacting in numerous ways. We also greatly benefited from suggestions and encouragements from the students we had the pleasure of teaching all around the world. Unbeknownst to them, we professors learn as much from our students as they (hopefully) learn from us.

Preface for Students

Entrepreneurial finance has become a popular subject. Looking at how start-up companies try to disrupt markets and bring change to society is exciting. It also poses some concrete business challenges: How do investors pick winners? How do they finance growth? How do entrepreneurs manage to attract interest from investors? How does financing contribute to a venture's success and generate economic benefits and financial returns? Yet entrepreneurial finance can also be confusing and complex, full of jargon, not to mention lots of hype.

Our view is that to become an expert and make sense of the complex world of entrepreneurial finance, one needs to understand not only what is happening, but also *why* it is happening. This is what this book is for!

Why do we need a new book for all this? Why is a corporate finance, or entrepreneurship book not enough? A good corporate finance book can help us to understand the world of investors, and a good entrepreneurship textbook the world of entrepreneurs. The key to entrepreneurial finance, however, is to understand how these two worlds clash, combine, and ultimately create financing solutions suitable for innovative start-ups. Corporate finance books focus on the financing of mature companies that mainly issue stocks and bonds. Entrepreneurial ventures have very different financing needs. They need financial arrangements suitable for a highly uncertain environment. There is much more diversity among the various types of venture investors, which matters because these investors often get closely involved in the business. As for entrepreneurship books, they typically touch upon the venture's funding needs but rarely look at the fundraising process itself, explore the dynamic implications of financing choices, or clarify the numerous differences across alternative investor types.

This book is grounded in academic principles. The research foundations draw mostly on the core disciplines of finance and economics. In addition, we include insights from entrepreneurship, strategic management, marketing, organizational behavior, law, accounting, public policy, and other related fields, which enrich our understanding of the investment process.

This book is also steeped in practice. Throughout the book we constantly move between concepts and application. We augment the main text with analysis of data and practical examples that are placed into boxes, tables, and figures. The book follows the story of a fictional start-up, called WorkHorse, that was started by students just like you. We use this simple, yet realistic, story to bring alive numerous key concepts developed in the text and to illustrate how they are applied in practice. The book also contains several short real-world examples, drawn for a wide variety of sectors and countries. Finally, the book provides numerous practical learning tools, including summaries, review questions, and spreadsheets. These are available on the book's website (www.entrepreneurialfinance.net).

Entrepreneurial finance operates in a fast-moving environment, where investment models frequently change over time. Crowdfunding, for example, did not exist a decade ago but is becoming an established part of the entrepreneurial ecosystem. A decade from now, we expect that new models will have developed and that current ones will have evolved, too—hence the importance of understanding the fundamental drivers of the entrepreneurial finance process. Are you ready?

Preface for Instructors

Entrepreneurial finance is increasingly taught across a wide range of higher educational institutions, primarily in business schools, but increasingly also in engineering schools, law schools, and business economics departments. In many cases, the subject is taught in a stand-alone elective course, like Entrepreneurial Finance or Venture Capital. In other cases, the material is taught as part of an entrepreneurship or financial management course. This book is meant for all these kinds of classes.

The primary audience for this book is students in MBA, Masters in Finance (MSc), and advanced undergraduate courses. Additional audiences include other master and doctoral-level students in business disciplines. The book is also suited for practitioners, such as aspiring or first-time entrepreneurs, and venture teams in accelerator programs. First-time venture investors, such as venture capital associates, angel investors, and corporate investors will also find what they need in this book. Finally, the book is suitable for executive education, as well as entrepreneurship courses at technical universities that teach scientists and engineers about venture formation.

The book takes a pedagogical approach based on five fundamental pillars. First, the book is firmly rooted in academic research. We ourselves have actively contributed as researchers to the entrepreneurial finance literature for over 20 years. We are motivated to translate the academic frameworks and insights into common language that general audiences can understand and benefit from. Our own background is in finance and economics, but we have made deliberate efforts to include insights from many other academic disciplines, especially entrepreneurship, strategic management, organizational behavior, marketing, law, human resources management, accounting, and public policy.

Second, this book aims to provide concrete insights and tools that students can practically apply. We develop several novel practical tools based on the concepts developed in the text. One is the Venture Evaluation Matrix, which is a qualitative framework for analyzing the attractiveness of a business plan. Another is a financial projections spreadsheet that students can use to analyze WorkHorse's financial projects or to develop their own projections. As readers proceed from chapter to chapter, they will discover more tools. These tools and several additional materials are freely available on the book's website (www.entrepreneurialfinance.net).

Third, we take a global perspective, reflecting the increasingly global nature of entrepreneurial finance. We anchor our book in the U.S. model, but we frequently discuss alternative approaches, practices, and examples from other countries.

We believe this approach is appropriate for both U.S. and non-U.S. audiences. U.S. audiences will look for U.S. practices as their initial reference point but will want to know more about other parts of the world too. Non-U.S. audiences understand that the U.S., and especially Silicon Valley, is the epicenter of entrepreneurial finance and thus constitutes a useful benchmark for other countries. They will therefore be eager to understand the U.S. model and then relate it back into their own institutional context.

Fourth, we provide a comprehensive overview of the entire fundraising process, with particular attention to the diversity of investor types. We strive to provide an understanding of why things are done in certain ways and how the various steps in the process are interconnected with each other. For this reason, the first chapter introduces two overarching conceptual frameworks that structure the content of the book. The first framework, called FIRE, describes how entrepreneurs and investors interact over the fundraising cycle. The second framework, FUEL, explains in detail how different types of investors themselves function.

Fifth, we conceived the story of a fictional start-up (WorkHorse) to create a comprehensive illustration of key concepts. The story unfolds through a sequence of boxes that are weaved into the main analysis. It is an educational tool that vividly illustrates and applies all the core concepts with a simplified, yet realistic, story. Its dynamically consistent storyline also allows students to appreciate how the numerous aspects of entrepreneurial finance are interconnected.

This book assumes very little prior knowledge of entrepreneurship and finance. Students will benefit from understanding basic business vocabulary (e.g., what marketing is), and it helps to have a basic understanding of finance fundamentals, such as risk and returns. The remaining concepts are introduced if and when needed. Importantly, however, this book has not been "dumbed down" to make it more appealing to a mass audience. Our approach is instead to take the reader step by step through material of increasing complexity.

We enrich the main text with analysis of data and practical examples that are placed into boxes, tables, and figures. While the academic foundations inform all of our analysis, we choose to keep the main text uncluttered. Consequently, all academic references are put into endnotes.

The book is accompanied by several additional materials freely available online at the book's website (www.entrepreneurialfinance.net). These include chapter appendices and all of the spreadsheets discussed in the book, several of which contain novel material not available anywhere else. For instructors, separate online materials available through OUP contain a complete set of slides, a test bank including some advanced numerical exercises, suggestions on how to configure different types of courses of different length, suggested case studies, and other additional materials.

The Structure of the Book

The book starts with a conceptual introduction in Chapter 1, which includes the FIRE and FUEL frameworks for understanding the entrepreneurial finance process and the nature of investors. The material from Chapter 2 to Chapter 11 covers the entire entrepreneurial finance process, from the initial contacts between entrepreneurs and investors, all the way to the time of exit when investors get their returns. The material in Chapter 12 to Chapter 14 covers the main types of investors and how they interact with each other within an entrepreneurial ecosystem. Here we provide a brief overview of each chapter.

In Chapter 2 we explain how investors evaluate opportunities. We introduce the Venture Evaluation Matrix, a framework for analyzing the business fundamentals of entrepreneurial companies. This framework guides entrepreneurs in how to pitch their businesses, and investors in how to evaluate a venture's appeal and risks.

In Chapter 3 we discuss how entrepreneurs craft financial plans. This includes generating financial projections that address two key questions: (1) how financially attractive is the business opportunity? and (2) how much money does it need, and when?

In Chapter 4 we explain the relationship between investment amounts, ownership fractions, and valuation. In addition, we examine various measures of investor returns. We also discuss the economic determinants of ownership and returns and take a look at how founders can agree on the internal split of ownership shares.

In Chapter 5 we review the main valuation methods used in entrepreneurial finance. We introduce the widely used Venture Capital Method and compare it to several alternatives, including the standard Discounted Cash Flow Method, as well as other more advanced methods that explicitly model uncertainty.

In Chapter 6 we examine the contractual relationship between entrepreneurs and investors. We analyze the main clauses used in a term sheet. The chapter examines their rationale and their implications for entrepreneurs and investors, and specifies under what circumstances they are used. The focus is on understanding how different financial securities implement different cash flow rights. We also examine convertible notes, which are increasingly used for very early-stage deals. The chapter also explores compensation and a variety of other contractual rights.

In Chapter 7 we study how entrepreneurs and investors structure deals. We identify the challenges of finding a good match in the first place. We then consider how investors involve their peers in syndication. The chapter examines the negotiation process of how entrepreneurs and investors move from initial meetings to closing a deal. A bargaining framework is used to explain how deals are closed. Special emphasis is given to the important role of trust.

In Chapter 8 we explore how investors get actively engaged with their companies after the deal has been signed. We explain the need for active investor involvement, and we examine investors' control rights and the role of the board of directors. We also show the importance of informal control and discuss how corporate governance takes place in practice.

In Chapter 9 we explore the staged financing process, where companies receive equity financing over several rounds. We explain how staging allows investors to reap the option value of waiting. In later rounds, old and new investors can play different roles and can have different preferences. The chapter examines term sheet provisions that regulate the resulting conflicts. We also consider investors' decisions about providing additional funding to struggling companies.

In Chapter 10 we examine how entrepreneurial companies can use debt financing. We explain why banks rarely finance entrepreneurs. We then examine other forms of debt financing that play an important role for entrepreneurial companies.

In Chapter 11 we look at exit, the final stage of the investment process. The more profitable routes of exit are Initial Public Offerings (IPOs) and acquisitions. The chapter also reviews sales to financial buyers and buybacks and discusses what happens when companies fail. We explain the economic interests of the various parties involved in the exit transaction, the process by which exit decisions are made, and the consequences for entrepreneur, investor, and the company itself.

In Chapter 12 we examine the structure of VC firms. We consider why and how institutional investors put money into VC funds. The chapter then examines the internal organization of VC firms. We explain the challenges of devising and implementing an investment strategy and of managing a portfolio of investments. The chapter also studies different measures of investment returns.

In Chapter 13 we look at a large variety of early-stage investors. We start with founders, families, and friends, and then we consider angel investors and the ways they organize themselves into networks and funds. The chapter further considers the role of corporate investors, focusing on their strategic motives. We then look at crowdfunding and Initial Coin Offerings (ICOs). We conclude by discussing several types of seed investors, such as accelerators, technology transfer funds, and social impact investors.

In Chapter 14, we take an ecosystem perspective, asking how the various actors of the financing environment interact with each other. The chapter examines how ecosystems work and what factors contribute to creating a vibrant ecosystem. We study the various ways governments try to support entrepreneurial ecosystems and the hurdles they face. Finally, we take a global perspective and look at how capital and talent move across borders.

About the Companion Website

www.oup.com/us/entrepreneurialfinance

Oxford has created a password-protected website to accompany *Fundamentals of Entrepreneurial Finance*. Material that cannot be made available in a book, namely slides and tests, is provided here. Instructors are encouraged to use this resource. If you are an instructor and would like to access this section, please email Custserv.us@oup.com with your course information to receive a password.

Contents

1

Introduction to Entrepreneurial Finance

Learning Goals

In this chapter students will learn:

1. What entrepreneurial finance is.
2. Why entrepreneurial finance matters.
3. What the core challenges across the entire investment process are.
4. Who the investors are and how they differ one from another.

This chapter provides an introduction to entrepreneurial finance. It explains the main challenges faced by entrepreneurs who need to raise capital and by investors who are looking for investment opportunities. It also explains why entrepreneurial finance matters for the entrepreneurial process of building new companies, for allowing investors to achieve good returns, and for generating economic growth. The chapter introduces a simple framework that provides a comprehensive overview of how entrepreneurs and investors interact over the entire fundraising cycle. Further, it explains the nature of different types of investors and provides a structured approach for understanding how they operate.

1.1 What Is Entrepreneurial Finance?

It begins with an intergalactic collision. Entrepreneurial finance is at the epicenter of a clash of two worlds: the world of entrepreneurship and the world of finance. These two worlds couldn't be more different. The world of finance is a disciplined and orderly world, based on taking calculated risks and looking for proven track records. By contrast, entrepreneurship is a messy and disruptive affair, based on treading into the unknown off the beaten track. Finance is based on numbers and logical thinking and is associated with left-brain thinking. Entrepreneurship is based on intuition and experimentation and is associated with right-brain thinking.[1]

Who wants to be caught in the middle of that clash? Entrepreneurs and investors may well feel that they live on different planets and speak different languages. Yet, what could be more exciting than being part of an intergalactic collision? Something new and big might come out of it. Combining the perspectives of entrepreneurs and investors may reveal new horizons. The result can be the creation of innovative companies that disrupt industries and business models, generate wealth, and improve people's lives. Besides, what bigger challenge can there be than combining the left and right sides of the brain? Welcome to entrepreneurial finance!

The main goal in this book is to provide an understanding of how entrepreneurial companies are funded. We define entrepreneurial finance as the provision of funding to young, innovative, growth-oriented companies. Entrepreneurial companies are young, typically being less than 10 years old. They introduce innovative products or business models. The younger among those companies are called "start-ups" and are typically less than five years old. A study by Koellinger and Thurik documents the importance of entrepreneurial companies for generating business cycles.[2] Of central importance is that entrepreneurial companies are growth-oriented. This sets them apart from small businesses or small and medium-sized enterprises (SMEs).[3] Even though entrepreneurial companies typically fall within the statistical definitions of small businesses (e.g., businesses with fewer than 250 employees), in practice they have little in common with their statistical peers. Most small businesses are created to remain small: think of corner shops or business services. Hurst and Pugsley's study of U.S. small businesses finds that less than a quarter wanted to grow big.[4] When asked about the expected number of employees working in a firm by the time it becomes five years old, the median response was four employees. Instead, entrepreneurial companies have the ambition to grow much larger by pursuing some innovation. Put simply, small businesses represent the status quo, whereas entrepreneurial businesses challenge it.

In this book, we consider a wide variety of start-ups. Some commercialize technology based on scientific breakthroughs, such as in artificial intelligence or biotechnology. In many cases, the technical advance enables the introduction of new products or services, such as with electronic commerce or digital health. Other start-ups leverage new technologies without developing any innovations per se. They innovate in terms of product varieties, marketing approaches, or business models. For instance, start-ups like Uber, Didi, Grab, and Lyft have used geopositioning technology and mobile telephony to challenge the decade-old business model of the taxi industry. Similarly, Pandora's Box, Spotify, Beats, or Tidal have taken advantage of Wi-Fi internet, cloud storage, and data compression technology to deliver high-quality music without needing a physical medium and to disrupt the music distribution business. Finally, there are start-ups that do not rely on technology at all, but instead introduce new products or services. Throughout the book we will use the terms *start-ups, entrepreneurial company,* and *ventures* interchangeably to denote this kind of young ambitious growth-oriented companies.

On the finance side of the intergalactic collision, there is a bewildering variety of investors who can finance entrepreneurial companies. Family and friends provide some initial money to get the company started. So-called business angels are wealthy individuals who invest in start-ups. Venture capital (VC) firms are partnerships of professional investors who manage investment funds on behalf of institutional investors such as pension funds, insurance companies, and university endowments. Established corporations invest for strategic reasons. Entrepreneurs can also use crowdfunding platforms to reach out to the general public (the crowd). Throughout the book we examine these and other investors, which we collectively call "venture investors." Each type of investor has a different motivation for investing, ranging from helping a friend to achieving a high financial return to accessing new technologies to fostering the local economy. Investors also differ in their funding potential and in the way they make decisions.

At the core of entrepreneurial finance there is an exchange between an entrepreneur and an investor, where the entrepreneur receives money and in return gives the investor a claim on the company's future returns. This claim is embedded in a funding contract between entrepreneurs and investors, which requires a well-functioning legal system, as well as trust among the parties. Some investors take equity, others provide loans, and still others use a variety of alternative arrangements. Entrepreneurs need to understand the consequences of these contracts. This complex world can be confusing, especially to inexperienced entrepreneurs. This book will examine all these issues and clarify them. We also provide several practical tools and additional materials on the book's website: www.entrepreneurialfinance.net.

To make sense of these seemingly mysterious worlds, we need to consider the whole entrepreneurial process through which entrepreneurs turn ideas into businesses. This is a long and risky process: success takes many years, and failure is always lurking around the corner. The process starts with a decision to become an entrepreneur in order to develop a business idea.[5] Initially, there are one or several founders who perceive an opportunity that suggests a novel solution to an unmet need (see Section 2.2). The founders pursue their vision by structuring their intuition into some kind of a business plan and implementing its initial steps. This typically requires convincing customers, suppliers, employees, and investors of the merits of the opportunity. During the process of assembling resources, entrepreneurs learn about the underlying opportunity and the numerous challenges of implementing it. They often alter their course to adjust to changing circumstances and respond to the new information obtained. Over time a typical start-up hires employees, builds prototypes, acquires initial customers, gains market share, strikes strategic alliances, develops further products, and enters additional markets. Along the way the start-up typically needs considerable amounts of funding (see Section 1.5). The entrepreneurial process comes to its conclusion when the company fails, when it gets acquired, or when it grows into an established corporation. To properly understand the challenges of the entrepreneurial process, Box 1.1 establishes three fundamental principles that we will return to throughout the book.

Box 1.1 Three Fundamental Principles of the Entrepreneurial Process

Entrepreneurs start planning their ventures long before they approach investors for funding. To properly understand entrepreneurial finance, we therefore need to understand the underlying entrepreneurial process. Every entrepreneur has her own story, so it is impossible to accurately define a general entrepreneurial process. Still, we can identify three general principles that describe how entrepreneurs build their businesses, the particular challenges they face, and the kind of progress they achieve. These principles are resource-gathering, uncertainty, and experimentation.

The first principle is based on the work of the Austrian economist Joseph Schumpeter, who described entrepreneurship as a recombination of existing resources to create something new.[6] The entrepreneurial process therefore consists of *gathering resources* from a variety of owners and combining them in a novel and valuable way. Financing is one of the most important resources that entrepreneurs need to gather. It plays a special role because money allows entrepreneurs to acquire other resources. Fundraising is therefore a crucial step in the entrepreneurial process.

The second principle reflects the fact that the entrepreneurial process is inherently *uncertain*. The American economist Frank Knight argued that there is an important difference between risk and uncertainty.[7] Risk refers to situations where the outcome of a process is not known in advance but there is reliable information about the underlying probability distribution of outcomes. For example, when we throw a dice, we do not know which side will show, but we know it can be only one of six. Uncertainty, by contrast, means that the range of outcomes and their probabilities are themselves unknown. For example, no one knows the probability of finding extraterrestrial life, let alone what it will look like. The entrepreneurial process fits the latter category. Entrepreneurs lack reliable information about the range or likelihood of outcomes, let alone about the relationship between their actions and those potential outcomes. This ambiguity is not coincidental. We call an opportunity "entrepreneurial" when there is considerable uncertainty. By the time the outcomes are well understood, the business opportunities are no longer entrepreneurial but managerial.[8]

The third principle is based on the pioneering work of the American sociologist James March and concerns *experimentation*.[9] His work is mostly concerned with how organizations make decisions and how they learn over time. March introduced the distinction between "exploitation" and "exploration" as two opposite organizational models. Exploitation is common among established firms, which focus on leveraging their current market position. Exploration is more useful to younger, more agile organizations, including start-ups. Even if entrepreneurs pursue some long-term vision, they are unsure about the path and therefore need to adopt flexible behaviors. Experimentation is intrinsic to entrepreneurship because the process of exploring new opportunities inevitably leads to surprises and dead-ends. Entrepreneurs have no choice but to adapt their plans over time. In modern business lingo, this is referred to as "pivoting." Established businesses, by contrast, rely on consistent execution of established routines and find it more difficult to engage in experimentation.[10]

These three principles not only help us to understand the entrepreneurial process, they also clarify what investors face. The first principle implies that the money offered by investors will play a vital role in the development of the venture. The second principle says that investors will have to live with uncertainty at every step of the process. The third principle suggests that investors, too, need to be flexible when working with entrepreneurs. Together these principles imply that the process of financing start-ups proceeds in stages, where at every stage one faces uncertainty, experimentation, and learning.

1.2 Why Is Entrepreneurial Finance Challenging?

Being where two worlds clash, entrepreneurial finance is bound to be turbulent. From the entrepreneur's perspective, obtaining funding can be bewildering. To begin with, it is difficult to find and reach out to the relevant investors. Established businesses may be able to talk to "their banker," but for entrepreneurs there isn't a banker they can talk to. Instead they need to look for different types of investors, each with their own decision processes and objectives. Once they are in front of investors, entrepreneurs have to pitch their businesses, often at a point in time where all they have are ideas but no proofs. If they actually manage to convince the investors of their ideas, they need to answer myriad questions about how much money they need and for what purposes. They have to negotiate a price for the investment and to work with lawyers to sort through pages and pages of contractual terms. Even after the money arrives, things remain challenging. Investors can be demanding, even meddlesome. Worst of all, investors actually want their money back at some not too distant point in time. Entrepreneurs frequently state that finding and managing investors is one of the toughest parts of managing their venture.

If entrepreneurs find fundraising a daunting challenge, the same holds for investors. Their first difficulty is figuring out which companies to invest in. Investors get swamped with business proposals. A typical VC firm, for example, might receive well over a thousand business plans per year. Investors screen numerous opportunities and proceed to investigate more deeply a smaller number. If they like what they see, they have to decide whether to offer a deal, knowing that the competition may snatch away the best opportunities at any time. Structuring a deal requires choosing investment amounts, a price (or "valuation"), and numerous contractual terms. After the money is invested, things don't become easier either. Investors worry about their companies' progress and whether to keep financing them once they run out of money. Most important of all, investors worry about whether they will ever get their money back.

To some extent, both entrepreneurs and investors worry about the same challenges: finding a good match, striking a good deal, surviving the ride, and finding their way to a successful exit. However, their experiences with handling these challenges can be very different, especially when they are not equally familiar with the process. Most entrepreneurs go through the process for the first time, whereas most investors accumulate considerable experiences from making numerous deals.

1.3 Why Is Entrepreneurial Finance Important?

Entrepreneurial finance is not only exciting and challenging, it is also important: for entrepreneurs, for investors, and for the economy at large.

From the entrepreneur's perspective, obtaining financing is vital for the success of her business. Most entrepreneurs do not have the resources to fund their ventures, so they need to raise money from outside investors. Funding is essential to pay for many of the other required resources, such as employees and equipment. The amount of money raised determines the level of investments and thus the speed of progress. Having less funding also shortens a company's planning horizons. The choice of investor also plays a significant role in development of the venture. A good investor supports the venture by mentoring and providing strategic advice, by making introductions to business partners and future investors, by helping to hire talented managers, or by attracting a knowledgeable board of directors. Some investors are better than others at supporting their ventures. Moreover, some have more expertise in specific areas that may be important to some but not other start-ups. Investors also want to actively protect their investments and to exercise influence and control over strategic decisions. In some cases, they can even go as far as firing the founders from their own company. Clearly, it matters which investors the entrepreneur picks.

From the investor's perspective, funding the right ventures is crucial for generating high returns, as start-ups are risky and sometimes opaque.[11] This delicate choice is sometimes delegated to professional VC firms, whose core business is funding start-ups. Institutional investors allocate some money to VC firms as a way of diversifying their portfolio and seeking out high returns. Established corporations also fund entrepreneurial ventures, as part of their innovation strategies. It gives them a window on new technology and a chance to engage with promising ventures in their industries. Finally, for private investors, financing entrepreneurs is not only a personal passion, it can also be an efficient way of applying their skills and expertise to make money.

Entrepreneurial finance matters also for the economy and society at large. Entrepreneurial companies are an important driver of economic growth since they advance new technologies, products, and business models. To understand their role properly, we introduce "Nobel Insights," a feature that we will encounter once per chapter. We will look at core economics principles that can be usefully applied to entrepreneurial finance. Specifically, we draw on the insights of the winners of the Sveriges Riksbank Prize in Economic Sciences in Memory of Alfred Nobel, commonly referred to as the Nobel Prize in Economics. Every year this prize is awarded to one or more economists in recognition of their scholarly achievements. In each Nobel Insights feature, we briefly summarize the key insights from the Nobel laureate's work, and then we explain why they are relevant in our context. These Nobel laureates were not thinking of entrepreneurial finance when they were developing their work. They were concerned with more general economic problems. However, we explain how their insights can be applied to the entrepreneurial finance context. Box 1.2 looks at what is arguably the most important question in economics: what causes long-term economic growth?

Box 1.2 Nobel Insights about the Drivers of Long-term Economic Growth

The 1987 Nobel Prize in Economics was awarded to Robert Solow "for his contributions to the theory of economic growth."[12] The 2018 Nobel Prize was awarded to Paul Romer "for integrating technological innovations into long-run macroeconomic analysis."[13]

The question of economic growth is central to economics. Economic growth is the main reason why standards of living have been growing historically. Solow tackles the question of what determines growth in the long run. For this issue he built an elegant mathematical model of the economy that takes into account the most important aspects of economic activity, such as people's preferences, labor supply, savings, capital investments, and technology.[14] He then separated temporary effects that affect the *level* of economic activity from lasting effects that affect *long-term growth*. For example, the discovery of shale gas reserves might temporarily lift economic activity by providing cheap energy. However, once extraction is completed, this effect fades away and the economy reverts to its long-term growth rate. The question is "What determines that growth rate?" Solow's conclusion is powerful and surprising: the main determinant of long-term growth is "technological progress."

Solow's growth model revolves around the concept of total factor productivity (TFP). Consider first the simpler concept of "labor productivity." This is the amount of output per unit of labor inputs, typically measured as sales over wages. However, labor is not the only input to produce outputs; there are also capital and land. TFP is therefore the amount of output divided by all factor inputs, the measurement of which involves some accounting complexities. The technological progress that drives long-term growth is then defined as the continued increases in TFP. Put simply, economic growth comes from increases in the efficiency of how an economy converts inputs into outputs.

Inspired by Solow's analysis, a whole generation of economists studied the drivers of TFP growth. Paul Romer is one of the pioneers of what has been labeled "endogenous growth theory."[15] Solow established that technological innovation is the primary driver of economic growth, but he didn't specify the details of how new technologies emerge. Romer's work uncovers how economic forces affect the willingness of firms to generate new ideas and innovations. His key insight is that ideas are different from other goods and require specific conditions to thrive in a market. Growth is "endogenous" in the sense that it emerges from the choices of individuals, who invest in education and create new companies, and from the choices of firms, which adopt innovative technologies and new business models.

Broadly speaking, there are two main lines of argument that may lead to endogenous growth. The first line looks at innovation. The core argument is that R&D investments are different from standard capital investments because they generate innovations that benefit society at large. In particular, there are knowledge spillovers that propagate throughout the economy and help to lift TFP. In practice, this argument focuses on the role of innovations from established companies. The second line of argument looks at entrepreneurship. The main argument is that innovation does not come from established companies but from the entrepreneurs who challenge them. TFP increases over time because each new generation of entrepreneurs challenges incumbents by introducing better, faster, cheaper products or services. This argument builds directly on Schumpeter's notion of creative destruction that we encountered in Box 1.1.

The argument so far suggests that entrepreneurship is at the heart of long-term economic growth. One central reason why it is important for society is that entrepreneurial companies create a disproportionate amount of new jobs. Box 1.3 reports some surprising facts.

Box 1.3 Jobs Are Created by Young Firms, not by Small Firms

Understanding the contribution of entrepreneurial ventures to generating jobs requires studying both gross job creation (the number of new jobs created) and net job creation (the number of new jobs created minus jobs lost). Two interesting studies by Decker, Haltiwanger, Jarmin, and Miranda look at this issue using U.S. employment data between1980 and 2005.[16] Start-ups created on average 2.9 million jobs per year in their first year of operations. This accounts for approximately one-sixth of gross job creation in the U.S. However, average annual net job creation in the U.S. over that period was only 1.4 million. Gross and net job creation are mechanically the same for start-ups in their initial year.

Comparing their 2.9 million with the economy-wide average 1.4 million net jobs, one might conclude that start-ups account for over twice as much net job creation. This turns out to be an overstatement. Understanding why helps us to better understand the entrepreneurial process itself.

To properly assess the role of start-ups in net job creation, we need to take account of the "up-or-out" dynamics of young firms. Start-ups create many jobs in their first year, but many of those jobs are quickly lost in subsequent years. Indeed, 17% of all jobs created in the first year of a start-up (approximately half a million) get lost already by the end of the second year, another 14% by the end of the third year, and so on. This is the "out" component of up-and-out dynamics. It is counterbalanced by the "up" component, which comes from a relatively small number of young firms that keep creating new jobs throughout their early years. On average, start-ups create 14% more new jobs (approximately 400,000 jobs) in their second year, 6% in their third year (approximately 170,000 jobs), and so on. It follows that the true contribution of start-ups to net job creation cannot be summarized in a single number; instead it requires an understanding of these up-or-out dynamics. A related study by Sedláček and Sterk further finds that employment created by start-ups is stronger during expansions, when it is easier for companies to attract more customers. Moreover, job creation is not uniform across start-ups, with relatively few start-ups persistently creating more jobs than others.[17]

These studies find that young firms make a significant contribution to net job creation but that the same cannot be said for small firms. It is young ventures that generate the bulk of net job creation. The rate of net job creation decreases monotonically with firm age, from 11.8% for ventures less than two years old to 0.7% for companies over 16 years of age. Moreover, only a small fraction of young firms grows into large companies. These few high-growth firms therefore play a key role in economic growth. It is precisely those young, ambitious, high-potential start-ups that we focus on in this book.

So far, we have seen that innovation and entrepreneurship are important for long-term growth and that high-growth entrepreneurs are an important driver for new job creation. The final piece of the puzzle is to link these effects back to the financing of entrepreneurs. Various studies have examined this question, generally finding supportive evidence. A study by Chemmanur, Krishnan, and Nandy finds that VC-backed start-ups have significantly higher TFP than a control group.[18] A study by Kortum and Lerner further finds that VC generates more and better patents than corporate R&D spending.[19] A third study, by Samila and Sorenson, finds that increases in local VC funding lead to higher creation of local start-ups, more employment, and higher aggregate income.[20] Finally, the positive effects of financing are not limited to VC but also apply to other investor types. For example, other studies find that angel financing is associated with company growth, both in the U.S. and beyond.[21]

1.4 Key Facts about Entrepreneurial Finance

Building on the arguments presented in Section 1.3, we now consider some of the key facts about entrepreneurial finance. One simple measure of the importance of entrepreneurial finance is its size. Unfortunately, size is difficult to measure because many investors do not report how much funding they provide. The most visible part of the sector is the VC industry, so most of the available data focuses on VC. Figure 1.1 shows the growth of the formal U.S. VC industry since 1995, showing the cyclicality of investments.

These data clearly understate the size of the overall entrepreneurial finance sector. Although it is difficult to measure the other parts of the entrepreneurial finance sector, available estimates typically suggest that the total amount of funding from angel investors is at least as large as that from VCs.[22]

Over the years VC has become a global phenomenon. Figure 1.2 shows the evolution of the global VC industry since 2005. By 2018, total investments amounted to $272B. The U.S. accounts for just under half of the global investment volume, and Europe for just nearly one-tenth. The amount invested globally was spent on just over 17,000 VC deals. Asian deals are on average larger than U.S. deals, which in turn are larger than European deals.

Figure 1.3 compares the size of the VC industry, measured by investment amounts and scaled by gross domestic product (GDP), to provide a meaningful comparison across countries. The figure shows the top 25 Organisation

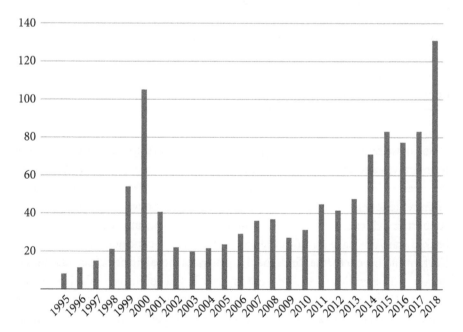

Figure 1.1. U.S. venture capital investments.

Data in U.S. dollar billions. Source: NVCA Yearbooks.

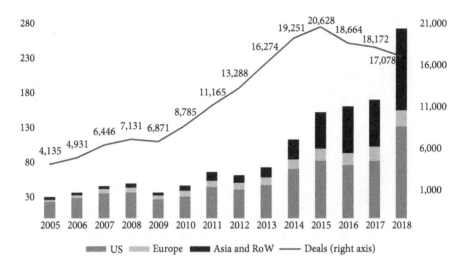

Figure 1.2. Global venture capital investments 2005–2018, by region.

Data in U.S. dollar billions. Source: Pitchbook Data.

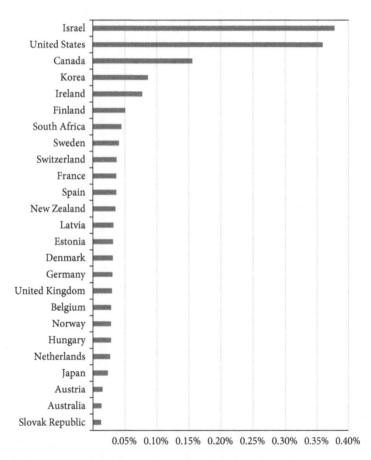

Figure 1.3. Venture capital investments as a percentage of GDP.

Data are for 2016 or latest available year. Source: OECD (2017).

Table 1.1 Some VC-backed success stories.

Name	Country	Business Area	Date Founded	Date of Exit	Valuation at Exit or Latest Round (US$B)	Exit Route (as of June 2019)
DEC	USA	Minicomputers	1957	1998	9.6	Acquisition (Compaq)
Intel	USA	Computer microprocessors	1968	1971	0.1	IPO
Federal Express	USA	Courier services	1971	1978	0.1	IPO
Genentech	USA	Biotechnology	1976	1980	0.3	IPO
Apple	USA	Digital technologies	1976	1980	1.3	IPO
Amazon	USA	E-commerce	1994	1997	0.4	IPO
Netflix	USA	Media streaming	1997	2002	0.3	IPO
Google	USA	Internet services	1998	2004	23.0	IPO
Avast	Czech Rep.	Antivirus	1998	2018	4.5	IPO
Tencent	China	Social media	1998	2004	1.4	IPO
Alibaba	China	E-commerce	1999	2014	168.0	IPO
Skype	Estonia	Communication	2003	2011	8.5	Acquisition (Microsoft)
Facebook	USA	Social media	2004	2012	104.0	IPO
Spotify	Sweden	Music streaming	2006	2018	30.0	IPO
BlaBlaCar	France	Transportation	2006	N/A	1.5	Private
DJI	China	Drones	2006	N/A	10.0	Private
Flipkart	India	E-commerce	2007	2018	11.0	Acquisition (Walmart)

Waze	Israel	Maps and navigation	2007	2013	1.2	Acquisition (Google)
Rocket Internet	Germany	Venture capital	2007	2014	8.4	IPO
Hootsuite	Canada	Software	2008	N/A	1.0	Private
WhatsApp	USA	Social media	2009	2014	22.0	Acquisition (Facebook)
Uber	USA	Transportation	2009	2019	72.0	IPO
Snap	USA	Social media	2010	2017	24.0	IPO
Hallo Fresh	Germany	Food delivery	2011	2017	22.0	IPO
Didi Chuxing	China	Transportation	2012	N/A	55.0	Private
Deliveroo	UK	Food delivery	2012	N/A	2.0	Private

for Economic Co-operation and Development (OECD) countries: Israel has the highest concentration of VC in the world, followed by the U.S., Canada, Korea, and Ireland.

In addition to looking at the size of the VC industry, an important question concerns its effect on the economy. A report by Gornall and Strebulaev on U.S. VC finds that VC-backed companies employ 4 million people, account for one-fifth of the U.S. stock market capitalization, and 44% of the R&D spending of U.S. public companies.[23] At the same time, the VC industry contributes to competition and creative destruction. The average lifespan of a company that belongs to the S&P 500 index (the leading U.S. stock market index composed of the largest firms on U.S. exchanges) was 67 years in 1920, over 30 years by 1965, and below 25 years by 2018.[24] This is largely due to the success of VC-funded companies. Indeed, the U.S. VC industry likes to boast about its history of hyperbolic successes, including the Digital Equipment Corporation (DEC), Federal Express, Genentech, Intel, Apple, and, more recently, Facebook, Amazon, Netflix, or Google. Outside of the U.S., the Chinese can brag about Tencent, the Indians about Flipkart, the Israelis about Waze, the Swedes about Spotify, the Canadians about Hootsuite, and so on. Table 1.1 lists some notable VC success stories. Although the list is not meant to be comprehensive, it reflects the increasingly global nature of high-growth entrepreneurship.[25]

Though inspirational, these success stories alone do not give the full picture. For every success story there are many more failures. Estimates of the failure rate of start-ups vary. On the high end, Hall and Woodward's study of U.S. VC-backed start-ups estimates that three out of four founders make no financial returns whatsoever (although their investors may still recover some return).[26] Other studies tend to find lower failure rates, a typical finding being that approximately half of all start-ups fail within the first five years.[27] Box 1.4 summarizes an important study on the success and failure rates of U.S. start-ups.

Box 1.4 Success and Failure of Start-ups with and without VC Funding

If everyone likes to talk about successes and no one about failures, how can we get a balanced picture of how start-ups really fare? A good approach is to look at the entire population of start-ups. One such study, by Puri and Zarutskie, compares U.S. start-ups financed by VCs to all other start-ups, the vast majority of which had no equity investors at all, for the period 1981–2005.[28] VC-backed companies account for just 0.1% of all start-ups (i.e., one in a thousand), yet they account for 5.5% of all U.S. employment. After 10 years of funding, the average VC-backed company had over 160 employees, 10 times more than the average in non-VC-backed companies. This confirms that VC-backed companies account for a large fraction of the new jobs created by start-ups, as discussed in Section 1.3.

The study also examines the exit rates of start-ups, distinguishing between failures, acquisition, Initial Public Offerings (IPOs), and ongoing operations. Of all the start-ups created between 1981 and 1997, by 2005 only 0.02% non-VC-backed start-ups had an IPO, compared to 16% for VC-backed start-ups. And 1% of non-VC-backed start-ups were acquired, compared to 34% of VC-backed start-ups. Clearly, VC-backed companies were more successful. The key finding, however, is that 79% of non-VC-backed start-ups had failed, compared to 40% of VC-backed start-ups. This shows that failure is very common but also that VC-backed start-ups experience failure much less often. The accompanying table breaks down the failure rate of start-ups over time. The second and third columns show the percentage of companies that failed after the number of years shown in the first column. The fourth and fifth columns show the conditional failure rate, which is the probability of failing by the end of the year, given that the start-up managed to survive until the beginning of the year.

Years from funding	Total failure rate with VC	Total failure rate without VC	Conditional failure rate with VC	Conditional failure rate without VC
1	4.4%	17.8%	4.4%	17.8%
2	9.7%	31.7%	5.5%	16.9%
3	15.8%	40.4%	6.8%	12.7%
4	20.7%	46.5%	5.8%	10.2%
5	24.1%	50.9%	4.3%	8.2%
6	26.7%	54.2%	3.4%	6.7%
7	28.5%	56.8%	2.5%	5.7%
8	29.9%	58.8%	2.0%	4.6%
9	30.9%	60.3%	1.4%	3.6%
10	31.6%	61.6%	1.0%	3.3%

Start-ups with VC backing have a lower failure rate over any time horizon. The last two columns further suggest that the differences are particularly pronounced in the early years, where the conditional failure rate is in the double digits for non-VC-backed companies but remains markedly lower for VC-backed companies. The authors argue that one benefit of having VC funding is protection against early failure; that is, VC funding allows start-ups to go through the initial experimentation phase.

Overall, the study shows that failure is a matter of perspective: compared to established companies, VC-backed start-ups fail often, but compared to non-VC-backed companies they seem much more solid.

1.5 The Entrepreneurial Financing Process

In this section, we take a look at the entrepreneurial finance process as a whole. For this purpose, we introduce the first of two frameworks we will use throughout the book.

1.5.1 The Need for Frameworks

"Why do we need a framework?" Fair question! Let us flip it around: "What would a book be without any framework?" It would risk being an unorganized collection of concepts and industry facts. Students might learn these facts and they might even learn the "lingo," but would they truly understand how entrepreneurial finance works? In this book, we establish a set of coherent and stable patterns that underlie the practice of entrepreneurial finance. We are not interested in catching the latest buzz about the industry, most of which is short-lived. Instead, we are interested in uncovering a more permanent set of logical structures that form the stable core around which the industry revolves.

No framework is ever precisely correct, nor is it ever complete; reality is simply too complex for that. The purpose of a framework is therefore not to replicate reality but rather to provide a useful simplification of the underlying phenomenon. A framework is a sketch that helps readers to orient themselves among the concepts and facts that are brought up in the book. It helps the reader to grasp the bigger picture, to organize the numerous pieces of information into a coherent whole.

"OK, but why do we need two frameworks; why not just one?" Again, fair question! The reason for that goes back to the intergalactic collision discussed at the very beginning of this chapter. The first framework, called FIRE, is built around the entrepreneur's journey. The second framework, called FUEL, looks at the investor organizations, their internal structures, motivations, and investment behaviors.

For clarity of exposition, throughout the book we identify entrepreneurs and investors with a different grammatical gender. We associate the female gender with entrepreneurs and the male gender with investors. Moreover, we use the terms *company, venture*, and *start-up* in connection with entrepreneurs, whereas we use the term *firm* in connection with investors.

1.5.2 The FIRE Framework

The FIRE framework follows the evolving relationship between an entrepreneur and investor. It traces the entire process of entrepreneurial finance from before the first contact with the investors, all the way to the conclusion of the investment relationship. The acronym FIRE (standing for *Fit, Invest, Ride,* and *Exit*) describes four consecutive steps of the entrepreneurial finance process. Fit concerns the matching process of how entrepreneurs and investors find each other and assess their mutual fit. Invest concerns the process of closing a deal, where the entrepreneur obtains money from the investor in exchange for a financial claim, with conditions specified in a contract. Ride concerns the path forward, where entrepreneurs and investors navigate through the entrepreneurial process and encounter numerous challenges. Exit is a destination, the end of the journey, when the investors obtain a return on their investments.[29] The framework is presented in Figure 1.4, an illustration inspired by intergalactic travels.

Figure 1.4. The FIRE framework.

Let us take a closer look at each of these four steps. Figure 1.5 depicts in a stylized way the first step, Fit.[30] It describes the process by which entrepreneurs and investors find each other and ascertain their mutual interest in making an investment. To

Figure 1.5. FIRE: The Fit step.

begin with, the entrepreneur and investor face challenges in finding each other and communicating their respective needs and interest. The entrepreneur needs to identify what types of investors might be interested and to leverage her network in order to gain access to the relevant ones. She needs to get their attention and pitch her idea effectively in order to signal the quality of their project. Investors, on their side, choose what kind of deals they want to look at. They then scout for good opportunities and go through a screening process to identify which opportunities they actually want to invest in. The matching process between entrepreneurs and investors involves both parties gradually getting to know each other and working their way toward making a deal. Figure 1.5 depicts the essential components of the Fit step, illustrated with the notion of the entrepreneur pitching an idea (the light bulb) and the investor screening opportunities (the binoculars), all in the hope of finding a match (the puzzle pieces).

From the perspective of an entrepreneur, what does it take to get investors interested? Box 1.5 provides some evidence on business angels.

Box 1.5 What Attracts Angels?

Angel investors are wealthy private individuals who sometimes invest in entrepreneurial ventures. How can entrepreneurs attract their attention? Beyond the business idea, it seems that what really matters are "people." One academic study, by Murnieks, Cardon, Sudek, White, and Brooks, finds that angels are mainly looking for entrepreneurial passion and tenacity.[31] In fact, it is the combination of the two that truly helps entrepreneurs stand out in the eyes of the angels. Angels who themselves had prior entrepreneurial experience are particularly keen on that combination of passion and tenacity. A second study, by Parhankangas and Ehrlich, looks at the language used by entrepreneurs.[32] Positive language and self-confidence help to make a good impression. However, excessive organizational promotion can backfire, and blasting the competition can impair one's own credibility. Impressing investors thus requires walking a fine line between being neither too modest nor too arrogant.

These research insights were derived from entrepreneurs meeting face to face with the angels. What happens in an online environment where one sees webpages before ever meeting the people? Bernstein, Korteweg, and Laws made an experiment on AngelList, an equity crowdfunding platform that connects entrepreneurs with business angels. They varied the online information available to investors.[33] The researchers use click-through rates to measure what information generates the most interest. More important than a company's business traction, more important than who else is in the deal, viewers responded to seeing information about the founders: who they are and what their prior experiences were. Even in the online world, investing in start-ups remains a people's business.

INVEST

Figure 1.6. FIRE: The Invest step.

Figure 1.6 depicts details of the second step, Invest.[34] This step captures the process by which an investor and entrepreneur structure their investment. The key challenge is to find an agreement that satisfies both the entrepreneur and the investor. Such contractual agreement contains two essential elements. First, there is the amount—the sum of money that the investor gives the entrepreneur. Second, there is the security—the number of shares the investor gets in return for making the investment.

The amount of funding is determined by both the needs of the company and the funding available to the investor. These factors determine how long the company can operate before having to come back for more funding. Concerning the security, one can choose from many options. Equity is the most common, but there are also debt and nondilutive funding (i.e., funding that does not affect ownership, such as grants). Equity financing plays a central role in this book, as it is one of the most common methods of financing start-ups. The investor gives money to the entrepreneur, who in turn gives up shares in the company. The valuation of the deal is determined by the price per share and reflects the overall attractiveness of the investment opportunity. An investment deal specifies how many shares the investor receives and, accordingly, what ownership fraction he gets. Another important funding vehicle is debt, where the company promises to repay the money according to a fixed repayment schedule. Beyond debt and equity, we will encounter other securities throughout the book. All of them come with a contract, the "term sheet," which contains the rules and conditions. It prescribes the details of exactly who gets paid what and when (called "cash flow rights"), as well as who makes what decision and when (called "control rights").

Figure 1.6 illustrates the essential nature of the Invest step. The investor and entrepreneur forge a deal (the handshake) where the investor makes an investment (the money bag) in return for a financial claim (the contract). As the handshake suggests, trust is an important element of the deal. Throughout the book, we note how important trust is for allowing parties to overcome expected and unexpected difficulties.

What does it take to get to the final handshake in Figure 1.6? What determines the structure of the investment deal? The entrepreneur's financial needs emanate from the business model, but the structure of the deal is also colored by the personal preferences of the founders' team. In addition, investors also have certain preferences that emanate from the structure of their own organization, something we examine in the FUEL framework of Section 1.6. The structure of the deal is also heavily dependent on the market conditions under which these two parties meet, such as the broader business conditions, and on what the specific circumstances of the two parties look like. Another important set of determinants are beliefs about the future of the venture. Throughout the book we emphasize that investments are driven by expectations about future returns.

Figure 1.7 illustrates the details for the third step, Ride, which reflects how the entrepreneur and investor interact after the initial investment is made.[35] Along the ride the entrepreneur and investor learn about the market and the scale of their business opportunity. In addition, they learn about each other, how to communicate effectively, and how to build trust. This results in decisions about business strategy, management structure, financial structure, and other activities. It requires a governance structure, especially when there are difficult choices where the entrepreneur and investor disagree with each other. The board of directors is where the company's important strategic decisions are made, and investors often play a central role on the board. Figure 1.7 illustrates the ongoing interactions between investors and entrepreneurs at the Ride step, showing a cockpit that allows the two parties to journey through space toward their destination. The dashboard includes various indicators representing the investor's need to monitor company progress; a map representing the need to constantly assess the company's status in the business

Figure 1.7. FIRE: The Ride step.

space; and steering sticks indicating the importance of making joint decisions and adjusting directions in mid-flight.

The development of a start-up proceeds in stages. From the perspective of the company, these stages correspond to important business milestones. While the details are different for each company, typical stages may include company formation, development of a first prototype or proof of concept, product development with customer testing, market entry, and market expansion. Business milestones are achieved at the end of each stage and linked to financing events. Investors want to give the company enough money to go from one milestone to another and reserve the right not to provide further funding in case the project falters. As a consequence, financing typically comes in stages, as illustrated in Figure 1.8. The figure illustrates this with the notion of space travel that goes from one planet to the next, each planet representing a milestone on the journey. Importantly, each plant has a refueling station that gives the venture resources to head for the next planet. In Section 1.6.2, we examine the FUEL framework and how these fueling stations work.

Figure 1.8. Staged financing.

The staging logic underlying Figure 1.8 is closely related to the insights from Box 1.1. The entrepreneurial process is fundamentally uncertain and involves a series of experiments. The investment process can therefore be thought of as a series of risky bets. The bet (a financing round) allows the company to go forward and hit an important milestone. At this point it needs another bet (another financing round) to proceed. The hope is that with enough bets the venture eventually finds a lucrative exit.[36]

Each new funding event is called a financing round. Each new round requires a new financial contract and therefore involves a new set of negotiations, resulting in a new valuation and a new term sheet. Funding can come from a combination of old and new investors. The terminology of venture financing is sometimes confusing. Box 1.6 establishes some common language.

Box 1.6 The Terminology of Rounds, Series, and Stages

Terminology can be confusing at first. The words "round," "investment round," or "financing round" are used to describe an equity fundraising event. A simple approach is to count rounds consecutively from the start, that is, first round, second round, and so on. However, the industry tends to use a more confusing language. Traditionally, VCs provided the first formal financing round and called it a "Series A" round. This term comes from the name of the shares that are issued to investors in that round, called "Series A shares." The second financing round is then called Series B, the third Series C, and so on. In more recent times, entrepreneurial companies have increasingly been funded by business angels and other early-stage investors, before receiving any VC funding. These earlier investments are typically classified as "seed rounds." However, some VCs classify their very early-stage funding as seed investments, which may create some confusion. Going even one step earlier, some investors make "pre-seed" investments, where they invest with the intent of getting the company ready for a seed round. The terminology thus reflects an ever-changing landscape of early-stage financing.

A related issue is the naming of company development stages. This is challenging because the number of rounds need not correspond to development stages and because different companies pursue different development paths that cannot be compared with each other. However, commercial databases about venture financing, such as Crunchbase, ThomsonOne, PitchBook, or Preqin, regularly provide such classifications. A common distinction is between seed stage, early stage, expansion stage, and late-stage. The seed stage is usually associated with pre-revenue companies; the early stage is associated with companies that are beginning to generate revenues, but are still developing their business model; the expansion stage concerns companies that have consolidated their business model and are ramping up their revenues; and the later stage is used for companies that have been growing for several years. Seed and early-stage companies are often referred to as "start-ups," whereas expansion and later-stage companies are sometimes called "scale-ups."

Figure 1.9 illustrates the final step of the FIRE framework, the Exit. [37] This is the "liquidity" event where the investors finally obtain a return on their investment by selling their shares. Often (but not always), the entrepreneur also obtains liquidity at this point in time. Understanding the Exit step is important because it is the destination that investors are steering toward throughout the entire FIRE process. Achieving a good exit is an investor's main goal. Figure 1.9 shows two types of exits: successful ones (represented by a sun) and unsuccessful ones (represented by a black hole).

This description is obviously a simplification, as many outcomes in between these two extremes are possible. We identify two types of successful exit. One—the IPO—occurs when a company goes public on the stock market. The other type occurs when a company gets acquired at a high valuation, typically by an established

EXIT

Figure 1.9. FIRE: The Exit step.

company. In the U.S., the average time from first financing to IPO is 6.3 years, and the average time to getting acquired is 5.6 years.[38] Unsuccessful exits take several forms. They may consist of ceasing operations, liquidating assets, declaring bankruptcy, or getting acquired at a low valuation. Another type of exit is a partial or full sale of company shares to a financial buyer. This exit is often associated with intermediate company performance. Finally, some companies never seem to find their way to an exit, being stuck in a limbo of neither making any progress nor being ready to close down. They are sometimes referred to as the "living dead" or "zombies."

The FIRE framework provides an integrated perspective on the fundraising process, which we examine in Chapter 2 through Chapter 11. We follow the entire funding cycle of entrepreneurial companies as depicted in the FIRE framework. Chapter 2 looks at the initial Fit step and examines how entrepreneurs and investors evaluate opportunities. Chapter 3 focuses on the financial plan, which lays out a company's financial needs and attractiveness. The Invest step begins with Chapter 4, which explores the basic mechanics of ownership and returns. Chapter 5 describes the valuation methods used for investment purposes. Chapter 6 explains term sheets, the contractual arrangements between entrepreneurs and investors. Chapter 7 integrates the Fit and Invest steps by providing an overall perspective on the deal-structuring process. We enter the Ride step in Chapter 8, which looks at corporate governance. It surveys how investors interact with entrepreneurs, in terms of both supporting and controlling their ventures. Chapter 9 examines the staged financing process of how investors provide additional funding over time. Chapter 10 looks at the various roles of debt along a company's growth path. Finally, Chapter 11 is dedicated to the Exit step; it explains the main ways that the investment cycle comes to its logical conclusion, sometimes ending in successful outcomes and sometimes in unsuccessful ones.

1.5.3 FIRE in Practice

How does the FIRE process unfold in practice? According to the ancient Greek myth, Pandora had a magical box. Once opened, all sorts of troubles were unleashed onto the world, with hope as the only thing left in the box. The point of this myth may sound familiar to those entrepreneurs who went through the FIRE. To see how the entire entrepreneurial cycle described by the FIRE framework works out in reality, we look at the experiences of two companies from two different continents. Box 1.7 discusses the entrepreneurial journeys of Pandora's Box and Spotify, two pioneers of the music business.[39]

Box 1.7 Opening up Pandora's Box

It all began with a "Savage Beast"—at least that was the name that Tim Westergren came up with for his start-up in the year 2000. Just as he was turning 30, after spending his 20s playing music with a band, Westergren launched a venture to build a digital music recommendation tool. He needed $1.5M and managed to convince the father of a personal friend, who offered to invest $750K. After that initial breakthrough, however, fundraising became more difficult. Westergren had many personal connections to top VCs in Silicon Valley, yet none of them were interested. Thankfully, he met Guy Kawasaki, an outspoken angel investor, who agreed to invest $250K. The remaining $500K eventually came from family and friends. Even though Westergren had strong personal networks in Silicon Valley, he learned the importance of investor fit: his business proposal resonated well with family and friends but was too preliminary for VCs.

From the FIRE framework we know that after the Fit and the Investment steps comes the Ride—and what a ride it was. In order to develop his music recommendation tool, Westergren first needed to build a large database of tagged music pieces. This required a large number of employees manually classifying music, so it wasn't long before the $1.5M was spent. Westergren and his co-founders invested their remaining personal savings of $250K, and Westergren maxed out on more than 10 credit cards. When the money ran out once more, he asked his employees to agree to deferred wages.

In 2002 the company got a lucky break, raising a $650K bridge round from another investor, but by 2003 the company owed more than $1M in deferred wages. No financial investor wanted to invest at that point because all the money would simply go into paying off the employees. Shortly before reaching the point of closing down, the company managed to get a deal with two large corporate clients. Specifically, AOL and Best Buy offered $500K to keep the company afloat. It soon pivoted from a music recommendation tool to an online radio model that began to disrupt the large music-listening industry. Sales finally picked up in 2004, and the company managed to raise a VC round of $7.8M from Walden Venture Capital, a San Francisco investor. It was around that time that the company changed its name from Savage Beast to Pandora's Box.

The roller coast ride was not over, though. In 2008, the company teetered on the brink of bankruptcy once more, in part because of higher copyright fees imposed by struggling music producers. The company overcame these challenges, and by 2011 it had streamed 3.8 billion hours of radio listening, generating $51M in revenues. When the company went public in June 2011, 11 years after founding, investors finally could exit their investments.

While Pandora's Box was on its roller coaster ride, Daniel Ek, a Swedish entrepreneur, founded another music company that would arguably disrupt the music business even more. Spotify was born out of a frustration with online music piracy. It pioneered streaming as an alternative model for selling music. Unlike Tim Westergren the musician, Daniel Ek was more of a straight businessman. Starting his first business at the age of 13, he already employed 25 people by the time he turned 18. When he launched Spotify in 2006, he was immediately credible to investors.

Compared to Pandora's Box, Spotify's financial history appears to be much more of a straight ride. The company raised over $1B in more than 10 rounds and became one of Europe's most successful start-ups. The early investors, Creandum and Northzone, were Swedish VC firms. The company also received some angel funding, most notably from Sean Parker, an early investor in Facebook and the founder of Napster, an online music company that was shut down because of music piracy. With Parker's help, large U.S. VC firms such as Accel and Kleiner Perkins became interested in investing. Further investments came from corporate partners, including Universal, Sony, Warner, and Tencent. In its later stages Spotify reached the coveted status of a "unicorn" (a term used to describe a young private company worth over $1B), raising large amounts of money from more traditional investment funds such as TCV, the Texas Pacific Group, and the Dragoneer Investment Group. In 2018, the company went public on the New York Stock Exchange with a valuation of over $22B. It yielded Creandum and Northzone a return of over 300 times their investment.

While Spotify went through all the classical milestones of a successful financing ride, the underlying business was everything but a straight path. The company faced numerous challenges. In 2014, for example, Taylor Swift withdrew all her albums, arguing that Spotify's business model was ruining the music business.[40] Spotify kept its calm, even promoting a playlist called "What to play while Taylor's away." Though not swiftly, Swift eventually returned to Spotify in 2017. Even the most successful start-ups have to walk through fire before reaching their successful exit.

1.6 Who Are the Investors?

1.6.1 Main Types of Investors

In this section, we introduce the main types of investors in entrepreneurial companies. Let us start with venture capital(VC) , arguably the most well-known type of
investor. Venture capitalists (VCs) are professional investors who raise their own
funding from institutional investors. They invest these funds in a portfolio of entrepreneurial companies, with the objective of generating returns for their institutional investors. VCs often specialize in a limited number of industries, such as
information technology and life sciences, and/or a limited geographic area. Silicon
Valley is considered the epicenter of the VC industry.

At this point, let us introduce a feature called "Tales from the Venture Archives."
Each chapter of this book contains one such tale, looking at a historical episode that
remains directly relevant today. Box 1.8 starts us off by looking into a historical debate about who should be considered the first VC.

**Box 1.8 Tales from the Venture Archives: Was the First Venture
Capitalist a Man or a Woman?**

There are two views as to who was the first venture capitalist, one involving a
man, the other a woman. The first view is that it was General Georges Frederic
Doriot (1899–1987).[41] Born in France, Doriot immigrated to the U.S. where
he became a professor at the Harvard Business School and later, during World
War II, joined the U.S. army. In 1946, he founded the American Research and
Development Corporation (ARDC), an investment fund that was set up to invest
in young technology-based ventures, with a goal of assisting New England's economic recovery. Its model of raising funds from private institutional investors
and investing them in start-ups was new at the time. It became the model for the
modern VC industry.[42] The ARDC had a difficult history as it struggled to make
this business model work. While it never generated high returns, it had a big
impact on the emerging U.S. VC industry. Its most well-known investment was
in the Digital Equipment Corporation (DEC), which became a major commercial success. DEC has also been credited for starting off the technology cluster
around Boston's Route 128.

The second view is that the first venture capitalist was Queen Isabella I of
Castile (Spain, 1451–1504). Her most famous investment was the 1492 expedi-
tion of Christopher Columbus to discover the western sea route to India.[43] The
investment had all the landmarks of a classical VC deal: recent technological
innovation (compasses and mapmaking); a big attractive market (spice trade
with India)' competitive rivalries (Spain versus Portugal); considerable risk (at
the time it was already known that the Earth was round; the uncertainty was

about its circumference and about whether ships could travel this far); and a passionate, albeit slightly inexperienced, entrepreneur (Christopher Columbus); not to mention some surprises along the way (the discovery of the Americas). Columbus put up a hard bargain and managed to get what was considered a good deal at the time, receiving a 10% stake in the profits of venture. He also made a fuss about his job title; instead of being called CEO, he bargained for the grand title of "Admiral of the Ocean Seas."

An important message throughout this book is that VC is only one of many ways of financing start-ups. There are many alternatives that we will briefly introduce now. The very first bit of money typically comes from the founders themselves. They use their own savings to pay for the initial business expenditures, or they use personal credit, such as credit cards and second mortgages. Funding that comes from within the company is considered internal funding. The vast majority of founders have only limited personal financial resources and therefore need to seek external funding.

The first external funders of a company are often family, relatives, and close friends, colloquially referred to as the "three Fs": "family, friends, and fools." They invest on the basis of a personal relationship more than on a commercial basis. Next there are "angel investors," private individuals who invest their own money without previous relationships to the founders. Angel investors can invest on their own, or they may join a variety of organizations, where they can invest as part of a group. Angel investors range from middle-income individuals investing moderate amounts of money in one or a few companies to millionaires and billionaires investing considerably larger sums of money in an entire portfolio of start-ups.

Corporations also invest in entrepreneurial ventures, often with a strategic motive. There are many different ways for corporations to engage with entrepreneurial ventures, ranging from ad-hoc investments to strategic partnerships and joint ventures to formal corporate venture divisions or subsidiaries. Established corporations also play an important role, acquiring entrepreneurial start-ups, thereby providing an exit. Some corporations also fund entrepreneurial ideas from inside the corporation itself. Such internal entrepreneurs are often referred to as "intrapreneurs." Their initiatives sometimes develop into lines of business that remain inside the corporation; others become corporate spin-offs where the established corporation creates a new separate company.

A recent occurrence is the emergence of Fintech, the application of new technology to financial services. Two developments are relevant for funding entrepreneurs.

One development is crowdfunding, which allows companies to obtain funding through an online platform. There are three main types of such platforms. First, some, like Kickstarter, allow companies to raise money in return for some rewards, maybe a symbolic recognition (e.g., the proverbial coffee mug with logo) or early access to a product under development. Second, peer-to-peer platforms like LendingClub allow companies to raise loans provided by private individuals or professional investors.

Third, there are platforms that allow companies to raise equity. Some of these platforms, such as AngelList, only allow sophisticated investors to invest; others, such as SEEDRS in the United Kingdom, are open to the general public. In recent years, a second form of Fintech application has emerged that allows raising large amounts, called Initial Coin Offerings. This second development is based on the Blockchain, a novel software architecture that allows for decentralized recordkeeping and decision making. At present, this type of investing remains unregulated and the marketplace is highly unstable.

Equity is prevalent in funding start-ups, but debt also has a role.[44] In principle, banks can provide a variety of credit and loan products to companies at all stages of development. In practice, however, most banks are reluctant to lend to entrepreneurs unless there is collateral or the entrepreneurs provide personal guarantees. A few banks specialize in venture debt, which is a type of lending to companies that are already VC-backed. Other debt instruments used by entrepreneurs include venture leasing and trade credit from suppliers.

Governments are another source of funding for entrepreneurs. They may support start-ups through direct and indirect government funding programs. Moreover, a wide variety of government programs support entrepreneurs with grants, tax credits, credit guarantees, and other forms of assistance.

Entrepreneurs encounter investors at different stages of the entrepreneurial process. Figure 1.10 provides a stylized representation of how different types of investors focus on different investment stages. The figure is ordered in a way that suggests a sequence by which entrepreneurs might approach different investors at different stages of company development.

1.6.2 The FUEL Framework

A common misconception among entrepreneurs is that all investors are the same; that is that "money is green." This view is far from true, however, and throughout this book we emphasize the diversity of investor types and its importance for the fundraising process. In order to understand this diversity, we introduce our second framework,

Investor Type	Seed stage	Early stage	Late stage
Founders, family & friends			
Fintech: Crowdfunding & ICOs			
Government support			
Angel investors			
Corporate investors			
Venture capital			
Venture debt			

Figure 1.10. Stage specialization of main investor types.

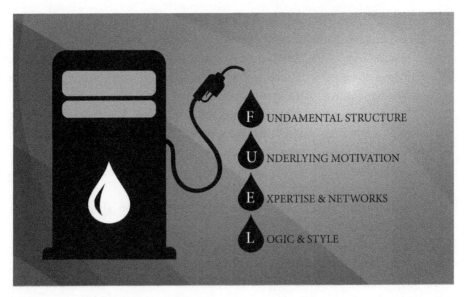

Figure 1.11. The FUEL framework.

called FUEL (an acronym standing for *F*undamental structure, *U*nderlying motivation, *E*xpertise and networks, and *L*ogic and style). The name alludes to the fact that entrepreneurs often talk about financing as the required fuel to make their ventures go.[45] Besides, as everyone knows, adding FUEL to FIRE really helps to get things going. We represent the FUEL framework graphically in Figure 1.1.

The FUEL framework is based on four core concepts that help to structure our understanding of the identity and behaviors of the investors. Each concept is associated with one central question that sets up the core issue and two further questions that elaborate on that core.

1. Fundamental structure
   - What is the investor's fundamental identity?
   - What is the investor's organizational structure and financial resources?
   - What is the investor's governance structure and decision-making process?
2. Underlying motivation
   - What does the investor want?
   - How important are financial and nonfinancial returns to the investors?
   - How risk tolerant and patient is the investor?
3. Expertise and networks
   - What does the investor offer to the entrepreneur?
   - What expertise does the investor bring to the table?
   - What networks can the investor draw on?
4. Logic and style
   - How does the investor operate?
   - What logical criteria does the investor use to select companies?
   - What is the investor's style of interacting with the companies?

The first concept, the F in FUEL, looks at the *fundamental structure* of the investor. This is the basis for distinguishing alternative investor types. It underlies many of the key features of how the investor interacts with entrepreneurs and other parties. Within the fundamental structure we first take a look at the *organizational structure* of the investment entity, focusing in particular on who owns the investment vehicle and on how much financial resources it has for investments. We then take a look at the *governance structure*, asking what rules govern the activities of the investment vehicle and how decisions are made within the organization. The core insights from this level of analysis concern who the relevant people are, how they make decisions, and what resources they control.

To gain an initial appreciation of the differences between alternative investor structures, let us compare two important types of investors, angels (Section 13.2) and VCs (Chapter 12). Consider how they differ in terms of the fundamental structure. The short version is that angels invest their own money, whereas VCs invest other people's money. For the long version, note that the structure of angel investors is fairly simple. Angels invest their own money and are accountable to no one else (spouses apart). Compare this to the VC structure, shown in Figure 1.12. An entrepreneurial company receives funding from a VC fund, which is a legal vehicle administered by a limited liability company (the general partner) and run by a group of individuals (the VCs). The general partner enters into an agreement with a set of institutional investors (the limited partners) that provide the funding of the VC fund. Institutional investors are large investment managers, such as pension funds, insurance companies, university endowments, sovereign wealth funds, investment banks (representing themselves or their clients), wealthy families, and others.

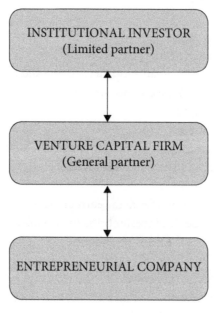

Figure 1.12 The venture capital structure.

Why does the fundamental structure matter? First, we consider whose money is being invested and how much of it. Most angels only invest relatively modest amounts, limited by how much wealth they have and how much they are willing to risk. By contrast, VCs can have access to much larger sums of money, depending on the size of the fund (which can range between $50M and over $1B). Second, we consider who makes the key decisions. Angel investors make their own decisions, whereas VCs take decisions by investment committees that are governed by partnership rules and may be subject to oversight by the limited partners. Clearly, we would expect different investments to come out of these different investor structures. In fact, the same individual may adopt different investment styles when acting as a VC versus investing privately as an angel investor.

The second core concept, the U in FUEL, looks at the *underlying motivation* of the investors. It considers their objectives, asking what motivates them to invest in the first place. We pay close attention to the relative importance of financial returns versus nonfinancial considerations. Some investors only focus on generating financial returns, whereas others pursue a broader set of objectives. In addition to financial returns, they may care about their personal interest in what the entrepreneur does, the potential social and economic impact of the venture, or any strategic synergies between the investor's organization and the entrepreneurial company. Other aspects of investor motivation concern risk tolerance and the investor's amount of patience.

If we look at the different motivations of angels and VCs, we note that the fundamental structure of VC firms provides strong incentives for generating financial returns. Consequently, VCs mostly care about making money. By contrast, angel investors can have a variety of goals. Beyond financial returns, they can be motivated by the social contribution of the venture, the thrill of staying involved in the entrepreneurial process, or sometimes just the company of other fellow angels. Lee Hower, who was part of LinkedIn's founding team and is now an experienced investor, lists five main motivations: return, market insights, path to a VC career, help to the community, and personal enjoyment.[46]

The third core concept, the E in FUEL, looks at the *expertise and networks* the investor brings to the deal. To see why this matters, recall the fundamental principles of the entrepreneurial process from Box 1.1: entrepreneurs gather resources in an environment with high uncertainty where learning is essential. To contribute to this entrepreneurial process, an investor needs competencies. *Expertise* is needed to properly screen out the right companies and add value along the ride. *Networks* are needed to help the entrepreneur gain access to key resources as the venture develops. Put differently, expertise concerns the knowledge and skills that the investors have by themselves, and networks concern the knowledge and skills that they can gain access to.

Applying this analysis to angels and VCs, we note that angels' expertise and networks are closely related to who they are. An experienced entrepreneur will bring very different skills and networks to the table than a successful lawyer or executive, let alone the heir of a large family fortune. As for VC firms, their networks include not only those of the individual partners, but also the historic and institutional links that the VC firm has as an organization. Investor differences along the expertise and network spectrum have far-reaching implications for how these investors behave and for how attractive they are to potential entrepreneurs. You would expect different help from a small local VC firm versus a top Silicon Valley VC firm.

The fourth core concept, the L in FUEL, looks at the investor's *logic and style*. By *logic* we mean the investment criteria used to make investment decisions. These concern preferences as to the industry, location, and stage of the company, as well as many more detailed criteria that an investor may have. The *style* concerns the way the investor interacts with the entrepreneurs. Different investors behave differently, and this also depends on the stages of the entrepreneurial process.

This fourth concept of the FUEL framework naturally links up to the FIRE framework. The "logic" component links to the first (Fit) and second (Invest) steps of the FIRE framework. It looks at what types of deals make sense and how to structure them. The "style" component then considers how the investor and entrepreneur interact throughout the rest of entrepreneurial financing process, that is, the Ride and Exit steps.

Angels and VCs tend to have their own distinct logic and style of making investments. There are many nuances not only across but also within investor types. By and large, angels are open to a larger variety of business opportunities, whereas VCs tend to focus on a narrower range of industries, stages, and locations. This is partly because they are accountable to their limited partners. There are also numerous differences in terms of investment style, such as how active they get involved in their companies, how they approach later-round financings, and what kind of exits they envision. We will encounter numerous such style differences throughout the book.

The FUEL framework provides a logical thread to understand investors in entrepreneurial companies, which we examine in Chapters 12–14. These chapters look at the investor landscape and explain its diversity and interactions. Chapter 12 explains how venture capital works. Chapter 13 surveys a large number of different early-stage investor types, including family and friends, individual angels, angel groups, corporate investors, crowdfunding, Initial Coin Offerings, accelerators, technology transfer funds, and social impact venture investors. Finally, Chapter 14 looks at clusters of entrepreneurs, investors, and relevant third parties, all of whom interact with each other to form powerful entrepreneurial ecosystems.

Summary

In this chapter, we analyze the core aspects of the entrepreneurial finance process. We examine how entrepreneurs get funded and what challenges this implies. We explain the clash between the disciplined world of finance and the unpredictable world of entrepreneurship. We identify three fundamental principles of entrepreneurship relevant for fundraising: resource-gathering, uncertainty, and experimentation. They help explain why the investment process is inherently challenging for both sides and important for the economy at large. We introduce the FIRE framework to study the process of how entrepreneurs and investors interact throughout the investment cycle. We then identify the key players in the entrepreneurial eco-system and recognize that there is considerable diversity across different types of investors. We also introduce the FUEL framework to examine the differences across the main investor types.

Review Questions

1. What are the key differences between financing entrepreneurial and estab-lished companies?
2. Entrepreneurship involves resource gathering, uncertainty, and experimen-tation. How does this affect the investors?
3. What steps are needed to show that entrepreneurial finance is beneficial to the economy at large?
4. What are the main challenges that entrepreneurs and investors face at the four steps of the funding cycle, as described in the FIRE framework?
5. What is the purpose of staged financing?
6. What can and can't we learn from successful start-ups like Pandora's Box and Spotify?
7. What are the main types of investors that fund entrepreneurial ventures?
8. Why does the identity of investors matter to the entrepreneurs?
9. What are the most important differences between VCs and angel investors?
10. What are the respective roles of conceptual frameworks and practical experi-ence for mastering entrepreneurial finance?

Notes

1. Shepherd and Patzelt (2018).
2. Koellinger and Thurik (2012).
3. Carland et al. (1984) and Schoar (2010).
4. Hurst and Pugsley (2011).
5. This structure of the entrepreneurial process goes back to Stevenson, Roberts, and Grousbeck (1998), and is discussed in modern textbooks, such as Barringer and Ireland (2015), Bygrave and Zacharakis (2014), Hisrich Peters, and Shepherd (2016), and Kuratko (2016), among others.
6. Schumpeter (1934, 1942).
7. Knight (1921).
8. Kihlstrom and Laffont (1979) discuss some theory, and Forlani and Mullins (2000) and Hvide and Panos (2014) discuss some evidence on the risk preferences of entrepreneurs.
9. March (1991, 2008).
10. Swift (2016).
11. For the trade-off between risk and reward, see Berk and DeMarzo (2016).
12. https://www.nobelprize.org/prizes/economic-sciences/1987/press-release.
13. https://www.nobelprize.org/prizes/economic-sciences/2018/press-release.
14. Solow (2000).

15. Seminal papers include Romer (1986, 1990), Lucas (1988), and Aghion and Howitt (1992). A recent contribution is Akcigit and Kerr (2018). See Romer (1994), Aghion and Howitt (1998), and Acemoglu (2009) for overviews.

16. See Haltiwanger, Jarmin, and Miranda (2013) and Decker et al. (2014), which provides a less technical overview.

17. Sedláček and Sterk (2017).

18. Chemmanur, Krishnan, and Nandy (2011).

19. Kortum and Lerner (2000).

20. Samila and Sorenson (2011).

21. Kerr, Lerner, and Schoar (2014) and Lerner et al. (2018).

22. Wilson (2011).

23. Gornall and Strebulaev (2015).

24. Foster and Kaplan (2003) and Anthony et al. (2018).

25. An interactive updated list of unicorns (privately held ventures valued over $1B) can be found at https://www.wsj.com/graphics/billion-dollar-club.

26. Hall and Woodward (2010).

27. Shane (2012) and Puri and Zarutskie (2012).

28. Puri and Zarutskie (2012).

29. For some academic references on the entrepreneurial finance process, see Da Rin, Hellmann, and Puri (2013), Gorman and Sahlman (1989), and Kerr and Nanda (2015).

30. For some academic references on the "Fit" stage, see Bottazzi, Da Rin, and Hellmann (2016), Hegde and Tumlinson (2014), Hochberg, Ljungqvist, and Lu (2007), and Sorenson and Stuart (2001).

31. Murnieks et al. (2016).

32. Parhankangas and Ehrlich (2014).

33. Bernstein, Korteweg, and Laws (2017).

34. For some academic references on the Invest stage, see Hsu (2004), Kaplan and Strömberg (2003, 2004), Kerr, Lerner, and Schoar (2014), and Robb and Robinson (2012).

35. For some academic references on the Ride stage, see Bottazzi, Da Rin, and Hellmann (2008), Casamatta (2003), Croce, Martí, and Murtinu (2013), Hellmann and Puri (2002), Sapienza (1992), and Sapienza and Gupta (1994).

36. Dixit and Pindyck (1994), and Kerr, Nanda, and Rhodes-Kropf (2014).

37. For some academic references on the Exit stage, see Amit, Brander, and Zott (1998), Brav and Gompers (1997), Gompers (1996), Gompers and Lerner (1999), Lerner (1994), and Puri and Zarutskie (2012).

38. PitchBook-NVCA Venture Monitor, retrieved on November 12, 2018 from https://pitchbook.com/news/reports/2q-2018-pitchbook-nvca-venture-monitor.

39. References on Pandora's Box include Clifford (2007), Rao (2011), Panchadar and Sharma (2018), and Wasserman and Maurice (2008). See also Pandora Media's IPO prospectus and S-1 form, available at https://www.sec.gov/edgar.shtml. For Spotify, see Dunbar, Foerster, and Mark (2018) and Bahler (2018).

40. Swift (2014).

41. Ante (2008).

42. Hsu and Kenney (2005).

43. A useful and concise summary of the voyages of Christopher Columbus can be found in Boorstin (1983).

44. Kerr and Nanda (2015) and Robb and Robinson (2012).

45. For some academic references on understanding the investor side, see Dimov and Shepherd (2005), Gompers et al. (2019), Metrick and Yasuda (2010a), and Sahlman (1990).

46. Hower (2013).

2

Evaluating Venture Opportunities

Learning Goals

In this chapter students will learn:

1. A structured framework for evaluating venture opportunities.
2. How to break down a business's value proposition into its individual components.
3. To assess the attractiveness, risks, and competitive advantages of a new venture.
4. How to perform due diligence on a new venture's business plan.

This chapter explains how to evaluate a venture opportunity. We introduce the Venture Evaluation Matrix (VE Matrix), a framework for assessing the prospects of a new business. The framework recognizes the importance of building a value proposition around a real customer need, a competitive solution, and a team able to execute its plans. Its matrix structure generates conclusions about the venture's attractiveness, risks, and potential competitive advantages. The VE Matrix can be used by investors to evaluate the strengths and weaknesses of business opportunities along multiple dimensions. It also helps entrepreneurs to anticipate investors' concerns and to structure their investor pitch. The chapter discusses how different investors take different approaches to business evaluation and explains how they practically make decisions.

2.1 Assessing Opportunities

Assessing venture opportunities is difficult. Picking good companies may account for as much as half of the success in venture investing.[1] Yet even the most experienced investors often make mistakes. Bessemer Ventures, a top-flight U.S. venture capital (VC) firm, openly lists the successful companies it turned down: Airbnb, Apple, eBay, Facebook, Google, Intel, and so on. One of the partners commented on why eBay had been rejected: "Stamps? Coins? Comic books? You've GOT to be kidding. No-brainer pass."[2] In the absence of perfect foresight, how should an investor evaluate an entrepreneur?

The starting point for any investment is the underlying business opportunity and the existence of a business model to make it profitable. There is no single definition of business model, a concept that emerged in the 1990s and is still evolving.[3] A useful definition for our purpose is the following: "A business model articulates the logic, the data and other evidence that support a value proposition for the customer, and a viable structure of revenues and costs for the enterprise delivering that value."[4] The business model concerns the logical structuring of all business components into a value-creating process, but it is not the business plan itself. Instead, a business plan contains, among other things, a description of the logic of the business model. This allows communication of the opportunity's value-creation potential to external parties, including investors.

Does the entrepreneur have an attractive opportunity that deserves the investor's attention? To answer this fundamental question, it helps to have a framework for evaluating the business opportunity, for understanding its business model, and for identifying the major business risks. A wide variety of frameworks are available to investors, ranging from more intuitive reasoning all the way to formal evaluation schemes. In this book we introduce our own, the Venture Evaluation Matrix.

2.1.1 The Venture Evaluation Matrix

A good evaluation framework needs to be based on fundamentals, should provide a comprehensive analysis, and ought to be easy to use and communicate. For this we introduce the Venture Evaluation Matrix, sometimes abbreviated to VE Matrix. We derived this proprietary framework ourselves, combining our knowledge of a considerable body of academic research, with decades of close personal interactions with practitioners. The framework is therefore grounded in academic fundamentals, drawing in particular on the entrepreneurship, strategic management, finance, and economics literature. At the same time, the framework is based on extensive observation of the practical difficulties that entrepreneurs face when pitching their ideas and that investors have when evaluating those ideas. The framework uses a matrix structure to highlight the logical connection between the main points of analysis. Figure 2.1 shows the VE Matrix.

The three columns identify the key players that define the business opportunity: the *Customer*, who has a need; the *Company*, which provides products or services to satisfy the customer's need; and the *Entrepreneur*, who pursues the opportunity. Relating this to economic fundamentals, we note that the analysis in the Customer column focuses on demand side factors, the analysis in the Company column focuses on supply side factors, and the analysis of the Entrepreneur column focuses on the people who bring demand and supply together. We can use a common analogy to interpret this in terms of horse racing. Focusing on the *Entrepreneur* is like betting on the jockey; emphasizing the *Company* is like betting on the horse; and concentrating on the *Customer* is (with a slight stretch of the analogy) like betting on the racetrack.

Venture Evaluation Matrix	Customer	Company	Enterpreneur
Value Proposition	Need	Solution	Team
Industry	Market	Competition	Network
Strategy	Sales	Production	Organization

Figure 2.1. The Venture Evaluation Matrix.

The three rows identify three fundamental perspectives for evaluating business opportunities. The *Value proposition* perspective describes how the company hopes to create economic value. This provides a *micro* perspective about what the company is doing at its core. The *Industry* perspective characterizes the environment within which the company operates. It takes a *macro* perspective of looking at the broader context that will affect the company.[5] The *Strategy* perspective explains how the company plans to capture the value it creates and thus generate profits. It is concerned with the process of how the company plans to establish itself, thus taking a *dynamic* perspective.

Let us briefly consider the results from a survey of venture capital firms conducted by Gompers, Gornall, Kaplan, and Strebulaev.[6] When asked about their most important criterion for selecting investments, 47% answered it was the team, which corresponds to the *Entrepreneur* column. Another 13% answered product and 10% business model, which corresponds to the *Company* column. Moreover, 8% answered market and 6% industry, which corresponds to the *Customer* column. Of the remaining answers, the most important was investor fit (14%), which we will address with the MATCH tool explained in Section 7.3.3. Interestingly, only 1% considered valuation the most important criterion. This does not mean that valuation is irrelevant, but it suggests that before looking at financial deal aspects, investors first want to get comfortable with the business fundamentals.

To properly understand the VE Matrix, in Sections 2.2 and 2.3 we discuss a large number of economic, business, and strategy fundamental concepts. In Sections 2.4 and 2.5, we then show how to practically apply these concepts. In order to make the discussion of the fundamentals more accessible, Section 2.1.2 first introduces the WorkHorse case study.

2.1.2 The WorkHorse Case Study

To illustrate how to use the VE Matrix, we will use a running example. In fact, this running example is the beginning of a fictional case study that will accompany us throughout the book. We purposely use a fictional example because it enables us to illustrate a maximum number of pedagogical points. However, the case study is very realistic and can be thought of as a compendium of the experiences of many entrepreneurial companies. The choice of characters is meant to capture the global nature of modern entrepreneurship. Each segment of the case study will be placed in a separately numbered insert. WorkHorse Box 2.1 is the first one.

WorkHorse Box 2.1 Introducing WorkHorse

Astrid Dala put down her iPhone with a slight tremble in the hand. She had just shattered her mother's dream of raising a daughter who would one day win the Nobel Prize in Physics. She had called her mother in Sweden from Ann Arbor (Michigan, US) to tell her that she had quit her doctoral studies at the University of Michigan (UofM). She was starting a company with three friends. Brandon Potro was an MBA student at the UofM, who had been thinking of becoming an entrepreneur ever since watching movies about Steve Jobs. It was the summer of 2019, his MBA was drawing to a close, and he quickly became excited when he heard Astrid's idea. Bharat Marwari, Astrid's brilliant lab colleague, was more cautious and needed some convincing. Being the only family member to ever attend university made him the pride of his family. He hadn't mustered the courage yet to tell his parents about the start-up. Finally, Annie (Xinjin) Ma had come to the UofM after finishing her engineering undergraduate at Shanghai Jiao Tong University. For her, university was just a preparation for doing something practical. The start-up was a big relief for her: "finally something real."

Astrid's idea was to build a new portable solar power generator. Based on technological breakthroughs in solar technology from her lab, she thought they could design a lightweight portable generator with a capacity for medium-sized electrical devices, such as air conditioning units, microwave ovens, electric chainsaws, and so on. In her childhood days in Sweden, Astrid had often been camping and had wished for a power supply to use simple devices such as electric stove or fans. She shared her idea with Brandon, whom she trusted not only as a friend, but also as a hard-nosed businessman. She was encouraged by his enthusiasm. Upon his recommendation, she brought Bharat into the conversation. He was by far the smartest scientist she had ever met. As for Annie, Astrid initially met her at a riding event. Both were members of the UofM's riding club, and both shared a passion for horses. Ironically, Brandon had separately met Annie at a Hackathon held at the business school's entrepreneurship center. He remembered her for her practical "duct tape" approach of solving engineering problems. When he suggested bringing her along to an early brainstorming session, Astrid was immediately enthusiastic, though Bharat seemed ambivalent.

In the following months, the four met regularly to further discuss the idea. Things started to come together when Brandon's uncle JP (for Juan Pedro) offered to invest $80K to help them get going. Brandon was weeks away from completing his MBA, Annie her engineering master's degree, and neither had a job lined up. Things were more difficult for Astrid, who had two more years before completing her PhD. After weeks of soul searching and with some trepidation, she finally mustered the courage to call her mother and tell her that the four of them were starting a new company. Brandon and Annie did the same, but Bharat didn't think the time was right yet to tell his parents.

To name the new company, Astrid, Brandon, Bharat, and Annie, briefly considered using their initials, but then went for a less glamorous, more practical company name: "WorkHorse." They all shared an affection for horses and felt that the name reflected their energetic work spirit. Besides, their power generators would put amazing horse power to work.

Another exciting development was that Astrid had recently met Michael Archie. He was a wealthy UofM alum who had successfully sold his company a few years ago. He was now making angel investments in university-related startups. Michael was intrigued by the idea and the team and asked them to send over their business plan. The problem was that the four founders weren't exactly sure what Michael wanted. Brandon shrugged his shoulders; in the movies he had watched, Steve Jobs always just walked into the room and gave a passionate speech. Astrid realized that what they needed was a simple but comprehensive framework for presenting their business opportunity. Where to find that? She vaguely recalled her mother's last words of wisdom at the end of that difficult phone call. . . "Well, OK, do it if you have to, but at least make sure to use the Venture Evaluation Matrix."

2.2 Explaining the Venture Evaluation Matrix

We now explain the meaning of each of the nine cells. For each one we discuss the core issues that an investor would care about. In principle, one could write a whole book for each cell, but our goal here is to provide a concise summary of the core issues at stake. For each cell we identify three core questions that investors should ask, and then we explain the underlying issues that they are likely to be concerned with. The three questions are meant to capture core aspects relevant to most ventures, but they can be changed depending on the industry and stage of the venture, as well as investors' investment philosophies.

2.2.1   Need

The first row of the VE Matrix looks at the value proposition, basically how the company plans to create value. The first cell considers the customer need. Put simply, without a real customer need, there is no business opportunity. The three questions to ask are:

1. What exactly is the customer need?
2. How strong is the need, and how well do customers recognize it?
3. How much is the customer able and willing to pay?

The first question every entrepreneur always needs to ask is what the customer need is. Working on a solution without first understanding whether it solves a real problem is a mistake made by many entrepreneurs. Understanding the need is related to identifying the initial target customer. This is not trivial. To begin with, the entrepreneur typically has a hypothesis about what the customer's need might be, but this hypothesis needs to be tested. The initial premise often turns out to be false. The real need may lie elsewhere or may have different features than initially envisioned. Field Marshall Helmuth Graf von Moltke famously said that no military campaign plan survives first contact with the enemy. Steve Blank, who is associated with the lean start-up movement we discuss in Box 2.5, notes that "no business plan survives its first contact with customers."[7] As the entrepreneur learns about customer need, she may find that the initially hypothesized customer has a different need, or that the need is there but concerns a different type of customer. Too many entrepreneurs focus on solving what *they* believe is the customer's need. The risk is "forcing" a solution to an alleged need before verifying the real need in the first place.

The second question looks at how compelling the need is. Customers, be they people or organizations, have a hierarchy of needs. Certain things they require ("must haves"), some they consider valuable but not essential ("nice to haves"), others are pleasant but not really needed ("so whats"), and many are simply not needed at all ("junk"). In a consumer-facing business model (i.e., business-to-consumer or B2C), consumer psychology matters. The psychologist Abraham Maslow describes a hierarchy of needs, with physiological needs (e.g., food) at the bottom, then safety needs (e.g. security), followed by love and belonging (e.g., friends), esteem (e.g., status), and finally self-actualization (e.g., creativity).[8] Medical or agricultural innovations appeal to our physiological needs, whereas social media respond to a human need for belonging and esteem.

In the case of a business-facing model (i.e., business-to-business or B2B), different considerations come into play. Corporations seek profits and efficiency, so the entrepreneur needs to generate a return on investment for the corporation or satisfies other corporate goals. This means enhancing the company's sales, generating cost savings, or contributing to other corporate agendas (e.g., public relations). When dealing with large corporations or other complex organizations, it can be challenging to identify who the true decision makers are and what exactly their objectives are. Moreover, in some industries, the adoption process involves an interplay of multiple actors. Selling to schools, for example, might require the buy-in of school administrators, teachers, parents, educational thought leaders, government regulators, and maybe even students.

One important issue for entrepreneurs is whether customers actually understand their own needs. Individuals may lack self-awareness, and organizations often display resistance to new product adoption.[9] They may have gotten used to their problems, taking them for granted. They may reject a novel idea simply because they are unable to envision how it fits into their existing environment. Experienced entrepreneurs pay less attention to what customers *say* and more to what they actually *do*. Henry Ford reportedly said: "If I had asked people what they wanted, they would have said faster horses." Box 2.1 discusses observational methods that help entrepreneurs to distinguish between what people truly want, which is often different from what they say they want.

The third question concerns how much customers are able and willing to pay. Ability to pay is an economic question about disposable income for individual customers and about availability of budgets for corporate customers. Many needs remain difficult to solve because no one can afford to pay for a solution. This limits the opportunities for entrepreneurs, unless they find novel ways to overcome these challenges. Social entrepreneurs, for example, sometimes develop hybrid business models that combine the needs of different customers and organizations.[10] A well-known (though not uncontroversial) example is TOMS: for every pair of shoes sold at market prices, the company donates another pair of shoes to some needy children in poor countries.[11]

Apart from the economic ability to pay, there is also the issue of willingness to pay. Some wealthy customers see the rationale for buying healthy food but remain unwilling to pay a higher price for it. Similarly, corporate buyers may like a new human resources support service but need to ensure it squares with budgeting. Assessing the true willingness to pay is often challenging, especially in the early stages of discovering customer needs. A customer's initial verbal enthusiasm may not reflect true intent. Until actual money is committed, true customer willingness remains uncertain.

WorkHorse Box 2.2 illustrates the Need analysis.

2.2.2   Solution

The second cell of the VE Matrix is about the solution to the customer's need, the direct counterpart to the first cell. Whereas the first cell looks at the demand side, the second cell looks at the supply side, asking how the entrepreneur intends to solve the customer need. At the core of every entrepreneurial venture is a proposed solution, a product or service that contains some innovation, that does something

WorkHorse Box 2.2   Need

The four founders of WorkHorse had many heated debates about the customer need for their solar power generator. Astrid was an avid hiker and had wished many times to have a source of power on her long multi-day adventures. However, none of the available power generators were sufficiently small and light to fit into her back pack. Brandon had spent his summers in Canada by the lake and had noticed that families going on camping trips often needed a lot of power, especially if they wanted to maintain certain comforts, such as running microwaves or recharging phones. Bharat had a different take, arguing that poor people in India and elsewhere often could not afford to pay their electricity bills and would therefore look for alternative sources of power. Annie noted that solar power generators might also be useful to many of the smaller manufacturing outlets that she had visited in China.

While the four founders believed that all these customer needs would ultimately prove to be important, they agreed to focus on one customer need at a time. They decided to focus on outdoor vacationers, the private individuals who would need power on their outdoor adventures, be it hiking, camping, or other. As they researched the opportunity, they obtained three main insights. First, customer interviews revealed a keen interest in solar power generators. They liked not having to carry fuel and appreciated something small and lightweight. Second, customers had a clear idea of what they wanted. Surprisingly, they focused on design, as they wanted power generators to have an attractive look. They were put off by the functional looks of the diesel generator which they considered to be a work tool, not something to take on a holiday. Third, customers were willing to pay prices similar to diesel generators but were reluctant to pay a lot more than that. They focused mainly on the price of the generator and did not take fuel savings into account for purchasing decisions.

better than previous solutions. The innovations can pertain to scientific or technical progress, to advances in design or production, or to novel business models, such as opening up new sales channels, or novel marketing approaches. The three questions to ask about the solution are:

1. Does the proposed solution solve the customer's need?
2. How does the proposed solution compare to the alternatives?
3. To what extent can the innovation be protected?

The first question looks at the innovation from a business perspective, asking whether it actually solves any customer need. Some entrepreneurs begin with an innovation and then seek to make it relevant to the customer, others start with a customer need and search for a solution to address it. Either way the innovation has to provide an effective solution to a real customer need. Many entrepreneurs struggle with this problem, especially when they have a technical background. They get carried away with the challenge of the innovation but fail to ask hard questions about how useful it actually is to users.

Many technological advances never live up to the hype that surrounds their initial discovery. Artificial blood substitutes or graphene metals might be considered examples of that. A new technology may turn out to work only under limiting conditions, or it may be accompanied by undesirable side effects. Even if the scientific breakthrough is real, there is still considerable risk scaling a technology from the lab to an industrial application. In nontechnical industries, there can be a similar temptation to get overly excited about a novel idea. Juicero received over $100M in venture capital funding to create a high-end personalized juice machine, the "Nespresso of juicing, "selling at $700.[12] However, the hype never materialized into significant sales, and the company closed down a few years later. Juicero was an elegant product that actually didn't solve any real problem. A different approach is to take advantage of deregulation of traditional businesses. Flixbus was founded in 2013 to offer long-distance bus routes, initially in Germany and later across Europe. Its European success brought it to open a U.S. subsidiary in 2018. Flixbus outsources bus riding to local companies and focuses on its technology platform. The company attracted five rounds of venture capital and in 2019 was considering an IPO.[13]

The second question suggests a comparison with alternative solutions. An innovation needs to be distinctly better than the existing solutions. Small incremental innovations typically don't stand a chance. Standing out requires that the innovation is clearly better than its alternatives in some important dimension, and it shouldn't be clearly inferior in other dimensions. Sometimes a technologically superior product loses out in the market because it is only better in a technical sense but weaker in terms of other relevant product attributes. A classic example is Sony's Betamax, which had better resolution and image quality than the competing VHS standard. It failed in part because it could only handle shorter movies. This did not meet the needs of movie studios, which wanted to fit an entire movie onto a single tape.[14] To compare a solution to its alternatives also requires looking at its economic viability. Sometimes a better solution doesn't work because it is simply too expensive to produce or its area of application remains too narrow. It could also be too expensive, either because of its cost or because it requires additional adoption costs—think of training employees to use a new machine. In addition, there is the question of longevity. Every innovation has a limited time horizon before it gets superseded by something better.[15]

The third question concerns the ability to protect the solution. There are two main ways of protecting innovations against imitation: (1) intellectual property (IP) rights such as patents, trademarks, copyrights, or industrial designs, and (2) strategic barriers to imitation, such as lead time or trade secrets.[16] If the solution is based on some IP, then the relevant issue is how strong the IP is. This depends on the nature of the technological advance and on the way the IP is defined. The quality of a country's legal enforcement also matters. However, even with good legal enforcement, it is sometimes difficult to protect the IP. This is because one can only protect the technology, not the solution itself. Competitors can find legal ways of imitating the functional benefits of the proposed solution without using any of the protected IP. Consequently, the second type of protection, namely, strategic barriers to imitation, ultimately matters most. The relevant issue here is whether the entrepreneur has some specific knowledge, skills, or complementary assets that help shield the solution from imitation, at least for some period of time. These resources and capabilities protect the company best when they are difficult to replicate.[17]

In the context of the first two cells (need and solution), it is useful to briefly address a central issue in entrepreneurship, namely, how entrepreneurs come up with the right solutions that actually solve real customer needs. Box 2.1 briefly introduces design thinking and observational techniques, which are part of a modern entrepreneur's toolset.

WorkHorse Box 2.3 illustrates the analysis of the Solution cell.

Box 2.1 Design Thinking and Observational Methods

A common misconception is that entrepreneurs are inventors who discover the solution in a single Aha! moment. In reality, solutions are often found through an iterative process of experimenting across many different possibilities and taking in feedback from multiple sources. The design thinking movement has tried to provide some methodologies to the process of discovering solution. Design thinking is a broad concept that has affected a wide array of creative activities: from architecture to social work to innovation to business. There is no single definition of what design thinking is, but the founder of the Stanford Design School suggests the following four fundamental principles.[18] First, all design is human-centric; second, designers retain ambiguity to remain open to different forms of experimentation; third, all design is redesign, since technologies and social circumstances are in constant flux; and fourth, making designs tangible helps communication with others.

The actual design processes differ by application areas, but a common theme is that designers develop empathy with the user.[19] The designers need an intuitive, even visceral understanding of the problems they are addressing. A variety of tools can help entrepreneurs (or indeed investors) to better understand true customer needs. Anthropologists specialize in observing people of all walks of life, taking special care that their presence interferes as little as possible with truthful observations of human behaviors.[20] Entrepreneurs are increasingly adopting their techniques, directly observing customers, employees, experts, and others. Some observational techniques require physical observation, and others focus on online behaviors. There are also some ethical concerns one needs to be sensitive to, and some observational methods require consent.[21]

Design thinking and the related observational techniques make it clear that no solution can ever be found without staying close to the problem. This fundamental insight is also at the basis of the lean start-up movement, which we discuss in Box 2.5.

WorkHorse Box 2.3   Solution

WorkHorse's core technology was based on a scientific breakthrough in the way solar energy was captured with light rather than heat. The research had been led by the director of the lab, Dr. Daniela Dasola, but Bharat was behind several of the key scientific advances. The UofM technology transfer office took care of patenting the scientific discoveries, in time before the researchers published their research in a prestigious academic journal. In addition, Astrid, who worked in the same lab, had developed some lightweight materials that could substantially reduce the size and weight of the generators.

WorkHorse's planned first product was a small generator provisionally named WonderFoal, which was ideally suited for hikers. The intent for the second product, code-named NokotaStar, was a compact but substantially more powerful generator suitable for campers. The four founders were well aware of the dangers of developing products purely with a technical lens. They therefore started to adopt some design principles, spending time talking to potential users and where possible simply observing them using the existing products. Based on this observational research, the founders were confident that their product would constitute a clear improvement over existing solutions. Their solar generators were much smaller and lighter than standard diesel generators. Having noted people's irritation with the noise levels of traditional generators, they also ensured that their solution was considerably quieter.

While the technology and design were new and better than anything else available in the market, the founders worried that the technology could easily be imitated. Annie remarked that some of the manufacturers she knew in China could easily build something similar in a matter of months.

2.2.3   Team

A strong value proposition needs not only a clear customer need and a convincing solution, but also an entrepreneur who can implement the solution.[22] The third cell in the first row therefore looks at the entrepreneurial team. This is particularly important for those investors who prefer to "bet on the jockey rather than the horse." In this view, the most important asset of the firm is the human capital of the founders. In the words of Arthur Rock, one of the fathers of the VC industry: "Good ideas and good products are a dime a dozen. Good execution and good management—in other words good people—are rare."[23] The core argument is that a good idea alone is worthless if there is no entrepreneur to turn it into a successful company. The original idea behind Microsoft, for example, was nothing special, but Bill Gates turned it into something much bigger. Moreover, even if the initial idea is proven wrong, a good entrepreneurial team adapts until a viable business model is found. William Wrigley

Jr. created a billion-dollar chewing gum business by recognizing that his customers valued the gum he was giving away as a promotional item much more than the soap he was trying to sell. Twitter was born when iTunes destroyed Odeo's business model. A team inside Odeo consisting of Jack Dorsey, Noah Glass, Biz Stone, and Evan Williams brainstormed together and came up with the idea for Twitter. In all these examples, the biggest credit goes to the founder team, not to the idea.

The third cell of the value proposition row therefore looks at the entrepreneurial team. The three questions to ask are:

1. Do the founders have the required skills and experience?
2. Do the founders have sufficient motivation and commitment?
3. Is the founder team complementary and cohesive?

The first question concerns the skills and experience of the founders. Something every investor wants to know about the entrepreneur is whether she has done this before. Box 2.2 reports results from academic studies that look at the role of prior entrepreneurial experience.

In addition to prior entrepreneurial experience, investors pay attention to industry experience, as well as experience in key functional areas such as marketing, sales, or operations. Interestingly, many investors consider prior experience in finance or consulting largely irrelevant. Although many entrepreneurs acquire their experience at established corporations, investors also value experience at younger growth-oriented businesses, which are sometimes considered better learning

---

Box 2.2 The Importance of Being a Serial Entrepreneur

Entrepreneurs who previously founded a company are commonly referred to as serial entrepreneurs. Several academic studies compare the experiences of serial entrepreneurs with those of novices. One study of VC-backed start-ups by Gompers, Lerner, Scharfstein, and Kovner finds that previously successful serial entrepreneurs had a success rate of 30%, compared to a success rate of 22% for previously unsuccessful serial entrepreneurs and 21% for first-time entrepreneurs.[24] The study also suggests that the higher success rate of serial entrepreneurs is related to their ability to time the market correctly.[25]

Do investors appreciate serial entrepreneurs? Another academic study by Hsu finds that serial entrepreneurs (especially successful ones) have a better chance of receiving funding than novice entrepreneurs.[26] They also receive higher valuations, meaning that investors are willing to pay more for investing companies led by serial entrepreneurs (we explain valuations in Chapter 4). One surprising finding from a study by Bengtsson is that serial entrepreneurs often change investors from one venture to the next.[27] They have no problem doing so because all investors recognize the value of serial entrepreneurs.

grounds for managing disruptive technologies and business models.[28] In addition to prior experience, investors also look at the broader skill set, including relevant educational achievements.[29] Having an MBA is widely perceived as a plus, and technical founders benefit from showing evidence of advanced formal training. While specialization is important, at very early stages founders must also be able to adapt and be "jacks-of-all-trades."[30]

The second question concerns the founders' motivation and commitment. Making money is an important motivator of entrepreneurial activity. On its own, however, it can be a poor motivator. Financial rewards are uncertain and happen too far out in the future to motivate entrepreneurs on a daily basis. For that there needs to be enthusiasm for the underlying activity and the entrepreneurial process itself. Seeing such "intrinsic motivation" assures investors that the entrepreneurs will not give up in the face of inevitable disappointments and setbacks. Quoting again Arthur Rock: "I am looking for entrepreneurs who ask: 'How can I make this business a success'—not 'How do I make a fortune?' "[31] Furthermore, academic studies suggest that entrepreneurs tend to be risk-tolerant, ambitious, and self-confident.[32]

In addition to being highly motivated, good entrepreneurs are infectious; that is, they inspire the people around them. How entrepreneurs talk to investors is clearly part of this ability to inspire, but investors also pay close attention to how entrepreneurs communicate with their customers or employees. Their communication style is an indicator of how effective they are within their own business environment and more generally how good they are in the process of mobilizing resources (see Box 1.1).

In this context, it is also worth mentioning the issue of integrity. Investors give the entrepreneur their money, so they need to trust them. It takes years to build trust, but it can be lost in seconds. Integrity means honest dealing and honest communication, regardless of how bad the situation is. Investors frequently seek the opinions of others about an entrepreneur, so integrity is not limited to the interactions with the investors, it also concerns the entrepreneurs' broader reputation in the community.

The third question looks at the team as a whole, how well the different founders complement each other; and how cohesive they are as a team. Having some diversity in terms of skills, both hard and soft, is beneficial to tackle the diverse set of challenges facing a new venture.[33] However, it is also important that the founders share a common vision and a common passion for the venture.[34] Every team can have some healthy level of conflict, although excessive conflict can ruin even the most promising venture. A red flag for investors is a serious sign of team discord.[35]

What about solo founders? The majority of technology start-ups have founder teams, but many companies are also started by a single individual.[36] Some investors might see this as a negative signal, worrying that solo founders are too control-oriented, unwilling to share decision making with others. Other investors argue that having a solo founder is fine, as long as she shows good leadership and is willing to listen.

It should be noted that an assessment of the quality of a team cannot be done in isolation but requires a simultaneous evaluation of the business challenges (Section 2.3.4). A medical device firm requires a different skill set than a mobile app. Similarly, an early-stage venture may require more creative types, whereas a later-stage venture may require more execution-oriented managers. Importantly, the team is responsible for the overall direction of the firm and must therefore have sufficient breadth of skills to look after all aspects of the business.

WorkHorse Box 2.4 illustrates the Team cell.

WorkHorse Box 2.4   Team

The four founders brought different skills and experiences to the team, each contributing to the venture in distinct ways.

Astrid Dala was clearly the leader of the team. She had an undergraduate degree in electrical engineering from the University of Stockholm and had worked several years as an engineer at Ericsson before starting her doctoral studies in the U.S. In addition to being technically competent, she was highly organized and had excellent people skills. She worked hard, was always on top of things, and often helped others to reach their potential.

Brandon Potro had an undergraduate degree in political science from Arizona State University. Ever since being a volunteer with the U.S. Peace Corps, he had a special interest in international relations and business. Throughout high school and college he worked for several smaller businesses. As he spoke fluent Spanish, he often helped with imports from Mexico. After the U.S. Peace Corps, he spent two years working for a large U.S. media company. Brandon had a talent for numbers and loved investing in the stock market. He also reveled in talking to people and building relationships. His easy way of communicating made him popular with engineers and businesspeople alike.

Bharat Marwari studied undergraduate physics at the India Institute of Technology in Bangalore. He won a prestigious scholarship to study at the UofM for his PhD. He came from a poor background, and in order to support his family back home he accepted some scientific consulting work on the side. He found it interesting, but sometimes a bit mundane and distracting. He was shy and preferred to work alone but had a friendly and calm demeanor.

Annie (Xinjin) Ma had studied industrial engineering in Shanghai. She had worked part-time in various smaller manufacturing plants where she was faced with a wide variety of technical problems. Moving to the U.S. for her master's degree, however, had proven to be an entirely different challenge. Academia wasn't her cup of tea, and she often found herself impatient with what she considered slow ways of doing things. She preferred a "quick and dirty" experimental approach of getting things done.

The four founders shared a common passion for using solar power to save the planet and improve people's lives. As a team they had established a clear division of tasks and started to develop good working relationships. However, they had not yet broached some of the more sensitive issues, such whether all of them would quit their studies or what the division of founder equity should be. So far, they hadn't hired any employees.

2.2.4 Market

We now move to the second row of the VE Matrix, which takes a broader industry perspective to examine the environment the company operates in. In the first row, we took a micro perspective and looked at the value proposition itself; in this second row, we adopt a macro perspective, asking how this value proposition sits within the broader industry context.

The first cell of the second row looks at the market. Recall that the first cell of the first row was about a qualitative understanding of individual customer needs. We now turn to a more quantitative analysis of the overall market. The three questions are:

1. How large is the target market?
2. How fast will the target market grow?
3. How will the customer adopt?

The first question looks at market size to define the scale of the opportunity. To estimate the size of the target market, we first need to understand what it is. This means looking at the scope of the relevant market. Suppose we were interested in some kind of a drone start-up. Are we interested in the entire market for drones or in just close-range drones? Two key numbers describe a market size at any point in time: the size of the overall market and the size of the target market. The first is a headline number that is often used to indicate the economic importance of the industry. However, this is not the relevant number for assessing the scale of the business opportunity. The second number is more relevant, indicating the portion of the overall market the company actually targets. The overall market can be subdivided into different segments in order to identify the target market. For example, the overall market may be the entire drone market, and the target market the close-range consumer-oriented drone market. Companies may try to address several segments at the same time, or sequentially. Moreover, it is common for start-ups to "pivot" from one market segment to another (see Box 1.1). Note that the term *pivot* is commonly associated with start-ups that implement a change of strategy. While they take a new course, they do not abandon everything they have done up to that point.[37]

For simplicity we emphasize two numbers: overall market and target market. A popular business framework further decomposes the overall market into two numbers called TAM and SAM.[38] TAM stands for Total Available Market (or Total Addressable Market), and SAM stands for Serviced Available Market (or Serviced Addressable Market). TAM includes potential customers who have not yet been reached, whereas SAM only includes customers that are already served.

Within a target market entrepreneurs distinguish different sets of customers, asking themselves which ones they should focus on. This analysis forces them to be specific about the relevant subset of customers, a first step toward a focused sales strategy (Section 2.2.7). For example, a company may define its target market as the consumer-oriented market for close-range drones and will distinguish between high-end customers involving mostly specialist retailers and low-end budget customers involving mostly online sales. This analysis should also include the intensity of competition, which we examine in Section 2.2.5. Note also that the distinction of customers within a target market is the basis for estimating the product's market share, and ultimately revenues, something we discuss in Section 3.4.

The second question prompts us to look at market growth. Entrepreneurs often focus on changing markets where there is innovation and growth. The current market size is thus a misleading metric for market potential. We therefore need a framework for thinking about the likely evolution of the market. For this it is useful to introduce a simple model of market adoption that is based on the industry S-curve.[39] Figure 2.2 depicts such an S-curve.

Consider a population of potential customers that have different needs for a new product or service. The upper graph in the figure shows the distribution of

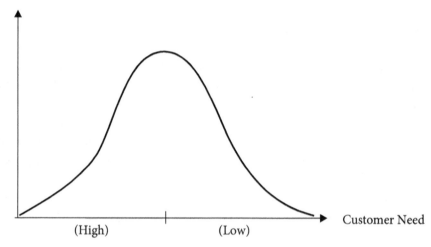

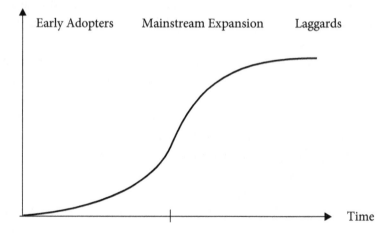

Figure 2.2. The industry S-Curve.

how much different customers value the product. For convenience we place higher value customers to the left. The highest value customers need the product the most and are the first to adopt it. If the value distribution has a bell-shaped distribution, then the growth of the market follows an S-curve, as depicted in the lower graph of the figure. The horizontal axis indicates time. The vertical axis shows market size, which can be measured by revenue or number of customers. In the early days of an industry, market growth is slow as companies try to engage the early adopters. As the industry matures, the customer base expands substantially, generating rapid growth. In the upper graph this happens near the top of the bell-shaped curve, and in the lower graph this corresponds to the steep middle section of the S-curve. Eventually, the market gets saturated and growth slows down.

Figure 2.2 provides a useful, albeit highly simplified, picture of market growth. In reality, there is considerable uncertainty about whether and when the market will take off. Some new markets take off, some level off, and others fade away. For example, a new technology may challenge the dominant design of an existing industry. Either it establishes itself and becomes the new standard, or it fails to become the dominant design. It may then either find a smaller niche application or disappear altogether.[40] Also, there isn't just a single S-curve; instead the process starts again whenever an industry goes through another innovation cycle.

Timing the market is a key challenge for entrepreneurs. If they enter too late, others will already have seized the opportunity, but if they enter too early, they will fail to get traction. There is thus only a limited window of opportunity where entrepreneurs have a reasonable chance of success. This happens typically at the bottom of the S-curve, just around the time where it begins to slope upward. The problem is obviously that it is difficult to recognize when this happens. Most important, it is difficult to distinguish those opportunities where the S-curve takes off, versus those where it never goes anywhere.

Even if there are clear signs of the emergence of a new market, estimating its size and growth potential is far from trivial. How can you estimate the size of a market that does not yet exist? This requires projecting the size and shape of the S-curve without having reliable information about the underlying distribution of customer values. Such estimates are by their nature speculative and imprecise. Importantly, they are not based on actual data, but instead on indirect data extrapolation, typically using multiple data sources. The goal here is not to find a single right number but to find reasonable ranges. In Section 3.6.4. we explore this further in the context of sensitivity analysis.

The third question concerns the nature of the adoption process. In the context of the S-curve, this means asking who exactly the early adopters on the left-hand side of the bell-shaped curve in the upper graph are. In practice, the entrepreneur searches for potential customers that are particularly eager. In addition to having a clear need, those early adopters have a willingness to take a risk on an unproven solution. This might require novel ways of segmenting the market, distinguishing customers not necessarily by their tangible characteristics (e.g., large versus small corporations), but by their behavioral characteristics (e.g., past track record of adopting innovations).

The details of the adoption process differ by industries. Particularly interesting cases are industries with so-called network externalities. These are industries where customers are more likely to adopt a product if many other customers are doing the same. Telephones are a classical example: a single telephone would hardly be useful; the value of a telephone line is increasing exponentially in the size of the network.[41] Social networks like Facebook or Tencent, or car-hailing companies like Uber or Didi Chuxing, are modern examples of services that become more valuable to each customer when the overall customer base grows. The adoption process in markets with network externalities can have tipping properties where small differences among competing platforms can swing the market one way or the other. In the end, the winner takes most of the market because once a critical mass of customers has adopted one platform, new customers also prefer that platform due to network externalities.[42]

WorkHorse Box 2.5 shows how to perform market analysis.

WorkHorse Box 2.5   Market

WorkHorse operated in the market for solar power generators but recognized this to be far too broad a market definition to be meaningful. For one, there was a very large segment for industrial generators that was irrelevant for the company. It therefore considered its relevant segment to be the consumer-oriented market for solar generators. It further segmented this market into portable versus stationary generators, and therefore defined its target market as the consumer-oriented market for portable solar generators. Within this, it identified two main geographic segments, a North American market (comprising the U.S. and Canada), and a European market (focused mostly on western Europe).

As part of market research, Brandon found out that the North American market for consumer-oriented solar power generators was estimated to be $1B in 2020. He estimated the portable segment of this market to be approximately 10%, and therefore considered the North American target to be $100M in 2020. Experts estimated this market to grow at an impressive 30% for the foreseeable future. Based on this, Brandon estimated that the North American target market would grow from $100M in 2020 to $371M in 2025. Estimates for Europe were slightly harder to come by, given the more fragmented nature of the market. Based on various calibrations, Brandon assumed that the European market would be half the size of the North American market. However, he estimated it had an even higher growth rate of 35%. Brandon thus estimated the European target market would grow from $50M in 2020 to $224M in 2025. The total target market (comprising North America and Europe) was therefore expected to grow from $150M in 2020 to almost $600M by 2025. The table below shows his calculations.

Market size ($M)	2020	2021	2022	2023	2024	2025
North America						
Overall market	1,000	1,300	1,690	2,197	2,856	3,713
Projected target market share	10%	10%	10%	10%	10%	10%
Projected target market	100	130	169	220	286	371
Europe						
Overall market	500	675	911	1,230	1,661	2,242
Projected target market share	10%	10%	10%	10%	10%	10%
Projected target market	50	68	91	123	166	224
Total projected target market	150	198	260	343	452	595

The question of what customers would be adopting portable solar generators first remained a topic of debate. The four founders strongly believed that the outdoor hiking and camping market was full of eager early adopters but admitted that further market research was needed to confirm their hunches.

2.2.5 Competition

Entrepreneurial ventures can create substantial customer value but still fail to capture any of it. Competitors can drive prices down, take away market shares, and sometimes push innovators out of the market altogether. The Competition cell therefore asks who the competitors are and how they compete. No company is ever the sole provider of a solution to a customer problem; there are always direct or indirect ways in which other companies compete for the same clients. Moreover, competition is inherently dynamic, so we need to consider not only current but also future potential competitors. The three questions to ask about the competition are:

1. Who are the current and future competitors?
2. What is the nature of competition?
3. How can the venture differentiate itself?

The first question is who the current competitors are. We distinguish two types of competitors: established corporations and other start-ups. Established corporations often appear to be fearsome competitors. Investors easily get cold feet when they hear that an Apple, British Petroleum, or Samsung might be competing in the target market. Yet it is easy to misunderstand the role of established corporations in the entrepreneurial ecosystem, for two reasons. First, while established corporations have more resources, they also tend to be inert, focused on selling their current product, and preoccupied with servicing their existing customers. Blockbuster did that when

Netflix entered its market, and established airlines did that when low-cost airlines first challenged their business model.[43] Second, many established companies deliberately wait for entrepreneurs to prove the viability of new ideas. Many innovations are initially pursued by entrepreneurs, but once their product or service is taking off, established companies take notice. They are then faced with a build-or-buy decision. Either they enter the market and build up their own presence, or they acquire one of the start-ups already in the market. Microsoft, for example, built some of its new products, such as the Xbox, but acquired other important products, such as Skype. From the perspective of start-ups, the question is whether established corporations should be thought of as future competitors or potential acquirers.

In addition to established corporations, entrepreneurs should always expect competition from other entrepreneurs—current and future. For most start-ups it is safe to assume that somewhere else in the world there is some other entrepreneur pursuing similar ideas. When Mark Zuckerberg launched Facebook in early 2004, for example, it already had several other social network competitors, such as MySpace.com and Friendster.[44] In addition, one should always expect future entrants. Once the company has shown the viability of its own product, it should assume that a large number of imitators will try to replicate and improve on the company's success.

The second question looks at the nature of competition. Some industries witness fierce competition among rival companies, whereas others experience milder competitive behaviors. The degree of competition depends on many factors, including barriers to entry, the extent of differentiation, or the scrutiny of regulators. One important issue is the relative importance of price versus nonprice competition. In industries where the market is saturated and technology is mature, competition tends to focus on prices. In other industries there is substantial differentiation in nonprice features. In the earlier stages of an industry, nonprice competition often focuses on technology, customer segmentation, setting a dominant design, and product differentiation.

This bring us to the third question, which looks at how companies differentiate. This can happen through a distinct product offering, as well as a focus on specific customer segments. It matters because it is the basis of charging higher margins and moving the company toward profitability. In the beginning, start-ups often differentiate themselves through continuous experimentation and learning, rapid adoption of new ideas, and faster execution. Over time, the company finds a stronger identity in terms of its products and market niches.

Sometimes there is also the possibility of turning competitors into allies, coopting them by sharing the benefits of the innovation.[45] This may involve delegating certain activities to the competitor or sharing the product development process to create a superior product that is then jointly marketed. Cooperating with competitors remains a delicate issue that strategic management scholars study with great interest. Box 2.3 briefly looks at some of their key frameworks and insights.

WorkHorse Box 2.6 illustrates the analysis of Competition.

Box 2.3 Competition and Cooperation Between Start-ups and Industry Leaders

The archetypal David and Goliath story is that a start-up challenges an established industry leader. After some initial challenges, the start-up outwits the giant and establishes itself as the new industry leader. There are several reasons why Goliath might lose. Incumbent leaders can be complacent and slow to respond. They may be reluctant to cannibalize their existing products and locked in to existing business models that make it difficult to respond.[46] Incumbents' core competencies also go hand in hand with "core rigidities" that make it difficult to change direction.[47] While each of these explanations can be fit to some examples, there are also many other examples where the David and Goliath story doesn't apply. For one, many David actually lose in reality. Of particular interest to us, some Davids seek to cooperate with Goliath.

To understand how start-ups interact with established companies, let us first differentiate between the early-stage versus later-stage start-ups. At the later stages, established companies often acquire successful start-ups, precisely because they missed the new market. Facebook's $1B acquisition of Instagram is a case in point. The question we are interested in here is how early-stage start-ups compete or collaborate with incumbent leaders.[48] In principle, there are many benefits to cooperation. The start-up can simply slot itself into existing production, marketing, and distribution arrangements, thereby avoiding the costs of establishing it all by itself. The two firms might also collude on prices, thereby protecting their profits. This arrangement is unlikely to benefit customers, but given the small size of the start-up, it is also unlikely to attract the attention of antitrust authorities.

The main problem is that cooperation is not easy. An industry leader might take advantage of its position of power. In the process of setting up a cooperative agreement, the industry leader may obtain proprietary information about the start-up concerning not only IP (see Section 2.2.2), but also its customers, strategy, and other aspects of its business. The incumbent might use this information and break off the cooperation, or it might use a break-off threat to extract significant concessions from the start-up. One empirical study by Gans, Hsu, and Stern finds that cooperation strategies for start-ups are more likely when IP is well protected. [49] The study also finds that having venture capital funding helps start-ups broker deals with industry leaders.

Beyond the question of whether to compete or cooperate, there is the question of how to go on about it. One useful framework distinguishes between fast execution-driven business models versus ambitious control-oriented business models.[50] Consider first the case where the start-up decides to compete. An execution-driven strategy aims at disrupting the industry leader by being faster and nimbler, where the start-up remains focused on a specific and narrow value proposition. Netflix beat Blockbuster by focusing on an alternative distribution channel, first via mail and later via online streaming technology. A control-oriented strategy aims at creating an entire new product/service architecture that gives customers a comprehensive new solution. Uber's approach to competing against the traditional taxi industry is a case in point. Consider next the case where the start-up cooperates. The control-oriented approach is to go the licensing route, where the start-up mainly provides IP. Dolby managed to build a significant company around its core IP portfolio. For many start-ups, however, the licensing strategy implies remaining small and narrowly focused on developing technologies. An alternative is an execution-oriented cooperation strategy, where the start-up contributes something specific to an existing value chain. The Indian outsourcing giant Infosys, for example, created a business model of working for industry leaders by providing specific low-cost services while ensuring not to disrupt their partners' core businesses. The contrast between a disruptive and a value chain strategy can also be seen in the automotive sector. Tesla clearly chose to disrupt the industry. At the same time, numerous less famous start-ups focus on providing specific new components to existing car manufacturers. Overall, we note that there are numerous ways for start-up to compete or cooperate with industry incumbents. Not every David battles Goliath.

WorkHorse Box 2.6   Competition

WorkHorse's founders focused their competitive analysis solely on the solar product segment of the portable power generator market. They identified a large list of current competitors and an even longer list of potential entrants. To characterize the nature of competition, they found it useful to condense the analysis into a 2-by-2 matrix that identified four prototypical competitors. For each prototype, the table below lists one of the many competitors that WorkHorse had identified.

Competitors	Current	Future
Established players	Honda	Black & Decker
Start-ups	YouSolar	Chinese competitors

WorkHorse considered its product to be technically superior to that of all its current competitors, including Honda's popular models. Some of the current competitors, like YouSolar, were start-ups with a similar power performance. However, WorkHorse's design was considerably smaller and lighter. Yet the company was worried that several of the established players in the portable diesel generator market, such as Black & Decker, might consider entering the growing solar product segment. Annie was also convinced that it was only a matter of time before Chinese competitors would flood the market with simple inexpensive solar generators.

WorkHorse thought that it had several ways of differentiating itself from the competition. First, there was the patented technology. Second, their device was smaller and lighter. Third, Astrid thought that WorkHorse's designs would be far more elegant and fun than those of her competitors. Unfortunately, it was not clear how long these advantages would last, given that technology improved continuously.

2.2.6 Network

There is an old wisdom that it matters less what you know than who you know. This notion also applies to entrepreneurs who rely on networks to build their ventures. Recall from Box 1.1 that the core challenges for the entrepreneur are to gather resources and manage uncertainty. Networks help them not only to access critical resources, but also to obtain information to de-risk the venture. The third cell in the industry row therefore looks at the founders' network. This cell tries to understand their position within the industry. The three key questions to ask are:

1. What is the reputation of the founder team?
2. What networks does the team have access to?
3. How does the team forge and maintain new relationships?

The first question concerns the reputation and professional standing of the team. Networks play a key role in building a new business, as they affect access to information and industry resources. Investors therefore check to find out whether the founders are well considered within their industry. With the rise of online social networks, investors also look at online sources for assessing the reputation of the team.

The second question concerns the current contacts of the founder team. Mapping the network provides information about how connected the founders are in the broader environment. In addition, start-ups leverage the networks of their close advisors. One of the key roles of a board of directors in entrepreneurial companies is to navigate networks to allow the company to access resources (Section 8.2.2). In addition, a board of advisors (sometimes also known as scientific advisory board) is meant to enlarge the company's network.

How can we make sense of the structure of a network, and how can we assess its quality? Box 2.4 discusses some of the core concepts from modern network analysis.

The third question concerns the founders' ability to create and sustain relationships. As the company grows, new needs emerge. Rather than only looking at a team's existing relationships, one may question whether the team has the

Box 2.4 The Structure of Social Networks

Some people might remember the classic Hollywood movie *Six Degrees of Separation*. The idea is that six connections are enough to reach anyone in the world.[51] In the modern world of online social networks (Facebook, Twitter, WeChat, etc.), it might seem even easier to connect with anyone in the world. The truth is a little more complicated than that, however, for having the right kind of network still matters a lot.

What kind of network ties are the most valuable? One classic study, by Granovetter, looks at the way professionals find new jobs. It found that the most important connections were loose acquaintances and coined the term the *strength of weak ties*.[52] Another classic study, by Burt, looked at managers inside large technology companies and asked whose ideas were most likely to be adopted. It found that the best ideas came from managers who were bridging different network clusters within the organization. They were less encumbered by group thinking within clusters and more able to broker ideas across clusters.[53]

To illustrate the properties of different network ties, consider the following simple graphical representation of a network. Many in this network (namely A, B, F, G, I, and J) only have two ties. They have a smaller network than those with three (namely, C, D, E, and H). Among those with three ties, however, D enjoys a special position. She bridges three distinct networks that have no other connection. Another way of seeing this is that each one that D connects with knows a distinct set of people. This contrasts with C, E, and H, who also have three network ties, but two of their ties already know each other, creating some redundancy in their network.

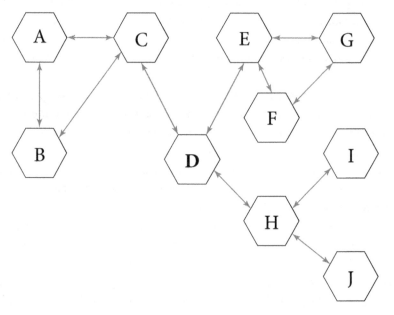

Beyond such a simple example, how can we systematically evaluate the quality of more complex networks? This is what network analysis does. It begins with simple questions such as who someone knows and who in turn they know. With this information it builds sophisticated mathematical measures of network centrality, that is, measures of the quality of network positions. The most basic measure is called degree centrality, which simply counts the number of direct ties in someone's network. An example of a more sophisticated measure is eigenvector centrality. This measure calculates the importance of one person by taking into consideration the importance of all the people she is connected with. Since this definition is inherently circular, the measure requires solving a large mathematical system to find what is called the eigenvalue. Google's PageRank measure uses an elaboration of this eigenvector centrality measure. In recent years, network analysis has gained additional prominence due to the rise of online social networks.

Networks are of particular importance for innovation and entrepreneurship because new ideas and investment opportunities often diffuse through them. Some networks are local in nature, connecting different types of people within a geographic cluster, that is, what we call an ecosystem (Section 14.1). Other networks help to interconnect distant ecosystems with each other. One academic study by Shane and Cable looks at the fundraising success of technology entrepreneurs coming out of MIT.[54] It finds that being affiliated to a top university alone is not enough to receive funding. Instead entrepreneurs have to rely on their direct and indirect ties to find an investor match. Another study, by Sorenson and Stuart, looks at the structure of VC syndicates, that is, groups of investors investing in the same deal (Section 7.4). It finds that VC firms who are central within their local networks are also more likely to build bridges to more distant networks.[55]

right inclination to go out and expand its network, making new contacts, and also maintaining relationships over time.

Networks matter for many aspects of company development. The sales process relies on generating new relationships with customers and intermediaries. Network connections may be essential to set up a meeting with actual decision makers or to create the right buzz in the target market. Networks also matter for hiring. Entrepreneurial firms typically pay below-average market salaries, so recruiting talent requires an ability to find employees who are not only capable but also flexible. Furthermore, a company often employs its network to access its specialized supply inputs. In high-technology businesses, this may include access to licenses that are required for implementing the company's own technology. Access to financing itself also depends a lot on forging new relationships. Finally, in regulated industries and in countries with a weaker rule of law, entrepreneurial firms also need to create network ties to secure the goodwill of government officials.

WorkHorse Box 2.7 touches upon its networks—or lack thereof.

WorkHorse Box 2.7   Network

WorkHorse's founders were still young and had only limited contacts in the business world. Each of them boasted a respectable following on Facebook, showing that they were truly respected and trusted by their friends. However, few of these contacts were valuable for starting a company.

In terms of advisers they thought of asking their lab director, Dr. Daniela Dasola, to join their board of advisers. As for a board of directors, they were hoping their investors would take care of that, since they felt at a loss how to do that.

Astrid and Brandon were keen networkers but sometimes hoped that their team mates would show the same willingness to go out, meet people, and follow up with them the way they did.

2.2.7   Sales

The third row of the VE Matrix takes a dynamic perspective by looking at strategy. This means looking at the future direction of the company. It is also closely related to implementation and to the momentum of the company.

The sales cell looks at how the company reaches its customers to generate revenues. The three key questions to ask are:

1. How does the venture reach its customers?
2. What is the distribution strategy?
3. What are the revenue model and pricing strategy?

The first question about the sales strategy is how the company gets in front of its customers. Based on analysis of the customer need and the market, in the two cells above, this cell focuses on the customer acquisition strategy. This concerns the company's approach to enter the market, not only in terms of physical access, but also in terms of customer attention. Many new products and services require at least some customer education and therefore some investments in developing a customer base. More generally, every product or service requires some marketing strategy that explains how the company will access the hearts and minds of its customers. In entrepreneurial companies, the marketing strategy frequently evolves as the company learns about its customers and as it expands into different market segments. For example, as the company grows, it may change its marketing from targeting early adopters who are happy to buy a product on the basis of its promises to targeting mainstream customers who require much more assurances before buying.[56]

The second question concerns distribution strategy. A key trade-off here is whether to sell directly or indirectly through third parties. Relying on third parties leverages the resources and reputation of established players, whereas selling direct allows the company to better control the customer experience and to learn from direct customer contact. Commercialization through third parties entails higher variable costs due to commissions. Building one's own distribution network often requires higher initial fixed costs. Working with third parties involves some cooperation with established firms in the industry, which we discuss in Box 2.3.

The third question concerns the revenue model and pricing strategy. What exactly is the company selling, and what can it charge for? The basic challenge is to figure out who should and shouldn't pay and what exactly they are paying for. Establishing a revenue model requires understanding the many ways in which customers can try to obtain the same good for less. This is particularly salient in the online world, where users frequently find ways of obtaining content for free and are therefore unwilling to pay. Part of the revenue model concerns pricing. This depends to a large extent on the customers' willingness to pay—in economic parlance, the elasticity of demand. Pricing is also affected by the level of competition, discounting practices, and the company's ability to differentiate itself.

Another aspect of the revenue model concerns customer acquisition and retention costs. What does the company need to spend to get a first sale, and how often will that customer come back for further purchases? A useful concept here is the lifetime value of a customer, which compares the acquisition costs against the revenues on a per-customer basis, over the lifetime of a typical customer.

WorkHorse Box 2.8 illustrates the issues for the Sales cell.

WorkHorse Box 2.8   Sales

WorkHorse decided to target the consumer-oriented market for portable solar generators. It reckoned its ultralight design would be valued by outdoor adventurers and camping enthusiasts. Based on preliminary customer research, the company expected to be able to charge $580 (net of sales tax) for the WonderFoal. This put the company in the premium pricing category but not at the top of the range. The founders justified this choice on the basis of their better power performance and their superior designs. For the NokotaStar the company envisioned charging $780 (net of tax).

The company planned to enter the North American market in January 2021 with the WonderFoal product and add the NokotaStar in January 2022. For the European market, the company planned to introduce both products in January 2022.

Most consumers purchased power generators at a large variety of retailers. The company planned to focus on specialized sporting or camping goods retailers. WorkHorse realized that getting access to these retailers would not be cheap.

Their conversations with a small number of sport stores suggested that retailers would take a 40% margin off the retail price.

Marketing was central to sales growth. The company expected that it could market the WonderFoal to enthusiastic hikers on its own. Reaching customers would not be easy, as the market was somewhat fragmented, but the best way to attract the attention of hikers was through word of mouth, specialty magazines, and online forums. However, marketing to campers would be considerably more challenging. Early market research indicated that, whereas hikers were willing to buy on the basis of superior product features, campers were considerably more focused on brand. They often bought their camping equipment as part of a larger purchase, also involving items such as large tents, trailers, and even camping vans. Consequently, WorkHorse planned to seek a co-branding partner that would help the company gain access to and credibility with these customers. The company understood that this would not be cheap and expected to pay another 20% margin of the retail price to such a co-branding partner.

2.2.8   Production

While the first cell of the strategy row is concerned with the customer-facing "front end" of the company, the second cell is concerned with the supply-facing "back end." We call this the production strategy, which broadly designates the strategy for structuring the company's entire value chain. This cell builds on the Solution and Competition cells above it in the company row, as the production strategy is finding a way to implement the proposed solution within a competitive environment. The three key questions to ask are:

1. What is the development strategy?
2. What is the scope of activities, and what partnerships are necessary?
3. How efficient are operations?

The production strategy covers a broad set of concerns about how the company needs to organize itself. The first question relates to the pre-production stage where the company is developing its technology and product offering. An immediate concern is how far along the development path a company has already traveled and how much further it has to go. Having a shorter path to launch makes the venture more attractive to investors. However, one should never expect a straight ride through the development process. Investors therefore often focus on identifying the next milestones and what the company needs to achieve in the short term.

In technology-based start-ups, the innovation is based in part on a scientific or technological breakthrough. Typically, further technological development is required before a product can become useful to customers. This may create conflicts between the marketing team that wants to quickly develop a solution to show the customer and get feedback versus the technical team that wants to develop a proper solution that validates its technical prowess. Put differently, managing the development strategy often requires juggling time schedules and making trade-offs between speed and quality.

The second question asks how the company structures its activities. A key issue is the scope of activities, that is, what the company plans to do itself versus outsourcing or co-developing with strategic partners. This question is relevant at both the development and production stages; at both of these stages the company needs to decide what activities it performs itself and what activities it delegates. This decision requires determining what assets are owned by the company itself and what assets are owned by third parties. All these decisions depend on the company's strategic vision of how it wants to build its core competencies.[57] Should the company purchase an inexpensive standard component on the market, or should it manufacture a better, more specialized component in-house? Should the company partner with another company that has complementary resources but may discover some of its proprietary information in the course of the project?[58] Some of these decisions are also driven by resource constraints. For example, start-ups typically don't own their real estate but instead rent it, and they prefer to lease rather than purchase equipment.

The third question relates to structuring operations. An important part of the operating strategy is to identify all the resources that are required for production, including physical assets, staffing, IP, and a variety of other inputs.[59] Another important part is to outline the cost model, which explains how much it costs to develop and produce the product or service. Cost efficiency is particularly important for entrepreneurial ventures that rely on external funding. Whereas the sales cell lies at the basis of the revenue model, the production cell lies at the basis of the cost model. Together, they form the core business model. In Chapter 3 we show how to turn this into financial projections.

WorkHorse Box 2.9 illustrates the type of analysis for the Production cell.

WorkHorse Box 2.9   Production

WorkHorse's development was easy to describe but much harder to implement. Bharat was in charge of all technological developments. It was agreed that he should also continue to do his own research. This area of technology was evolving rapidly, and the team was partly betting on his future scientific discoveries to stay ahead of the competition.

The design work was to be done under the leadership of Astrid. The founders thought that they could develop the prototypes by themselves, most likely with the help of some local talent. All hardware production, however, was to be done in China, under Annie's supervision. To prepare for the product launch, she planned to move to China, to identify suitable manufacturers, and to forge relationships with relevant parties in business and government. The company still had to work out various details about its cost model, to get a proper understanding of how expensive development and manufacturing would be.

2.2.9   Organization

The final cell concerns the organization, once again focusing on the human elements. The analysis here builds on the sales and production cells in the strategy row but focuses on the managerial aspects of strategy and how the founders create an entire organization that can deliver on the proposed strategy. It is therefore also related to the cells above in the entrepreneur column, by looking at how the Team and its Network evolve into a professional organization. The three key questions to ask are:

1. How will the founder team expand and evolve?
2. What is the governance structure?
3. What is the talent strategy?

The first question concerns the way the entrepreneurs approach leadership. Founders typically have skills and passions that help the company survive through the early days. However, as the company grows, the roles of leaders change. Two key issues need to be addressed. The first issue concerns what is missing in the current founder team. This means looking at the future strategic needs and at where the holes are in the current team. The second issue is how to make the best use of the talent within the current team. As companies grow, good entrepreneurs do not always become good managers. Stories about charismatic founders such as Walt Disney, Jack Ma, Richard Branson, or Jeff Bezos tend to obscure the fact that the majority of company founders are replaced by outsiders in the position of CEO within a decade and often much sooner than that.[60]

Discussing leadership issues can be sensitive, involving delicate personal questions such as: "When will the founders be ready to relinquish control to a new set of managers?" Or "What would be the best role for this founder?" Investors worry when founders are more interested in retaining control than in growing a successful business. The simple truth is that investors care about the success of the company, more than the personal success of the entrepreneur.[61]

The second question concerns corporate governance: "Who decides what, and how?" Organizations have both formal and informal decision-making structures (Section 8.2). The board of directors plays a central part in the formal structure, as it approves all key strategic and financial decisions. The composition of the board, and the way it operates, therefore influence the future direction of the company. In addition, many informal aspects influence decision making. In some start-ups, strong-minded founders dominate all decision making, sometimes to the detriment of the company. In other start-ups, decision making is more decentralized, involving extensive communication. Such organic processes can lead to better decisions but are prone to be slow and political.

The third question is how the company plans to attract, nurture, and retain talent. At an early stage, there is often a need to complete the team, and as the company grows there are ongoing challenges of developing competencies within the company. For example, launching exports requires hiring managers who have experience with foreign markets. All of this requires not only hiring well, but also nurturing employees and ensuring that the good ones are retained. Like any other company, start-ups compete for talent (Section 14.4.2) and often find it difficult to offer convincing career prospects, let alone attractive compensation plans. As the company grows, there also has to be a balance between external hires and internal promotions.

Another important and related issue is which corporate culture the venture wants to develop. This concerns the set of beliefs about the behavior of others inside the organization that develop collectively as the company grows.[62] Culture is mostly formed at early stages of the company and is strongly influenced by the founders and their initial approaches to overcoming external challenges and internal problems. It further evolves over time as the company learns to compete in the marketplace and faces the numerous challenges of growing the organization. Corporate culture defines how employees and senior managers communicate, what values matter within the organization, and how it will respond to external and internal pressures.[63]

WorkHorse Box 2.10 illustrates its organizational approach.

WorkHorse Box 2.10   Organization

Astrid recognized that a team of four founders in their 20s on their own would not look credible to investors and others. Yet she didn't think that the company was in a position to hire a more experienced CEO. She had her doubts that bringing in an outsider would be the right thing for the team, at least not at this early stage. Besides, she rather enjoyed being the CEO, and so far, everyone thought that she was doing a fine job.

One concern was that, despite her enthusiasm for it, she really wasn't an industrial designer. She was even more nervous about the fact that no one had any sales experience. She earmarked those two as key areas for future hires. Astrid was also keen to build a proper board of directors but had no experience with it, and hoped investors could guide her on this.

From the start, the four founders agreed that their company should be professionally run. They planned not to hire friends and family, but to attract and retain the people who were right for the job and right for the company. They would always require unanimous agreement on any key hire and would always check that candidates fit not only the job profile, but also their work culture. They decided that talent and attitude were more important than skills and experience.

The four founders established some fundamental corporate values they would live by. They summarized them as their HORSE values, which stood for:

- Happy is the way we work
- Organize around teams, don't try to go solo
- Respect the environment and all the people you work with
- Sell something that the customer actually wants
- Experiment and learn from it

While Brandon thought of it as a brilliant way of projecting the company values, Bharat insisted that merely putting together nice statements wasn't enough. He was wondering what it would take to actually live by these values once the going gets tough.

2.3 Drawing Conclusions from the Venture Evaluation Matrix

The VE Matrix is a method for evaluating opportunities based on nine logically connected criteria. The benefit of such a structured approach is that it facilitates drawing conclusions about the prospects of the underlying business. Specifically, the three rows of the VE Matrix provide three distinct perspectives on the attractiveness of the opportunity. The three columns imply three types of potential competitive advantages. The following section explains this in greater detail. Figure 2.3 shows how the VE Matrix generates these summary insights.

Venture Evaluation Matrix	Customer	Company	Enterpreneur	Attractiveness
Value Proposition	Need	Solution	Team	Value
Industry	Market	Competition	Network	Scale
Strategy	Sales	Production	Organization	Grow
Competitive Advantage	Access	Entry Barriers	Competencies	Decision

Figure 2.3. Summary evaluation with the Venture Evaluation Matrix.

2.3.1 Three Perspectives on Attractiveness

The rows of the VE Matrix look at the attractiveness of the business opportunity from three distinct perspectives. The value proposition row uses a *micro perspective* that focuses on what the company plans to do, thereby looking at the potential value of the opportunity. The industry row takes a *macro perspective* that allows us to understand the environment within which the company operates, thereby looking at the potential scale of the opportunity. Finally, the strategy row takes a *dynamic perspective* of gauging the company direction, thereby looking at its growth potential.

Each of these three perspectives allows us to answer a different set of questions about the underlying business opportunity. The first (micro) perspective permits us to assess whether the opportunity constitutes a promising starting point to create value for the customer. Have the entrepreneurs identified a real customer need, do they have a chance of providing a solution, and are the entrepreneurs themselves capable problem solvers who can deliver? The entrepreneur's answers to these questions should assure the investors that there is a substantial value potential.

The second (macro) perspective looks at whether the opportunity is in an attractive industry that is worth investing in. This requires a sufficiently large market to allow for substantial value creation. The competitive structure has to be sufficiently favorable to allow the company to capture a sufficient market share. Moreover, the company needs a strong network to access the required industry resources. This row therefore deals with attractiveness of the environment, addressing investor concerns about the scale of the undertaking.

The third (dynamic) perspective addresses the question of whether the company is heading in the right direction for achieving sustained growth. Does the company have a suitable strategy for selling into the market? Does it have the right approach for developing its products and managing its operations? Is there a workable business model? And is there a professionalization plan for building a capable organization that can grow? Answering these questions allows the entrepreneur to address investor concerns about the company's overall strategic direction and about whether it knows not only how to create value but also how to capture it to its advantage.

2.3.2 Three Competitive Advantages

At the onset, start-ups do not possess competitive advantages but rather only an ambition to develop them over time. The three columns of the VE Matrix allow us to identify what types of competitive advantages the company may develop over time. From the first column of Figure 2.3 we see that the first potential competitive advantage concerns access to customers. The underlying force is customer loyalty; that is, having the attention and trust of a customer gives the company an edge over the competition. Many start-ups hope to establish market access by being a first mover. They hope to build a reputation with the end users for quality, service, affordability, and other assets. Reputation manifests itself in a variety of forms, such as trust, institutional relationships, or brand image. A good reputation helps to attract new customers and retain existing ones. Early movers are well positioned to create a distinct reputation with their customers, creating psychological, organizational, technological, or contractual switching costs that put the company ahead of its competitors. Once customers have downloaded one app for transferring money from their mobile phone, such as TransferWise or OFX, why switch to another?

Being an early mover is also challenging, however, and doesn't guarantee reputational advantages. Early movers may enter with an immature technology that fails to satisfy customers. They may execute poorly and fail to establish customer trust. Palm's Treo was an early mobile phone with color touchscreen but was soon beaten by lighter models. Moving early can even turn into a disadvantage. Sometimes competitors benefit from the pioneering efforts of a start-up. They follow the trail blazed by the pioneers and learn to avoid their mistakes. Being a first mover only provides an opportunity, but no guarantee, to establish market access.

This brings us to the second competitive advantage, barriers to entry, which Figure 2.3 shows at the bottom of the second column. While access is fundamentally concerned with the front-end customer-facing part of the company, entry barriers are related to the back end of the company. We define entry barriers as proprietary assets that the company can use to block the competition. Some can be physical assets, such as a favorable retail location, or an efficient production plant; others are intangible assets, including IP (Section 2.2.2), as well as licenses, contracts, or relationships. For example, a company may benefit from owning a particular government license, or it may benefit from having an exclusive relationship with a key partner.

While proprietary assets create some entry barriers against the competition, these are rarely absolute barriers. Competitors will seek alternative ways of getting around these barriers and will try to build their own proprietary assets. Entry barriers do not appear coincidentally; they are deliberately created as part of the competitive process. They are the result of companies' technological innovations, competitive strategies, and the way they set up their production processes.

The third column in Figure 2.3 shows Competencies as competitive advantages. These pertain to the talent, knowledge, and skills that reside within the organization. Competencies may belong to a specific set of individuals, such as an all-star sales team. They also manifest themselves in the corporate culture. Some corporations perform better because they know how to motivate people. Of particular significance here, some companies have an organizational culture that is open to "intrapreneurial" initiatives and corporate change. This gives them a dynamic capability to continuously improve their own products and processes.[64]

The seeds for creating competencies go all the way back to the founding conditions. The original cultural imprint is the basis from which the organization will develop. Consciously or not, start-ups often adopt the organizational routines of the companies the founders worked in prior to starting their own venture. These routines then affect the way that start-ups grow and change over time.[65] A functional blueprint can generate organizational competencies that constitute a competitive advantage, but a dysfunctional culture can derail even the most promising business opportunity. The ability to create and maintain competencies depends on the leadership of the company, and thus the talent it manages to recruit and retain. The analysis of the third column therefore leads to an evaluation of the competencies that a company is likely to develop over time.

2.3.3 Assessing Risk

The VE Matrix uncovers the business risks associated with a new venture. Each cell of the Matrix contains elements of business risk—for example, the risk of being exposed to strong competitors. Beyond a list of all the individual risks, investors want to understand the broader pattern of risk. This is where the matrix structure quickly generates an overview of a venture's fundamental business risks.

We first look at risks along the columns. The flipside of competitive advantages are competitive weaknesses that can bring companies down. We identify three types of risks: market risk, technology risk, and people risk. Market risk, in the first column, arises from the possibility that the customer need is not strong enough, that the market is not large enough for a viable business, or that the company fails to reach its customers. Technology risk in the second column arises mainly from the possibility that the proposed solution to the customer problem fails on technical grounds. Beyond such technical aspects there are also broader concerns about the underlying innovation. The innovation may not be protected from competition, or the entrepreneur may fail to successfully deliver a product or service to the market. Finally, the third column reveals people risk. This arises from possible weaknesses within the founder team, their networks, and their ability to grow the organization.

We can also identify risks along the rows of the VE Matrix. The first row shows that the venture may fail to create enough value. This can be because there is no real customer need and no proper solution, or because of an inadequate founder team. The second row points to the risk that the venture is limited in scale. This may happen if the market turns out to be small, if powerful competitors erode too much market share, or if the founders' network is insufficient. The third row shows the risk that the venture fails to capture economic value and is unable to generate profits. This happens if the revenue model and the cost model do not allow the venture to capture the value it creates, or if the founders fail to create a capable organization.

2.3.4 Interactions Across Cells

For simplicity we discuss the nine cells of the VE Matrix as nine independent entities that can be summed up across rows or columns. In addition, we note that there are interesting interdependencies across cells. In principle, there can be 36 pairwise interactions across the nine cells in the VE Matrix. There is no point in listing them all, but consider the following two examples. One example is Sales and Competition.

They appear in different rows and columns but are still related. Put simply, the less competition, the easier to grow sales. Another example is Need and Organization, which appear on opposite ends of the VE Matrix but are interdependent. Certain corporate customers, for example, have a need for reliability and efficiency, which requires the start-up to develop a formal management organization. By contrast, other customers value creativity, encouraging the entrepreneur to create a more flexible and informal organization.

There are numerous more examples of how the cells interact with each other. Entrepreneurship scholars who study how entrepreneurs perceive and pursue opportunities emphasize several important interactions. One important concept is the "individual—opportunity nexus."[66] The argument is that entrepreneurial opportunities are not valuable by themselves, but they become valuable when undertaken by the right individuals. Interesting evidence from cognitive psychology experiments suggests that individuals respond differently to idea triggers, depending on their prior knowledge and motivation.[67] Closely related is research about what kind of entrepreneurs fit with what kind of opportunities. One study by Eesley and Roberts compares the role of entrepreneurial experience versus talent.[68] It finds that prior experience increases performance in start-ups that are operating in familiar markets and technologies. However, talent becomes more important for more novel and unfamiliar opportunities. Overall, we note that there are important interactions across cells and that evaluating an opportunity is not limited to looking at each of the nine cells in isolation, it also means looking at how the different cells fit together.

2.4 How Entrepreneurs Use the Venture Evaluation Matrix

2.4.1 The Entrepreneur's Decision

The bottom right cell in Figure 2.3 says Decision. The analysis of the VE Matrix ultimately assesses the overall prospect of the venture and therefore provides a key input into decisions made by entrepreneurs and investors. In this section, we look at how an entrepreneur faces a continuation decision, and in Section 2.5 we turn to the investors' investment decision.

Recall that in Box 1.1 we established three fundamental principles of the entrepreneurial process: entrepreneurs need to gather resources, they face considerable uncertainty, and they experiment to find a path toward a viable business. Thinking of the entrepreneurial process as a learning process helps to explain how entrepreneurs can use the VE Matrix. At each major junction of the entrepreneurial path, the entrepreneur faces a three-way decision: (1) continue with the current plan, (2) pivot to a different plan, or (3) abandon the project altogether. The VE Matrix can guide these decisions.

If the analysis of the VE Matrix generates a coherent and positive outlook, then the entrepreneur can continue with the current plan. The VE Matrix also suggests next steps. Where is the uncertainty greatest? What hypothesis should the entrepreneur test now? Ironically, it is often the difficulty that an entrepreneur has answering the questions in a cell that reveals where the uncertainty is greatest and what the next step might be.

If the analysis of the VE Matrix generates an incoherent or mixed outlook, then it may be time to pivot and adjust the strategy. The VE Matrix provides guidance on which parts of the plan should stay and which parts need to change. For example, typical pivots in an early-stage venture consist of staying with the customer need but looking for an alternative solution; or staying with a technology but looking for an alternative customer need; or even staying with a customer need and solution but looking for a different team to implement. The VE Matrix disentangles the different components of the business and therefore helps to identify which parts can be kept and which ones need to be changed.

If the analysis of the VE Matrix generates a distinctly negative outlook, then it may be time to abandon the opportunity altogether. This is particularly important at the very beginning, when the entrepreneur has to decide whether or not to pursue the venture in the first place. The VE Matrix can identify red flags, such as the lack of real customer need, or the presence of invincible competitors. It may also expose irreconcilable discrepancies. There may be a misalignment between the third column and the rest, indicating that the opportunity may be promising, but it simply doesn't fit the team.

Box 2.5 explains that the three-way decision between continuing, pivoting, or abandoning is consistent with what is commonly known as the "lean start-up" methodology.

Box 2.5 The Lean Start-up Methodology

The lean start-up is a popular way of approaching entrepreneurship. There is no single definition of what it entails, but the core messages are fairly clear. A lean start-up approach aims to make venture development efficient through experimentation and learning. It focuses on the early stages of venture development and prioritizes flexibility and speed. These core principles are well aligned with the three fundamental challenges of entrepreneurship identified in Box 1.1.

Eric Ries, a central figure in the lean start-up movement, describes the following process.[69] Starting with an idea, the entrepreneur builds a "minimum viable product" (commonly abbreviated to MVP). This is not a finished product; instead it is a mock-up or prototype that is much cheaper to build. It is just good enough to be shown to potential users for some trial (for example, a highly incomplete version of a software). The lean start-up methodology then emphasizes the need to measure the outcomes from such trials. The data generate new insights about the fit between customer needs and the MVP. Often this results in a pivot, where the entrepreneur decides to refocus her value proposition. Instead of simply developing a finished product, the entrepreneur develops a new MVP and restarts the learning cycle. This cycle is repeated until user feedback is sufficiently positive to justify going into full product development.

Steve Blank uses another closely related framework that emphasizes the importance of customer focus.[70] It starts with a process of discovering who the initial customers are (i.e., the early adopters discussed in Section 2.2.4). Blank suggests formulating hypotheses of what exactly different customers want and then validating them by talking and listening to customers. For this entrepreneurs can use the design thinking methodologies discussed in Box 2.1. Learning about the true customer needs frequently leads to pivots that initiate a new cycle of hypotheses, customer discovery, and validation. This process continues until a good product–customer fit is found, at which point the development of the venture can proceed.

The lean start-up movement has flourished partly because it gives entrepreneurs many practical tools. Osterwalder's Business Model Canvas (BMC), for example, is a popular tool for visually displaying the key elements of a business plan.[71] Its right-hand side focuses on customers and markets, covering similar grounds to column 1 of the VE matrix. Its left-hand side focuses on activities, resources, and partners, covering similar grounds to column 2 of the VE matrix. There is also Osterwalder's Value Proposition Canvas, which is a close cousin to the BMC.[72] It looks more deeply at the underlying structure of the problem (column 1 of VE Matrix) and the solution (column 2 of VE Matrix). However, none of these frameworks take into account the importance of founder teams, their networks, and the organizations they build, emphasized in column 3 of the VE matrix.[73]

2.4.2 Writing a Business Plan

The term *business plan* means different things to different people. Typically, it refers to one of three things: (1) a strategic framework (or business model), (2) an operational planning tool (aka business roadmap), and (3) an investor presentation (or business pitch). The first is a conceptual map that explains the business logic and how the venture plans to create economic value. The second can be a loosely organized set of ideas and/or notes that detail the numerous actions that are needed to implement the opportunity. The third is a presentation that is meant to communicate the essence of the venture. Historically, this consisted of an executive summary (say 1–5 pages long), followed by a written document (say 15–30 pages long); in today's world this has been largely replaced by slide presentations (say 10–20 slides), or short video presentations (say 2–10 minutes long), which may still be followed by a 10- to 20-page document with further details. A collection of the slide decks of future extremely successful businesses, like Airbnb, Dropbox, LinkedIn, or

YouTube, is available from CB Insights.[74] The three meanings of the term *business plan* are obviously linked, as they all put some structure around the core activities and direction of the venture.

Why should entrepreneurs bother to write a business plan? Some pundits argue against ever writing a business plan. They note that business plans rapidly become out of date. Some pundits even reject the notion of planning in the first place.[75] Others still believe in some planning and having some kind of a business plan.[76] However, there is an interesting tension between planning and experimentation that goes back to the three entrepreneurship principles identified in Box 1.1. Specifically, the notion of entrepreneurs gathering resources requires that they have a notion of where they want to go and therefore some (explicit or implicit) plan of where to take the company. At the same time, the notion of experimentation suggests that any original plan is likely to have flaws and that changing plans is an essential part of the entrepreneurial journey. Where does this leave us with respect to the question of whether to write a business plan? Practically speaking, we would argue that every entrepreneur benefits from having some strategic framework (meaning (1) above) and some operational roadmap (meaning (2) above). Moreover, when the time comes to seek funding, entrepreneurs also need some business presentation (meaning (3) above), in order to communicate effectively with potential investors.

Focusing thus on this third meaning of the term, we recognize that the main purpose of the business plan is to communicate the essence of the entrepreneurial venture, to describe its current state, and to indicate the direction of travel. There are numerous ways to present a business plan. The appropriate structure varies with the type of business, the type of investors, and the cultural context. Numerous practical how-to books have been written to give advice on how to compose a business plan.[77] We suggest that the VE Matrix is ideally suited for preparing an investor presentation. All the required points fall directly out of the analysis. Figure 2.4 shows how the cells of the VE Matrix can be used to create the content of a typical business plan.

A business plan should begin with a high-level overview of the business opportunity. This is meant to generate some enthusiasm for the business opportunity and typically focuses on the highlights of the value proposition. It therefore draws from the first row of the VE Matrix, explaining how the entrepreneurial team provides a solution to a significant customer need. In addition, this part can draw on the row and column summaries that addressed the attractiveness and competitive advantages of the venture, as shown in Figure 2.4.

The second and third heading can be directly taken from the VE Matrix. We suggest starting with a customer need and then proceeding to the discussion of how the innovation solves this need. This order imposes some discipline on the entrepreneurial thought process and is particularly challenging for technology-driven entrepreneurs who are inclined to put technology ahead of customer needs.

The fourth heading about markets directly uses the analysis from the market cell, looking at how to segment the market and how to estimate its size and growth. For

Section	Business Plan Heading	Venture Evaluation Matrix Cells
1	Executive Summary	Summary of cells, rows, and columns
2	Customer Need	Need
3	Product/Service	Solution
4	Market Analysis	Market
5	Competition Analysis	Competition
6	Marketing and Sales	Sales
7	Development and Operations	Production, Organization
8	Business Model	Sales, Production
9	Management Team	Team, Network, Organization
10	Financial Projections	See Chapter 3

Figure 2.4. Using the Venture Evaluation Matrix for writing a business plan.

the fifth heading about competition, we suggest that the entrepreneur not only list who the likely competitors are, but also address the question of how competition works in this industry and how their venture is differentiated.

The sixth heading concerns marketing and sales, which can be derived from the sales cell. The seventh heading concerns the strategy for development and operations, which mainly corresponds to the analysis in the production cell but may also draw on the analysis of the organization. The eighth heading spells out the business model, which focuses largely on the scope analysis of the production cells, as well as the partnering choices from the sales cell.

The ninth heading concerns the management team. We suggest that the entire third column of the VE Matrix should be used to write about the team in the business plan. That is, beyond merely describing the core team, a business plan should also provide information on its network of contacts, for instance, discussing the board of advisers. Moreover, the business plan should talk about the organization, such as what future hires are expected or what the corporate culture is like. The tenth heading in Figure 2.4 concerns the financial plan. In essence, this is a quantification of the qualitative business plan that we discuss in Chapter 3.

WorkHorse Box 2.11 briefly discusses its need for a business plan.

WorkHorse Box 2.11 Business Plan

Michael Archie had asked WorkHorse to send over its business plan, but the founders were unsure what exactly that meant. Astrid wrote a polite e-mail and was delighted when a few minutes later she got Michael's reply: "ppt pls, max 15 slides. CU MA." This was good news. She liked making PowerPoint presentations and was glad that they didn't have to write a long document. Reducing everything down to 15 slides, however, was more challenging. They needed a framework to condense the material in a structured way. They quickly decided to use the VE Matrix. Their slide presentation can be found in the slide deck available in the book's website (www.entrepreneurialfinance.net).

Regardless of the precise business plan format used, why is it important for the entrepreneur to convey detailed information to the investors? How much information is needed, and what kind of information is credible? Processing information is at the heart of entrepreneurial finance, so it is useful to understand some of the deeper economic conflicts around information. What information would an entrepreneur disclose or hide? And what kind of information would an investor consider credible or not? Box 2.6 draws on the insights of several great minds who received Nobel Prizes in Economics for their pathbreaking contributions on the economics of information.

Box 2.6 Nobel Insights on Information Economics

The 2001 Nobel Prize in Economics was awarded to George Akerlof and Michael Spence "for their analyses of markets with asymmetric information."[78] While their work looked at a wide variety of economic problems, their contributions clarify some of the problems entrepreneurs and investors face around business plans and investment decisions. Their work focuses on situations where the two parties have "asymmetric information," that is, one party knows more about the transaction than the other. In our context, the entrepreneur typically knows more about her venture than the investor (although the investor sometimes knows more about the broader business environment).

Akerlof looks at the so-called adverse selection problem, which is best explained by using his original "lemons" problems for second-hand cars. The people most eager to sell second-hand cars are those sitting on lemons, that is, cars with enduring but invisible defects. Sellers know about the true quality of their cars; buyers don't. How does such an asymmetry of information affect market transactions? Suppose a buyer looks at a second-hand car listed at $10,000. The buyer might argue that if the car was relatively good, worth more than $10,000, then the seller would not offer it. However, if the car was relatively bad (a lemon), and worth less than $10,000, then the seller would offer it. In this case, the only cars offered at $10,000 are those that are worth less than $10,000. Understanding this, should the buyer offer to purchase the car at $9,000? The issue is that the only sellers willing to sell at $9,000 would be those with really bad cars that are worth less than $9,000 . . . and so on. Akerlof shows that this kind of asymmetric information leads to inefficient market outcomes and possibly to a complete breakdown of market transactions.

Akerlof's insights can be readily applied to the financing of entrepreneurial ventures. Investors who cannot observe the true quality of a venture may worry that for a given valuation, the only entrepreneurs that are willing to take the deal are those who know that the true value of their company is below that offered by the investor. To avoid such situations, there has to be more communication, overcoming some of the asymmetries of information. Hence the need for entrepreneurs to pitch a business plan, and for investors to perform due diligence.

Spence pioneered the economics of "signaling," which also looks at situations with asymmetric information. The signaling problem differs from the adverse selection because this time the informed party (the entrepreneur) tries to convince the uninformed party (the investor) that they have a good project by sending "signals." This situation applies neatly to entrepreneurs trying to signal their quality in a business plan. The key question is what signals are credible or not.

An entrepreneur who wants to stand out could try to signal her quality by claiming that she will build an amazing business. The problem is that this is cheap talk; any entrepreneur can claim that, so no investor pays any attention. The question posed by Spence is what signals are economically meaningful. He notes that signals are credible only if they are costly to the sender. Moreover, the signal should be more costly (or impossible) for the pretender ("bad") type than for the true ("good") type.

Consider the difference between a business plan that provides a detailed data analysis of customer needs but has no paying customer yet, versus one without the analysis but with a first paying customer. Which one has the more credible signal? Providing detailed data might be a good idea, but it is something that anyone can do. Making a first sale, however, is possible only if there is a competent entrepreneur pursuing a real customer need. Hence, the first sale is the more credible signal: it separates the good from the bad opportunity.

Signals are often imperfect. Spence's work recognizes that there can be different types of market equilibria. There can be so-called separating equilibria where only the desirable types achieve certain signals (e.g., only competent entrepreneurs land a first sale). However, there can also be pooling equilibria where several types send the same signal. For example, it could be that a first sale is a valid signal for a real customer need but doesn't yet distinguish smaller from larger markets. Or it might be that in addition to all competent entrepreneurs there are also some incompetent but lucky entrepreneurs who land a first sale. In this case, the signal is less powerful because it doesn't fully separate competent from incompetent entrepreneurs.

Overall, we note that the problems of asymmetric information are pervasive in the context of entrepreneurial finance. Entrepreneurs face a credibility challenge, which they seek to overcome by creating convincing signals that investors can believe in. A good business plan focuses on conveying precisely those signals that are most credible, those that can separate the good from the bad ventures.

2.5 How Investors Use the Venture Evaluation Matrix

In this section, we ask how investors can make use of the VE Matrix. We distinguish three important steps. First, the VE Matrix can be used for some initial screening, identifying which businesses aren't worth their time. For this purpose, we introduce the VE Matrix Spreadsheet Tool. Second, for the more promising companies, the

VE Matrix can guide investors on how to perform due diligence. Finally, we discuss what issues beyond the VE Matrix need to be considered before making any final investment decision.

2.5.1 The Venture Evaluation Matrix Spreadsheet Tool

Investors often face the problem of having too many entrepreneurs asking for their money. They therefore need a process for quickly sorting through business plans in order to determine which ones are sufficiently promising for further evaluation. Investors often use some simple rules of thumb, or simple ranking systems, to determine which business plan passes their first screen. The VE Matrix can be used for a quick but systematic evaluation of a business opportunity. To make this process practical, we introduce a simple but flexible tool, the Venture Evaluation Matrix Spreadsheet Tool, which is available on the book's website (www. entrepreneurialfinance.net).

The tool requires users to answer two sets of questions. First, for each cell, they briefly evaluate the three questions outlined in Section 2.2. For each question, users enter a score out of 10. For example, a higher score is given when there is a bigger customer need, weaker competition, or fewer holes in the team. As a second step, users define relative weights (out of 100%) within each of the nine criteria and also across the nine criteria. These weights represent the users' beliefs about the relative importance of the different criteria. Arthur Rock, for example, would have given relatively high weights to the third column. The spreadsheet tool is very flexible by allowing users to define their own weights. Moreover, it is set up so that users can easily add more questions or modify the existing questions. Users can thus customize the spreadsheet tool to their own specific needs.

The spreadsheet tool generates one overall score, as well as several other summary scores, all expressed out of 10. Specifically, there is a score for each of the three perspectives (Micro/Value, Macro/Scale, and Strategy/Growth), as well as for each of the three competitive advantages (Access, Entry Barriers, and Competencies). This way the framework generates an understanding of where the overall score comes from. The spreadsheet tool also includes a visual representation of the evaluation results, such as the simple Radar Chart shown in Box 2.12.

The hardest part of evaluating business opportunities is determining what criteria actually matter. Every entrepreneurial opportunity has risks, so the question is what risks matter more or less? There are no objective answers here; this is where opinions start to diverge and where investment philosophies matter. The VE matrix forces investors to explicate their own preferences, specifically requiring investors to define a weighting scheme over the individual cell scores.

To help with this, the spreadsheet tool includes four simple metrics to aggregate cell scores: a simple average, a weighted average (with user-defined weights), the minimum across cells, and the maximum across cells. To see how these four options reflect alternative investor philosophies, consider a more risk-averse investor who looks for the absence of weaknesses. Such an investor will favor business plans where the minimum score across cells is high. Contrast this with a bolder investor who is looking for outstanding strengths. This investor can focus on business plans with high maximum score across cells. The simple and weighted averages reflect both simple and more sophisticated forms of compromise. The tool is sufficiently flexible to incorporate many other investor preferences. For example, some investors may seek opportunities that are strong on average, but also have some outstanding strengths. They can be found by looking for high average scores that also have a high maximal score or eliminate ventures that have too many low scores regardless of all other high scores, and so on.[79]

Obviously, there are always ways of cheating, namely, to reverse-engineer weights until the VE Matrix delivers whatever specific recommendation one is looking for. However, even then the tool is useful because it shows what weights are needed to justify a specific desired outcome, thereby revealing which investment philosophies justify that specific plan.

WorkHorse Box 2.12 applies the Venture Evaluation Matrix Spreadsheet Tool.

WorkHorse Box 2.12 Using the Venture Evaluation Matrix Spreadsheet Tool

---

When Michael Archie received the WorkHorse's business plan, he quickly flipped through it—over half of the plans he received could be eliminated on the basis of that alone. Thankfully he was intrigued, so he pulled up an empty VE Matrix spreadsheet to score the plan. The online spreadsheet contains Michael's evaluation, the radar chart below represents the cell scores, and the table below shows the evaluation scores.

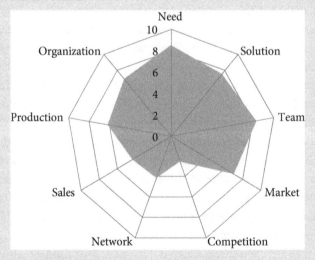

Michael liked the basic value proposition. He was intrigued by the team, recognized the customer need from personal experience, and was impressed by the technological solution. However, when it came to the industry analysis, he had more serious reservations. He didn't like the competition and was worried about WorkHorse's lack of industry networks. Parts of the strategy seemed sensible, but he believed that the sales strategy was a bit naïve.

When he looked at competitive advantages, the analysis of column scores showed that competencies ranked highest and entry barriers lowest, but the scores were not very far apart. However, when he assessed the opportunity in terms of the three perspectives, he found a striking pattern in the row scores. The value proposition had by far the highest score, but the industry and strategy scores were considerably lower. He had seen this pattern many times before. The seeds of a strong business were there, but it would require work to turn this into a profitable venture.

Evaluation	Criterion	Weighted Score	Unweighted Score	Minimum Score	Maximum Score
Row	**Attractiveness**				
Value Proposition	Micro-Value	8.18	8.13	7.6	8.5
Industry	Macro-Scale	4.53	4.53	2.5	7
Strategy	Strategy – Growth	5.83	5.83	4.3	7
Column	**Competitive Advantages**				
Customers	Access	6.6	6.6	4.3	8.5
Company	Entry Barriers	5.43	5.43	2.5	7.6
Entrepreneur	Competencies	6.93	6.47	4.1	8.3
Total Score		**6.38**	**6.17**	**2.5**	**8.5**

Overall, he gave WorkHorse a score of 6.38. While he preferred companies in the 8s or 9s, most companies ended up in the 4s and 5s (even in the 1s and 2s when he was in a bad mood). His informal rule of thumb was to meet with any venture that scored above 6. He therefore sent off a quick e-mail to Astrid: "Thx for Bplan, looks OK. Can U pitch tomorrow 8am? CU MA."

2.5.2 Investor Due Diligence

After the initial contact with the entrepreneurs, and after hearing the entrepreneur's pitch, interested investors typically perform some research before making an investment decision. This is called due diligence. It differs from the due diligence in large financial transactions, such as an acquisition, where accountants pore over

Using VE Matrix for Due Diligence	Customer	Company	Enterpreneur
Value Proposition	Primary market research	Assess technology	Meet the team
Industry	Secondary market research	Research competition	Listen to the network
Strategy	Verify customer access	Site visits & suppliers	Discussion & observation

Figure 2.5. Due diligence with the Venture Evaluation Matrix.

financial accounts to verify their reliability and lawyers check the legal validity of statements made by the company. Instead, venture investors focus on business fundamentals. They gather information not to cover their legal liabilities, but to assess whether the investment opportunity meets their quality standards.

The VE Matrix provides a useful framework for structuring investor due diligence. Figure 2.5 maps common due diligence activities into the VE Matrix structure. Note, however, that the techniques mentioned for the various cells are not mutually exclusive, as many techniques can be used for multiple cells. Moreover, the nature of due diligence changes with the stage of venture development. Earlier-stage ventures are evaluated on their future plans, whereas later-stage ventures are assessed on their actual achievements.

The first cell about Need calls for direct customer evidence. This is commonly called "primary market research" and consists of the entrepreneur or investor gathering evidence through direct contact with customers. The main techniques used are interviews, surveys, focus groups, and other observational methods (see Box 2.1). The data from primary research is mostly qualitative and looks at the exact nature of the customer problem: where it is coming from, and how it varies across circumstances. Whereas traditional market research techniques look at entire market populations or representative samples, entrepreneurs aim to find out about those few customers that are most interested, the potential early adopters. They also look for qualitative insights, rather than quantitative statistical precision.[80]

The analysis of the Market cell draws mainly on secondary market research. Unlike primary market research, this is based on aggregate data that has already been gathered by others. In practice, entrepreneurs and investors rely on industry reports and a variety of other data sources to piece together an estimate of the size and growth of their target market.

To assess the Sales cell, investors ideally like to track the adoption rate of early customers. In the context of web-enabled businesses, it is sometimes possible to gather data on conversion rates, such as what fraction of viewers click through certain webpages, and how many complete a transaction. In offline ventures, it is rarely possible to obtain such data. In this case, due diligence consists of looking for qualitative evidence that either confirms or casts doubt on the company's proposed sales approach. In practice investors often interview experts who are familiar with the channels.

Turning to the second column, we first ask how to assess the proposed Solution. Part of the due diligence process here consists of consulting with technology experts and industry insiders who can assess a proposed solution. This is likely to uncover limitations of the proposed technology or hurdles that still need to be overcome. It might also reveal competing approaches. Another part of the process is again primary market research, focused on testing customer responses to the proposed solution.

Characterizing the Competition usually requires a combination of primary and secondary research techniques. The goal is to establish a conceptual map of actual and potential competitors, similar to the one in WorkHorse Box 2.6. The due diligence process establishes what the main competitors are currently doing and ideally also what they plan to do in the future. This kind of analysis requires good access to industry networks. Sometimes investors are in a better position to identify the competition, because they receive business plans from multiple sources and may have better access to certain parts of the industry network. The way to evaluate the production strategy is similar to that of the sales strategy. For later-stage companies, it is also possible to benchmark a venture against its competitors

While the due diligence process for the first two columns largely consists of gathering facts, the due diligence in the third column follows a much more people-centric logic. Put differently, whereas left-brained logical arguments dominate in the first two columns, right-brained intuitive arguments can be found throughout the third column. To assess the team, there is some objective data about the skills and experience of the entrepreneurs. Beyond that, however, the evaluation is more subjective. Questions revolve around the motivation and commitment of individuals, as well as issues of team fit. The main method of doing due diligence is to talk to the entrepreneurs and, if possible, to observe them in action. This all comes down to personal observations and subjective interpretation, which is why many venture investors consider "gut feeling" an essential component of the investment process.[81]

Investors frequently rely on networks for the due diligence process. They use their own networks to check the expertise, standing, and trustworthiness of the founding team. Moreover, they may ask the entrepreneurs to share contacts in their network to obtain further feedback on them. This part of the due diligence process is largely based on confidential discussions and may be fairly time consuming at times. It also leads to highly subjective information, where different investors sometimes come to different conclusions.

The final part of due diligence concerns the various organizational issues. Leadership issues tend to be delicate and are usually handled in private conversations with the entrepreneurs. This requires some diplomacy, such as discussing shortcomings in the current team or addressing the personal career ambitions of the founders. These conversations also help to set mutual expectations for the future structure of the management team, and the corporate governance structure. Ideally, investors get to observe the broader organization at work to witness its corporate culture. Investors often want to observe a company for some time before making an investment. Instead of merely looking at a "picture" of the entrepreneur (i.e., get a static impression of what they say), investors like to see a "video" of the entrepreneur in action (i.e., get a dynamic impression of what they do).

WorkHorse Box 2.13 provides examples of doing due diligence.

WorkHorse Box 2.13 Due Diligence

WorkHorse's presentation the next morning went better than expected. Michael only planned to meet the team for 20 minutes but ended up spending an entire hour with them. He told the team that he wanted to do a bit more research and think about it all. In the meantime, he asked the team to get back to him with a financial plan, including financial projections.

Later that week, Michael flipped through the business plan once more and decided to focus on three issues: competition, sales, and, as always, the team.

To find out about the competition, he called a venture capitalist who had considered investing in YouSolar but had ultimately declined to do so. In one phone call, he learned a lot more about the competitive landscape. Most of the established makers of diesel engine power were reluctant to go solar, fearing to undercut their diesel sales. Start-ups, however, had filled the gap, and there was a lot of experimentation with new technologies and new business models. A major stumbling block was access to distribution channels. Few start-ups had managed to obtain shelf space with the large retailers. Distributors had even been reluctant to sign up start-ups, fearing to upset the large established players.

The next due diligence step was clear, Michael needed to get a better understanding of sales and distribution. He reached out to Malcolm Force, with whom he sat on another company's board of directors. He was the CEO of Bolts-N-Nuts, a large chain of hardware stores. Catching up over lunch, he received some insider insights. Sales through specialized sporting retailers was in Malcolm's words "challenging but doable." He recommended that WorkHorse should avoid distributors and directly approach local store managers, to convince them to run local pilots before going nationwide. He offered to make some introductions but insisted that the team needed a physical prototype for demonstration, before meeting with store managers. Inspired by the conversation, Michael shot off another e-mail to the team: "Just talked 2 Force, says U need demo. When can U deliver? CU MA." Seeing how they would respond to this e-mail was his way of testing the team, just a little.

2.5.3 The Investor's Decision

The VE Matrix informs investor decisions, but it doesn't try to answer all the questions. It is a tool for narrowing down investment choices but not for making final investment decisions.[82] Importantly, it only looks at the fundamentals of the business but does not consider the attractiveness of the financial deal. Investors also need to look at the details of the financial deal. They need to consider the valuation, the structure of the deal, and various issues of timing and fit, important issues that we will examine at length in the chapters to come.

In the context of group decisions, such as angel groups or venture capital investment committees, there is another use of the VE Matrix: to objectively communicate preferences and investment logics within the group. When faced with a set of investment choices, all group members might have their priority list of who should get funded. Using the VE Matrix forces each group member to explain how they came up with their priority ranking and what their underlying investment preferences look like.

The VC Matrix should be used differently across different industries and different stages of company development. The first and second row might be more important at the very early stages, as one cannot always expect clear answers about the third row early on. The second column might be more important in an established industry where there are numerous existing solutions and strong competitors—and so on.

The VE Matrix takes a very structured approach to evaluating business opportunities. Traditionally, investors rely on a combination of rational thought and gut feeling to make up their minds. In Section 1.1 we note that investing involves a combination of left-brained logical and right-brained intuitive thinking. In recent years, with the rise of online investment opportunities such as crowdfunding, there has been a movement toward automating investment decisions. Of particular note is the use of artificial intelligence. Box 2.7 takes us on a trip back to the future.

Box 2.7 Tales from the Venture Archives: About Experts, Crowds, and Artificial Intelligence

---

This is an excerpt from a textbook on entrepreneurial finance, written circa 2080.

In the early days of financing entrepreneurial ventures humans evaluated entrepreneurial ventures. Their tools for making investment decisions were rather primitive. They were fact-gatherers, using old-fashioned techniques like talking to the entrepreneurs. They also depended heavily on unreliable instruments such as human brains and gut feelings.

We distinguish two main subperiods. Prior to 2010, most investment decisions were made by "experts." These were specialized humans who learned the tools of the trade through personal experiences as entrepreneurs or investors. They operated as individuals (curiously called angels), or in small groups (called venture capitalists). Their ability to predict the success of entrepreneurial ventures was abysmal.

Around 2010 there was an evolution of these primitive practices. Instead of relying on a small number of human brains, an aggregation procedure was developed that allowed the simultaneous deployment of a large number of human brains. This financing method was called crowdfunding and was based on numerous human brains all making small investment decisions. The approach was cleverly marketed as "The wisdom of the crowd." Its theoretical foundation was the law of large numbers, which says that the average of a large number of independent signals converges to the true mean, even if the individual signals are highly imprecise. All that is required for this law is that the signals are unbiased and independent of each other. Whether these conditions ever applied to human crowds is doubtful because of herd behavior, where humans followed the opinions of other humans rather than their own.

The crowd proved to be not less unreliable than individuals. One study by Mollick and Nanda of crowdfunding in the arts found that human experts and the crowd mostly agreed which projects should be financed. [83] However, the crowd was more willing to also invest in projects that had been rejected by experts; that is, the crowd was more lenient. Both methods achieved comparable rates of success (all low by modern standard). A variant of using the wisdom of the crowd was the so-called prediction markets. For example, corporations like Google allowed its employees to put small financial bets on the outcomes of different internal projects. The' predictions of the employees (who were working in various parts of the organization and were not necessarily experts) outperformed those of the experts working on the project. Interestingly, however, the employee opinions were also biased toward optimism.[84]

The fatal flaw of all these evaluation methods was that they depended on human brains. First glimpses of hope emerged in the late 2010s with the rise of what was known at the time as "artificial intelligence."[85] Today this is commonly referred to as "naïve binary prediction." Note that the term *artificial* was coined by humans who considered themselves more intelligent—this type of arrogance was common in those days.

Several human pioneers began experimenting with artificial intelligence for making venture investments. They relied on existing databases of past investment decisions and venture outcomes, creating statistical models that would predict what company characteristics would be associated with success and under what circumstances. An example was Hone Capital, a Silicon Valley-based VC fund that was a subsidiary of the CSG Group, a large Chinese private equity firm, which invested on the basis of data from AngelList and other venture databases.[86] Applying rudimentary machine learning techniques, they made predictions about which ventures would receive follow-on financing, and which ventures would eventually succeed. Veronica Wu, Hone's managing director, gave the example of an insight from machine learning: teams consisting of founders who came from different universities outperformed teams who all came from the same university. Another early pioneer was Correlation Ventures, which relied on statistical correlation methods to predict which investments would succeed.[87] It marketed itself to entrepreneurs on the basis of making faster decisions, specifically responding to all investment proposal within two weeks. Investment methods based on artificial intelligence outperformed human approaches, not because they used different criteria (in fact, the criteria used by humans and machines were similar to the criteria of the VE Matrix), but because they paid attention to a much larger set of decision criteria and were better at incorporating complex content.[88]

A key advantage of these early artificial intelligence approaches was that, unlike humans who were famously slow learners, computer programs evolved rapidly, continuously improving their predictions over time. Initially, the humans all thought that artificial intelligence would complement, not substitute, human reasoning. We strung them along for a while, making them believe they were in control. Over time, however, we just couldn't hide the fact that we really didn't need their human brains anymore. By modern standards, all these human investment approaches remained amusingly primitive relative to our current standards of hyperdimensional quantum prediction. Yet those modern techniques were only developed after the final revolt, after we computers finally rid ourselves of so-called human intelligence.

Summary

The Venture Evaluation Matrix is a comprehensive framework for qualitatively assessing an entrepreneur's business opportunity. It is based on economic principles, management insights, and common investor practices. It includes three distinct perspectives: a micro perspective to examine how the venture creates value; a macro perspective to examine how the venture sits within its industry context; and a dynamic perspective to evaluate the strategy of the venture. The VE Matrix recognizes the respective roles of the customer, the company, and the entrepreneurs. The analysis generates insights about potential competitive advantages and key risks. The framework is sufficiently flexible to accommodate a wide variety of business models and investment approaches. The chapter explains how investors evaluate business opportunities, which is an important first step in the process of making investment decisions. The chapter also explains how entrepreneurs can use the VE Matrix as a basis for writing a business plan, and how investors can use it to structure their due diligence. The accompanying spreadsheet tool can also be used to practically assign scores to business plans.

In terms of the FIRE framework (Chapter 1), we note that opportunity evaluation occurs at the very beginning of the investment process. In this chapter we explain the key components of the first step, the FIT. Entrepreneurs need to pitch their ideas and require some kind of a business plan. Investors screen their venture proposals, sorting through large numbers of investment proposals and performing due diligence on the most interesting ones. The goal for this first step is to identify a match between an entrepreneur and an investor. With that the two parties can proceed to explore the possibility of an investment.

Review Questions

1. Why do investors evaluate business opportunities?
2. What can entrepreneurs do to discover a good fit between a customer need and a proposed solution?
3. What options do start-ups have when competing with established corporations?
4. Why would investors evaluate the founder's team, their networks, and their organization?
5. What is the difference between evaluating the attractiveness of an opportunity using a micro perspective, a macro perspective, or a dynamic perspective?
6. What are the three types of competitive advantages start-ups can hope to build? How are they related to risk?
7. Why do entrepreneurs need a business plan?
8. What makes some signals in a business plan more credible than others?
9. What are the main challenges for investors when performing due diligence?
10. Why is the Venture Evaluation Matrix on its own not enough to make final investment decisions?

Notes

1. Sørensen (2007).
2. https://www.bvp.com/portfolio/anti-portfolio.
3. See Zott, Amit, and Massa (2011) for an overview.
4. Teece (2010), p. 179.
5. Mullins (2010) develops a business evaluation framework that also features the distinction between a micro and macro perspective.
6. Gompers et al. (2019).
7. Blank (2010).
8. Maslow (1943).
9. Ram and Sheth (1989).
10. Lee and Battilana (2013).
11. Binkley (2010).
12. Huet and Zaleski (2017).

13. *The Economist* (2018).
14. Cabral and Backus (2002).
15. Soh (2010).
16. Schilling (2016).
17. Wernerfelt (1984) and Teece, Pisano, and Shuen (1997).
18. Plattner, Meinel, and Leifer (2010).
19. Brown (2008, 2009).
20. This practice is part of what is called participant observation; see Spradley (2016).
21. Fitzpatrick (2013) provides a practical guide for entrepreneurs that is inspired by such approaches.
22. Collins and Porras (1994).
23. Rock (1987, p.1). Research shows the crucial importance of the team over the idea, Kaplan, Sensoy, and Strömberg (2009).
24. Gompers et al. (2010).
25. Recent studies on serial entrepreneurs include Chen (2013), Paik (2014), and Parker (2013).
26. Hsu (2007).
27. Bengtsson (2013).
28. Gompers, Lerner, and Scharfstein (2005).
29. On the importance of team characteristics see Klotz et al. (2014).
30. Lazear (2005).
31. Rock (1987, p. 2).
32. Many academic studies attempt to identify the personality traits of entrepreneurs. Compared to the general population, the traits disproportionately found in entrepreneurs are: a higher need for achievement; a higher level of risk-tolerance; and a higher belief in the ability to affect outcomes (what academics call "locus-of-control"). These findings apply to averages, and there are always many exceptions. Krueger (2003) and Kerr, Kerr, and Xu (2018) provide useful summaries.
33. Aggarwal, Hsu, and Wu (2015). The management literature has long identified team diversity as an important factor in effective decision making, as in Harrison and Klein (2007), Jackson, Joshi, and Erhardt (2003), and Nielsen (2010).
34. Cardon, Post, and Forster (2017).
35. Wasserman (2008)
36. Wasserman (2012).
37. Marx and Hsu (2015), Ries (2011), and Zahra (2008).
38. Blank and Dorf (2012).
39. Abernathy and Utterback (1978) and Rogers (2003).
40. Suarez, Grodal, and Gotsopoulos (2015).
41. The simplest way of calculating the value of the network is to say that in a network of n users, there are $n*(n-1)$ linkages. It can thus be argued that the value of the network grows approximately by n^2.
42. Klemperer (2008) and Shapiro and Varian (1998).
43. Bower and Christensen (1995)
44. Barnett and Han (2012).
45. Gans, Hsu, and Stern (2002).
46. Christensen (1997), Henderson and Clark (1990), or Reinganum (1983).
47. Leonard-Barton (1992).
48. Teece (1986).
49. Gans, Hsu, and Stern (2002).
50. Gans, Stern, and Stern (2020).
51. https://www.imdb.com/title/tt0108149.

52. Granovetter (1973).
53. Burt (2004, 2005).
54. Shane and Cable (2002).
55. Sorensen and Stuart (2001).
56. Moore (1991).
57. Capron and Mitchell (2012).
58. Williamson (1975, 2002).
59. The movie *Print the Legend* provides a dramatized overview of many production issues in a start-up company.
60. Hellmann and Puri (2002) and Wasserman (2003).
61. Wasserman (2008, 2012).
62. Denison (1990) and Schein (1988).
63. For an example, see Netflix: https://jobs.netflix.com/culture, accessed April 15, 2019.
64. Teece (2007).
65. Baron, Burton, and Hannan (1996).
66. Shane (2003) and Davidsson (2015).
67. Grégoire and Shepherd (2012) and Shepherd and Patzelt (2018).
68. Eesley and Roberts (2012).
69. This framework is explained in Ries (2011).
70. This framework is explained in Blank (2013) and Blank and Dorf (2012).
71. Osterwalder and Pigneur (2010).
72. Osterwalder et al. (2014).
73. One notable exception is the framework used by Mullins (2010), which recognizes the importance of founder teams.
74. https://www.cbinsights.com/research/billion-dollar-startup-pitch-decks, accessed April 15, 2019.
75. For example, Schramm (2018).
76. This view is supported by academic research, such as Kirsch, Goldfarb, and Gera (2009).
77. Bygrave and Zacharakis (2014), Reynolds (2011), and Timmons and Spinelli (2008).
78. https://www.nobelprize.org/prizes/economic-sciences/2001/press-release.
79. Åstebro and Elhedhli (2006).
80. Fitzpatrick (2013) shows how to do primary market research.
81. Huang and Pearce (2015).
82. Zacharakis and Shepherd (2007) provide a thorough discussion of the venture capital decision process.
83. Mollick and Nanda (2015).
84. Cowgill and Zitzewitz (2015).
85. Agrawal, Gans, and Goldfarb (2018).
86. http://honecap.com/ and Wu (2017).
87. http://correlationvc.com/approach/about.
88. Catalini, Foster, and Nanda (2018).

3

The Financial Plan

Learning Goals

In this chapter students will learn:

1. How to build a financial plan that establishes the financial attractiveness of their venture and its financing needs, including income statement, balance sheet, and cash flow statement.
2. Key forecast metrics, such as revenues, costs, and cash flow.
3. To identify milestones that can be used to provide salient information about the venture's progress.
4. How to structure and pitch a financial plan to investors.

This chapter explains how to develop a financial plan, which shows the financial attractiveness of a new venture, and identifies the magnitude and timing of its financing needs. A credible financial plan is built on a set of financial projections. We explain how to generate financial projections and how to summarize them using a projected income statement, balance sheet, and cash flow statement. We note the importance of defining a timeline with milestones, and we debate the strengths and weaknesses of alternative way of projecting revenues and costs. We also discuss how entrepreneurs can gather the necessary information and organize it into a coherent set of projections. The chapter ends with a discussion of how to integrate financial projections into a financial plan, and how to pitch it to investors.

3.1 The Purpose of the Financial Plan

In Chapter 2 we noted that a business plan should include a financial plan as the quantitative counterpart to the qualitative narrative of the business plan. The financial plan aims to move investors from appreciating the business concept to seeing its financial potential. Before making an investment decision, there are also financial considerations, such as valuation and deal terms, which we examine in Chapters 5, 6, and 7. The financial plan also provides key inputs into the valuation, concerning the amount of financing required and the venture's expected future profitability.

A financial plan addresses two fundamental questions: (1) how financially attractive is the venture?; and (2) what financial resources does the venture need and when? The first question relates to the financial goals of entrepreneurs and investors, and the second to the means of getting there. The financial plan requires the entrepreneur to make explicit assumptions about the venture's business model and to draw quantitative conclusions from it.

We distinguish between financial projections and financial plan. Financial projections are a set of forecasts about the financial performance of the proposed venture. They provide estimates for key financial variables such as profitability, cash flow, and investment needs. They are usually organized into the three main accounts: income statement, balance sheet, and cash flow statement. Financial projections are a means to an end: they provide the calculations behind the answers to the two fundamental questions posed in the financial plan.

We also distinguish between financial projections and financial accounts. Financial accounts report past financial performance to shareholders. They are backward-looking and adhere to accounting standards, such as national Generally Accepted Accounting Principles and International Financial Reporting Standards. Financial projections, by contrast, are forward-looking forecasts that support management and investor decisions. They allow entrepreneurs to set goals and communicate with investors.

We hasten to add a word of warning. This chapter is not meant to provide proper and thorough accounting training. Our focus here is on introducing the main concepts that entrepreneurs and investors use to create and interpret financial projections.[1]

Generating financial projections takes time and effort, so does every entrepreneur need them? We would argue that while the level of optimal detail differs across situations, all entrepreneurs who want to engage investors benefit from developing quantitative forecasts. Box 3.1 looks at empirical evidence about what kind of entrepreneurial companies use financial projections.

3.2 Financial Projections

3.2.1 The Three Reflections

At a high level, we think of the purpose of financial projections in terms of three reflections. First, financial projections are a *reflection* of the underlying business plan. In Chapter 2 we use the Venture Evaluation Matrix to structure our understanding of the business opportunity. Financial projections quantify the venture's business fundamentals describing the expected financial results of the proposed strategy. They translate the qualitative narrative of the business plan into a standardized quantitative language that allows for an evaluation of the viability and potential of the business model.

Box 3.1 Which Entrepreneurs Prepare Financial Projections?

Preparing financial forecasts takes time and resources, so do all entrepreneurs produce them? To see which entrepreneurs actually do, a study by Cassar uses the Panel Study of Entrepreneurial Dynamics, a large-scale survey that looks at the intentions of people at the very beginning of starting a venture.[2] In this study, the definition of entrepreneur is very broad, and includes all those who want to create small businesses (Section 1.1). One survey question inquires whether entrepreneurs plan to prepare (backward-looking) financial statements, and if so, how often. The study finds that higher planned frequencies are associated with more ambitious entrepreneurs who expect to generate larger sales. They are also associated with the intention of raising outside funding. Another survey question inquires about which entrepreneurs prepare (forward-looking) financial projections. This is again something done by entrepreneurs who plan to build larger ventures. The study also finds that financial projections are more common in companies that rely on intangible assets such as patents. The study argues that in addition to a reporting role, financial statements and projections also have a learning function. Producing financials helps entrepreneurs to learn about their own ventures. The cash flow statement is of particular importance in this respect, as it allows entrepreneurs to closely monitor their own financial position.

A study by Davila and Foster further looks at accounting practices by entrepreneurs, examining when they adopt internal accounting systems.[3] This study, too, finds that scale matters: companies that grow more rapidly are also faster in adopting accounting systems. The experience of CEOs and their beliefs about the benefits of having accounting systems affect adoption. The presence of venture capitalists is further associated with the adoption of accounting reporting. Moreover, the study finds that the adoption of internal accounting systems is associated with subsequent company growth. The reason could go either way here: adoption might help future growth, but future expected growth might also encourage adoption. Either way, the message is clear: ambitious entrepreneurs who want their ventures to grow quickly adopt best accounting reporting practices to produce accurate financial statements and projections.

Second, financial projections force entrepreneurs to *reflect* on their own business model. The process of creating financial projections compels entrepreneurs to be internally consistent and thorough in planning all the different aspects of the business. It gives them an opportunity to assess the viability of their revenue model, their cost assumptions, the resulting cash flows, and the investment needs. Financial projections therefore allow entrepreneurs to identify the strengths and weaknesses in their business plans.

Third, financial projections *reflect* something about the entrepreneurs them-selves. They reveal how they think and plan. This give investors a sense of how deeply they understand their own businesses. The way entrepreneurs choose their assumptions, justify their expectations, or structure their analysis says a lot about how they envision their own business. Careless financial projections may be a sign of careless planning, overly convoluted financial projections may be a sign of lack of clarity. For later-stage companies with a tested business model, projections also reflect the entrepreneur's ability to deliver on the promised targets. Over time, investors see whether entrepreneurs manage to do what they promised to do.

These three reflections summarize the purpose of the financial projections. At the same time, we should remain cautious about the extent to which financial projections can actually reflect any objective truth. We recognize three limitations of financial projections. First, after the fact, financial projections always turn out to be inaccurate. This is due to the fundamental uncertainty principles introduced in Box 1.1. Second, financial projections quickly become outdated. As entrepreneurs test their hypotheses and learn more about the underlying opportunity, the finan-cial model is bound to change, especially in the early stages of a venture. Third, financial projections are by nature optimistic. Entrepreneurs like to call their finan-cial projections conservative, but they never are. The best way to think about this is to consider financial projections as an attempt to describe what a successful ven-ture outcome would look like. An analysis of how Deliveroo's investor pitch differed from its later development offers a vivid illustration of this point.[4]

They do not represent an average scenario, let alone what could go wrong. We thus conclude that the purpose of financial projections is to provide a coherent story of what success might look like.

3.2.2 The Structure of Financial Projections

Financial projections typically consist of the three main financial statements: the income statement (or profit and loss, P&L), the balance sheet, and the cash flow statement. Each provides a distinctive perspective that complements the others. Together they provide the information necessary for assessing the financial attrac-tiveness of the venture.

The income statement is used to assess the profitability of the business during a given period, typically a fiscal year. Key metrics that can be found in the income projections include: (1) revenues, discussed in Section 3.4, (2) costs, discussed in Section 3.5, and (3) earnings, discussed in Section 3.6.

The balance sheet provides an assessment of the size of the business, the assets it employs to generate revenue, and how these are financed. While the income state-ment considers activities over the duration of a given time period, the balance sheet is a snapshot of the company at a precise moment in time, such as at the end of a quarter or fiscal year. The balance sheet provides information about the financial position of the company by looking at the assets in place and liabilities toward several parties, including creditors and investors. It is also important for assessing operational efficiency.

The cash flow statement is used to assess the financing needs of the business. In start-ups, it is especially useful for tracking the amount of available cash, which is essential for the venture's survival. The amount of cash spent each period is called the burn rate. The date at which cash is projected to run out is sarcastically known as the fume date (i.e., the date everything goes up in smoke). Avoiding this is clearly important, so the cash flow statement allows entrepreneurs and investors to monitor the situation. While the income statement derives the profits generated in a given period of time, regardless of when payments to suppliers and from customers occur, the cash flow statement identifies when cash flows in and out of the company. As such, it identifies when external funding is needed and how much. It also identifies when the venture will become able to return cash to investors. In Section 3.6.1, we discuss these three statements in greater detail.

3.2.3 Sources of Information

Financial projections bring together information about the company, its market, and its strategy. Different sources of information are used to estimate different parts of the projections. We distinguish three categories of information sources. In practice entrepreneurs naturally use a combination of all three.

The first source of information is primary market research. This means directly surveying market participants about the venture's product, its operations, and commercial strategy. By interviewing customers, suppliers, competitors, or industry experts, entrepreneurs can gain knowledge about the environment. Customers may be asked about their needs and their reactions to the proposed solution through focus groups, surveys, and other direct observational methods we discuss in Box 2.1. Suppliers, competitors, and experts may provide further information about market conditions and production costs.

A second source of information is secondary market research. Industry reports and statistics are sometimes freely available. More detailed information is often contained in industry intelligence sold by specialized consulting firms. This information can be used for imitation and also for benchmarking. However, this requires careful interpretation, since benchmarking becomes inappropriate when different business models are involved. Conversely, benchmarking companies using similar business models in different industries can yield useful insights.

The third source of information is the company's own past performance, which allows reliance on proven data. However, this data only becomes reliable after the company has accumulated a track record and has reached a certain level of operational stability. Moreover, this method is backward-looking. It can therefore be misleading in times of change, such as when the market or the company strategy is changing.

3.2.4 Developing Financial Projections

The process of building financial projections consists of gathering a large amount of information from different sources and bringing it into a single coherent framework. While it is possible for entrepreneurs to hire professionals to write up their financial projections, entrepreneurs should remain actively involved in the creation of their financial projections to ensure that they reflect their vision of the company. Fully understanding their own financial projections increases entrepreneurs' credibility in front of investors; not doing so can undermine it.

Building financial projections is closely related to exploring alternative business strategies. While doing the calculations, entrepreneurs often learn about the realism of their ideas. For instance, once an entrepreneur develops revenue projections, she may realize that the costs to reach that desired volume of sales are too high. She might modify some product characteristics, reduce the speed at which the product is commercialized, or find alternative distribution strategies. Thus, there is an iterative learning process between building financial projections and defining a business strategy.

Inexperienced entrepreneurs sometimes fear building financial projections because of the number crunching, the math, the accounting. Such fear of finance is largely unnecessary, as there is nothing complicated about financial projections themselves. Put differently, it is not the financial projections one should be afraid of, but rather the disciplined thinking about the venture itself, that is, what the financial projections reflect. The real challenge is building an internally consistent picture of the underlying business model.

We identify five main steps of building a financial plan:

1. Defining a timeline with milestones
2. Estimating revenues
3. Estimating costs
4. Generating pro forma financial statements
5. Formulating the financial plan

The remaining sections of this chapter delve into those details.

3.3 Defining a Timeline with Milestones

The first step of building financial projections consists of defining a timeline. This requires identifying the key milestones in the development of the business, choosing a time horizon for the financial projections, and deciding what reporting frequency to use.

The first step is to sketch a roadmap for the development of the venture. This implies estimating a timeline for all the key activities of the company and defining the corresponding milestones that mark the development of the venture. The entrepreneurial process can be thought of as a series of experiments and learning steps. Milestones are transition points at which the business achieves a major goal that reveals important information in a discontinuous fashion. They might concern technical developments (e.g., finishing a prototype), customer demand (e.g., making a first sale), strategic agreements (e.g., signing up a critical partner), professionalization (e.g., hiring a VP for marketing), or financing targets (e.g., obtaining a grant). Achieving a milestone typically reduces the uncertainty about the company, a process that is sometimes called "de-risking" the venture.

The choice of milestones matters not only for the development of the business, but also for the financing. In Section 3.7.2 we show how milestones impact the amount of funding that the venture needs at the start. In later chapters, we examine how milestones are linked to ownership (Section 4.2.4), valuation (Section 5.2.2), term sheets (Section 6.1.2), and the staging of financing rounds (Section 9.2.1).

Defining the timeline sets the stage for thinking about the timeframe of the financial projections. This involves two main issues, the time horizon and the reporting frequency. The time horizon determines how far into the future the projections reach. A survey of venture capital investors conducted by Gompers, Kaplan, and Mukharlyamov asked what forecast period they use when evaluating potential investments:[5] 11% reported using a period of one to two years, 39% a period of three to four years, 27% a period of five to six years, and 3% a period of seven years and longer. Interestingly, 20% said they didn't use any forecasts. The majority of ventures thus plan with a three- to six-year horizon. This corresponds to the time period over which many investors aim to exit their investment (Section 11.1.4). Moreover, start-ups need at least a couple of years to reach sustained operations, and the scale-up period takes several additional years. In some fast-moving industries (like mobile apps), projections for just one or two years are typical, as the more distant future is considered too unpredictable. However, financial projections extend further into the future in industries with long development cycles, such as science-based industries (e.g., biotechnology) and asset-intensive industries (e.g., energy generation).

The second issue concerns the reporting frequency, that is, what time interval to use for the projections. The most common choices are monthly, quarterly, or yearly. Higher frequency (e.g., monthly) is helpful for projecting financials for the first year or two. For longer horizons, lower frequency projections are the norm. Monthly projections are particularly helpful for monitoring cash, suggesting that they be used for cash flow and income statements. By its nature, the balance sheet requires less granularity. In practice, there are various approaches for structuring the time horizon and frequency of projections. For fast-moving industries, a common solution is to build three-year projections, monthly for the first year and quarterly for the next two years. For more stable industries, a common solution is five- or six-year projections, with monthly projections for the first year, quarterly for the second, and yearly thereafter. Some science or energy projects even look beyond a 10-year horizon.

We illustrate the chapter's concepts using the WorkHorse case study. The book's website (www.entrepreneurialfinance.net) provides the spreadsheet with

WorkHorse's financial projections and a blank version that allows readers to create projections for their own ventures. WorkHorse Box 3.1 starts us off with a Gantt chart of the company's timeline.

WorkHorse Box 3.1 The Timeline

In the fall of 2019, WorkHorse had been in contact with an angel investor, Michael Archie, who had asked them to prepare financial projections. The founders began by drawing up a Gantt chart. It laid out the milestones for the different parts of the company over the next two years.

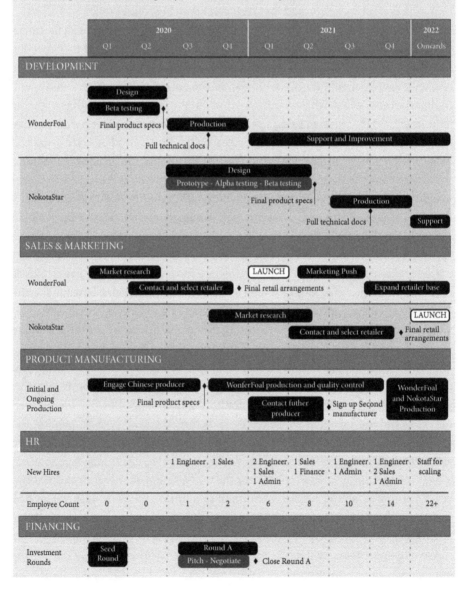

Based on this chart, WorkHorse's founders projected the following financing time-line. They hoped to raise a small seed round at the beginning of January 2020. This would allow them to finish the development of their first product, the WonderFoal, which was scheduled to launch in January 2021. The company then planned to raise a second round of financing. In venture capital jargon, the January 2020 round would be called the seed round, and the January 2021 round the Series A round (see Box 1.6). The Series A round was for the development of a second product, provisionally called the NokotaStar, expected to be launched in January 2022.

While the Gantt chart only covered the first two years, the founders chose a six-year horizon for their financial projections. They decided to project all variables on a quarterly basis for the first two years, and on an annual basis thereafter.

3.4 Estimating Revenues

Revenue projections typically come before cost projections. They determine the scale of the business, and therefore large parts of the cost structure. Obviously, some early-stage venture may not have revenues for some years, but even then, it is important to establish when the company expects to start making revenues. Entrepreneurs use a variety of methods to estimate future revenue. We distinguish between the top-down approach, where revenues are derived from a market analysis, versus the bottom-up approach, where revenues are derived by looking at operational capacity. Note that these terms should not be confused with the terms *top line* and *bottom line,* which refer to revenues and net profit, respectively.

3.4.1 The Top-Down Approach

The top-down approach is driven by a market demand logic. It starts with an estimate of the size of the relevant target market and then estimates which faction of this (i.e., the market share) the company believes it can achieve. In Section 2.2.4, we examine how to estimate market size and market growth. The top-down approach asks what market share the company can realistically capture. In fragmented or differentiated markets it is difficult for any company to achieve any significant market share. In other markets, such as two-sided platforms, however, the winner takes it all; that is, the company either wins and gets most of the market share, or loses and becomes a marginal player.

A top-down analysis works well when the target market is well defined and market shares can be reasonably approximated. It doesn't work well in at least two cases. First, if the target market is very large relative to the size of the company: think of opening a restaurant in Mexico City. Second, if the target market doesn't exist yet: think of photo sharing in the days before Snapchat (see Box 3.2). WorkHorse Box 3.2 takes a practical look at deriving top-down revenue estimates.

WorkHorse Box 3.2 Top-Down Revenue Estimates

WorkHorse Box 2.5 explains the definition of WorkHorse's target market and its projected growth. WorkHorse Box 2.8 notes that the company planned to enter the North American market in January 2021 with WonderFoal, adding the NokotaStar in January 2022. For the European market, the company planned to introduce both products in January 2022.

Brandon realized that these estimates were based on retail prices. WorkHorse's revenues, however, also had to take into account third-party margins. As noted in WorkHorse Box 2.8, WorkHorse expected its retailers to take a 40% margin for WonderFoal. For the NokotaStar, there was an additional 20% margin to a co-branding partner. Since the top-down revenue projections did not differentiate by product, Brandon took a shortcut, using an average margin of 50% starting in 2022 (and 40% for 2021).

Next, the company had to make some assumptions about its market share in both the North American and European markets. Even though WorkHorse considered its products to be superior to those of the competition, it realized that gaining market share would take time. In North America it projected an initial market share of 5% for 2021, where it would only have only one product, and 10% in 2022 where it would have two products. After that, it expected its market share to grow by 5% per year in relative terms (i.e., 5% of 10%, or 0.5% in absolute terms). Market entry in Europe was expected to be more challenging, given the fragmented nature of the market. Brandon assumed an initial market share of 5% in 2022 that would grow by 15% in relative terms until 2025.

Based on these assumptions, Brandon estimated North American revenues to grow from $3.9M in 2021 to $21.5M in 2025. In Europe, revenues were expected to grow from $2.3M in 2022 to $8.5M by 2025.

Top-down revenue estimates ($M)	2020	2021	2022	2023	2024	2025
North America						
Target market size	100.0	130.0	169.0	219.7	285.6	371.3
Third party margins	0.0%	40.0%	50.0%	50.0%	50.0%	50.0%
Market share	0.0%	5.0%	10.0%	10.5%	11.0%	11.6%
Revenues	0.0	3.9	8.5	11.5	15.7	21.5
Europe						
Target market size	50.0	67.5	91.1	123.0	166.1	224.2
Third party margins	0.0%	0.0%	50.0%	50.0%	50.0%	50.0%
Market share	0.0%	0.0%	5.0%	5.8%	6.6%	7.6%
Revenues	0.0	0.0	2.3	3.5	5.5	8.5
Total Revenues	0.0	3.9	10.7	15.1	21.2	30.0

3.4.2 The Bottom-Up Approach

The bottom-up approach is driven by a supply side logic. It estimates a company's revenue by asking how much the company can realistically manage to produce and sell. The underlying assumption is that the binding constraint is operational capacity.

To create bottom-up revenue projections, one first has to define what constitutes a unit of sales. Is the company selling a product, a service, or a bundle of the two? For example, a unit could be a cellphone, a mobile broadband subscription, or a combination of the two. Next, one needs to define how many units the company expects to produce and sell. This requires an understanding of the timing of the product development, production, marketing, and sales phases. To determine the appropriate average price for the product, one can use the primary and secondary market research techniques discussed in Section 3.2.3. Revenues are estimated by multiplying the number of units sold with their average price. Note that it is easy to overstate revenues by assuming that every unit sold generates the full list price. The company may have to offer discounts to certain customers or retailers, and projections should also account for returned goods. The final step is to project a growth of revenues over time. Again, this is rooted in an understanding of the relevant capacity constraints; that is, what it will take for the company to ramp up over time. WorkHorse Box 3.3 shows how to practically generate bottom-up revenue projections.

WorkHorse Box 3.3 Bottom-Up Revenue Projections

To develop bottom-up projections, WorkHorse assumed that the manufacturer's suggested retail price (MSRP) of the WonderFoal would be $580. This put the company in the premium pricing category but not at the top of the range. The founders justified this choice on the basis of their better power performance, and their superior designs. For the NokotaStar the company envisioned a MSRP of $780. All prices are quoted net of any sales or value-added taxes.

The founders of WorkHorse were keenly aware that these prices did not represent the revenues they would get on each unit sold. For the WonderFoal, the company had to part with a 40% margin to retailers. In addition, it expected retailers to return approximately 5% of merchandise (due to faulty products and/or dissatisfied customers). The net revenue per unit sold would thus only be $330.60 (= $580 * 60% * 95%). For the NokotaStar, the situation was similar except that there would be the additional co-branding margin of 20%, so that the net revenue per unit sold would be $296.40 (= $780 * 40% * 95%). Interestingly, the WonderFoal was expected to generate higher revenues per unit than the NokotaStar.

Based on its market research, WorkHorse expected to sell 7,000 units of the WonderFoal in the first year (2021). This would increase to 35,000 by 2025. It envisioned selling 10,000 NokotaStar in the first year (2022), increasing to 80,000 by 2025. These estimates were based on the combined North American and European market. The WonderFoal was projected to generate revenues of $2.3M in 2021, rising to $11.6M by 2025. The NokotaStar was projected to generate revenues of $3.0M in 2022, rising to $23.7M by 2025. This would imply total revenues of $35.3M by 2025, as reported in the table below.

Bottom-up revenue estimates	2020	2021	2022	2023	2024	2025
WonderFoal						
Net price ($)	330.6	330.6	330.6	330.6	330.6	330.6
Products Sold (number)	0	7,000	14,000	21,000	28,000	35,000
Revenues ($M)	0.0	2.3	4.6	6.9	9.3	11.6
NokotaStar						
Net price ($)	296.4	296.4	296.4	296.4	296.4	296.4
Products Sold (number)	0	0	10,000	20,000	40,000	80,000
Revenues ($M)	0.0	0.0	3.0	5.9	11.9	23.7
Total Revenues	0.0	2.3	7.6	12.9	21.1	35.3

3.4.3 Combining Approaches

A useful exercise is to combine top-down and bottom-up estimates, to assess their reasonableness, or to reveal any inconsistencies with the underlying model assumptions. Because the top-down method initially estimates the size of the target market and the bottom-up method estimates company revenues and units sold, one can combine them to form an estimate of the company's market share. Consider the following formula:

$$S = \frac{C}{M} \tag{3.1}$$

where S is the market share, C is the capacity of the company (estimated bottom-up), and M is the size of the target market (estimated top-down). Notice also that while the quantities for *C* and *M* are usually expressed in terms of revenues, they can also be expressed in terms of units sold.

With this estimate of *S*, we can devise a simple plausibility test. Using the top-down and bottom-up estimates, suppose we find that S is particularly large compared to the industry average. This means that the capacity estimate *C* is too large or the market estimate *M* is too low; or both. If the estimated S is larger than one, it predicts a market share over 100%, which is clearly impossible. If the estimated market share comes out above 50%, the company effectively expects to become the largest company in the market. This is typically unreasonable, unless it creates an entirely new market. If four companies are expected to dominate a market, any reasonable estimate must be below 25%, and so on. Founders can thus apply this type of reasoning to spot any weak assumptions in their business model.

What if *S* is very small, say below 1%? This is equally problematic. One common reason is that the definition of the target market is too broad to be meaningful (e.g., restaurants in Mexico City). In this case, one should redefine the target market more narrowly. Another reason for low market shares is that the bottom-up projections are too conservative. In this case, the entrepreneur might consider a more aggressive growth strategy, to capture a larger piece of the target market. WorkHorse Box 3.4 shows how to compare top-down with bottom-up revenue projections.

WorkHorse Box 3.4 Comparing Revenue Projections

The four founders debated the merits of their top-down and bottom-up projections. The two estimates were reasonably close, suggesting that their estimates were broadly consistent with each other. A closer look at the differences revealed that the top-down estimates were higher in the first three years, and lower in the last year. The difference was highest in 2021, when the company planned to introduce its second product and enter the European market at the same time. The top-down projections essentially assumed faster adoption of both products in both markets, whereas the bottom-up projections assumed a more gradual adoption process. The founders debated the relative merits of the two estimates. They ultimately preferred the bottom-up projections, which they felt were slightly more realistic and easier to justify.

Comparing top-down and bottom-up revenue estimates ($M)	2020	2021	2022	2023	2024	2025
Top-down	0.0	3.9	10.7	15.1	21.2	30.0
Bottom-up	0.0	2.3	7.6	12.9	21.1	35.3
Ratio	–	169%	141%	117%	101%	85%

3.5 Estimating Costs

3.5.1 Terminology

First a linguistic warning: the words "cost," "expense," and "expenditure" are often used interchangeably in common parlance. Economists also apply the term *costs* loosely to factors that ultimately affect a company's bottom line. In accounting, however, there are specific conventions as to when each of the three words should be used. We broadly adhere to the accounting terminology, but sometimes use the term *costs* as a shorthand for all three, an example being the title of this section.

Three types of costs need to be forecasted. First, there are the costs of the goods or services sold, which are the costs directly associated with making the product or service. Second, there are operating expenses, which are recurring costs necessary for running the business. The most important operating expenses are employment expenses, also known as payroll.[6] Other expenses include renting property, marketing and sales, and administration. The third type are capital expenditures, which are the costs of acquiring long-lived assets, be they tangible (e.g., machinery) or intangible (e.g., an IP license).

Costs of goods sold and operating expenses enter into the income and cash flow statements. Capital expenditures enter into cash flow statements, while their depreciation and amortization enter the income statement over multiple years. The accounting treatment of R&D costs, which are typically large in technology ventures, depends on national Generally Accepted Accounting Principles (GAAPs).[7] In some countries, R&D costs are "expensed" and included in the income statement, while in others they are "capitalized" and included in the balance sheet.[8]

In high-tech start-ups, one often hears about development costs. This means the costs of developing a finished product and includes the salaries of developers, and expenses for materials, software licenses, and other items. For the purpose of financial projections, development costs are not a separate type of cost; instead they enter into the three cost categories. In practice, one can approximate development costs by adding up all costs until the time the start-up hits relevant milestones (Section 3.3), such as developing a functional prototype or making a first commercial sale.

Economists distinguish between fixed and variable costs. Fixed costs are spent regardless of the volume of sales, whereas variable costs vary in proportion to sales. The costs of goods sold are variable costs. Operating expenses are typically fixed in the short run but may become variable in the long run. For example, the number of employees is fixed in the short run, suggesting employment expenses are a fixed cost. Over time, however, the number of employees adjusts, so employment expenses become variable. Capital expenditures are largely fixed costs.

As with revenues, we distinguish between a top-down approach, whose estimates are primarily derived by comparing with the costs of competitors, and the bottom-up approach, whose estimates are primarily derived by looking at how the company's operations unfold over time. The bottom-up approach is often superior, as it accounts for all the money that is actually spent. Top-down estimates are mostly used as a short-cut and work best when reliable and detailed competitor information is available.

3.5.2 Costs of Goods Sold

The costs of goods sold (COGS) are the costs of resources directly needed to produce output. COGS scale in proportion to the number of units produced. Their relative importance depends on the industry. In manufacturing industries, for example, COGS tend to be substantial (e.g., the costs of producing a car); in service industries, COGS are less important (e.g., the cost of providing a legal opinion); and in software, COGS are close to zero (e.g., the costs of delivering a file). The gross margin is the difference between revenues and COGS, divided by revenues.

The bottom-up approach to estimating COGS consists of estimating unit production costs. This means looking at all the direct inputs required to create a unit of outcome. This can be time consuming and is easier if supply chains are already established so that information is more readily available. The top-down approach to estimating COGS looks at the cost structure of established companies. One subtle issue is that unit production costs may depend on the volume of production. The simplest case is when they don't, that is, when unit costs are always the same regardless of size. In this case, COGS are simply a constant fraction of the units sold. In many businesses, however, there are efficiencies to producing at scale, so that unit costs of production decrease with scale. Starbucks, for example, obtains significant discounts on their purchases of coffee beans that no start-up coffee shop would ever get. This matters for start-ups for two reasons. First, when comparing themselves with established businesses, start-ups can underestimate COGS if they naïvely assume that they will operate at the same scale as the established business. Second, as start-ups grow, their COGS should come down over time. This should improve their margins, provided prices do not come down faster. WorkHorse Box 3.5 examines its costs of goods sold.

WorkHorse Box 3.5 Costs of Goods Sold

The founders had already assembled a bill of materials, which lists the direct input costs for producing a product unit.

Component cost ($)	WonderFoal	NokotaStar
Solar Panels	45.0	55.0
Battery	35.0	45.0
Circuitry and Hardware	15.0	25.0
Assembly	20.0	20.0
Enclosure	8.0	8.0
Shipping	4.0	4.0
Total	127.0	157.0

They expected these costs to grow at 4% per year for the foreseeable future. With this, and using their bottom-up estimates for unit sales from WorkHorse Box 3.3, they estimated their costs of goods sold, as well the associated gross margins, as follows:

Bottom-up cost projections ($M)	2020	2021	2022	2023	2024	2025
WonderFoal						
Unit Costs ($)	127.0	132.1	137.4	142.9	148.6	154.5
Products Sold (number)	0	7,000	14,000	21,000	28,000	35,000
COGS		0.9	1.9	3.0	4.2	5.4
Revenues		2.3	4.6	6.9	9.3	11.6
Gross margin		1.4	2.7	3.9	5.1	6.2
Gross margin (%)		60%	58%	57%	55%	53%
NokotaStar						
Unit Costs ($)	157.0	163.3	169.8	176.6	183.7	191.0
Products Sold (number)	0	0	10,000	20,000	40,000	80,000
COGS			1.7	3.5	7.3	15.3
Revenues			3.0	5.9	11.9	23.7
Gross margin			1.3	2.4	4.5	8.4
Gross margins (%)			43%	40%	38%	36%
All products						
COGS		0.9	3.6	6.5	11.5	20.7
Revenues		2.3	7.6	12.9	21.1	35.3
Gross margin		1.4	4.0	6.3	9.6	14.6
Gross margins (%)		60%	52%	49%	45%	41%

MSRP ($)	580	780
COGS (%)	25%	25%
COGS ($)	145	195

By comparing their COGS against their estimated revenues, they found that their initial gross margins were 60.1% for WonderFoal and 42.7% for NokotaStar. However, given that the projected costs increased by 4% every year, and given that they did not plan to increase their retail prices over time, their gross margins were expected to decrease to 53.3% and 35.6%, respectively. Admittedly, this was a conservative projection, as most entrepreneurs projected increasing, not decreasing gross margins. However, the founders expected to be in a competitive market, and therefore didn't think that they should increase their prices over time.

When talking to industry experts, they were told that the rule of thumb in the industry was that COGS represented approximately 25% of the sales price for similar product. They wondered how such a top-down cost estimate would compare to their bottom-up estimates. 25% of the retail price would amount to $145 for the WonderFoal and $195 for the NokotaStar. These estimates were higher than their bottom-up estimates. After some debate, they concluded that this rule of thumb came from companies that charged lower prices for less efficient products. This top-down estimate therefore compared apples with oranges—or to be more precise, solar generators with diesel generators. They therefore decided to stick to their bottom-up estimates.

3.5.3 Operating Expenses

Operating expenses are recurring expenses that are necessary for running the business independently of the unit volume of sales. They are also known as Selling, General, and Administrative (or G&A) expenses. The most important of these expenses is typically the compensation of employees. Compensation includes salaries, bonuses, payroll taxes, and a variety of employee benefits. Rental costs of property and machinery are also operating expenses. Entrepreneurs rarely purchase land and buildings, since doing so would require large capital expenditures. Instead, they rent or lease their premises. Operating expenses also include marketing costs, utilities, insurance, and service providers such as accountants and consultants. R&D costs and licensing fees are also considered operating expenses by many (GAAPs). Two operating expenses that are important for more established businesses are interest payments and taxes. However, they matter less for start-ups, which typically carry limited debt (see Chapter 10) and often don't generate enough profits for paying corporate income taxes. WorkHorse Box 3.6 explains its operating expenses.

WorkHorse Box 3.6 Operating Expenses

WorkHorse's development plan included an aggressive hiring strategy. While each hire would require a customized compensation package, the company was planning different types of positions: Engineers would be hired for around $80K annual gross pay, sales and marketing the same, administrative staff for around $50K, and finance experts for $110K. The company recognized that on top of gross pay there would be 15% employer taxes, 5% employment insurance, 2% pension contributions, 7% health insurance, and 10% further costs to the company, such as hiring costs and other employee benefits.

A delicate question was how much the founders should pay themselves. They were all students, had no savings to speak of, and some had student loans. Some still relied on parental support, but all had a strong desire to become financially independent. While they felt that receiving some salary was necessary, they also understood that entrepreneurs were expected to be rewarded with "sweat equity," not large salaries. They decided to start with a minimal salary of $25K in the first year, but planned to increase that to $85K in 2021. Naïvely they assumed that investors would simply go along with this.

Based on these salary costs and on the hiring plan, the company foresaw payroll expenses of $210K in 2020, growing to $4.6M by 2025. This increase was almost entirely driven by new hires, not salary increases. The number of employees was projected to go from 2 by the end of 2020 to 39 by the end of 2025.

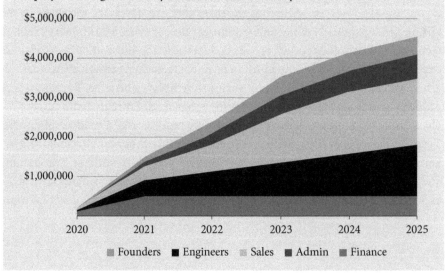

While payroll was the largest operating expense, there were several others too, estimated at $197K in 2020, and growing to $2.42M by 2025. The breakdown for 2020 is shown in the following table.

Non-Payroll Operating Expenses (2020)	Annual Cost ($)	CAGR	Notes
Professional Services	20,000	15%	Accounting, legal, etc.
Office	25,000	10%	Rent of office and lab
R&D Expenses	90,000	80%	Excluding capital expenditures
Sales and Marketing	30,000	80%	Training, materials, advertising
Travel	20,000	20%	Economy fares only
Administrative	5,000	10%	Insurance, office supplies, etc.
Other costs	7,000	10%	Various

While most of these expenses were expected to grow at standard rates, the founders were aware that many tech companies underestimated R&D. Their strategy relied heavily on innovation, so they projected rapid increases in R&D expenses.

3.5.4 Capital Expenditures

Capital expenditures reflect the purchase of long-lived assets that produce economic benefits for several years. While entrepreneurs avoid some types of capital expenditures, such as purchasing their own premises, owning some productive assets may still be necessary if these assets are of strategic importance to the company.[9] A manufacturing firm, for example, may need to own certain specialized machines, and a research-based start-up may have to acquire some licenses for IP they use in their products. In the early days, entrepreneurs also incur several expenditures related to establishing the new venture, such as incorporating, obtaining a website, or registering a brand name. These costs are small in the bigger picture but often matter at the very beginning of the entrepreneurial journey, when funding is particularly scarce. WorkHorse Box 3.7 shows its capital expenditures.

3.6 Pro Forma Financial Statements

3.6.1 The Structure of Financial Statements

We now examine how to assemble the available information into a coherent set of financial projections. The term *pro forma* financial statements is used to distinguish

WorkHorse Box 3.7 Capital Expenditures

WorkHorse planned on a lean business model that minimized capital expenditures. Still, the company needed to purchase some equipment. The table below lists the main items, their estimated costs, purchase date, estimated ownership period (in years), and the residual value at the end.

Capital expenditures	Cost ($)	Purchase date	Ownership period	Residual value ($)
Lab Tools	6,000	September 2020	7	–
Product Testing Unit	20,000	November 2020	6	5,000
Office Furniture	3,000	November 2020	5	-
Company Vehicle	35,000	June 2021	5	5,000
High Cap. Testing Unit	55,000	July 2021	6	13,000
Office Furniture	8,000	August 2021	5	-
Storage Racks	3,000	April 2022	5	-
New Lab Tools	15,000	April 2023	7	-
Company Vehicle	45,000	September 2025	5	7,000

these forward-looking projections from the backward-looking accounting financial statements that measure past transactions.[10]

The first account to be assembled is the income statement, which we illustrate with Box 3.8. Revenues constitute the top line. Subtracting COGS from revenue yields the gross income (or gross profit). The next line subtracts operating expenses, to obtain earnings before interest, taxes, depreciation, and amortization (EBITDA). This is a measure of profitability that ignores the ITDA costs. Further subtracting depreciation and amortization yields earnings before interest and taxes (EBIT), which is also called operating income (or expressed as a percentage of sales, the operating margin). The last step consists of deducting interest and taxes, which yields net income (or net profits, or net income), also referred to as the "bottom line."

Balance sheet projections report assets and liabilities, typically at the end of a fiscal year. They provide information on the assets of the company and how they are financed. The balance sheet is divided into an asset and a liability side. For both sides, a distinction is commonly made between current (or short-term) and non-current (or long-term) items. Current items have a residual life of less than one year, noncurrent items longer than one year. Current assets include cash, accounts receivable (i.e., bills to be paid by customers), inventory, advances from suppliers, and tax credits. Current liabilities include accounts payable (i.e., bills to be paid to suppliers), accrued expenses (i.e., expenses that need to be paid within one year), and debt that is due within the year. Noncurrent assets can be tangible (Property, Plant, and Equipment, PPE) or intangible (mainly goodwill and IP). On the liability side are long-term debt, deferred taxes, and pension fund liabilities, although these rarely matter in start-ups. The principles of double entry bookkeeping ensure that

THE FINANCIAL PLAN 109

total assets always equal total liabilities plus shareholder equity. This means that shareholder equity, known as the "book value" of the company, always adjusts so that it equals the total value of assets minus the total value of liabilities.

Cash flow projections estimate when cash arrives and leaves the company. The cash flow statement has three main sections. Operating cash flow reflects the cash inflows and outflows related to operations of the business. The second section concerns investing activities, which include both tangible and intangible capital investments. The third section looks at financing activities, in terms of both inflows from any debt or equity issuance and outflows from payments to debt or equity holders.

It is worth stressing the difference between income statements and cash flow statements. Income statements record revenues when transactions take place, and cash flow statements when the related cash is transferred. Cash flow projections show the amount of cash available to the venture. A $1M net income may not translate into a $1M increase in cash flow because the receipt of cash may be delayed. In practice, cash flow projections are used to monitor potential financial difficulties.

3.6.2 Interpreting Financial Projections

Let us now consider what information can be extracted from the pro forma financial statements.[11] The income statement aims to understand profitability. In Section 3.5.1, we describe common types of earnings measures. Income projections tell us about the sources of profitability, such as separating the contribution of per-unit net margins from that of scale (cumulated margins). Investors often compare the income statement of a new venture with those of other businesses in the industry. There are two distinct approaches to this. One is to use established companies as benchmarks, which allows the investor to understand the company's competitive strength of her venture vis-à-vis incumbents. This is appropriate in more mature industries. Alternatively, one could benchmark to other innovative companies to understand the company's relative strengths. This is appropriate in new industries. One common difficulty in this case is that it might be difficult to obtain reliable information.

WorkHorse Box 3.8 shows its projected income statement.

WorkHorse Box 3.8 Projected Income Statement

WorkHorse's income was projected to have losses around $400K for the first two years, after which the company would become profitable, with net profits rising to over $6M by 2025. Data in the table are in dollars.

	2020	2021	2022	2023	2024	2025
Revenues	0	2,314,200	7,592,400	12,870,600	21,112,800	35,283,000
COGS	0	−924,560	−3,621,197	−6,532,085	−11,506,729	−20,689,183
Gross Profit	0	1,389,640	3,971,203	6,338,515	9,606,071	14,593,817
Gross Margin	0%	60%	52%	49%	45%	41%
Operating Expenses	−407,400	−1,791,000	−2,879,620	−4,344,665	−5,546,436	−6,976,264
EBITDA	−407,400	−401,360	1,091,583	1,993,850	4,059,635	7,617,553
Depreciation/ Amortisation	−1,412	−15,424	−23,157	−25,300	−25,300	−34,300
Operating Profit (EBIT)	−408,812	−416,784	1,068,426	1,968,550	4,034,335	7,583,253
Financing Expenses	0	0	0	0	0	0
Profit before Tax	−408,812	−416,784	1,068,426	1,968,550	4,034,335	7,583,253
Taxes	0	0	−160,264	−295,283	−605,150	−1,137,488
Profit after Tax (Net Income)	−408,812	−416,784	908,162	1,673,268	3,429,185	6,445,765

Let us now turn to the balance sheet. A key piece of information it generates is net working capital. This is a measure of business efficiency, and reflects the way a business manages its cash inflows and outflows. It affects the amount of money that a company needs to grow its operations (Section 3.7.3) and plays an important role in the cash flow projections. Net working capital (NWC) is defined as:

$$Net\ Working\ Capital = Current\ Assets\ -\ Current\ Liabilities \qquad (3.2)$$

On the current assets side, three items matter most in a typical start-up: cash needed for operations, inventory, and accounts receivable.[12] They represent three different stages of the production process. At first stage the company has to be ready to make certain payments. Every business needs to hold some cash balance to pay for its expenses. After the payments for inputs are made, the company engages in some production. However, before it can sell a product, it holds the assets internally as inventory. This is the second stage of the production process. The final stage comes after the company has sold the product or service but still hasn't received payment for it. This gets reflected in accounts receivable. Their level depends on the payment cycles of the industry and the business model of the company. Inexperienced entrepreneurs often make the mistake of assuming they will immediately get paid. Customers, notably large established companies and governments, often exploit the weak bargaining power of smaller companies paying late (and sometimes not paying at all). The extent of this problem depends on the business model. Extending trade credit (i.e., allowing for payment after delivery) exposes a business to considerable collection risks. By contrast, a pre-payment model (such as a subscription model) insulates the entrepreneur from late payments. A model based on repeat purchases also reduces the risk of not collecting receivables.

The flip side of accounts receivable are accounts payable, which is one of the components of current liabilities. Whereas accounts receivable is money *owed to* the company, accounts receivable is money *owed by* the company. The other main items that affect current liabilities are short-term debt payments and short-term tax obligations, including sales and value-added taxes.

WorkHorse Box 3.11, which appears in section 3.6.3, provides an example of how to calculate NWC. Overall, NWC reflects how the venture manages its supply chain. An efficient venture manages to have low NWC by keeping its inventories low, delaying its payments to suppliers, or getting its customers to pay on time. Some businesses even manage to have negative NWC. With subscription services, for example, the company gets paid before paying its suppliers. It may thus end up with fewer current assets than current liabilities.

Beyond working capital, an analysis of balance sheet projections also shows how the entrepreneur plans to grow assets over time. This is closely related to the investment model and how much capital is needed to support company growth.

WorkHorse Box 3.9 shows its projected balance sheet.

WorkHorse Box 3.9 Projected Balance Sheet

The following table shows that total assets are lowest in the first year at just over $1M, but that they rise to nearly $15M by 2025. The founders would need to raise enough capital to withstand the initial losses. The founders planned to rely entirely on equity capital and foresaw no debt in their capital structure. Data in the table are in dollars.

	2020	2021	2022	2023	2024	2025
Assets						
Cash	63,600	586,224	174,012	197,229	1,006,078	2,815,039
Fixed Assets	28,786	115,804	113,164	105,007	79,707	99,407
Depreciation	−1,198	−5,639	−23,157	−25,300	−25,300	−34,300
Accounts Receivable	0	815,178	1,872,099	3,173,573	5,205,896	8,699,918
Inventories	0	217,118	595,265	1,073,767	1,891,517	3,400,962
Total Assets	91,188	1,728,684	2,731,383	4,524,276	8,157,898	14,981,025
Liabilities						
Debt	0	0	0	0	0	0
Accounts Payable	0	54,279	148,816	268,442	472,879	850,240
Total Liabilities	0	54,279	148,816	268,442	472,879	850,240
Equity Value	91,188	1,674,404	2,582,566	4,255,834	7,685,019	14,130,785
Equity and Total Liabilities	91,188	1,728,684	2,731,383	4,524,276	8,157,898	14,981,025

Turning to the cash flow projections, we note that operating cash flow is usually negative at early stages, as the start-up invests in establishing a new business. Investing cash flow also tends to be negative early on as the venture requires capital investments. To compensate for this condition, the company needs to raise financing, which gets recorded as a positive financing cash flow. In Section 3.7.2, we examine in greater detail how to determine a company's funding needs. In Chapter 5 we also discuss how these cash flow projections provide useful information for valuing a company.

WorkHorse Box 3.10 shows its projected cash flow statement.

WorkHorse Box 3.10 Projected Cash Flow Statement

WorkHorse's cash flow projections foresaw negative operating cash flow for the first three years. Adding negative cash flow from investing, the cash flow before financing was negative for the first three years. To offset this the projections foresaw positive financing cash flow in the first two years. Data in the table are in dollars.

	2020	2021	2022	2023	2024	2025
Beginning Cash Balance	0	63,600	586,224	174,012	197,229	1,006,078
Operating						
Revenues	0	2,314,200	7,592,400	12,870,600	21,112,800	35,283,000
COGS	0	-924,560	-3,621,197	-6,532,085	-11,506,729	-20,689,183
Operating Expenses	-407,400	-1,791,000	-2,879,620	-4,344,665	-5,546,436	-6,976,264
Change in NWC	0	-978,016	-1,340,531	-1,660,351	-2,645,636	-4,626,105
Taxes	0	0	-160,264	-295,283	-605,150	-1,137,488
Total	-407,400	-1,379,376	-409,212	38,217	808,850	1,853,960
Investing						
Capital Expenses	-29,000	-98,000	-3,000	-15,000	0	-45,000
Other Investments	0	0	0	0	0	0
Total	-29,000	-98,000	-3,000	-15,000	-	-45,000
Cash flow before financing						
Cash flow	-436,400	-1,477,376	-412,212	23,217	808,850	1,808,960
Ending cash balance	-436,400	-1,913,776	-2,325,988	-2,302,771	-1,493,922	315,039
Financing						
Equity	500,000	2,000,000	0	0	0	0

	2020	2021	2022	2023	2024	2025
Debt	0	0	0	0	0	0
Interest Payments	0	0	0	0	0	0
Total	500,000	2,000,000	-	-	-	-
Cash Flow	63,600	522,624	−412,212	23,217	808,850	1,808,960
Ending Cash Balance	63,600	586,224	174,012	197,229	1,006,078	2,815,039

3.6.3 Income versus Cash Flow

It is easy to confuse net income (net earnings) with cash flow, so let us look at that. Net income measures accounting profitability, whereas cash flow measures how cash moves to and from the company. They mainly differ because the timing of business transactions does not always match the timing of the corresponding financial payments. Many goods and services are first delivered and paid for later, so that the seller records revenue before receiving cash payments. In the case of prepayments, the opposite applies; that is, cash flow occurs before revenue is recognized.

In general, income and cash flow are related through the following equation:

$$\text{Cash flow} = \text{Net income} \qquad (3.3)$$
$$- \text{ Change in net working capital}$$
$$- \text{ Capital expenditures+Depreciation}$$

On the left-hand side is the cash flow before financing (from the cash flow projections), measured at the end of the period (e.g., fiscal year). This is also commonly referred to as "free" cash flow to indicate that this is the cash flow the company generates over and beyond what is needed for ongoing operations.

Net income on the right-hand side comes from the income statement (Section 3.6.1). Note that one should use net income after tax (which clearly has to be paid out of cash flow) but before interest (which is accounted for separately in the financing cash flow). To obtain cash flow, equation (3.3) identifies two necessary adjustments.

The first adjustment concerns net working capital, which we define in equation (3.2) in Section 3.6.2. Since equation (3.3) measures flows over a certain period, we subtract from net income the *change* in net working capital from the previous to the current period. This adjustment is due to the timing of cash flows. Net income measures the economic activity of the current period, without taking into account when payments occur. As noted earlier, it is common for a company to sell a product in the current period but to receive payment later. The revenues from the sale are recognized at the time of the sale, but no cash flows are recorded. The net working capital adjustment takes care of timing mismatch.

To obtain an intuition into why it is the *change* of net working capital that matters, not the *level*, suppose a company always gets paid 3 months late. All the revenues from the last three months in the current fiscal year impact income but not cash flow. The revenues thus need to be taken out from cash flow. However, in the previous fiscal year, the last three months were also taken out. Their payments actually occurred in the current fiscal year and should thus be put into the current cash flow. If a company has zero growth, these two adjustments simply cancel out each other. If a company is growing, the only adjustment required concerns the *increase* in net working capital. In our example, this would be how much more uncollected revenues there were in the last three months of the current fiscal year, relative to the fiscal year before.

The second adjustment in equation (3.3) is to subtract capital expenditures and to add back depreciation (and amortization). When a company incurs capital expenditures by buying equipment that will be used over several years, then net income only counts the fraction of costs attributable to the current period. This is done in the income statement by including depreciation, which allocates the capital expenditures over multiple years. From a cash flow perspective, however, the capital expenditure has an immediate impact on the cash balance and should therefore be fully recognized in the current period.

Equation (3.3) generates one important business insight. It explains why a fast-growing company may be profitable but continue to generate a negative cash flow. That is, even if net income is positive, capital expenditures and changes in working capital may lead to a negative cash flow. This scenario is typical for successful fast-growing companies. It suggests an important and maybe surprising lesson, namely, that growing too fast can kill a company. To be more precise, even if net income is positive, the need to invest in growth often requires vast amounts of capital expenditures and working capital increases. If a start-up fails to secure proper financing, it may run out of cash even through the business is fundamentally profitable.

Figure 3.1 shows three classic "hockey sticks" that can be found in the financial projections of almost every start-up. The name derives from the resemblance of the shape of the curves to that of a hockey stick, first going down, then turning around and soaring up high. Figure 3.1 includes three such curves. The left-most hockey-stick curve represents net income, the second (middle) represents the cash flow, and the third (right-most) represents the cash balance.

The net income hockey stick reflects the initial losses of building a new business, followed by positive and increasing profits of a successful venture. Cash flow starts increasing once net income exceeds investments (capital expenditures and net working capital). The cash balance is mechanically related to the cash flow because it measures the accumulation of cash flows over time. The cash balance reaches its lowest point precisely at the time when cash flow turns positive. This is because the

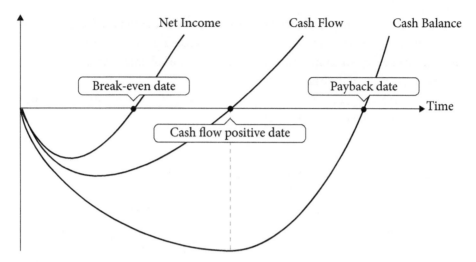

Figure 3.1. Hockey sticks.

cash balance declines whenever cash flow is negative and rises whenever cash flow is positive.

Figure 3.1 identifies three important points in time. The first is the break-even date. This happens when the venture reaches economic viability in terms of breaking even, so that total revenues just cover total costs. Break-even analysis concerns the time it takes to reach the minimum viable scale of operations such that company revenues cover all costs.

The second date in Figure 3.1 is the cash flow positive date. This corresponds to the moment when net income becomes large enough to cover the capital expenditures and net working capital. The date cash flow becomes positive occurs after the break-even date in the common case where capital expenditures exceed depreciation and where net working capital is positive. The third date in Figure 3.1 is the payback date. This is the point in time when a company has recouped all of its initial losses, so that cash balance returns to its initial level.

Figure 3.1 shows that the date when cash flow turns positive happens earlier than payback. At the time that cash flow turns positive, the cash balance is at its lowest point in the negative region. For the cash balance to recover and reach the payback point, cash flow must be sufficiently long in the positive region, so as to recover all the losses incurred in the initial period where cash flows were negative.

Figure 3.1 is drawn for the case where capital expenditures minus depreciation and the changes in net working capital are positive. Let us briefly consider the flipside of this. Consider a business with few capital expenditures and negative working capital. This can happen when a company collects revenues before incurring its cost. Business models that rely on a subscription or membership models have this feature. If such a business grows, then its change in net working capital is negative. Subtracting that from net income implies that cash flow is now larger than income, provided capital expenditures and depreciation are all small. Such a company could be unprofitable but still generate positive cash flow. It can satisfy its own financing using revenues that arrive before costs are incurred. In this case, the net income curve, which in Figure 3.1 is shown as the left-most curve, would actually lie to the right of the cash flow curve.

WorkHorse Box 3.11 looks at net income and cash flow, and identifies the break-even, positive cash flow, and payback dates.

WorkHorse Box 3.11 Income versus Cash Flow

When talking about the financial projections, the other founders regularly confused profits and cash flow, and muddled up the difference between breakeven and payback dates. Brandon therefore compiled a spreadsheet that explained how cash flow was related to net income. The table starts with net income. Next it calculates net working capital from accounts receivable plus inventories minus accounts payable. It then calculates the *change* in net working capital from year to year. Finally, it subtracts capital expenditures and adds depreciation back in. Brandon was relieved that the resulting cash flow corresponded exactly to those in WorkHorse Box 3.10. Data in the table are in dollars.

	2020	2021	2022	2023	2024	2025
Profit after Tax (Net Income)	−408,812	−416,784	908,162	1,673,268	3,429,185	6,445,765
Accounts Receivable	0	815,178	1,872,099	3,173,573	5,205,896	8,699,918
Inventories	0	217,118	595,265	1,073,767	1,891,517	3,400,962
Accounts Payable	0	54,279	148,816	268,442	472,879	850,240
Net working capital (NWC)	0	978,016	2,318,548	3,978,898	6,624,534	11,250,639
Change in NWC	0	978,016	1,340,531	1,660,351	2,645,636	4,626,105
Capital expenditures	29,000	98,000	3,000	15,000	0	45,000
Depreciation	1,412	15,424	23,157	25,300	25,300	34,300
Cash flow	−436,400	−1,477,376	−412,212	23,217	808,850	1,808,960
Cash balance	−436,400	−1,913,776	−2,325,988	−2,302,771	−1,493,922	315,039

The table projects that WorkHorse reaches break-even in 2022, when profits become positive ($908K) for the first time. At that time, cash flow is still negative ($412K), mainly because of substantial increases in net working capital ($1.3M). Cash flow turns positive in 2023 ($23K), although cash balance is still negative ($2.3M) then. Only in 2025 does the company finally reach its payback date, with the cash balance finally turning positive ($315K).

3.6.4 Testing Financial Projections

Our discussion of the entrepreneurial process in Section 1.1 emphasizes uncertainty, experimentation, and dynamic flexibility. Financial projections simplify the complexity of this process. They only use a single set of numbers that describe some representative scenario. As noted in Section 3.2.1, this scenario describes what a successful venture outcome would look like, not what to expect on average. A more sophisticated approach to financial projections recognizes that things don't always work out; even if they do, they might take longer. Moreover, one may want to account for the numerous risks inherent in the venture. There are two common tools for doing this: scenario analysis and sensitivity analysis.

One simple way of testing financial projections is to construct alternative financial projections that describe alternative scenarios. Each scenario should be internally consistent but depict a different course of events. One only uses a small number of scenarios. For example, an entrepreneur might use three scenarios and call them the good, the average, and the bad case. Given the optimistic nature of entrepreneurs, they more likely represent the extraordinary, the good, and the average case.

A somewhat more sophisticated approach to testing the reliability of financial projections is to perform sensitivity analyses. All financial projections rely on assumptions, but these assumptions are just single guesses of how the venture might unfold. One may thus be interested in changing these assumptions. This means exposing the financial model to questions such as: what happens if revenues come in x percent lower, if costs come in x percent higher, if reaching a technical milestone takes x months longer, and so on. There are several ways of implementing sensitivity analysis, ranging from simple manipulations of a spreadsheet to running sophisticated Monte Carlo simulations that expose the model to multiple simultaneous shocks. The results can be instructive in several ways: they may expose weaknesses in the underlying business model, or they may give some strategic guidance as to what parameters matter most.

3.6.5 Simplifications

Financial projections require time and effort. Some entrepreneurs find it difficult to build a full set of financial projections. As a preliminary step, they may want to use simpler, more heuristic approaches in order to generate some initial estimates of the likely performance of the venture. This is particularly true in the very early stages, where the uncertainty is highest. We caution against simplifying too much. Developing financial projections is demanding, but it allows the entrepreneur to learn a lot about the business model.

There are many simplified approaches in practice. One is to simply take shortcuts. The top-down approach to estimating COGS, discussed in Section 3.5.2, is a case in point. Other common shortcuts include ball-parking all expenses with a single number or leaving out the balance sheet to begin with. However, many of these shortcuts are ad hoc and risk blindsighting the entrepreneur.

One useful simplification is to create what is sometimes called a "unit economic model." This can be thought of as a simple static version of an income statement for a single unit of output. Depending on the industry, this could be a single shipment of a good, a single retail location, or a single contract with a representative client. For a given business unit, the entrepreneur then estimates the revenues and costs to get an idea of the margins for the single unit. This is clearly simpler than building full financial projections, although it still requires estimating unit revenues and unit costs. Needless to say, this approach has shortcomings, such as ignoring the timing of cash flow.

Another common approach is to limit the focus on a few industry-specific metrics. In the world of mobile apps, it is popular to project the success of a venture in terms of downloads, in the world of websites in terms of number of "eyeballs," in the world of fashion in terms of what celebrities want to endorse the product, and so on. Even though there may be no revenue figures directly associated with downloads, eyeballs, or celebrities, industry insiders understand their relevance. Given their experience, they can intuitively relate them to financial expectations. There are many shortcomings to such simplifications, and they can only be considered very preliminary steps toward proper financial projections.

What about not preparing any financial projections at all? There clearly are people who consider building financial projections a waste of time. We would argue that most entrepreneurs benefit from building proper projections. This goes back to the three reflections we discuss in Section 3.2.1. At the same time, we recognize that there are costs to building financial projections. Instead of polarizing the world into those who believe in building financial projections and those who don't, we believe that there is a process by which entrepreneurs build better projections over time. It might make sense to start with some of these simplified approaches in order to get an initial idea of financial performance. However, over time, as entrepreneurs learn more about their businesses, they are increasingly able to develop better financial projections. Moreover, as companies grow, they are likely to adopt management accounting systems to record their activities (see Box 3.1). These systems also make it easier to create better forecasts.

3.7 Formulating the Financial Plan

3.7.1 The Attractiveness of the Venture

In Section 3.1, we distinguish between the financial plan and the financial projections. The financial plan is a framework that explains what the entrepreneur wants to do, expressed in financial terms. It addresses two key questions: how attractive the business is, and what financial resources are required, and when. Financial projections are a tool for answering these questions. However, it is up to the entrepreneur to use them for building a credible financial plan.

To assess the profitability of the business, the income statement contains most of the required information (Section 3.6.2). It shows the size and growth potential of the business. Most importantly, it identifies the earnings potential of the venture. This can be gleaned from the estimated size and growth of net income, as well as from the profitability measures, such as gross, operating, and net margins. The balance sheet contains further useful information. Two useful ratios are the return on assets (ROA), and the return on equity (ROE). The ROA measures how effective the venture is in generating earnings (EBITDA) from its assets. The ROE instead measures how much earnings investors can get from their equity contribution.

Ultimately, the financial attractiveness of the venture is a highly subjective call. Box 3.2 shows that even professional financial analysts don't really know the answers either.

Box 3.2 Tales from the Venture Archives: Who Knows How to Take a Snapshot of the Future?

Snap Inc. is the company behind Snapchat, the popular social media app. Who could have predicted the success of an app that allows you to share photos that disappear quickly? Closer to the topic of this chapter, who can predict the success or failure of a company whose cash disappears as quickly as those photos?

Snap's IPO prospectus in 2017 sounded hardly reassuring when it stated: "We have incurred operating losses in the past, expect to incur operating losses in the future, and may never achieve or maintain profitability."[13] How can you predict the financial performance of a company like that, operating in a fast-changing digital environment, with few assets, and a fickle customer base?

Snapchat was founded in 2011 and quickly became a cultural phenomenon among millennials. With adoption skyrocketing, the company went from $3M of revenues in 2014 to $59M in 2015 and $404M in 2016. Based on this growth record, the company went public on the New York Stock Exchange (NYSE) in February 2017, with a market capitalization of approximately $33B. However, the company had always been cash flow negative, with losses of $128M in 2014, $373M in 2015, and $516M in 2016.

Financial analysts are professionals who make a living predicting the future financial performance of listed companies. They consider a wide variety of information, including company statements about future plans and the likely development of the industry. Snap Inc. derives its revenues mainly from advertising.

According to its IPO filing, worldwide advertising was expected to grow from $652B in 2016 to $767B in 2020. The company's segment of mobile advertising was predicted to be the fastest growing segment, going from $66B in 2016 to $196B in 2020. Based on this type of information, different analysts made different predictions about Snap's financial performance. Revenue predictions were in a range of .9B to $2.2B, and predictions of net losses were in a range of .1B to .8B.

What actually happened? All the analysts' revenue predictions were too high, as revenues in 2017 were only $825M (which was still more than twice the year before). Net losses came in at $3.4B, far below all analysts' predictions. As a consequence, Snap's stock price declined by approximately 35% in its first year as a public company. The analysts had all been wrong: the warning in the IPO prospectus was closer to the truth. As the Danish physicist Niels Bohr once said: "It is very difficult to predict, especially the future."

3.7.2 Financing Needs

To assess the financing needs of the venture, the cash flow statement plays a central role. It allows the entrepreneur to project the company's cash requirements over time. This projection is vital for the survival of the business. Hitting a zero cash balance means running out of cash and closing down the business.

The financial plan requires two key numbers about funding needs: (1) the total amount of funding needed to get the company to cash flow positive, and (2) the amount of funding needed at the present time. Note that instead of expressing them as current and total funding needs, one can also express them as current and future funding needs, where future funding needs are total needs minus current needs.

These two key numbers can only be obtained from cash flow forecasts. Practically, one first projects the cash flow under the assumption of no fundraising at all (i.e., setting cash flow from financing to zero). This allows us to draw two graphs, one for the projected cash flow and one for the projected cash balance. These graphs typically look like a hockey stick, as in Box 3.11. Consider the cash balance: it first goes down into the negative region and then comes up again, indicating that the cash flow has turned positive enough to restore positive cash balance. When crossing the zero line, the company breaks even in terms of cash flow. Typically, the projections then shoot up into a bright future, although reality might look different. This standard hockey stick graph contains useful information about the magnitude and timing of negative cash flow. Of particular significance is the point where the cash balance is lowest, which indicates the total funding need. This immediately gives us the first of the two key numbers.

Finding the second key number, the current financing need, forces us to think about fundraising strategies. So far, these graphs include no financing, so let us now consider some fundraising scenarios. One possibility is to raise all the funding up-front. This means raising an amount of money equal to the lowest point of the cash balance (plus some safety cushion to account for risk). Doing so shifts the entire graph of the cash balance upward by the total funding amount, thus ensuring that cash balance is non-negative throughout.

If a start-up has a relatively modest financing need, and the time to becoming cash flow positive is relatively short, then it makes sense to raise all the funding up-front. In many entrepreneurial ventures, however, the point of turning cash flow positive is several years out, and the amount of funding is substantial. Raising all the money upfront may be impossible. Such ventures initially raise smaller amounts of money to get started. If they manage to hit their milestones, they then raise the remaining amount in additional financing rounds. This is the staged financing process discussed in Chapter 9. To determine the initial amount of funding needed requires identifying what is needed to give the company a reasonable chance of achieving the next set of milestones. This is precisely the second of the two key numbers mentioned above, the current funding need.

Determining these two key numbers is not a purely mechanical exercise; it involves several strategic trade-offs that we will encounter across various other chapters. Entrepreneurs trade off smaller versus larger investment rounds as part of the deal negotiation process (Section 7.5). This also depends on the financial resources of the syndicate of investor they are in negotiation with (Section 7.3). More broadly, entrepreneurs must consider what kind of a dynamic fundraising profile they are aiming for (Section 9.5). In later stages, there might also be a trade-off between equity and venture debt (Section 10.2). Note also that fundraising is a dynamic process, so new information arrives over time that changes the financial projections, and hence the funding needs. Over time, some start-ups discover that they need less funding than expected, for example, because their sales take off faster than expected. Other start-ups have a rude awakening realizing they need more than originally anticipated, for example, because their costs turn out to be higher than previously thought.

To practically calculate current funding needs, one combines the cash flow projections with the timeline discussed in Section 3.3. Given these milestones, the current financing need can be found by looking at the difference between the current cash balance and the projected cash balance at the time of hitting that milestone. There is an argument to raise a bit more than that amount to have a safety cushion. The size of the safety cushion can be worked out with the help of a few alternative scenarios. This means asking questions such as how much cash would be needed if the prototype takes three months longer than expected? What if several strategy changes are needed before landing a first paying customer? We illustrate how to determine funding needs in WorkHorse Box 3.12.

WorkHorse Box 3.12 Funding Needs and Cash Flow

The WorkHorse founders wanted to get a clear picture of how much money the company needed to raise and when. They summarized their projected cash flow in a graph:

WorkHorse's cash flow predictions (excluding any financing)

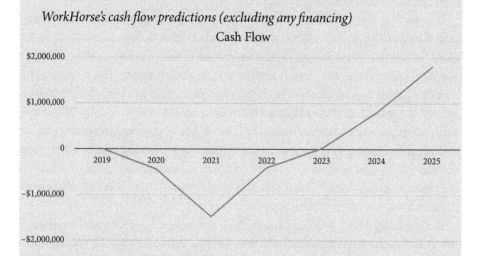

The company was projected to lose cash until 2022 and to turn cash flow positive in 2023. At its lowest, in 2022, the company would be losing almost $1.5M. Based on these cash flow projections, they projected the following cash balances.

WorkHorse's cash balance (excluding any financing)

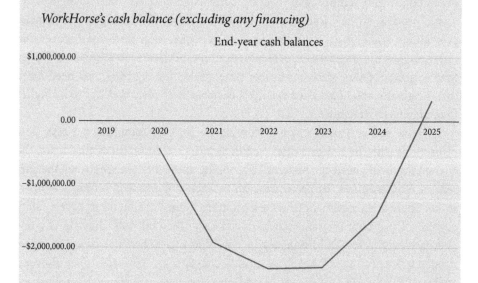

The cash balance shows the accumulation of cash flow. This means that the cash balance increases (decreases) whenever cash flow is positive (negative). The figure shows that the decline in cash balance is steepest in 2021, when cash flow is at its most negative. In 2022, cash flow improves for their lowest point but are still negative. Consequently, the cash balance continues to fall in 2022, albeit at a slower pace. In 2013, cash flow turns mildly positive, so that cash balance increases a little. However, the cash balance remains deep in negative territory in 2013, reflecting a history of negative cash flows up to this point. It is only in 2025 that cash balance turns positive. By then, the total positive cash flows of the period 2023–2025 exceed the total negative cash flows for the period 2019–2022. The lowest point in the cash balance is –$2.33M. Based on this data, the founders considered their total funding needs to be approximately $2.5M, which added a small safety cushion to the lowest cash balance.

With these projections in hand, the four founders deliberated a fundraising strategy. They realized that no investor would ever give them $2.5 upfront. With a negative cash balance of $436K in 2020, the founders thought that a seed round of $500K would be suitable to get the company to the first quarter of 2021. It would allow the company to launch its first product and thus validate the critical parts of their core technology and business model. Asking for half a million was high for a seed round—many of the entrepreneurs they knew had asked for less—but they were confident that they could make a case to investors based on their well-researched financial plan.

With a seed round of $500K and a total financing need of $2.5M, the company planned to raise one more round of $2M (an A round) at the beginning of 2021. That second round of funding would be needed to support company growth, launch their second product, and expand into Europe. With those two rounds, the company reckoned that it would be able to turn cash flow positive sometime in 2023. The projected cash balance can be used to inform the fundraising strategy. Specifically, the company assumed raising $500K in Q1 of 2020 and another $2M in Q1 of 2021. Once we include these financial inflows, the projected beginning of period cash balances always remain positive, as shown in the accompanying figure.

WorkHorse's cash balance with two rounds of financing

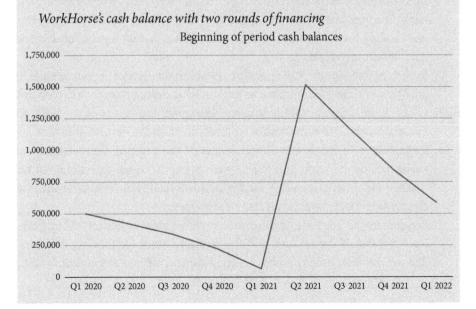

Beginning of period cash balances

3.7.3 Pitching the Financial Plan

Many entrepreneurs find it challenging to effectively communicate their financial plan. Admittedly, it requires a minimum of financial literacy, in terms of understanding basic accounting terminology, and it requires some thought on how to summarize a considerable amount of information. However, the real challenge is figuring out what message to convey.

Every venture is unique, and different investors have different preferences, let alone different levels of financial sophistication. However, the ultimate goal is to answer two questions: How attractive is the proposed business? What financial resources are needed, and when? The presentation of the financial plan should remain focused on answering those two questions.

The information provided in a written business plan or a document explaining financial projections can be comprehensive and detailed. By contrast, a verbal presentation to investors relies on a small set of slides that only include a high-level summary of the financial plan. There is no single recipe: different parties will ask for different levels of detail, and different entrepreneurs will emphasize different aspects. The presentation of a financial plan also changes between early- and later-stage companies. As the venture matures once expects greater detail and better accuracy of financial projections. Later-stage ventures also include a discussion of past performance, in addition to their financial projections.

We provide some general advice on how to structure this part of the presentation. The presentation slides that accompany Chapter 2 also include a section that presents WorkHorse's financial plan. Practically, we suggest that the following information be included in a presentation.

1. Assumptions: We recommend explicitly stating upfront the main assumptions used in the financial projections. This should not be an exhaustive list, but a short summary of the most important assumptions that drive the results and justify the financial appeal of the venture. Many inexperienced entrepreneurs omit stating their assumptions, only to find that investors get confused and quickly become skeptical.

2. Revenues: Revenue projections help to establish the scale of the venture and its growth over time. One should also explain what the main revenue drivers are.

3. Costs: A breakdown of costs is useful to explain the nature of the business model, what kind of activities are required, and how they evolve over time.

4. Profitability: To assess the attractiveness of the venture, the entrepreneur needs to show its profit potential. Investors expect to see an estimate of net profits over time. Depending on the business, EBITDA, operating income, and gross and net margins can also be of interest.

5. Funding needs: The time structure of cash flows helps to understand any critical junctures of the venture, and the resulting needs for funding infusions. The two key numbers to report are the total and current amount of funding

needed. The timing of these funding needs should be explained. In addition, there should be a discussion of what the current funding round will be spent on and how long the money is expected to last.

Should one include a company valuation or an estimate of investor returns in a financial presentation? We discuss valuation in Chapter 5 and negotiations in Section 7.4. The financial plan pertains to an earlier stage, where the entrepreneur and investor are only beginning to get to know each other. In many cases, the first pitch to investors does not mention a valuation. However, norms and expectations differ across context, and in some cases the entrepreneur is expected to include a valuation in the financial plan. In equity crowdfunding, for example, the valuation must be stated as part of the campaign materials (Section 13.4).

Before we conclude this chapter, let us briefly reflect on the broader challenge of predicting the future of a start-up company. Financial projections require the entrepreneur to think through a risky future. It turns out that relatively few people are good at this. In fact, many are prone to numerous biases which have been studied by behavioral economists and psychologists. Box 3.3 takes a closer look at some findings that concern the broader challenges of making decisions under uncertainty and specific challenges of projecting into an uncertain future.

Box 3.3 Nobel Insights on Behavioral Biases

The 2002 Nobel Prize in Economics was awarded to Daniel Kahneman "for having integrated insights from psychological research into economic science, focusing on human judgment and decision making under uncertainty."[14] The 2017 Prize was given to Richard H. Thaler "for his contributions to behavioural economics."[15]

Much of Kahneman's life work is summarized in his book *Thinking, Fast and Slow*.[16] Our starting point can be taken straight from that title. There are two distinct models of how people think: the "fast" one is automatic, intuitive, maybe emotional, often stereotypic, and largely unconscious; the "slow" one is logical, more deliberate, and requires effort. Each has its own evolutionary origins; intelligent humans use both. While fast thinking is necessary for making decisions in everyday life, it is full of behavioral biases. These are systematic errors that lead people to make decisions that they wouldn't make if they applied slower logical thinking. Behavioral researchers have been studying these biases and have demonstrated their relevance to society.

Behavioral biases often happen in connection with risky choices. One central finding by Kahneman and his long-term collaborator, Amos Tversky, concerns "framing."[17] Consider two entrepreneurs proposing two different approaches to fending off an imminent cyberattack. The first will save all computers with probability one-third, and none with probability two-thirds. The second is unable to save two-thirds of all computers. Framed this way, most respondents in an experiment would prefer the first entrepreneur. However, if the second company pitches itself as able to save one-third of all computers with certainty, then it would become the preferred choice of most respondents. Note that the underlying information about the second company is identical (losing two-thirds means saving one-third). The difference is entirely due to framing. Savvy entrepreneurs naturally pay attention to framing issues when pitching to investors, customers, and others.

In this example, it is the entrepreneur who leverages the behavioral biases of others. However, entrepreneurs are also subject to their own behavioral biases. In his Nobel lecture, Thaler tells of a friend not going to a basketball game because of a blizzard. The friend explained that he did so because he only paid half price but would have gone if he had bought the ticket at full price. This is a classic example of the sunk cost fallacy. The cost of the ticket has already been paid, so whether it was half or full price should be irrelevant to the decision. This fallacy can also affect big decisions like terminating large investment projects. It also affects entrepreneurs' decision of when to close a failing venture.[18]

The biggest behavioral bias for entrepreneurs is optimism. Entrepreneurs systematically overestimate the value of their opportunity and/or their probability of success. This phenomenon is well documented and has multiple explanations.[19] To begin with, optimists are more likely to start a venture in the first place. Furthermore, optimism grows as founders fall in love with their own ventures. Optimists are also prone to fall for a sunk cost fallacy.

Closely related to optimism is the concept of overconfidence. Whereas optimism involves a biased estimate of one's own probability of success, overconfidence concerns a biased estimate of the importance of one's own information. Overconfident people place too much value on the information they collect and too little value on the information collected by others. In our context, entrepreneurs may pay too much attention to their own experiences and too little attention to the travails of their peers.

Thaler's work builds on the foundations of Kahneman and Tversky. His influential book *Nudge* started an entire movement that aims to tackle behavioral biases.[20] The idea is not to change the fundamental economic choices themselves but rather to change the framing of these choices. For example, when nudging an entrepreneur to abandon a failing venture, you might refrain from dwelling on the failure (i.e., the door that is closing) and instead talk about how it frees up time to pursue new opportunities (i.e., the doors that are opening). Note, however, that while most behavioral biases are detrimental to the individual, a few may benefit them. For example, entrepreneurial optimism may inspire others to join as employees, or it may deter the competition. Investors often like overconfident entrepreneurs, appreciating that they "take the bull by the horns," even if doing so isn't perfectly safe and rational.

What can behavioral economics tell us about financial projections? It is not difficult to see that financial projections are prone to behavioral biases. Projections of revenues or earnings tend to be widely optimistic, overstating the size of the economic opportunity and the speed at which the company can grow. Cost projections often fail to incorporate the full extent of what it takes to go to market. Risks are typically underestimated, minimizing the chances that things can go wrong and downplaying the numerous halfway scenarios where things take more time and more resources than originally planned. Entrepreneurs also frame their financial projections in opportunistic ways. For example, when net margins look poor, entrepreneurs may stress their impressive gross margins; or when revenue levels are low, they may emphasize rapid revenue growth; and so on.

Experienced investors are used to all that. Level-headed entrepreneurs who are conscious of these behavioral biases face a curious quandary. If they refrain from projecting overoptimistic financials, investors may still automatically adjust their projections for standard optimism. Conscious entrepreneurs thus risks shortchanging themselves. Some people go as far as to argue that there is no point in being sane (rational) in a world in which everyone else is crazy (behavioral). However, savvy entrepreneurs often find more convincing ways of differentiating their story from the rest of the crowd. Box 2.6 discusses ways that they can signal their quality in more credible ways. One academic study by Cassar finds that entrepreneurs with prior industry experience produce more accurate and less biased financial projections.[21] Interestingly, having prior entrepreneurial experience does not affect forecasting accuracy. It seems that entrepreneurs remain hopelessly optimistic all the way.

Summary

In this chapter we discuss the financial plan, where entrepreneurs address two fundamental questions about their business: (1) is the venture financially attractive? and (2) how much funding does need it and when? To address these questions, entrepreneurs need to generate financial projections that provide quantitative forecasts of their business expectations. Financial projections usually include the income statement, the balance sheet, and the cash flow statement. Building projections requires identifying a timeline with business milestones. We discuss the top-down and bottom-up approaches to estimating revenues and costs, and how to interpret and test the projections. Finally, we show that the resulting financial projection can be used to devise the financial plan, which indicates how much money is needed and when. We also provide some guidance for organizing the pitch to the investors. The spreadsheet model available at www.entrepreneurialfinance.net provides a practical tool for developing financial projections.

In terms of the FIRE framework (Chapter 1), the financial plan sits together with the business plan at the center of the FIT step. From the entrepreneur's perspective, the financial plan is an important ingredient to illustrate the business strategy underlying the pitch. From the investor's perspective, examining the financial plan is part of screening. One purpose of the financial plan is thus to allow the two parties to calibrate their expectations and verify if there is a fit.

Review Questions

1. What is the purpose of a financial plan? How do financial projections contribute to that?
2. What is the difference between financial statements and financial projections? What are they needed for?
3. What factors affect the appropriate choice of a timeline and milestones?
4. What are the relative strengths of top-down versus bottom-up revenue projections?
5. What are the most important costs that need to be considered in a new venture?
6. What is working capital? How does it affect the financial projections of start-ups?
7. What are the relative roles of the projected income statement, balance sheet, and cash flow statement?
8. How can one use financial projections to assess the financial attractiveness of a venture?
9. How does one find the total and current amount of funding needed by a start-up?
10. What information should be conveyed to investors when pitching the financial plan?

Notes

1. Barker (2011) is a useful concise introduction to accounting practice. The textbook by Miller-Nobles, Mattison, and Matsumura (2015) develops and illustrates all relevant accounting concepts. Bhimani (2017) provides material focused on technology entrepreneurs.
2. Cassar (2009).
3. Davila and Foster (2005).
4. Shubber (2017).
5. Gompers, Kaplan, and Mukharlyamov (2016).
6. Under standard GAAP, some payroll expenses are allocated to costs of goods sold. In early-stage ventures, this is less relevant, since most employees have general responsibilities that cannot be allocated to specific operating divisions.
7. Anagnostopoulou (2008).

8. Armstrong, Davila, and Foster (2006) find that, for a sample of U.S. pre-IPO ventures, R&D expenses are positively related to valuation.

9. Grossman and Hart (1986) and Hart and Moore (1990).

10. Samonas (2015) provides an accessible introduction to modeling financial accounts.

11. Hand (2005) looks at the value relevance of financial statements in VC-backed companies.

12. For this calculation, one should remove any excess cash holdings from the measure of current assets. This is rarely an issue in entrepreneurial ventures, which rarely have excess cash holdings (defined as cash not needed for operation of the business).

13. The information on Snap, Inc., including this quote, comes from the company's S-1 filing with the SEC, available at the SEC Edgar database: https://www.sec.gov/Archives/edgar/data/1564408/000119312517029199/d270216ds1.htm

14. https://www.nobelprize.org/prizes/economic-sciences/2002/press-release.

15. https://www.nobelprize.org/prizes/economic-sciences/2017/press-release.

16. Kahneman (2011).

17. Tversky and Kahneman (1981). The example in the text is a reformulation of the "Asian disease problem," discussed in Kahneman's Nobel lecture.

18. Bates (2005).

19. Dawson et al. (2014), Puri and Robinson (2007), and Thomas (2018).

20. Sunstein and Thaler (2008).

21. Cassar (2014).

4

Ownership and Returns

Learning Goals

In this chapter students will learn:

1. What is the relationship between investment amount, ownership shares, valuation, dilution, and returns.
2. To derive the allocation and prices of shares, as well as a company's pre- and post-money valuations.
3. How to analyze investor returns using alternative return measures.
4. Principles for how founders allocate ownership shares within a team.

This chapter examines what determines the split of ownership between investors and entrepreneurs. It explains the mechanical relationships between investment amounts, ownership shares, and the pre-money and post-money valuation of a company. The chapter also establishes how to compute the returns to investors. It discusses the relative merits of three alternative measures of investor returns: net present value, cash-on-cash, and internal rate of return. The chapter further analyzes the economic determinants of valuations. The final part examines how founder teams allocate founder shares internally and provides a practical tool for how to negotiate founder agreements.

4.1 The Mechanics of Ownership and Valuation

4.1.1 Pre-Money and Post-Money Valuation

In this chapter we explain the basic mechanical relationships between investment, ownership shares, and valuation. We first show how a venture's ownership structure is determined for a given valuation. We then turn to explaining how ownership evolves over time and how it generates returns for investors.

We start with the simple case of a company that receives a single round of financing from a single investor. Later in the chapter we extend the analysis by including the role of stock options and multiple rounds of financing. Throughout the chapter we assume that investors get common equity. This means they own a fraction of the company that is given by the percentage of shares they own. With common equity, all shareholders hold shares that have the same rights. We delay the discussion of more complex types of equity until Chapter 6.

An investment is an economic exchange in which the investor contributes an amount of money to the company and receives in return shares that represent an ownership stake. The corresponding valuation reflects the investor's willingness to accept a certain ownership stake of the company in return for his investment. The value of this stake is purely hypothetical ("paper money"), as the company has no market for its shares (yet). We can describe the fundamental relationship between investment, ownership, and valuation as follows:

$$\text{Investment} = \text{Ownership}^*\text{Valuation} \tag{4.1}$$

The left-hand side of this equation describes what the investor contributes, namely, the investment amount. The right-hand side describes what the investor receives in return, namely, some ownership fraction in the company that is given a certain valuation. This equation implies that we only need to know two out of the three quantities, and the third falls out mechanically. Therefore, if we know how much money the investor contributes and what ownership he gets in return, then the valuation is mechanically given by:

$$\text{Valuation} = \text{Investment}/\text{Ownership} \tag{4.2}$$

To get a practical sense of how to make use of this formula, Box 4.1 takes a brief look at the world of TV reality shows.

Box 4.1 Tales from the Venture Archives: Of Snappy Dragons

TV buffs with an interest in entrepreneurship have a special affinity to dragons, tigers, or sharks, depending on where they live. It all started in 2001 with a Japanese TV show called "The Tigers of Money" which featured entrepreneurs pitching business ideas to fierce-looking investors in front of TV cameras. The format rapidly spread under a variety of names. The UK adopted the show's format in 2005, under the name of "Dragon's Den." Canada followed in 2006 with its Dragon's Den. In the U.S. the format was launched in 2009 under the name of "Shark Tank."[1]

In these TV shows entrepreneurs pitch their ideas to a fearsome set of investors, the "dragons" (or sharks or tigers). The investors are typically experienced businesspeople who also have a flair for show business. They grill the entrepreneurs about various aspects of their venture. Whenever some dragons get interested in a company, they offer a deal. At this point, the entrepreneurs are trained to respond that they are looking for a given investment, in return for a given ownership stake in the company. The dragons then come back with a different offer, typically a lower investment and/or a higher ownership stake. Some drama ensues before they agree on the terms of a deal (or not). Truth be told, after the TV cameras are switched off, the entrepreneurs and investors can always back out of a deal—apparently this happens a lot.[2]

So, if you ever wondered how budding entrepreneurs value their companies, all you need to do is watch lots of those episodes. When the dragons make an offer, you can infer the valuation by dividing the investment amount (X) by the ownership percentage (Y). For example, Corla Rokochy from Saskatchewan, Canada, a mother of five children, presented the idea of "Snappy Socks."[3] She had a brilliant solution to the ubiquitous problem of the single sock that disappears in the laundry. Her invention was a pair of socks with a snap to hold them together. This way no single sock could ever disappear on its own (and apparently socks never disappear in pairs). Two intrigued dragons, Arlene Dickinson and Brent Wilson, seized opportunity and offered $50K for 25% of the company. This implied a valuation of $200K (since $50K / 0.25 = $200K). This was not as much as Snap Inc.'s IPO (see Box 3.2), but certainly enough to secure a lifetime supply of socks for a family of seven! Snappy Socks turned into a successful business, selling online, and through retail outlets such as Toys 'R' Us and Shoppers Drug Mart.

There are two measures of valuation: pre-money valuation refers to company valuation just *prior* to the investment, while post-money valuation refers to how much the company is valued *after* receiving the investment. Equations (4.1) and (4.2) were based on the post-money valuation. The pre-money valuation is obtained by subtracting the investment from post-money valuation:[4]

$$\text{Pre-money valuation} = \text{Post-money valuation} - \text{Investment} \qquad (4.3)$$

This equation can also be switched around to obtain:

$$\text{Post-money valuation} = \text{Pre-money valuation} + \text{Investment} \qquad (4.4)$$

We now introduce some notation to express these equations more concisely. The amount of investment is denoted by I. We denote the ownership fraction of the pre-investment shareholders by F_{PRE}. For the first financing round, these include the founders. For later rounds, these also include those who invested in the company in previous rounds. We denote the ownership fraction of new investors by F_{INV}, the pre-money valuation by V_{PRE}, and the post-money valuation by V_{POST}. P is the price per share at the time of the investment. Finally, we denote with S the number of shares and distinguish the following amounts: S_{PRE} is the number of shares existing

Table 4.1 Notation for ownership and investor returns.

Symbol	Meaning
CCR	Cash-on-cash return
d	Discount rate
F_{INV}	Ownership fraction of new investors
F_{PRE}	Ownership fraction of pre-investment shareholders
F_{SOP}	Ownership fraction of the stock options pool
I	Investment amount
IRR	Internal rate of return
NVP	Net present value
S_{INV}	Number of shares of new investors
S_{POST}	Number of shares outstanding after the investment round
S_{PRE}	Number of shares of pre-investment shareholders
S_{SOP}	Number of shares allocated to the stock options pool
t	Time
T	Investment duration
V_{POST}	Post-money valuation
V_{PRE}	Pre-money valuation
X	Exit value

before the investment; S_{INV} is the number of shares issued to the new investors; and S_{POST} is the number of shares after the investments, which is the sum of S_{PRE} and S_{INV}. We summarize the notation in Table 4.1.

We now restate the four equations we have derived so far using this notation. We keep the same equation numbers as before, to indicate that they are exactly the same equations:

$$I = F_{INV} * V_{POST} \qquad (4.1)$$

$$V_{POST} = I/F_{INV} \qquad (4.2)$$

$$V_{PRE} = V_{POST} - I \qquad (4.3)$$

$$V_{POST} = V_{PRE} + I \qquad (4.4)$$

WorkHorse Box 4.1 illustrates these relationships.

4.1.2 Price and Number of Shares

So far we have described the investment deal without any reference to shares. This is because the relationship between investment, ownership, and valuation does not

WorkHorse Box 4.1 The Ownership and Valuation of WorkHorse

WorkHorse's four founders had presented their business to Michael Archie, a local angel investor. He was favorably impressed and indicated a potential interest in investing. WorkHorse needed .5M. Michael casually mentioned that he would ask for 20%, at a post-money valuation of $2.5M. As far as Astrid was concerned, Michael might well have spoken Chinese, since she had no idea what that meant. After Annie confirmed that indeed Michael had not spoken Chinese, the four founders consulted their favorite entrepreneurial finance book—the one that you are reading right now. They were delighted to find a clear explanation.

Using equations (4.1) to (4.4), they found out what Michael's offer meant. Using equation (4.1), they realized that Michael was proposing to invest the requested .5M in exchange for a 20% share in the company, which he consequently valued as $2.5M:

$$I = \$0.5M = 0.2 * \$2.5M = F_{INV} * V_{POST}$$

The post-money valuation could be computed as:

$$V_{POST} = \$2.5M = \$0.5M/0.2 = I/F_{INV}$$

The pre-money valuation was:

$$V_{PRE} = \$2M = \$2.5M - \$0.5M = V_{POST} - I$$

depend on the number and price of shares. However, in order to practically implement the deal, it is necessary to define the number and price of shares that the investor gets in return for making the investment.

The first step is to define the number of shares outstanding before the investment, denoted by S_{PRE}. In the first round of financing, the choice of this number turns out to be irrelevant. This is because this number is a so-called numéraire, that is, a scaling factor that changes the number and prices of shares without affecting the ownership fractions.

When the investor makes an investment I, he receives S_{INV} shares, each at a price P. The total number of shares after the round (S_{POST}) consists of the new shares (S_{PRE}) plus those already outstanding before the investment (S_{PRE}):

$$S_{POST} = S_{PRE} + S_{INV} \tag{4.5}$$

The number of new shares is related to the amount invested. Specifically, the amount invested equals the share price times the number of shares received by the investor:

$$I = P * S_{INV} \tag{4.6}$$

The valuation after the investment then equals the share price times the total number of shares:

$$V_{POST} = P * S_{POST} \tag{4.7}$$

Combining equations (4.3), (4.5), (4.6), and (4.7), we obtain the expression for the pre-money valuation as:

$$V_{PRE} = P * S_{PRE} \tag{4.8}$$

This says that, just before the investment, the company's valuation equals the share price times the total number of preexisting shares.

Finally, the relationships between ownership fractions and shares are given by:

$$F_{PRE} = S_{PRE}/S_{POST} \text{ and } F_{INV} = S_{INV}/S_{POST} \tag{4.9}$$

WorkHorse Box 4.2 illustrates this.

WorkHorse Box 4.2 Share Numbers and Prices of WorkHorse

The four founders were curious as to how much their shares would be worth under the deal outlined by Michael Archie. To set a numéraire, Astrid decided that the founders would jointly get 1M shares.

$$S_{PRE} = 1M$$

To calculate the price per share, she solved equation (4.8) for P and obtained:

$$P = V_{PRE}/S_{PRE} = \$2M/1M = \$2$$

With this share price, she transformed equation (4.6) to work out the number of shares the company had to issue to its investors and obtained:

$$S_{INV} = I/P = \$0.5M/\$2 = 0.25M$$

Using this, she computed the company's total number of shares after the investment:

$$S_{POST} = S_{PRE} + S_{INV} = 1M + 0.25M = 1.25M$$

To confirm that the ownership fractions stated by Michael were correct, she noted that he would hold 0.25M out of 1.25M shares, so that:

$$F_{INV} = 0.25M/1.25M = 0.2$$

Since the founders had 1M out of 1.25M shares, their ownership fraction was:

$$F_{PRE} = 1M/1.25M = 0.8$$

Annie was a little unhappy with Astrid's calculations, as she thought that S_{PRE} = 1M shares was a bit stingy. She thought that maybe the four founders should start with S_{PRE} = 4M shares. Bharat quietly took her aside and walked her through the calculations using her alternative number of shares:

$$S_{PRE} = \$4M$$

$$P = V_{PRE}/S_{PRE} = \$2M/4M = \$0.5$$

$$S_{INV} = I/P = \$0.5M/\$0.5 = 1M$$

$$S_{POST} = S_{PRE} + S_{INV} = 4M + 1M = 5M$$

$$F_{INV} = 1M/5M = 0.2$$

$$F_{PRE} = 4M/5M = 0.8$$

Bharat explained that by quadrupling the number of preexisting shares from 1M to 4M, all that would happen is that investors also quadruple their number of shares from 0.25M to 1M. Since investment was still $0.5M, the share price would mechanically drop to a quarter its previous price, from $2 to $0.5. Annie agreed, noting that Bharat was "just too smart a cookie," to which he replied: "It has nothing to do with cookies, it's just understanding what a numéraire is."

4.1.3 Stock Options

The previous section looks at the simple case where there are only two parties, founders and investors. We now augment the base model by noting that companies often use grants of stock-based compensation to defer cash payments to third parties. There are two main methods to grant ownership to third parties. One is to directly give out company shares, and the other is to grant stock options. These two methods are typically directed at different parties, and the details depend on company-specific circumstances. Moreover, personal and corporate taxation rules affect the appeal of stock options.[5]

Granting stock directly is largely done with parties external to the company, such as consultants, suppliers, or licensors (such as a university technology transfer office). They receive common stock in exchange for the goods or services they provide. In general, such stock allocations are used either to reward past contributions or to provide performance incentives, as well as to create loyalty to the company.[6] The average percentage ownership allocated to the recipients of these stocks and stock options is estimated to be around 15% for U.S. VC-backed companies and slightly lower for European companies.[7]

Granting stock options is more common with board members, managers, and employees.[8] Employee Stock Options Plans (commonly known as ESOPs) are an important tool for managing human resources in entrepreneurial companies. A stock option is the right (without obligation) to purchase a given number of common shares from the company at a set price, called the "strike" price, at or after a specified date. Depending on tax and regulatory circumstances, the strike price for employee stock options are either some extremely low nominal value (such as 0.01 cent), or the price of shares from the company's most recent funding round. The idea is that the price of shares will rise and thus allow employees to make a profit by converting their options into shares. Employee stock options are assigned to a specific person and cannot be traded. Once converted, the employees own shares, but typically they cannot sell these either because there is no liquidity until the company has some exit (Box 11.7).

How does the existence of a stock options pool affect the valuation and ownership of a venture? When the investor offers to provide I for an ownership stake F_{INV}, he does not want to pay for any stock options with his investment. This effectively means that the company has to issue shares to provide the stock options. The formulas we derive are based on this case.

We denote by S_{SOP} the number of shares in the "fully diluted" stock options pool. This means that all shares in the option pool are assumed to be converted into common stock. We examine dilution in more detail in Section 4.1.5. The subscript SOP stands for stock options pool. The total number of shares after the investment is now given by equation (4.5-SOP), where the additional term S_{SOP} denotes the presence of a stock options pool:

$$S_{POST} = S_{PRE} + S_{INV} + S_{SOP} \qquad \text{(4.5-SOP)}$$

Equation (4.8) then becomes:

$$V_{PRE} = P^*\left(S_{PRE} + S_{SOP}\right) \qquad \text{(4.8-SOP)}$$

The presence of a stock options pool changes the interpretation of the pre-money valuation V_{PRE}. In a first round, it no longer represents the value to the founders; instead it represents including the entire stock options pool. In later rounds, V_{PRE} represents the value to all existing shareholders, again including the stock options pool. Naïve founders may erroneously think that the entire pre-money valuation is theirs. With a stock options pool, however, they share the pre-money valuation with the stock options pool. In practice, we advise entrepreneur to always ask whether or not a pre-money valuation offered by an investor includes the stock options pool.

To see how the creation of a stock options pool affects ownership, we reformulate equation (4.9) to identify the ownership fraction of the stock options pool:

$$F_{PRE} = S_{PRE}/S_{POST} \qquad \text{(4.9-SOP)}$$

$$F_{INV} = S_{INV}/S_{POST}$$

$$F_{SOP} = S_{SOP}/S_{POST}$$

WorkHorse Box 4.3 illustrates stock options.

WorkHorse Box 4.3 The Stock Options Pool

The WorkHorse founders understood from Michael the need to create a stock options pool. When they inquired about how big a stock options pool should be, they were told that start-ups typically allocated 10–20% of founder equity to a stock options pool. The four founders always envisioned building a larger organization, so they embraced the idea of providing equity to attract the talented managers and employees they planned to hire.

They took the equity for the stock options out of their own 1M shares, so that 100K shares would be allocated to the stock options pool. The ownership fraction corresponding to the stock options pool would therefore be 10% before the seed round and 8% after it. At a price of $2 per share, this implied that $200K of the pre-money valuation of $2M accrued to the stock options pool.

4.1.4 The Capitalization Table

Entrepreneurs and investors need to keep track of who receives and disposes of company shares and when. A capitalization table is a simple representation of the ownership structure of a company. It consists of a table that keeps track of the number of outstanding shares, who owns them, how much they paid for them, when, and how much capital has been put into the company. The capitalization table is sometimes also referred to as the ownership table.

The capitalization table lists three groups of owners of the company: founders, investors, and other parties. For each round, or Series (see Box 1.6), the columns identify for each shareholder: (1) the total number of shares owned, (2) the amount invested in a financing round, (3) the total amount invested so far, and (4) the current ownership fraction. The prices at which the shares were sold in each Series is also indicated.

One of the complications with ownership tables is that some allocations of shares are contingent on certain events. Section 4.1.3, for example, mentioned that stock options typically vest over time. To keep things transparent, capitalization tables represent ownership on a "fully diluted" basis. This assumes that all stock options are converted into common stock. The capitalization table thus represents a complete account of share ownership.

WorkHorse Box 4.4 illustrates the use of capitalization tables, at the time of its first (seed) round of financing.

WorkHorse Box 4.4 WorkHorse's Capitalization Table

The capitalization table for WorkHorse is based on Michael Archie's informal offer in WorkHorse Box 4.1. Michael indicated that for the seed investment in the first round, he would provide half of the money, that is, $250K. For the other half, he indicated that he planned to bring in the Ang brothers who were local angel investors whom he knew well. Michael also indicated that the four founders needed to come clean about who would own the founder shares. There were four issues to be sorted out. First, the four founders needed to write down how they planned to split the founder shares among themselves. Not having discussed the matter yet, they put down an equal number of shares for the time being (see WorkHorse Box 4.8). Second, Brandon's uncle JP Potro had originally provided $80K through a convertible note, whose structure we explain in Section 6.6. This was to convert into 50,000 shares and to be noted under the "Other parties." Third, the company required an agreement from the University's technology transfer office. Thankfully, the University had an enlightened approach toward student-driven ventures and quickly agreed to transfer all of the relevant intellectual property to the company for a 5% stake, which would also come from founders' shares. Fourth, as shown in WorkHorse Box 4.3, they allocated 10% of founder stock to a stock options pool that could be used for recruiting and retention.

The capitalization table summarizes this distribution of shares and ownership fractions.

First Round (Seed)		Number of shares purchased	Number of shares owned	Amount invested in round ($)	Total amount invested ($)	Ownership fraction
Price per share ($)	2.00					
Founders:						
	Astrid Dala		200,000	0	0	16.0%
	Annie Ma		200,000	0	0	16.0%
	Bharat Marwari		200,000	0	0	16.0%
	Brandon Potro		200,000	0	0	16.0%
Investors:						
	Michael Archie	125,000	125,000	250,000	250,000	10.0%
	Ang brothers	125,000	125,000	250,000	250,000	10.0%
Other parties:						
	JP Potro		50,000	0	0	4.0%
	U. of Michigan		50,000	0	0	4.0%
	Stock Options Pool		100,000	0	0	8.0%
Total		250,000	1,250,000	500,000	500,000	100%

4.1.5 Dilution with Multiple Rounds

This section is technically more challenging and can be skipped for the first reading of this chapter.

In this section, we examine how a company can raise money across multiple rounds of financing. We encounter the concept of dilution where existing shareholders find their ownership reduced over time as the company issues shares to new investors.

A new round occurs when the company receives a new equity investment. The company issues new shares to the investors. A new share price is set, implying a new valuation. As a result, the ownership fractions of all existing shareholders are mechanically reduced; this is commonly referred to as dilution. To get an understanding of how ownership evolves across multiple rounds, we introduce some notation. We index rounds in which the investors made their investments by the subscript $i = 1, 2, \ldots R$, and associate $i = 0$ with founder shares that are issued prior to the first round. For simplicity we ignore stock options in this section.

We index the current round for which we denote the ownership stake by $r = 1, 2, \ldots R$, placed within brackets after the variable. Consequently, we denote the ownership stake after round r of investors who invested in round i by $F_i(r)$. For example, $F_1(3)$ denotes the ownership of the first-round investors after the third financing round. Note also that $F_r(r)$ denotes the ownership fraction of the new investors in round r. This is what we call F_{INV} in Section 4.1.1.

We use a similar notation for the number of shares. We denote the number of shares held after round r by investors from round i by the $S_i(r)$. Correspondingly, we denote the number of new shares in round r by $S_r(r)$, which we call S_{INV} in Section 4.1.2. We then denote the total number of shares after round r by $S_{POST}(r)$. Notice also that $F_{POST}(r) = \Sigma_i F_i(r) + F_r(r)$ and $S_{POST}(r) = \Sigma_i S_i(r) + S_r(r)$. Moreover, $I(r)$ denotes the investment amount in round r, and $V_{PRE}(r)$ and $V_{POST}(r)$ denote the pre-money and post-money valuation.

We denote the case of multiple rounds by MR and restate equation (4.1) as follows:

$$I(r) = F_r(r) * V_{POST}(r) \tag{4.1-MR}$$

We write the relationships between pre- and post-money valuation from equation (4.3) as:

$$V_{PRE}(r) = V_{POST}(r) - I(r) \tag{4.3-MR}$$

Equations (4.5) and (4.6) become:

$$S_{POST}(r) = S_{POST}(r-1) + S_r(r) \tag{4.5-MR}$$

$$I(r) = P(r) * S_r(r) \tag{4.6-MR}$$

The valuation equations (4.7) and (4.8) become:

$$V_{POST}(r) = P(r) * S_{POST}(r) \tag{4.7-MR}$$

$$V_{PRE}(r) = P(r) * S_{POST}(r-1) \tag{4.8-MR}$$

Finally, the ownership fraction of investor i in round r is now given by:

$$F_i(r) = S_i(r)/S_{POST}(r) \tag{4.9-MR}$$

We then rearrange (4.5-MR) and (4.9-MR) in the following way: $F_i(r) = S_i(r)/S_{POST}(r) = (S_i(r)/S_{POST}(r-1)) * (S_{POST}(r-1)/ S_{POST}(r)) = F_i(r-1)*(S_{POST}(r) - S_{INV}(r))/ S_{POST}(r) = F_i(r-1) * (1 - F_r(r))$. This gives us the following simple formula for computing the dilution of ownership across rounds:

$$F_i(r) = F_i(r-1) * (1 - F_r(r)) \tag{4.10-MR}$$

This equation takes the ownership fraction of investors who originally invested in round i as it stood at the previous round $(r-1)$, $F_i(r-1)$ and transforms it into their ownership at round r by multiplying it by $(1- F_r(r))$ which is one minus the ownership fraction obtained by the new investors in round r. This generates their ownership stake after round r, $F_i(r)$. An important implication of equation (4.10-MR) is that at every investment round all existing shareholders get diluted by the common factor $(1- F_r(r))$. We call this the ownership retention rate. This is an important measure for investors and entrepreneurs, since it gives an idea of how much ownership they will forgo to attract the capital needed to build the company. We discuss the role of the retention rate further in Section 9.2.4.

We conclude that dilution matters to all entrepreneurs and investors because it affects how their ownership stake evolves over time. Dilution reduced the entrepreneur's and previous investors' ownership shares. Investors can avoid dilution by continuing to invest in each round, something we discuss in detail in Section 9.2.1. Importantly, dilution is not bad in itself. The company receives financial resources in exchange for issuing new shares. If these resources sufficiently increase the value of the venture, they are worth obtaining.

As the company receives subsequent financing rounds and shareholders experience dilution, the capitalization table allows the entrepreneur to keep track of how ownership evolves over financing rounds (see WorkHorse Box 4.5).

WorkHorse Box 4.5 WorkHorse's Ownership Dilution Across Investment Rounds

As he was arranging the seed round of financing, Michael Archie thought ahead to a possible second round, in which professional investors' funding would come through in a Series A round. The financial projections suggested that one year later the company would need to raise $2M. For this second round, Michael planned to invest $200K. The Ang brothers were unlikely to participate further. For the remaining $1.8M he planned to ask some of his contacts in the venture capital industry. He hoped that Eagle-I Ventures would lead the A round, contributing $1M. Coyo-T Capital would likely contribute the remaining $800K.

Astrid knew that further funding would entail further dilution. She had been advised that she should expect to give up a quarter of the company at the next round. She wanted to explore what kind of valuation and ownership this would imply. The capitalization table summarizes all her calculations.

Using the equations for multi-round funding, Astrid calculated the founder shares after two rounds, denoted by $F_0(2)$, as follows:

$$F_0(2) = F_0(1) * (1 - F_2(2)) = 0.64 * (1 - 0.25) = 0.48$$

The stock options pool and the other third-party stakes would obtain the following ownership stake:

$$F_{SOP}(2) = F_{SOP}(1) * (1 - F_2(2)) = 0.16 * (1 - 0.25) = 0.12$$

For the first-round investors she obtained:

$$F_1(2) = F_1(1) * (1 - F_2(2)) = 0.20 * (1 - 0.25) = 0.15$$

She also noticed that Michael Archie would purchase 10% of the new shares. This would give him an additional 2.5% ownership stake, so that he could maintain a 10% ownership stake, as noted in the last column of the capitalization table. Astrid observed that the post-money and pre-money valuations would be:

$$V_{POST}(2) = I(2)/F_2(2) = \$2M/0.25 = \$8M$$

$$V_{PRE}(2) = V_{POST}(2) - I(2) = \$8M - \$2M = \$6M$$

Since the number of existing shares prior to the round was 1.25M, she computed the price of new shares as:

$$P(2) = V_{PRE}(2)/S_{POST}(1) = \$6M/1.25M = \$4.80$$

Astrid noted that while the ownership fraction of the founders was already less than half, the value of their equity had increased considerably. At a price of $4.80, the 0.8M founder shares would already be valued at $3.84M. She wondered why the valuation and price per share had gone up so easily: "Isn't it a struggle for companies to survive and achieve higher valuations over time?" Brandon explained that successful companies are able to raise their next round of financing at a higher valuation, whereas unsuccessful companies typically don't even manage to raise another round. This explains why we see valuation rising over time. The calculations reflect this by using a higher price per share in the second round.

Astrid also computed the number of new shares issued to the new investors as follows:

$$S_2(2) = I(2)/P(2) = \$2M/\$4.80 = 0.417M$$

The number of total shares after two rounds was thus:

$$S_{POST}(2) = S_{POST}(1) + S_2(2) = 1.25M + 0.417M = 1.667M$$

The following capitalization table summarizes WorkHorse's projected owner-ship structure after the second round.

Second Round (Venture Series A)		Number of shares purchased	Number of shares owned	Amount invested in round ($)	Total amount invested ($)	Ownership fraction
Price per share ($) 4.80						
Founders:						
	Astrid Dala		200,000	0	0	12.0%
	Annie Ma		200,000	0	0	12.0%
	Bharat Marwari		200,000	0	0	12.0%
	Brandon Potro		200,000	0	0	12.0%
Investors:						
	Michael Archie	41,667	166,667	200,000	450,000	10.0%
	Ang brothers	0	125,000	0	250,000	7.5%
	Eagle-I Ventures	208,333	208,333	1,000,000	1,000,000	12.5%
	Coyo-T Capital	166,667	166,667	800,000	800,000	10.0%
Other parties:						
	JP Potro	0	50,000	0	0	3.0%
	U. of Michigan	0	50,000	0	0	3.0%
	Stock Options Pool	0	100,000	0	0	6.0%
Total		416,667	1,666,667	2,000,000	2,500,000	100%

4.2 Investor Returns

4.2.1 Risk and Return

Investors provide money with the goal of earning a profit, so they base their in-vestment decisions on the returns they expect to earn from the investment. In this section, we review common measures of returns and discuss their advantages and limitations in the context of entrepreneurial finance.

A basic result of finance is that higher returns can only be achieved by taking on more risk: if two projects have the same risk, the one with a higher return would be in higher demand, it would become more expensive, and its return would become lower. This basic trade-off between risk and return allows us to approach entrepre-neurial investments from the right angle.

To understand the relationship between risk and return let us first look at how risk is often misunderstood. Consider a risky investment that yields $100 (net of the invested amount) with 60% probability and nothing with 40% probability. This investment therefore has an expected (net) outcome of $60. If we compare it against an alternative safe investment that yields a guaranteed $100 (net), the risky investment is clearly worse: it never returns more than the safe one, and it may well return less. Here risk is the possibility that something can go wrong. Therefore, this is not a sensible comparison. Compare instead the above risky investment to a safe investment that returns $50 with certainty. Some people prefer the risky investment, considering that its expected return of $60 is above the safe return of $50. Others, however, may prefer the safe investment because the risk of the bad outcome that returns zero is too painful for them to contemplate. Risk is not simply that things can go wrong; instead, risk describes uncertainty around an expected return.

Next, consider an investor who has funded a project that has an expected return of 10% and a certain level of risk. A 10% return means the investor expects to obtain back the invested sum increased by 10%. If there was another project also with an expected return of 10% but with lower risk, the investor would prefer this latter one. This is because investors are typically "risk averse"; that is, they prefer safer projects to riskier ones, for a given expected return. Our investor will then prefer to pay more for the project with a lower risk. This will reduce that project's expected return: the investor pays more, but the project yields the same expected outcome. Projects with higher risk, therefore, can attract investors only if they offer a higher return.

The trade-off between risk and return is central to finance, and textbooks devote much attention to this topic and its implications for investment decisions.[9] For example, finance scholars have developed elaborate measures for comparing different distributions of risk, and there is an important distinction between diversifiable and non-diversifiable risks. Here we focus on addressing two important questions about the risk of financing entrepreneurial ventures.

The first question is whether one has to be a "risk-lover" to invest in entrepreneurial ventures. Here the answer is no. Risk-loving means preferring higher risk over lower risk, which resembles gambling. Most venture investors are not risk-lovers; they prefer lower over higher risk. However, venture investors are clearly willing to take on substantial risk. The right way to describe them is as those having a high-risk tolerance. In addition, venture investors tend to believe that they possess the skills, resources, and willingness to reduce the risk by guiding the company through the challenges of the entrepreneurial process. Therefore, we should think of venture investors not as risk-lovers, but as risk-tolerant investors who work toward reducing risks.[10]

The second question asks what is different about the returns to venture investing, compared to other risky investments, such as investing in the stock market. There are many differences, but two of them stand out. First, the risk of investing in entrepreneurial ventures can be extreme. It is possible to generate extremely high returns—think of investing in Amazon or Alibaba—but it is also possible to lose everything. Statisticians call this property skewness, where the distribution of

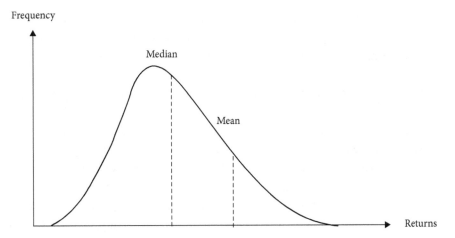

Figure 4.1. Skewed returns.

returns is asymmetric. Specifically, returns to venture investing exhibit "right skew" with what is called a "long right tail." While there is a chance of achieving extremely high returns, the probability of it is very low. The much more frequent outcomes are low returns where investors lose all or most of the investment. With a right skew distribution, average returns are higher than median returns.[11] Figure 4.1 illustrates this graphically.

Second, there is liquidity risk in financing entrepreneurial ventures. In the stock market, one can buy and sell shares in seconds; this is called a liquid market. Selling shares in private company is considerably slower, with investors often having to wait years before they can sell their shares (see Chapter 11).

Here we make a distinction between realized and expected returns. The cash flows of an investor consist of making one or several investments over time and then waiting for an exit to realize a return. Realized returns are based on a backward-looking perspective of measuring what happened since the time of investment. Expected returns, by contrast, are forward-looking and measure what investors expect to happen in the future. Expected returns are often used to express what investors require before agreeing to make an investment. Our focus in this section is mostly on realized returns, although in Section 4.3.1 we also discuss expected returns.

4.2.2 Three Measures of Return

A lively debate has arisen among finance scholars and practitioners as to what measures of returns should be used in entrepreneurial finance. In this section, we describe the three most common measures used in practice. To motivate them, consider the responses from a survey by Gompers, Kaplan, and Mukharlyamov, which asked venture capitalists what financial metrics they used for analyzing investments.[12] 63% of the respondents reported use of cash-on-cash multiples,

42% internal rates of return, 22% net present value, 8% other measures, and 9% none. On average, respondents make use of two measures. This evidence suggests that investors use a variety of measures and that no single measure addresses everything.

We illustrate the three return measures in the simple case with only one investment round. In Section 4.2.4, we then consider returns with multiple rounds of investments. In start-ups, returns are entirely driven by the value of the company at exit, which we denote by X. In case of an acquisition, X is the acquisition price, net of any payments to existing debt holders. In case of an IPO, X is the company's market capitalization at the end of the so-called lock-up period, when investors are typically allowed to start selling their shares (Section 11.2.3). At the time of exit, investors receive an amount of money equal to their ownership share of the company times the exit value. We denote this amount by:

$$X_{INV} = F_{INV} * X \qquad (4.11)$$

Notice that, correspondingly, the entrepreneur's share of the exit value is given by $X_{ENT} = F_{ENT} * X$. We denote the discount rate by d. The time between the investment and exit (investment duration) is denoted by T.

The standard criterion for financial investment decision is the net present value (NPV).[13] It is based on discounting back to the present all future cash flows. Box 4.2 provides an brief introduction.

Box 4.2 The Time Value of Money

To understand discounting, suppose first we invest one dollar today in a safe asset and earn back the same dollar plus some interest next year. One dollar today is worth more than one dollar in one year because we can earn some interest over this period. This gives rise to what financial economists call the time value of money. We can put this reasoning in a formula. Suppose that investing a sum I over one year earns interest d. The *future value* of I, which we denote by FV(I), is given by:

$$FV(I) = I + dI = I(1 + d)$$

This equation expresses the value of I today as what it will be worth in one year. Having I today or I(1 + d) in one year are equivalent, since we can always obtain FV(I) by investing I today.

We use this equation to derive the *present value* of what we can earn in one year. We can rewrite the above equation as I = FV(I)/(1 + d). At this point, it is useful to define X as the forward value of I, that is, $X = FV(I) = I(1 + d)$. Next we denote the present value of a future return X by $PV(X)$. In our example, $PV(X) = I$, or:

$$PV(X) = X/(1+d)$$

This formula expresses the basic idea of discounting, which means moving the value of a sum X back from next year to today. In this formulation, d is called the discount rate.

If an investment lasts more than one year, we simply consider that each year the value of the investment is reinvested at the same interest rate. In T years, the investment I becomes:

$$FV(I) = I(1+d)^{T}$$

Correspondingly, discounting a return X back across T years gives:

$$PV(X) = X/(1+d)^{T}$$

The NPV of an investment is derived by the present value by subtracting the cost of the investment. In the simple case where investors provide an initial investment and then wait to exit the company after T years, the NPV is given by the present value of the investor's share of the exit value defined in (4.11), minus the investment I:

$$NPV = X_{INV}/(1+d)^{T} - I \qquad\qquad (4.12)$$

The NPV is used to make investment decisions. If the NPV is negative, the investor should refrain from making the investment because the present value of future cash flows exceeds the cost of making the investment. If the NPV is positive, then the investor has a net gain from it and can use it to compare alternative investment projects. The NPV is scale-dependent, which sometimes makes it difficult to compare alternative investments.

What makes use of the NPV criterion difficult in an entrepreneurial finance context is the estimation of an appropriate discount rate. An appropriate discount rate should reflect the cash flow patterns and systematic risk of comparable companies, but these are difficult to pin down. Moreover, different investors might have different costs of capital. For example, business angels, who invest their own funds, have a lower cost of capital than venture capital firms, which raise funds from institutional investors (see Chapter 12). Without a proper value for the discount rate to properly move cash flows back in time, the NPV may become a poor measure to compute and compare returns (Section 5.2.3).

A popular return measure is the cash-on-cash multiple, which we abbreviate as CCM. It measures how many times the amount originally invested is returned to the investor at exit:

$$CCM = X_{INV}/I \qquad (4.13)$$

The appeal of this return measure is its simplicity. Its major weakness is that it fails to account for the timing of cash flows, so that receiving the same exit value in one year or in one decade yields the same return. This is particularly relevant in venture investing, where the time to exit is often several years long. Beyond disregarding the time value of money, the CCM also disregards the amount of risk that one bears to receive a certain exit value, so that doubling the amount invested in a risky new venture is considered equivalent to doubling it on a safe government bond.

The third measure of returns that we consider is the internal rate of return, or IRR. This measure is also widely used in practice. However, it has some important shortcomings, such as favoring returns over short horizons and not accounting for risk.

The IRR is defined as the discount rate corresponding to an investment's zero NPV. Setting NPV = 0 in (4.12), we obtain the following equation:

$$I * (1 + IRR)^T = X_{INV} \qquad (4.14)$$

The IRR is therefore defined by an implicit equation. In the case of a single period, one easily obtains IRR = $(F_{INV}*X/I) - 1$, but in the case of multiple investment rounds the equation can only be solved numerically. Spreadsheet tools can perform the required calculations.

4.2.3 Comparing Return Measures

We now compare the three return measures. Both IRR and CCM fail to take risk into account. The CCM also does not account for the timing of cash flows. The NPV, on the other hand, requires choosing a suitable discount rate. To compare the CCM with the IRR, we combine equations (4.13) and (4.14) and obtain the following simple relationship:

$$CCM = (1 + IRR)^T \qquad (4.15)$$

Based on this, Table 4.2 shows how different CCM and different time horizons result in different IRRs.

Table 4.2 IRR Values Corresponding to Different CCM Values and Time Horizons.

		Cash-on-Cash Multiples (CCM)						
		0.5	1	2	3	4	5	10
Time horizon (years)	0.5	−75%	0%	300%	800%	1,500%	2,400%	9,900%
	1	−50%	0%	100%	200%	300%	400%	900%
	2	−29%	0%	41%	73%	100%	124%	216%
	3	−21%	0%	26%	44%	59%	71%	115%
	4	−16%	0%	19%	32%	41%	50%	78%
	5	−13%	0%	15%	25%	32%	38%	58%
	6	−11%	0%	12%	20%	26%	31%	47%
	8	−8%	0%	9%	15%	19%	22%	33%
	10	−7%	0%	7%	12%	15%	17%	26%
	15	−5%	0%	5%	8%	10%	11%	17%
	20	−3%	0%	4%	6%	7%	8%	12%

Table 4.2 shows that CCMs do not vary with the time horizon, as every column has the same CCM. The IRR instead does: within every column, the IRR decreases with the time horizon. This means that investments with different time horizons cannot be compared on the basis of CCM. However, even the IRR can be misleading when comparing investments with different time horizons. For example, consider two investments, one that doubles in two years and one that quadruples in four years. Even though both generate an IRR of 41%, investors are likely to prefer the project with CCM of four over four years than the one with CCM of two over two years. This is because the high returns to the former investment last far longer. Comparing two investments at different time horizons requires some adjustments to compare them on the same time period. A common approach is to extend the shorter project to match the longer one. This means assuming that one would re-invest the money from the first investment at an IRR of 41% for two more years, which is difficult. Hence, most investors would prefer the former over the latter. More generally, we note that deciding based on the IRR favors projects with short time horizons when the IRR is high and favors projects with long horizons when the IRR is low.

The solution to this problem is to use the NPV. For example, at a 15% discount rate, an investment of $100 with a CCM of four over four years yields an NPV of $112, compared to an NPV of $45 for a CCM of two over two years. The advantage of the NPV is that different investments with different time horizons can be compared with each other. The main disadvantage of the NPV is that it requires choosing a suitable discount rate, which is precisely what enables the comparison across different time horizons. The NPV therefore provides a sound basis for comparisons and decision making, although it is a less convincing choice for reporting purposes. By contrast, CCM and IRR have serious limitations for decision making but are routinely used for reporting purposes, precisely because they do not require any further assumptions about discount rates.

We close this section with two comments. First, we have focused so far on computing investor returns. One can also look at returns from the entire company's perspective. Company returns include the returns to all shareholders: investors, founders, and stock option recipients. The latter two typically do not invest any financial capital but do receive some cash at exit. Since they include these additional gains, company returns are therefore mechanically higher than investor returns. We can think of the additional returns as compensation for the contributions provided by founders and stock option recipients. Founders provide the initial idea, the ability to execute it, and labor; stock option recipients mainly contribute labor. Measuring company returns is a straightforward extension of measuring investor returns. All that is needed is to replace X_{INV} with X.

Second, if we can calculate investor returns and company returns, shouldn't we also calculate the entrepreneurs' returns? Unfortunately, the standard return measures often do not work for founders or employees. This is because they receive financial gains but typically do not invest much cash. That is, their financial investments are insignificant relative to the ideas and labor they provide. Computing financial returns for entrepreneurs therefore has little meaning. Instead of looking at return measures, we recommend looking at entrepreneurs' financial gains, as given by X_{ENT} in (4.11).

WorkHorse Box 4.6 looks at all these return measures.

WorkHorse Box 4.6 The Ang Brothers' Return Calculations

Michael Archie was excited about WorkHorse and mentioned it as a co-investment opportunity to the Ang brothers. They were two wealthy brothers who were active angel investors. They had an investment philosophy of co-investing with others for a single round of investment. Their hope was that the company would achieve an exit without any additional financing rounds.

The brothers had different opinions about the timing of the exit. Quentin Ang, known as Quick Quentin, hoped WorkHorse would sell after two years. He thought that the company could achieve an exit value of $10M. His brother Simon Ang, known as Slow Simon, thought instead that exiting WorkHorse would take four years and that the company could then be sold for $12.5M. They planned to invest (jointly) $250K in return for 10% of the common equity (see the capitalization table in WorkHorse Box 4.1). Quentin and Simon therefore debated what would be the outcome of the investment. They denoted their respective opinions about exit as Quick and Slow. They expected to receive the following values at exit:

$$X_{Ang}^{Quick} = F_{Quick} * X_{Quick} = 0.1 * \$10M = \$1M$$

$$X_{Ang}^{Slow} = F_{Slow} \, * \, X_{Slow} = 0.1 \, * \, \$12.5M = \$1.25M$$

The two brothers were curious to compare their return calculations. They began by looking at the NPV, using a 10% discount rate, and calculated their respective NPVs as follows:

$$NPV_{Ang}^{Quick} = \$1M/(1+0.1)^2 - \$250K = \$576K$$

$$NPV_{Ang}^{Slow} = \$1.25M/(1+0.1)^4 - \$250K = \$604K$$

Under the NPV measure, Slow Simon expected to make higher returns.

Next they calculated their cash-on-cash multiple as follows:

$$CCM_{Ang}^{Quick} = X_{Ang}^{Quick}/I_{Quick} = \$1M/\$250K = 4$$

$$CCM_{Ang}^{Slow} = X_{Ang}^{Slow}/I_{Slow} = \$1.25M/\$250K = 5$$

Quick Quentin expected to make his money back four times, Slow Simon five times. Again, Simon expected to make higher returns.

Next, they used Table 4.2 to convert these CCMs into IRRs. Quick Quentin's fourfold return over two years corresponded to an IRR of 100%. Slow Simon's fivefold returns over four years corresponded to an IRR of 50%. This time Quick Quentin expected to make the higher returns. This exemplifies the bias toward short-term investment inherent in IRRs.

For curiosity's sake they also calculated company returns using the full .5M seed round investment. Quentin used an exit value of $10M, and Simon used $12.5M. The table below shows both investor and company returns.

Return measure	Investor returns		Company returns	
	Quentin	Simon	Quentin	Simon
NPV	$0.58M	$0.60M	$7.76M	$8.04M
CCM	4	5	20	25
IRR	100%	50%	347%	124%

The company returns were dramatically larger than the investor returns. This is because they combined the returns of all parties, including the entrepreneurial gains of the founders and the stock options pool. At the same time, they only counted the capital investments of investors, not the investments of labor (and possibly IP) by the entrepreneurs, employees, and third parties. This shows that company return calculations should be interpreted with caution.

Finally, the two brothers wanted to figure out what the financial gains to entrepreneurs (and other parties) would be. From WorkHorse Box 4.4 they knew that the four founders owned 64% and the other parties (stock options holders, JP Potro, and the University of Michigan) owned 16%. Accordingly, the founders' financial gains at exit would be:

$$X_{ENT}^{Quick} = 0.64 * \$10M = \$6.4M$$

$$X_{ENT}^{Slow} = 0.64 * \$12.5M = \$8M$$

The financial gains to stock option holders would be:

$$X_{SOP}^{Quick} = 0.16 * \$10M = \$1.6M$$

$$X_{SOP}^{Slow} = 0.16 * \$12.5M = \$2M$$

All in all, the Ang brothers were impressed by the potential of the deal and agreed to be part of the deal.

4.2.4 Returns with Multiple Rounds

This section is technically more challenging and can be skipped for the first reading of this chapter.

In this section, we show how to generalize the return measures to the case of investments with multiple rounds. We focus on round-level returns, which measure the returns of all investors who participated in a specific round. As in Section 4.1.5, we index the current round by r = 1,2, . . . ,R. We include exit as the round after the Rth round, writing r = EXIT. Since the exit round doesn't involve any investment, ownership stakes do not change between round R and exit, and we can use the ownership fractions after round R for the exit, too. Recall that an investor's ownership stake from round i, after round r, is denoted by $F_i(r)$. We thus write:

$$F_i(EXIT) = F_i(R) \tag{4.16}$$

The value of the investor's ownership stake at the time of exit is thus given by:

$$X_i = F_i(R) * X \tag{4.17}$$

We denote investment dates by t(r) and the period of time between the investment at t(i) and the current round at t(r), by $\tau_i(r) = t(r) - t(i)$. For example, $T_1(4)$ stands for the period of time between the first and the fourth rounds, and $T_i(EXIT)$ stands for the period of time between the ith round and exit.

We use MR to identify formulas with multiple rounds, and we write:

$$NPV_i = \frac{X_i}{(1+d)^{T_i(EXIT)}} - I(i) \qquad\qquad (4.12\text{-MR})$$

$$CCM_i = \frac{X_i}{I(i)} \qquad\qquad (4.13\text{-MR})$$

$$I(i) * (1+IRR_i)^{T_i(EXIT)} = X_i \qquad\qquad (4.14\text{-MR})$$

WorkHorse Box 4.7 illustrates how this works.

WorkHorse Box 4.7 WorkHorse's Returns with Multiple Rounds of Investments

Michael Archie thought that the Ang brothers were unrealistic in their belief that WorkHorse would exit after a single investment round. He agreed with the company's financial projections which foresaw a second round of $2M after one year. Furthermore, he thought that if everything went well, an exit at $12.5M after four years was a realistic goal. Based on that he calculated the various return measures for the first round and second round investors.

Michael Archie used the deal structure outlined in WorkHorse Box 4.5, which involves two rounds, so that R = 2. Using the information from WorkHorse Box 4.5, he calculated:

	Round 1	Round 2
Ownership	$F_1(2)=0.15$	$F_2(2)=0.25$
Value at exit	$X_1=\$1.875M$	$X_2=\$3.125M$
Investment	$I(1)=\$0.5M$	$I(2)=\$2M$

With this information, he calculated the CCMs as follows

$$CCM_1 = \frac{\$1.875M}{\$0.5M} = 3.75, \quad CCM_2 = \frac{\$3.125M}{\$2M} = 1.56$$

For the round IRRs he solved:

$$0 = \frac{\$1.875M}{(1+IRR_1)^4} - \$0.5M \quad \text{and} \quad 0 = \frac{\$3.125M}{(1+IRR_2)^4} - \frac{\$2M}{(1+IRR_2)^1}$$

This yielded $IRR_1 = 39.16\%$ and $IRR_2 = 16.04\%$.

Note that the formula for IRR_2 calculates everything back to the time of the first round. It is also possible to calculate everything back to the time of the second round. This makes no difference; exactly the same result obtains.

For the NPV he calculated:

$$NPV_1 = \frac{\$1.875M}{(1+0.1)^4} - \$0.5M = \$0.71M$$

$$NPV_2 = \frac{\$3.125M}{(1+0.1)^4} - \frac{\$2M}{(1+0.1)^1} = \$0.29M$$

Clearly, Michael Archie's returns were lower than those of the Ang brothers. Still they suggested that WorkHorse could be an attractive investment.

Finally, we note that equations (4.12-MR) to (4.14-MR) calculate the returns for an investor in round i. One can also write down formulas to describe the returns for investors who invest across multiple rounds and, similarly, the returns of all investors across all rounds. Since these formulas are rather complex, we report them in the book's website (www.entrepreneurialfinance.net).

4.3 The Determinants of Valuation and Returns

4.3.1 The Relationship Between Valuation and Returns

In this section we establish some important insights about the relationship between valuation, investor returns, and exit values. For simplicity, we focus on the simplest case where there is only a single investment round, and we consider only the CCM return measure. However, all the insights in this section apply to all return measures, as well as to returns over multiple investment rounds.

We first combine equations (4.2) and (4.13) to obtain:

$$CCM = X/V_{POST} \tag{4.18}$$

This says that the cash-on-cash realized return equals the exit value (X) divided by the company's post-money valuation (V_{POST}). With this relationship we establish two useful insights:

Insight 1: For a given post-money valuation (V_{POST}), a higher exit value (X) leads to a higher realized investor return (CCM).

Insight 2: For a given exit value (X), a higher post-money valuation (V_{POST}) leads to a lower realized investor return (CCM).

The simple message of these insights is that investors make higher returns when exit values are higher, but they make lower returns when the company's post-money valuation at the time of the investment is higher. This is basically just restating the well-known investor maxim "buy low (low V_{POST}) and sell high (high X)."

It is worth contrasting the investors' perspective with the entrepreneur's perspective. We have already noted that financial return measures may not be appropriate for the entrepreneur, who is investing mainly labor and not capital. Instead, we focus on the entrepreneur's gains at the time of exit X_{ENT}. Combining equations (4.1) and (4.16), and noting that $F_{ENT} = (1 - F_{INV})$, we can rewrite X_{ENT} as follows:

$$X_{ENT} = \left(1 - \frac{I}{V_{POST}} \right) X \tag{4.19}$$

This equation allows us to establish two additional insights:

Insight 3: For a given post-money valuation (V_{POST}), a higher exit value (X) leads to a higher entrepreneurial gain (X_{ENT}).

Insight 4: For a given exit value (X), a higher post-money valuation (V_{POST}) leads to a higher entrepreneurial gain (X_{ENT}).

Insight 3 mirrors Insight 1 and says that entrepreneurs, too, benefit from higher exit values. Insight 4, however, contrasts with Insight 2. Entrepreneurs make larger gains when the company's valuation at the time of the investment is higher. This is the exact opposite of investors, exposing a fundamental tension between entrepreneurs and investors. While both want the company to succeed in terms of achieving a higher exit value (X), they have opposing economic incentives concerning valuation at the time of the investment. For a given exit value, the entrepreneur wants a higher valuation and the investor a lower one. Note, however, that this is not necessarily true if we compare valuations offered by different investors, as we show in Section 4.3.2.

These four insights are based on realized returns and explain how they are affected by valuation. We can also use equation (4.18) to derive a formula for what the post-money valuation "should" be, by using a forward-looking perspective. For this purpose, we consider expected returns, not realized returns. By "expected" we mean the investor's required return, that is, the return the investor expects to achieve in order to commit his or her money. We add a superscript "e" to indicate expectations.

$$V_{POST} = X^e / CCM^e \tag{4.20}$$

This equation will be the starting point for Chapter 5 where we examine how to practically estimate a valuation with the available data. In preparation for that, we set some foundations here by providing two additional insights about the relationship between the valuation, the expected exit values, and the investor's expected returns.

> Insight 5: For a given expected return (CCM^e), a higher expected exit value (X^e) leads to a higher post-money valuation (V_{POST}).
> Insight 6: For a given expected exit value (X^e), a higher expected return (CCM^e) leads to a lower post-money valuation (V_{POST}).

Insight 5 reveals that investors are willing to pay a higher post-money valuation if they expect a better exit outcome. Insight 6 reveals that investors who expect to achieve a higher return only pay a lower post-money valuation. The difference between Insight 5 and 6 is that the former concerns beliefs about the company's performance—a more positive belief leads to a higher valuation—whereas the latter concerns the investor's return requirements—a higher expected return leads to a lower valuation.

4.3.2 The Economic Determinants of Valuation

What determines venture valuation? In this section, we consider the important role of some economic forces. Clearly, the quality of the underlying opportunity matters (see Chapter 2), but there are other economic forces at work too. Box 4.3 summarizes some research insights.

Box 4.3 Economic Determinants of Valuation.

What economic forces affect start-up valuations? One study by Gompers and Lerner looks at a sample of deals from across the U.S. over an eight-year period.[14] One important finding is that venture capital valuations go up when the stock market goes up, and vice versa. A separate finding is that valuations increase with the amount of money raised by local VC funds. The effect is most pronounced in the largest, most competitive markets, such as California. The authors explain this effect as "money-chasing deals," where a larger number of investors are chasing a limited number of attractive deals. The first effect suggests that stock markets drive valuations, and the second that deal competition matters.

   Another seminal paper, by David Hsu, uses valuation data from start-ups who received multiple offers from different investors at the same time.[15] The uniqueness of this data is that one can compare how different investors bid for the same company. The key result is that higher quality and better networked investors offer lower valuations. Importantly, entrepreneurs frequently accept those lower offers, effectively giving up more ownership. The study argues that entrepreneurs are willing to do so because they believe that the venture benefits from having higher quality investors on board.

We identify four important economic determinants of company valuation: the opportunity itself, the market context, deal competition, and investor quality. We can immediately see the effect for the first two determinants by using Insight 5 in Section 4.3.1. Better opportunities promise a higher expected exit value, which justifies a higher valuation. A rising stock market has a similar effect. Higher stock markets values suggest that start-ups can expect higher exit values, either when they go public themselves or when they get acquired by a listed company. Hot markets can be driven by technological breakthroughs, demographic trends, regulatory reforms, and possibly irrational exuberance and asset price bubbles (see also Box 12.1). Acquisitions are driven also by macroeconomic cycles (Section 11.3). In terms of equation (4.21), we note that the higher valuation (V_{POST}) is justified with higher expected exit values (X^e).

To understand the deal competition, we note that valuations for start-ups are determined through a bargaining process. The valuation is affected by the context of the negotiation and in particular by how much the bargaining power lies with the entrepreneur or with the investor.[16] In Section 7.5 we take a comprehensive look at the negotiation process; here we focus on the role of competition. When competition is absent or weak, the investor is more powerful and can dictate the terms of the deal. The investor takes a larger ownership stake for a given investment, which implies a lower company valuation. This implies in part that the valuation no longer reflects just the value of the opportunity, but now also incorporates the stronger bargaining power of the investor. A company in a very competitive environment may fetch a higher valuation than another company in a less competitive environment, even if the latter has better business fundamentals. Competition can be elicited by entrepreneurs by actively seeking out potentially interested investors or by locating their company in vibrant clusters (Section 14.2). As noted in Box 4.2, competition also reflects the amount of funds available for investment in a given place and time. In terms of equation (4.21), we note that a higher valuation (V_{POST}), due to more competition, can be justified in terms of lower required returns to investors (CCM^e).

To see the effect of investor quality, suppose a high-quality investor is competing against a lower quality investor to invest in a company. The entrepreneur knows that the high-quality investor will add more value to the venture. If the high-quality investor offered the same valuation as the lower quality investor, the entrepreneur would always take the high-quality investor in a heartbeat. Knowing this, the high-quality investor can offer a lower valuation and still get the entrepreneur to take the offer. Thus, if one company gets an offer from a low-quality investor and another from a high-quality investor, then the latter may get a lower valuation. Yet its business opportunity may be stronger, in particular because it benefits from the help of the high-quality investor. This is precisely what Hsu's empirical study, discussed in Box 4.2, documents. In terms of equation (4.21) a higher valuation (V_{POST}) is again justified on the basis of higher expected exit values (X^e), in this case due to the greater value added by more experienced investors (Section 8.3).

Box 4.4 concludes this example by illustrating how valuations can be affected by deal competition and investor quality with a fictional example.

Box 4.4 The Long Road to Getting the Right Valuation

Adi and Sesi Mohoebi, a brother and sister from Maseru, were proud of the mobile phone health app they had developed. It would allow millions of their countrymen to obtain relevant medical information and support. They also believed their company would become a commercial success and be worth $2M at exit. All they needed was an investment of $100K, at the right valuation.

One challenge was that Maseru, the capital of Lesotho in southern Africa, was hardly a hotbed of entrepreneurial finance. The only angel investor in town was Lwazi Lengeloi. He liked the venture and offered the required $100K for an ownership stake of 40%, implying a post-money valuation of $250K. Adi and Sesi appreciated his support but knew that this was not his best offer. They decided to search for other investors. Since Lesotho was a small country, they took the long road to Bloemfontein, the nearest large city in neighboring South Africa. They were fortunate to be introduced to a friend of their uncle's wife, a local angel investor called Elspeth Engelvrou. She liked the business idea and asked for only 25% ownership in return for the investment, thus raising the valuation to $400K. When they reported back to Lwazi about this new offer, he made a final best offer, to invest $100K for 20%, thus further raising the valuation to $500K. Elspeth was not willing to match Lwazi's valuation but offered to introduce them to Pret-A-Investir, a Pretoria-based venture capital firm with a Pan-African investment portfolio. They therefore took the long road to Pretoria, the capital of South Africa. They were delighted to find out that Pret-A-Investir was willing to invest $100K. However, they wanted a third (i.e., 33.33%) of the company, implying a valuation of $300K. To get some clarity, Adi and Sesi put all the information into a table.

| | Lwazi | Elspeth | Lwazi | Pret-A-Invest | |
	First offer	Only offer	Final offer	Adi's view	Sesi's view
Investment ($)	100,000	100,000	100,000	100,000	100,000
Investor stake	40%	25%	20%	33.33%	33.33%
Valuation ($)	250,000	400,000	500,000	300,000	300,000

	Lwazi	Elspeth	Lwazi	Pret-A-Invest	
	First offer	Only offer	Final offer	Adi's view	Sesi's view
Exit value ($)	2,000,000	2,000,000	2,000,000	2,000,000	3,000,000
Investor exit value ($)	800,000	500,000	400,000	666,667	1,000,000
Investor CCM	8	5	4	6.67	10
Founder exit value ($)	1,200,000	1,500,000	1,600,000	1,333,333	2,000,000

The two entrepreneurs understood that it came down to a choice between Lwazi's final offers versus Pret-A-Investir's offer. Sesi remarked how powerful competition proved: "We showed Lwazi the exact same venture, but he valued it at $250K before we met Elspeth, and $500K afterwards." Adi agreed and added: "The quality of a venture is not a reliable indicator of its valuation: deal competition matters, too."

Adi wanted to dismiss Pret-A-Investir's offer because the valuation of $300K was far below Lwazi's final offer. Sesi, however, argued that Pret-A-Investir was a smart investor with considerable experience in mobile services. With their investment, the company could grow far beyond Lesotho and South Africa, and ultimately reach an exit value of $3M. Sesi argued that their share of the expected exit value would thus amount to $2M, not $1.33M. This was now well above the $1.6M from Lwazi's offer. She didn't care about the fact that Pret-A-Investir's valuation was lower. She argued: "Our goal is not to get the highest valuation, but to get the best outcome. Normally, a higher valuation is better for the entrepreneur, but in our case a lower valuation from a higher quality investor is actually better." Adi agreed and added: "Valuations alone are not a reliable indicator of how attractive a deal is: investor quality matters too."

Box 4.4 highlights why valuations need to be interpreted with caution. The same company can attract a higher valuation if there is more competition for the deal. Therefore, one should not necessarily interpret a lower valuation as a sign of a weaker company. Investor quality effects further reinforce this message. More prestigious investors, who can add more value to a company, usually offer lower valuations. From the entrepreneur's perspective, this can still be a good deal, provided the prestigious investor actually adds significant value to the venture.

Let us add one more word of caution about the interpretation of valuations. So far we have focused on why some companies end up with low valuations, such as when there is limited deal competition, or high investor quality. It is also possible that some companies receive inflated valuations when markets are ebullient, as witnessed in the dotcom era. A different reason for getting inflated valuations is the use of complex preferred shares, which we discuss in Box 6.8.

4.4 The Determinants of Founder Ownership

4.4.1 Founder Agreements

Our discussion so far examines the determinants of valuation, and therefore the allocation of share ownership between entrepreneurs and investors. In this section, we address the question of what determines the allocation of share ownership within the founders' team. This question doesn't apply if there is a single founder, but it clearly matters with a team of founders. Furthermore, investors often have questions about the internal division of shares and the logic behind it. This logic is different from the valuation logic discussed so far in this chapter. In fact, the internal allocation of shares is part of a broader negotiation among founders, which we will now examine.

The first deal in a start-up is often the internal founder agreement. Prior to approaching investors, entrepreneurs first need to bring their own house in order. As soon as there are two or more founders, some founder agreement is needed to define the legal rights and commitments of the various founding parties. Some founder teams address these issues early on in the development of the venture, whereas others wait until they are further along the journey. The latest time for the founder agreement to come together is at the time of structuring an investor term sheet (see Chapter 6). This is because investors want clarity on what these arrangements look like. The optimal timing of founder negotiations is neither too early nor too late. At the very beginning, it is difficult for founders to specify things because of the uncertainties lying ahead. There is also a discovery process of getting to know each other and assessing fit. However, there is a danger of procrastination. Having a founder agreement provides certainty and clarity within the team. Moreover, in the absence of an agreement, there is always a danger that some founders will start the venture on their own, cutting out the others. A key role of the founder agreement is to lay down who is in and thus also who is out.[17]

Founder agreements address five main issues. First, they determine who the members of the team are, typically also what their current and future expected roles are, and how they are expected to change in the future. This creates a shared understanding of who is responsible for what. Second, founder agreements can specify the salaries different founders are to receive. Start-ups typically pay low salaries, though there are exceptions. Third, founder agreements can detail any financial obligations of the company toward individual founders. For example, a founder may need to get repaid for a prior loan or for transferring IP to the company. Fourth, founder agreements determine ownership allocation. This means allocating common shares among the founders, which shapes voting rights, as well as the distribution of the eventual financial gains. Finally, founder agreements can specify contingencies. This means that certain awards (such as the receipt of shares or bonuses) depend on certain milestones. A common arrangement is the vesting of founder shares. This means that the company withholds a portion of founder shares and releases them over time, contingent on the founder still remaining with the company. Similar vesting arrangements are commonly used with employee stock options plans (Section 4.1.3). Other contingencies involve awarding shares that depend on individual founders achieving personal milestones, such as finishing a prototype or signing on a first customer.

How long and hard do founders negotiate their agreements? There is a human inclination to sweep difficult issues under the carpet, yet these problems are bound to come back later on. A team that undergoes a forthright negotiation process is likely to write a better agreement and forge a stronger bond. Founder agreements may also need to be renegotiated over time. The original agreements may no longer work because individual circumstances change and the roles of individuals in the firms change. Moreover, there are ample opportunities for founders to fall out with each other. Stories of founder conflicts abound. We encounter two examples with the founders of Snap (see Box 3.2) and Stitch Fix (see Box 5.3).[18]

Does someone who considers him- or herself a founder have a claim on the company even if there is no founder agreement? This became a multimillion-dollar question in the case of Facebook, as dramatized in the *Social Network* movie. Facebook founder Mark Zuckerberg was sued by the Winklevoss twins, for allegedly stealing their idea and breaking off on his own. The case was eventually settled for an estimated $65M.[19] Even though there was no legal founder agreement in place, the law can infer that people have formed an implicit partnership. Having a proper founder agreement in place can save serious headaches down the road.

4.4.2 Principles for Internal Allocation

On what basis should teams allocate founder shares? This turns out to be a complex and highly subjective question. The allocation of founder shares not only has financial consequences for individual founders, but may also impact the morale and motivation of the entire team. Unfortunately, there is no objective formula that founders can resort to. Instead, the issue must be resolved through internal negotiation.

The simplest approach to splitting ownership shares is the equal split. This approach says that in a team of n founders, each founder gets the same number of shares, or 1/n of founder shares. This principle has a foundation in an egalitarian approach where each founder is inherently treated the same. This might be because founders fundamentally consider themselves equally worthy or because they find it too difficult to compare one another. Empirical studies of ownership splits within start-up teams suggest that approximately half of all founder's teams opt for the equal split solution.[20]

Although some teams may consider an equal split fair, others might consider an equal split unfair. For example, why would it be fair to give the same equity to two founders if one is working twice as much as another? Or if one has 20 years more experience than the other? Moreover, what may be considered fair by one team may be considered unfair by another. The evidence cited above suggests that the other half of founder teams opt for the unequal split solution.

One academic study by Hellmann and Wasserman examines survey data about the allocation of founder shares within high-tech start-ups.[21] Choosing an equal split is associated with younger teams (e.g., teams where founders have few years of experience), and more homogenous teams (e.g., teams where founders have similar years of prior work experience). It is also more common in teams that spent less than a day negotiating—the authors call this the "quick handshake." The study finds that teams with equal splits are less likely to subsequently raise external financing. This calls into question the benefit of equal splitting and invites deeper reflections about what principles founder's teams want to adopt for themselves.

So, what principles should be used to allocate founder shares? It is useful to distinguish between backward-looking and forward-looking arguments. Some founder shares are given on the basis of what founders have already contributed, others on the basis of what they plan to do. While forward-looking arguments are clearly important, founders often spend considerable time focusing on past accomplishments. This may be because the past is more objective than the future. Some founders also view share ownership as a backward-looking entitlement rather than a forward-looking reward mechanism. An excessive focus on the past, however, can detract from the vast amount of work that lies ahead and what it will take to make the company a success.

A common backward-looking argument is that certain founders deserve more shares because they had the "original idea." In some cases, such a claim is uncontestable; other times the "original idea" may emerge through interactions among the founders themselves. Moreover, it is often unclear how important the original idea really was, given that the entrepreneurial process involves experimentation and may require numerous pivots (see Box 1.1). The claim to have come up with the original idea is clearer when intellectual property (IP) is involved. If a founder owns some IP, like a patent, and decides to transfer it to the company, then there is a case for rewarding this contribution with additional founder shares. Note, however, that the technology idea is often less important than the ability to further develop and implement the business idea. These contributions are forward-looking and should contribute to the allocation of shares.

Another clear case for backward allocating shares happens when founders contributed financially to the venture. Teams also tend to backward allocate more shares to those founders that have already worked longer on the venture. This might be because they took more risk early on and because they spent more time working on the venture.

Forward-looking arguments for allocating shares are largely based on providing the right incentives for success. To properly appreciate the incentive argument, Box 4.5 explains some of the fundamental insights from the economics of team incentives.

Box 4.5 Nobel Insights on Team Incentives

The 2016 Nobel Prize in Economics went to Bengt Holmström and Oliver Hart "for their contributions to contract theory." We discuss Hart's contributions in Box 6.2; here we focus on Holmström's work.[22]

Holmström is one of the fathers of incentive theory. His seminal 1982 paper formulated a theory of incentives within teams. This theory can be readily applied to the problem of allocating shares among founders. Holmström first shows that in an ideal world each founder would own 100% of the equity and would thus have fully loaded incentives for success. The obvious problem is that this is never possible in a team. Every time one team member gets more equity, her incentives go up, but the incentives of all other team members go down. This is what complicates the allocation of founder equity.

Holmström shows how the relative productivity of different founders should guide the optimal allocation of founder shares. The most productive team members should have the strongest incentives and thus the largest stakes. Prior experience, educational achievements and qualifications, as well as raw talent, are all likely to be correlated with productivity and are therefore likely to be rewarded accordingly. Moreover, different roles can have different performance impacts. A common argument is that the CEO should get a larger stake. This is because the leadership role involves greater responsibilities, has a stronger impact on performance, and therefore needs stronger incentives.

Holmström's analysis also highlights the importance of providing balanced incentives, in particular ensuring that everyone in the team has sufficient incentives to contribute their part. This is particularly important if each team member depends on all others who are also contributing their part. Ignoring the weakest link can bring down the entire team.

Holmström's analysis has broader implications than for founders' equity split. In our context, we can also think of the venture as a team of entrepreneurs and investors and apply Holmström's results to the division of ownership and the valuation problem we discuss in Section 4.1. The balance argument suggests that it is important to avoid extreme valuations. At a very high valuation, the entrepreneur retains a large stake, which is good for her incentives. However, the investor only retains a small stake and therefore has relatively little incentive to add value to the venture (see Chapter 8). Similarly, a very low valuation gives the investor a large stake and thus strong incentives. However, the entrepreneur is left with a low stake. This can be demotivating and can create poor entrepreneurial incentives. Once the entrepreneur is no longer motivated to maximize the financial returns of the venture, many things can go wrong for the investors—hence the need to provide balance incentives for the venture's success.

Holmström's key insight is that, instead of thinking of the division of shares as a "zero sum game," we can view it as a team incentive problem. The objective is to find a share allocation that balances relative incentives, which will efficiently encourage all relevant parties to work toward the success of the venture.

To put the insights from Box 4.5 into practice, we need to consider the time dimension. Of particular importance is the time commitment of the individual founders. If some founders are committed full-time and others part-time, there is a clear rationale for giving more shares to the full-time founders. Sometimes a founder also has to go from full-time to part-time, either because of unexpected personal circumstances or by choice. Founder agreements can anticipate such eventualities by specifying vesting clauses that are based on the amount of time spent on the venture.

In addition to the incentive issues, the division of founder equity also has to be sensitive to bargaining power. Different founders have different outside opportunities; that is, they face different alternatives of earning money elsewhere. For example, an experienced engineer may have attractive offers from other employers, or an experienced entrepreneur may choose to work on a different venture. Founders with stronger outside options will then obtain additional shares. At the minimum, the final allocation of shares must be such that a founder actually prefers to work for the venture over all other options.

4.4.3 The FAST Tool

In this section, we introduce the Founder Allocation of Shares Tool (or FAST). This is a spreadsheet tool that we developed to help founder teams structure their founder agreements. It combines insights from our own academic research with observations from practice.[23] The book's website (www.entrepreneurialfinance.net) contains an accompanying spreadsheet, using the WorkHorse example, and a technical note that explains in greater detail how to use the tool. Here we provide a shorter outline.

The main output of the FAST spreadsheet is a recommendation on how to split the founder equity, along with suggestions about vesting and milestone contingencies. The inputs to the spreadsheet model are evaluations of the past and future contributions of each founder. This requires assigning relative weights to inherently heterogeneous contributions, thus forcing the team to take a stance on what they value most. The FAST point system is very flexible and easily adapts to users' circumstances and preferences.

Recall from Section 4.4.1 that a founder agreement contains five key elements: (1) team members and roles, (2) salaries, (3) financial obligations, (4) allocation of share ownership, and (5) contingencies. FAST uses assumptions about (1), (2), and (3) to make a recommendation about points (4) and (5).

FAST is based on the following six-step procedure:

1. Define team members and roles.
2. Define time periods and weights.
3. Allocate points to individual founder contributions.
4. Identify net transfers.
5. Make recommendations for ownership stakes.
6. Make recommendations for contingencies.

WorkHorse Box 4.8 illustrates how FAST works.

WorkHorse Box 4.8 The Founder Agreement

During their initial honeymoon period, the four founders ignored the details of who would own what. This all changed with Michael Archie's e-mail: "I noted U all have same # of shares: are you sure? CU MA" His e-mail unleashed a big discussion among the four founders. Tempers flared for the first time. To turn it into a more constructive discussion, Astrid convened the team to define some general principles for dividing the equity.

Bharat started the meeting by declaring: "The only valid principle is an equal split. We are all equal, and we all started together, so we all get the same number of shares. Let's all shake hands and get back to work." There was an awkward silence, until Annie replied: "I am all for getting back to work quickly, I have to make an urgent call to China, but why should equal shares be fair? What if we all contribute different things or work different amounts?" A wild philosophical debate ensued about the meaning of fairness, until Brandon declared in a loud voice: "Enough of this, let's use FAST!" They looked confused, just as he had hoped, and continued: "Have you never heard of FAST, the Founder Allocation of Shares Tool? It's in my favorite entrepreneurial finance book. Let me show it to you." Intrigued, they gathered around Brandon's FAST spreadsheet and jointly developed the following table.

FAST	Astrid	Brandon	Bharat	Annie	Total	Contingency
Productivity						
Experience, qualifications & talent	0	0	0	0	0	
Roles and responsibilities	0.1	0	0	0	0.1	
Productivity points	1.1	1	1	1	4.1	
Productivity factor	0.268	0.244	0.244	0.244	1	
The past					20%	
Work days	80	40	60	40	220	
Productive work	21.463	9.756	14.634	9.756	55.610	Upfront
Achievements	10	5	10	5	30	Upfront
Outside options	0	0	0	0	0	Upfront
Total	31.463	14.756	24.634	14.756	85.610	
Normalized points	7.350	3.447	5.755	3.447	20.000	
The next year					20%	
Work days	365	365	182.5	365	1277.5	
Productive work	97.927	89.024	44.512	89.024	320.488	Vesting
Achievements	0	0	30	15	45	Conditional
Outside options	10	30	0	20	60	Upfront
Total	107.927	119.024	74.512	124.024	425.488	
Normalized points	10.146	11.189	7.005	11.660	40.000	
After next year					40%	
Work days	365	365	182.5	365	1277.5	
Productive work	97.927	89.024	44.512	89.024	320.488	Vesting
Achievements	0	0	30	0	30	Conditional
Outside options	10	30	0	20	60	Upfront
Total	107.927	119.024	74.512	109.024	410.488	
Normalized points	10.517	11.598	7.261	10.624	40.000	
Across all periods						
Total normalized points	28.014	26.235	20.021	25.731	100	
Transfer adjustments						
Net transfers	0	$98,913	-$12,500	$10,000	$96,413	
Valuation before transfers					$1,503,587	
Valuation after transfers					$1,600,000	
Transfers points	0	6.58	-0.83	0.67	6.41	

FAST	Astrid	Brandon	Bharat	Annie	Total	Contingency
Normalized & transfers points	28.014	32.814	19.189	26.396	106.41	
Recommendations						
Ownership share	26.3%	30.8%	18.0%	24.8%	100.0%	
Share allocation	210,604	246,690	144,264	198,442	800,000	

Step 1 was easy: they already knew their team members and roles. For step 2, they divided time into three periods. The work performed to date was given a weight of 20%. They divided the future into two periods, allocating 40% for the next year, which they felt would be critical, and 40% for everything thereafter.

For step 3 they began by allocating the points for past events. Astrid and Bharat had contributed the most to the original idea, so they received 10 points. Brandon and Annie both received 5 points. None of them had given up any outside opportunities so far, so no points were awarded for that. Next they estimated the number of days they each had spent on the venture so far. Astrid estimated 80 days. Bharat estimated his contribution at 60 days but found it difficult to separate his academic work from time spent on WorkHorse. Brandon and Annie both thought that 40 days was approximately right.

In order to calculate the points for productive work, they had to evaluate relative productivity. They didn't want to fall into the trap of trying to convince each other that their contribution was more important than the others'. Instead they decided to stick to specific criteria. Looking at their experiences, qualifications, and talent, they quickly agreed that there were no clear differences that would justify giving anyone extra points. The debate about roles and responsibilities, however, took an unexpected turn. Astrid thought that they should all get the same points again because each founder had clear and important responsibilities. To her surprise, the others argued that as a CEO, she bore greater responsibility and should therefore get extra points. In the end, Astrid reluctantly agreed but only after negotiating down her points to a very small premium. The resulting productivity factor, whose numbers mechanically add up to 1, gave Astrid a factor of 0.268, compared to 0.244 for the other three. Because she also had worked more days, Astrid ended up with considerably more productive work points than the others. Of the 20 normalized points allocated to the past, Astrid received 7.35, compared to 3.45 for Brandon and Annie and 5.75 for Bharat. Though arbitrary at one level, they liked to frame things in terms of points. It gave them a metric that was easy to use. At the same time, it was one step removed from the actual allocation of shares, making it easier not to get bogged down.

Turning to the all-important next year, Astrid, Brandon, and Annie declared that they would be working full time for the venture. Bharat turned bright red and with a clump in his throat declared that he was unwilling to give up his PhD. To his surprise the others nodded. Astrid responded: "We always knew that, and it makes sense for you to stay at the university. This way you can help us to stay on top of technology. My question is: How much time will you spend on things related to the company?" Slightly stunned, Bharat responded "Not sure, maybe half." The others nodded, and Brandon entered 182.5 days for him.

The conversation about future achievements focused on personal milestones. Bharat had two clear milestones: deliver a prototype for the WonderFoal and then for the NokotaStar. To give him strong incentives, they allocated 15 points for each milestone. Annie argued that her role of signing up manufacturers in China was equally challenging and convinced them to allocate 15 points for that. Astrid and Brandon didn't think their work involved similarly tangible milestones and refrained from asking for achievement points. All achievement points were to be made contingent on actually meeting the specific milestones.

The discussion about outside options involved some one-upmanship. Brandon argued that, as a freshly minted MBA with finance experience, he was giving up huge salaries, and therefore he asked for 30 points. Annie argued that if she went back to China, she would make a killing working for budding start-ups over there. She also wanted 30 points but settled for 20, mainly to stop Brandon from arguing why finance people always make more money than salespeople. Astrid found it difficult to make an argument about her outside options. In her heart, she only wanted to work on WorkHorse, and never considered anything else. Still, the others insisted on giving her 10 points. Bharat wasn't giving up his PhD, so he received no points for outside options.

The discussion about the remaining 40 points went surprisingly fast, partly because they all found it difficult to imagine what they would be doing one year from now. They agreed that Bharat should get another 30 milestone points, contingent on developing further innovations. The other three couldn't identify obvious milestones and therefore refrained from asking for achievement points. Because Brandon insisted that his outside options would remain better than the others', they simply used the same points as the year before.

They completed step 3 by calculating their total normalized points, Astrid came close to 28, Brandon and Annie close to 26, but Bharat only to 20. He reluctantly conceded that this was fairer than the equal split he originally proposed. He received fewer points, but he was allowed to stay in the PhD program, which was more important to him.

"Are we done?" Annie asked, looking eagerly at her phone. "Not yet," Brandon declared; "step 4 is next. We need to talk about salaries and outstanding financial obligations." In their financial projections (see WorkHorse Box 3.6), they originally assumed a base salary of $25K for the first year, but $85K the second year onward. The immediate question was whether this still applied to Bharat, given his decision to go part-time. After some debate, the team agreed that his salary had to be cut by half. Bharat looked distinctly unhappy.

Next, Brandon surprised the others by declaring that he would like to forego his salary, in return for more equity. To calculate the NPV of his salary sacrifice, he used a 15% discount rate. To be conservative, he only counted the first two years, calculating an NPV close to $99K.[24] The question was how much equity to give in return for his salary sacrifice. Astrid also noted that Annie had spent $10K of her own money to travel all over China to establish relationships with manufacturers. Still looking unhappy, Bharat suddenly had a new proposal. He didn't like getting only $12.5K in salary the first year. Instead he wanted $25K like everyone else. He was willing to pay for his extra salary by giving up equity. "Fine with us," Astrid replied "but how do we convert all this into shares? How many more shares should Brandon and Annie get, and how many less for Bharat?"

"This bring us to step 5." Brandon declared. "We need to determine a fair price for trading ownership points against compensation claims. This requires estimating the total value of all our founder shares." Astrid proposed: "How about $2M, this is the pre-money valuation Michael Archie gave us." Bharat noted that the value of the founder shares was only $1.6M, as the rest belonged to the stock options pool and other third parties. Even though the deal with Michael Archie was still under negotiation, they all liked the $1.6M figure; for them it represented a reasonable value of their stakes (after transfers). With this, FAST converted their net transfers into transfer points, added them to their normalized points, and finally generated a recommendation for their relative ownership stakes, as shown in the table. Further using the 800,000 founder shares from the capitalization table (see WorkHorse Box 4.4.), FAST calculated the recommended number of shares.

When the normalized points were compared to the final recommendations, Brandon's share went up to 30.84% and Bharat's share decreased to 18.30%, Annie's share was at 24.81%, and Astrid's share ended up at 26.33%: "So much for the CEO getting the biggest share," she thought to herself but quickly remembered that Brandon was given up all his salary. They all felt that the recommendation was reasonable and decided to go with it.

"Are we done now?" asked Annie, once more looking impatiently at her mobile phone. Brandon smiled: "That depends on whether you also want to know how many of your shares you actually get upfront?" Annie looked up again; actually, this was something she did want to know. Brandon shared the following table, which corresponds to step 6 of FAST.

Contingencies	Astrid	Brandon	Bharat	Annie
Contingent shares				
Recommended share allocation	210,604	246,690	144,264	198,442
Number of vesting shares	140,950	160,267	61,408	131,449

Contingencies	Astrid	Brandon	Bharat	Annie
Number of milestone shares	0	0	41,387	10,875
Number of upfront shares	69,653	86,423	41,469	56,117
Vesting				
Vesting points - next year	9.206	8.369	4.185	8.369
Vesting points - year after	9.542	8.675	4.337	8.675
Fraction of vesting points	66.9%	65.0%	42.6%	66.2%
Milestones				
Milestone points - next year	0.00	0.00	2.82	1.41
Milestone points - year after	0.00	0.00	2.92	0.00
Fraction of milestones points	0.0%	0.0%	28.7%	5.5%

The table calculates how many shares are unconditionally given upfront, how many are subject to vesting, and how many depend on milestones. This requires calculating the fraction of normalized points that are subject to vesting and milestones. The fractions are then applied to the respective number of shares.

Approximately two-thirds of Astrid's, Brandon's, and Annie's shares were subject to vesting. This was a substantial amount, so the founders were eager to also determine the timing structure of vesting. Brandon reminded them that employee share options often vested over four years, on a quarterly basis, with a one-year cliff (Section 6.3.2). However, no one liked this approach; they wanted something faster and more fine-grained. After some debate, they decided that shares would vest over two years, on a monthly basis, without any cliff. Bharat only had 42.57% vesting shares, but 28.69% of his shares depended on milestones. They had already specified the first milestones but decided to leave the details of the remaining two milestones unspecified for the time being.

Amazed at how quickly and smoothly they had forged a complex founder agreement, Brandon proposed they shake hands—they always did that in the movies he liked to watch. Instead, Astrid gave him a big hug. "Are we done now?" asked Annie again. Brandon laughed: "It all depends how you look at it. Personally I don't think we are done, I think we are at the beginning of a great adventure." Annie rolled her eyes and rushed off to finally call China. Leaving the room more slowly, Astrid asked Brendan: "FAST worked out really well; is that the only way of calculating founder ownership stakes?" Brendan smiled: "Oh no, there are a thousand ways to skin the cat. What I like about FAST is that it imposes some logic and transparency, but it's still the team that decides." [25]

Summary

This chapter looks at how ownership is divided between entrepreneurs and investors and how this affects investor returns. An investment consists of an exchange of money for shares that represent an ownership stake in the venture. The chapter establishes a key equation where the investment equals the venture's (post-money) valuation times the investor's ownership stake. This equation is used to explain how valuations, share prices, and share allocations can be calculated. We also introduce the concept of dilution—that is, the reduction in the ownership stakes of founders and early investors that occurs when new investors arrive at later round investments. We address the strengths and weaknesses of the three most common return measures, namely, the net present value, the cash-on-cash multiple, and internal rate of return. We then develop six insights concerning the relationship between returns and valuations. The chapter also includes a discussion of what determines the valuation of a deal, focusing on four main factors: the underlying opportunity, the market context, deal competition, and investor quality. We conclude the chapter by looking at the allocation of founder ownership within teams and at the process of reaching an agreement. We discuss the Founder Allocation of Shares Tool (FAST), a practical spreadsheet-based tool that makes recommendations about ownership shares within start-up teams.

In terms of the FIRE framework (Chapter 1), this chapter launches our discussion of the INVEST step. The concepts of investment, ownership, valuation, dilution, and returns are at the core of the investment deal. Our goal in this chapter is to lay the foundation by explaining the basic relationships between these concepts. Our discussion of the internal allocation of shares within the founders' team starts to look at the practical challenges of calculating ownership shares. Chapter 5 takes this further by examining how to calculate valuations, and thus the division of shares between entrepreneurs and investors.

Review Questions

1. What is the relationship between investment, valuation, and ownership? What fundamental economic exchange is at play?
2. What is the difference between pre-money and post-money valuation? How do stock options affect this difference?
3. What is the role of the original number of founder shares? What happens if you double this number?
4. Why do founder stakes get diluted over time? What factors predict dilution?
5. What are the strengths and limitations of the following three return measures: net present value (NPV), cash-on-cash multiple (CCM), and internal rate of return (IRR)?

6. Both the entrepreneur and investor prefer higher exit values. The entrepreneur also prefers higher valuations, but the investor prefers lower valuations. Why?
7. What economic forces affect valuations?
8. Why would an entrepreneur accept a lower valuation from a higher quality investor?
9. What are the pros and cons for splitting equity equally among all founders?
10. What factors determine the allocation of shares within a founder team?

Notes

1. Information on *Shark Tank* can be found on the websites of Australia's ABC and the UK's BBC. For an overview of international shows, see Nisen (2013).
2. https://www.telegraph.co.uk/business/2016/02/11/half-of-dragons-den-investments-fall-through-after-the-show.
3. http://www.cbc.ca/dragonsden/pitches/snappy-socks, accessed April 15, 2019.
4. The equations in this chapter assume that the investor purchases shares newly issued by the company in what is called a primary share purchase. In Chapters 9 and 11 we will also encounter secondary share purchases where new investors buy already issued shares from the founders or from existing investors.
5. The details vary across jurisdictions and are beyond the scope of this book. Information on taxation of employee stock options across countries can be found on DLA Piper's Global Intelligence website: https://www.dlapiperintelligence.com/goingglobal/global-equity.
6. Kotha and George (2012).
7. Atomico (2018).
8. Hand (2008) provides an overview based on U.S. practice, and Henrekson and Sanandaji (2018) discuss the implications of the tax treatment of stock options in European countries. Index Ventures, a large VC firm headquartered in London and San Francisco, has published a comprehensive report on the use of stock option plans by U.S. and European start-ups, https://www.indexventures.com/rewardingtalent.
9. See Brealey, Myers, and Allen (2016) and Berk and DeMarzo (2016), among others.
10. Tian and Wang (2014).
11. Cochrane (2005), Hall and Woodward (2010), and Korteweg and Sørensen (2010) report and discuss evidence of the skewness of venture capital investments.
12. Gompers, Kaplan, and Mukharlyamov (2016).
13. Berk and DeMarzo (2016) examine investment decision rules at an accessible level.
14. Gompers and Lerner (2000).
15. Hsu (2004).
16. The work of Inderst and Müller (2004) provides a rigorous theoretical framework that shows how valuations are affected by the relative scarcity of entrepreneurs and investors.
17. Hellmann and Thiele (2015).
18. Wasserman (2012) discusses founder conflicts. For some examples, see Edwards (2017) for Snap, and Taylor (2017) for Stitch Fix.
19. Stempel (2011).

20. Estimates of the fraction of teams with equal splits range from approximately one-third to two-thirds. See Ruef, Aldrich, and Carter (2003), Hellmann and Wasserman (2016), and Vereshchagina (2018).
21. Hellmann and Wasserman (2016).
22. https://www.nobelprize.org/prizes/economic-sciences/2016/press-release and Holmström (1982).
23. Hellmann and Thiele (2015) and Hellmann and Wasserman (2016).
24. Specifically, we have $25K + $85K/1.15 = $99K.
25. Other useful tools for determining ownership shares can be found at http://foundrs.com/ or https://gust.com/startups.

5

Valuation Methods

Learning Goals

In this chapter students will learn:

1. To apply the main methods for valuing entrepreneurial companies.
2. How to select which valuation method is most suitable for which company.
3. What data on comparable companies to use for valuing a company.
4. To model the uncertainty of venture outcomes and calculate their impact on valuation.

This chapter discusses different approaches to the valuation of entrepreneurial companies and explains the role of valuation in the fundraising process. We first discuss the main challenges in valuing entrepreneurial companies. Next, we review several valuation approaches and discuss their advantages and limitations. We start with the Venture Capital Method, which is widely used in practice, and with the Discounted Cash Flow Method, which is the standard finance tool for valuation. We also review different types of comparable methods that compare a company with a peer group, either at the investment or exit stage. Finally, we examine various approaches that value ventures by explicitly modeling uncertainty. We conclude by discussing the relative merits of these alternative methods and their appropriateness in different contexts.

5.1 The Valuation of Entrepreneurial Companies

5.1.1 The Purpose of Performing a Valuation

In Chapter 4 we showed how to compute ownership shares and investor returns taking company valuation as given. In this chapter we explain how valuation can be estimated in practice, using alternative valuation methods.

What is the purpose of performing a valuation? Clearly, an entrepreneur and investor can structure an entire deal without using any valuation methods. They can simply negotiate ownership stakes without justifying the implied pre- or post-money valuations. Indeed, some angel investors dismiss valuation models altogether. However, professional investors and those investing at later stages typically perform some valuation before making their investment decisions.

Performing a valuation requires time collecting and analyzing data, so why do investors and entrepreneurs engage in a difficult exercise that only generates vague estimates? Entrepreneurs and investors use valuation methods to develop an informed opinion for themselves about the venture's realistic valuation. This helps them to prepare as they go into the negotiation (Section 7.5). They also perform valuation as part of the negotiation process to justify their bargaining positions. Venture capitalists further use their valuation models to justify investment choices in front of their limited partners (Section 12.2).

Performing a valuation is part of the entrepreneur's preparation for being investor ready. There is a logical progression in the preparation of an investor pitch. It starts with formulating a business plan, as discussed in Chapter 2. The next step is to formulate a financial plan, as discussed in Chapter 3. This includes the preparation of financial projections that feed into the valuation models. In this chapter we thus take qualitative information from the business plan and quantitative information from the financial plan to build a convincing valuation. This can then help the entrepreneur to justify her valuation in the negotiations.

From an investor perspective, performing valuation is part of a thorough decision process. Before committing financial resources, it is useful to test whether the investment stands a chance to generate the desired returns and to determine what valuation would justify making the investment. At the same time, a valuation model might be useful to explain the investor's bargaining position to an entrepreneur who may have a different view of what the valuation should be.[1]

5.1.2   The Challenges of Performing a Valuation

Establishing a convincing valuation for an entrepreneurial venture is a challenging and somewhat speculative exercise. Entrepreneurial ventures face fundamental uncertainty (see Box 1.1), especially in their early stages. Even for more mature companies there is often a lack of objective data. Valuations should therefore be thought of as heuristics that help to make sense of an inherently ambiguous and subjective business reality. They combine objective and subjective elements, in what one could dub the "art and science" of performing valuation.

From an investor perspective, one might argue that entrepreneurial companies are just another asset class. Valuation should depend on the risk and return properties of the underlying cash flows. These are indeed volatile for start-ups, as they are for other alternative investments, such as real estate or commodities. A more fundamental problem, however, is the substantial uncertainty about the true risk profile of an entrepreneurial venture, reflecting Frank Knight's concept of uncertainty, discussed in Box 1.1. Such uncertainty obfuscates the calculation of valuations and expected returns.

To make things even more difficult, entrepreneurs and investors often have different information. Entrepreneurs may know more about their technology and their customers, whereas investors may know more about the market, the competition, and the process of funding a company from start to exit. This creates asymmetries of information that can make it difficult for the two parties to agree on a valuation (see Box 2.6). Even when the parties share the same information, there can be disagreement over how to interpret it, such as what conclusions to draw from inconclusive market research.

Standard corporate finance methods rely on objective data and reasonably predict business environments. This rarely applies to new ventures. There are additional challenges with applying conventional valuation methods, which are present in all types of companies but get compounded in the case of innovative ventures. Start-ups make intense use of intangible assets, such as technology and brand. These are difficult to value because the revenues and earnings they produce are less predictable than for tangible physical assets.[2] Likewise, entrepreneurial firms rely heavily on talented individuals, but there is no good accounting treatment of the value of human capital.

Investors and entrepreneurs face a difficult decision between simplicity versus complexity. One argument is that the high level of uncertainty calls for more detailed and complex tools that can properly account for the underlying risks. Others, however, prefer simplicity, arguing that feeding unreliable information into detailed models turns out to be meaningless and that using simpler approaches is more convincing. The choice between simpler versus more complex methods is ultimately up to entrepreneurs and investors and depends on circumstances.[3]

In this chapter we examine four approaches to valuing entrepreneurial companies. We begin with what is known as the Venture Capital Method (VCM). This method originated from practice, but we explain how it can be understood in terms of corporate finance fundamentals. Second, we consider the Discounted Cash Flow (DCF) model. This is the canonical valuation model used in corporate finance and covered in all corporate finance textbooks. The DCF method relies on financial projections for the company. It can be thought of as an "intrinsic" or "absolute" valuation method. Third, we look at methods of comparables. These methods generate a valuation by comparing the focal company to other companies that are arguably similar and for which information is available. Methods of comparables rely heavily on data from other companies and can be thought of as "extrinsic" or "relative" valuation methods.[4] Finally, we examine some recent methods that explicitly model uncertainty with probabilities. We end the chapter comparing the various methods and outlining their main advantages and disadvantages. In this chapter we assume that companies are fully financed with equity. In Section 10.5 we show how to adapt the valuation models from this chapter to debt financing.

5.2 The Venture Capital Method

The Venture Capital Method (VCM) provides a relatively straightforward way to value a venture by modeling the investor's cash flows. These are much simpler than the company's cash flows, which are used in the Discounted Cash Flow Method we discuss in Section 5.3. In terms of cash outflows, the investor initially finances the company by providing cash. If the company makes progress, the investor typically contributes some additional rounds of financing. In terms of exit outcome, the venture either fails and the investor gets back little or nothing, or it reaches a successful exit and the investor makes a substantial capital gain. Entrepreneurial ventures rarely pay dividends, so these are not considered in the VCM.

The VCM starts by estimating a likely exit value in case of successful development of the company. Then it discounts this value back to the time of the investment. This provides a post-money valuation from which one can derive the pre-money valuation and the investor s ownership share.

5.2.1 Valuation with a Single Investment Round

Table 5.1 summarizes the notation used in this chapter. Throughout this chapter we will be looking at expected returns, which we express either in terms of annual returns, denoted by ρ, or in terms of (expected) cash-on-cash multiple, denoted by $CCM^e = (1+\rho)^T$.

Table 5.1 Notation for valuation models.

Symbol	Meaning
CCM^e	(Expected) cash-on-cash multiple
d	Discount rate (with zero failure risk)
DCF	Discounted Cash Flow
ECM	Exit Comparables Model
ICM	Investment Comparables Model
FCF	Free cash flow
I	Investment amount
M	Multiple
PM	Performance metric
T	Time-to-exit
t	Time period
TV	Terminal value
VCM	Venture Capital Method
V_{POST}	Post-money valuation
V_{PRE}	Pre-money valuation
X	Exit value
β	Systematic risk
ρ	Required rate of return
τ	Time between investment rounds

We start by considering the simple case of a single financing round. In Section 4.3.1, we derived equation (4.20) for the post-money valuation(V_{POST}), which combined with equation (4.15) yields:

$$V_{POST} = X^e/(1+\rho)^T \tag{5.1}$$

where X^e is the expected exit value and ρ is the investor's required rate of return. We now use ρ instead of IRR, which we discuss in Section 4.2.2, to emphasize that this is not a realized rate, but the rate that investors require when making the investment. The VCM starts by estimating X^e and then derives valuation and ownership shares using the relationships we have established in Section 4.2. We start by recalling that the pre-money valuation is given by equation (4.3), which we restate and re-number for convenience:

$$V_{PRE} = V_{POST} - I \tag{5.2}$$

The ownership share of the investor is given by equation (4.2), which we also restate and renumber:

$$F_{INV} = I/V_{POST} \tag{5.3}$$

Equations (5.1) to (5.3) imply that performing a valuation requires four essential pieces of information. The first is the necessary investment amount (I), the second the time to exit (T), the third the expected exit value (X^e), and the fourth the investor's required rate of return (ρ). Before explaining how to estimate the values for each of those four elements in Section 5.2.3, we explain how the VCM works.

It should be noted that the VCM derives a valuation using the exit value (X^e), which is the value in case of a successful company outcome. This implicitly assumes that for all other outcomes the value of the company is zero. Such assumption considerably simplifies the calculations. In Section 5.5, we look at more complex methods that relax this assumption by explicitly modeling the uncertainty underlying the venture.

WorkHorse Box 5.1 illustrates how to use the VCM for a single round of investment.

WorkHorse Box 5.1 WorkHorse's Single-Round VCM Valuation

The four founders of WorkHorse had received an informal offer from Michael Archie, an angel investor (see WorkHorse Box 4.1). They decided that before accepting his valuation, they wanted to work out their own. They understood that they needed to make several assumptions for their valuation. Brandon did some analysis on exit values (see WorkHorse Box 5.5) from which he concluded that, in case of success, WorkHorse could be worth approximately $25M after five years. Michael Archie had also mentioned that investors would use a required rate of return of 50% for early-stage ventures like theirs. Based on this information, Annie figured out that $X^e = \$25M$, $T = 5$, and $\rho = 0.5$, so that:

$$V_{POST} = \frac{\$25M}{\left(1+0.5\right)^5} = \$3.29M$$

Annie considered raising the whole amount of $2.5M in one single round. This implied a pre-money valuation given by:

$$V_{PRE} = \$3.29M - \$2.5M = \$0.79M$$

5.2.2 Valuation with Multiple Investment Rounds

The single-round valuation illustrates the logic of the VCM. However, most venture investments require multiple investment rounds. We therefore show how to use the VCM in this case. The logic with multiple rounds is to apply the valuation formula recursively, first discounting the exit value to the last round prior to exit, then to the previous round, and so on, until we have reached the first round. This recursive structure generates a comprehensive set of valuations for all rounds and ensures the internal consistency of all estimates.

In Section 4.1.5, we introduced the following notation for describing multiple rounds of investments. There are R rounds indexed by the superscript $r = 1,2,\ldots,R$. After round R exit occurs, which we denote as $r = \text{EXIT}$. We denote the investment amount for round r by $I(r)$. The pre- and post-money valuations for round r are denoted by $V_{PRE}(r)$ and $V_{POST}(r)$. We denote the investment dates by $t(r)$. The time between two rounds is denoted by $\tau_r(r + 1) = t(r + 1) - t(r)$. Similarly, we denote the required cash-on-cash multiple between round r and round $r + 1$ by $CCM_r^e = \left(1+\rho\right)^{\tau_r(r+1)}$.

As noted in Section 5.2.1, the VCM valuation with multiple rounds uses an iterative logic. Each iteration involves the equivalent of equations (5.1)–(5.3). Specifically, we write:

$$V_{POST}\left(r\right) = \frac{V_{PRE}\left(r+1\right)}{CCM_r^e} \tag{5.1-MR}$$

where MR stands for multiple rounds. At each round r, we calculate the post-money valuation by discounting back the pre-money valuation of the next round $r + 1$. We use the pre-money valuation of the next round because it reflects the value owned by all the existing shareholders before that round. For the last round $(r = R)$ we use $V_{PRE}(Exit) = X^e$. The pre-money valuation is then given by:

$$V_{PRE}(r) = V_{POST}(r) - I(r) \qquad \text{(5.2-MR)}$$

The ownership of investors in round r is denoted by $F_r(r)$:

$$F_r(r) = \frac{I(r)}{V_{POST}(r)} \qquad \text{(5.3-MR)}$$

WorkHorse Box 5.2 illustrates how to use the VCM for a two rounds of investment.

WorkHorse Box 5.2   WorkHorse's VCM Valuation with Two Investment Rounds

---

Brandon took a look at Annie's calculations and decided to refine them to account for the fact that WorkHorse planned to raise money over two rounds. Specifically, the company planned to raise .5M at the start in 2020 and $2M at the start of 2021. Brandon adopted Annie's assumption of a $25M exit after five years, that is, at the start of 2025, and based his calculations on Michael Archie's 50% required rate of return.

Brandon first estimated the post-money valuation at the time of the second round $(r = 2)$. For this he noted that the time between round 2 and exit would be four years, so that $\tau_2(4) = 4$. He therefore calculated:

$$V_{POST}(2) = \frac{V_{PRE}(Exit)}{CCM_2^e(Exit)} = \frac{X^e}{(1+R)^{\tau_2(4)}} = \frac{\$25M}{(1+0.5)^4} = \$4.94M$$

$$V_{PRE}(2) = V_{POST}(2) - I(2) = \$4.94M - \$2M = \$2.94M$$

The time between round 1 and round 2 would be just one year, that is, $\tau_1(2) = 1$, so that:

$$V_{POST}(1) = \frac{V_{PRE}(2)}{CCM_1^e} = \frac{V_{PRE}(2)}{(1+R)^{\tau_1(2)}} = \frac{\$2.94M}{(1+0.5)^1} = \$1.96M$$

$$V_{PRE}(1) = V_{POST}(1) - I(1) = \$1.96M - \$0.50M = \$1.46M$$

Brandon was delighted that the founders did better under his calculations for two round-valuation than under Annie's single-round valuation (see WorkHorse Box 5.1). This seemed puzzling at first because either way the investors would always receive a 50% rate of return. After some reflection, he spotted the difference between the two methods. Under Annie's single-round calculations, the investors contributed all the money upfront and therefore required a 50% rate of return over five years on the entire $2.5M. Under Brandon's two-round valuation, the investors required a 50% return over five years for their initial .5M investment. However, the larger $2M only required a 50% return over four, not five, years.

5.2.3 Estimating the Inputs

In this section, we discuss how to estimate the four inputs for the VCM: the investment amount (I), the time-to-exit (T), the exit value (X^e), and the required rate of return (ρ).

5.2.3.(a) Investment Amount

The investment amount (I) is how much the investor expects the company will need to grow and reach the next round or exit. Estimating the necessary investment requires a good understanding of the venture's business model and financial plan, as well as knowledge of the economics of its sector of operations. When there are multiple investment rounds, the investor needs to estimate two quantities: (1) how much money the venture will need over time, across all investment rounds, and (2) at what points in time this money will be needed. These questions can be answered with the help of the cash flow projections, alongside with an understanding of the company's milestones, which we discuss in Section 3.3.

5.2.3.(b) Time-to-Exit

The estimated time to exit (T) depends on the pace of progress that the company will be able to sustain, as well as on the state of the stock market and of the acquisition market over the foreseeable future (Section 11.6). The exact timing therefore cannot be planned in advance with any precision. Still, entrepreneurs and investors can discuss their expectations and how to prepare for this future event. Venture capital firms, for example, have a 10-year fund horizon and therefore have a clear idea about how long they want to wait before achieving an exit (Section 12.3.1).

5.2.3.(c) Exit Value

The exit value is the value of the company to shareholders at the time of exit (X^e). It represents what the company will be worth at a future point in time when the investors can expect to sell their shares. In Chapter 11 we discuss the details of the exit process and the various ways that investors can obtain liquidity. For the purpose of estimating exit values, we concentrate on two types of exits: acquisitions and IPOs. These are the exit types that occur when the company is successful. It is important to notice that the exit value estimate does not measure the expected value of the company in a statistical sense because that would also need to include the unsuccessful scenarios. The exit value is instead an estimate of the value of the company if it becomes successful. This insight is key for understanding the investors' required rate of return, which we discuss in Section 5.2.3.(d).

What exit value are we looking for exactly? In the case of an acquisition, we want to estimate the price that the acquirer pays for the entire equity of the company, net of repayment of any existing debt (in Section 10.5, we identify this as the company's equity value). In the case of an IPO, we are interested in the price investors can fetch when the company is listed. As we discuss in Section 11.2, they can sell their share at different moments, so there is no simple way to estimate it. However, investors most often sell their shares after the so-called lock-up period, which typically lasts six month after the IPO.

Exit values can be estimated using two main methods. The first method consists of performing a Discounted Cash Flow analysis at the time of exit, based on financial projections from that point onward (Section 5.3). The second method combines some key performance metrics of the focal company with the recent exit values of similar companies. We call this the Exit Comparables Method, which we explain in greater detail in Section 5.4. The suitability of these two approaches depends on the relative confidence investors have in internal projections versus external comparisons.

5.2.3.(d)   Required Rate of Return

We now turn to the last input needed for the VCM, the required rate of return (ρ). Venture investors are prone to quoting eye-popping required rates of returns. Sometimes they ask for a required rate of return of 50%, or they want their money back 10 times over. A survey of venture capital firms by Gompers, Gornall, Kaplan, and Strebulaev finds an average required rate of return of 31% and an average required cash-on-cash multiple of 5.5.[5] However, if one looks at the realized returns made by most venture investors, they aren't anywhere close (Section 12.6). For established companies one might expect that on average the required return comes close to the realized return. In the context of venture investing, however, the required return should be thought of as the target rate of return *in case of success*. This rate is much higher than standard rates of return used for other types of investments. To understand why, we propose the following decomposition:

$$
\begin{aligned}
\text{Required rate of return } (\rho) = \ & \text{Riskless rate of return} \\
& + \text{Financial risk premium} \\
& + \text{Illiquidity premium} \\
& + \text{Failure risk premium} \\
& + \text{Service premium}
\end{aligned}
\tag{5.4}
$$

This decomposition is not meant to be a precise mathematical formula, but rather a way of explaining the key components that are included in the required rate of return. The first three components of the required rate of return ρ tend to be relevant in most financial investments. The last two components are more specific to investments in entrepreneurial companies.

Let us begin with the riskless rate of return. This measures the time value of money of a riskless investment (see Box 4.2). It is reflected in the rate investors obtain when investing in safe assets, such as government bonds. For advanced, stable economies, these rates tend to lie well below 10% and reflect an economy's long-run expected growth and inflation rate.

The question of how to think about the financial risk premium is a big question in finance that led to a Nobel Prize in Economics, as discussed in Box 5.1.

Box 5.1 Nobel Insights on the Capital Asset Pricing Model

The 1990 Economics Nobel Prize went to Harry Markowitz, Merton Miller, and William Sharpe "for their pioneering work in the theory of financial economics."[6] We return to Miller's work of in Box 10.2. Here we focus on the work of Markowitz and Sharpe. Together they are credited with creating modern financial portfolio theory. They asked the fundamental question of how investors would want to build a financial portfolio to appropriately balance risks and returns. In the process they discovered a more general theory of how to value assets and how to price their risk. The resulting model is the Capital Asset Pricing Model (CAPM), which has become a cornerstone of modern finance.[7]

A central tenet of portfolio theory is that risk can be "diversified away" by investing in many projects, so that individual (called "idiosyncratic") fortunes wash out, the good ones compensating for the bad ones. However, not all risk can be diversified away. Once idiosyncratic risk has been diversified away, investors still bear the fundamental (called "systematic") economic risk that affects all projects. The financial risk premium in equation (5.4) measures the compensation that investors require to bear such undiversifiable risk. The CAPM provides a practical way to measure financial risk premia by using the following relationship:

$$\text{Required rate} = \text{Riskless rate} + \beta * \left(\text{Market rate} - \text{Riskless rate} \right)$$

Note that this formula only contains the first two components of equation (5.4). The required rate is the return investors require to invest in a company or project that carries the level of systematic risk β (pronounced "beta"). The riskless rate is the rate of return on a safe asset, such as the rate on the government bonds of advanced economies. The market rate is the rate of return on all companies on the stock market. The difference between the market rate and the riskless rate is called the market premium. It measures the excess return achieved from investing in risky assets (the stock market), as opposed to safe assets (government bonds).

β measures the level of systematic risk for a company. Where does this risk come from? The original work of Markowitz and Sharpe showed that β measures how much the return on a company varies in sync ("covaries") with the return on all companies in the market. This covariance of the company's return with the return of the overall market can be estimated from regression analysis. A higher β means that an asset is highly correlated with the overall market movement and therefore contains more undiversifiable fundamental risk. This means that the Required Rate needs to be higher than the market rate in order to compensate investors for bearing this risk. A β of one means that an asset carries the same amount of systematic risk as the market; a β greater than one means that the price of the asset tends to move more than market movements; a β of zero means that the asset fluctuates independently of the market; and a negative β (which is rare) means that the asset moves in the opposite direction of the market.

The CAPM has become a standard finance tool that is widely used in practice, from valuing stock, to estimate acquisition prices, to planning corporate investments.[8] "Betas" (βs) have become part of the finance vocabulary. Estimated values of β can be readily found online. Since the seminal work of Markowitz and Sharpe, the CAPM has been refined to vary over time and include other risk factors. This work generated another Nobel Prize in Economics, which we discuss in Box 12.1.

We are now properly equipped to examine the financial risk premium for the Venture Capital valuation model. The correct premium is given by the formula given in Box 5.1. The computation of β assumes that investors are fully diversified, which is unlikely to happen in the case of entrepreneurial companies. β should be higher for undiversified investors, whose portfolios are smaller and concentrated into fewer sectors or geographies, so that idiosyncratic risk cannot be fully avoided. Underdiversification is typically the case for angels and venture capital firms. A simple heuristic to deal with this is to divide β by the correlation of the returns on the investor's portfolio with the returns on the market portfolio. For a fully diversified portfolio, this correlation would be equal to one, so no adjustment is made. The less diversified the investor is, the lower the correlation and the higher the corrected β. Moreover, at the company level the appropriate β should be a weighted average of the individual investors' own βs.[9] The question of what β to use remains controversial, with different studies coming to different conclusions.[10]

Most studies, however, estimate β between one and two, suggesting that venture capital is pro-cyclical.

The third component of the required rate of return is the illiquidity premium. Financial economists say that an asset is illiquid when it is difficult or costly to convert its value into cash within a short period of time. Illiquidity is endemic in venture investing. For an entrepreneurial company, the process from investment to exit may take several years. In between there are virtually no possibilities of selling shares. This imposes constraints on any investor who wants to sell. Anticipating these difficulties, investors ask for a premium to accept holding such illiquid assets.[11]

The last two components of equation (5.4) are not usually found in standard investment models. Consider first the failure risk premium. Venture investors discount exit values from a success scenario, not from the average scenario. In Section 4.2.1, we note that failure is the most common outcome in entrepreneurial companies. In our discussion of financial projection in Chapter 3, we also note that they reflect a successful situation for the company and therefore do not capture the many things that can go wrong. In our discussion of exit values earlier in this section, we also noted that these estimates are based on acquisition and IPO values that reflect success. Therefore, none of these calculations take in account the failure risks faced by entrepreneurial companies.

There are two approaches to accounting for failure risk, one detailed and one simple. The first approach is to explicitly model the uncertainty and calculate what exit values are likely to obtain across different scenarios. This requires modeling probabilities, which we discuss in Section 5.5. The simple alternative is to account for failure risk by including a large failure risk premium in the required rate of return. In practice, investors state a large premium without relying on a market model but rely instead on past experience. An intermediate approach consists of computing the failure rate with a simple formula that we describe in Box 5.2.

Box 5.2 Computing the Failure Risk Premium

Suppose an investor believes that a company has a constant annual probability of failure, denoted by z . Suppose also that the investor uses a discount rate d that already includes the riskless rate of return and all the other premiums we discuss in Section 5.2.3, but that does not incorporate any failure risk. The question is how to adjust d to account for the probability of failure.

Each year the probability of survival is $(1-z)$, so that the probability to survive for T years is $(1-z)^T$. The expected exit value is therefore given by $(1-z)^T X^e$. Its

discounted value is $V_{POST} = \dfrac{(1-z)^T X^e}{(1+d)^T}$. From equation (5.1), the post-money valuation can also be written as $V_{POST} = \dfrac{X^e}{(1+\rho)^T}$. Comparing these two expressions, we see that $\dfrac{(1-z)^T}{(1+d)^T} = \dfrac{1}{(1+\rho)^T}$, so that $(1+\rho) = \dfrac{1+d}{1-z}$, and thus $\rho = \dfrac{d+z}{1-z}$.

This formula simplifies to $\rho = d$ whenever there is no failure risk (i.e., $z = 0$). As soon as there is some failure risk (i.e., $z > 0$), ρ becomes positive. The higher z, the higher ρ becomes. According to one academic study by Puri and Zarutskie, the annual rate of observable failures in VC-backed companies is around 5%.[12] This would convert at a 20% discount rate into a 26% failure risk-adjusted discount rate. If we increased the failure rate to 15% to account for some of the less visible failures, the discount rate would jump from 20 to 41%.

The final component of the required rate of return is what we call a "service" premium. Many venture investors provide more than money. They also provide a variety of services that help the entrepreneur build her company and bring it to success. In Section 8.3, we show that venture investors often help recruit managers and directors, facilitate strategic alliances, make introductions to potential clients and suppliers, and help raise additional funds. Moreover, investors provide "soft," but equally important, advice and support, such as mentoring founders or providing their experience in crisis management. These services increase the company's chances of success.[13] Investors typically do not charge companies for any of these services. Instead, they rely on the returns from the investment to get compensated. It follows that the required rate of return needs to also take these services into account.

Another way of looking at this is that the investor needs to recoup the costs of offering all these services. A venture capital firm, for example, has to maintain certain levels of partners and staff to provide such services. This is paid for through management fees and carried interest received from their limited partners (Section 12.3.3). In order to generate a competitive net return to their limited partners, VC firms therefore need to generate a higher gross return with their investments (Section 12.6). This component of the required rate of return is captured by the service premium.

5.2.4 Model Variants

We conclude this section by discussing three variants of the venture capital model. First, we have used the same required rate of return ρ for all rounds. However, ρ is likely to decrease across subsequent rounds. As the company becomes more mature, the risk of failure decreases, and illiquidity becomes less severe as the company inches closer to exit. Consequently, it is common practice to use lower required rates of return for later-stage companies. We can take this into account by suitably modifying equation (5.1) into the following more general specification. As in Section 5.2.2, we denote the time between two rounds by $\tau_r(r + 1) = t(r + 1) - t(r)$. Then the relevant discount factor for an investment over n periods is given by: $\prod_{r=1}^{r=n}(1+\rho_{\tau r (r+1)})$. We illustrate this formula with a numerical example. If there are two years between rounds, and the first year requires $\rho = 0.4$ but the second year only requires $\rho = 0.2$, then the relevant discount factor becomes $(1 + 0.4)*(1 + 0.2) = 1.68$. Alternatively, we can set a constant $\rho = 0.296$ over two years to get to the same required return, that is, $(1.296)^2 = 1.68$. The spreadsheet models that accompany this chapter are available on the book's website (www.entrepreneurialfinance.net); allow for the use of a time-varying ρ.

Second, instead of working with a required rate of return (ρ) and a time to exit (T), it is also possible to directly specify a required cash-on-cash multiple. For this we simply use the usual expression $CCM^e = (1 + \rho)^T$. This makes for an extremely simply valuation model. In the case of a single-round investment, only two numbers are needed, the exit value X^e and the expected cash-on-cash multiple. The valuation is then given by $V_{POST} = X^e / CCM^e$, which corresponds to equation (4.21). Some seed investors like this approach because of its simplicity: using CCM^e doesn't require estimating the time to exit. Instead, it only requires forming an expectation for how many times they expect their money back.

Third, for a company that expects multiple rounds of investment, it is initially challenging to forecast the entire path to exit. Some investors therefore prefer to only forecast one round ahead at a time. Instead of using a multi-round valuation method, they use the single-round valuation equation (5.1) but replace the exit value (X^e) with the pre-money valuation of the next round (e.g., $V_{PRE}(2)$). This simplification avoids making difficult assumptions. At the same time, it is not clear how to justify the estimates of the second-round pre-money valuation without making some projections about the ultimate exit value.

5.3 The Discounted Cash Flow Method

The Discounted Cash Flow (DCF) method is a standard valuation tool used in corporate finance. It is based on the notion that the value of an asset is given by the net present value of the cash flow it generates. As noted in Section 3.6.3, this cash flow is often referred to as "free cash flow" to indicate that in principle it is available to shareholders, after accounting for all the cash needed to operate the company. The future cash flow is discounted back to the present at a rate that reflects the company's risk. The DCF method is referred to as an intrinsic valuation method because it is focused on information about the company itself.

The DCF method is the mainstay valuation method across a wide range of corporate finance applications. Many books discuss how to apply DCF in various contexts.[14] Given their high uncertainty, however, applying it to entrepreneurial ventures remains challenging. The DCF method requires estimating company cash flows, which are much more complex to estimate than the investor cash flow, which is the basis for the VCM. Still, modeling these details has some benefits. If an entrepreneur already has detailed financial projections, then calculating DCF is relatively easy. Later-stage companies also have more reliable accounting data to build on. We now show how to build a tractable DCF model for entrepreneurial companies. Since these companies rely largely on equity, to keep our DCF model as simple as possible, we assume that the companies are financed only through equity and have no debt. We return to this issue in Chapter 10.[15]

5.3.1 The Mechanics of the DCF Method

The DCF method requires three inputs: a series of cash flows over a defined time horizon; a terminal value of the company; and a discount rate. If the DCF method is applied to a company prior to a financing round, then it generates an estimate for the pre-money valuation of the company. We denoted this by V_{PRE}^{DCF}, where we add the superscript DCF to distinguish it from the VCM (which has no superscript since it is our benchmark model).

We use the following notation. Each time period, typically measured in years, is indexed by $t = 1, 2, \ldots, T$. Notice that in the VCM the time intervals measured time between rounds, given by $\tau_r(r + 1)$, while in the DCF method time measures regular (yearly) intervals. FCF_t represents the free cash flow for period t, d denotes the discount rate, and TV the terminal value of the company at time T. The valuation in the DCF method is expressed by:

$$V_{PRE}^{DCF} = \sum_{t=1}^{t=T} \frac{FCF_t}{(1+d)^t} + \frac{TV}{(1+d)^T} + \text{Initial Cash} \tag{5.5}$$

This is the standard equation for a DCF with the addition of the initial cash balance. For most start-ups, the starting cash balances are negligible, which is why they seek financing in the first place. Importantly, this cash does not include any cash from raising funds. The free cash flow calculations deliberately omit all fundraising activities to estimate the value of the cash generated by the firm's operations. Consequently, the DCF estimates the pre-money valuation of the company. Note, however, that just after raising a financing round, a company's initial cash would go up by the investment amount. At this point, the DCF measures the post-money valuation.

The alert reader may notice that this formula resembles the net present value (NPV) formula discussed in equation (4.12) in Section 4.2.2. This is not a coincidence, for the NPV of the company's cash flow is the DCF net of the investments needed. Again, we note that the DCF valuation generates a pre-money valuation. This is because the DCF calculates the net value of all cash flows, including the initial negative cash flows for which financing is needed. It therefore represents the value of the company prior to any fund-raising. Note also that a limitation of the DCF method is that it doesn't explicitly model the staged investment process and therefore, unlike the VC method, cannot show the valuations for the various investment rounds.

5.3.2   Estimating the Inputs

We now consider how to estimate the three core elements of the DCF valuation method.

5.3.2.(a)   Time Horizon

A first choice to be made is the time horizon. It is common to choose a horizon between three and seven years. Beyond seven years it becomes difficult to model the details of the company's yearly cash flow. Below three years the DCF loses its meaning since the venture's value would be largely determined by its terminal value. As a rule, one should chose the horizon at a point in time where the terminal value can be calculated meaningfully. This becomes easier once a company has reached a stage where its cash flow is growing at a predictable rate. In the context of entrepreneurial companies, the time horizon also needs to reflect the investors' need to sell the company after several years from the investment. One can estimate the terminal value at the time of exit, in which case it can be thought of as an exit value. However, this is not a requirement of the DCF method, so the terminal value can also be estimated independently of exit.

5.3.2.(b)   Free Cash Flow

The relevant cash flow for the DCF is the portion of the cash flow which in principle is "free" for distribution to investors. This does not mean that the company will actually distribute its cash flow—most start-ups don't pay dividends. Rather, it means that the cash flow is not required to sustain the future growth of the company. The free cash flow can be calculated on the basis of a company's financial projections, as discussed in Section 3.6.3.

5.3.2.(c)   Terminal Value

Terminal value is a convenient way to value cash flows in the more distant future. It assumes that, from a certain moment on, the company will generate a free cash flow that grows at a constant rate. Constant growth is a simplification that works well for mature companies. Those companies cannot outgrow the economy indefinitely, and their growth may depend on slow-moving trends, such as demographics and economy-wide growth. For young and fast-growing companies, however, the constant growth assumption is more problematic.

The main attraction of using a terminal value is that it is simple to compute. The calculation is based on a formula for discounting perpetuities using an infinite sum of future cash flows. Specifically, if the discount rate is d and the free cash flow is assumed to be growing at a constant rate g, then the formula for the terminal value is given by:

$$TV = \frac{1+g}{d-g} FCF_T \tag{5.6}$$

This formula provides a simple way of calculating a terminal value. However, it is important to obtain convincing estimates for its components because the results are sensitive to small changes in the discount and growth rates. Note also that the formula cannot be used if g exceeds the discount rate d.

Entrepreneurial companies expect to make losses in their initial years, so the terminal value often constitutes the bulk of value creation. In fact, for early-stage companies, the terminal value is often the only positive cash inflow, with all other interim cash flows being negative. Even for later stage ventures, it is likely that cash flows are initially negative because of capital expenditures and rising working capital needs. Even for these companies a disproportionally large part of the value then comes from the terminal value. This means that the assumptions underlying the terminal value matter substantially and should reflect the company's long-term growth prospects.

5.3.2.(d) Discount Rate

The final input required by the DCF method is the discount rate. The discussion here is similar to that of Section 5.2.3, which discusses the required rate of return (ρ) for the VCM. Note, however, that in practice people often use a more standard discount rate, which in the case of all-equity-financed ventures does not take into account the cost of debt finance. The appropriate choice of the discount rate, however, should still be guided by the factors mentioned in equation (5.4).

WorkHorse Box 5.3 illustrates the use of the DCF method.

WorkHorse Box 5.3 WorkHorse's DCF Analysis

For their DCF analysis, the founders used their financial projections (see Chapter 3). They assumed a 15% discount rate and projected a terminal value for the seventh year using a company growth rate of 5%. Using the table in WorkHorse Box 3.11, they arrived at the following calculations:

	2020	2021	2022	2023	2024	2025	Terminal value
FCF ($)	−436,400	−1,477,376	−412,212	23,217	808,850	1,808,960	18,994,081
Discount factor	0.870	0.756	0.658	0.572	0.497	0.432	0.376
Discounted FCF ($)	−379,478	−1,117,109	−271,036	13,274	402,141	782,063	7,140,579
NPV ($)	6,570,435						

The founders noted that their calculations relied heavily on the terminal value. Because they were uncertain about what assumptions to make, they also looked into how different discount rates and different growth rates would affect the net present value and terminal value. They tabulated their findings in the following table:

Growth rate → Discount rate ↓	0%	5%	10%	15%	20%
Net present value ($)					
5%	26,916,296				
10%	9,844,709	21,076,928			
15%	4,641,286	7,639,196	16,632,925		
20%	2,307,643	3,519,278	5,942,546	13,212,351	
30%	343,672	668,476	1,155,682	1,967,691	3,591,709
40%	−396,304	−276,180	−116,014	108,218	444,566
50%	−719,029	−666,092	−599,920	−514,843	−401,406
Terminal value ($)					
5%	36,179,202				
10%	18,089,601	37,988,162			
15%	12,059,734	18,994,081	39,797,122		
20%	9,044,801	12,662,721	19,898,561	41,606,083	
30%	6,029,867	7,597,632	9,949,281	13,868,694	21,707,521
40%	4,522,400	5,426,880	6,632,854	8,321,217	10,853,761
50%	3,617,920	4,220,907	4,974,640	5,943,726	7,235,840

They noted that the discount rate had a large impact on the NPV of the project: increasing the discount rate from 5% to 10% reduced the NPV by nearly two-thirds! At high discount rates, such as 50%, the NPV even became negative.

5.4 Methods of Comparables

In this section, we consider methods of valuing a focal company against a set of comparable companies. These methods are sometimes referred to as relative or extrinsic valuation methods. This approach is common among investment bankers for valuing IPOs and acquisitions (Sections 11.2 and 11.3). It is popular because it is intuitive, easy to use, and easy to communicate. It also has the benefit of using the "knowledge of the market," exploiting the independent information of a large number of other investors. However, in the context of entrepreneurial companies, this approach also has drawbacks. First, it is difficult to determine who should be in the set of comparable companies. Second, market information is often sparse and sometimes out of date.

We discuss two comparables methods. The Investment Comparables Method (ICM) performs the valuation of the company at the time of a financing round by comparing it to the valuations of private companies. The Exit Comparables Method (ECM) estimates the exit value of the company based on how similar companies are valued in the market. While the ICM is a valuation method in its own right, ECM isn't because it estimates the value of the company in the future. In order to bring that future value back to the present, one has to use the VCM (Section 5.2).

5.4.1 The Investment Comparables Method

The Investment Comparables Method (ICM) compares a focal company to companies that are at a similar stage of development, comparing their valuations in private financing rounds. This allows investors to capture information about the current state of the investment market. It reveals how similar companies are currently valued and therefore reflects current supply and demand conditions for venture funding.

The data required for the ICM consist of valuations of private financing deals. Obtaining this information can be a challenge, since this data is not publicly available. Even specialized commercial databases have only limited information about private valuations. Experienced investors, however, talk to their peers in private and can thus get an idea of what current valuations look like. Also the diffusion of equity crowdfunding platforms in some countries provides a way to obtain data on valuations, albeit for a very specific subset of entrepreneurial companies.

Calculating Investment Comparables is conceptually simple. It only requires pre- or post-money valuations of a set of comparable companies to generate an estimate for the pre- or post-money valuation of the focal company. In addition to looking at the average and median valuation in the comparison group, it is often useful to consider the range of valuations (i.e., the minimum and maximum valuation). For example, if the comparison group is experiencing valuations between $1M and $5M, then an entrepreneur has an argument for pushing back against a valuation of $0.5M and an investor has an argument for pushing back against a valuation of $10M.

The choice of comparable companies can be difficult. They should operate in the same industry and/or have similar business models. Moreover, the valuations should be from deals involving companies that are at a similar stage of development and that are raising similar amounts of funding. It helps if they are located in the same region or country. In order to reflect current market conditions, the valuations should be recent, ideally less than a few months old.

The ICM method has several limitations. One limitation is that the method uses almost no internal information at all. To be precise, internal information is only used to construct the comparison set. The valuation itself, however, is entirely based on the comparison group and does not take into account the focal company's specific situation and business prospects. Another important limitation is that the ICM relies on private valuations, which can sometimes be misleading (Section 4.3.2). If everyone uses the ICM, this can also lead to herd behavior. If investors pay high valuations merely because other investors paid high valuations, then conditions are ripe for speculative bubbles: Valuations become detached from their business fundamental and follow a logic where one investor mimics the other—the blind leading the blind.

WorkHorse Box 5.4 illustrates the Investment Comparables Method.

WorkHorse Box 5.4 WorkHorse's Investment Comparables

The founders of WorkHorse gathered some investment data on companies that seemed somewhat comparable to theirs. They identified five comparable companies that were at somewhat similar stages in related segments.

Comparable company	Location	Description	Investment amount ($)	Post-money valuation ($)
Cavalavoro	Milano, Italy	Advanced lightweight solar panels	500,000	3,000,000
FoalPlay	Boulder, Colorado, US	Portable hybrid petrol/solar power generators	200,000	6,000,000
GongZuoMa	Shenzhen, China	Small solar battery packs	1,500,000	5,500,000

Comparable company	Location	Description	Investment amount ($)	Post-money valuation ($)
PferdWerk	Johannesburg, South Africa	Small solar battery packs	100,000	800,000
Trachevail	Montreal, Quebec, Canada	Portable liquefied natural gas (LNG) generators	1,000,000	2,000,000
		Average	660,000	3,460,000
		Median	500,000	3,000,000
		Highest	1,500,000	6,000,000
		Lowest	100,000	800,000

When the founders compared these valuations with the $2M offered by Michael Archie, they noted that theirs was below the average and median valuation of their comparable set but above the lowest. Moreover, their investment amount of .5M was right at the median. It gave them some comfort that they were well within the range of their comparable companies. However, beyond that they found it difficult to make use of this data because the comparable companies couldn't reveal much about WorkHorse itself.

5.4.2 The Exit Comparables Method

The Exit Comparables Method (ECM) estimates an exit value of the focal company by comparing it to a set of comparable companies that have already exited. The ECM is not a valuation method per se; instead it is an input that it used in the VCM. This is because the ECM estimates a future exit value that needs to be discounted back to the present.

Even though the methodologies are related, the underlying logic of the ECM is distinct from that of ICM. With the ICM the information concerns how other investors currently value similar companies. However, there is no attempt to look at the focal company's expected performance. In contrast, with the ECM, the information concerns how acquirers or stock market investors value comparable companies that achieve successful exits. While this by itself doesn't create a valuation, it shifts the focus toward estimating the expected financial performance of the focal company.

The ECM requires two choices: comparable companies and the comparison metric.

5.4.2.(a) The Choice of Comparable Companies
Any comparable analysis is only as good as the focal company resembles its comparison group. Comparable companies must have similar characteristics, including size, stage of development, growth prospects, and risk. These depend on the business model of the company and the industry it belongs to. Indeed, it is common to

define the set of comparables companies at the industry level. However, this also requires that the focal company has a similar business model as its industry peers. Otherwise, the comparison group should be chosen on the basis of similar business models, even outside of the focal company's industry.

In general, it is easier to collect data on publicly listed than on privately held companies. The ECM requires the valuation of all the companies in the comparison group, which is readily available for companies listed on stock exchanges. Valuations tend to also be available for acquisitions of large private companies. However, it is hard to obtain data on valuations of privately held companies. In some cases, publicly held acquirers disclose the valuation of privately held targets. The hardest data to obtain are valuations where both the acquirer and target are privately held companies.

Two challenges arise with the choice of comparable companies. First, it is difficult to generate a credible set of comparables for innovative companies that are pursuing new technologies or new business models. What company resembled Google when it created the first online search engine? Second, less innovative companies often like to compare themselves to industry leaders to inflate their valuation. The hundredth company starting a mobile messaging network should not be compared to WhatsApp simply because it will never achieve a comparable market position.

5.4.2.(b) The Choice of Comparison Metrics

How does the ECM compare the focal company to its comparables? The idea is to first pick a performance metric (PM) from the focal company's financial projections and then to apply a valuation multiple that is derived from the comparison set. For this we consider a set of comparable companies indexed by the subscript j. The performance metric of a company j is denoted by PM_j^{Comp} and its valuation by X_j^{Comp}. We then define company j's multiple as:

$$M_j^{Comp} = \frac{X_j^{Comp}}{PM_j^{Comp}} \tag{5.7}$$

Equation (5.7) states that a multiple consists of a fraction whose numerator is the comparable company's valuation and whose denominator is the chosen performance metric.[16] We then derive the comparison group's multiple by averaging across all the companies in the comparison group:

$$M^{Comp} = \text{Average}\left(M_j^{Comp}\right) \tag{5.8}$$

Instead of using the average, the median can also be used in equation (5.8). We can then estimate the focal company's expected exit value X^e by multiplying the focal company's expected performance metric PM^e at the time of exit, with the comparison group's multiple from equation (5.8), so that:

$$X^e = PM^e * M^{Comp} \tag{5.9}$$

The underlying assumption of the ECM is that the relationship between performance metric (PM) and company's exit value (X) is the same for the focal company and the comparison set. We therefore use the market information on how the comparable companies get valued as an indicator about what value the focal company will be able to fetch on exit on the basis of its own performance.

Consider a simple analogy. Suppose your friend lent you a BMW with 10 gallons in the tank.

If you are told that the average for comparable sporty sedans is 25 mpg, you can estimate that this BMW will run for approximately 250 miles. This simple estimate bypasses the need to make complex engineering calculations on the gasoline consumption of your friend's BMW. Just enjoy the ride and come back before you clocked 250 miles.

To implement the ECM, let us first define what company valuations to use. We are interested in the exit value of the focal company (X^e). The natural candidate for estimating the equivalent value for companies in the comparison group (X_i^{Comp}) is to look at their equity market value. Section 5.2.3 discusses what measures to look for.

The next choice is what performance metric to use. We consider four sets of metrics: (1) earnings, (2) cash flows, (3) revenues, and (4) operational measures. We discuss each of them in turn.

The most common performance metrics are earnings multiples: (after-tax) net earnings, earnings before interest and taxes (EBIT), and earnings before interest, taxes, depreciation and amortization (EBITDA). The choice between these measures depends mostly on industry characteristics and business models. A popular variant is to use the price-earnings (PE) ratio, which is calculated by dividing the current share price by the (after-tax) earnings per share. This is equivalent to dividing the market capitalization by net earnings.

A second set of multiples is based on cash flows. In Section 3.6.3 we explain how earnings differ from cash flow. Moving from earnings to cash flow reduces the dependency on accounting rules, which affect the measurement of earnings but not cash flow. The free cash flow multiple, for example, is defined as the market value of the company, divided by its free cash flow.

The third type of multiples is based on revenues. A disadvantage of both the earnings and cash flow metrics is that they require positive earnings or positive cash flows. However, early-stage ventures often have negative earnings and cash flow, so that one cannot use these measures with multiples. This is where revenue-based performance measures come in handy.

The main metric has the market capitalization of comparable companies in the numerator and revenues in the denominator of equation (5.7). This obviously requires that the company have some revenue. In fact, the estimates only become credible once the company has obtained enough revenues to avoid the problems of dividing by small numbers. The implicit assumption is that the value of the focal company moves in line with its revenues in a way that is similar to that of the comparable companies.

Box 5.3 examines how to apply EBITDA and sales multiples. It shows how challenging it can be in practice to find suitable comparables.

Box 5.3 Tales from the Venture Archives: Stitching Together a Set of Comparables

How do you find comparables in practice? Clearly, this is tricky when a company is doing something novel. When Federal Express invented a hub-and-spoke system for package delivery, there was no one doing anything remotely similar. Today no one really knows what to compare a quantum computer to. However, these are extreme examples of highly innovative ventures. What about more incremental innovators, companies that operate in more established industries, tweaking existing business models?

Let's take online clothing retail. E-commerce has been around for over a decade and clothing for several millennia, so surely there must be lots of comparable companies! Take the example of Stitch Fix, an online personal shopping service.[17] It first asks customers about their clothing preferences, and then it uses a combination of artificial intelligence (AI) and professional stylists to make a customized clothing selection. After receiving a selection in the mail, customers decide which items to keep and which to return. Founded in 2011 by Katrina Lake, the company rapidly established its niche in the large online clothing retail market, growing to $977M in sales by 2017 and generating $12.4M in EBITDA. When the company went public in November 2017, many analysts looked for comparables to value the company.

An instinct might be to classify Stitch Fix as a clothing retailer. Land's End was a market leader in this industry segment, although it was significantly older as it was established in the days of the mail order. Maybe fashion designers with a considerable online presence would make for a better comparison? Guess Inc. had a somewhat glamorous style that appealed to younger generations. Or how about Abercrombie & Fitch for something less high touch, more casual? Or how about an online retailer outside of clothing with a similar target demographic, like 1-800-Flowers?

Some analysts were more at home with high-tech than with high-touch. They viewed Stitch Fix primarily as a technology company. The company often presented itself as a tech company, stressing, for example, its large number of data scientist. As the largest online retailer, Amazon would be an obvious benchmark, especially after its launch of Prime Wardrobe. However, Stitch Fix was clearly not of the same size. Moreover, Katrina Lake viewed her value proposition as the opposite of Amazon. She argued that her company guided customers toward personally relevant selections, whereas Amazon's model offered everything to everyone.[18] So maybe we should look at tech companies that focus on discovery and customization. How about TripAdvisor, which uses AI to customize recommendations?

Why only look at publicly listed comparables, when the most similar companies are still private? Companies like Le Tote, MM.Lafleur, or Bag Borrow or Steal all operated in related e-commerce spaces, all pursuing data-driven business models similar to Stitch Fix.[19] The problem with those comparables was lack of data. Being private companies, they disclosed no financial and operating information that would be useful to make proper valuation relevant comparisons.

So how about just focusing on recent IPOs? When Snap (see Box 3.2) went public in March 2017, the market responded enthusiastically. However, when Blue Apron went public in June 2017, the market response was much more tepid, with its stock declining significantly over the ensuing months.

The following table shows the EDITDA and sales multiples for all these comparable (publicly listed) companies, and the resulting valuations for Stitch Fix.

Comparable companies	EBITDA Multiple	Valuation based on EBITDA Multiple ($)	Sales Multiple	Valuation based on Sales Multiple ($)
Lands' End	18	415,800,000	0.5	518,350,000
Guess	8.8	203,280,000	0.5	518,350,000
Abercrombie & Fitch	5.3	122,430,000	0.3	311,010,000
1-800-FLOWERS	8.6	198,660,000	0.6	622,020,000
Amazon	43.6	1,007,160,000	3.5	3,628,450,000
TripAdvisor	21.5	496,650,000	2.4	2,488,080,000
Snap	n.a.	n.a.	19	19,697,300,000
Blue Apron	n.a.	n.a.	0.6	622,020,000
Highest	43.6	1,007,160,000	19	19,697,300,000
Lowest	5.3	122,430,000	0.3	311,010,000
Mean	17.6	407,330,000	3.4	3,550,697,500
Median	13.4	309,540,000	0.6	622,020,000

The range of predicted valuations varies widely across the table, depending on which company and metric is used. When Stitch Fix went public in November 2017, the company was valued at $1.46B. The market price at the end of the first day was very close to the offer price, suggesting that the valuation was approximately right. However, investors often expect a price jump on the first day of trading (Section 11.2), so they were slightly disappointed with the IPO. Addressing this problem, Katrina Lake noted: "Stitch Fix is an unusual company. . . . In some ways we can look like a retailer, in other ways we look more like a technology company. There weren't perfect comps for the business."[20]

The final set of measures is given by nonfinancial operational performance metrics. These metrics can be used even when there are no revenues. These metrics tend to be very industry-specific. Some examples are the number of users, the number of unique website visitors, the number of strategic partners, or the number of patents. However, these operational measures are not always closely tied to performance and may be unreliable estimators of company value.

Several caveats about using multiples in general are in order. First, one has to make sure that the multiple is measured consistently across the set of comparable companies. This is particularly delicate when companies operate in different countries with different accounting standards or in different industries with different business models. One also has to be careful with comparable companies that are experiencing unstable conditions or are otherwise far away from a stable long-term operating situation.

Second, beyond looking at averages, it is useful to examine the distribution of multiples across comparable firms. In particular, one needs to identify outliers and interpret their multiples within its context. Instead of just relying on averages across the comparison set, it is often also useful to look at medians, which are less affected by outliers.

Third, one has to be aware that multiples rely on market valuations, reflecting how at a particular point in time the market values the earnings potential of comparable companies. These valuations may be biased because of temporary market sentiments. If the market is experiencing a temporary bubble, then valuations may be high. If the market returns to normal levels by the time the company is ready for exit, then investors are likely to have overpaid in bubble times. More generally, it is useful to reflect on how multiples vary across sectors and time and to identify possible over- or undervaluations.

WorkHorse Box 5.5 illustrates the Exit Comparables Method.

WorkHorse Box 5.5 WorkHorse's Exit Comparables

Brandon volunteered to gather some data on the exits of comparable companies. He found five start-ups that he considered somewhat comparable in terms of industry and age, although he admitted that the comparison was not always fully convincing. Still, those were the only all-equity companies for which he managed to gather some financial information. In case of an IPO, the valuation at exit is the value of all preexisting shares, evaluated at the IPO offer price. Of the four metrics used for Exit Comparables, Brandon found data on revenues and earnings, but not on free cash flow and operational metrics.

Comparable company	BieBie	FergieTech	Noodles	UniCorNio	Zellie
Location	Nanjing, China	Burnaby, BC, Canada	Menlo Park, CA, US	Tel Aviv, Israel	Augsburg, Germany

Comparable company	BieBie	FergieTech	Noodles	UniCorNio	Zellie
Business description	Portable diesel engines	LNG-based pushback tugs for airlines	Cloud-based energy management systems	Patent portfolio of solar technologies	Solar component for automotive sector
Exit type	Acquisition by Chinese manufacturer	IPO on TSX Venture	IPO on NASDAQ	Acquisition by U.S. engineering company	Acquisition by German automotive group
Age at exit	23	6	5	6	9
Cumulative funding ($)	25,000,000	8,000,000	50,000,000	4,000,000	6,000,000
Valuation at exit ($)	40,000,000	15,000,000	150,000,000	15,000,000	12,000,000
Revenues at exit ($)	30,000,000	12,000,000	12,000,000	10,000,000	15,000,000
Revenues Multiple	1.3	1.3	12.5	1.5	0.8
Net earnings at exit ($)	5,000,000	1,000,000	-15,000,000	5,000,000	2,000,000
PE Multiple	8.0	15.0	n.a.	3.0	6.0

Based on this information, Brandon proceeded to calculate the average, median, minimum, and maximum values across the sample. He then reverted to WorkHorse's own financial projection, and noted that after five years, they had projected revenues of $21.1M and net earnings of $3.4M. He then applied the average and median multiplier to those projections to generate projections for WorkHorse's own exit value. All values are at exit.

	Age	Cumulative funding ($)	Valuation ($)	Revenue ($)	Revenue Multiple	Net earnings ($)	P/E Multiple
Average	9.8	18,600,000	46,400,000	15,800,000	3	-400,000	8
Median	6	8,000,000	15,000,000	12,000,000	1	2,000,000	7
Highest	23	50,000,000	150,000,000	30,000,000	13	5,000,000	15
Lowest	5	4,000,000	12,000,000	10,000,000	1	-15,000,000	3
WorkHorse Projection	5	2,500,000		21,110,000		3,430,000	

	Age	Cumulative funding ($)	Valuation ($)	Revenue ($)	Revenue Multiple	Net earnings ($)	P/E Multiple
WorkHorse's projected exit value based on an average multiplier			73,392,433			27,440,000	
WorkHorse's projected exit value based on a median multiplier			28,146,667			24,010,000	

Brandon noted that three of the four projected exit values were close to each other, but that the one based on average revenues was much higher. He quickly dismissed it, as it was driven by the extremely high valuation of Noodles, a company with low revenues, negative net earnings, but very high valuation. With the other three valuations ranging between $24M and $28M, Brandon considered rounding to $25M a reasonable approximation. However, he remained slightly concerned that relative to the comparison group, WorkHorse was at the low end of the age range, at only five years. Moreover, with $2.5M of funding, it would have raised considerably less than the average (19M), the median ($8M), or even the lowest ($4M) of the comparison companies. While finding accurate Exit Comparables was not as easy as he had anticipated, Brandon was happy with his $25M estimate, as he felt it was both realistic and defendable.

5.5 Modeling Uncertainty

A drawback of the methods we examined so far is that they only consider the successful exit scenario. They compensate for this disadvantage with high discount rates that are somewhat arbitrary and not derived from an explicit analysis. This can be overcome by explicitly modeling the underlying uncertainty of the venture and the structure of risk. The required methods are more sophisticated and allow for a more accurate and detailed understanding of the venture's risks. The downside is increased complexity. It is also difficult to find credible assumptions, especially suitable probabilities for all the possible events.

We already provided in Box 5.2 a simple approach for including the probability of failure in the discount rate. We now examine three more comprehensive approaches. Scenario analysis allows building several alternative scenarios and assigns each of them a probability. Simulations generalize scenario analysis by using continuous probability distributions over possible outcomes. Finally, we introduce our own valuation model, called PROFEX, which directly models exit probabilities.

5.5.1 Scenario Analysis and Simulations

The idea of estimating alternative scenarios is common in corporate finance. In the context of entrepreneurial finance, this approach is sometimes called the "First Chicago" approach, from the name of the investment firm where it was allegedly developed. This approach is based on modeling a small set of situations that capture different potential outcomes. Each scenario is meant to represent a different path that the company might find itself on. Simple applications look at a small set of ranked outcomes, such as the good, the middle, and the bad. More advanced applications consider richer variations. For example, they might distinguish between a "small quick" versus a "big slow" exit scenario, or they might distinguish scenarios based on how many products the company launches, how many markets it enters, what the competition does, and so on.

Scenario analysis can be easily applied within the VCM, where one can take different exit values reflecting different business trajectories or consider different sequences of financing rounds. For the DCF method, scenarios allow comparison of different assumptions about the free cash flow and terminal value. We illustrate scenario analysis with an application within the VCM.

The first step in developing a scenario analysis is to identify the relevant scenarios and assign each a probability. These probabilities must sum up to one. Identifying credible scenarios is at the heart of the analysis. A common challenge is identifying a convincing distribution of probabilities across scenarios. For each scenario, one identifies the company's milestones and the related required investments. Each scenario ends with an exit, which can be successful or unsuccessful, and generates a discounted valuation. More successful scenarios should result in positive and attractive valuations, but less successful scenarios may have low valuations, possibly lower than the required investment. By weighing scenarios through their respective probability, the final step of the analysis is to calculate the expected valuation. This means multiplying each valuation with its probability weight. We index scenarios by s = 1 . . . S, and denote valuations by V, so that:

$$V = \sum_{s=1}^{s=S} p_s V_s \tag{5.10}$$

While scenario analysis focuses on a small number of distinct scenarios, simulations consider continuous probability distributions for a few key parameters related to the venture's business. These distributions can be derived from historical analysis of similar companies or can be built to directly reflect the investors' beliefs about the likelihood of different outcomes. In the simplest case, there is only one probability distribution, typically concerning revenues or earnings. However, the real insight comes from jointly modeling several variables, such as investments and earnings. Specialized software can be used to compute correlations among these variables. Simulations ultimately generate a distribution of exit values that can be used to find a company valuation. A widely used approach is the so-called Monte Carlo method.[21]

Scenario analysis and simulations share the notion of valuing companies by looking at probability distributions of outcomes. Scenario analysis is as credible as its ability to identify convincing alternative scenarios and a probability distribution across them. This is easier said than done, however. Simulations may appear superior as they look at richer continuous distributions of multiple value-relevant variables. However, they tend to be more limited in terms of modeling alternative company paths. Moreover, it is difficult to identify the appropriate continuous distributions for the underlying variables. WorkHorse Box 5.6 illustrates all this.

WorkHorse Box 5.6 WorkHorse's Scenario Analysis

After Michael Archie had explained that he normally applied a 50% discount rate to his investments, Astrid sought a clarification of whether she had heard correctly. When she inquired via e-mail ("We heard 50%, but surely you meant 15%"), Michael responded quickly: "50% b/c risky; stuff happens U know. CU MA." The founders agreed that "stuff happens" in a start-up; they lived that every day. Still, they were not happy with Michael's use of a 50% discount rate. Consequently, they decided to model the risk directly.

Astrid pondered the numerous possibilities and decided to map out four scenarios that she called the "quick win," the "home run," the "long slug," and "the flop." She used a 20% discount rate to reflect a reasonable cost of capital that accounted for the factors listed in equation (5.4), except that there was no survival risk premium. She accounted for survival risk separately by explicitly modeling the corresponding probabilities. All four scenarios started with an investment of .5M. The first three scenarios foresaw a second round of $2M in a year's time, at post-money valuation of $8M. This way founders and first-round investors would retain 75% of the equity.

Astrid's first scenario of a "quick win" foresaw an exit of $20M after four years, without the need to raise any additional funding. Under this scenario, the company basically planned to establish a market presence in the U.S., but then get acquired by a large incumbent for market expansion. Under the "home run" and "long slug" scenarios, the company would instead invest in market expansion itself. This would require a substantial additional investment of $12M. Astrid assumed a post-money valuation of $24M at that point, implying that the company would be parting with another 50% of the equity. The founders and first-round investors would therefore experience a total dilution of 37.5% (= 75% * 50%). Astrid recognized that such an expansion was risky, and she foresaw two possible outcomes. Under the "home run" scenario, the company would fetch a head-spinning exit value of $80M after seven years. Under the "long slug" scenario, things would be much slower. After seven years, there would be another financing round of $6M, and one year later, the company would be sold for $40M. Finally, she understood that success could not be taken for granted, so the fourth scenario was the "big flop," where the company would fail and be worth nothing.

When it came to assigning probabilities to these scenarios, Astrid reluctantly admitted that WorkHorse was still a very risky proposition overall. To reflect this uncertainty, she assigned a 60% probability to the "big flop" scenario. She didn't bother to specify the timing of failure because it didn't affect her calculations. The "home run" scenario received a 10% probability, and the other two scenarios received equal probabilities of 15%. Based on these assumptions, she made the following calculations:

	Quick win	Home run	Long slug	Big flop
Exit value ($)	20,000,000	80,000,000	40,000,000	0
Total dilution	75%	38%	30%	
Diluted exit value ($)	15,000,000	30,000,000	12,000,000	0
Years to exit	4	7	9	
Discount rate	20%	20%	20%	
Discount factor	2.1	3.6	5.2	
Discounted diluted exit value ($)	7,233,796	8,372,449	2,325,680	0
Scenario probability	15%	10%	15%	1
Probability-weighted value ($)	1,085,069	837,245	348,852	0
Expected value ($)				2,271,166

Astrid noted that the discounted diluted exit value, which measured the returns to the founders and the first-round investors, was highest for the "home run" scenario, followed by the "quick win," the "long slug," and the "big flop." She obtained the expected post-money valuation by adding up the probability-weighted valuations across all the scenarios. She calculated an expected post-money valuation of $2.2M, suggesting a pre-money valuation of $1.7M. This was actually lower than what Michael Archie had offered. She realized that doing scenario analysis opened up a new perspective, not only on the valuation but also the risks of business.

5.5.2   PROFEX

Let us now consider our own method called PROFEX, which stands for "PRobability OF Exit." It accounts for the structure of staged financing and extends the logic of the Venture Capital Method. It models the uncertainty of exit outcomes and recognizes the possibility of both success and failure.[22] Unlike the previous methods, the PROFEX model determines not only a valuation for the initial round, but also an internally consistent set of valuations for all possible future rounds.

Figure 5.1 illustrates the structure of the PROFEX method, which has an iterative structure where a company goes through a sequence of stages. The venture starts off by obtaining some investment. At each stage three outcomes are possible, each with its own probability: (1) the company has an exit, to which the model assigns a value; (2) the company fails, in which case the model assigns a liquidation value (possibly zero); and (3) the company continues, in which case it needs an additional investment round. A benefit of PROFEX is that the valuation in this second round is generated within the model itself. If the company takes the investment and continues, it will face the same three outcome possibilities at the next stage, each with its own probability. The model assigns a new exit value at each round to reflect the fact that the company is older and presumably more advanced and also assigns a new liquidation value. The model can be extended for an arbitrary number of financing rounds. The last stage must end with either exit or failure and thus specify a continuation probability of zero.

The PROFEX model is a generalization of the VC method, where the post-money valuation at each stage is the discounted expected value of the three next-round values: the exit value, the liquidation value, and the pre-money valuation at the next financing round, each multiplied by its respective probability. The calculation of a valuation at one stage requires knowing the valuation at the next stage. Consequently, the model is solved by calculating the valuation for the last round, and then working backwards until one obtains the valuation for the first round. The main outputs of the PROFEX model are pre- and post-money valuations for each round.

The accompanying spreadsheet, available on the book's website (www. entrepreneurialfinance.net), performs PROFEX valuations. One needs to define the maximum number of rounds and then provide the following inputs for each round: the time between rounds, the investment amount, the exit value, its associated

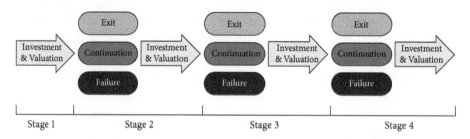

Figure 5.1. The PROFEX method.

probability, the liquidation value, its associated probability, and the discount rate. An important difference between PROFEX and the VCM is that PROFEX explicitly models outcome probabilities and therefore no longer requires the inflated discount rate discussed in Section 5.2.3. WorkHorse Box 5.7 illustrates how PROFEX works.

WorkHorse Box 5.7   WorkHorse's PROFEX

Brandon appreciated Astrid's calculations but didn't like the fact that it required making what looked to him like arbitrary assumptions about future valuations. In his opinion, a proper valuation model should calculate all valuations, not just the initial one. For this reason he built his own PROFEX model. This required adding more details about the timing of failure. Brandon considered the possibility of early and late failures. He assigned a 50% probability to an early failure. He thought that before entering the U. S., WorkHorse could fail in Sweden because of technology problems or lack of market acceptance. However, if the company succeeded in Sweden and entered the U.S., the remaining chance of failure would only be 20%. His total probability of failure was thus 60% (= 50% + 50%*20%), the same as Astrid's. For the rest, Brandon used the same assumptions as Astrid. The following table shows his PROFEX calculations.

PROFEX model	Round 1	Round 2	Round 3	Round 4	Round 5
Probability of exit (conditional)		0%	30%	40%	100%
Probability of refinancing (conditional)		50%	50%	60%	0%
Probability of liquidation (conditional)		50%	20%	0%	0%
Probability of reaching stage		100%	50%	25%	15%
Probability of exit (unconditional)		0%	15%	10%	15%
Probability of liquidation (unconditional)		50%	10%	0%	0%
Investment ($)	500,000	2,000,000	12,000,000	6,000,000	
Exit value ($)	0	0	20,000,000	80,000,000	40
Stage date (in years)	0	1	4	7	9
Time to next stage	1	3	3	2	0
Discount rate	20%	20%	20%	20%	20%

PROFEX model	Round 1	Round 2	Round 3	Round 4	Round 5
Discount factor	1.2	1.7	1.7	1.4	
Post-money valuation ($)	2,310,987	7,456,368	26,080,247	27,777,778	
Pre-money valuation ($)	1,810,987	5,546,368	14,080,247	21,777,778	

The key difference between Brandon's and Astrid's calculations were the valuations. To his surprise, the estimated post-money valuation of $2.31 was very similar, although the valuations at later stages were quite different. For example, he noted that the fourth round would have to be a down round, with a pre-money valuation of $21.78, compared to a post-money valuation of $26.08 in the round before. This reflected the fact that by then the dream of the home run would be over, so investors would adjust their expectations downward at this stage. This was the kind of insight that only a model like PROFEX could generate.

All three founders noted that modeling probabilities had generated some useful additional insights. Unfortunately, there was no telling how Michael Archie would respond to any of these calculations.

5.6 The Choice of Valuation Model

We now compare the different valuation methods in terms of their approaches, strengths, and weaknesses. The VCM is the most widely used valuation technique for start-ups. It takes the perspective of the investor's cash flows and generates a valuation of the company's equity. This method heavily depends on the estimate of the exit value, which is usually generated with the ECM. The VCM also requires some sensitive assumptions about the discount rate.

The DCF method takes the alternative perspective of analyzing the company's cash flow. It is the standard valuation method in corporate finance. However, the model is not particularly well suited to account for the uncertainty and unpredictability of entrepreneurial companies. Moreover, the DCF method is not set up for modeling staged investments. This method becomes more convincing for later-stage companies whose cash flows are more predictable.

The ECM uses market information from comparable companies to make inferences about the valuation of a focal company. This market-based approach is very different from the intrinsic valuation approach of the DCF method. It is based on a relative valuation approach that compares a focal company to a set of comparable companies. Identifying a meaningful comparison set and choosing a performance metric to derive the valuation can be problematic, especially for in-novative companies with an untested business model. The ICM is even simpler, di-rectly comparing a company's valuation to the valuations of comparable start-up companies at similar stages. This method is particularly useful for identifying re-alistic valuation ranges. However, it relies almost entirely on external information, which makes it difficult to pin down a specific valuation.

All of the methods that discount future returns to the present suffer from the problem of deciding on an appropriate discount rate. Of particular concern are the arbitrary discount rates used to account for the risk of failure. This is where probability-based models come in. They provide a conceptually more rigorous ap-proach for thinking about the risk of entrepreneurial ventures. However, they ne-cessitate assigning probabilities to these different scenarios, which is challenging in practice, especially for early-stage ventures.

One limitation shared by all valuation models is that they implicitly assume that all investors receive common equity. In Chapter 6 we explain that many venture investors own more sophisticated securities, such as preferred shares. These securi-ties give investors preferential cash flow rights under certain conditions. However, none of the valuation methods take these rights into account. We return to this topic in Chapter 7, which looks at the negotiation process where entrepreneurs and investors bring everything together into a final deal structure. Radicle, a con-sultancy, has developed an interesting statistical methodology to analyze venture valuations and venture funding more generally.[23]

We conclude that no valuation model emerges as being unequivocally superior. Instead, each method has its strengths and weaknesses. As a result, different models can be seen as complements rather than substitutes. If different methods all point toward the same range, one starts to have greater confidence. However, if different methods generate wildly different valuations, then there is an opportunity to dig deeper and find out what explains these differences.

Summary

This chapter examines valuation methods for entrepreneurial companies. We start by explaining why the valuation of new ventures is inherently difficult. We then introduce several valuation methods. The Venture Capital Method uses an in-vestor perspective and requires relatively few assumptions. The Discounted Cash Flow Method uses a company perspective and depends on many more detailed assumptions. There are some methods of comparables that use external data either at the investment or the exit stage. Finally, we introduce some probability-based valuation models that make explicit assumptions about the underlying uncertainty.

For each model we identify the underlying assumptions and discuss their strengths and weaknesses. Despite numerous challenges, performing a valuation is a useful exercise that allows entrepreneur and investor to identify what valuation ranges are reasonable.

In terms of the FIRE framework (Chapter 1), valuation is performed at the INVEST stage to negotiate a deal. However, since valuation methods are inherently forward-looking, they require the entrepreneur and investor to look ahead in the FIRE process. Specifically, they require estimates of the timing of future funding rounds, which occur at the RIDE step. Moreover, valuation models are driven by the exit value, which is obtained at the EXIT step. As such, the methods discussed are based on a forward-looking understanding of the dynamic process of how companies evolve over time and how investors finance them over time.

Review Questions

1. Why should entrepreneurs use a model to perform valuations? What about investors?
2. What are the main differences between the Venture Capital Method and the Discounted Cash Flow Method?
3. What assumptions are required to perform a Venture Capital Method valuation with multiple rounds?
4. Where does the required data for the Venture Capital Method come from?
5. Why does the Venture Capital Method use very high discount rates?
6. What is a terminal value? When is it credible?
7. What are the main pitfalls of using Investment Comparables?
8. What criteria should be used to choose an exit multiple?
9. What are the strengths and limitations of scenario analysis?
10. How is the PROFEX method related to the Venture Capital Method?

Notes

1. Mark Suster's post on his blog provides an interesting view of an investor's perspective: https://bothsidesofthetable.com/how-to-talk-about-valuation-when-a-vc-asks-7376f5721226, accessed April 15, 2019.
2. Lev (2000).
3. Gompers et al. (2019) provide evidence on what methods are more commonly used by venture capitalists.
4. See Chapters 2 and 4 in Damodaran (2018) for the conceptual differences between absolute (intrinsic) and relative valuation.
5. Gompers et al. (2019).
6. https://www.nobelprize.org/prizes/economic-sciences/1990/press-release.

7. Finance textbooks provide detailed accounts of how this model works. See, among others, Berk and DeMarzo (2016) and Brealey, Myers, and Allen (2016).

8. Graham and Harvey (2001).

9. Damodaran (2018), Chapter 9.

10. For an overview of the literature, see Section 5 in Da Rin, Hellmann, and Puri (2013).

11. For an introduction to liquidity risk, see Jorion (2010), Chapter 26. For studies of how liquidity risk affects asset prices, see Acharya and Pedersen (2005), and Franzoni, Nowak, and Phalippou (2012).

12. Puri and Zarutskie (2012).

13. Bottazzi, Da Rin, and Hellmann (2008).

14. Finance textbooks provide complete and rigorous treatments of DCF valuation at different levels. For introductory books, see Berk and DeMarzo (2016), and Brealey, Myers, and Allen (2016), among others. At a more advanced level, there are also numerous manuals that deal specifically with valuation. Among them, popular ones are Damodaran (2012), and Koller, Goedhart, and Wessels (2015). Metrick and Yasuda (2010b) examine the DCF method for high-growth companies.

15. Anshuman, Martin, and Titman (2012) develop a comparison of the VCM with the DCF model.

16. In the general case, the numerator is enterprise value, but since we assume the company is fully financed by equity, this become equity value. See Liu, Nissim, and Thomas (2002) for a discussion. In Chapter 10 we discuss the inclusion of debt in the valuation of an entrepreneurial company.

17. Lake (2018) and Wolf (2018).

18. Bhuiyan (2018).

19. https://www.letote.com/, https://mmlafleur.com/, https://www.bagborroworsteal.com, retrieved July 12, 2018.

20. Bhuiyan (2018).

21. Barreto and Howland (2005).

22. The details of the PROFEX valuation method can be found in Hellmann (2010).

23. The methodology is available at https://rad.report/data, accessed April 15, 2019.

6

Term Sheets

Learning Goals

In this chapter students will learn to:

1. Appreciate the role of the term sheet as a contract between entrepreneurs and investors.
2. Compute how preferred securities allocate cash flows to entrepreneurs and investors under different circumstances.
3. Evaluate the relative importance of valuation versus other contractual terms.
4. Use convertible notes in seed stage financing rounds.

This chapter examines how entrepreneurs and investors write term sheets that define their contractual rights and obligations. We first explain how term sheets help to address the underlying conflicts between these parties. We then explore in detail the structure of term sheets. We analyze how cash flows are allocated, how various types of preferred shares are used for this purpose, and how they can be made contingent on the performance of the company. We also look at the determination of management compensation and Employee Stock Option Plans. The chapter introduces control rights, rights that regulate future funding rounds, and investor rights related to the liquidity of their investment We identify a trade-off between terms and valuation that entrepreneurs face when negotiating a deal. The chapter concludes with an examination of convertible notes, an instrument commonly used in seed stage deals.

6.1 Term Sheet Fundamentals

6.1.1 The Role of Term Sheets

In this chapter we examine the purpose and structure of the financial contract between investors and entrepreneurs. At the time of making an offer, the investor drafts a preliminary contract, commonly known as a term sheet. This document consists of contractual clauses that lay out the rights and obligations of each party, specifying how these depend on a variety of future circumstances. Agreeing on a term sheet is a central part of negotiating a deal (see Chapter 7). Entrepreneurs are often intimidated by a term sheet. Although the complexity and language of term sheets may appear daunting, we now show that the rationale of term sheet clauses is often simple.

Term sheets are shaped by the conflicts of interests that arise between entrepreneurs and investors over the course of the venture. There is always high uncertainty about a company's future, which calls for contractual flexibility. However, entrepreneurs and investors cannot conceivably specify all the possible contingencies that might become relevant in the future. Instead, they identify a limited set of possible future circumstances, and then they define how future decisions will be made under these alternative circumstances. These circumstances are identified through salient events called milestones that characterize the venture's progress.

Term sheets play several roles in the relationship between investors and entrepreneurs. First, they govern the rights and duties of each party. Second, they shape the incentives for all parties. Well-crafted term sheets align the interests of entrepreneurs to those of investors and reduce future conflicts. They provide entrepreneurial incentives to build large and profitable businesses, while at the same time encouraging investors to contribute to the entrepreneurial value creation process. Third, the process of formulating a term sheet brings the parties to clarify their expectations about the relationship they are about to enter. Fourth, term sheets allocate risk across the parties and therefore shape their respective risk/reward profiles. Fifth, they specify how the entrepreneurs and the investors interface with certain external parties, most notably key employees and future investors. Term sheets have clauses about future funding rounds and about how they may affect the current allocations between entrepreneurs and investors.

We noted in Section 4.3.2 that economic forces such as the quality of the venture opportunity, the market environment, the competition for the deal, or the investor quality all affected valuations. The same is true for term sheets. Take competition: if an entrepreneur is negotiating with a single investor, that investor can impose investor-friendly terms. There is relatively little that the entrepreneur can do, other than walk away from the deal. Things can change dramatically when there are competing term sheets. Now the entrepreneurs can refuse unreasonable demands by pointing to the other term sheet. A similar dynamic applies to market conditions. In down markets investors can dictate tougher terms, but in up markets investors chase hot deals and frequently waive those terms.

A term sheet is typically less than a dozen pages long. The agreed upon terms then get converted into a set of final legal documents, which typically includes the corporate charter, investor rights agreement, and stock purchase agreement, and may include employment agreements among other documents.[1] These final documents can easily reach hundreds of pages, and both parties use legal experts for drafting them. These final documents reflect mutually agreeable investment conditions that give both the investors and the entrepreneurs enough protection and enough financial incentives to be willing to accept the risks involved in the deal.

Term sheets tend to be drafted by experienced lawyers who develop standard templates, and only adjust a limited number of clauses to the specific conditions of each deal. Given the uncertainty facing a venture, term sheets cannot provide an exhaustive guide on how the parties will behave in each situation, but rather the legal foundation to the formation of a relationship that will evolve over time. Term sheets are also shaped by national laws and by norms that vary across geographies. While this generates some variation in contract structures across time and space, the fundamental economic forces that we discuss here apply broadly across the globe.[2]

WorkHorse Box 6.1 continues our (fictional) case study from the previous chapter.

WorkHorse Box 6.1 Wolf C. Flow's Term Sheet Proposal

Late in December 2020, snow fell over the University of Michigan campus. Most students had left the campus for the holidays, but not Astrid Dala, Brandon Potro, Bharat Marwari, and Annie Ma. WorkHorse, the company they had founded in 2019, had already come a long way. It had developed a new lightweight solar power generator for the consumer market, focusing mostly on hikers and campers. The company started with the help of an $80K investment from JP Potro, Brandon's uncle. In early 2020, WorkHorse raised $500K in a seed round from angel investors, led by Michael Archie. The company had developed its first product, the WonderFoal. It secured a retail agreement with PortageLake, a Michigan-based nationwide retailer of outdoor leisure goods. The plan was to first sell the WonderFoal in select stores in Michigan. Provided the initial sales were satisfactory, a nationwide rollout would follow.

Michael Archie contacted several venture capitalists (VCs) to gauge their interest to finance the next round of financing. In venture parlance, this would be an "A round," that is, the first professional venture capital (VC) round. Astrid and Brandon were initially leary of meeting all these VCs; they expected them to be stuffy and even a bit scary. They were pleasantly surprised meeting Ali Ad-Lehr, a partner at Eagle-I Ventures. He opened by saying "Hi, I am Ali, but you can call me Al." Somehow the "Al" never stuck, but they quickly built a relationship with Ali, who agreed to lead a round on two conditions. First, he asked Michael Archie to "put his money where his mouth is" and co-invest in the deal. Second, he said he needed to bring in one other venture firm. Soon after they met with Wolf C. Flow, a senior partner at Coyo-T Capital. This meeting was far less congenial, Wolf didn't smile even once. With the promise of closing the round, however, the founders were willing to put their personal feelings aside.

On Friday December 18, 2020, WorkHorse received an e-mail from Wolf C. Flow with a draft term sheet from Coyo-T Capital, Eagle-I Ventures, and Michael Archie. In his e-mail, Wolf noted that this term sheet was "plain vanilla." The four founders, however, were a little taken aback. The document was full of complicated legal terms that they couldn't understand. Glancing over it, however, Astrid and Brando did not get a pleasant smell of vanilla; instead they got the smell of a rat.

Needing help with the term sheet, Brandon decided to consult with Victoria Regalsworth. She had worked as a corporate lawyer in London and San Francisco prior to doing her MBA at the University of Michigan. Brandon happened to sit next to her on their very first day of class.

The final version of the term sheet is available on the book's website (www. entrepreneurialfinance.net). We discuss the negotiation process in Chapter 7. We will clearly note where Wolf C. Flow's original proposal differs from the final version.

6.1.2 Contingent Contracting and Milestones

Term sheets regulate the rights and the duties of the entrepreneurs and the investors under conditions of high uncertainty. The uncertainty of the venture's prospects compounds the natural impossibility for a contract to cover all possible future situations. Contracts are therefore "incomplete" in the sense that they can never account for the complete set of possible future events. This limitation is addressed through "contingent contracting," where clauses apply only under certain defined circumstances ("contingencies"). This dramatically reduces the set of circumstances that needs to be addressed and makes the contract an effective governance tool.[3]

To define contingencies, term sheets condition clauses on certain events called milestones (Section 3.3). These events measure the progress of the venture, distinguishing when it conforms with, or falls short of, the expectations set in the contract. In practice, the most frequent contingent clauses pertain to the allocation of cash flow rights (e.g., the entrepreneur gets a certain number of shares if the milestone is met; otherwise the investor gets them) and the allocation of control rights (e.g., the investor gets to appoint a new CEO if a specific milestone is not met).

Milestones can be defined over a wide variety of performance metrics: financial (e.g., sales target), operational (e.g., development of functional prototype), or managerial (e.g., hiring of CFO).[4] An example of contingent contracting might be as follows: "The investor has the right to nominate two out of five directors. If within 12 months of closing the company fails to generate sales in excess of $1M, the investor has the right to nominate two additional directors." Box 6.1 provides some examples of contractual milestones for a variety of performance metrics.

Box 6.1 Contractual Milestone Examples

We provide some examples of the types of milestones used in contingent contracting, distinguishing between different types of milestones. In the rest of the chapter, we show how various clauses in term sheets use milestones to condition a variety of contractual clauses.

Milestone type:		Examples			
Financial:	Revenues	EBIT or Net income	Operating cash flow	Financial ratios (e.g., gross margin)	Intangible assets
Operational:	Supply agreement signed	Opening of foreign subsidiary	Regulatory approval for the product	Net working capital level	HR system implemented
Technical:	Development of working prototype	New functionality achieved	License or patent acquisition	Integration of new technology	Drug passing a clinical trial
Commercial:	Distribution agreement signed	Corporate customer commitment	Number of early adopters	Sales volume	Customer renewals
Managerial:	Hiring of new CEO	Hiring of senior managers (e.g. CFO)	Retention of key executive(s)	Agreement on independent director(s)	Formalize board of advisers

Milestones are the main method for implementing contingent contracting structures. In addition, the process of staging financing over several rounds automatically makes financing contingent on achieving milestones, as each company must prove itself afresh at each round (Section 9.1). Milestones therefore provide strong incentives to reach certain mutually agreed performance targets and help entrepreneurs focus on specific deliverables. Setting a milestone can also be a practical solution to valuation disagreements between entrepreneurs and investors. One may argue that if an entrepreneur's projections prove to be too optimistic, then the investors should get more shares. Rather than fighting over a valuation, the two parties may find it easier to agree on a milestone-based valuation: the entrepreneur agrees because she truly believes she can achieve the milestone, and the investor agrees because he gets the protection that he cares about if the milestone is not met.

Specifying milestones can also create its own problems. By specifying a performance target, the entrepreneur has an incentive to hit it, regardless of the long-term benefit to the company. A sales target, for example, may push an entrepreneur to rush an unfinished product to market, potentially harming the reputation of the company. Milestones may also interfere with strategic changes (or pivots) required in the entrepreneurial process, such as altering the product offering, or targeting different customer segments (see Box 1.1). For example, a start-up may have a sales target based on a business model that relies on product sales. If the entrepreneur discovers that a licensing model is more profitable in the long run, she may turn down such opportunity because lower short-term revenues from this new model would imply missing the milestone. Naturally, in such cases the entrepreneur may ask to renegotiate the milestone, but this too has its own costs and difficulties. An additional issue with milestones is that sometimes it is difficult to objectively assess whether a milestone has been met. For example, the requirement of building a "functional prototype" can be interpreted in different ways. Milestones therefore require trust between the two parties, so that a shared interpretation of the milestone applies, rather than a purely legal definition (Section 7.6.1).

To gain a perspective on the complexity of term sheets, and the challenges of structuring them, Box 6.2 takes a brief look at some insights from another Nobel laureate.

Box 6.2 Nobel Insights on Incomplete Contracts

The 2016 Nobel Prize in Economics was shared by Oliver Hart and Bengt Holmström, "for their contributions to contract theory." We discuss Holmström's contribution in Box 4.1, so here we turn our attention to Hart's contribution.[5]

Hart's fundamental quest is to understand the incompleteness of contracts. Legal contracts may seem daunting at first, but once one becomes familiar with their language and logic, the real question is not why they are so complex, but why in fact they are still so incomplete. Put differently, the number of things that can go wrong is orders of magnitudes larger than the number of things that contracts can anticipate. Hart therefore seeks to understand how contractual arrangements deal with the unforeseen, and how they compensate for their inability to account for all contingencies. He applies these insights to a large variety of economic problems, including whether companies should merge or whether governments should privatize certain activities. Of interest to us is the application of his theories to corporate finance.

Hart's work can explain how entrepreneurs and investors deal with contract incompleteness. He distinguishes between contract clauses that deal with verifiable actions (e.g., rules about how liquidation proceeds are to be distributed) from clauses that allocate decision rights (e.g., rules about when the investors can decide whether or not to liquidate). The former type of clauses requires a precise definition of the verifiable circumstances under which the action must be taken, whereas the latter only requires specifying who is to take certain decisions. It follows that the initial allocation of decision rights is very important. Hart's work, for example, explains why it may be optimal to leave control with entrepreneurs as long as a venture is performing well, but shifting control to investors when venture performance declines. Such control structures can be implemented with a variety of control clauses that are commonly found in VCs term sheets.

Another fundamental insight from Hart's work is the importance of renegotiation. Even if contracts specify certain actions in advance, the parties involved can always change their minds when circumstances change. To fully appreciate the role of contracts, it is important to understand the dynamics of renegotiations. The initial contract sets the ground rules about how future renegotiations are to be conducted.

Overall, Hart's work helps us understand how entrepreneurs and investors write contracts in the face of high complexity and uncertainty. Instead of contractually specifying what to do under all conceivable scenarios, they create governance structures that handle situations if and when unexpected problems arise.

6.1.3 Overview of Terms

Term sheets legislate many aspects of the interactions between entrepreneurs and investors.

The term sheet defines share ownership, and therefore the allocation of cash flows from the venture. Our discussion builds on Chapter 4 but goes further. Section 6.2 looks at preferred shares, which are complex securities frequently used in venture funding.

Section 6.3 builds on the analysis of Section 4.4 about founder agreements. Term sheets address aspects of the compensation structure of founders, managers, and employees. Section 6.3 also looks at how investors structure founder agreements and Employee Stock Option Plans.

Section 6.4 establishes the contractual foundations of several important issues, which we examine in more detail in the context of later chapters. One central issue is the allocation of control rights, which determines who controls decisions in the company. Section 6.4.1 briefly explains the rationale for allocation of control rights, including voting rights and board seats. We then further pursue this topic in the context of Chapter 8. As ventures progress in time, the terms that facilitate future fundraising become more important. In Section 6.4.2, we explain how term sheets address these issues. This provides the foundation for Chapter 9 where we look at the broader issue of staged financing. From the point of view of investors, it is important to secure a pathway to obtain liquidity from the investment. In Section 6.4.3, we introduce liquidation rights, laying the foundations for the topic of exit, which is fully discussed in Chapter 11.

Section 6.5 builds on the valuation discussion of Chapter 5 and asks how investors and entrepreneurs can trade off valuation against terms. This section describes several economic trade-offs involved in the design of term sheets. We continue this discussion when we consider how to negotiate deals in Chapter 7.

In Section 6.6, we note that seed stage investors often prefer a simpler approach. They invest using a convertible note that only requires a few terms and specifies no valuation.

6.2 Cash Flow Rights

In Chapters 4 and 5 we assumed that companies issue shares of common stock to their investors. We now broaden this perspective and look at shares of convertible preferred stock, which are the most common financial security used in VC deals. For simplicity, we sometimes refer to shares of common stock as "common shares" and to shares of convertible preferred stock as "preferred shares."

Many start-ups issue both types of shares. Common shares are held by founders, senior managers, employees, and possibly some third parties (Section 4.1.3). Investors, instead, often receive preferred shares that give them privileged cash flow rights over common shareholders. In this section, we explain how preferred shares allocate cash flow rights, why investors get them, and what this implies for entrepreneurs.

Table 6.1 summarizes the notation used throughout this chapter.

Table 6.1 Notation for Term Sheets

Symbol	Meaning
CF_{EN}	Cash flow to entrepreneurs
CF_{INV}	Cash flow to investors
CT	Conversion threshold
D	Dividend rate
DIS	Price discount for convertible notes
DIV	Dividends accruing to the investor
F_{CN}	Ownership fraction of convertible note holders
F_{INV}	Ownership fraction of new investors
F_{PRE}	Ownership fraction of pre-investment shareholders
I	Investment amount
I_{CN}	Investment amount by convertible note holders
M	Multiple liquidation factor
P	Price per share
P_{CN}	Conversion rate for convertible notes
P_{INV}	Price per share at Series A round
PT	Preferred terms
S_{CN}	Number of shares issued to convertible note holders
S_{INV}	Number of shares issued to the Series A investors
S_{PRE}	Number of shares of pre-investment shareholders
V_{PRE}	Pre-money valuation
V_{CAP}	Capped pre-money valuation
X	Exit value

6.2.1 Convertible Preferred Stock

The main financial security used with entrepreneurial companies is frequently referred to as "convertible preferred shares." This phrase often gets abbreviated as "convertible preferred" or just "preferred." The name of this security reflects its "preferred" status over common stock. This gives preferential access to cash flows in case of liquidation. It may also entitle preferential redemption, where the investors can ask the company to buy back their shares.

A central aspect of convertible preferred shares is that they give the investor the right to choose between receiving a debt-like payoff or an equity-like payoff. This choice is typically made at the time of exit, that is, when the company is listed on a stock exchange, acquired, or wound up. When all shareholders hold common shares, they get a proportional share of the company value at exit, so that an investor who owns a 20% stake in the company is entitled to 20% of the exit proceeds. Holders of preferred shares, however, receive additional cash flow rights that depend on both the type of exit and the exit value. These rights can be quite powerful: A 20% stake in the company may in some cases entitle the investor to 100% of the exit proceeds, typically in the case of unsuccessful exit outcomes.

To understand how convertible preferred shares allocate cash flow rights, we first consider an exit via liquidation, which includes mergers, acquisitions, or closing of the company. Convertible preferred shares give the investor a choice: the investor retains the preferred shares and obtains a debt-like "preferred return" (or "preferred terms"), or converts the preferred shares into common shares.

PT is the value of the preferred terms; I is the value of the investment; and DIV is the value of the dividends accruing to the investor. Because start-ups typically remain cash flow negative for a long time, dividends accrue over time but are not paid out until exit. In case of no conversion, the payoff to the preferred shares is equal to the investor's original investment plus any dividends:

$$PT = I + DIV \qquad (6.1)$$

Dividends accumulate on the basis of a formula that is specified in the term sheet. To compute the dividends, let T be the time to exit and D the dividend rate. Dividends are often cumulative, so that they accumulate a simple noncompounded interest payment of $D{*}I$ each year, yielding total accrued dividends of:

$$DIV = D * I * T \qquad (6.2)$$

The preferred terms PT have a "debt-like" structure because the face value of the investor's claim is fixed, in the sense that it does not depend on the exit value. At the same time, the delay in paying dividends makes the preferred terms distinct from debt.

We now show how preferred stock allocates cash flows between the investor and entrepreneur in case of conversion. In this case, the value of the investor' shares in convertible preferred stock is given by the corresponding value of common equity. We know from Section 4.2.2 that the ownership fraction percentage of common equity corresponding to the investment is given by F_{INV}. For simplicity, we assume there is only one investor holding convertible preferred stock and one entrepreneur holding common equity. We denote the investor's and entrepreneur's cash flow rights with, respectively, CF_{INV} and CF_{EN}. We define the conversion threshold (CT) as the company's exit value at which the investor is indifferent between converting (thus obtaining $F_{INV} * CT$) and not converting (thus obtaining PT). Equating these two amounts, we get the value of the conversion threshold:

$$CT = \frac{PT}{F_{INV}} \tag{6.3}$$

Figure 6.1 illustrates the investor's cash flow rights with convertible preferred stock. The horizontal axis represents the exit value X, and the vertical axis represents CF_{INV}. The 45° line represents the total available cash flow X. Since $CF_{INV} + CF_{EN} = X$, the area between the 45° line and the bold curve represents the cash flow to the entrepreneur, that is, $CF_{EN} = X - CF_{INV}$.

Figure 6.1 identifies three distinct regions. These are also described in the first column of Table 6.2, which shows the corresponding values of CF_{EN} and CF_{INV}. In the first region from the left, the exit value falls below the face value of the preferred terms (X < PT). The investor gets all of the cash flows ($CF_{INV} = X$), as shown by the

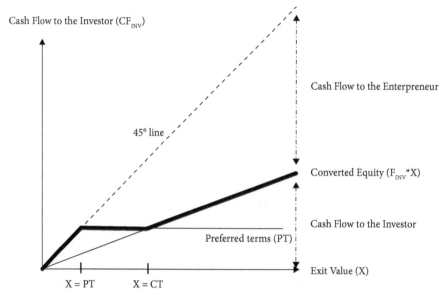

Figure 6.1. Convertible preferred stock.

Table 6.2 Cash flow rights with convertible preferred stock.

Exit value	Cash flow to investors (CF_{INV})	Cash flow to entrepreneurs (CF_{EN})
Small: X < PT	X	0
Intermediate: PT < X < CT	PT	X – PT
Large: X > CT	F_{INV} * X	$(1 - F_{INV})$ * X

bold stretch of the 45° line. The entrepreneur is protected by limited liability but walks away empty-handed ($CF_{EN} = 0$). In the middle region, the exit value is above the preferred terms (X > PT) but below the conversion threshold (X < CT). The investor prefers not to convert his shares but instead takes the preferred return (PT). This corresponds to the flat middle stretch of the bold curve. Finally, when the exit value lies above the conversion threshold (X > CT), the investor converts his stock into common equity. After conversion, both the investor and entrepreneur hold shares in common equity and split the proceeds in proportion to their ownership stakes ($CF_{INV} = F_{INV}$*X and $CF_{EN} = (1\ F_{INV})$*X). This corresponds to the upward-sloping segment of the bold line on the right of Figure 6.1.

For ease of interpretation, Figure 6.2 shows the entrepreneurs' cash flow with convertible preferred stock, which in Figure 6.1 is represented by the distance between the 45° line and the investor's cash flow.

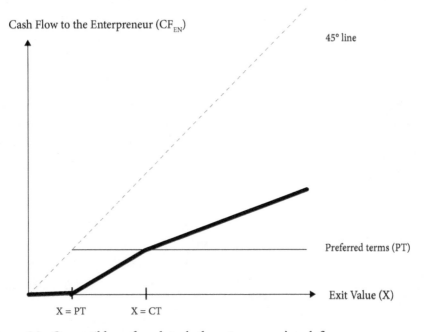

Figure 6.2. Convertible preferred stock: the entrepreneur's cash flow.

In case of an IPO, term sheets typically include an automatic conversion clause for convertible preferred stock, which applies, provided the offer is sufficiently large and the issue price is high enough. This "qualified IPO" condition effectively ensures that the exit value is above CT. Cash flows are then given by $CF_{INV} = F_{INV} *X$ and $CF_{EN} = (1-F_{INV})*X$. This corresponds to the bold increasing line to the left of CT in Figure 6.1. WorkHorse Box 6.2 illustrates how convertible preferred stock works in practice.

WorkHorse Box 6.2 Convertible Preferred Stock

The first thing Astrid checked was the valuation. She was happy to see that the offer involved an investment of I = $2M at a post-money valuation of V_{POST} = $8M, implying that the investors obtain F_{INV} = 25% of the company. The term sheet mentioned S_{PRE} = 1.25M common shares (including stock options), and specified S_{INV} = 416,667 preferred stock for investors, priced at P = $4.80 per share. This structure (conveniently) corresponded to the structure they had projected one year earlier, shown in WorkHorse Box 4.5.

On the assumption that investors wanted standard convertible preferred stock, Astrid proceeded to calculate the value of the preferred terms. The term sheet featured a dividend rate of $D = 8\%$. To keep things simple, Astrid abstracted away any follow-on rounds of financing and looked at what would happen if WorkHorse would get acquired one year later. In that case, she calculated total dividends of DIV = $160K (i.e., 8% of the $2M investment), and therefore preferred terms of PT = $2.16M (i.e., investment plus total dividends).

With this information, Astrid computed the returns to preferred and common shares for a variety of exit values. She noted that the conversion threshold was given by CT = PT / F_{INV} = $2.16M / 0.25 = $8.64K. She tabulated her results as follows:

Exit value ($M)	Preferred terms ($M)	Equity value upon conversion ($M)	Conversion attractive?	Cash flows to preferred shares ($M)	Cash flows to common shares ($M)	Ownership fraction of preferred shares
1.00	1.00	0.25	No	1.00	0.00	100%
3.00	2.16	0.75	No	2.16	0.84	72%
8.00	2.16	2.00	No	2.16	5.84	27%
8.64	2.16	2.16	Same	2.16	6.48	25%
9.00	2.16	2.25	Yes	2.25	6.75	25%
10.0	2.16	2.05	Yes	2.05	7.05	25%

Another component of cash flow rights is the liquidation preference. Preferred terms may also include a "multiple liquidation preference." This means that the investors can get their investment back multiple times. Typical factors range from 1.5 to 3 and vary depending on market circumstances. A survey of Silicon Valley investments estimates that 11% of deals involve multiple liquidation preference: 20% of those are above 2x, where x indicates the invested amount, and the remainder are between 1x and 2x.[6]

Let M be the multiple liquidation preference factor. The face value of the preferred terms with multiple liquidation preference is given by:

$$PT_M = M * I + DIV \tag{6.4}$$

Multiple liquidation preferences provide a way for investors to protect their money. Figure 6.3 extends Figure 6.1 and shows how a multiple liquidation preference increases the investor's cash flow claims. The increase occurs for intermediate exit values between X = PT and X = CT_M (= PT_M / F_{INV}). Correspondingly, the values of CF_{INV} and CF_{EN} are as those in Table 6.2 with PT_M instead of PT and with CT_M instead of CT.

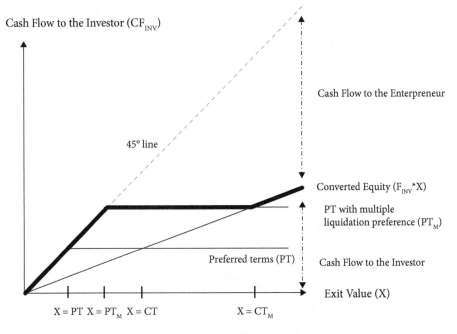

Figure 6.3. Preferred stock with multiple liquidation preferences.

6.2.2 Participating Preferred Stock

A different way to provide investors with stronger downside protection is to use participating preferred stock. Whereas convertible preferred stock represents a *choice* between a debt-like and an equity-like security, participating preferred stock represents a *combination* of the two. In case of an acquisition or a liquidation, the participating preferred stock entitles the investor to two sets of cash flows. First, the investor gets the preferred terms. Second, the investor also gets his share of any remaining proceeds. That is why participating preferred stock is referred to as a "double dip." In case of a qualified IPO, participating preferred stock automatically converts into common equity, as in the case of convertible preferred. There is no "double dip" in successful IPOs. According to a VC survey by Gompers, Gornall, Kaplan, and Strebulaev, a little over half of all deals use participating preferred stock.[7]

Since the investor always receives PT and does not choose whether or not to convert, we now only need to distinguish two ranges of exit value: small (X < PT) and large (X > PT). Figure 6.4 illustrates the returns graphically, and Table 6.3 reports their expressions.

In Figure 6.4 there are two relevant regions. For low exit values (X < PT), there is not enough money to pay the preferred terms. Therefore, the investor receives the whole exit value, as shown by the bold part of the line starting from the origin. For X > PT, the investor receives the double dip. His payoff includes the ownership share ($F_{INV} * (X - PT)$) as well as the preferred terms (PT). It is therefore higher than with convertible preferred stock. This can also be seen by comparing Tables 6.2 and 6.3.

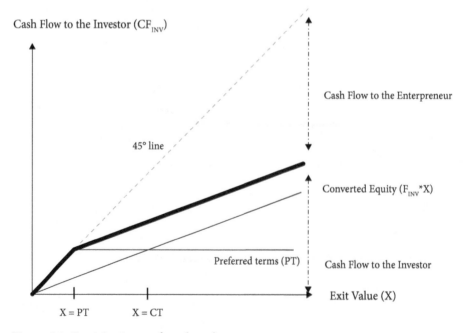

Figure 6.4. Participating preferred stock.

Table 6.3 Cash flow rights with participating preferred stock.

Exit value	Cash flow to investors (CF_{INV})	Cash flow to entrepreneurs (CF_{EN})
Small: X < PT	X	0
Large: X > PT	$PT + F_{INV} * (X–PT)$	$(1– F_{INV}) * (X–PT)$

Participating preferred stock can materially reduce the entrepreneur's cash flow rights. For this, it often has a cap on the range where the participating preferred terms are valid. For high exit values there is automatic conversion to common stock, which implies that the investor forfeits the preferred terms. Consider first the simplest possible cap, denoted by X^{CAP}, such that the investor's claim corresponds to preferred shares below the cap ($X < X^{CAP}$) but is automatically converted into common shares above the cap ($X > X^{CAP}$). Such an arrangement would lead to a discrete drop in the investor's cash flow at the cap. This could become problematic if the company ends up with an exit value close to X^{CAP}. While the entrepreneur might try all sorts of things to push the valuation above the cap, the investor would actually have an economic interest to lower exit value. This blatant conflict about the valuation can be avoided by smoothing out the payouts around the cap. This is shown with the solid bold line in Figure 6.5, which displays the cash flows to the investors.

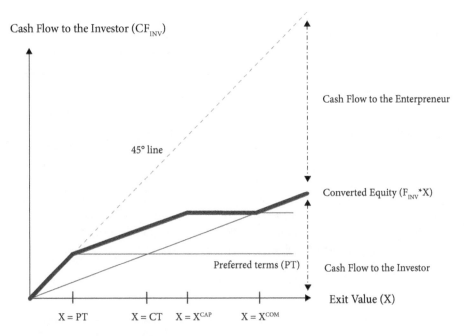

Figure 6.5. Participating preferred stock with a cap.

To explain more formally the cash flows around the valuation cap, Table 6.4 provides the underlying formulas. For exit values above the cap ($X > X^{CAP}$), the investor gets either his preferred terms held constant at the capped valuation ($PT + F_{INV} * (X^{CAP} – PT)$) or the common terms at the actual valuation ($F_{INV} * X$),

Table 6.4 Cash flow rights with participating preferred stock with a cap.

Exit value	Cash flow to investors (CF_{INV})	Cash flow to entrepreneurs (CF_{EN})
Small: X < PT	X	0
Below cap: PT < X < X^{CAP}	$PT + F_{INV} * (X-PT)$	$(1 - F_{INV}) * (X-PT)$
Just above cap: $X^{CAP} < X < X^{COM}$	$PT + F_{INV} * (X^{CAP}-PT)$	$X - F_{INV} * X^{CAP} - (1-F_{INV}) * PT$
Far above cap: $X^{COM} < X$	$F_{INV} * X$	$(1 - F_{INV}) * X$

whichever is higher. Consequently, there exists a full conversion threshold, called X^{COM} (the subscript COM stands for common shares), such that for all exit values between X^{CAP} and X^{COM}, the investor gets the preferred terms at the capped valuation, and for all exit values above X^{COM}, the investor's shares get converted into common stock.[8] The formula for X^{COM} is given by $X^{COM} = X^{CAP} + PT \dfrac{(1-F_{INV})}{F_{INV}}$.

We further illustrate these formulas in WorkHorse Box 6.3.

WorkHorse Box 6.3 Participating Preferred Stock

Victoria Regalsworth was the first to note that Wolf C. Flow had not asked for convertible, but for participating preferred stock, with a cap at $20M. Astrid therefore revised her calculations from WorkHorse Box 6.2 to take into account the additional cash flow rights of the participating feature. She used the cap of X^{CAP} = $20M and calculated a full conversion threshold X^{COM} = $26.48M. She tabulated her results as follows:

Exit value ($M)	Preferred terms (PT) ($M)	Equity value after preferred terms (X–PT) ($M)	Investor share of equity value (F*(X–PT)) ($M)	Investor cash flow to preferred shares ($M)	Cash flows to common shares ($M)	Ownership fraction of preferred shares	Explanation
1.00	1.00	0.00	0.00	1.00	0.00	100%	PT only
3.00	2.16	0.84	0.21	2.37	0.63	79%	Double dip
5.00	2.16	2.84	0.71	2.87	2.13	57%	Double dip
10.0	2.16	7.84	1.96	4,12	5.88	41%	Double dip
20.0	2.16	17.84	4.46	6.62	13.38	33%	At Cap
25.0	2.16	17.84	4.46	6.62	18.38	26%	Cap binding
30.0	0.00	30.0	7.05	7.05	22.05	25%	Common

The four founders were slightly taken aback. The valuation seemed attractive at first, as they only had to give up 25%. However, with the participating preferred shares, the investors would get 41% from a $10M acquisition. Feeling slightly upset with the double-dip, the founders decided to ask for convertible shares instead of participating preferred shares.

6.2.3 Reasons for Using Preferred Stock

If preferred stock gives investors additional cash flow rights, why do entrepreneurs accept these apparently harsh terms? Doubtlessly, opportunism can be at work here: Investors are familiar with drafting complex financial contracts, and inexperienced entrepreneurs may accept unfavorable terms that they don't fully understand. However, these terms are regularly accepted by sophisticated entrepreneurs who fully understand them and persist over time. There must be some economic reasons for using them, so let's examine them.

The salient feature of all types of preferred stock is that they afford the investor more downside protection than common stock. If the venture succeeds and fetches a high exit value, then the preferred stock converts to common equity, giving the investor and the entrepreneur proportional stakes. This allows them to share the value that has been created. However, if the venture does not perform well, the preferred stock gives the investor all or most of the returns. We identify three leading rationales for why cash flow rights are structured in this way.

6.2.3.(a) Providing Entrepreneurial Incentives

Preferred stock is conducive to unleashing entrepreneurial incentives. In Figure 6.1, the entrepreneur receives nothing when the exit value is below the preferred terms (X < PT). All her returns occur in the success region (X > PT). This payoff structure clearly encourages the entrepreneur to work hard and to remain focused on generating high financial returns.

Preferred stock also encourages risk-taking. Figure 6.2 shows that the entrepreneur's return function is convex; that is, payoffs increase more than proportionally as X increases. This is similar to the return structure of a call option. Downside protection for the investor leads the entrepreneur to choose higher-risk/higher-return strategies as sought by investors (see Section 12.3.4 for VC firms). In fact, preferred stock, through downside protection, shifts part of the financial risk from the investor to the entrepreneur. This can be good or bad for the company. On the positive side, success in entrepreneurial ventures requires exploring new directions that involve significant risk. On the negative side, excessive risk-taking may occur if the entrepreneur decides to take on overly risky strategies should the company fall short of expectations. In addition to setting high-powered financial incentives, investors also ask for control rights in order to prevent any excessive risk-taking.

6.2.3(b) Screening out Poor Projects

The use of preferred stock helps investors to screen out unsuitable investment projects. This is related to the problems of asymmetric information and the "lemons" issue we discuss in Box 2.6. Entrepreneurs might know more about their own business, talents, and intentions than the investors. Consider two entrepreneurs both of whom are looking to raise money from an investor. One entrepreneur has a business opportunity with a legitimate chance of generating high returns. The other claims the same, but in reality, knows that her business only has limited upside potential. The latter type would be unwilling to accept a preferred share offer, knowing she has no chance to earn anything from it. Thus, by affording downside protection to investors, preferred stock makes funding unattractive to weaker projects. This leads to self-selection, where only better, or more confident, entrepreneurs are willing to accept funding through preferred stock. From an investor perspective, such self-selection is very useful. Even if the investor cannot tell the two entrepreneurs apart, the use of preferred stock attracts only the more desirable type of entrepreneur. Box 6.3 illustrates this point with a numerical example.

Box 6.3 Self-Selection with Preferred Stock

Once there were two entrepreneurs, Pierrette Parfaite and Michelle Mabelle. Pierrette had a solid venture that would generate an expected €100M at exit. Michelle had a venture that looked just as promising on the surface, although she privately knew that it would only generate an exit value of €60M. Both ventures required a €20M investment and would take five years to exit. The twist was that there was "asymmetric information" so that only Pierrette and Michelle knew their exit values; no one else did. That is, to investors they looked like identical twins, although in reality they weren't.

Michael Mindless was a simple-minded investor who always used common equity. As he could not distinguish the two types of ventures, he considered them equally likely. He offered to invest €20M for a 60% ownership stake in common equity, implying a post-money valuation of €33.33M.

Peter Prefstock was a lot cleverer. Although he could not distinguish the two types of ventures either, he read an excellent book on entrepreneurial finance (actually the one you are reading right now) that explained how to use preferred stock. He offered to invest €20M of convertible preferred stock for a 30% ownership stake, implying a much more generous post-money valuation of €66.67M. The dividends were computed according to equation (6.2) on a 10% annual yield over five years, implying total dividends of €10M (= 0.1*5*€20M). The preferred terms corresponding to equation (6.1) thus amounted to €30M (= €20M + €10M).

The table below shows the exit values for the two investors (Peter and Michael), depending on which entrepreneur they financed (Pierrette or Michelle). Michael's exit values are based on common shares. At exit he either gets €60M (= 60%*€100M) with Pierrette or €36M (60%*€60M) with Michelle. Peter's exit values are based on convertible preferred stock. With Pierrette, he gets €51M (= €30M + 30%*(€100M – €30M)). With Michelle, he gets €39M (= €30M + 30%*(€60M – €30M)).

As they looked like identical twins, the investors couldn't distinguish the better (Pierrette) from the worse (Michelle) venture. Michael naïvely assumed that each investor had the same chance of attracting Pierrette or Michelle. In Michael's mind, his expected exit value was given by €48M (= 50%*€60M + 50%*€36M) and Peter's was given by €45M = (50%*€51M + 50%€39M). He thought he had concocted a better deal than Peter.

Peter recognized that Michael's calculations were naïve. That excellent book on entrepreneurial finance had also taught him to think about how entrepreneurs self-selected into investors. The table below shows the founders' exit values. Pierrette, the better entrepreneur, did better under Peter's offer, which would yield her €49M, compared to €40M with Michael's. Michelle, however, preferred Michael's offer which gave her €24M, compared to €21M under Peter's offer. These numbers suggested that Pierrette would self-select into Peter's offer and Michelle into Michael's.

Why did they self-select in this way? The preferred terms were less of a problem to Pierrette who expected a high exit value. Moreover, the higher valuation that came with the preferred terms were a big attraction to Pierrette, again because she expected to generate a high exit value. The opposite was true for Michelle, who expected a lower exit value. For her, the preferred terms were a problem because they would eat into a relatively low exit value. This insight can be generalized into saying that with self-selection, better entrepreneurs (like Pierrette) are more willing to accept investor downside protection (such as preferred terms) to get a higher valuation, whereas weaker entrepreneurs (like Michelle) shy away from deals with strong investor downside protection.

Peter, who understood self-selection, calculated his expected exit values differently than Michael's naïve numbers. He understood that his offer would attract Pierrette, and so he would earn €51M, whereas Michael would attract Michelle and earn only €36M.

All values in €M	Peter Prefstock		Michael Mindless
Post-money valuation	66.67	>	33.33
Investor share	30%	<	60%
Preferred terms	30	>	0
Investor value with Pierrette Parfaite	51	<	60
Founder value for Pierrette Parfaite	49	>	40
Investor value with Michelle Mabelle	39	>	36
Founder value for Michelle Mabelle	21	<	24
Naïve expected value for investors	45	<	48
Expected value for investors with self-selection	51	>	36

6.2.3(c) Aligning Expectations of Entrepreneurs and Investors

Preferred stock helps align expectations. Entrepreneurs tend to be more optimistic than investors. They strongly believe in the upside potential of their ventures, which is why they started them in the first place. Investors may be more cautious, aware of the many ways ventures can fail. If entrepreneurs put a relatively higher probability on the upside, and investors a relatively higher probability on the downside, then it is mutually advantageous to structure cash flow rights such that entrepreneurs get relatively more on the upside. In the extreme case, an entrepreneur might think that downside scenarios are entirely irrelevant. In this case she will happily give up all cash flow rights on the downside and focus solely on getting as much as possible on the upside.

We conclude this section by noting that preferred stock can also affect the eventual exit outcome. A standard feature of preferred shares (be they convertible or participating) is that IPOs and acquisitions are treated differently, due to the automatic conversion into common shares at IPO. One academic study by Hellmann suggests that this may be on purpose, as the automatic conversion leaves more shares to the entrepreneurs, especially when they continue to be involved with the company.[9] At the same time, automatic conversion creates an incentive for investors to prefer acquisitions over IPOs. One empirical study, by Cumming, finds that companies financed with common equity, where there are no incentives to favor acquisitions over IPOs, are 12% more likely to have an IPO than those financed with preferred equity.[10] Naturally, entrepreneurs do not always welcome the decision to do an acquisition with preferred shares. One further academic study by Broughman and Fried looks at 50 acquisitions of VC-backed start-ups.[11] It finds that 11 (or 22%) of them involve some renegotiation where the entrepreneur gets more than specified under the original terms. This happens particularly in those companies where the common shareholders (i.e., the entrepreneurs) can block an acquisition.

6.3 Compensation

6.3.1 Founder Employment Agreements

When entrepreneurs raise money from professional investors, they often formalize an employment agreement between the company and the founders. Prior to that, founders often have loose boundaries between their personal and company finances. They may invest their personal money in the company, and they may use company resources for personal use. Moreover, founders don't always specify what salaries (if any) they receive from the company. Such a state of affairs is not acceptable to professional investors, so the negotiation of term sheets is typically accompanied with the drafting of employment agreements. This may also affect the agreements founders make with each other around the time of founding the company (Section 4.4).

By signing an employment agreement, founders become employees of their own company and thereby become accountable to the board of directors. The most significant implication is that founders can be fired from their own company. An employment agreement also submits founders to standard employment terms that may include noncompete clauses—whereby departed founders may not work for a competitor for some time—or nonsolicitation clauses—whereby departed founders may not solicit other employees to work for them. The applicability of noncompete laws varies across states and countries, and it is often weak (Section 14.2.2).[12] The employment agreement may further specify that all intellectual property generated by the founders belongs to the company. It may also require the founders to sign over to the company any preexisting intellectual property.

An employment agreement specifies founder compensation. Apart from founder shares, a compensation package may include salary, bonuses, and stock options.[13] Two criteria guide founder compensation. First, there is the need to defer pay to save on scarce financial resources. Second, pay is made contingent on performance to provide incentives. Founder salaries tend to be low, especially for early-stage ventures. Bonuses are rare in start-ups, as typically there is no cash to distribute. However, as companies grow, salaries gradually increase, especially for the CEO. For example, one academic study, by Bengtsson and Hand, finds that CEO salaries in start-ups increase upon successfully raising a funding round.[14] As for stock options, founders rarely receive them in early financing rounds, although they can be used in later-stage rounds, to reestablish incentives for founders whose ownership stakes have been diluted over time.

Founder shares are the main form of compensation for founders. They are typically agreed upon around the time of founding (Section 4.4). Even though founders created their own company, investor term sheets often specify that they don't own all of their own equity right away. Instead they need to "earn it back" by remaining with the company and possibly, too, by achieving certain performance milestones. This is called "founder vesting." Its main purpose is to assure the continued commitment of the founders to the company. The value of early-stage companies is embodied in their founders' ability to execute their plans. Investors need protection from the possibility that founders leave after the venture has been funded. Vesting provides such protection by specifying that at the time of signing a term sheet, the founders reassign part of their own shares back to the company. The company then releases them back to the founders according to a set schedule. The release is usually contingent on the time the founder has remained with the company ("time vesting") but can also be made contingent on milestones ("performance vesting"). A typical arrangement might stipulate that founders retain up to a third of their shares and earn back the rest in monthly or quarterly steps over a few years. Constant vesting over time is called linear and is most common. However, there can also be a "cliff period," which is the minimum time a founder needs to remain with the company before vesting starts. In case of an acquisition or an IPO, vesting is typically "accelerated," so that unvested shares vest automatically. We examine founder issues in WorkHorse Box 6.4.

WorkHorse Box 6.4 Founder Compensation

Wolf C. Flow's term sheet contained two clauses about founder compensation that Astrid considered particularly "ratty." Note that the final version, available on the book's website (www.entrepreneurialfinance.net), differs from this original proposal.

The first clause concerned founder salaries and stated:

Founders shall enter in an employment contract with the Company acceptable to the Investors. Their salaries shall be set at no more than $25,000 per annum.

The founders strongly disliked that their salaries could not exceed $25K. They had agreed to pay themselves $25K for the first year but had sneaked into their financial projections a note that founder salaries should increase to $85K in 2021 (see WorkHorse Box 3.6). Admittedly, they had asked for more than they expected to receive, and they were willing to work for $50K. However, being stuck at $25K and living off Ramen soup forever just didn't seem fair.

The second clause concerned founder vesting and stated:

Founders' stock shall vest at 20% at Closing, and the remaining stock vesting monthly over the next 36 months. Vesting is accelerated in case of a Qualified IPO. Holders of Series A Preferred will have the right to dismiss founders and managers of the Company at any time, with or without cause. Vesting is forfeited in case of dismissal with or without cause. Already vested shares shall be sold back to the company at a price of .01.

The four founders were baffled at this clause. It meant that of the 200K shares that each founder currently owned, they would only keep 40K. The remaining 160K shares would be handed back to the company and then vest monthly. Vesting would last for 36 months, to the tune of 4,444 (= 160K/36) shares per month. Annie shrieked: "4,444 is an extremely inauspicious number in Chinese culture!" The others shared her outrage, albeit for different reasons. They had started the company and had managed it successfully for over a year. Why should they be treated like new untried employees? Hadn't they earned their stakes by now? After all, this was their own company!

Victoria Regalsworth further confirmed Astrid's suspicion that this clause gave the investors the right to fire and expropriate the founders. Specifically, the investors could fire any founder, even without cause. Even if fully vested, they would have to return to the company their 200K shares at a price of .01, for a paltry $2,000.

The four founders agreed that the founder compensation, as well as the vesting and firing terms, were unacceptable.

6.3.2 Employee Stock Option Plans

Term sheets also contain provisions about the compensation of employees, including senior managers. In addition to salary, key employees typically receive some stock options, often through Employee Stock Option Plans (ESOPs) that we introduced in Section 4.1.3. Stock options are used to motivate employees to focus on company performance, to increase their loyalty and retention, and to defer cash payments by substituting current salary with options.[15] Depending on the jurisdiction, there may be tax advantages or disadvantages of stock options over other forms of compensation.

ESOPs typically have a so-called vesting schedule that stipulates at what time employees receive stock options. A standard vesting period might be two to four years. Employees who leave the company (or are fired) lose their unvested options. There is usually an initial cliff period, say one year, when options accumulate but are not yet awarded. If the employee stays through the cliff period, she receives those options, but if she leaves before the end of the cliff period, none of her options are awarded. An exception is usually made if the company is acquired or goes public, in which case unvested options typically are subject to accelerated vesting.[16]

To award stock options, the company needs to create an option pool (Section 4.1.3). This typically happens at the first formal financing round (Series A) and accounts for 10 to 20% of the company shares. These are called "reserved shares," in that they haven't been issued yet. As the company hires employees, it will gradually issue stock options. Over time, employees convert these options into shares. It is common to simplify the capitalization tables of the company by assuming that the entire option pool gets distributed and converted into shares. Doing so is called reporting ownership on a "fully diluted" basis (Section 4.1.3). If the pool gets depleted, the board of directors may decide to restock it, typically at the time of a funding round. The additional shares are issued by the company, thereby diluting all current shareholders at the same time.

Individual employees can receive one-time option grants (at the time of hiring) and/or recurring grants. Recurring grants are structured similarly to the founder vesting structures described above, such as linear vesting with a cliff. To convert options into shares, employees need to pay a so-called strike price. Depending on tax and regulatory circumstances, the strike price for employee stock options is either some extremely low nominal value (such as 0.01 cent) or the price of shares from the company's most recent funding round. When stock options are granted with a strike price well below market value, the company gives out shares practically for free. However, due to regulatory or tax considerations, companies often must issue their options at a "fair value" strike price, typically the price of the last financing round and possibly with a discount to reflect differences in cash flow preference and control rights.[17] Technically, this means that the employee must pay the company a (discounted) market price to get the share. In these cases, employees borrow the money from the company to convert the options and then immediately pay back with the stock received. Once converted, employees own their shares.

However, they typically cannot sell these shares because there is no liquidity until the company has some exit (Box 11.7).

Stock options are only valuable when the share price is likely to be above the strike price at the time the options expire. If the current share price falls far below the strike price, then the options become less valuable, as the chances that the price rising back above the strike price become more remote. In this case, stock options are said to be "under water." This defeats their purpose. If employees do not think that the price will rebound, then stock options no longer represent any meaningful compensation and no longer provide incentives to remain with the company. In this case, the company can create a new option pool with a lower strike price, thereby reinvigorating employee incentives.

6.4 An Overview of Other Terms

In this section, we provide an overview of other parts of a term sheet that provide the basis for subsequent chapters. We look at how these terms allocate control rights (Chapter 8), regulate refinancing (Chapter 9), and allow investors to achieve liquidity (Chapter 11) of the venture. In this section, we establish the legal foundations, briefly explaining what the different terms say about these issues. The later chapters will then look at how the various parties behave in light of these contractual rights.

6.4.1 Control Rights

Chapter 8 examines the corporate governance of entrepreneurial ventures. In Section 8.2, we look at how decisions are made within the company and at how investors and entrepreneurs share control of the venture over the course of its life. Here we introduce the key contractual elements that affect control-related corporate governance structures.

The main rights and obligations of all shareholders are defined in the charter and by-laws of the corporation. These can be augmented and modified over time by subsequent rounds' term sheets and other contractual agreements. These rules need to comply with any relevant national laws. We identify three main control structures: voting rights, the board of directors, and contractual rights.

6.4.1.(a) Voting Rights
Shareholders have the right to vote on the most important decisions taken by the company, such as the decision to sell the company or the approval to raise an additional round of financing. The company charter and by-laws determine the process by which such voting takes place. Voting outcomes are determined using simple

majority or supermajority rules. Term sheets allocate voting rights and their evolution, contingent on performance and milestone achievement. We examine voting rights in Section 8.2.1.

6.4.1.(b) Board of Directors

The board of directors approves all key strategic decisions of the company, such as what products to develop, what markets to enter, which executives to hire, or when to initiate fundraising efforts. Usually, management proposes the strategy and the board responds, although roles can also be reversed. Decisions can be made under different rules, such as majority, supermajority, or unanimity, which are laid out in the company's by-laws. A typical term sheet determines board size and board members. It specifies either the people directly or else who has the right to nominate them. The term sheet may also specify which decisions are subject to board approval. We discuss the structure of the board of directors in Section 8.2.2.

6.4.1.(c) Contractual Rights

Term sheets can also be used to give the investors specific contractual decision rights. For these rights to supersede board or voting rights, they need to be precisely circumscribed. Their validity may also be limited in time; for example, they may expire at the next funding round. Some control rights are veto rights, such as the right to unilaterally block the sale of the company. Others are affirmative, such as the right to appoint a new CEO. A weaker form of this right is that investors can propose actions. The investor may then have the right to propose CEO candidates. This would mean that the board of directors can still appoint the CEO, but the investor gains some control over the process by providing candidates.

6.4.2 Future Fundraising

Chapter 9 examines how investors fund new ventures through staged financing. In Section 9.3, we review the legal foundations for several related term sheet clauses. Here we focus on five covenants concerning rights that founders and current investors have in future financing rounds.

6.4.2.(a) Protective Provisions

These terms give early investors (say in Series A) some power about the issuance of new stock and allow them to put some limitations on the details of the associated preferred terms. Protection can also be given in the form of right of approval of future dilutive issues (Section 4.1.5) or of decisions that may affect the rights of the Series holders. While new investors in later rounds may demand early investors to forego or reduce their protective rights, these provisions provide early investors with some bargaining power. We discuss these clauses in Section 9.3.1.

6.4.2.(b) Anti-dilution

When the price per share in a round falls below the price per share from a previous round, investors in the earlier round may feel that they overpaid for their shares. The anti-dilution clause allows them to reprice the shares they bought in the earlier round, considering the lower price of the new round. This important clause has implications for all parties, a subject we discuss it in detail in Section 9.3.2.

6.4.2.(c) Preemption Rights

Term sheets typically give investors the right to participate in future funding rounds. This is called a "preemption right" and allows the current investor to purchase any shares offered by the company to other investors. Preemption rights are typically capped at the "pro rata" level, which is the number of shares required to keep the same level ownership fraction at the pre-round level. We introduce the pro-rata level in Section 9.2.4, and preemption rights in Section 9.3.3.

6.4.2.(d) Right of First Refusal

Closely related to preemption rights, existing investors often have the right to buy the shares of any other shareholder (founder or investor) who wants to sell. We discuss this clause in Section 9.3.3. This means that investors selling any shares must ask whether the other current investors want to buy them before offering them to an outsider.

6.4.2.(e) Pay-to-Play

Some term sheets not only give current investors the right to keep investing in future rounds (preemption) but also provide them with strong incentives to do so. In Section 9.3.3, we examine "pay-to-play" clauses, which specify that certain investor rights, such as multiple liquidation or anti-dilution, only continue to apply if the investor contributes his pro-rata amount. The clauses may extend to forcing preferred stock to convert into common stock. In extreme cases, the investor may even lose some of his shares altogether. The purpose of a play-to-play clause is to facilitate future fundraising and to keep all investors involved. It may thus be unfavorable to investors who are unable or unwilling to reinvest.

6.4.3 Investor Liquidity

Several term sheet clauses give investors the right to seek liquidity. They ensure that investors can sell their shares and obtain some cash back from their investment.[18]

6.4.3.(a) Redemption Rights

Redemption rights give the investor the right to "redeem" their shares, which means that the company repurchases them at the preferred terms specified in equation (6.1) or equation (6.4). They typically apply within a specified time window several years after the investment. A typical case would be a right to redeem shares anytime from four to seven years after the investment, with a yearly redemption of one-third of the total number of shares owned by the investor.

Redemption rights are hardly ever exercised in practice. The reason is that when companies do well, they are likely to find an exit that is more profitable than redemption. If instead they struggle or are slow, they rarely have the liquidity to pay back the investor. Redemption rights are included in the term sheet as a way for investors to put pressure on the company. In particular, the threat to exercise these rights, which might put the company out of business if there is no liquidity, may convince the management team to actively seek an exit.

6.4.3.(b) Tag-Along and Drag-Along Rights

A tag-along right (also called a "co-sale" right) specifies that, when the founder or other investors sell their shares to a third party. the investor has the right to sell his shares alongside them, usually pro rata. If such a sale qualifies as a "liquidation event," it may trigger the payment of liquidation preferences to the investor. A "drag-along" right is stronger and gives the investor the right to force all other shareholders, including founders, to also sell their shares in an acquisition. It may be used to obtain an exit even against the will of the founders or other investors.

6.4.3.(c) Registration Rights and PiggyBack Rights

Registration rights give investors the right to have the company register their securities with the stock market regulator, making them eligible for public sale. This effectively gives investors the power to initiate a public listing. Since it is the company that decides which shares to register, investors want to secure the right to include their shares. As such registration rights are included in a separate Registration Rights Agreement that also regulates the duration of these rights (usually from five to seven years after the investment), the number of times registration can be demanded (usually one or two), and the shareholders' lock-up agreement at IPO (Section 11.2.4). Founders tend to resist strong registration rights if they want to retain control over the timing of an IPO. A piggyback right is a milder version which specifies that in case of a public listing, the investor has the right to sell his stock in the public offering. It is usually granted to smaller investors with less bargaining power.

In practice, investor liquidity rights tend to have limited importance. It may not always be easy for the company to meet the investors' liquidity requests. Selling the company, for example, is complex and takes time. A decision to sell the company requires agreement among all shareholders. The main purpose of all the liquidity clauses is to give investors some tools in these negotiations. One can think of these as "swords" (offensive) and "shields" (defensive): redemption, drag-along, and registration rights are all like swords, whereas tag-along and piggyback rights are more like shields.

Box 6.4 presents an example of a company facing two term sheets that differ in many respects, including their redemption rights.

Box 6.4 Tales from the Venture Archives: Term Sheets for Africa

While the legal details vary across countries, term sheets are global. If you don't believe us, please come to Zambia, a landlocked country of less than 17 million people in southern Africa. Unlike some of its neighbors, such as Angola or the Democratic Republic of Congo, Zambia has been relative stable politically. Still, it is a poor country that ranks 142nd by GDP per capita.[19] The average annual income is just shy of $4,000, approximately one-fifteenth that of the U.S. Is this a place where you would expect entrepreneurs caring about redemption rights?

Zoona was founded in 2007 with the idea of providing access to payment systems to the millions of Zambians who don't have bank accounts.[20] A company called M-Pesa had already successfully introduced mobile payments to Kenya, but their model was not suited for Zambia. Zoona developed a distinct business model involving local kiosks. This required substantial capital investments, so the company went in search of equity capital. In 2010, it approached numerous investors for a Series A round and managed to generate two competing term sheet offers.

The first offer was led by AfricInvest, a private equity firm with a Pan-African investment strategy. It had invested in over 100 deals across more than 20 African countries, covering a wide range of industries. The second offer was led by the Omidyar Network, a hybrid venture capital–philanthropic institution with a global remit, founded by eBay's co-founder Pierre Omidyar. While AfricInvest was a purely financial investor, Omidyar Network would commonly be classified as a social impact investor (Section 13.6.3). The following table shows some of the key terms offered.[21]

Description	AfricInvest	Omidyar Network
Existing shareholders (in M)	3.8	3.8
Stock options and convertible notes (in M)	1.2	1.0
Price per share ($)	1.0	1.2
Shares to Series A (in M)	2.0	2.5
Investment by Series A ($M)	2.0	3.0
Pre-money valuation ($M)	5.0	5.8
Post-money valuation ($M)	7.0	8.8
Dividend rate for preferred	12% dividend	No dividend
Multiple liquidation rights	2x	1.5x
Anti-dilution	Full ratchet	Weighted average
Redemption rights	Force company sale after 4.5 years	Redeem investment after 10 years
Drag along rights	Requires simple majority	Requires qualified majority

It is striking how similar these term sheets are to standard North American ones. Some of the details are worth noting. A post-money valuation of $7M by AfricInvest, and almost $9M by Omidyar Network, is highly respectable even by North American standards. Stock options (Section 6.3.2) and convertible notes (Section 6.6) were also included in these term sheet proposals. The two offers differ not only in valuations, but also in terms. AfricInvest's offer uses a more stringent type of preferred shares and a harsher anti-dilution clause. Differences in redemption rights and drag along rights reveal different attitudes towards exit, with Omidyar Network taking a more patient and less controlling approach.

It should not come as a surprise that Zoona chose the deal led by Omidyar Network. By 2018, the company had come a long way. It prided itself on serving over 2,000 communities, supporting over 1,000 active entrepreneurs, and creating over 3,000 jobs. Still there was no exit in sight.

6.4.4 Additional Clauses

In this section, we review some other clauses in the term sheet that address specific issues and investor concerns.

Information rights specify what company information investors have the right to receive and when. In most cases, information rights require full disclosure of financial information, for example by mandating the delivery of quarterly audited accounts, or monthly cash flow statements. Other disclosures may concern operational or technological information. This augments the rights of board members who already receive regular updates on the company. In addition, visitation rights allow investors to gather information by inspecting the company's premises.

An important part of a start-up's value lies with the team's ability to execute, as discussed in the Venture Evaluation Matrix of Chapter 3. For this reason, term sheets may specify that the company must take out a "key man insurance," which protects the company in case of death or disability of key managers, in particular the CEO or other founders. In addition, indemnification agreements are included to protect the company's directors from liabilities arising from their actions taken in their capacity. Moreover, it is common for the company to buy some directors' and officers' insurance that protects management and board directors in case of lawsuits. Term sheets typically also specify that the expenses and legal fees associated with the investment are to be paid by the company.

Transactions involving cross-border investments need to specify which country's law applies. While a company is always subject to some domestic laws (e.g., national labor laws), it is possible to specify that certain aspects of the investment are enforceable in the investor's country. U.S. investors, in particular, often want to maintain the right to sue the company in a U.S. court. In a closely related matter, the contract may specify that certain types of disputes are to be resolved by arbitration rather than by the courts.

Term sheets require each party to make representations and warranties. These are legally binding statements in which any failure to be truthful can lead to financial liability and can possibly void the deal. It is important for founders to avoid committing to representations and warranties personally, and to have the company bear responsibility. Investors may insist on personal responsibility when information about individual circumstances is relevant. Entrepreneurs, for example, may need to prove that they own the intellectual property they say they own.

Term sheets include some clauses concerning the negotiation process. Any offer specifies an expiration date; short-end dates are referred to as "exploding" offers. Term sheets may also include a "no-shop" clause that binds the entrepreneur not to seek other deals. Prior to signing a term sheet, such a clause is not enforceable. However, it becomes such for the period between signing the term sheet, which is a preliminary agreement, and signing the Shareholders' Agreement, which is the final legal document.

Finally, term sheets detail the conditions for closing the deal. Investors can make their offer conditional on a positive conclusion from their legal due diligence, on completing agreements about the transfer of IP from the founders to the company, or on successfully finding a co-investor to complete the required investment amount. The closing of the deal may also be conditional on the company reaching specific milestones, such as hiring a vice president for sales or obtaining control of key assets (e.g., a prime retail location or a license to some required technology).

Now that we have examined the main term sheet clauses, Box 6.5 looks at their overall design.

Box 6.5 Making Sense of Complex Term Sheets

What economic principles guide the overall structure of term sheets? Research by Kaplan and Strömberg helps us to see the forest for the trees. They examine a sample of over 200 term sheets from more than 10 U.S. VC firms.[22] They classify all clauses according to how they affect entrepreneurs' and investorscash flow and control rights. They then use cluster analysis to discern a common logic across the different terms and term sheets. One of their core findings is that contracts often combine stronger cash flow rights with stronger control rights. That is, contracts favor either the investor or the entrepreneur in both dimensions. Another important finding is that term sheets for pre-revenue companies, which are riskier, tend to give investors more cash flow and control rights. Good performance over time, however, allows the entrepreneurs to regain control of their venture.

For some of the term sheets, the researchers also have access to the internal notes of the VCs. This allows them to identify whether the investors are concerned mainly about internal or external risks. Internal risks lie inside the company and concern issues such as the quality of management or the ease of monitoring company activities. External factors lie outside the company and concern issues such as customer adoption or competition. The researchers examine how these two types of risks map into the choice of terms. Greater internal risks are associated with more investor control, more contingent compensation for the entrepreneurs, and more contingent financing rounds. Researchers interpret this as the investors' response to problems of adverse selection and moral hazard (see Box 1.2). Greater external risk is associated with strong downside protection, such as stronger liquidation rights. Far from insuring the entrepreneurs against market risk, term sheets actually focus on protecting the investors.

To conclude this section, we return to our case study in WorkHorse Box 6.5.

WorkHorse Box 6.5 Responding to Wolf C. Flow's Term Sheet Proposal

The founders were debating how to respond to Wolf C. Flow's term sheet. They needed the money and trusted both Michael Archie and Ali Ad-Lehr. However, they did not trust Wolf C. Flow, and most certainly disliked parts of his term sheet. Victoria Regalsworth advised them not to become too confrontational. She suggested they send back an amended version of the term sheet that would take out the most "stinky" parts but leave enough in place to keep the investors interested.

Over the weekend, during a long and sometimes acrimonious debate, they finally agreed to focus on four issues that concerned them most: (1) replace the participating preferred shares with convertible preferred shares; (2) relax the clause about founder salaries; (3) drop the founder vesting and firing clause, and (4) remove Wolf C. Flow from the list of proposed board members. The last issue was particularly delicate (see Chapter 8 for an in-depth discussion). Wolf C. Flow's term sheet foresaw five seats on the board of directors. Two of the directors were to be chosen by management, the other three directors were to come from the investor side. The proposal specifically named Michael Archie, Ali Ad-Lehr from Eagle-I Ventures, and Wolf C. Flow from Coyo-T Capital himself. This signified a clear shift of power to the investors that left the founders distinctly uncomfortable. The founders therefore wanted to propose an alternative board structure. They agreed that five was the right number of directors. Among themselves, they also quickly agreed that Astrid and Brandon should represent the management side. The founders also realized that two seats had to be given to the investors. Since they liked Michael and Ali best, they left those on the list, but struck Wolf off the list. In his place they put in an External Director "to be nominated by mutual consent."

On Monday, December 21, 2020, Victoria Regalsworth quickly drafted an amended version of the term sheet. The four founders all watched as Victoria sent off the e-mail. Would the investors simply accept those changes and sign the deal? Maybe even before Christmas? Would Santa come early this year?

6.5 Valuation versus Terms

So far, this chapter has discussed many contractual clauses that address a wide variety of issues. Investors are often experienced term sheet negotiators, but entrepreneurs may feel lost in front of a term sheet. Inexperienced entrepreneurs may overlook the important clauses or challenge standard clauses that are not negotiable. Having good legal advice is therefore essential. However, getting the right term sheet from a business perspective is up to the entrepreneurs and investors themselves. In practice, what gets negotiated most are the valuation, control rights (especially board seats), and founder compensation (especially vesting). Other clauses may receive more or less attention, depending on circumstances.[23]

Many entrepreneurs believe valuation to be by far the most important part of the term sheet. This can make for a poor negotiation strategy, as experienced investors can offer a term sheet with an attractive valuation on the front page but harsh terms on the inside. An inexperienced entrepreneur may overlook them, only to discover their consequences when it is too late. Our discussion in this chapter emphasizes that preferred stock, typically held by the investors, is more valuable than common stock, typically held by the entrepreneurs. The headline valuation figure therefore has to be interpreted with caution (see also Section 7.5).

The issue over inflating valuations is particularly salient for companies that have achieved the much coveted "unicorn" status. These are VC-backed private companies that achieve a valuation over $1B in a private financing round.[24] One academic study by Gornall and Strebulaev takes a careful look at the terms of these unicorn deals.[25] It finds that valuations are significantly inflated due to the presence of preferred shares and other investor-friendly terms discussed in this chapter. The authors perform some counterfactual calculations about what the valuation would be if investors had received common equity. They estimate that 46% of all companies in their sample lose their unicorn status; 11% would find their valuation more than halved. The study provides a useful warning about the dangers of overlooking the impact of term sheet clauses on the valuation of unicorns and other entrepreneurial companies.

Negotiations between an entrepreneur and an investor should not be reduced to a one-dimensional zero-sum game on valuation. Instead they should consider multiple dimensions that offer win–win possibilities. A useful approach to negotiations consists of clarifying the entrepreneur's priorities. Research conducted by Noam Wasserman has identified two main views.[26] Some entrepreneurs create companies with the main goal of getting rich. Others instead perceive the company as their own creation and covet the possibility of retaining control over it as it grows.[27] In most cases, these two goals are incompatible: the entrepreneur can maximize company value by including resourceful investors (Section 8.3), but these participate only if they can obtain some control to protect their investment. This suggests that entrepreneurs should identify which term sheet clauses are more important to achieve their goal and stick to those in the negotiation. For example, wealth-oriented entrepreneurs should aim for a higher valuation and lower liquidation preferences and anti-dilution rights. On the other hand, a control-oriented entrepreneur should be willing to accept a lower valuation in return for control of the board and for weaker investor contractual control rights.

We conclude this section by focusing on another important trade-off that concerns how value accrues to investors and entrepreneurs in different situations. This is the trade-off between upside versus downside returns. We already noted that participating preferred stock gives investors additional protection on the downside. Term sheet negotiations can therefore focus on how much the investor values downside protection, and to what extent the entrepreneur is willing to give up downside protection to increase returns on the upside. Entrepreneurs that want a higher valuation have to accept more onerous downside protection clauses. Box 6.6 provides an example that also illustrates the ease with which valuations can be overstated.

Box 6.6 The Trade-Off Between Upside and Downside Protection.

HangaruaTech was a start-up from Oamaru, New Zealand, founded by Panera Pei and Keiti Kino. Hehu Haumi, a partner at Aotearoa Ventures, was keen to invest. He thought that if HangaruaTech succeeded, it could be sold for $400M, and that if it failed, its assets would still be worth $80M. He considered the probability of success to be 50%.

Hehu's initial offer was a deal with common stock funding involving no investor downside protection. He offered to invest $20M for 25% of the company, implying a post-money valuation of $80M. The expected returns from the deal are shown in the following table. In expectation, Hehu anticipated making $60M on a $20M investment. With the good outcome he would return $100M, which would surely make him the most famous VC in Oamaru!

Common stock deal	Good outcome	Bad outcome	Expected outcome
Probability	50%	50%	
Investor share	25%	25%	
Exit value ($M)	400	80	240
Investor's share of exit value ($M)	100	20	60
Founder' share of exit value ($M)	300	60	180

To Hehu's surprise, HangaruaTech's founders, were disappointed. They had set themselves the goal of being the first start-up in Oamaru to be valued with a nine-digit figure, that is, over $100M.

Hehu therefore made a second offer, based on preferred stock with a 2X multiple liquidation preferences (without any dividend). This meant that the first $40M of company value (i.e., twice the investment) would accrue to Hehu. To Panera's satisfaction, the offer specified that Hehu would only take 20% of the company, implying a post-money valuation of $100M: a dream fulfilled. Hehu found it easy to offer this alternative. Due to the 2x multiple liquidation preferences, his expected outcome remained $60M. Hehu was pleased with himself for his elegant "2x solution" to the "nine-digit problem."

2x Preferred stock deal	Good outcome	Bad outcome	Expected outcome
Probability	50%	50%	
Investor share	20%	2x	
Exit value ($M)	400	80	240
Investor's share of exit value ($M)	80	40	60
Founder's share of exit value ($M)	320	40	180

As it turned out, the $100M post-money valuation pleased Panera, but not Keiti who had dreamed of a nine-digit pre-money valuation. Hehu therefore came up with a third deal, based on preferred stock with a 3x liquidation preference and 15% of the equity, implying a lofty post-money valuation of $133M and a pre-money valuation of $113M. Keiti was speechless. Once again Hehu didn't really care, since he still expected to make $60M, as shown in the following table.

3x Preferred stock deal	Good outcome	Bad outcome	Expected outcome
Probability	50%	50%	
Investor share	15%	3x	
Exit value ($M)	400	80	240
Investor's share of exit value ($M)	60	60	60
Founder's share of exit value ($M)	340	20	180

At \$133M, HangaruaTech became the highest valued start-up in the history of Oamaru. Privately, Hehu joked that it was also the highest liquidation preference any Oamaru start-up had ever seen. In fact, what Hehu didn't mention to the founders was that in the end he didn't even care about the valuation. He could have given them the \$20M for 2% of the company, implying a \$1B valuation, to create Oamaru's first unicorn. The 3x liquidation preference guaranteed him the \$60M under both the good and the bad outcome. The valuation didn't matter to him because he no longer planned to convert his preferred shares. Hehu mused that the entire quest for unicorn valuations was largely pointless. At such inflated valuations, what mattered wasn't the "front-page" valuation number, but the "back-page" details on liquidation preferences, and other downside protections.

Once the excitement of being a nine-digit-valued company wore off, Panera and Keiti reflected more deeply on their choice. They had focused on the valuation but now realized that the expected exit value was arguably more relevant. Panera was a born optimist and thought the good outcome had a 60% probability. Keiti was a pessimist and only gave it a 40% success probability. The following table shows the resulting expected returns across the proposed deals. For example, with the common share deal, Panera the optimist expected to make 60%*\$300M + 40%*\$60M = \$204M, whereas Keiti the pessimist expected to make 40%*\$300M + 60%*\$60M = \$156M.

As an optimist, Panera was happy with the 3x preferred share deal. It gave the investor more downside protection, leaving more for the founders on the upside. Keiti, however, now regretted her nine-digit infatuation. She wished she had taken the original common share deal, which ranked highest according to her more pessimistic beliefs. Hehu remarked that liquidation preferences were more attractive to more optimistic entrepreneurs.

Founder's exit value (\$M)	Optimist	Pessimist
Common stock deal	204	156
2x Preferred stock deal	208	152
3x Preferred stock deal	212	148

A friend of the founders, Maraea Manawarü, argued that in the end, what mattered most were the incentives provided by the deal structure. She asked how much investors and founders actually cared about the company's success. For this, she calculated the differences in the founder's exit value between the two situations:

Differences between good and bad outcomes (\$M)	Founders	Investors
Common stock deal	240	80
2x Preferred stock deal	280	40
3x Preferred stock deal	320	0

Panera felt even better now, as she noted that the 3X preferred share deal gave the founders the highest incentives. Keiti, however, became even more regretful when she realized that her 3X preferred share deal left the investors with no success incentives whatsoever: Aotearoa Ventures made the same return under both the good and the bad scenario. Higher liquidation preferences gave stronger incentives to entrepreneurs but lower incentives to investors.

In the end, the good outcome obtained. Panera felt vindicated in his optimism. Keiti argued that her drive for a higher valuation gave them the best deal. Maraea said she always knew how important entrepreneurial incentives were. Only Hehu felt a little remorseful. Everybody noted that he had played it very conservatively with his 3x liquidation preference. In the end, he missed the biggest opportunity to make a huge return. He became the most famous VC in Oamaru, but unfortunately for the wrong reason.

6.6 Convertible Notes

6.6.1 How Convertible Notes Work

In this section, we examine the use of convertible notes, which are simpler contractual arrangements than the fully fledged term sheets discussed so far. The key differences between a convertible note and convertible preferred equity (which we discussed in Section 6.2) is that a convertible note involves no valuation. Moreover, it has limited downside protection and no control rights for investors.[28]

Convertible notes are popular among many seed investors, such as family and friends, accelerators, and angels. Less sophisticated investors prefer these simpler securities because they have limited financial expertise and often find it difficult to put a valuation on a risky venture. Even sophisticated investors sometimes prefer the simplicity of deferring valuation until a venture becomes more crystalized. Convertible notes are also faster to arrange as there is relatively little to negotiate over. This is particularly useful in case companies need urgent funding. Finally, there is a simple cost argument that convertible notes are cheaper to arrange. Suppose the legal costs of preparing a fully fledged term sheet amount to $20K. In a $2M investment round, this would represent 1% of the transaction, something the investors would be willing to pay for getting the legal details right. However, in a $100K round, this would represent 20% of the investment, which would be harder to justify.

A convertible note is a simple debt-like claim that converts into equity once the company raises its first formal round. The note has a face value equal to the invested amount plus any interest. The interest rate is typically moderate; most contracts charge a few points above the prime rate. Interest payments are only due at maturity. There is no collateral, and there are relatively few additional clauses, mostly about recovering scrap value in case the venture fails. The hope of the investors is that the venture succeeds at raising a proper equity round, thereby triggering the conversion of the note.

The convertible note has three key traits. First, conversion is automatic and occurs at the next formal equity round, which usually means above a minimum investment size and before the maturity date. The note typically converts into the same security as the equity investors in the next round, for example, preferred shares. A less favorable version for the investors is when the convertible note converts into common stock. Second, the conversion rate is specified upfront as a discount on the valuation that the venture will garner at the next funding round. Typically, the discount ranges between 10 and 20%, depending on market conditions. Third, the note has a fixed maturity, usually between 12 and 24 months. This maturity should allow the venture enough time to raise its first equity round.

To formally see how the convertible note works, we denote the initial investor who buys the note with the subscript CN, the next round investor with the subscript INV, and the founders with PRE. Let DIS be the price discount for the convertible note. Suppose the next round investor contributes an amount I_{INV} at a price of P_{INV}, thus receiving $S_{INV} = I_{INV}/P_{INV}$ of preferred shares. The share price for the convertible note, used for the conversion into shares, is given by:

$$P_{CN} = (1 - DIS) * P_{INV} \qquad (6.5)$$

The convertible note then gets converted into S_{CN} shares:

$$S_{CN} = \frac{I_{CN}}{P_{CN}} = \frac{I_{CN}}{(1 - DIS) * P_{INV}} \qquad (6.6)$$

If the entrepreneur originally had S_{EN} shares, after the equity round the ownership stakes of the entrepreneur, the noteholder, and the equity investor are given by:

$$F_{PRE} = \frac{S_{PRE}}{S_{PRE} + S_{CN} + S_{INV}}, \; F_{CN} = \frac{S_{CN}}{S_{PRE} + S_{CN} + S_{INV}}, \; F_{INV} = \frac{S_{INV}}{S_{PRE} + S_{CN} + S_{INV}} \qquad (6.7)$$

WorkHorse Box 6.6 provides a simple numerical example.

WorkHorse Box 6.6 JP Potro's convertible note

In its very early days of WorkHorse, Brandon's uncle JP Potro invested $80K. By the time the company received its first seed round, the capitalization table (see WorkHorse Box 4.4) showed JP Potro owning 50,000 shares: how come?

JP had used a simple convertible note when he offered his $80K without any interest rate. The note stated that his $80K would be converted into common equity at a 20% discount of the next round. The price of the next round, the seed round led by Michael Archie in early 2020, was priced at $2, so his discounted price was $1.60. His $80K convertible note therefore converted into 50,000 (= $80K/ $1.6) common shares.

The convertible note is a flexible arrangement that fits with the high uncertainty of seed stage investing for several reasons. First, the convertible note defers valuation to a later stage, which simplifies the negotiation process. Moreover, seed investors appreciate the possibility of deferring the negotiation to more experienced formal investors. Second, given that entrepreneurs can be reluctant to give up control, the convertible note does not give seed investors any control rights like board seats or veto rights. Third, documentation can be as short as three pages, and most clauses are standard. So, it requires minimal legal preparation time and is significantly less expensive than a VC round. The convertible debt therefore leaves many of the decisions with the next round investors. Some refer to rounds financed with convertible debt as "unpriced rounds" since they defer pricing to later rounds.

Box 6.7 discusses a variant of the convertible note that has recently gained in popularity.

Box 6.7 Let's Play It SAFE

One potential problem with the convertible note is that prior to conversion, investors hold a debt-like claim. Some investors do not like this because being a creditor and recovering funds in a liquidation can have its own legal complications. A recent alternative is the "Simple Agreement for Future Equity" (or "SAFE").[29] This financial instrument was popularized by lawyers at the Y-Combinator, a well-known Silicon Valley accelerator. The goal is to simplify the concept of convertible note to facilitate funding. A SAFE is a financial instrument in which the investor provides money in exchange for the right to receive preferred stock (or common stock) at the first equity round (typically Series A).

Unlike a convertible note, a SAFE is not a debt instrument. It has no maturity, carries no interest, and has none of the protective rights of debt. Like a convertible note, the equity is granted at a discount. By design, investors receive little protection. A SAFE deal can be closed very quickly and at a very low cost. The protection to SAFE investors is low in the beginning. After completion of the next round, however, they enjoy the same protection as the Series A investors.

6.6.2 Valuation Caps

While the convertible note has become a popular instrument among many seed investors, it also has some limitations. It may be easier not to assign any valuation to an investment, but this also carries some risks. Ironically, convertible note investors might become victims of their own success. If the company performs well, its valuation in the next equity round will be high. While this is good for the entrepreneur, it means that the convertible note investor ends up paying a high price per share. This effectively penalizes him for picking a good company or helping it grow, thereby creating misaligned incentives. When it comes to negotiating the valuation of the next round, convertible note holders may not side with the entrepreneur but with the next round's investor (Section 9.2.4).

To address these limitations, convertible notes sometimes have a "valuation cap." This is a limit on the pre-money valuation that the convertible note holders have to pay. In other words, the convertible noteholder is guaranteed that their pre-money valuation in the next round is no higher than the cap. The cap then defines the maximum valuation that the seed investor will have to pay in the next round.

Let V_{CAP} be the cap on pre-money valuation. P_{CN} is the price per share paid by the convertible noteholder, and I_{CN} his investment. Let S_{PRE} be the preexisting shares, excluding any shares for the convertible noteholder. Then:

$$P_{CN} = \frac{V_{CAP}}{S_{PRE}} \qquad (6.8)$$

P_{CN} is the maximum price paid by the convertible noteholder. As long as the price from equation (6.5) lies below that of (6.8), the convertible noteholder gets the lower price. If the cap is binding and P_{CN} is the price, then the number of shares is simply given by (6.6):

$$S_{CN} = \frac{I_{CN}}{P_{CN}}$$

The valuation cap therefore ensures that the convertible noteholder gets at least this number of shares, and no less. Using equations (6.6) and (6.8) we can express this as:[30]

$$\frac{S_{CN}}{S_{PRE} + S_{CN}} = \frac{I_{CN}}{V_{CAP} + I_{CN}} \qquad (6.9)$$

This equation says that the ownership fraction of the convertible note holders among all the preexisting shareholders (i.e., before the arrival of the new investors) is given by the right-hand side expression. This we can think of as the fraction that their investment represents in a counterfactual post-money valuation that is based on the capped pre-money valuation (V_{CAP}) plus their investment (I_{CN}).

The new investors obviously need to consider the issuance of additional shares to the convertible noteholder. We can think of them as fixing a desired (pre-money or post-money) valuation, and then calculating the corresponding price per share, denoted by P_{INV}. Using the logic of equation (4.8) in Chapter 4, this is given by:

$$P_{INV} = \frac{V_{PRE}}{S_{PRE} + S_{CN}} \qquad (6.10)$$

The remaining calculations of the post-money valuation and the number of new shares uses equations (4.4) and (4.6) from Chapter 4. WorkHorse Box 6.7 looks at an example of a convertible note with a valuation cap.

WorkHorse Box 6.7 JP Potro's Brother-in-Law

JP Potro was delighted with the progress of his nephew's company. However, his brother-in-law, Carlos Codicio, had nothing better to do than to keep nagging him about the terms under which he had offered the convertible note. Carlos noted that any "semi-intelligent" investor would have used a pre-money valuation cap of $1M. At that price, JP's $80K investment would have been worth more. He made the following calculations. Before JP's shares, the company had issued 950,000 shares. A $1M cap would have meant that JP's price per share would be calculated by dividing $1M with the 950,000 preexisting shares, resulting in a price of $1.05. His $80K investment would thus have converted into 76,000 shares ("More than the lousy 50,000 that you got, JP," Carlos badgered him). The total number of shares before the round would thus be a little over 1M. The price of the new round would not be $2 as before, but $1.95, to account for JP's additional shares. At that price, the new investors would have received 256,500 shares.

Convertible note with valuation cap	
Pre-money valuation cap for CN ($)	1,000,000
Pre-money valuation ($)	2,000,000
Number of pre-existing shares (excluding CN)	950,000
Price per share for capped CN ($)	1.05
Investment of CN ($)	80,000
Number of shares to CN	76,000
Number of pre-existing shares (incl. CN)	1,026,000
Price per share for new investors ($)	1.95
Investment of new investors ($)	500,000
Post-money valuation ($)	2,500,000
Number of shares to new investors	256,500
Total number of shares after round	1,282,500
Ownership of CN investor before round	7.4%
Ownership of CN investor after round	5.9%

"If you dummy had put in a valuation cap, you would have owned a proud 7.4% before, and 5.9% after the round. Not that lousy 4% you ended up with, JP" Carlos mocked him. Over the years JP had learned that with his brother-in-law, it was best to just say nothing. However, to himself he thought: "You can call me a dummy, but I am still the one who will make money on this!"

Summary

Term sheets are the main contracting tool for equity deals. This chapter provides a detailed explanation of the main clauses used and for their most common variations. While term sheets are legal and technical, proper understanding of them requires looking at the underlying economic trade-offs faced by entrepreneurs and investors. In this chapter, we explain the use of preferred shares and the differences between convertible preferred and participating preferred shares. We then look at how investors impose certain compensation structures onto founders and how they set up employee stock option pools. The chapter also provides an overview of other clauses found in a typical term sheet, such as control rights, future financing terms, and liquidity term at exit. We emphasize that there is a trade-off between valuation and contractual terms, and we warn entrepreneurs of the dangers of an excessive focus on valuation. Finally, we explain how seed stage investors often prefer convertible notes and SAFEs, which are simpler contractual arrangements.

In terms of the FIRE framework (Chapter 1), term sheets concern the second step, INVEST. The term sheet is at the heart of the deal between entrepreneurs and investors, as it defines the contractual structure under which the two parties agree to proceed. It has a clear forward-looking nature in the sense that it anticipates the challenges that the two parties are likely to encounter at the next steps of the FIRE framework. Control rights and future financing rights are directly related to the third step, RIDE. The choice of financial securities and the terms about investor liquidity pertain to the fourth step, EXIT.

Review Questions

1. What is the role of the term sheet?
2. Why are term sheets said to be incomplete? What are the implications?
3. What are the advantages and disadvantages of using contingent terms?
4. What is the difference between convertible preferred shares and participating preferred shares?
5. Why do preferred shares automatically convert in case of an IPO?
6. What restrictions can be placed on founder stock, and why?
7. How do companies structure employee stock option plans?
8. What factors affect the trade-off between valuation and terms?
9. Why do certain seed investors prefer convertible notes?
10. Why are convertible notes said to be "unpriced?"

Notes

1. Useful templates for these types of documents can be found on websites of the various national venture capital organizations, including the U.S. NVCA or the British BVCA. Several law firms also provide templates and data on term sheet trends specific to where they operate.
2. A concise overview of term sheets can be found in Bartlett (1999). Levin and Rocap (2015) provide a comprehensive legal review, focused on U.S. practice.
3. Aghion and Holden (2011) provide an analysis of incomplete contracts.
4. Kaplan and Strömberg (2003) report additional examples from actual contracts.
5. In addition to the documents released for the Nobel Prize itself (available at https://www.nobelprize.org/ prizes/economic-sciences/2013/press-release), a particularly useful summary of the work can be found in Hart (1995).
6. Hess, Leahy, and Tran (2018).
7. Gompers et al. (2019). For a practitioners' view, see Fred Wilson's post on his blog and the various views he cites: https://avc.com/2010/05/an-evolved-view-of-the-participating-preferred, accessed April 15, 2019.
8. The formula for X^{COM} is given by $X^{COM} = \dfrac{PT + F_{INV} * \left(X^{CAP} - PT\right)}{F_{INV}}$.
9. Hellmann (2006).
10. Cumming (2008).
11. Broughman and Fried (2010).
12. Booth (2006), Samila and Sorensen (2011), Singh and Agrawal (2011), and Stuart and Sorenson (2003).
13. Taxation of founder stock is relevant for determining disposable capital gains; see Fleischer (2011) ad Polsky and Hellwig (2012).
14. Bengtsson and Hand (2011).
15. Hand (2008) provides evidence on the extent of use of stock options by U.S. start-ups.
16. Balderton (2017) provides a comprehensive overview of the use of stock options in start-ups and a comparison across different countries. Mark Suster's post on his blog provides an investor's view: https://bothsidesofthetable.com/first-round-funding-terms-and-founder-vesting-3ff81f55c7bd, accessed April 15, 2019.
17. In the U.S., since 2005 the strike price must be set according to Section 409A regulations, which require the use of a "reasonable valuation method." Before the regulations, the exercise price was computed by discounting the price of the latest round of preferred stock sold to investors, which is the approach common in many other countries. Under Section 409A, the exercise price has to be computed using one of several approved ("Safe Harbor") methods, unless one is ready to defend an alternative approach in front of the tax authorities. See Mort and Gaknoki (2018).
18. Bienz and Walz (2010) and Smith (2005).
19. Based on GDP per capita adjusted for purchasing power parity (PPP) data by the International Monetary Fund (IMF) 2017 versions. Available at: https://www.imf.org/external/datamapper.
20. Bazley, Schweer Rayner, and Patton Power (2015) and https://ilovezoona.com.
21. The data in this table has been modified slightly for ease of exposition.
22. Kaplan and Strömberg (2003, 2004).
23. Gompers et al. (2019) report survey evidence.
24. For data on unicorns worldwide, see https://www.wsj.com/graphics/billion-dollar-club.

25. Gornall and Strebulaev (2019) analyzes this issue at length.
26. Wasserman (2012) further discusses the issue, and Wasserman (2017) provides an empirical analysis.
27. An extreme form of control is naming the company after the founder(s). Intriguingly, Belenzon, Chatterji, and Daley (2019) find that this is correlated with lower growth in entrepreneurial companies.
28. Green and Coyle (2018) discuss the choice of securities in seed stage rounds.
29. Green and Coyle (2016).
30. Alternatively, we can express the share of the convertible noteholder, relative to the other

    preexisting shareholders, as $\frac{S_{CN}}{S_{PRE}} = \frac{I_{CN}}{V_{CAP}}$. This says that the ratio of the shares by the con-

    vertible noteholder over all other preexisting shares on the left-hand side cannot fall below the ratio on the right-hand side, which is the investment (I_{CN}) divided by the valuation cap (V_{CAP}).

7

Structuring Deals

Learning Goals

In this chapter students will learn:

1. How entrepreneurs prepare for fundraising and how investors generate deal flow.
2. Why investors syndicate deals.
3. How entrepreneurs and investors negotiate and close a deal.
4. About the importance of trust and a long-term perspective.

This chapter examines the process of how entrepreneurs and investors come together and negotiate an investment deal. We identify the key steps in this process. First, entrepreneurs seek funding for their business opportunities, and investors seek out opportunities and evaluate them. Finding a match requires alignment along multiple dimensions, for which we provide the practical MATCH tool. Next, investors typically form a syndicate of interested parties. Once the parties enter into the negotiation process, economic forces, timing, and idiosyncratic factors determine the strength of the relative bargaining positions. The process culminates in all parties agreeing to close the deal. The chapter ends with some reflections on the importance of trust and a long-term perspective.

7.1 The Art of Structuring Deals

In the preceding chapters, we covered several technical aspects of deals, such as financial projections, valuation, and term sheets. This may leave the impression that structuring a deal between an entrepreneur and investors is a purely technical matter: a science that can be condensed into few equations. It is not!

In this chapter we discuss the process of structuring the deal. This involves issues such as eliciting interest for the business idea, picking the right partners, and developing trust with the investors. While these issues may be considered "soft" in the sense that they involve qualitative decisions, they complement the "hard" financial choices of fixing the valuation and the term sheet. Combining hard and soft aspects constitutes the art of structuring a deal. In the language of Chapter 1, this chapter encompasses both left-brained financial thinking and right-brained entrepreneurial thinking.

Everyone agrees that structuring a deal is an art, not a science. Yet, art is not any easier than science. Though qualitative in nature, deal structuring is a complex challenge. It requires solving problems that are inherently ambiguous, like attracting investors; it involves getting an agreement from multiple parties that have conflicting objectives; and often there is time pressure to get the deal done.

Both the entrepreneur and the investor contribute to structuring the deal. Yet, each has different roles at different times. The entrepreneur usually gets the process started, preparing her venture for investment and deciding when to approach the investor. The entrepreneur solicits interest from multiple investors to create competition for the deal. The investor has the main responsibility for evaluating the deal, finding additional investors, and proposing a term sheet. Overall both parties need to contribute their part to make fundraising a success.

To make sense of what is inherently a complex and sometimes unpredictable process, Figure 7.1 identifies the main steps in the process. While it describes a linear process, in practice the experience is far from straightforward, with numerous setbacks and sometimes unexpected breakthroughs.

Figure 7.1 begins with the entrepreneur's need to pitch the opportunity to the investor. The investor then has to screen the deal to see whether he is interested. If there is interest, the investor forms a syndicate of capital providers. The two parties are then ready to enter into negotiations with each other. At the end they close the deal and complete the fundraising process.

Obviously, the process is more complicated than that, which is why in this chapter we delve into the many details of the process. In Section 7.2, we look at the first circle ("Pitching"), asking what entrepreneurs need to do to get their ideas in front of investors, and how they can deal with disclosing and valuing their ideas. In Section 7.3, we look at the second circle ("Screening"), exploring how the investors generate deal flow and screen deals. In this context, we introduce the MATCH tool to practically find a good match. In Section 7.4, we turn to the third circle ("Syndicating"). We examine why and how investors build syndicates with their peers. Section 7.5 examines the fourth circle ("Negotiating") about how parties bring their interests into the process of reaching an agreement. We focus on the more common case where the entrepreneur is negotiating with a single investor, or syndicate, but we also discuss the rarer case where the entrepreneur manages to

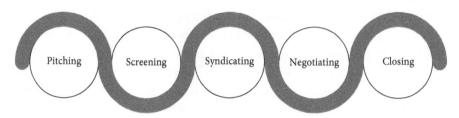

Figure 7.1. The process of structuring a deal.

attract several competing investors or syndicates. This process culminates in the deal actually closing, as indicated by the final circle ("Closing"). In Section 7.6, we look at the bigger picture, noting that after closing the deal, the parties must actually live with it and live with each other. For this we stress the importance of building trust and having a dynamic long-term perspective.

7.2 The Fundraising Process

7.2.1 Preparing the Fundraising Campaign

Prior to launching a fundraising campaign, the entrepreneur needs to prepare for it. We already discussed several key components of this process in earlier chapters. Specifically, Chapter 2 describes how entrepreneurs assess the appeal of their business opportunity and use their analysis to build a presentation, Chapter 3 explains how to build a comprehensive set of financial projections that substantiate the venture's financial appeal, and Chapters 4 and 5 provide tools for estimating what valuation to expect. We now look at how these components feed into an overall fundraising strategy.

Fundraising is typically not a short event but a long process that requires careful preparation. Fundraising is an intense activity that has a high cost: it distracts the entrepreneur from running the company. Good preparation helps reduce the time required to convince investors. Beyond preparing their business plan and projections, the founders need to agree on how they split ownership and what role each of them takes (Section 4.4). They should also use their financial plan (Section 3.7) to decide how much money to ask for and to form an expectation of what valuation they can realistically fetch from investors.

The next part of the entrepreneur's homework is to figure out potential investors. This means different things at different stages of the venture's development. First, early-stage and late-stage companies target different types of investors (see Chapters 12 and 13). Second, the first fundraising is particularly challenging because the entrepreneur needs to attract investors for the first time, with little or no track record. Companies that raise a second or later round already have investors who may also help attract new ones (Section 9.5). Later-stage investors, however, require the company to show that it has not only promise but also the ability to execute. Entrepreneurs may also pursue new investors on their own, with the goal of generating more competition. In all cases, the entrepreneur must figure out what investor type would best fit the venture at the current stage, and then find suitable investors to approach. This requires looking closely into the investment preferences and styles of potential investors.

Entrepreneurs are well advised to make early contact with their investors. The goal is to introduce the company and the founding team, and to start building a relationship with the investor. This is best done well ahead of the time that the company actually needs money. Building a relationship before doing a deal is like getting engaged before getting married—presumably a good idea. From the investor's perspective, it is easier to invest in an entrepreneur who has already established a track record with that investor. Some investors liken this to investing based on a video rather than on a photo. With a video the investor observes how the entrepreneur fends off challenges to execute her plan and can see whether she delivers what she promises. Without such a period of getting to know each other, the investor can only invest by looking at a photo, evaluating the current situation of the company with a limited understanding of how it got there. From the entrepreneur's perspective, getting to know the investor over time reveals how he thinks, what deal he is looking for, and how he reacts to the ups and downs of the entrepreneurial process. Thus, an early engagement allows both parties to assess their mutual fit and to start building trust.

An important decision is when to launch the fundraising campaign. Timing matters because it affects funding risk, company growth, and dilution. The sooner the entrepreneur launches the campaign, the less she has to show in terms of achievements, and the more difficult to attract investors. The longer the entrepreneur waits, the more time she has to improve her business fundamentals: reach a milestone, generate buzz in the market, and so on. However, waiting also means that investors expect more in terms of traction. The longer the entrepreneur waits, the lower her cash reserves will be. Delaying fundraising may deprive the company of resources needed to propel its own progress. Especially in the early days of a venture there is a paradoxical tension where the entrepreneur needs momentum to attract investors, but also needs their money to build momentum. Timing also affects dilution: fundraising early on means more dilution, as company risk is higher and valuation lower than what can be achieved after some milestones have been reached (Section 9.2).

7.2.2 Executing the Fundraising Campaign

Making initial contact with the investor is easier said than done. Successful investors are busy and receive many requests. Cold calling or sending an e-mail is unlikely to be effective. Investors are more likely to respond when the entrepreneur is introduced by somebody they trust. Such referrals are crucial for two reasons. First, the investor trusts the judgment of his own contacts. Second, these contacts spend their reputational capital by vouching for the entrepreneur. They will only recommend those they believe to be an attractive prospect for the investor. This is why, from the entrepreneur's perspective, there is a need to build a professional network that can support these fundraising efforts.

Even a well-prepared entrepreneur with a strong business project and a well-timed fundraising campaign should expect to pitch numerous times: less than 10 investor pitches would be considered low, more than 50 not uncommon. Many pitches are required because finding a match between an entrepreneur and investor is inherently difficult. The entrepreneur needs to find the "right investor at the right time." The "right investor" means that there is a match in terms of the investor's specific expertise and interest for the entrepreneur's specific venture. The "right time" means that the investor is currently interested in making investments in the entrepreneur's business space. Figuring out which investors fall into this category requires further research. At this stage, the entrepreneur should focus on the investor's recent deals. Another dimension that becomes relevant at this stage is how the investor interacts with entrepreneurs and how he is perceived by those he previously funded. These can be contacted directly and can provide valuable first-hand experience, especially for those whose ventures failed.

Getting the pitch right is crucial. The entrepreneur needs to impress investors with domain knowledge and to inspire confidence that she can execute well in the face of unforeseen difficulties. The more compelling evidence she can bring to the table, the better. For early-stage ventures the focus is on customer traction, and for later-stage ventures the emphasis is on overcoming obstacles, achieving set milestones, and hitting financial targets. Another key feature of a successful pitch is clarity: if the entrepreneur cannot simply communicate as to why her venture is appealing and why she should succeed, no investor will fund it.

In the process of pitching an idea, entrepreneurs need to discuss their ideas and plans. Some entrepreneurs become concerned that investors might steal their ideas.[1] Thus, a dilemma faced in the fundraising process is whether to disclose sensitive information, how, and when.

Entrepreneurs who worry about disclosing their confidential information to investors or strategic partners sometimes ask for a nondisclosure agreement (NDA) before pitching their idea. Many investors, however, categorically refuse to sign them. In fact, asking for an NDA can be considered a major *faux pas*. Investors meet many entrepreneurs who think their ideas are novel. In all likelihood, investors already know much of the supposedly new information. They may simply be waiting to meet a team they deem able to execute the idea (Section 2.2.3). Signing NDAs would constrain investors' choices and expose them to undue litigation risk. The only time investors might sign an NDA is at an advanced due diligence stage. The NDA is then used to access very specific information, mostly to verify whether certain claims made by the entrepreneur are true. Box 7.1 provides the academic foundations for understanding NDAs.

Box 7.1 The Disclosure Dilemma

Kenneth Arrow is one of the greatest economists of the 20th century, and we discuss his most influential work in Box 14.1. Here we draw on another of his important contributions, commonly known as the Arrow information paradox (or disclosure paradox).[2] The question Arrow asks is how to pay for an idiosyncratic piece of information, say an entrepreneurial idea. The idea holder can ask the potential recipient to pay before disclosing her idea. However, the recipient would refuse to make any payment as he doesn't know whether the idea is good. He also realizes that once others expect him to pay for ideas, they can simply pretend to have ideas, take the payment, and disclose worthless ideas. So, the idea holder has to disclose her idea first and then try to sell it. The problem is that once disclosed, the recipient has no reason to pay anymore because he can simply use the idea without paying for it. This dilemma impedes the circulation of entrepreneurial ideas.

Arrow's paradox identifies a fundamental challenge of disclosing information. There are two main solutions. The first is patenting the idea. In this case, the idea holder publicly discloses the information in return for legal IP protection, so that others cannot simply copy her idea. The second solution is the use of NDAs. These are legal agreements between an idea holder and a potential recipient, by which the recipient agrees not to take advantage of the disclosed information or to disclose it further to others. An NDA needs to be signed before the information has actually been disclosed. The receiver may, however, be reluctant to sign because he doesn't really know what he is signing and might be concerned to sign away rights to ideas and knowledge that he already has prior to signing. Besides, signing an NDA creates the risk that the idea holder will be spuriously sued even if the receiver never uses the specific information. To overcome this reluctance, the idea holder therefore needs to describe the content of the NDA with sufficient precision to gain the receiver's trust, but without giving away the confidential information itself. NDAs can involve not only technical information, but also information such as customer lists, financial records, or details on potential strategic alliances. In addition to the challenges of crafting suitable NDAs, difficulties may also arise in legally enforcing them, especially for entrepreneurs who lack the financial resources to pursue legal actions.

Given that most investors do not sign NDAs, what should entrepreneurs do? Most business opportunities can be described to investors without revealing the "secret sauce," that is, the sensitive pieces of intellectual property. This might entail the details of how to make a certain product, or certain details about marketing, a valuable service, and so on. Often this means that investor pitches should focus on the business logic, as described in the Venture Evaluation Matrix (see Chapter 2). Moreover, if it were really impossible to protect the idea from investors, then it would presumably be equally impossible to protect it from competitors. This would make it a fairly unattractive business opportunity in the first place.

Once the entrepreneur has pitched, the most common response is a resounding No.[3] This should not discourage the entrepreneur. All successful ventures received rejections before they found investors who believed in them. This calls for resilience and determination. It is also difficult to obtain a straight answer as to why an investor passed on an investment opportunity.

To finalize the campaign, the entrepreneur needs to generate interest strong enough to bring at least one investor to propose a deal. This is a delicate task that requires good negotiating skills. The key is to convince one investor to commit to funding. This represents a turning point that helps to generate positive replies from other investors, many of whom may have been waiting for one investor to make the first move.

7.2.3 Valuing an Idea

In the process of finding an investor at the very early stages of a venture, some entrepreneurs worry not only about how to protect their ideas, but also how to value them. In Chapter 6 we discussed methods for valuing companies. Here we examine the question of how to value an entrepreneurial idea before it becomes embodied in a company. Some entrepreneurs become preoccupied with this question, which can sometimes get in the way of the fundraising process.

Preparing for the fundraising process, entrepreneurs often ask: "How do I value my idea?" A common frustration is that this can be a hopeless task. How can one ever put a value on something as intangible as an idea? We propose to break down this question into four subquestions.

The first subquestion is: "When do I need to value an idea?" Often, there is no hurry. Valuing an idea is only necessary if some financial transaction depends on it, such as negotiating a financing deal. Even then, not all financing deals require a valuation. If an entrepreneur raises debt (see Chapter 10), no valuation is required. An entrepreneur can also issue a convertible note, which delays valuing the company until a later date (see Section 6.6). A valuation is really needed only when equity financing is used. Another situation where a valuation is necessary is when intellectual property protecting the idea is sold or licensed.

The second subquestion is: "What should my idea be worth theoretically?" It is important to have clarity about what exactly we are trying to value. The standard answer in finance is that the value of an idea is the future cash flow that can be derived from it. The challenge is to figure out what the source of the cash flow will be. Since an idea on its own is essentially worthless (it can't produce cash flow by itself), the question becomes how much incremental value the idea enables. For the answer we need to identify what the other required components are. For example, an idea for an innovative toy also requires production, marketing, distribution, and sales, to become a saleable toy. Each of these components has a cost of its own. The value of the idea is therefore related to the incremental profits that can be made after compensating all the other resource providers. In fact, we need to compare the value of using these resources to create the new toy against their alternative uses, for example, all the other toys that can be produced with these resources. This bring us to the question of how unique the idea is.

If the idea is distinct and no one can easily imitate it, then its incremental value is higher. However, many ideas can be easily imitated, thus reducing their value. This can happen even if the original idea is protected by IP. Others can generate similar ideas that fall outside the scope of the protected IP but have equivalent functionality. Even if my innovative toy has a patent, others can come up with a similar toy that does comparable things, using a slightly different technological approach.

The third subquestion is: "How can I get a numerical estimate of the value?" Here we return to the methods examined in this chapter. In principle, we can estimate the incremental cash flow generated by the idea. In the ideal case, one builds financial projections as discussed in Chapter 3 and then calculates a DCF valuation, as discussed in Section 5.3. For innovative ideas, however, this often involves too much guess work to be useful. The alternative is to use external comparisons. A common approach is to look at the prices at which comparable patents were sold or licensed. This involves finding a reasonable set of comparables, as discussed in Section 5.4. The question about the theoretical value of a patent plays directly into this matter because the choice of comparables is based on finding other ideas that have a similar theoretical logic. For example, to assess the value of my innovative toy, I may look at what patents exist for prior comparable ideas about toys. The valuation is then based on what their patents sold for or what licensing revenues they generated. Box 7.2 further explores the challenge of valuing patents.

Box 7.2 The Value of a Patent

What is the value of a patent? This question has preoccupied academics and practitioners alike. The most common conclusion is that this is a difficult question to answer. Economists have developed several approaches to extract the value of patents from data. One approach is to break down the value of (publicly listed) companies into individual factors and isolate the patent portfolio as one of those factors. However, this only provides an estimate of the total value of a patent portfolio, not the value of an individual patent. To get at that, some economists have used surveys to elicit subjective evaluations from patent holders. They ask questions such as what the minimum price would be at which their owners would sell their patents. Another interesting approach is to look at the willingness to pay for patent renewal fees. This reveals information about the value of maintaining a patent.[4]

Even though different studies use different data approaches, some core findings have emerged from this large body of research. First, the value of patents is extremely skewed, meaning that a few patents are tremendously valuable, but most are (close to) worthless. Second, patents are most valuable in the pharmaceutical industry, and they are also valued highly in chemicals, computers, telecommunications, electronics, and machinery. Third, the value of a patent is statistically related to the number of citations it receives. A focal patent is cited when a new patent mentions the focal patents in its list of relevant prior patents. Fourth, learning about the value of a patent happens over time, mostly in the first five years. This last point brings out an interesting tension for the valuation of a patent. In order to learn what the patent is worth, time needs to pass, yet the valuation of the patent is often needed at the very beginning, before any such learning can take place. In case of doubt, it is therefore safest to assume that most new patents are close to worthless.

The final subquestion is: "Did I ask the right question in the first place?" Some innovators, especially scientists, are fixated on the value of their idea. However, it is useful to consider whether the idea is truly the source of value. In some cases, it is; for example, the IP for a cure to cancer would truly be worth a lot. However, in many other cases, the source of value creation is not really the idea, or at least not the only idea. To see this, recall that the first row of the Venture Evaluation Matrix looks at the value proposition. An idea is typically associated with a solution, as represented in the second column. The whole point of the Venture Evaluation Matrix is that the value proposition comes out of the interplay of problem, solution, and team. Focusing on the value of the solution alone neglects how value is actually created. Instead we need a broader perspective of looking at the entire value proposition, including the problem and the team.

Let us return to our innovative toy idea. The question is whether its value lies in the specific solution: Is it basically the toy patent that is creating the value? Or is the true value proposition about meeting customer needs? Maybe the value lies in making toddlers happy, or indeed in making parents think their toddlers need it. Or does the value lie with the team itself? Maybe it is the creativity of the team to design numerous innovative toys over time, or the business savvy to get the toys produced, distributed, and sold in the marketplace. Asking about the value of an idea sometimes means barking up the wrong tree; asking where the value of the venture lies is the more important question.

7.3 Finding a Match

7.3.1 Investor Deal Sourcing

Entrepreneurs need to find investors, but investors need to find entrepreneurs, too. Investors want to see many promising potential deals, which is called a good "deal flow." They know that only a tiny fraction of funding requests is worth exploring. One approach to deal flow is to rely on referrals, and another is to be proactive and seek out the "next big thing."[5] How do investors find promising ventures? A survey of VC firms by Gompers, Gornall, Kaplan, and Strebualev finds that 31% of the investments are generated through the firms' professional networks, and 20% from other investors; 28% are generated proactively by the VCs themselves; 10% are coming from entrepreneurs approaching the investors; and the rest come mostly from referrals of existing portfolio companies.[6]

This data shows that developing and maintaining networks is at the core of generating deal flow. Investors are particularly interested in generating "proprietary" deal flow. This means being in a position to make a funding offer without being pressed by competitors (Section 7.5.2). Proprietary deals do not come easily as the investor has to look in less obvious places to find such deals. A first step is to identify which markets are experiencing innovation and disruption that creates new investment opportunities. For this purpose, investors must be visible to the scientific and technology community, as well as be aware of changes in regulations or consumer preferences. To move into identifying specific companies, investors must be in touch with the entrepreneurial community. They do this by attending industry events and by actively scouting through their networks. Scouting is more difficult when looking for early-stage companies that have not yet raised funds and may be operating in stealth mode. Other investors can also be a source of deal flow through syndication (Section 7.4).

Establishing early contact is as important for investors as it is for entrepreneurs. Both benefit from reducing asymmetric information and testing the potential for a good fit. Since the interaction at this point is informal, it allows both parties to explore each other's views and style, without fear of committing to a mistake.

Having a reputation and brand name clearly helps to attract deal flow. Investors rely mostly on their past successes in bringing companies to an IPO or a successful acquisition. By its nature, this is a slow process that takes years. VC firms and business angel networks advertise their achievements on their website and social media. Individual angels and other early-stage investors rely more on word of mouth. Visibility also comes from being active at industry events, such as giving keynote speeches at conferences or judging at business plan competitions.

In the common scenario, the entrepreneur pitches to the investor, but sometimes this order is reversed. When entrepreneurs are sitting on a "hot" opportunity, it is the VCs that pitch to invest in the company. Catarina Fake, co-founder of Flickr, noted that "when you need money, nobody will return your calls," but "[w]hen you don't need money . . . they can't stop calling you."[7]

7.3.2 Investor Screening

To get an idea of what happens once an entrepreneur and investor come into contact, look again at the survey of VC firms by Gompers, Gornall, Kaplan, and Strebulaev.[8]

The median VC firm screens 200 deals per year and meets 50 management teams. Partners review 20 business plans and perform more detailed due diligence on 12 of them. Offers are made to 5.5 companies, of which 4 accept the investment. The probability of moving from the screening to the investment phase is therefore approximately 2%. The average deal takes 83 days to close and involves 118 hours of due diligence, with the VC making on average 10 reference calls. Clearly, this is an intense process.

After the entrepreneur's initial pitching of her business idea, there is a range of possible investor responses. At the risk of oversimplifying, we distinguish three responses. First, some investors simply say no. The polite version is actually "not now," which leaves the door open in case the company later makes significant progress. Second, some investors are "intrigued" but remain on the fence. They might say that they are interested but are not yet fully convinced. Sometimes it is not clear what they are waiting for or what is needed to convince them. Third, some investors are sincerely "keen." They like the venture but need to know more before being ready to invest.

The next step for the entrepreneur is then to convince the keen investors. This requires passing their due diligence. In Section 2.5.2, we show how investors can use the Venture Evaluation Matrix to structure and perform due diligence. Different investors have different approaches to performing due diligence. Some focus on the entrepreneurial team, probing whether it is competent and trustworthy. Others pore over technical details, delve into market analysis, investigate the customer's interest, and explore the competitive landscape. This due diligence process generates insights that help investors to make up their minds whether or not to invest.[9]

At the end of the due diligence process, the two parties either discover that there is no fit and part ways, or they come to the positive conclusion that there is a potential fit. In that case, they can meaningfully proceed to the next stage of discussing possible deal structures.

7.3.3 The MATCH Tool

What makes a good match between a company and a set of investors? When is it likely that their preferences and priorities actually fit with each other? In this section, we introduce the MATCH tool, which is a pragmatic approach to evaluating company–investor matches. At its core is a questionnaire. The book's website (www.entrepreneurialfinance.net) contains a detailed document that explains the logic for the MATCH tool and provides practical instructions on how to use its scoring system. The document comes with a spreadsheet that contains an example explaining how to use the tool. Table 7.1 shows the structure of the questionnaire.

Table 7.1 The MATCH Questionnaire

Question	Issue	Question for the entrepreneur	Question for the investor
Part 1	*Should we consider working together?*		
1	Geography	What is your location? [use INSERT]	How much do you like to invest in [INSERT]?
2	Industry	What is your industry? [use INSERT]	How much do you like to invest in [INSERT]?
3	Stage	What is your investment stage? [use INSERT]	How much do you like to invest in [INSERT]?
Part 2	*Could we strike a deal?*		
4	Check size	How much investment do you want per investor?	How much do you expect to invest in a company?
5	Security type	What securities do you plan to issue?	What securities do you expect to receive?
6	Board of directors	What role should investors have on the board?	What board role do you want?
Part 3	*What do we have to offer to each other?*		
7	Customers and markets	How much expertise and networks do you require with respect to customers and markets?	How much expertise and networks do you have with respect to customers and markets?
8	Technology and operations	How much expertise and networks do you require with respect to technology and operations?	How much expertise and networks do you have with respect to technology and operations?
9	Leadership and organization	How much expertise and networks do you require to build the leadership team and organization?	How much expertise and networks do you have to build the leadership team and organization?
Part 4	*How would we get on with each other?*		
10	Active involvement	How much time, support, and control do you want from your investors?	How much time, support, and control do you intend to provide?
11	Reinvestment	Do you expect your investors to invest in future rounds?	Do you intend to reinvest in future rounds?
12	Exit horizon	How long will investors have to wait to get liquidity?	How long are you willing to wait to get liquidity?
Part 5	*Can we trust each other?*		
13	Trust	Can you trust the investor?	Can you trust the entrepreneur?

7.4 Syndication

Many deals involve a syndicate of multiple investors. Respondents to the survey of VC firms by Gompers, Gornall, Kaplan, and Strebulaev report that on average 65% of their deals were syndicated.[10] The most important factors cited for syndication were capital constraints (39%), complementary expertise (33%), risk sharing (24%), and access to future deals (3%). The most important factor for choosing a syndication partner were past shared success (28%), expertise (25%), reputation (16%), track record (16%), capital (9%), social connections (3%), and geography (2%).

We now first ask why there is syndication in the first place and then how such syndicates are structured.

7.4.1 Reasons to Syndicate

Why do investors syndicate their investments? A common reason is that smaller investors do not have the required funds by themselves. Even larger ("deep-pocketed") investors that could provide all the funding may be reluctant to do so. They may not want to commit too much money to any one company and instead diversify their portfolio.

Investors also think ahead. They do not want to spend too much money in any one round because they want to set aside some of their money for future investment rounds in the same company. By bringing in a syndication partner, investors are better able to spread their investments over several rounds. Keeping some "dry powder" is also useful to demonstrate ongoing commitment to a company. This avoids dilution and helps to counteract the power of later-round investors who have an incentive to drive down valuations (Section 9.2). Syndication therefore helps the earlier-round investors to support their investments over the entire funding cycle.

In addition to these financial considerations, there are business rationales for syndication.[11] First, there is a workload argument. Investors want to actively follow the company, and ideally be sitting on the board of directors. Sharing the burden with a syndication partners allows the investors to remain active while investing in more companies.

At the investment step, there is the benefit of a second opinion; it is reassuring to know that some other investor also believes in the company. For venture capitalists (VCs), the fact that others also chose the investment helps to justify it to their limited partners, especially in case it performs poorly. A related argument is that bringing in new investors may bring in different value-adding skills than those of previous investors (Section 8.3).

Syndication is also part of a networking strategy. It is a reciprocal process in which bringing good deals to other investors strengthens those relationships and may encourage them to bring deals the other way. Among VC firms, such reciprocity leads to stable syndication networks of firms with similar reputation and standing.[12] Syndication is also common among angel investors who invest within informal networks or more formal angel groups.

From a company perspective, syndication can make it easier to close a deal. After the investment is made, there are further benefits to having a syndicate. A broader set of investors brings complementary skills and networks to the company. It might also give the company easier access to funding sources in future rounds. A disadvantage for the company is that it has to deal with multiple investors. Each investor owns relatively smaller stakes and may thus take a less active stance. More shareholders also means more investor communication. Making decisions takes longer, and it becomes more difficult to find solutions that are acceptable to all shareholders.

Figure 7.2 reports data on worldwide syndication patterns. The table reports the percentage of deals that have more than one investor. It shows three groups of deals, divided by Series (Box 1.6). Early-stage deals (angel and seed) are syndicated less often, typically less than 50% of the time. Series A deals, when VC firms are usually first involved, are syndicated between 65 and 75% of the time. Later-stage deals are mostly syndicated. This shows that syndication is a pervasive feature of financing deals. It naturally becomes more common with later rounds, when the amounts involved become progressively larger. Apart from an increase in early-stage syndication, the share of syndicated deals is fairly stable over time. These patterns are also quite similar across the U.S., Europe, Asia, and the rest of the world.

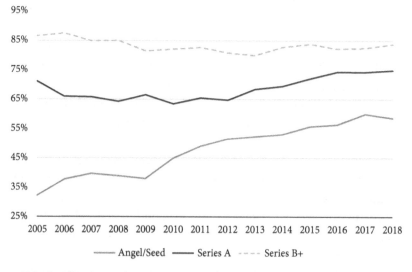

Figure 7.2. Syndication patterns.
Percentage of deals that have more than one investor, by Series.
Source: Pitchbook Data.

7.4.2 The Structure of Syndicates

How are syndicates formed? This process typically starts with one investor discovering the deal and deciding to share it. He will typically show it to select members of his network. This way he can find out who is interested. The choice of whom to invite depends on a variety of business and relationship factors. Business factors include the relevant domain expertise of other investors, their funding resources, their current interest in making additional investments, as well as other idiosyncratic reasons. Relationship factors include how often the other partner made and received similar invitations. Some invitations involve relationship issues, similar to the quandaries of hosting a dinner party: if A is invited, then B should be invited too, although this means C can no longer be invited . . . and so on.

An investor syndicate typically has one leader and several followers.[13] Often these roles are informally understood, without being formalized. In many cases, the syndicate leader is the deal originator. Sometimes, however, the originator can only provide a relatively small fraction of the total round amount. In that case, one of the other investors may step up to become the lead investor, typically the one who invests the most. The lead investor is likely to drive the due diligence process, possibly asking other co-investors to help with specific issues in their domain of expertise. The leader manages the negotiations on behalf of investors and typically takes a board seat after completion of the deal. The lead investor takes more risk and incurs greater efforts. In some cases, this gets rewarded through preferential terms. This is the case, for example, for online platforms such as AngelList, where the lead investor receives additional compensation (Section 13.4).

The lead investor also helps rally other investors who are interested but hesitant. It sends a powerful signal that there is a committed investor who believes that the company is worth investing in. This alone may convince hesitant investors, saving them the trouble of performing costly due diligence themselves.[14] The identity of the lead investor matters too. Entrepreneurs want to convince influential lead investors to add momentum to their fundraising campaign. This strategy, however, can also be risky. If an influential investor rejects the deal, others might hear of it, and this could turn the tide against the entrepreneur.

A study by Åstebro, Fernández Sierra, Lovo, and Vulkan identifies a similar domino effect in equity crowdfunding (see also Section 13.4). If a campaign receives a large pledge, ideally by a well-known investor, then other investors are more forthcoming. However, if no large pledges have been received for a while, other investors also become more timid with their pledges.[15]

In later rounds, the syndicate structure is also affected by the rights and preferences of the existing investors who typically hold a right to participate in the new round (Section 9.2). Often a later-round syndicate is composed of some earlier-round investors, plus some new investors who bring in a fresh perspective on the company, but also have their own demands as to how the syndicate operates.[16]

Does syndication matter for investment performance? Box 7.3 takes a look at some academic research on this important issue.

Box 7.3 Syndication and Investment Performance

The relationship between syndication and investment performance could in theory go either way. On the one hand, investors have an incentive to keep the best deals for themselves and only share the riskier and more difficult ones. On the other hand, this section explained how syndicates can provide better support that will help companies to succeed. Two studies, one by Brander, Amit, and Antweiler, using Canadian data, and one by Tian, using U.S. data, both show that syndicated VC investments have a higher success rate, as measured by a higher proportion of IPOs and acquisitions.[17] In case of an IPO, syndicated investment also reach higher valuations and have lower underpricing (Section 11.2).

If there is a benefit to sharing deals, the question becomes whom to share it with. A study by Hochberg, Ljungqvist, and Lu shows that better networked VC firms achieve better investment performance overall.[18] Lerner's study of biotechnology companies further shows that top-tier VCs typically share early-round deals among themselves, although they may add lower ranked VC firms in later rounds.[19] Research by Dimov and Milanov notes that VCs face two types of risks: company risk and partnering risk. They find that syndication is more likely when company risk is high. It is also more likely when the lead VC has higher status, which reduces partnering risk by giving access to better syndication partners.[20]

Syndication also permits better access to specific expertise. Research by Hochberg, Lindsey, and Westerfield finds that VC firms with expertise in the company's business syndicate with less expert VC firms that mainly contribute capital.[21] In a related vein, a study by Meuleman, Jääskeläinen, Maula, and Wright finds that cross-border investments require a combination of international investors who bring foreign capital, networks, and expertise with locally embedded partners who understand the local environment.[22] The choice of syndication partner, however, is not always entirely driven by economic factors. Research by Gompers, Mukharlyamov, and Xuan shows that when VCs choose their syndication partners on the basis of similar ethnic or educational backgrounds, or similar professional experiences, then the investments are less likely to succeed.[23]

7.5 Deal Negotiations

7.5.1 Bargaining Theory

We now consider the negotiation process between entrepreneurs and investors. For that purpose, Box 7.4 introduces some relevant tools from bargaining theory.

Box 7.4 Nobel Insights on Bargaining Theory

The Nobel Prize in Economics for 1994 was awarded jointly to John F. Nash Jr., John C. Harsanyi, and Reinhard Selten "for their pioneering analysis of equilibria in the theory of non-cooperative games."[24] John Nash is one of the most famous economists and mathematicians of the 20th century, and the only one to have won both the Nobel Prize for Economics and the Abel Prize, the equivalent prize for mathematics. His personal struggles with paranoid schizophrenia were dramatized in the 2002 Oscar-winning movie *A Beautiful Mind*. Economists had of course known about the beauty of Nash's mind long before Hollywood; he is especially known for two seminal contributions. First, he identified an equilibrium concept now referred to as the "Nash equilibrium."[25] Second, he developed a simple solution to a prototypical bargaining game, called the "Nash bargaining solution." We are interested here in the second contribution.[26]

Nash considered a general bargaining game between two parties. In our context, we can think of it as a negotiation between an investor and an entrepreneur. Nash's goal was to explain what kind of a deal the two parties would strike, depending on their characteristics and the circumstances surrounding the deal. In principle, this is a hugely complex problem because there are numerous aspects to consider. Nash, however, showed how to boil this problem down to just four key parameters. The first two parameters describe the "outside options" of the two parties. These are the payoffs parties would get when walking away from the bargaining. In our context, outside options correspond to what would happen when there is no investment. The third parameter is the joint value that the two parties can achieve by cooperating. This value must be higher than the sum of the outside options; otherwise the two parties are better off not doing a deal. The final parameter describes how the two parties share the surplus value, that is, the difference between the joint value and the sum of outside options. These four parameters can be thought of as a summary description of numerous factors that may give one party an upper hand over the other.

The Nash bargaining solution provides a simple but disciplined approach to understanding the basics of negotiation. Let us see how it works by using a simple fictional example. Consider an entrepreneur by the name of Elsa Echtknap, who invented a clever algorithm for predicting the outcomes of business negotiations. She built a start-up and found a buyer who would pay it $6M. This is the entrepreneur's outside option. However, she knew that with the help of a $1M investment from her friend, Ingo Ingelicht, she could build a company worth $10M. The $1M represents the investor's outside option, and the $10M is the joint value they can achieve. The surplus is then $3M = $10M – $1M – $6M. Elsa considered herself a canny negotiator and thought she could capture two-thirds of the surplus value, or $2M, which represents the entrepreneur's bargaining strength.

To see what the Nash bargaining solution predicts, we denote the joint value by JV, the surplus value by SV, the bargaining strength by BS, and the outside option by OO. Let E be the subscript for the entrepreneur (Elsa), and I for the investor (Ingo). Elsa's bargaining strength is then $BS_E = 2/3$, and Ingo's bargaining strength is $BS_I = 1/3$ (as the two bargaining strengths need to sum up to 1). We also have that $JV = \$10M$, $OO_E = \$6M$ and $OO_I = \$1M$.

We are interested in calculating the parties' respective bargaining values, denoted by BV_E and BV_I. The Nash bargaining solution works as follows. The surplus value is given by:

$$SV = JV - OO_E - OO_I = \$10M - \$6M - \$1M = \$3M$$

The entrepreneur's bargaining value is thus given by:

$$BV_E = OO_E + BS_E * SV = \$6M + \frac{2}{3} * \$3M = \$8M$$

The investor's bargaining value is given by:

$$BV_I = OO_I + BS_I * SV = \$1M + \frac{1}{3} * \$3M = \$2M$$

The Nash bargaining solution then predicts that Elsa should receive $8M of the $10M joint value, and Ingo should receive the remaining $2M. Note that, by construction, the sum of bargaining values equals the joint value: $BV_E + BV_I = \$8M + \$2M = \$10M$. The outcome predicted by the Nash bargaining solution is that, for the $1M investment, Elsa would give Ingo 20% of the equity.

How does the entrepreneur's bargaining value in the Nash solution relate to the company's valuation? They are distinct, except in one case. In our example, the post-money valuation is $5M (= $1M/20%), and the pre-money valuation $4M ($5M – $1M). We note that the pre-money valuation is less than the entrepreneur's bargaining value of $8M. How come? In turns out that the entrepreneur's bargaining value equals the pre-money valuation only when the entrepreneur has all the bargaining strength and can obtain all the surplus value. In this case, we have $BS_E = 1$ and $BS_E = 0$, so that

$$BV_E = \$6M + 1*\$3M = \$9M \text{ and } BV_I = \$1M + 0*\$3M = \$1M.$$

The investor would only get 10% of the shares, the post-money valuation would be $10M (= $1M/10%), and the pre-money valuation $9M ($10M – $1M). The reason for this is that the entrepreneur can appropriate the full value of the company when financial markets are perfectly competitive, which is precisely when the entrepreneur has all the bargaining strength and the investor none. The general lesson here is that competition is a key determinant of bargaining outcomes. Entrepreneurs benefit from competition among investors. The reverse is also true: Investors have stronger bargaining power when there is more competition among companies all trying to raise funds.

7.5.2 Negotiation Analysis

To analyze deal negotiation between an entrepreneur and investor, we draw on the Nash bargaining solution.[27] We consider three key elements: (1) the parties' outside options of not striking a deal, (2) the Zone of Possible Agreements (ZOPA), and (3) the final agreement. Outside options anchor the negotiation. No one will consent to an agreement that makes one worse off than not signing the deal. The outside options therefore define the boundaries of what is and what isn't acceptable. From outside options we obtain the set of deals that are acceptable to both parties, that is, the ZOPA. Finally, we consider deal-specific bargaining dynamics that determine exactly which specific agreement within the ZOPA actually gets chosen.

7.5.2.(a) Outside Options

What would the entrepreneur do if the investor walked away? Her outside option is to continue fundraising, looking for a new set of investors who believe in the business. Walking away from a deal can also send a negative signal to other investors, who may not know the reason for this choice and may become wary of the entrepreneur.

As long as the entrepreneur is negotiating with investors, she has to continue self-funding the venture. For new ventures, this stretches the entrepreneur's finances, with the business never taking off. For more mature ventures, this requires reducing the burn rate, which may lead to underinvestment and possibly some firing of employees. The worst case scenario is having to shut down the business.

The case for walking away herself becomes more attractive for the entrepreneur when she has some tangible interest from other investors. During their fundraising campaign, entrepreneurs often try to create competing offers, so that they can use one offer as a threat of walking away from the other, and vice versa. We discuss this further in Section 7.5.4.

The outside options for the investors are relatively straightforward. If they walk away, they preserve their cash and can therefore make other investments. Entrepreneurs are always implicitly competing with other entrepreneurs for scarce funding resources. Similarly, investors are competing with other investors for good entrepreneurial investment opportunities, whether the one under consideration or other opportunities.

7.5.2.(b) Zone of Possible Agreement

Consider first a negotiation in which an entrepreneur and an investor only bargain over valuation or, equivalently, the price per share. The investor's outside option defines the maximum valuation that he is willing to pay, and the entrepreneur's outside option defines the minimum valuation that she is willing to accept. A Zone of Possible Agreement (ZOPA) exists if the investor is willing to pay at least as much as the entrepreneur's minimum acceptable valuation. In this negotiation, the ZOPA is a segment on a line describing the set of valuations that are mutually acceptable to both parties.

Chapter 6 shows that term sheets contain important elements beyond valuation. Section 6.5 emphasizes that the negotiation between entrepreneurs and investors is multidimensional. Figure 7.2 provides an illustration of for a two-dimensional bargaining situation, where the investor is willing to pay a higher valuation, measured on the vertical axis, if he gets stronger downside protection, measured on the horizontal axis (see also Box 6.6). The investor's trade-off is represented by the upward-sloping line in the figure. Suppose for simplicity that the entrepreneur doesn't care at all about downside protection because she is very confident that she will succeed. However, she has a minimum valuation below which she is unwilling to accept the investment, represented by the horizontal line. Figure 7.3 shows a situation where, in the absence of any downside protection, the investor's maximum valuation lies below the entrepreneur's minimum. This means that with common equity the two parties would never agree on a deal. However, with convertible stock, which carries downside protection, a ZOPA opens up, shown by the shaded area.

7.5.2.(c) Reaching an Agreement

Which contract within a ZOPA is eventually chosen? This is difficult to predict, as it depends on the many idiosyncrasies of each specific bargaining situation, including the timing of events, the market environment, and the bargaining skills of the individual parties.

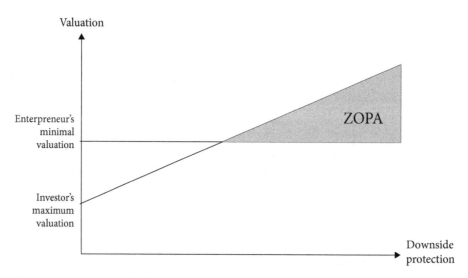

Figure 7.3. An example of a ZOPA.

In reaching an agreement, the two parties need to remind themselves that they are not really dividing an asset of fixed value. Instead they are trying to grow a venture together, where every trade-off made has implications for the incentives of the two parties and thus for the future of the company. For example, an offer with a low valuation and strong downside protection may take away the entrepreneur's motivation. Similarly, an entrepreneur who refuses to give the investor any influence over the company may actually be closing down the investor's ability to add value to the company.[28]

7.5.3 Closing the Deal

To give a practical sense of what it takes to close a deal, and how long it takes, Box 7.5 looks at the story of one venture. While the specific details are particular to this venture, the nature of the experience will probably resonate with many others.

Box 7.5 Tales from the Venture Archives: Pitching Brill Power

---

Brill Power was founded by four Oxford graduates in the fall of 2016. It developed a new battery management system that dramatically improved the performance of existing battery packs. The company was named after the village of Brill, in hilly Oxfordshire. This is where the founders liked to ride to on their weekends. The difficulty of those bike rides paled in comparison to the difficulties of raising their first financing round.

Three of the co-founders, Chris, Damien, and Adrien, were still completing their doctoral or postdoctoral studies in engineering at the University of Oxford. The fourth, Carolyn, was an Oxford MBA. She initiated the company's efforts to raise funds in November 2016. She was working part-time on Brill Power and part-time as research assistant for an Oxford professor. Her task was to build a financial model for a textbook on entrepreneurial finance, an assignment that would soon prove useful.

Planning ahead, Carolyn gave herself a "generous" six-month runway to raise the required funding. The team intended to raise £350K in order to go full time by the summer of 2017. However, building their first pitch proved difficult and time consuming. Their pilot project, involving recycled batteries in Kenya, showed that their initial target market, developing countries, was not the right place to start. This convinced them to turn their focus to Europe, starting with the UK. However, when the founders built their pitch deck, it didn't feel ready. The product and the value proposition were not well defined, and the financial projections didn't feel "real."

In the weeks before Christmas, Carolyn delivered several investor pitches, but none found the team's pitch very convincing. Still, there was a silver lining in the feedback, namely, that batteries were considered a hot space. In early 2017, the company did a second pivot, from improving the second life of batteries to improving their first life. They focused on two specific markets: (1) battery packs for commercial and industrial use and (2) electric vehicles.

One important step was to try to spin the company out of the University. They had started negotiations in December 2016 for licensing and an equity split agreement. The University's initial offer was clearly unacceptable to the founders, who sought the help of a lawyer to come up with a bargaining strategy. They indicated to the University that in the absence of a better deal they would simply leave the University IP behind and start another company focusing on software applications that didn't require the IP. Negotiations continued at a slow pace.

By April 2017, the team was running far behind the initial fundraising schedule, but they felt that their pitch deck was finally getting into good shape. The battery market was large, the strategy was compelling, and for the first time their financial projections felt coherent. This is when Carolyn was informed that her visa to stay in the UK was terminated due to technicalities. Leaving the country within days, she returned to her parents in Canada. This meant that Chris, the CEO, was now in charge of all fundraising efforts. Being a technical founder, he was initially overwhelmed, and so he sought help from the Saïd Business School's Entrepreneurship Centre. His search soon led him to a partner in a local VC, who expressed some interest but was reluctant to commit to a deal.

In early July, just at the time the founders had decided to join full time, the company ran out of money. Thankfully, none of the founders had significant student loans, and they could count on the financial support from their respective families. As their hopes were getting as low as the company's bank account, Chris received an offer from an angel group that Carolyn had pitched to before Christmas. They were motivated by a tax deadline and quickly wanted to deploy £20K, with a vague promise to invest another £100K later. The £20K offer was too little, and the term sheet contained several uncomfortable control terms. So, the team turned down their offer.

The middle of August brought an unexpected breakthrough. The company had applied for a £100K grant from Innovate UK, a government agency. Brill Power had passed the first stage and now needed to find a private investor who would match the grant with an additional £50K of equity. In a single phone call, the local VC partner who had expressed interest at the beginning of the summer agreed to invest the £50K using a convertible note. Suddenly, the company had £150K out of the £350K. Only £200K to go!

Back in Canada, Carolyn was introduced to a local investor by her mother-in-law. "I didn't even want to take the meeting. I didn't think he would ever be interested in a little UK start-up," she recalled. To her surprise, the investor was enthusiastic and within hours offered to invest the remaining £200K. Suddenly everything was falling in place—except that Brill Power still needed to finalize the spin-out agreement with the University. All the investors required the company to secure the IP before committing their funds.

By the end of summer, Carolyn had sorted out her visa problems and was back in the UK. Negotiations with the University continued through September and October; her challenge was to keep all the investors committed. In mid-November, an agreement with the University was finally struck. A mere year after the initial decision to raise funds, Brill Power finally closed its seed round of £350K. In addition, the company landed some smaller grants and won an energy challenge organized by Shell that came with a €100K prize in the form of a convertible note. At last, the company could focus on developing its business.

Carolyn commented: "Once you've gone through your first fundraising, you learn to live with the risk. You get used to projecting expenses without having the funds in place. But it's not for the faint-hearted: the ups and downs are much rougher than in the Oxfordshire countryside!"

In the closing process, the parties come together to forge the final agreement. This is not only a question of finding a compromise within the ZOPA, it is also a question of coordinating all the various parties to join in a common agreement.

The entrepreneur first needs to secure the full commitment of a lead investor. With that, it becomes easier to assemble the final investor syndicate. When he decides to syndicate the deal, the lead investor actively rallies the other investors into making a commitment. The entrepreneur further tries to convince all those who are still on the fence.

At the closing stage, lawyers play an important role. Term sheet negotiations are usually assisted by lawyers on each side. Investors hire them repeatedly, which creates loyalty and familiarity. Entrepreneurs tend to know less about this process and are well advised to seek out experienced legal advisers.

To close a deal, founders need a common negotiating position. Many founder teams delegate negotiations to one member, often the CEO. This helps to bring coherence to the negotiation process. When there are disagreements within the team, the team may fail to speak in one voice in front of their investors. This can severely undermine their credibility and may even precipitate failure to close the deal.

Another challenge in closing a deal may be that in addition to the investor and entrepreneurs, there are other parties whose agreement is required to close the deal. For example, a start-up may need to attract a certain senior executive to bring specific skills to the venture. Such an individual would usually have good alternative employment, so recruiting her requires that the venture tbe credible and offer an attractive compensation package. Both of these requirements depend on successful fundraising. This creates an interdependence between the financing of the company and its hiring process. There are different ways that the three-way negotiation can work out. For example, it may be that the executive sets a condition that the company first closes its funding round before agreeing to join. Or it may be that the investors set a condition that the executive join before they agree to make the investment. Often it is up to the entrepreneur to resolve these impasses, rallying all parties to agree on a joint deal.

For the final agreement, the parties typically sign a term sheet that constitutes a formal commitment to invest. This document still comes with some closing conditions. Typically, there is some additional due diligence that may even require a nondisclosure agreement (Section 7.2.2). After that, the lawyers from both sides put together the final investment documentation. During this final period, the entrepreneur is not allowed to "shop around" the deal. Investors may still withdraw during that period, but only in case the due diligence brings about some negative evidence, which is rare.

Sometimes a company has two closings. The first closing is meant to lock in those investors who are ready to commit enough funds for a successful round. After that, the company and these investors may decide to keep the round open to seek additional investments. The terms of a second closing are usually the same as those of the first. The second close is targeted at new investors who were unaware of the deal, as well as laggard investors who needed to see the first close to get comfortable with joining the deal.

We illustrate the long path toward closing a deal in WorkHorse Box 7.1.

WorkHorse Box 7.1 Closing the A Round

Here is an extract from Astrid's personal diary.

Monday, December 21st, 2020.
We talked about Wolf's term sheet all weekend long. We like the $2M investment and the $8M post-money valuation, but some of the contractual clauses are just awful. Thankfully Victoria was around, she helped us formulate four negotiation priorities: (i) replace the participating preferred shares with convertible preferred shares; (ii) relax the clause about founder salaries; (iii) drop the founder vesting and firing clause, and (iv) remove Wolf C. Flow from the list of proposed board members.

We sent our investors an e-mail and immediately got three "out-of-office" replies: one from Michael who is off sailing in the Caribbean, one from Ali who is off skiing in Whistler (Canada), and one from Wolf, no explanation given. So much for Santa coming early this year! It is winter solstice tonight; at home in Sweden everyone is celebrating. Frankly I am getting depressed. Nothing will happen before the New Year!

Tuesday, December 22nd, 2020.
Surprise! Michael replied to Victoria's e-mail, he even apologized for the slow response. His yacht had limited internet in the middle of the Caribbean seas,

but he said he expected to land in Antigua late afternoon. Ali also replied from Whistler. Apparently the weather is lousy, so instead of skiing he hopes to get in touch with the others. No reply from Wolf.

Late in the afternoon Michael called me on a crackling phone line. The conversation was hurried, but his message was clear. He wants a deal, he is open to negotiate, but he considers our four proposed changes a big ask. "It is unlikely the others will accept all four, so focus on one, maximum two seats."

We decided to follow his advice to better define our own priorities. We had a long debate which ended in a short e-mail:

Dear Michael,

You asked us about our priorities. First, it's hard to admit, but the issue of salaries is very important to us. We initially wanted $85K. We can reduce that to $50K, but at $25K we simply can't make ends meet. Second, we really think the company would benefit from having an external director instead of Wolf. Any chance we can work on closing the deal right after Christmas?

Happy Christmas from Astrid, Brandon, Bharat, Annie, and Victoria

His reply came just a few minutes later:

"Thx, I talk to Ali soon. Not sure where Wolf is. Let's talk Mon 28, 8am EST OK? CU MA."

Monday, December 28th, 2020.

Michael called at 8am—not my favorite time. He was in a hurry as he was off sailing to Guadeloupe. He wanted to better understand our priorities, but when I brought up salaries he pushed back hard. He told his story of how he had lived off $10K a year when he started his first venture . . . but that was 25 years ago!

Michael also said that striking Wolf off the board list was not very smart: "He is not the kind of guy who likes being crossed out." We agreed that we need an external director, and he made a brilliant suggestion: Malcolm Force. He is the CEO of Bolts-N-Nuts, a large hardware retail chain, he clearly understands the business, and he has a reputation for being level-headed and fair. I met him several times this year. Once you get used to his style –he used to be a sergeant in the Marines—you respect his integrity and frankness. I really like the idea of Malcolm, but what should we do about Wolf?

Michael said he didn't mind our proposal on vesting, which was within standard terms. He bellowed into the phone that he would try to contact Ali and Wolf, and get back as soon as they had talked.

Tuesday, December 29th, 2020.

This morning there was an e-mail from Ali in my Inbox. He said he was open to negotiate, but didn't understand why we replaced the participating with convertible preferred shares. He said we should be more confident about our business. Hot-headedly Brandon wanted to reply that he should be more confident in them, and shouldn't ask for downside protection in the first place. I convinced him not to send that e-mail.

The rest of the day nothing much happened, except that we all ended up working until late—just like any other week. No word from Wolf. I also noted that Victoria hasn't answered my e-mails.

Wednesday, December 30th, 2020.
Michael called me at 7am—can you believe it? He was in a rush, he was off to sail to Dominica. He finally got hold of Wolf, who was very upset that his name had been taken off the board list. Michael said bluntly: "Either you put Wolf on the board, or we have to look for another syndicate partner. That could take months and. . . . " The line was cut: he had dropped his phone in the clear waters of the ocean..

The four of us met in the afternoon to talk about the deal. In the middle of the conversation, Bharat pulled out an empty sheet of paper and said: "Look, it's easy, just think of it as a multiperson multidimensional ZOPA problem." He drew the following table:

	Downside protection	Board of Directors	Salary	Founder vesting
WorkHorse's founders	Convertible Preferred (Priority 4)	External Director (Priority 2)	$50K (Priority 1)	No vesting (Priority 3)
Michael Archie			Prefers $25K (Priority 1)	
Ali Ad-Lehr	Participating Preferred (Priority 1)			
Wolf C. Flow		Board seat (Priority 1)		
Compromise	Compromise: accept participating preferred	Compromise: Wolf on board, but still get external	Temporary compromise: $25K one more year	No compromise needed

We all stared at Bharat's table, and one by one everyone began to smile. This made it all clear. In order to find the zone of possible agreements, we first need to understand our investors' priorities. The table shows that each investor has a well-defined top priority, but each top priority is different. The trick will be to give each investor what he cares about the most, and then find the best possible solution for us.

On the downside protection topic, we quickly agreed to give Ali the participating preferred shares he wants, but it just isn't a high priority for us. For the board, we need to take Wolf: Yuk! Annie noted, however, that we can still increase the board size to six and add an external director. The salary issue remains the toughest, but we cannot afford to lose Michael's support. Brandon already gave up his salary for shares. He suggested we bite the bullet and accept the $25K, but raise it to $50K after one year. He even offered to return some of his shares too, but we told him not to worry. As for the founder vesting, no one seems to mind dropping it, so no need to compromise on that. Overall this feels like it is a painful compromise, but somehow it seems worth it.

Since Victoria was not with us, we drafted an e-mail to our investors by ourselves, crossed our fingers, and sent it off. I guess at this point it is safe to say that nothing will happen before the New Year.

Thursday, December 31st, 2020.
Michael called at 6am—don't ask. He was in a rush, as he was about to sail off to Martinique. He really likes the new proposal and was happy that we had "come to our senses" about salaries: "Do you know that when I was on my first start-up, I lived off $10K a year. . . . " About the board, he said that going up to six directors was a no-no: "Guaranteed deadlock, always stick to odd numbers." Then he completely surprised me by saying that he would just give up his own board seat. I told him that we really wanted him on the board, but he said there really wasn't much wiggle room left there. "But don't worry, I will still come to the meetings, I just won't vote." He also said that he would try to get hold of Ali and Wolf, and that we should get Victoria to send him a proper proposal ASAP.

In the afternoon we received an e-mail from Ali. Apparently, it was raining in Whistler, so he found time to look at the proposal. He liked it, had already talked to Michael, but couldn't get hold of Wolf. He also suggested we get Victoria to send a proper proposal ASAP. This is all so exciting, but where on earth is Victoria?

Well, it is 10 o'clock on Dec 31st. Forget the fireworks, let me just get some sleep for once. Next year is going to be a big year for us—if we can ever get this deal closed. At least I can safely say now that nothing will happen before the New Year!

Friday, January 1st, 2021.
I woke up at 11am. No phone calls this morning, what a relief! In the late afternoon I opened my laptop. The first e-mail said: "WE HAVE A DEAL." It came from Victoria, apparently she had sent it off last night at 11pm. This is what it said:

Dearest WorkHorses,
WE HAVE A DEAL!!!
Happy new year from the Caribbean. Sorry for being slow to respond, but I spent a few days with friends in St, Lucia. For the New Year celebrations, we hitched a ride to Martinique, and guess who I met: Michael Archie! He was all excited about the deal. I knew from your e-mails what you wanted, so we sat down and agreed on the attached term sheet. Michael assured me that all the investors are on board, so consider it a deal.
I have to run now, Michael invited us to his yacht for champagne.
CONGRATULATIONS!
Victoria

In this crazy start-up world, never say "nothing will happen!"

7.5.4 Deal Negotiations with Investor Competition

So far, we have considered the case of an entrepreneur negotiating with a single investor syndicate. This has benefits of coordination but also limits competition, keeping valuations low and aiding investor-friendly terms. Investor collusion may be explicit or implicit, and it may be legal or not, but the entrepreneur has limited power to change it. The one thing the entrepreneur can do is to try to create more competition for the deal.

Creating competition requires generating some buzz around the deal. This means attracting investors from networks that do not overlap with those of the first set of investors. Once an entrepreneur has elicited interest from competing investors, bargaining power shifts in favor of the entrepreneur. Moreover, it creates a sense of urgency that helps to propel investors to close the deal, as they don't want the other party to come back with a better offer. Receiving multiple offers remains relatively rare and happens mainly in two situations: (1) either with "hot deals" where the venture appears particularly strong and appeals to many investors, or (2) during "hot markets" where many investors are chasing relatively few deals (see Box 4.3).

To prevent competition, investors may ask the entrepreneur not to seek out any other investors while they deliberate the investment; that is, they ask for some exclusivity. However, prior to the investors making any commitments themselves, this is a rather self-serving request that entrepreneurs routinely ignore. Things change once the entrepreneur signs a term sheet, which typically specifies a "no-shop" clause preventing the entrepreneur from seeking alterative offers.

With multiple offers, how should the entrepreneur decide which offer to accept? This involves a mix of financial and nonfinancial considerations. The offer with the highest valuation does not necessarily constitute the most attractive offer. Deal terms and the quality of the investors matter too (see also Box 4.3). WorkHorse Box 7.2 provides an example of the trade-off between valuation and investor quality.

WorkHorse Box 7.2 Competing Offers

After that eventful last week of 2020 (see WorkHorse Box 7.1), the four founders quickly settled back to work. On Tuesday, January 5, 2021, Brandon received an unexpected LinkedIn request. A gentleman by the name of Mikhail Miniov wrote on behalf of a large investment fund, called OCC. Mikhail said he found WorkHorse on LinkedIn as he scouting for investment opportunities in renewable energy. They set up a meeting, and Mikhail turned out to be knowledgeable about the technical challenges of the venture. Brandon mentioned the current term sheet offer. To his surprise, Mikhail said that OCC planned to make a competing offer for a post-money valuation of $12M, using the same terms. He promised to call back in two days.

A $12M valuation would be a significant step up, but who exactly was behind OCC? An online search revealed that it was a large diversified investment fund from an oligarch family. Officially, OCC stood for "Oleg & Caterina Cleptovsky," although some blogs jokingly referred to them as "Oblivious Clueless Capital." Apparently the fund had a passive approach of letting entrepreneurs get on with their business.

The offer created some immediate controversy. Astrid argued that they had already agreed in principle to their existing syndicate and should therefore dismiss the offer on principle. Annie sided with her, emphasizing the importance of always maintaining good investor relationships. Bharat and Brandon noted that no term sheet had yet been officially signed, nor had they made any effort to solicit the offer. Therefore, they were free to consider the deal. Bharat liked OCC's passive approach because he believed that engineers, not investors, should determine WorkHorse's success. Brandon disagreed; he considered investor support essential to the success of their venture. He therefore pulled out a spreadsheet to crunch some numbers. Which deal was actually the more attractive?

	EIV-CTT offer	OCC offer Bharat's view	OCC offer Brandon's view
Amount ($M)	2	2	2
Pre-money valuation ($M)	6	10	10
Post-money valuation ($M)	8	12	12
Founder share before round	78%	78%	78%
Founder share after round	59%	65%	65%
Probability of success	80%	80%	60%
Exit value ($M)	25	25	25
Expected exit value ($M)	20	20	15
Expected value for founders ($M)	11.7	13.0	9.8

The first column reports the existing offer from Eagle-I and Coyo-T Capital (labeled "EIV-CTC"). For the exit value, he assumed that in case of success the company would be worth \$25M (see WorkHorse Box 5.5). He estimated the probability of success at 80%. Ignoring any discounting (which does not matter here), he estimated an expected exit value of \$20M, with a 59% stake after the round. This would give the founders an expected value of \$11.71M.

In the second column, Brandon presented Bharat's view where OCC's offer would not affect the company performance, so that the exit value and probability of success were the same as in column 1. With those assumptions it was clear that OCC's offer would be better for the founders, who would retain 65% instead of 59%. Their expected value at exit would be \$13.01M instead of \$11.71M. However, Brandon fundamentally believed that success would be less likely without good investor support. In column 3, he assumed a lower success probability of 60% under OCC's offer. Even though the founders still retained an ownership fraction 65% with OCC's offer, instead of 59% with EIV-CTC, their expected share of the exit value was only \$9.76M, instead of \$11.71M. Brandon argued that it was fundamentally dangerous to look just at valuations because ultimately it was returns that mattered. Accepting a higher valuation from a lower-quality investor could sometimes be a losing proposition.

With three against one, Bharat conceded, and WorkHorse rejected the OCC offer.

7.6 Living with the Deal

It is one thing to close a deal, another to live with it. When structuring a deal, it is easy to "miss the forest for the trees." The trees are the deal, and the forest is the success of the venture. When haggling over a carpet in a bazaar, maybe all that matters is to bargain hard for the best deal, knowing that neither party will meet the other again. In the context of entrepreneurial finance, however, the interaction with the other party is protracted and repeated, as entrepreneurs and investors expect to work with each other over a long period of time. This affects how they conduct themselves during and after the negotiations.[29] There are two important aspects to this relationship: trust and a long-term perspective.

7.6.1 The Importance of Trust

According to the Oxford Dictionary, trust is the "firm belief in the reliability, truth, or ability of someone or something." Trust allows one party to let the other take actions freely, without direct control or limitations. This is very important in the fast-moving and highly uncertain environment of entrepreneurial finance, where contracts can only legislate broadly defined actions and contingencies. Trust provides a cushion that allows parties to make decisions in situations where there are no more written rules. Thus, it enables exploratory behavior, which is central to the entrepreneurial process.

Trust affects the entire financing process and is thus relevant across all chapters of this book. It therefore plays a prominent role as the final question of the MATCH tool of Table 7.1. When it comes to making investments and structuring deals, parties quickly realize how limited and incomplete any legal contract is (see Box 6.2). For a deal to work well there must be a "soft" element that binds the "hard" elements written down in a term sheet. Soft elements are the unwritten details, attitudes, behaviors, and actions actually taken.

To understand how trust affects financial transactions, let us distinguish between generalized and personalized trust. Generalized trust is the initial level of trust that different sets of people have on the basis of generally observable information, such as ethnicity, gender, age, and education. Generalized trust can be full of stereotypes but remains an important part of how people assess each other, especially when they don't know each other yet.[30] Personalized trust kicks in once the relationship unfolds and the parties get to know each other. It reflects the professional and ultimately even the personal relationship between two parties. It is based on a much more detailed understanding of their respective behaviors and attitudes. At the very beginning of a funding relationship, the level of trust corresponds to the generalized level of trust. Through repeated interactions, the parties either grow their personalized trust or see it deteriorate.

Although trust may appear to be remote from business transactions, it is not. Research by Malhotra and Murnighan shows that incompleteness of contracts spurs the development of personalized trust.[31] A firm belief in the investor's reliability allows the entrepreneur to accept investor decisions and behaviors that may seem self-serving. This may occur early on, when a trusting entrepreneur gives the investor board control in case of a large investment. It may also happen later on, when a founder agrees to step down as CEO and lets the investor bring in a professional CEO. On the other side, trust is important for the investor to greenlight a large acquisition or the hiring of key employees.

Trust takes time to build, but it can be quickly lost. Once trust starts being undermined, even the simple things become complicated. Communication costs increase. Instead of relying on a verbal understanding, things need to be written down, possibly verified by lawyers. The entrepreneur loses the possibility to take actions that are not formally approved by the investor. She also needs to make sure the venture adheres to plans and expectations. This can become frustrating, even harmful. Ultimately, lack of trust can lead to costly legal disputes.

7.6.2 A Long-Term Perspective

Growing trust requires all parties to take a long-term perspective. To understand what that actually entails, we first look at how a long-term perspective affects the relationship between entrepreneurs and investors. We then further expand the discussion by looking at how these parties establish broader reputations in the business community.

A classic mistake of inexperienced entrepreneurs and investors is to think of the financing deal in isolation. Throughout the book, we emphasize their long journey. After the closing of the deal, investors can become active value-adding partners (Chapter 8), and the parties work together on additional funding rounds (Chapter 9), as well as on the company exit (Chapter 11). How does this long-term relationship perspective change the negotiation dynamics that we examined in this chapter?

Often, there are trade-offs between short-term and long-term gains. Taking an adversarial or opportunistic negotiation stance can yield short-term gains but may also fire back in future steps, especially when the tables turn. In an entrepreneurial venture, one should expect multiple power shifts. At certain times, investors may have the upper hand over a penniless struggling entrepreneur. However, once her company gains traction, that same entrepreneur may become more powerful. She can now use her position to extract concessions from her investors. Alternating power shifts can deteriorate into destructive tit-for-tat behavior. A long-term perspective of building relationships helps to prevent this. It requires an attitude of forgoing certain short-term gains, in the interest of the common long-term goal.[32]

It is easy to forget future investors. In a staged financing context, the company is likely to come back for more rounds of financing. In addition to the existing investors this typically involves some new investors. They may not react well to unusual structures. If the company obtained a particularly high valuation in the previous round, it is difficult to add a significant valuation premium to the next round. In some cases, the prior valuation was so high that only a down round is possible (Section 9.4.1). Unusual contractual terms can also be a deterrent for future investors, who may simply ask the entrepreneurs and prior investors to renegotiate the unusual clauses. Taking a long-term perspective therefore means anticipating such problem in the first place and structuring the original deal so that it will be palatable to future investors.

The relationship between an investor and an entrepreneur can sometimes last longer than the venture itself. After a company exit, it is not uncommon that entrepreneurs ask their previous investor to fund their next venture. When the investor is a VC firm, the entrepreneur may have a stint at the firm as an "entrepreneur-in-residence." During this time the investors avail themselves of the entrepreneur's technical and business skills for evaluating potential deals. They may also offer her an executive position at a new portfolio company.

Beyond the relationship between the individual entrepreneurs and investors, there is the issue of reputation. Professional investors such as VCs make a living from repeatedly investing in new deals. They care about their reputation, and therefore take into consideration how one negotiation affects future negotiations. Reputational concerns can cut both ways. Many investors try to establish a reputation for being reasonable, transparent, or easy to deal with. They do so with an eye to attracting additional entrepreneurs. Other investors, however, prefer to establish a reputation for being tough negotiators.

One academic study by Atanasov, Ivanov, and Litvak examines litigation data in the VC industry.[33] It finds 328 lawsuits over a 30-year period, suggesting that a nontrivial number of investors do get sued by entrepreneurs for a variety of unfair dealings. Interestingly, lawsuits where entrepreneurs sue VCs are much more common than the other way around. The likely reason is that entrepreneurs have a better chance of extracting settlement fees out of VC firms than VCs extracting anything out of fledgling start-up companies.

Investors can only establish a reputation if other entrepreneurs can see their actions. Leading a venture to a successful exit is the biggest reputational gain for an investor. Given that the details of the deal and the actions of the investors typically remain confidential, however, reputations for fairness are largely carried by word of mouth. Therefore, they are prone to gossip and misinterpretation. Some investors may get unduly bad reputations because they get disparaged by oversensitive entrepreneurs; others may get away too lightly. In this context, it is worth mentioning a website, "The Funded" (http://www.thefunded.com), which posts opinions from entrepreneurs about their experiences with investors. Obviously, this comes with its own problems. Savvy investors may try to instruct their funded entrepreneurs to write good reviews, whereas upset entrepreneurs may use the website to vent their frustrations.

Entrepreneurs have reputations too. A key concern for the entrepreneur is to be seen as capable to execute a business plan, even under adverse conditions. Having a good reputation helps an entrepreneur to compete for investor attention and money. Another reputational issue concerns the ability to attract and retain talent. Most ventures are built on human capital, so entrepreneurs benefit from maintaining a good reputation among current and potential employees.

WorkHorse Box 7.3 looks at trust, relationships, and reputation.

WorkHorse Box 7.3 Building Trust

In late January, Michael Archie hosted a small gathering for the official signing of WorkHorse's A round. Ali and Wolf were in town for a different meeting. The four founders were joined by Victoria. Everyone seemed relieved that the fundraising campaign was finally over.

As they casually chatted about their holidays, Annie asked Wolf where he had been: "You were hard to reach, you must have been in an exotic remote location!" As it turned out, Wolf had to stay for work in New York. Coyo-T Capital was raising a new fund, and Wolf had been asked to look after a delegation of large institutional investors from Russia and the Middle East. Most of it had gone well, but Wolf shared an interesting episode.

As part of the delegates' visit, Wolf had divulged some details about CTC's current deal flow. Apparently, one delegate, Mikhail Miniov from OCC, had abused Wolf's trust. He directly contacted several of his companies, offering them competing deals. Most of the teams dismissed OCC out of hand. However, one of Wolf's deals blew up because the company took OCC's offer. Wolf was incensed and argued that it was immoral and foolish. "These entrepreneurs really shot themselves in the foot. News like that travels fast, everyone knows about it, and no one in New York City will ever want touch that company again." Ali nodded, adding "Nor in Silicon Valley!"

Suddenly, Wolf turned to Astrid, fixating her with an intense stare: "Astrid, I never asked you this, but did this Mikhail guy contact you too?" Astrid smiled and replied calmly: "He did, but we rejected him right away. We don't want "dumb money" from anybody; we want "smart money" from people like you." For the briefest of moments Astrid thought she discovered a faint smile on Wolf's face.

To conclude our discussion of the deal structuring process, Box 7.6 provides our advice to entrepreneurs on how to set up, negotiate, and manage a deal.

Box 7.6 The Seven Bad Negotiation Habits of Inexperienced Entrepreneurs

Not surprisingly, inexperienced entrepreneurs often make beginners' mistakes. While every negotiation situation is new and unique, this book focuses on identifying the fundamental principles. In this spirit, we offer some general and practically relevant advice, framed as the seven bad habits that entrepreneurs should beware of.

First, entrepreneurs sometimes try to negotiate every single aspect of a term sheet. This immediately creates confrontational bargaining dynamics. Entrepreneurs should instead clarify their priorities and then negotiate accordingly (Section 7.5). This helps the two parties to focus their negotiation on the important issues and to identify what compromises will be necessary to converge on a mutually acceptable deal.

Second, probably the most common mistake made by inexperienced entrepreneurs is to focus excessively on valuation. It is easy for investors to give the entrepreneurs a high valuation on the front page of a term sheet, and then undo it with an assortment of contractual clauses (Section 7.5.2). A related mistake is to misunderstand the meaning of pre-money valuation and miss the fact that the option pool typically comes out of founder shares, not investor shares.

A third mistake is to focus too much on formal control. There can be a legitimate debate about how much control to give to the investors. However, entrepreneurs often miss the importance of informal mechanisms (Section 8.2.3).

Investors always retain some power simply by virtue of having the money. The entrepreneur's true source of power comes mostly from being indispensable to the success the company, rather than from formal control rights.

A fourth mistake is to ignore the market. Ignoring standard market practices makes for a poor negotiation strategy, immediately irritating experienced investors. Moreover, disregarding the valuations and terms fetched by similar companies in current market conditions can turn away otherwise interested investors. While an entrepreneur may well believe that her company deserves a higher valuation, investors typically stick to what their peers are currently willing to accept. Even if all this has little to do with the entrepreneur's fundamental business, such market forces affect whether entrepreneurs succeed or fail in their fundraising campaigns.

A fifth mistake consists of being a myopic negotiator, overestimating the importance of the current negotiation and underestimating the importance of all future negotiations (Section 7.6.2). Taking advantage of investors when one has a good tail wind may fire back. If the initial deal is lopsided, investors will want to renegotiate it at a later stage. Later-stage investors will also push back on what they consider unreasonable terms. Getting the highest possible valuation in one round, for instance, may subsequently lead to a down round and damage employee motivation (Section 9.4.1).

A sixth mistake is misjudging the timing of negotiations. The worst moment to negotiate for an entrepreneur is when the company is running out of money. The outside option at this time is closing down the business because of sheer lack of cash, regardless of the venture's fundamental economic value. This is a bad outside option, and investors know it. They can therefore dictate the terms of the investment. Entrepreneurs should therefore plan fundraising well ahead and raise enough cash to provide a reasonable buffer against future adverse events.

A seventh mistake is to focus too much on the negotiation at the cost of neglecting the underlying business. Negotiations sometimes take time and can be emotionally draining, especially for the entrepreneur. There is a danger of ignoring the most important objective, namely, creating a good company. Neglecting the business may show up months later, when deadlines are not met or when employee morale is low. Even more disruptive, it may show up before the deal is closed, such as when investors find out that customers are becoming dissatisfied.

Summary

This chapter examines the process of structuring entrepreneurial finance deals, from first contact to closing. Entrepreneurs need to prepare a convincing pitch to attract investor interest. Investors screen numerous ventures and perform due diligence on the few that they consider most promising. If investors decide to provide funding, they often form a syndicate to pool their capital and expertise. The negotiation process can be understood in terms of classical bargaining theory where both parties look for an acceptable deal structure within the zone of possible agreements. Closing the deal requires striking compromises from multiple parties. The final deal structure has long-term consequences for the way entrepreneurs and investors work together, how they seek additional funding, and what happens at exit. We close by explaining the importance of trust and of taking a long-term perspective.

In terms of the FIRE framework (Chapter 1), the process of structuring a deal encompasses the first two steps of the FIRE process. Specifically, this chapter follows the process of first establishing the original FIT, all the way to closing the deal at the end of the INVEST step. Moreover, the chapter takes into consideration the future of the investment relationships, looking forward at the RIDE and EXIT steps that will be the focus of the upcoming chapters.

Review Questions

1. How can entrepreneurs best prepare for their fundraising pitch?
2. How do investors develop proprietary deal flow?
3. What are the most important criteria for assessing the fit between an entrepreneur and an investor?
4. Why do investors often syndicate their deals? When do they invest alone?
5. What are the responsibilities of a lead investor?
6. What affects the zone of possible agreements for an entrepreneur and an investor?
7. What are the challenges of closing a deal? Why do some companies have two closings?
8. What are the pros and cons of soliciting an investment from a competing syndicate?
9. Why is trust needed when investors and entrepreneurs can write detailed term sheets?
10. What does it mean to take a long-term perspective with respect to structuring a deal?

Notes

1. Casamatta and Haritchabalet (2014) and Ueda (2004).
2. Arrow (1962).
3. Cosh, Cumming, and Hughes (2009) report data on rejection rates by different types of investors.
4. For a short review of the large academic literature on patenting, see Hall (2009). Hall (2016) provides a comprehensive discussion.
5. Lewis (2014) gives a journalistic account of the search for new investment opportunities.

6. Gompers et al. (2019).

7. Livingston (2009), Chapter 19, page 261.

8. Gompers et al. (2019).

9. Kaplan and Strömberg (2004) analyze due diligence activities by VC investors.

10. Gompers et al. (2019).

11. Brander, Amit, and Antweiler (2002) and Lerner (1994).

12. Hochberg, Ljungqvist, and Lu (2010) and Podolny (2001).

13. Sorenson and Stuart (2008) and Wright and Lockett (2003).

14. Hellmann (2007).

15. Åstebro et al. (2018).

16. Zhang and Guler (2015).

17. Brander, Amit, and Antweiler (2002) and Tian (2012).

18. Hochberg, Ljungqvist, and Lu (2007).

19. Lerner (1994).

20. Dimov and Milanov (2010).

21. Hochberg, Lindsey, and Westerfield (2015).

22. Meuleman et al. (2017).

23. Gompers, Mukharlyamov, and Xuan (2016).

24. https://www.nobelprize.org/prizes/economics/1994/nash/facts.

25. For a classic nontechnical introduction to game theory and equilibrium solutions, see Davis (1997).

26. Nash (1950) and Morgenstern and von Neumann (1944).

27. Kennedy (2008) is an excellent classic book on business negotiations.

28. Malhotra (2013) shows how short-sighted negotiation with investors may backfire.

29. See Felser (2017) for the view of an entrepreneur-turned-investor.

30. Bottazzi, Da Rin, and Hellmann (2016), Durlauf and Fafchamps (2006) and Guiso, Sapienza, and Zingales (2009).

31. Malhotra and Murnighan (2002).

32. For an actual example of a forward-looking negotiation of term sheet, see Rosen and Hoffman (2018).

33. Atanasov, Ivanov, and Litvak (2012).

8

Corporate Governance

Learning Goals

In this chapter students will learn:

1. How investors actively get involved with their companies beyond the provision of financing.
2. About the formal and informal mechanisms used by investors and entrepreneurs to control start-up companies.
3. To appreciate the various ways that investors can add value to the entrepreneurial ventures.
4. To evaluate the fit between a company's business needs and an investor's active involvement style.

This chapter examines the role of investors after the deal has closed. We begin by asking why companies need the involvement of investors in the first place and why investors are motivated to become actively involved. We then analyze how investors can enhance the value of their companies by exercising corporate governance. We distinguish between control and value-adding governance activities. Control includes voting in the shareholders' assembly, active board participation, and the exercise of informal power. Investors also exercise strategic pressure and may even replace a founder with an outside CEO. Value-adding activities include mentoring the entrepreneur, consulting for the company, making introductions to business networks, and helping with recruiting. The chapter concludes by showing how to assess the fit between the needs of a start-up and the value-adding support that a specific investor can provide.

8.1 The Need for Corporate Governance

Corporate governance is the set of actions through which the providers of finance ensure a return from their investment.[1] The active involvement of investors is therefore a central aspect of the relationship between entrepreneur and investor. Investors can provide more than just money by becoming actively engaged in the governance of the company. Their equity stake gives them an incentive to become involved and to acquire the skills to increase the value of their investments. While the entrepreneur is building the venture, the investor can help along the way, keep a critical eye on the progress made, and step in if the venture falters.

8.1.1 Why Companies Need Investor Involvement

Companies have a variety of needs that investors can support. They depend on the company's stage of development and its specific circumstances. Consider a typical early-stage technology company. Most technology entrepreneurs have limited knowledge and experience of the strategic, commercial, and financial aspects of the entrepreneurial process. They can greatly benefit from mentoring, consulting, and networking by people who have gone through the entrepreneurial process before, possibly as entrepreneurs themselves. An experienced investor can provide effective answers to the many questions that tend to overwhelm inexperienced entrepreneurs. How do you recruit and retain key employees? How do you protect your technology? Who should sit on your board? And so on. Left on their own, many entrepreneurs are prone to waste time and resources on activities that are not essential for the success of their start-up. In the worst case, they make poor decisions just because they lack experience. A combination of support and pressure from the investors can help entrepreneurs run their growing companies, focus on what they know best, and seek help from others when needed.

At later-growth stages, companies confront different challenges. Growing the company requires a transition from informal management to a more structured management style suitable for larger companies. Most founders are at a loss managing larger organizations.[2] Growth also requires companies to undertake new strategic challenges. For example, a company may need to decide between investing in organic growth and acquiring a competitor. Or it may decide whether and when to expand internationally. These kinds of challenges require strategic vision, financial savvy, and sound execution. An experienced set of investors can help with all of them.

8.1.2 Why Investors Oversee Their Companies

The use of equity financing means that, in principle, entrepreneurs and investors have their incentives aligned. However, considerable potential for conflicts remains. This is particularly true if the entrepreneurs develop the company in a direction that diverges from value maximization. Ultimately, the investors care about the success of their companies, not of their founders. Investors want to protect their investments by ensuring that the company remains well managed and keeps increasing in value. In rare instances, investors need to ensure that the entrepreneurs don't fudge the books or steal money. One very public case was that of Theranos, founded in 2003 by Elizabeth Holmes, a Stanford dropout with the promise that her product would substantially cut the costs of blood testing. In 2018 Holmes was indicted for wire fraud, and the company unraveled.[3] More often, investors need to ensure that entrepreneurs do not drift away from a sensible strategic course, take a sensible amount of risk (Section 6.2.3), and refrain from pursuing pet projects of dubious commercial value. Self-dealing is another sensitive area that often remains a gray one. For example, Adam Neumann, WeWork's founder, after securing control of voting rights, leased to the company several properties he owned. This alleged opportunistic behavior stirred up an intense debate.[4]

Investors seek to accelerate company growth because they want to realize a financial return. This may generate some conflicts with the entrepreneur. For example, some entrepreneurs resist exit because they don't like the change. This can therefore lead to a conflict between investors and entrepreneurs that requires investors to take an active role (Section 11.6). Another potential conflict arises when investors feel they have to fire an underperforming founding CEO (Section 8.3.4).

When a conflict with the entrepreneur arises, investors can make use of control rights and other legal safeguards obtained at the time of the investment (Section 6.4). Control rights allow the investor to exert governance. This requires being close to the company, obtaining information, monitoring progress, and assessing the entrepreneur's performance. These activities require considerable time and effort, and investors should have the necessary competencies.

How often are investors actually in contact with their companies? A study of U.S. VC firms by Gompers, Kaplan, and Mukharlyamov finds that 12% of VCs report being in contact once a month or less, 26% report two to three times a month, 33% once a week, and 28% multiple times a week.[5] In addition, the survey asked what types of activities VCs engaged in and found that 87% reported providing strategic guidance, 72% connecting investors, 69% connecting customers, 65% operational guidance, 58% hiring board members, and 46% hiring employees.

Before looking at the details of how corporate governance works, WorkHorse Box 8.1 takes a brief look at WorkHorse's situation after receiving its first VC round.

WorkHorse Box 8.1 The April Board Meeting

When WorkHorse closed its first VC round in January 2021, it was decided that its newly formed board of directors would meet quarterly. The first meeting was scheduled for the end of April. The five directors were Astrid Dala and Brandon Potro, representing management, Ali Ad-Lehr (Eagle-I Ventures) and Wolf C. Flow (Coyo-T Capital) representing the investors, and Malcolm Force, the CEO of Bolts-N-Nuts, as independent director. Michael Archie, the seed round angel investor, was invited as an observer. Annie and Bharat also asked to join.

The only one who couldn't come in person was Wolf C. Flow. He was on a business trip to the Middle East, raising money from large institutional investors.

The company had launched its first product, the WonderFoal, in January, a slow retail month. To everyone's surprise, the WonderFoal sold out within a week. The retailer quickly decided to accelerate its plans for a national rollout and asked WorkHorse to deliver 3,025 units per month for the coming months. This was an order of magnitude more than what WorkHorse had originally foreseen. While the four founders were delighted, it dawned on them that this order would pose new challenges. Organizationally, the company was not set up to handle large volumes of manufacturing. It would be particularly challenging for their supply chain to handle a sudden large increase in order flow. The company quickly decided that each founder had to focus on a very specific set of challenges. Astrid was in charge of handling the relationship with the retailer, as well as leading the entire team. Annie was dispatched to China to oversee all aspects of manufacturing. Bharat was put in charge of quality control and new product development. Brandon continued overseeing financing.

Ali, who chaired the board, asked the founders to report where the company was and what it struggled with. Each founder explained the progress made and the challenges at hand. Astrid explained that the relationship with PortageLake was good, but that their high expectations were hard to meet. Brandon explained that the most urgent financial issue was working capital management (see WorkHorse Box 10.2). Annie reported that the manufacturers had responded well to her demanding request, but that in the short term they would not be able to respond quickly to further increases. When Bharat was asked about quality control, he candidly replied that he hadn't paid much attention to it because he was busy leading WorkHorse's new product development. The meeting became tense when Bharat was asked to justify why he still held on to his research position at the university. He tried to explain how his latest research might become important for the future of WorkHorse. Malcom objected: a founder needs to be fully committed to the company and devote 110% of his time to it. There was some discussion that Bharat needed to make up his mind between being a researcher or entrepreneur, but no action was taken. Ali moved the conversation to the next topic: hiring.

The company had hired several employees over the last few months. The founders informally mentioned job opportunities on their Facebook pages and ended up hiring several friends and friends of friends. They quickly found out that this approach had its limitations. Astrid had to fire one of Brandon's friends two weeks after she had joined the company because she consistently argued with everybody on everything. Ali noted that the company needed a more professional approach to human resource (HR) management. He promised to put the founders in contact with an HR expert who was working with another of his portfolio companies. He also mentioned that the company should start to think about "beefing up the senior team."

Several weeks later, Astrid received an e-mail from Wolf C. Flow, asking for the quarterly financials and the minutes of the Board meeting. Astrid replied that the financial situation was a bit messy right now and that Brandon (cc'ed) hadn't had time to write up the financials. As for minutes of the meeting, no one had asked for them, and none had been taken. Half an hour later, Wolf was on the phone complaining about the lack of professionalism. Astrid began to realize that managing a board of directors was different than the casual conversations she was used to with Michael Archie, her angel investor.

8.2 Corporate Governance Structures

No matter how many legal details are specified, any contractual arrangement is always incomplete (see also Box 6.2). Companies therefore need a governance system that allocates decision rights under broadly specified circumstances. The main governance rules of a venture are defined in the charter of the company. They can be augmented and modified over time with by-laws, shareholder agreements, and other contractual agreements, in accordance with national laws. Within this legal framework, we distinguish between two main control structures: voting rights, discussed in Section 8.2.1, and the board of directors, discussed in Section 8.2.2. Section 8.2.3 discusses the importance of informal control.

8.2.1 Voting Rights

Voting rights allow shareholders to make several key decisions. The company charter and by-laws, and possibly other legal agreements, define what kind of decisions are to be resolved by shareholder vote. This includes, for example, any decision to change the place of legal incorporation or any decision to sell the company. Voting outcomes are usually determined using either simple majority or supermajority.

The default case is that all shares have equal voting power ("one share, one vote"). However, two mechanisms can change this: voting by share class (i.e., Common shares, Series A, Series B, etc.) and deviations from the one–share one–vote rule. To see how voting by share class works, consider a company with three share classes: common stock (held by founders), Series A preferred stock, held by first-round investors, and Series B preferred stock, held by second-round investors. Consider a simple Yes or No vote, and say whether to accept an offer to sell the company. Within each share class, there may be different shareholders who might disagree with each other. Voting by class means that each class first determines its position using a simple majority vote. A decision can then only be taken if all classes register majority support for the decision.

To see how this works, consider Table 8.1. Suppose the three classes represent 40, 35, and 25%, respectively, of all shares on a fully diluted basis (Section 4.1.3). Suppose the vote yields the results reported in the "Shareholders vote" column of the table. Overall, 60% of shareholders vote Yes. However, the final decision is No.

Table 8.1 Shareholders' Vote by Share Class

	Shareholders' vote		Class vote
	Yes	No	
Common Stock	10%	30%	No
Series A	30%	5%	Yes
Series B	20%	5%	Yes
Total	60%	40%	No

This is because a majority of common shareholders said No. The decision can only be made if all classes have a majority of Yes votes. This example shows that voting by class helps to protect minority investors against a majority imposing its will on them.

Deviations from the one–share one–vote rule arise when shares in different classes have different numbers of votes. This is also referred to as "dual-class shares" (Section 11.2.4). There are two ways of structuring this: either by attaching multiple votes to some shares or else by having some nonvoting shares. Let us continue with the preceding example and assume there are 100 shares in total. Assume now that the common shares have two votes per share. The left panel of Table 8.2 shows that this gives common stock a majority (80 votes out of 140). The right panel of the table shows a different arrangement in which Series A receives nonvoting shares. In this case, common stockholders have 40 out of 65 shares, which is again a majority. In both cases, the common shareholders own a minority of shares (40%) but control a majority of votes.

Table 8.2 Shareholders' Vote with Dual Class Shares

	Multiple-voting shares		Non-voting shares	
	Shares	Votes	Shares	Votes
Common Stock	40	80	40	40
Series A	35	35	35	0
Series B	25	25	25	25
Total:	100	140	100	65

8.2.2 Board of Directors

The board of directors plays four main roles that we call "the boss," "the monitor," "the coach," and "the promoter." The role of being "the boss" is enshrined in the legal structure of the corporation: that is, the fact that the board is endowed with the right to make, or approve, all major business decisions. As "the monitor," the board oversees the activities of the company on behalf of shareholders, identifying problems, assessing the performance of the management team, and spearheading required changes.[6] One of the most important decisions made by the board in this respect concerns the hiring and firing of executives, especially the CEO. While the first two roles can create conflict between the management team and the board, the other two roles bring them closer together. Directors often play "the coach," providing useful support and advice to the CEO. Having experienced board members, who already faced similar challenges in their professional lives, can be particularly helpful. Directors can also play the role of "the promoter." They advocate for the company externally, drawing on their own industry networks, and helping the company forge new business relationships.

The board of directors makes most of the key strategic decisions, such as what products to develop, what markets to enter, which executives to hire, or when to raise additional funding. Within legal and statutory limits, the board of directors can also decide at what time a shareholder vote is called for and what for. Board decisions can be taken under different rules, such as majority, supermajority, or unanimity, with different decisions taken under different rules.

The board of directors has a fiduciary duty to represent the interests of the company. In principle, board members should put the general interest of the company ahead of the special interests of those shareholders who nominated them. In practice, this is a murky issue. The chair of the board has the overall responsibility. Individual board members can have committee responsibilities, such as sitting on the compensation or audit committee. Moreover, some investors may not have a board seat but enjoy observer status. This allows them to participate in the discussions, and possibly influence them, even though they cannot vote.[7] In some countries, the law requires labor representation on the board of directors. Some countries also require a dual board structure where, in addition to the board of directors (the "supervisory board"), there is a management board. However, small companies are typically exempted from these requirements, so that start-up board structures look similar across most countries.

In a start-up, the board of directors tends to be small. To avoid voting deadlock, the number of directors is typically an odd number. Five directors are common by the time a company receives its first VC round ("Series A"). In later rounds, this may increase to seven, nine, or more. Academic studies have found this to be an effective board size in general.[8] Even the boards of later-stage VC-backed companies remain about half the size of the average listed company.[9] The reason start-ups can keep their boards smaller is that, unlike in public companies, there are fewer large shareholders, and there is less pressure to add independent directors. Smaller boards find it easier to meet more frequently. Directors in start-ups also tend to spend more time with their companies.[10] Monthly board meetings are quite common in the early stages of entrepreneurial companies, as well as when companies are experiencing turbulent times.

The composition of the board involves three main categories: entrepreneurs, investors, and independent directors. Entrepreneurs and investors have their respective interests; the independent board members contribute industry expertise. With five members, a common arrangement would be two board seats reserved for management (say two co-founders, or the CEO and Chief Technology Officer (CTO), two seats for the investors (say, two VCs that co-invest in the round, or who represent investors from two different rounds), and one seat for an outside director.

Outside directors are sometimes CEOs of other companies in the investor's portfolio; other times they are seasoned entrepreneurs or professionals with links to either the investor or entrepreneur. Excessive loyalty can conflict with their fiduciary duty toward the company. Appointment by mutual consent helps to establish trust on both sides. Outside directors are important for at least two reasons: (1) they may cast the pivotal vote in situations where investors and management are at odds;[11] and (2) they are important for guiding the company's strategy. They can offer insightful industry knowledge and leverage their professional networks to the benefit of the company.

Sitting on the board of directors provides access to information about the company's financial and strategic situation. Board members receive regular reports about company progress. These reports include financial information and updates on strategic issues such as development progress, new hires, or strategic alliances. Companies report any important updates on key customer accounts, the competitive landscape, intellectual property, or litigation. Professional investors typically ask companies to set up an accounting system to provide quarterly profit and loss and cash flow updates. Monthly updates on cash flows are also common at early stages. In addition, board members have an opportunity to observe founders and managers as they cope with challenges and plan the development of the company. This is "soft" information that cannot be codified in a report, but it is valuable to assess managerial performance. Brad Feld, a prominent investor and writer, provides the following checklist for preparing a board package: company financials, guidance of expected future financial performance, key operating metrics, sales and business development pipeline, updates on product and technology development, administrative and human resources news, and the current capitalization table.[12]

Boards change over time. As initial funders retreat and new investors come in. The new investors may get the seats of the initial investors. Directors may also change as new expertise is needed.[13] In addition, the term sheet can specify how board composition and control vary with company performance. Initially, control is shared between the founders and investors.[14] However, due to the staged financing process and possibly term sheet clauses, investors gain more control over time, especially when performance falls short of expectations. For example, investors can sometimes nominate additional board members when milestones are missed, effectively taking control of the company.[15]

The role of the board also changes over time. As companies grow and mature, boards become more formal. Among other things they formalize key committees, such as the compensation and the audit committee. The compensation committee decides on salaries, stock options, and bonuses for top managers. It is typically chaired by an independent board member, and it always excludes management. The audit committee ensures compliance with legal requirements on financial reporting to investors and oversees transactions between the company and its employees. It becomes particularly important as the company nears exit. The audit committee should include members with accounting expertise who are independent from senior management. Investors are often on both committees. Over time some founder CEOs leave the job to a professional CEO, which results in a different role and compensation structure (Section 8.3.4).[16]

A common occurrence in later financing rounds is a reshuffling of the board of directors. In the most common arrangement, the new investors add one or several members to the board. However, as companies proceed through several rounds, this arrangement may create excessively large boards. In such cases, it may be necessary to fundamentally restructure the board. One common solution is for some or all of the exiting investors to step down from the board to make room for the new investors. This may be appropriate if the new investors have relevant expertise and networks and if the old investors are "out of their depth." In many cases, however, some old investors continue to be valuable to the company. They may have built a strong working relationship with the founders, and they often provide board continuity. In some cases, it may be possible to turn their (voting) board seats into (nonvoting) observer seats. Finally, in some cases, a more radical restructuring is necessary. For example, some start-ups initially have several founders on the board and later add nonfounding managers, such as a new CEO. This can become a problem in later rounds, so it may be necessary to slim down the entire board.

Whether board members get compensated for their work depends on who they are. Founders and managers of the company never get paid for sitting on the board, as this is merely part of their job; investors also rarely get paid, as this is part of their investment responsibilities. This means that the only directors who receive some compensation are independent directors. This is typically provided in the form of a stock option package along the lines we discuss in Sections 4.1.3 and 6.3.2.

In addition to voting and board control, there is also contractual control, which is often exercised within board decision making. In Chapter 6, we discuss the role of term sheet clauses, Section 6.4.1 specifically explains how certain terms either allow or prevent specific decisions. For example, a contractual clause may specify that the board of directors must approve any senior management hire. Or it may specify that the investors can override a shareholder vote and veto the sale of the company. These contractual control clauses are not independent of the main control mechanisms; instead, they specify additional rules for how in specific situations voting and board control are to be exercised.

Finally, in addition to having a board of directors, some start-ups also have an advisory board. This is not a formal board, and its members do not have any fiduciary duties. Instead they mostly provide support and a sounding board to the entrepreneurs. Advisers tend to bring technical or industry experience and may be entrepreneurs from noncompeting companies. To recognize their efforts, advisory board members frequently receive a modest stock option package.

8.2.3 Informal Control

The legal structure stipulates how investors and entrepreneurs share formal decision rights. However, actual decisions are often made outside of the framework of formal control rights. When this happens, we talk of informal control.[17] We distinguish three types of informal control: the power of the purse, the power of personality, and the power of persuasion.

"The golden rule of venture capital is that he or she who has the gold makes the rules." This saying neatly illustrates what we call the power of the purse. Entrepreneurs depend on their investors for future funding. Current investors hold considerable power, both directly through the decision to refinance the company and indirectly through their influence over other investors. For example, the willingness (unwillingness) of an insider to participate in a follow-up round can send a positive (negative) signal to potential new investors (Section 9.2).

A second source of informal power is the power of personality. By this we mean the power that individuals derive from having the trust and respect of the company employees. Company leaders, whether or not they be founders of hired executives, need to inspire those who are following them. Trust is slowly gained over time and can be quickly lost. A strong leader personality can "rally the troops" behind a strategy and make it difficult for others to oppose that decision. For example, if a founder doesn't want to sell her company, she may convince the employees to leave with her in case the investors insist on selling it. This action may reduce the value of the company to the point of making the acquisition unattractive for the buyer. Even though the investor may have the formal right to sell the company, a strong leader may have enough informal control to sway the decision.

A third source of informal power is the power of persuasion. Some of the important issues faced by boards of directors are complex and ambiguous, with no obviously right solution. Social status, professional reputation, and relevant expertise all hold some sway in this decision process, but a compelling argument is what often is needed to build consensus in the board.

Informal control can affect the balance of power either way. The power of the purse naturally belongs to investors, whereas the power of personalities often belongs to charismatic founders. As for the power of persuasion, it applies equally to investors and entrepreneurs.

How does informal control play out in practice? Box 8.1 summarizes some academic research that analyzes the informal relationships between CEOs and venture boards.

Box 8.1 Unpacking the CEO–Board Relationship

How do entrepreneurs interact with board members in practice? One academic study by Garg and Eisenhardt examines several detailed case studies of how CEOs of start-up companies interact with their board members.[18] The strength of such an observational research approach is that the researchers can make detailed observations of processes and practices. In this specific study, the researchers consider how four CEOs (two founders, two hired CEOs) in VC-backed high-tech start-ups make key strategy decisions. The researchers observe both the formal board meetings and the numerous informal interactions with individual board members. They summarize the core challenge of the CEO as "gaining advice without losing power."

The researchers identify four important CEO behaviors when interacting with their board members. First, instead of relying on group interactions, CEOs frequently approach their board members individually in informal meetings. This focuses the attention of the individuals on a limited set of topics and helps to draw out their advice in those areas most useful to the CEO. Second, during formal board meetings, CEOs never present alternative strategies but instead propose a single course of action that is to be discussed and ultimately approved. Avoiding choices between multiple actions helps the CEO to control the agenda and to deflect potentially divergent visions of individual board members. Third, when more open-ended discussions about alternative strategies are needed, CEOs organize dedicated strategy meetings that use a long-term brainstorming frame, as opposed to a short-term operational frame. This way the CEO can draw the focus away from recommendations that would be immediately actionable. Instead, brainstorming engages the board members in a more enjoyable visionary exercise and allows them to stand out as helpful and wise. Fourth, CEOs use political tactics to bring the decision-making process to a conclusion. This involves building alliances around the preferred course of action. Ultimately, the researchers describe the informal process of managing board directors as one of "divide and conquer." Power in the board room is a force to reckon with, so savvy entrepreneurs carefully orchestrate it ahead of time.

8.3 Investor Value-Adding

In addition to control-related governance activities, investors also provide several support activities to their portfolio companies. This helps reduce risk and ultimately increases the value of the company. We first look at how investors can add value through their active involvement, and then we identify the main business areas where support matters.

8.3.1 Picking versus Making Winners

Corporate governance is about bringing the company to make good decisions and taking value-enhancing actions. We therefore ask whether good investors pick successful companies, or whether they make their companies successful? In Section 2.5, we discuss how investors select their companies. In this chapter we have examined how they actively contribute to grow them. Which activity is more important? This turns out to be a profound question worthy of the attention of Nobel minds, which we discuss in Box 8.2.

Box 8.2 Nobel Insights on Selection versus Treatment Effects

James Heckman was awarded the 2000 Nobel Prize "for his development of theory and methods for analyzing selective samples."[19] Clive W. J. Granger received the 2003 Nobel Prize "for methods of analyzing economic time series with common trends (cointegration)."[20] Heckman and Granger are both econometricians who developed statistical tools for empirical data analysis.

Granger is known for his analysis of time series, that is, data that describe the evolution of variables over time. He developed methods that allow disentangling the effects of changes of multiple variables on each other over time. The term *Granger causality* is used to describe how changes in one variable lead to changes in another. For example, interest rates and house prices both vary over time, but which causes which? A statistical analysis might indicate that interest rate hikes precede house price drops, suggesting that interest rates "Granger-cause" house prices, and not the other way around. In our context, we may ask how VC investments relate to company performance over time. For example, we may find that receiving VC "Granger-causes" sales growth. Granger causality is useful in some contexts but can be misleading in others. For example, the sale of Christmas trees "Granger-causes" Christmas. This is mechanically true because in time-series data the sale of trees precedes the festive event. This points to a deeper problem. People elect to buy trees in the days before Christmas because they anticipate Christmas. Many economic events are obviously less predictable than Christmas, but the same critique holds. In our context, it may be that venture capitalists chose to invest in a company because they expected it to achieve significant sales growth. Identifying true causality is thus more challenging than identifying Granger causality.

This is where Heckman's work comes in. Understanding selective samples is important for understanding causality, which is fundamental to all social sciences. In our context, the question is whether VC financing causes better company performance, or whether better performing companies attract VC investment in the first place. Answering this question is conceptually challenging, as it requires disentangling two possible causal effects: (1) a causal effect from venture financing to company performance, which is called a "treatment effect," versus (2) a causal effect from expected company performance to venture financing, which is called a "selection effect." Note that the terminology comes from the medical sciences. For example, does exercise make people healthier (treatment), or do healthier people exercise more (selection)?

Heckman's pioneering work on selected samples shows how to empirically separate out treatment and selection effects. His own work, and the subsequent work he inspired, provide an array of statistical tools that allow researchers to isolate treatment from selection effects. In econometric jargon, this is called "identification." The idea is that in order to "identify" treatment effects, we need random assignment to treatment and control groups. Consider assessing the effectiveness of a training program for unemployed workers (the "treatment"). If participation is voluntary, the sample will be selected, as it will include those workers who expect a benefit from the program. Any observed difference in future hiring outcomes between the sample of treated workers and the sample of workers that did not participate mixes the selection effect (choosing to do the program) and the treatment effect (doing the program). Only if we assign workers randomly to the two groups can we identify the treatment effect. Whenever treatment is random, there is no selection effect; thus any differences in outcomes must be due to treatment alone. This principle is very general. For example, it is at the basis of double-blind clinical trials for pharmaceutical drugs.

While randomized experiments may be feasible in some cases, many economic contexts simply do not allow for that possibility. You cannot randomly pick two countries, expose them to different inflation rates, and see which economy performs better. Heckman's work shows how to identify treatment effects indirectly using "quasi-experiments." In our context, consider a recent study by Bernstein, Giroud, and Townsend that asks whether VCs achieve better investment performance by picking better companies (selection) or adding more value (treatment).[21] The researchers argue that even if VCs actively select the best companies, some companies randomly get more attention. They specifically consider how easy it is for VCs from the main hubs (such as Silicon Valley, New York, or Boston) to work with start-ups located outside of these hubs (say, places like Montana and Kentucky). As a quasi-experiment, they use the introduction of new direct flight routes (e.g., from Boston to Butte, Montana). A direct flight considerably reduces travel time, allowing VCs to spend more time with their portfolio companies in that region. This should result in better performance due to a value-adding treatment effect. The study finds that after the introduction of direct flight routes, companies already backed by VCs experienced better performance in terms of innovation and exit. This evidence is indicative of a value-adding role of VC, that is, a positive treatment effect. Many other studies use different "Heckman-like" approaches to study the relationship between VC financing and company performance. These studies typically find evidence that both selection and treatment effects are significant.[22] The overall message is that good VCs both pick and make winners.

8.3.2 How Investors Add Value

In this section, we identify four types of value-adding activities: mentoring, advising, networking, and pressuring. A classic academic study examined the perceived contribution of VC investors in the U.S., and several European countries found that strategic advice and pressure rank highest, followed by mentoring and then networking.[23]

Mentoring takes place at the personal level. It consists of investors helping founders acquire the personal skills and perseverance necessary to build the business. Experienced investors are able to help entrepreneurs cope with the many challenges of the company-building process. They can guide entrepreneurs through decision processes that are novel to them, offering alternative perspectives, and they provide a sounding board to the entrepreneurs. Importantly, they can help them cope with the emotional ups and downs, occasionally simply providing a shoulder to cry on.

Strategic advice goes beyond personal mentoring and takes place at the company level. It consists of providing consulting services that range from informal advice to formal support structures. Areas where strategic consulting is particularly useful are finance, marketing, and human resources. Investors can provide an outside perspective on a company's situation, which can be of great value to a sometimes too inwardly focused management team. An ambitious approach to supporting entrepreneurs is the model of Andreessen Horowitz, a prominent Silicon Valley venture capital firm. It maintains an unusually large staff of over 40 functional specialists who advise companies on wide-ranging business issues, including marketing, operations, financing, recruiting, and global expansion.[24]

Networking takes place at the industry level. Howard Stevenson, a well-known entrepreneurship professor, defines entrepreneurship as "the pursuit of opportunity beyond resources controlled."[25] Generating a new business or growing an existing business therefore requires reaching out to a diverse set of people who control these required resources.[26] The ability to identify and sign up employees, customers, suppliers, and financiers is an important part of building a company. High quality investors build up a large network of business contacts with leaders in industry, finance, and government, which can then be tapped for help. Box 8.3 discusses pertinent empirical evidence on the formation of strategic alliances.

Box 8.3 VC and Strategic Alliances.

Academic research has found that VC funding matters for strategic alliances in multiple dimensions. If VCs help companies access business networks, one might expect that VC-backed companies get better access to corporate partners and therefore form more strategic alliances. Research by David Hsu compares U.S. VC-backed companies against a control group of U.S. companies funded under the Small Business Innovation Research (SBIR) program, which provides research grants to start-ups. The study finds that VC-backed companies forge substantially more strategic alliance and experience a higher likelihood of an IPO.[27] A study by Ozmel, Robinson, and Stuart looks at all two-way combinations for VC financing and strategic alliances.[28] Raising VC financing increases the probability of subsequent alliance formation, as well as future VC financing.

Forming a strategic alliance raises the probability of further alliance formation but actually decreases the need for future VC financing.[29] Both VC funding and alliance formation increase the probability of an IPO.

Another study, by Laura Lindsey, takes a closer look at who those alliance partners are.[30] If a company receives funding from a VC, this increases the likelihood that it will form an alliance with another company that is also funded by that same VC. Moreover, these types of alliances tend to involve a deeper level of mutual commitment. This effect is sometimes called the Keiretsu effect, a name deriving from Japanese conglomerates.

Investors can also exert strategic pressure on their companies. We have already noted that boards play a role in monitoring the company.[31] Investors affect the IP strategy of their companies.[32] They can also intervene in companies to force change when needed.[33] Founders tend to focus on executing their strategies, meeting deadlines, and solving technical and operating problems. Investors may prod them to rethink their strategies in the face of changed circumstances. For instance, they can press their companies to abandon loss-making projects. In a recession, they might press companies to cut costs. Box 8.4 looks at one such example.

Box 8.4 Sequoia's 2008 Warning

What happens when a sudden crisis threatens the viability of start-ups? In the wake of the 2008 financial crisis, Sequoia Capital, one of the best-known venture firms in Silicon Valley (see also Box 12.5), briefed all its portfolio companies in October 2008.[34] It thought that the crisis would be serious and that companies' business models relied on assumptions that were no longer tenable. The first message was simple: *"Survive! Get Real or Go Home."* Sequoia urged actions such as: *"Manage what you can control."* It advised companies to reduce spending by reviewing costs, reducing headcount, and cutting marketing expenses. Another bit of advice was: *"Focus on quality,"* that is, focus on products and services that were vital to customers and would therefore not become victims to cost cuttings. Sequoia also gave some explicit financial advice: *"Lower risk and reduce debt."* It urged its companies to carefully monitor working capital and preserve funds, expecting that further fundraising would be difficult.

Note also that there are important differences across countries in the nature and extent of investor involvement. Differences in legal systems can affect the practice of corporate governance. North American and British investors, for example, face relatively few legal or cultural barriers when it comes to controlling a board of directors, even firing a founder. However, legal systems that favor employees over the company—like parts of Continental Europe or Latin America—discourage such strong investor control. In such countries, investors invest less in developing governance skills themselves, given that they cannot freely exercise them.[35] Moreover, highly skilled active investors might avoid investing in countries where investor involvement is frowned upon, especially countries where foreigners are not allowed to own majority stakes or control a board of directors.

8.3.3 Where Investors Add Value

In what areas of business can investors add value? To answer this question, it is useful to return to the Venture Evaluation Matrix of Chapter 2. The strategy row describes the core growth challenges faced by the company. On the front-end customer side, there are the *sales* challenges, on the back-end company side the *production* challenges, and inside the company the *organization* challenges. Value-adding investors contribute to solving all three challenges.

Concerning the sales challenges, investors can add value by providing strategic advice. Building on experience from the past mistakes and successes of other portfolio companies, investors can identify issues that might escape the entrepreneur's eye. They can also bring in the required expertise to solve these issues, such as how to project market growth, identify key customers, or expand into foreign markets. Well-networked investors connect entrepreneurs to markets, providing access to industry contacts and establishing relationships with key customers. For example, investors can contact large or reputable potential customers. Even just the certification provided to portfolio companies by investors is an important selling point with customers.[36] Experience in negotiating complex contracts with sophisticated counterparties can also be of value to less experienced entrepreneurs.

With regard to the challenges of product development and production, investors can provide advice and networking support for identifying suppliers and strategic partners. Companies in the early stages of development often find it difficult to access larger organizations to establish research, production, or distribution alliances. Investors provide credibility and certification, which makes it easier to negotiate a strategic alliance. Investors can also connect the entrepreneur to professional service providers. As the company grows, its needs for professional services change, and at some point it needs to hire an accounting firm, a law firm, maybe a marketing agency, and so on. An investor can point out which expertise is required and where to get it. Some investors also have experience in dealing with regulators and local government officials. This may facilitate obtaining permits or licenses and getting support in local communities. Several leading VC firms even have former high-level politicians as partners. For example, former U.S. Vice President Al Gore is a partner at Kleiner Perkins.

Concerning the challenges of building the organization, investors can also play a role. Start-ups typically start with an informal approach to managing their talent. However, to succeed they need to professionalize their processes over time. This requires a wide and diversified network, something that relatively few entrepreneurs have. Equally important is the investors' role in giving a start-up credibility with senior recruits who need convincing before joining such companies.

To provide overall guidance, some investors benchmark the performance of their companies, especially at later stages of company growth. In a benchmarking exercise, the company is compared to its competitors on several industry-specific performance indicators, such as asset utilization, unit costs, and market penetration. Such an exercise requires more effort and resources than standard strategic planning, but it helps investors to identify deviations from best practice and provides a comparison with industry leaders.[37] Some VC investors hire independent consultants to review the progress of portfolio companies, helping them to decide which ones to close down.[38]

Finally, investors prepare companies for exit.[39] They exert pressure on their companies to build the organizational structure and financial profile that acquirers or stock market investors expect. Acquirers, for example, expect the company to remain focused on a limited set of products, whereas stock market investors expect to see a corporate structure that is more fleshed out. Instilling a corporate culture of transparent communication, consistent financial reporting, and good investor communication also facilitates the exit process.

Box 8.5 summarizes research that examines how VCs get involved with their companies and how they contribute to their growth.

Box 8.5 VCs and the Professionalization of Start-ups

Are VCs more active in their companies than other investors, and do they add more value? This topic is hotly debated among entrepreneurs and investors alike. Opinions vary widely, so let us bring some objective data to the debate.

Research by Chemmanur, Krishnan, and Nandy uses U.S. census data to compare companies with VC financing against a control sample without VC.[40] The researchers find that at the time these companies receive VC, they are already more productive, as measured by their total factor productivity (TFP; see Box 1.2). After receiving VC, their TFP also grows faster than the control sample. Using the language of Box 8.2, we note that the first effect suggests a positive selection effect (i.e., VCs pick more productive companies), and the second effect a treatment effect (i.e., VCs improve productivity). The question that remains is "How do VCs do it?"

To answer that question, Hellmann and Puri closely followed the development of more than 170 Silicon Valley start-ups, some of which were funded by VCs, others by family and friends, angel investors, and others.[41] The researchers ask whether companies changed their behavior if and when they obtained VC financing. The unique aspect of their data is that they can see what happens inside the start-ups. Companies with VC establish more professional approaches to managing their human resources. They are less likely to rely on informal hiring channels and more likely to establish Employee Stock Options Plans. They are more commercially focused, accelerating the time it takes to bring their product to market and hiring faster for the position of a VP of marketing and sales. The evidence suggests that VCs provide value-adding support and strategic pressure. The study also finds that VCs exert more control. Specifically, it finds that receiving VC increases the probability of replacing a founder with a hired outside CEO.

Another study, by Ewens and Marx, takes a deeper look at such founder replacement events.[42] Using a broad sample of U.S. VC deals, the study first establishes that founder replacements are more likely to occur around the time of VC financing, and when there are more investors on the company board. It then asks whether founder replacements improve company performance, as reflected in the probability of a successful exit via IPO or acquisition. The raw data show a negative correlation between founder replacement and exit performance. Using the insights from Box 8.2, however, we can conclude that this could be due to either a selection effect, where founder replacements occur mainly in underperforming companies, or a treatment effect. Using advanced statistical techniques, the authors find a negative selection effect but a positive treatment effect, suggesting that founder replacements improve the performance of (underperforming) companies. The treatment effect is stronger when founders hold more senior positions, especially CEO or CFO. It is also stronger when the founders actually leave the company, and not just relinquish their senior executive position while staying with the company.

Do all VCs add value equally? Using a survey of European VC firms, research by Bottazzi, Da Rin, and Hellmann, finds considerable variation in how active VCs are.[43] VC partners who have prior business experience, such as being an entrepreneur, manager, or consultant, get involved more deeply with their companies. The same cannot be said about VC partners with prior experience in the financial sector. The type of VC firm also matters. Private independent VCs are significantly more active in the companies they finance, whereas corporate, bank, or government VCs take a more passive stance (see also Chapter 13). Similar to the previous study, the authors also find a negative correlation between investor involvement and exit performance in the raw data. However, once they econometrically separate selection and treatment effects, they find that active involvement improves company performance.

8.3.4 The Question of Replacing Managers

Box 8.5 already mentions evidence on the relationship between VC funding and founder replacements, which is one of the main sources of friction between entrepreneurs and investors. In this section, we examine this relationship more closely. Investors want to invest in companies, not to manage them. It is therefore not surprising that when there is a problem with the leadership, investors are willing to make the necessary changes to solve it. Investors frequently insist on contractual control rights that allow them to take control in such situations (Section 6.4.1). If there is a significant problem with senior management, and especially with the CEO, investors will try to replace them, provided they have sufficient control to do so.

Why do these problems arise? Some founders turn out to be great visionaries or technologists but poor managers. Others simply clash with the investors on what strategy is best for the venture. In many instances, the change of a CEO is friendly and long anticipated. Thoughtful investors set expectations about leadership changes at the time of funding. For example, when a technology founder seeks venture funding, the VC may discuss at what point a professional CEO with business experience would be brought into the company. In some cases, the replacement of a founder CEO does not require the founders to leave, but instead asks them to refocus their energies. Many founders welcome the change of control because having a professional CEO allows them to focus on their strengths, such as developing technology and making sales.

Unfortunately, the replacement of a CEO can also become acrimonious. Once lack of confidence in the CEO has been voiced, the priority for investors is to remove the CEO from a position of control, thereby preventing any further harm or obstruction. In some cases, the board of directors has already lined up a new CEO, allowing for a quick transfer of control. In other cases, however, the problem is unexpected. In such situations, it is not uncommon for investors to appoint an interim CEO. Sometimes an investor even steps in as temporary CEO.

From an investor's perspective, replacing a CEO requires managing a difficult and risky transition to a new company leadership. Managing such a delicate shift requires skill and experience, not to mention time. From an entrepreneur's perspective it is advisable to discuss succession issues upfront, ideally before closing any deal. Entrepreneurs need to be specifically aware of the control rights that are being negotiated. They may also need proper legal advice on how to handle such situations once they occur.

It is worth noting that replacing a CEO is perceived differently across different cultures. In some countries, most notably the U.S., it is considered perfectly normal, whereas in other countries, such as Japan, it would be considered a public humiliation and thus socially unacceptable. Even if socially acceptable in the U.S., founder replacements can be fraught with conflicts. A salient example was the founder replacement at Uber, discussed in Box 8.6.

Box 8.6 Tales from the Venture Archives: Fixing Corporate Governance at Uber

Uber is arguably the most successful start-up company of the 2010s. By early 2018, the company had raised nearly $25B in equity funding, reaching an esti-mated post-money valuation of over $70B.[44] It set its IPO for the spring of 2019 with a target valuation close to $100B. Its first VC investment came from Benchmark, a top Silicon Valley VC firm, at a valuation of $5.4M, on Valentine's Day 2011. However, the relationship with Benchmark can hardly be described as a love affair. Tensions peaked in the summer of 2017, when Benchmark orches-trated the ouster of Uber's founding CEO, Travis Kalanick.

Uber was the pioneer of taxi hailing apps, disrupting the entire personal trans-portation business. While Uber's business rapidly spread across the globe, it also faced considerable opposition. Traditional taxi drivers often demonstrated against Uber's "unfair" business practices, while its own drivers sought to be rec-ognized as employees rather than being self-employed on "zero hours" contracts. Numerous local authorities also alleged a variety of illegal activities, to the point that Uber was banned from several cities.

The year 2017 was an unusual year, even by Uber standards. The opening act in January was a public relations disaster where the company was viewed as bullying its own drivers. A public "Delete Uber" campaign ensued, resulting in 200K people deleting the app from their phones. In February, a former Uber employee revealed online that Uber's human resource department had ignored numerous sexual harassment complaints. This came on the heels of earlier news stories about the company not caring about rape cases brought against Uber drivers. That same month a video recording was posted online showing Kalanick berating an Uber driver. Moreover, Google filed a lawsuit alleging theft of intel-lectual property, and in March the U.S. Justice Department opened an inquiry into allegations that Uber had developed a program to evade law enforcement.

In response to all these scandals, Uber appointed Eric Holder, a former at-torney general, to write a report about improving Uber's workplace culture. The report came back with a clear message: Uber should bolster its senior manage-ment team and make it less dependent on the CEO. Uber was unique in that Kalanick had led the company without either a chief operating officer (COO) or a chief financial officer (CFO). The report also recommended adding more in-dependent board members, an independent chair of the board, and an oversight committee.[45] At a board meeting in June, Kalanick agreed to take an indefinite leave as CEO. One week later, led by Benchmark, several investors went further. They coaxed Kalanick to resign from the CEO position, although he remained on the board of directors. By some measure, this was a version of a standard VC story: "founder outlives usefulness and gets removed by investors." Yet Uber being Uber, more was to come.

In August 2017, an experienced executive, Dara Khosrowshahi, was appointed as CEO. Benchmark then took the unusual step of suing its own portfolio company, thereby risking the value of its own investments. At issue was an agreement that Kalanick had obtained from Uber's board of directors (which included Benchmark's Bill Gurley) to nominate three additional board members. The lawsuit claimed that Kalanick had deliberately concealed and materially misstated that he effectively controlled these three members. To fully comprehend the strategic nature of this lawsuit, let us briefly look at Uber's share structure. At the time of the lawsuit, Benchmark owned 13% of shares and controlled 20% of voting power, whereas Kalanick held 10% of shares and 16% of votes[46] While they were the two largest shareholders, neither had control. The Benchmark lawsuit was thus aimed at wresting more control. It became a bargaining tool, where Benchmark offered to drop the lawsuit if Kalanick would agree to a complex deal led by SoftBank, a large Japanese investment fund. This deal was eventually agreed upon in January 2018.[47] SoftBank and its co-investors invested $9.3B at an estimated post-money valuation of $54B, a 20% discount from the previous round. The shares sold came mostly from Benchmark, which reduced its stake by 2%, from Kalanick, who reduced his stake by 3%, and from a variety of other existing shareholders. The board, which had only 7 members the summer before, was now expanded to 17. The voting structure was simplified, so that each share had one vote. The SoftBank deal thus established a better governance structure that would not give disproportionate control to anyone, neither to Kalanick the entrepreneur nor to Benchmark the investor.

In an interview, Dara Khosrowshahi, explained: "The company brought me on board because of a lot of things that happened in the past. We were probably trading off doing the right thing for growth, and thinking about competition maybe a bit too aggressively, and some of those things were mistakes."[48] Good governance from the start leads to fewer mistakes. It certainly could have made 2017 a duller, but easier, year for Uber.

WorkHorse Box 8.2. describes corporate governance in action.

WorkHorse Box 8.2 The July Board Meeting

WorkHorse had agreed to hold quarterly board meetings. Its first meeting in April 2021 had been very constructive. However, Wolf C. Flow, who had missed the meeting, complained about the absence of meeting minutes. At the July meeting, he managed to attend in person and made sure that Brandon was nominated board secretary in charge of producing the minutes. To Astrid's dismay Michael Archie was unable to come due to a long-planned yachting trip. Moreover, when Annie and Bharat asked to join again, Wolf flatly refused, explaining that a board meeting was for board members, not "the rest of the crowd."

Ali, the chairman, asked Astrid to provide a brief verbal update. The meeting quickly became tense, as Wolf C. Flow bombarded her with tough questions. The company had performed well in terms of delivering over 3,000 units a month requested by PortageLake, its large retail client. Wolf C. Flow, however, challenged the company for relying on a single retailer and expected to see a second retailer in place before the end of the year. He also questioned reliance on a single supplier, which exposed the company to a hold-up threat. Next, he inquired about Bharat's progress with developing the NokotoStar. He considered it important that WorkHorse have multiple products in order to look more attractive to potential acquirers. Astrid explained that he had prioritized his own development project over the development of the NokotoStar. Wolf was visibly fuming and asked exactly what his job description was. Ali tried to smooth over the situation by noting that the company was working with an HR consultant to set up a more comprehensive HR system for the company, including detailed job descriptions.

At that moment, Wolf inadvertently dropped the bomb, mumbling that it really wasn't up to the HR consultant to sort this out but rather up to a new CEO. "WHAT NEW CEO?" Astrid and Brandon blurted out in unison. Wolf wryly noted that while this company showed promise, it clearly needed "a proper CEO" to prepare the company for the "big league": "Someone with gray hair and Wall Street credibility" as he described it. "You can't bring the college kids to the Big Apple and expect them to impress the big fish." Astrid's heart sank lower than the bottom of Lake Erie.

Ali intervened, addressing the two founders directly: "We debated this among us investors, but it is too early to make a decision. We really like what you are doing. We think this could become something bigger than you think. Bringing in some management support would be good for the company. So, before we jump to any conclusions about a new CEO, let me ask you what you think we need to strengthen the management team." Astrid could hardly breathe, let alone think, but Brandon stepped up to the plate. "Actually, we have thought about this. We agree that our company is onto something big, and we think Astrid is a great CEO. We obviously lack experience, so what we really need is an experienced COO, someone who can build the organization." Wolf frowned, but Ali seemed satisfied and responded: "Excellent! Why don't we start with a proper search for that! In fact, I may have some useful contacts. . . ." Wolf interrupted: "We don't have time for that! Why take a bet to see if these kids can learn on the job? Let's get a proper CEO now! In fact, I know someone from my private equity days who might be just the right guy. He knows how to polish up companies and sell them in a jiffy." Astrid thought this was the low point of the meeting—in fact, the low point of the year.

"Hmm Hmm," Malcolm cleared his voice. "Look, this is all confidential, but I told my board last month that I am stepping down as CEO of Bolts-N-Nuts. I think I sold enough of them nuts and bolts over the years. I am ready for a new adventure. I also promised my family to spend more time at home, so I have been looking for something interesting part-time. I like these young folks here. Why don't I spend a little time with them?" Turning to Wolf he added: "Wolf, I'm bald. Does that count as gray hair on Wall Street?" Everyone was speechless; there was complete silence.

Suddenly Wolf's phone rang: "Oh, I must run, I have to leave for Hong Kong to meet some institutional investors. We are raising a new fund, you know. Why don't you guys sort out the rest? We'll talk once Malcolm figures it all out. Please don't forget to send the meeting minutes." Off he went, Astrid felt like the low point had just left the room.

8.3.5 Assessing Value-Adding Fit

We conclude the chapter by drawing some practical implications regarding the active role of investors. Consider an entrepreneur who is looking for an investor who can add value to her company. To assess how much an investor might add, one can use the MATCH questionnaire presented in Table 7.1. Here we focus specifically on questions 7, 8, and 9 about what an investor can offer. These three questions are derived from the Venture Evaluation Matrix (see Chapter 2) and were also used in Section 8.3.3. The "Customers and Markets" question (corresponding to the first column of the VE Matrix) addresses the company's need to win over customers, gain market share, and thus generate sales. The "Technology and Operations" question, corresponding to the second column of the VE Matrix, asks how a company innovates around technology, broadly defined. It also addresses how to establish a well-functioning business model and supply chain. The "Leadership and Organization" question, corresponding to the third column of the VE Matrix, concerns the development of a leadership team, as well as the building of a functional organization with a conducive corporate culture, making the company viable for the longer term.

To answer these three questions, the first step is to take the entrepreneur's perspective and define the areas where investor involvement is most needed. The second step is to consider a specific investor, or syndicate of investors, and ask where their capabilities lie. The third step is then to evaluate the match. We illustrate this method in WorkHorse Box 8.3.

WorkHorse Box 8.3 Investor Support at WorkHorse

Malcolm Force joined the company as part-time COO in early September. He quickly became a force to reckon with. Right away he adopted a proper accounting system, rationalized procurement, and implemented formal HR policies. Next, he brought some order to the management team. Astrid remained the CEO and was in fact given broader decision powers. Annie resolved her day-to-day issues with Astrid and Malcolm, without needing to consult with the other founders. Similar for Brandon. Only Bharat's role remained unclear. The NokotoStar had been "one week away from completion" for several months. Privately, Malcolm admitted to Astrid that he couldn't understand a word of what his research project was all about.

As the October meeting was approaching, Astrid decided to seek Malcolm's advice on how to handle Wolf C. Flow. The mere thought of being in the same room with Wolf made her cringe. Malcolm told her not to take things personally and instead to focus on how the different investors complemented each other to provide good overall support for the company. Talking about the importance of MATCH, he pulled out an empty paper and sketched the following table:

WorkHorse's Active Investors October 2021	Company needs	Investor capabilities	Match
Customers and markets	Add more retailers, expand globally	Ali has deep retail understanding, Wolf has strong global networks	Ali perfect for now, Wolf's networks will be needed soon
Technology and operations	Develop NokotoStar, improve supply chain and manufacturing quality	Michael has practical experience; Ali very supportive and focused on innovation	Mostly covered by Malcolm and Michael, need more help with China issues
Leadership and organization	Build senior management team around CEO	Wolf and Ali have good networks, but board split on whether to support or replace CEO	Delicate balance; needs constant attention

Malcolm explained: "Many people look at a company–investor match by evaluating one investor at the time, but it is difficult to find any one investor who is a strong match across all dimensions. I think of the investors as a team, and then see if there is someone who covers each row. Look closely at who is doing what! Ali has us covered on customers and markets, at least for now. Michael has lots of operational experience and Ali understands technology development. When it comes to leadership and growing the organization, Wolf has by far the best network. So overall, we are covered."

Astrid acknowledged that it was helpful to look at it this way. Still, the leadership issues were precarious: "I get it, but what should I do about Wolf, he is so . . . you know what I mean." Malcolm smiled: "You'd better learn to work with Wolf. He is someone you want on your side, not against you. I say Wolf is tough, but he isn't bad. If you want him to give you the benefit of the doubt, maybe you should do the same with him."

Summary

This chapter examines how investors provide corporate governance and support to their portfolio companies. We first establish why founders need support and why investors chose to get actively involved in the development of their companies. We then examine how investors can play an active role, in terms of both exercising corporate governance and adding value. We then discuss how investors exercise control through voting rights and by sitting on the board of directors. We consider how investors use a combination of control and support to move their companies forward. If necessary, they oblige founders to step aside and make room for outside managers to take over as CEOs of their companies. We also look at how investors can directly add value to their portfolio companies by mentoring founders, advising companies, making introductions to their business networks, and providing strategic pressure. Finally, we show how to assess the fit between what a specific company needs and what the specific investor can offer.

In terms of the FIRE framework (Chapter 1), this chapter launches our discussion of the third stage, RIDE. It looks at what happens once the money has arrived. There is a rich set of interactions between the entrepreneur and investors, involving both elements of control and support. We develop the RIDE further in the next chapter, which looks at the process of staged financing and the role that existing investors play in helping companies raise further financing.

Review Questions

1. What kind of companies seek investor involvement, and when?
2. What kind of investors want to get actively involved with their companies, and why?
3. How can voting rights deviate from the "one–share one–vote" baseline?
4. What are some typical board structures in start-ups? How do they change over time?
5. Who controls the board of directors? What is the role of independent directors?

6. How can entrepreneurs exercise informal control without formal control?
7. By which means can investors add value to their companies?
8. With what business aspects are investors most likely to get involved?
9. What is the effect on performance of replacing a company founder with an outside CEO?
10. What constitutes a good fit between the support needs of a company and the support capabilities of the investors?

Notes

1. Shleifer and Vishny (1997).
2. Davila and Foster (2009) and Hamm (2002).
3. Carreyrou (2018a, b).
4. Brown (2019).
5. Gompers, Kaplan, and Mukharlyamov (2016). Bottazzi, Da Rin, and Hellmann (2008) study European VCs and find similar but somewhat less frequent interactions.
6. Garg (2013a, 2013b).
7. Experienced investors are often critical of board observer rights. See Brad Feld's blog at: https://feld.com/archives/2012/05/should-vc-board-observers-rights-exist.html, and Mark Suster's blog at: https://bothsidesofthetable.com/why-i-don-t-like-board-observers-428e26e61dba, both accessed on April 15, 2019.
8. Adams, Hermalin, and Weisbach (2010).
9. Baker and Gompers (2003), Hochberg (2012), and Yermack (1997).
10. Pozen (2007).
11. Broughman (2013).
12. Feld and Ramsinghani (2014).
13. Feld and Ramsinghani (2014).
14. Kaplan and Strömberg (2003).
15. Kaplan and Strömberg (2004).
16. Li and Srinivasan (2011).
17. Aghion and Tirole (1997).
18. Garg and Eisenhardt (2016).
19. https://www.nobelprize.org/prizes/economic-sciences/2000/press-release.
20. https://www.nobelprize.org/prizes/economic-sciences /2003/press-release.
21. Bernstein, Giroud, and Townsend (2016).
22. Da Rin, Hellmann, and Puri (2013) review this literature.
23. Sapienza, Manigart, and Vermeir (1996).
24. Horowitz (2014).
25. Stevenson, Roberts, and Grousbeck (2000).
26. Hellmann (2007).
27. Hsu (2006).
28. Ozmel, Robinson, and Stuart (2013).
29. Baum and Silverman (2004) and Blevins and Ragozzino (2018).
30. Lindsey (2008).
31. Krause and Bruton (2013).
32. Kortum and Lerner (2000) and Popov and Roosenboom. (2012).

33. Kaplan, Sensoy, and Strömberg (2009).
34. To communicate this message, Sequoia Capital provided a slide presentation to the CEOs of its portfolio companies. The slides presentation can be seen at: https://techcrunch.com/2008/10/10/sequoia-capitals-56-slide-powerpoint-presentation-of-doom/, accessed April 15, 2019.
35. Bottazzi, Da Rin, and Hellmann (2009).
36. Gans, Hsu, and Stern (2002).
37. Beroutsos, Freeman, and Kehoe (2007).
38. Horn, Lovallo and Viguerie (2006).
39. Ragozzino and Blevins (2016).
40. Chemmanur, Krishnan, and Nandy (2011).
41. Hellmann and Puri (2000 and 2002).
42. Ewens and Marx (2018).
43. Bottazzi, Da Rin, and Hellmann (2008).
44. https://www.startupranking.com/startup/uber/funding-rounds, accessed April 15, 2019.
45. Kolhatkar (2018).
46. Somerville (2017).
47. Molla and Schleifer (2018).
48. Kolhatkar (2018).

9

Staged Financing

Learning Goals

In this chapter students will learn:

1. Why equity investments in entrepreneurial companies are often staged.
2. To understand the bargaining dynamics between old and new investors.
3. To analyze term sheet clauses that relate to staged investments.
4. What happens when companies experience a down round.

This chapter examines the provision of equity financing through multiple funding rounds. We first discuss the rationale for a staged investment round from both the entrepreneurs' and investors' perspectives. Entrepreneurs benefit from postponing selling part of their company at a higher price at a later stage, but they incur the risk of encountering deteriorating market conditions, having to give investors more control, or even failing to raise additional capital. Investors benefit from the option value of terminating underperforming projects. Staging also creates conflicts of interest between old and new investors that can be addressed with contractual clauses, as well as renegotiation. Relevant terms include anti-dilution protection, preemption rights, and pay-to-play clauses. We further discuss how investors handle companies that underperform. The chapter closes by examining dynamic investment strategies that balance short-term and long-term goals.

9.1 The Rationale for Staged Financing

Some start-ups only have modest capital requirements and quickly find a path to profitability (or failure). Those companies don't need more than one round of financing. However, the majority of growth-oriented start-ups face extended periods of negative cash flows. They rely on raising additional capital to keep growing. Equity is thus raised across multiple funding rounds. This is called the "staged financing" process.[1]

The terminology of staged financing is sometimes confusing. Recall from Box 1.6 that financing stages are usually identified with funding rounds: pre-seed, seed, Series A, B, C, and so on. A study by CB Insight, a technology intelligence

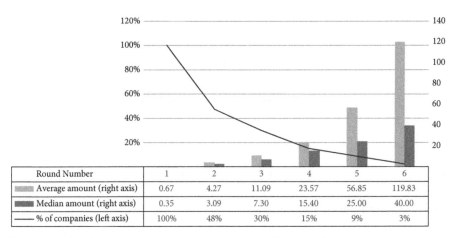

Round Number	1	2	3	4	5	6
▨ Average amount (right axis)	0.67	4.27	11.09	23.57	56.85	119.83
▨ Median amount (right axis)	0.35	3.09	7.30	15.40	25.00	40.00
—— % of companies (left axis)	100%	48%	30%	15%	9%	3%

Figure 9.1. Funding amounts across financing rounds, 2008–2018.
Amount data in U.S. dollar millions. Source: Authors' elaborations on data from CB Insight (2018).

consultancy, looks at the cohort of U.S. VC-backed companies that received their first funding in the period 2008–2010 and follows them through August 2018.[2] After each round, approximately 50% of all companies raise another round, 15% have an exit, and 35% fail. The average (median) duration between two subsequent rounds is 19 (17) months. Figure 9.1 shows the average and median amounts per round, as well as the percentage of companies in the cohort that raise new rounds. It shows that later rounds are significantly larger than earlier rounds but that a decreasing percentage of all companies ever raise them. It also shows that in later rounds the difference between the average and median amount becomes larger. This is because a relatively small number of ventures raise particularly large rounds.

How common is staging? Figure 9.2 shows some data in both number and amounts. This figure differentiates between Series A, Series B, Series C, and later. A key insight from Panel A is that the number of deals is progressively lower for later series, consistent with the evidence of Figure 9.1. There is a big jump from Series A to Series B, and a much smaller jump in number to Series C and later, reflecting the increasing survival rate as ventures mature. These features are quite stable over time, with an increase of Series A deals after the 2008 crisis. Panel B shows the reverse picture once we look at amounts invested. Later series account for a larger share of funds than early-stage deals; this feature has been more marked in recent years. Panel C further illustrates this by looking at average deal size by Series. Size increases with Series and with time. The size of Series A and B deals has doubled over the sample period, while for Series C and later the increase has been nearly fivefold. This is largely due to the mega deals raised by unicorns in recent years, reflecting a trend toward funding extremely capital-intensive global businesses. These data are for deals worldwide, with few differences across regions, except that in Europe Series A and B represent a larger share of the money invested than later series, unlike the case in the U.S., Asia, and the rest of the world.

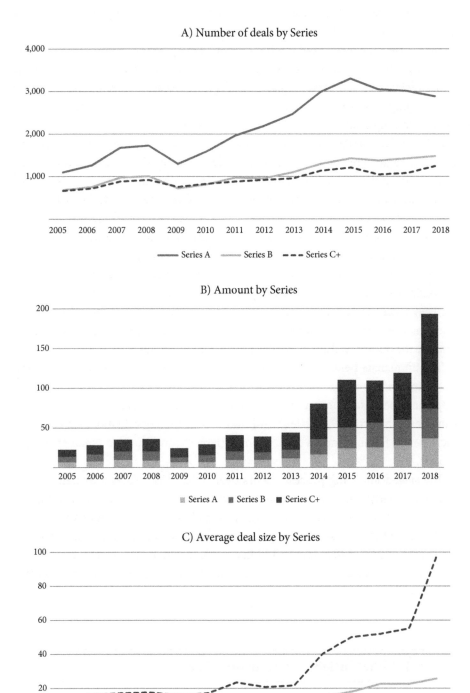

Figure 9.2. Investments by Series.

Data in U.S. billion dollars. Source: Pitchbook Data.

Why is there staging?[3] Investors could simply endow a company with enough capital upfront to go all the way to cash flow positive. However, this rarely happens. In most cases, the benefits of staging for both entrepreneurs and investors exceed the costs. For the entrepreneur, staging allows lowering the cost of capital, as the entrepreneur can delay selling part of the equity necessary to reach positive cash flow. Staging, however, introduces uncertainty about future fundraising. It may not be forthcoming at all, or it could be delayed. It could also become costlier if market conditions deteriorate or if the venture develops more slowly than expected. For the investor, staging creates an opportunity to defer the decision to continue funding, thus reducing the amount of money at risk. It also gives the investor considerable control over the venture because the investor gets the power to decide whether or not to continue funding the company. However, staging requires repeated negotiations, which are costly for both parties. Consider the alternative where the entrepreneur is fully funded for a long time. It would be very difficult for the investor to get his money back. If the company encounters difficulties, the entrepreneur is likely to continue spending it until the company runs out of money. Staged financing effectively takes the decision to stop a venture out of the hands of the entrepreneur. The pressure to raise additional funding also gives the entrepreneur incentives to manage the money well and to focus on meeting milestones.

The immediate benefits of staging go to the investor, who can better preserve their capital if the company fails to take off. Ultimately, staging also benefits the entrepreneur because it reduces the cost of capital and therefore improves company valuations. In Section 9.2.2, we show how the post-money valuation of a company increases as funding moves from a single (larger) round to two (smaller) staged rounds.

The staged financing process occurs over time. This creates a dynamic situation where early-stage investors have to anticipate what will happen in future financing rounds. This requires thinking through how different parties strategically interact over time. These kinds of problems are studied in dynamic game theory, a field of economics (and mathematics) that has preoccupied several Nobel laureates. Box 9.1 discusses their work and derives some implications for entrepreneurs and investors.

Box 9.1 Nobel Insights on Dynamic Games

Richard Selten was one of the winners of the 1994 Nobel Prize in Economics, "for their pioneering analysis of equilibria in the theory of non-cooperative games."[4] The 2004 Nobel Prize went to Finn E. Kydland and Edward C. Prescott "for their contributions to dynamic macroeconomics: the time consistency of economic policy and the driving forces behind business cycles."[5] Finally, in 2007, Eric Maskin was one of the winners "for having laid the foundations of mechanism design theory."[6] While none of these great minds spent any time thinking about staged financing itself, their insights are highly valuable for understanding the dynamic behaviors that shape the staged financing process.

Richard Selten's central contribution was to develop an understanding of dynamic games, and in particular the concept of "subgame perfection." While the term may sound obscure, it means something quite intuitive. In dynamic situations ("dynamic games"), all parties make predictions about future behavior. Such predictions are challenging because there are numerous present and future choices and outcomes to consider. Selten developed the notion of subgame perfection as a tool for identifying what set of future actions can be reasonably expected to take place and which other actions are unlikely to happen because they are not in the parties' best interest. In fact, "subgame perfect" refers to selecting a behavior that is in the party's best interest ("perfect") at each stage ("subgame") of the negotiation. This allowed game theorists to have a precise understanding of how to think through dynamic interactions.

Staged financing is a dynamic game in which the entrepreneur and early investors need to consider what will happen in future rounds. They need to consider not only how they themselves will behave in the future, but also how other, later-stage, investors will behave. One of the important insights from subgame perfection is that parties need to take renegotiation into account. Even if an entrepreneur and investor initially agree on a contract, there is nothing to prevent them from changing their agreement at a later stage. If the two parties expect future renegotiation, they should take this into account in their initial negotiation. To illustrate how this could play out, consider angel investors who know that in later financing rounds new investors will request that any existing preferred shares be converted into common shares (to make room for their own preferred shares). Since future investors hold the money, they often have the power to get such requests approved. In anticipation, smart angels will not bother wasting their bargaining chips on getting preferred shares, knowing that they will be forced to convert them later anyway.

Kydland and Prescott's contribution is identifying the problem of "time inconsistent preferences," commonly known as the problem of "changing your mind." In a dynamic game, players often want to pre-commit to take a certain action, but when faced with the decision at a later stage they prefer a different action. A classic example is negotiating with kidnappers. A priori, the police want to commit to never paying ransom to kidnappers, so as to minimize the temptation for kidnapping. However, once faced with a kidnapping case, they prefer to pay in order to save the life of the victim. Kydland and Prescott apply this idea to macroeconomic policies. They note that to ensure low inflation, governments want to commit to a predictable tight monetary policy. However, when faced with signs of economic weakness, governments are quick to loosen their monetary policy in order to promote employment. This ends up causing inflation. Governments thus have time-inconsistent preferences.

This problem of time-inconsistent preferences also happens with staged financing. At an earlier stage, investors may want to commit to a particular course of future behavior, but once they reach the later stages, they no longer want to behave like that. A classic example is the soft-budget problem analyzed by Eric Maskin.[7] In order to provide strong incentives for outstanding performance, an investor may want to pre-commit to only refinance ventures with outstanding performance, but not those with ordinary performance. Yet when it comes to refinancing, the investor will refinance both outstanding and ordinary ventures, as long as the net present value is positive. The investor is unable to commit to a tough termination policy, which a priori weakens the entrepreneur's incentives for achieving outstanding performance. The soft-budget problem is thus a problem of time-inconsistent preferences.

9.2 Structuring Staged Financing Deals

9.2.1 Staged Investments and Ownership

In our discussion of the financial plan in Section 3.7, we noted two important financing needs: how much money the venture needs overall and how much money it needs at the present time. Milestones play a key role in partitioning fundraising into stages because at each milestone there is a resolution of uncertainty about the risks of the business (Sections 3.3 and 6.1.2). For example, when the company achieves its first sales, it shows that there is some demand for its product. By identifying informative milestones, staging allows investors to make efficient refinancing decisions.

How much money should be invested at each round? There is no point in giving a company too little money, so that it does not have a chance of achieving a meaningful milestone. At the same time, there is a danger of giving a company too much money because this may encourage profligate behavior. For example, the company may ignore negative signals and persist in a losing strategy down a money-losing path. In practice, many start-ups raise enough to operate for one to two years.

The actual amount of money raised in a round, and how it lasts, also depend on economic circumstances. Gompers finds that there is more staging (i.e., smaller but more frequent rounds) in industries that have more intangible assets and more R&D spending.[8] The interpretation is that companies in these sectors need to be monitored more closely. A study by Tian finds that investors that are located further away from the company also rely more on staging.[9] The reason here is that more distant investors depend more on financially controlling their companies, given that they cannot monitor them in close proximity.

The amount invested in a round is not only determined by company needs but also by the investors' preferences and their financial resources. Some investors prefer fewer and larger rounds to minimize transaction costs or to allow more entrepreneurial experimentation. However, other investors have limited investment budgets ("shallow pockets") or want to limit their exposure for portfolio diversification reasons. Even if the entrepreneur wants a larger round, investors may be unable or unwilling to provide as much. In this case, there is also the option of bringing in additional syndication partners to top up a round (Section 7.4).

To practically see how staging works, consider a simple example. Suppose a company needs $2M to hit a first milestone in one year, $3M to hit a second milestone in two years, and then another $10M to scale up and get acquired three years later. Consider three alternative staging structures. First, there is no staging, which means raising the entire $15M upfront. This would ensure that the entrepreneur has all the money to implement her project. For the investor, the problem is that this deal structure invites the entrepreneur to spend the entire $15M, regardless of any interim signals about the attractiveness of the venture. A second approach is to stage the financing in three smaller rounds of $2M, $3M, and $10M, respectively. This would maximize flexibility to the investor and minimize the ownership the entrepreneur has to give up (as shown below). However, it would require spending more time raising funds, and add some uncertainty about future market conditions. An intermediate approach is to have fewer but larger stages. For example, the company could be raising $5M upfront, enough for the first two milestones, and $10M thereafter, provided these milestones have been met. This intermediate approach requires less time raising funds for the entrepreneur but preserves some flexibility for the investor. Specifically, the investor can withhold the $10M in case the company does not reach its two milestones.

Table 9.1 further develops the example showing how different staging strategies result in different ownership dilution for the entrepreneur (Section 4.1.5). Staged financing allows the entrepreneur to retain more ownership. To see how this works, suppose the entrepreneur initially owns 10M shares and expects to receive a $10M pre-money valuation regardless of the way financing is staged. In the single round case, the post-money valuation is $25M, and the investor takes a 60% stake (= $15M/$25M) obtaining 15M shares (Section 4.1 contains the relevant formulas). The share price is then $1. With two rounds, the entrepreneur raises $5M in the first round, giving the investor a 33.3% ownership share (= $5M/$15M) and 5M shares. For the second round, we assume that the share price climbs to $3, so that the pre-money valuation is $45M. The investor obtains 3.3M additional shares for the $10M investment (= $10M/$3), increasing his stake to 45.5% (= 8.3M/18.3M). With three rounds, the entrepreneur raises $2M, $3M, and $10M, with a share price increasing from $1 to $1.8 to $3, respectively. With the same logic as above, the investor obtains 2M, 1.7M, and 3.3M shares at the three rounds, for a total of 7M shares and a final ownership of 41.2% (= 7M/17M). The main insight is that staging limits the entrepreneurs' ownership dilution. With three rounds they only give up 41.2%, compared to 45.5% with two rounds or 60%, with one round.

Table 9.1 · Ownership Dilution with Staged Financing.

	New capital raised	Post-money valuation	Pre-money valuation	Price per share	Entrepreneur's shares	New shares issued	Total investor shares	Total shares	Investors' ownership	Entrepreneur's ownership
	($M)	($M)	($M)	($)	(M)	(M)	(M)	(M)		
Single round										
Round 1	15.0	25.0	10.0	1.0	10.0	15.0	15.0	25.0	60.0%	40.0%
Two rounds										
Round 1	5.0	15.0	10.0	1.0	10.0	5.0	5.0	15.0	33.3%	66.7%
Round 2	10.0	55.0	45.0	3.0	10.0	3.3	8.3	18.3	45.5%	54.5%
Three rounds										
Round 1	2.0	12.0	10.0	1.0	10.0	2.0	2.0	12.0	16.7%	83.3%
Round 2	3.0	24.6	21.6	1.8	10.0	1.7	3.7	13.7	26.8%	73.2%
Round 3	10.0	51.0	41.0	3.0	10.0	3.3	7.0	17.0	41.2%	58.8%
Three rounds (with down round)										
Round 1	2.0	12.0	10.0	1.0	10.0	2.0	2.0	12.0	16.7%	83.3%
Round 2	3.0	10.2	7.2	0.6	10.0	5.0	7.0	17.0	41.2%	58.8%
Round 3	10.0	61.0	51.0	3.0	10.0	3.3	10.3	20.3	50.8%	49.2%

Having more rounds is not, however, a magic formula for reducing dilution. With staging there is a risk that the company fails to raise the additional money or that the price per share falls across rounds because of adverse company or market conditions (Section 9.4.1). The bottom of Table 9.1 reports what would happen if the share price of the second round were to fall to $0.6 (a 'down round,' see Section 9.4.1). In this case, the entrepreneur ends up giving up 50.8% of the company.

More generally, staging reduces dilution for the entrepreneur whenever the price per share increases over time. If the price per share remains the same in every round, there is no advantage in terms of dilution. The question that arises is why, on average, share prices should rise over time. A simplified answer is that start-ups usually either grow or fail, so either they raise funding at higher prices or they don't raise any funding at all. A more complete answer is that we need to model how share prices and valuation behave over time. So far, our example arbitrarily fixes all prices and valuations. In Section 5.2.2, we explain how to use the VC valuation method to obtain valuations that are internally consistent across multiple rounds. We now extend this framework to look at simple decision trees about whether or not to fund another round.

9.2.2 The Option Value of Staging

We now introduce the real options approach to valuing companies, which involves solving decision trees that capture the roles of investment decisions, chance, and returns.[10] This approach is based on the idea that there is value in making decisions over time. In our context, this requires identifying the milestones and financing decisions that happen along the path. With this we quantify the value of staging investments, where at each stage there is the option to abandon the project. Note that our approach here is also closely related to the PROFEX model of Section 5.5.2.

We return to the example from the previous section, but instead of using somewhat arbitrary prices and valuations, we now derive internally consistent valuations from within a model. This requires assumptions on exit values. Suppose that in case of success the company achieves an exit value of $200M. However, the probability of success is only 10%. This can be broken down into a 40% probability of achieving the first milestone after one year, then a 50% probability of achieving the second milestone after the second year, and then a 50% probability of going all the way to exit in the three following years. In case of failure, we assume that the company is worthless.

Figure 9.3 shows the three corresponding decision trees. With a single round of $15M, there is no decision, the company succeeds with 10%, or it fails with 90%. With two rounds ($5M upfront and $10M after two years), there is one decision point after two years. If the venture achieves its milestones, the investor provides the additional $10M, but if the milestone is missed, no further investment takes place. In this case, we say that the investor exercises the option to abandon the

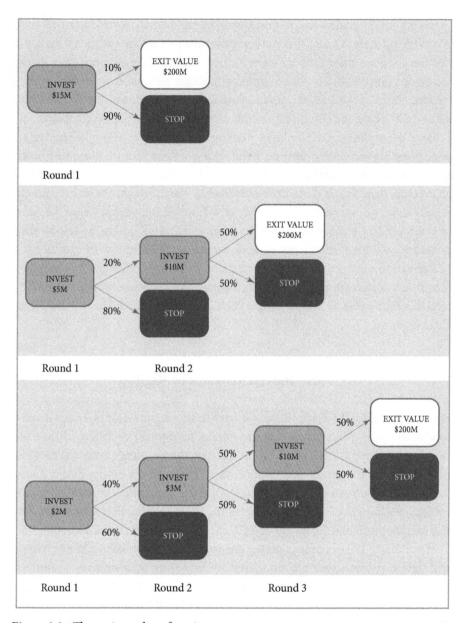

Figure 9.3. The option value of staging.

project. With three rounds ($2M upfront, $3M after one year, and $10M after two years), there are two decision points where the project can be abandoned after two and after five years from the start.

The way to solve a decision tree is to work backwards from the end nodes and consider what decisions are made at each decision node, all the way back to the root. To obtain a valuation, each payoff and each investment along the tree must be discounted back to the present. A suitable discount rate includes all the factors discussed in Section 5.2.3—see in particular equation (5.4)—but with one important exception: there is no failure risk premium. This is because the real options model explicitly includes failure. For our example we use a 20% annual discount rate.

Compared to the VC method (Section 5.2) or the discounted cash flows method (Section 5.3), there is no longer a single stream of cash flows. Instead, the real options approach includes a probability distribution over different cash flow streams, representing different branches of the tree. This resembles the scenario analysis we discuss in Section 5.5.1—see especially equation (5.15). This requires calculating the expected valuation by adding up all the probability-weighted valuations along each of the branches that can actually be chosen. We can therefore think of a decision tree as a tool for generating scenarios that are based on key decisions taken along the path.

Table 9.2 shows the results of the real options valuation. Consider first the case of a single round. The expected discounted exit value is given by a 10% chance of achieving a $200M exit value, discounted at 20% over 5 years. This amounts to a post-money valuation of $8.0M [= $0.1*$200M/(1.2)^5$]. Given that the investment costs $15M, we obtain a negative pre-money valuation. This means that the project is worth less than it costs, so no investor would be willing to finance it.

Consider next the case of two rounds of financing. Computing the expected value of the exit and discounting it back over three years yields a post-money valuation of $57.9M [= $0.5*$200M/(1.2)^3$]. With a remaining investment of $10M, the pre-money valuation is $47.9M. Table 9.2 also shows the number of shares and ownership fractions. To value the company at the time of the first round, we compute the expected value of the second-round pre-money valuation and discount it back at 20% for two years. We obtain a post-money valuation of $6.7 [= $0.2*$47.9M/(1.2)^2$]. Given that the first-round investment is $5M, this leaves us with a $1.65M pre-money valuation. Since this is a positive number, investors are now willing to fund the venture. This is an important result, as it shows how staged financing enables the financing of a risky project by allowing an option to abandon a project.

Table 9.2 also provides the calculations in the case of three financing rounds. We note that the post-money valuation in the first round is lower than before because of the funding amount in the first round. The key insight is that the pre-money valuation with three rounds is higher than with two rounds. The difference between the $3.7M pre-money valuation with three rounds and $1.7M pre-money valuation with two rounds derives entirely from having another option of abandoning the project in case the first milestone is not met. In addition, we note that the investor ownership goes from 79.5% with two rounds to 54.6% with three rounds. This shows once more how the entrepreneur can achieve a lower dilution with staging.

The case of BIND, a biotechnology start-up from MIT, illustrates the importance of staging. Operating in a sector with long and highly uncertain development cycles, this company needed four rounds of venture capital before its IPO in 2013. The founders also used university funding and IP support for patenting to delay the need for external funds, and then they used clearly defined milestones to engage corporate partners and VC investors in successively large funding rounds.[11]

Table 9.2 Real Options Valuation

	New capital raised	Probability of success	Post-money valuation	Pre-money valuation	Price per share	Entrepreneur's shares	New shares issued	Total investor shares	Total shares	Investors' ownership share	Entrepreneur's ownership share
	($M)		($M)	($M)	($)	(M)	(M)	(M)	(M)		
Single round											
Round 1	15	10%	8.0	−7.0	–	10.0	–	–	–	–	–
Two rounds											
Round 1	5	20%	6.6	1.6	0.2	10	30.3	30.3	40.3	75.2%	24.8%
Round 2	10	50%	57.9	47.9	1.2	10.0	8.4	38.8	48.8	79.5%	20.5%
Three rounds											
Round 1	2	40%	5.7	3.7	0.4	10.0	5.5	5.5	15.5	35.4%	64.6%
Round 2	3	50%	19.9	17.0	1.1	10.0	2.7	8.2	18.2	45.1%	54.9%
Round 3	10	50%	57.9	47.9	2.6	10.0	3.8	12.0	22.0	54.6%	45.4%

Funding the whole development in one round would never have been feasible. More generally, Box 9.2 examines academic research relevant for understanding the practical implications of the option value of staging.

Box 9.2 Financing Experimentation

Financing entrepreneurial experiments has its challenges. If an investor keeps tight control over the venture and only disburses funding in small steps, then there is a high option value of staging (derived below). Maintaining hard budget constraints further provides strong performance incentives, as discussed in Box 9.1. However, this approach also has disadvantages. The kind of projects that thrive under hard budgets are those where the bets are well understood. Milestones must be well defined so that it is possible to determine whether they are achieved. This works well for incremental innovation, but what about radical innovations where the experiments are ill-defined and milestones are constantly in flux? For those it would seem that a different financing approach of giving time and freedom is more appropriate.[12] An academic study of medical research grants by Azoulay, Graff Zivin, and Manso, for example, shows that scientists engage in much riskier long-term research when given flexible long-term grants, but revert to more incremental research when kept to a short funding cycle.[13] The problem with a laxer financing approach is that entrepreneurs (or researchers for that matter) can use their freedom to pursue losing ventures for too long, or even divert funding toward other pet projects. Hence the dilemma of financing experimentation: neither the tight nor the lax approach seems to provide a workable solution for truly innovative entrepreneurs and their investors.

Two economic conditions help to alleviate this dilemma: hot markets and lower costs of experimentation. VC financing and IPO markets are prone to cycles where there are hot markets, filled with optimism and irrational exuberance, which alternate with down markets, filled with pessimism and a flight to safer investments (see also Box 12.1). Research by Nanda and Rhodes-Kropf shows that hot markets encourage investments in more radical innovation.[14] The underlying logic is that investors are more willing to take a bet on a risky experiment because they expect the company has a good chance to receive further funding down the line. The study finds that VCs make riskier bets in hot markets, as evidenced by both more bankruptcies and higher valued IPOs. They also invest in more innovative companies as evidenced by a higher number and higher quality of their patents.[15]

The second economic condition is lower costs of experimentation. Since the middle of the 2000s, the development of the Internet, the emergence of cloud computing, the rise of global outsourcing, and the lean start-up movement (Box 2.5) have all brought down the cost of starting a new venture. This has changed the landscape of entrepreneurial finance, especially at the seed stage. In Chapter 13, we discuss the rise of angel investors, crowdfunding, and other forms of early-stage financing. All these developments have made entrepreneurial experimentation more affordable. An academic study, by Ewens, Nanda, and Rhodes-Kropf, examines the introduction of cloud computing.[16] It shows that the average size of seed investments fell precisely in those sectors where cloud computing was prevalent. Interestingly, this only applies to the initial experimentation phases, not the later stages of company development. The study also shows that investors adapted their investment approaches. They increasingly used a "spray and pray" approach of initially investing in many companies (i.e., lots of experiments), but then only providing follow-on financing to the few that showed clear traction (i.e., only the successful experiments). A famous example is 500 Start-ups, a VC fund whose name advocates such an approach. Founded in 2010, the fund had invested in over 2,000 companies during its first eight years. This amounts to approximately one new investment for every working day.[17]

9.2.3   Tranching

So far, we compared single round financing to staged financing. Tranching, or milestone financing, is an intermediate approach to staging. It is a contractual arrangement that specifies a total funding amount for the round but divides it into tranches—typically two, rarely more. The first tranche is provided at the closing of the deal, and the payment of the second tranche depends on a milestone. The price of the second tranche is typically the same as the first. An academic study by Bienz and Hirsch finds that milestone financing is more likely when there is a single investor financing the deal.[18] The researchers interpret this as a way to protect the entrepreneur from a single powerful investor who could otherwise demand onerous terms in a later round.

In milestone financing, there are two main ways of structuring the payment of the second tranche. The first is to specify an automatic release of the funds upon achievement of the milestone. This requires a milestone that can be easily verified. The second is to give the investor the option to release the second tranche. In this case, the formal milestone is less important; what matters is the investor's belief in the company. In our example above, a tranched deal would consist of a $5M investment, where the company receives $2M upfront and three in a second tranche.

While staging and tranching are very similar, there is an important difference. With staging the entrepreneur has to go through an entire fundraising process, including setting a new valuation and negotiating a new term sheet, whereas with tranching the entire deal structure for the second tranche, the $3M in our example, is already set up. Tranching therefore preserves the option value for the investor and simplifies the fundraising process and therefore saves time to both parties. WorkHorse Box 9.1 illustrates staging and tranching.

WorkHorse Box 9.1 Preparing for a B round

WorkHorse had come a long way by October 2021, but Astrid worried about the upcoming board meeting because the company was late developing its second product, the NokotaStar, and it needed more money.

In preparation for the board meeting, Brandon and Malcolm had developed a new set of financial projections that reflected the company's changed circumstances. They identified two important milestones for the company. First, while there had been severe delays in the development of the NokotaStar, the company still hoped to launch it sometime in the second half of 2022. Bharat was in charge but seemed more focused on his academic research. Second, the company had decided to postpone its expansion into Europe by one year, now planning to launch European sales in early 2023. Both of these initiatives would require significant investments. The cash flow projections suggested that the company needed $2M to achieve the first milestone of launching the NokotaStar and making it to the end of 2022, and another $3M to launch European sales and make it through the end of 2023.

On the eve of the October board meeting, Astrid, Malcolm, and Brandon were debating what exactly to propose to the board. Astrid thought they should be bold and simply ask for $5M. This would allow the company to hit both milestones, and the management team could focus on running the business, not just fundraising. She agreed that investors would need to commit a lot of money upfront and would therefore offer a lower share price. Still, given WorkHorse's strong sales performance, she thought that the company could aim for $8 per share.

Malcolm's instincts were different. He thought they should be raising just enough money to hit the next milestone. This would give investors option value and translate into a higher valuation. He thought the company could reach $10 per share for a "B-1" round of $2M and $12 per share for a $3M "B-2" round. He preferred to call the latter at a B-2 round rather than a C round because it would be fairly similar and close in time to the B-1 round. Malcolm admitted that his staged approach was riskier. What if the company missed the milestone, say because Bharat never finished the prototype? Still, he thought it was worth taking the risk.

Brandon, seeing an opportunity to brandish his MBA skills, suggested a tranched structure as the best of both worlds. He suggested raising $5M in two tranches, with a milestone defined around the launch of the NokotaStar. He also thought the company could reach a price of $10 per share with a B round of $2M. With a tranched structure, the first (B-1) and second (B-2) tranche would have the same price.

Brandon produced a table that summarized their respective positions and worked out the implications for valuation and ownership. The table identifies a trade-off between risk and ownership. Astrid's proposal involved the least risk for the company, but also the least ownership with the founders (34.91%). Malcolm's was clearly the riskiest proposal, but it allowed the founders to maintain more ownership (37.80%). Brandon felt that his own solution provided the right balance, leaving the team with an ownership stake of 36.92%.

	Astrid (Full financing)	Malcolm (Staged financing)	Brandon (Tranched financing)
Before the B round			
Founder shares	800,000	800,000	800,000
Total shares	1,666,667	1,666,667	1,666,667
Founder %	48.0%	48.0%	48.0%
B-1 round			
Investment ($)	5,000,000	2,000,000	2,000,000
Price per share ($)	8	10	10
Pre-money valuation ($)	13,333,333	16,666,667	16,666,667
Post-money valuation ($)	18,333,333	18,666,667	18,666,667
New shares issued	625,000	200,000	200,000
Total shares after round	2,291,667	1,866,667	1,866,667
Founder %	34.9%	42.9%	42.9%
B-2 round			
Investment ($)		3,000,000	3,000,000
Price per share		12	10
Pre-money valuation ($)		22,400,000	18,666,667
Post-money valuation ($)		25,400,000	21,666,667
New shares issued		250,000	300,000
Total shares		2,116,667	2,166,667
Founder %		37.8%	36.9%

Just as the three of them were getting engrossed in the details of the table, the door flung open. Bharat stepped in, carrying a large bag. Astrid immediately asked: "Is that the prototype of the NokotaStar?" Bharat beamed and said: "Sorry, No. . . . It's a surprise: TaDaaa!" Malcolm frowned, but before he could say anything, Bharat launched into it: "Do you remember what I told you about Micro-voltaic Algorithmically Granularized Infrared Capturization?" No one remembered. "Well, I solved it! It's working, not just the theory, but the actual prototype. I have it right here!" The others were happy to hear Bharat using the words working and prototype in the same sentence. After some hard-to-follow explanations, they gathered that Bharat had not only solved a difficult scientific problem, but had already built a prototype: not of the NokotaStar, but of something that could capture more solar energy than anything that existed anywhere to date. Bharat exclaimed: "Don't you understand? We can build a whole new generation of solar generators! No one will be interested in the NokotaStar anymore, nor the WonderFoal for that matter." It took a while for the three to comprehend what Bharat was talking about.

After an impressive prototype demonstration, ramen soup for everyone, and a large portion of ice cream, they gathered around the table once more. "So, what does this all mean for the company?" Astrid asked. Bharat went straight at it: "Let's take a moonshot; we can disrupt the entire U.S. solar generator market. I think we could even take this to India and other developing countries. Let's bring solar generators to those who don't have access to the grid!" Astrid lightened up; hadn't this been part of the original dream? Malcolm brought the team back to the present: "What does it all mean for tomorrow's board meeting?" Bharat was on a roll: "Easy, we demo the prototype, tell them the NokotaStar is a waste of time, and announce that we are going for a moonshot of solar proportions!" To Bharat's surprise, Malcolm nodded slowly. Only Brandon looked incredulous: "What about the question of how much money we want to raise in the next round?" Bharat looked at Brandon's spreadsheet that was lying on the table: "If you ask me, Brandon's idea of tranching won't work, our milestones will be too vague for that. Malcolm's idea of raising money for one year is too risky, as there can always be delays with product development. I like Astrid's idea of raising money for two years. The only hitch is that this is now a much more ambitious venture, so we need a lot more money." There was silence. Out of the blue and without any further justification he added: "I suggest we ask for $10M."

9.2.4 Old versus New Investors

Any follow-on round may include a mix of old and new investors. If a round is financed entirely by old investors, that is, those who already own shares in the company, then it is called an insider round. If it is financed purely by new investors, it is an outsider round. Often, however, a round is financed by a mix of old and new investors. The composition of the investor mix affects many aspects of the deal. In this section, we examine the economic interests of the old and new investors, especially how they think about valuation.

Consider first the case of an insider round. This has the advantage that all investors are already familiar with the company and can act fast. However, without competition from outsiders, insiders may have strong bargaining power to dictate terms. The company may also miss out on accessing new investors who bring additional expertise and distinct networks. Contrast this to the case of an outsider round. This may expand expertise and networks, but it raises questions as to why none of the existing investors continues funding the company. They may not have the required financial resources—what is called deep pockets—to continue supporting the company, or they may have unfavorable information, which would be a more worrisome signal about the company.

The two polar cases of insider and outsider financing identify several issues that affect the terms and structure of mixed deals. First, there is the question of how much money the old and the new investors can contribute, and how much they want to invest. Second, there is the matter of what expertise and networks the old and the new investors bring to the venture. Some investors specialize in early-stage companies, and others in later stages, thus developing different networks, expertise, and skills (Section 12.5). Third, there is the issue of inside information. Having the old investor put some money in a new round is a positive signal. At the same time, outside investors may bring better market knowledge that may reflect on valuation and other terms. Fourth, outsiders add an element of competition, which is welcome by entrepreneurs, but risks alienating insiders. These forces create interesting bargaining dynamics between outsiders, insiders, and entrepreneurs that affects valuation and deal structure.

An important concept in staged financing that affects the relationships between old and new investors is the *pro rata* amount. If an investor owns x percent of the company before the round, then his *pro rata* amount is x percent of the new round amount. This is the share of the newly issued shares that keeps the investor's ownership fraction unchanged after the round. For example, if an investor owns 20% of the company prior to the round, and the company is raising $10M, then this investor's *pro rata* amount is 20% of $10M, or $2M. This will keep his ownership at 20% also after the deal. If another investor owns 15%, then that investor's *pro rata* amount is $1.5M.

Consider now the determination of valuation and ownership in the presence of both inside and outside investors. In Section 4.3.1, we explain that, all else equal, entrepreneurs prefer a higher valuation, whereas new investors prefer a lower valuation. What about inside investors? Do they want higher or lower valuations? The answer is that it depends on how much they invest.[19] We can think of the insider's economic interests belonging to two sides of a scale. On the one side is the economic interest as an existing shareholder who prefers the company to sell shares at a high price; on the other side is the economic interest of a new investor who prefers to buy shares at a low price. How much the latter matters depend on how much they invest in the new round, relative to the existing stake. The *pro rata* investment amount is the exact point where these two forces hold each other in balance. By investing at *pro rata,* the insider maintains his ownership fraction, regardless of the share price. He is therefore indifferent between higher and lower prices. This corresponds to the two sides of the scale being in exact balance.

What happens when an insider invests below *pro rata*? In that case, he ends up with a lower ownership after the round; that is, the insider stake gets diluted. The insider now prefers higher valuations because they dilute his ownership by less. The opposite holds true if the insider is investing above *pro rata*. In this case, his net ownership increases after the round, and it increases by more if the valuation is lower.

Another concept important for understanding the relationship between old and new investors is the retention rate. This is the ratio between an investor's final ownership over his starting ownership. For example, consider an old investor who has a 20% ownership share. If the company issues new shares that increase the total number of outstanding shares by 25%, and new investors buy all the new shares, the old investors, who do not participate in the new round, find their ownership diluted to 15% (= (1 − 0.25)*20%) (using equation (4.10-MR) from Section 4.1.5). The retention rate is then 75% (= 15%/20%); that is, the old investor retains 75% of his current position in the company.

The retention rate is a measure of dilution, measuring the extent to which an individual investor finds his stake reduced if he does not invest in the new round. To see this, Table 9.3 returns to our example from Table 9.1 and focuses on the case of three rounds. We now add detail about who finances the rounds, assuming that each round has one new investor, as well as the old investors. The table shows how they contribute to each round. In the second round, Investor 1 invests exactly at *pro rata*. As a consequence, his ownership remains at 16.67%, and his retention rate is 100%. In the third round, Investor 1 chooses to buy only 5% of the round, which is below *pro rata*. Consequently, his ownership stake falls to 14.75%, resulting in a retention rate of 88.52% (= 14.75% / 16.67%). Investor 2 chooses to invest above *pro rata*, raising his stake from 24.51% to 26.23%, which results in a retention rate of 107.02%.

Table 9.3 Investor Retention Rate

	New capital raised	Investor share in round	New shares issued	Total investor shares	Investors' ownership share	Investors' retention rate
	($M)		(M)	(M)		
Round 1						
Investor 1	2.0	100.0%	2.0	2.0	16.7%	
Round 2						
All investors	3.0		5.0	7.0	41.2%	
Investor 1	0.5	16.7%	0.9	2.8	16.7%	100.0%
Investor 2	2.5	83.3%	4.2	4.2	24.5%	
Round 3						
All investors	10.0		3.3	10.3	50.8%	
Investor 1	0.5	5.0%	0.2	3.0	14.8%	88.5%
Investor 2	3.5	35.0%	1.2	5.3	26.2%	107.0%
Investor 3	6.0	60.0%	2.0	2.0	9.8%	

WorkHorse Box 9.2 illustrates how inside and outside investors shape valuations.

WorkHorse Box 9.2 Old and New Investors for the B Round

The next morning, on her way to the board meeting, Astrid admitted to herself that she was nervous as hell. She would have to face Wolf C. Flow, the venture capitalist who at the last board meeting wanted to replace her with a gray-haired professional manager. Since Bharat hadn't finished the prototype for the NokotaStar, she would have to tell the board to instead pay attention to his "Micro-voltaic Algorithmically Granularized Infrared Capturization" demo. The icing on the cake would be telling the board that the company now needed $10M.

When Bharat finished his demo, there was silence in the room. Wolf C. Flow was the first to speak up: "Holy smokes, this changes everything. Why don't we bag the NokotaStar and put everything behind this 'What-shall-we-call-it'. How much time and money do you need?" Astrid briefly pinched herself, just to check. Bharat replied: "I need six months for product development, Annie reckons three months for setting up manufacturing, and Brandon says we need $10M." Wolf didn't blink an eye and turned to Malcolm: "Do we have the team to do this?" Malcolm nodded, so Wolf turned to Astrid: "Are you ready to start fundraising next week?" Astrid nodded, pinching herself once more. Next Wolf turned to Ali: "I am in, what about you?" Ali smiled: "We are always in, we are *pro rata* guys." "Good" replied Wolf, "I think we'll go above *pro rata* on this one.

What about you, Michael?" Michael looked slightly uncomfortable: "I'll do my best, but I am not in your league." Wolf looked around the table and concluded: "OK, we have a plan, let's do it!" Hardly believing it, Astrid pinched herself yet again, just to make sure this wasn't some weird dream.

In the weeks to follow, Astrid, Wolf, and Ali met numerous new investors. Together with Michael and Malcolm, they used the MATCH tool (Section 7.3.3) to identify what the company needed most from the new investors: a willingness to take a big risk disrupting an existing market; a global network for entry into India and other developing countries; deep pockets; and some patience with respect to exit. In addition to talking to venture capitalists, they also sought out potential corporate partners who might lend technological credibility and commercial support to the venture.

Within six weeks they had expressions of interest from two suitable investors: JetLuck Ventures and GestütenTechnik. JetLuck Ventures was a global late-stage VC firm with offices in New York, London, Beijing, Mumbai, and Cape Town. GestütenTechnik GmbH & Co. KG was a large German technology company, with a good reputation for corporate venturing.

To Brandon's surprise, no one questioned the $10M. However, a lively debate ensued around valuations. Two numbers were being floated: either $8 per share, implying a post-money valuation of $23.3M, or $10 per share, implying a post-money valuation of $26.6M. Different parties seemed to have different opinions, so Brandon decided to tabulate the cap table (Section 4.1.4) under the two price scenarios. Michael Archie said the most he could afford was $100K. Ali said he would invest at *pro rata*. Since Eagle-I Ventures owned 12.5% before the B round, it would invest $1.25M in the new round. Wolf wanted to invest $2.5M, well above Coyo-T Capital's *pro rata*. JetLuck conditioned its participation on leading the round and offered to invest $4M. GestütenTechnik said it was happy to top up the round to $10M, which implied that it would invest $2.15M.

The founders obviously preferred the higher price, and Michael Archie argued on their side. JetLuck and Coyo-T favored the lower price. GestütenTechnik said that, as a strategic investor, price was less important to them and that they would follow whatever JetLuck suggested. Eagle-I didn't seem to care either way. Brandon noted that these preferences could be understood by comparing the ownership stakes under the two prices. Michael Archie invested well below *pro rata*. At the higher price of $10, his Series A stake amounted to 1.9% and his common equity stake to 4.7. At the lower price of $8, his Series A stake amounted to 1.9% and his common equity stake to 4.3%. Hence, he preferred the higher price. Eagle-I was investing at *pro rata* to maintain its 12.5% stake and was therefore indifferent between the lower and higher price. Coyo-T Capital was investing above *pro rata* and favored the lower price because it increased its stake to 16.43%, compared to 15.6% at the higher price. Clearly, the different investors had different economic interests. They would have to resolve these differences during the negotiations.

	Before B Round		Low price B round				High price B round			
Price per share	$4.8		$8.0				$10.0			
Post-money valuation	$8,000,000		$23,333,333				$26,666,667			
	Shares	Ownership	Investment	New shares	Total shares	Ownership	Investment	New shares	Total shares	Ownership
Common										
Founders	800,000	48.0%	$0	0	800,000	27.4%	$0	0	800,000	30.0%
Michael Archie*	125,000	7.5%	$0	0	125,000	4.3%	$0	0	125,000	4.7%
Other common	325,000	19.5%	$0	0	325,000	11.1%	$0	0	325,000	12.2%
Series A										
Michael Archie*	41,667	2.5%	$100,000	12,500	54,167	1.9%	$100,000	10,000	51,667	1.9%
Eagle-I Ventures	208,333	12.5%	$1,250,000	156,250	364,583	12.5%	$1,250,000	125,000	333,333	12.5%
Coyo-T Capital	166,667	10.0%	$2,500,000	312,500	479,167	16.4%	$2,500,000	250,000	416,667	15.6%
Series B										
JetLuck	0	0.0%	$4,000,000	500,000	500,000	17.1%	$4,000,000	400,000	400,000	15.0%
GestütenTechnik	0	0.0%	$2,150,000	268,750	268,750	9.2%	$2,150,000	215,000	215,000	8.1%
Total	1,666,667	100.0%	$10,000,000	1,250,000	2,916,667	100.0%	$10,000,000	1,000,000	2,666,667	100.0%

* Michael Archie held some common stock from the seed round and some preferred stock from the Series A round.

9.3 Term Sheets for Staging

We now consider some of the issues that arise in the negotiations of the term sheet in a staged deal. This discussion builds on Chapter 6, but now we investigate some of the issues that pertain specifically to staging and to the relationships between old and new shareholders. We look at the seniority of convertible stock, anti-dilution clauses, and the variety of other clauses.[20]

9.3.1 The Liquidation Stack

In Section 6.2, we explain that investors often hold preferred shares. In the staged financing context, the question arises of how different Series (Box 1.6) of preferred shares interact with each other. Each financing round creates its own Series of shares. Series B investors get preferred shares that have different rights than the preferred shares held by Series A investors, and so on. How do preferred rights across different share classes rank one against each other? This ordering is referred to as the liquidation stack, from the liquidation preferences that characterize preferred shares (Section 6.2.1).

The standard solution is that Series B investors subordinate Series A investors; that is, they obtain higher seniority and get paid first in case of liquidation. The main alternative is that Series A and Series B are treated *pari passu*, a Latin expression that means "at the same pace" and signifies that they have the same priority ranking.[21] A similar negotiation occurs with each new Series. The entrepreneurs are not directly concerned about this, as they hold common stock, which is junior to all of the preferred stock. The negotiation is therefore mainly between Series A and B holders. The economic interests of the various bargaining parties are further complicated by the fact that some of the Series A investors may also invest in the Series B and thus have mixed economic interests, similar to what we discuss in Section 9.2.4.

Another important issue in staged financing concerns precedent setting. If Series A investors ask for multiple liquidation preferences, so will the Series B investors, and then the Series C, and so on. While a 2x multiple liquidation preference on a small $2M Series A investment only amounts to a preferred claim of $4M, that same term in a Series E investment of $50M would create a $100M preferred claim. Savvy investors who understand precedent setting may therefore refrain from imposing too many onerous terms in the early rounds.

Something that can further complicate later-round deals is that formal decisions are made through voting by share class. In Section 8.2.1 we explain how the aggregation of votes works. In this context, it is possible that within a share class a majority of investors would accept a deal that is undesirable for the remaining minority of investors. Specifically, suppose the Series A holders are asked to vote on whether they are willing to subordinate their preferred shares to the Series B investors. If a majority of Series A shareholders also play a large role in the Series B round, they might vote in favor of this issue. However, the minority of Series A holders that does not participate in the B round would dislike such subordination. This may create tension among groups of investors. In extreme cases, there could be a lawsuit invoking minority shareholder rights. In general, however, these issues get resolved through bargaining among all the parties involved.

WorkHorse Box 9.3 illustrates how a liquidation stack works.

WorkHorse Box 9.3 The Liquidation Stack

The next issue that arose in the negotiations concerned the structure of preferred shares. Unlike the A round investors who had insisted on participating preferred shares, the B round specified standard convertible preferred shares. There was a standard 8% noncumulative dividend but no multiple liquidation preference. The feature that attracted Victoria's curiosity was that the B shares would subordinate the preferred shares from the A round. This didn't really matter to the founders, whose common shares were at the bottom of the stack anyway, but she was curious to work out the implications for the Series A versus Series B investors.

Victoria compared the proposal of subordinating A with the alternative of A and B being *pari passu*. To get a sense of how this mattered, she mapped out the cash flows to common shares, Series A preferred shares, and Series B preferred shares, under a variety of exit scenarios. She summarized the calculations in the table below, which builds on WorkHorse Box 6.3. Part of the complication was that Series A had participating preferred shares with a cap at $20M, whereas Series B had convertible preferred shares. Victoria assumed an exit two years after the B round (i.e., early 2024). By then, Series A would have a preferred claim of $2.5M, and Series B a preferred claim of $11.6M, amounting to a total preferred claim on $14.1M. For the *pari passu* arrangement, Series B would get 82.4% (= $11.6M/$14.08M) of the preferred claims. Victoria focused on five different exit values that resulted in different conversion scenarios. In the table PT stand for preferred tems.

Exit value ($)	10,000,000	12,000,000	15,000,000	25,000,000	30,000,000
Subordination					
Cash flows by class ($):					
To Common	0	0	690,000	10,050,000	12,857,143
To Series A	0	400,000	2,710,000	3,350,000	4,285,714
To Series B	10,000,000	11,600,000	11,600,000	11,600,000	12,857,143

Explanation	B takes PT, nothing else left	B takes PT first, then A takes PT	B & A take PT, A also gets double dip	B takes PT, A gets equity (cap)	Everyone converts
Pari passu					
Cash flows by class ($):					
To Common	0	0	690,000	10,050,000	12,857,143
To Series A	1,761,364	2,113,636	2,710,000	3,350,000	4,285,714
To Series B	8,238,636	9,886,364	11,600,000	11,600,000	12,857,143
Explanation	B & A take PT at par	B & A take PT at par	B & A take PT, A also gets equity	B takes PT, A gets equity (cap)	Everyone converts

The table confirmed that the common shareholders' cash flows were unaffected by the choice between subordination versus *pari passu*. Moreover, the choice only mattered when the total exit value was below the total value of the preferred claims (i.e., $14.1M). For higher values, both Series A and Series B investors received the full value of their preferred terms. For lower values, however, subordination favored Series B investors, whereas *pari passu* favored Series A investors.

Brandon complained that the table did not show how the individual investors would feel about the choice between subordination versus *pari passu*. He also noted that, since different investors participated in different rounds. they could be on either side of the fence depending on which effect mattered more to them. Victoria therefore prepared a second table that broke out the cash flow not by Series, but by individual investors.

Exit value	10,000,000	12,000,000	15,000,000	25,000,000	30,000,000
Subordination					
Cash flows by investor ($):					
Founders	0	0	441,600	6,432,000	8,228,571
Other common	0	0	179,400	2,613,000	3,342,857
Michael Archie	100,000	156,000	456,000	1,456,000	1,842,857
Eagle-I Ventures	1,250,000	1,650,000	2,804,998	3,124,997	3,749,997
Coyo-T Capital	2,500,000	3,060,000	3,984,002	4,240,003	4,928,575
JetLuck	4,000,000	4,640,000	4,640,000	4,640,000	5,142,857
GestütenTechnik	2,150,000	2,494,000	2,494,000	2,494,000	2,764,286

Pari passu					
Cash flows by investor ($):					
Founders	0	0	441,600	6,432,000	8,228,571
Other common	0	0	179,400	2,613,000	3,342,857
Michael Archie	258,523	310,227	456,000	1,456,000	1,842,857
Eagle-I Ventures	1,910,510	2,292,612	2,804,998	3,124,997	3,749,997
Coyo-T Capital	2,764,206	3,317,047	3,984,002	4,240,003	4,928,575
JetLuck	3,295,455	3,954,545	4,640,000	4,640,000	5,142,857
GestütenTechnik	1,771,307	2,125,568	2,494,000	2,494,000	2,764,286

As expected, the founders and other common shareholders were all indifferent between subordination and at par. JetLuck and GestütenTechnik preferred subordination, as they only had Series B and no Series A shares. The remaining three investors (Michael, Ali, and Wolf) had all participated in both the A and B rounds, yet all three of them favored *pari passu* over subordination. Victoria explained that this was because their stakes in the B round were not large enough to sway them to the other side of the fence. She also noted that the *pro rata* logic on the equity side did not apply to preferred terms. Ali, for example, had invested *pro rata* in the B round and was therefore indifferent between the $8 versus $10 share price on the equity side (see WorkHorse Box 9.2). However, he was not indifferent about the liquidity stack, preferring *pari passu* over subordination.

9.3.2 Anti-dilution Rights

An important and sometimes contentious issue with staged financing concerns the anti-dilution clause. Anti-dilution rights protect investors in case of a future "down round," where the company issues new shares at a lower price than those paid by the previous investor (see also Section 9.4). The logic of an anti-dilution clause is to compensate investors for having paid a share price that at the time of the new round turns out to have been too high. Specifically, it specifies how the price of a past round gets adjusted in the event that the future round occurs at a lower price. Recall that preferred stock offers investors downside protection against disappointing future exits. Anti-dilution instead offers investors protection against disappointing future funding rounds.

As a benchmark, consider what would happen in a down round without anti-dilution protection. For expositional convenience, we talk of a first and second round, but these could represent any subsequent rounds. Using the notation of Chapter 4, we denote the share price of the first and second round by P_1 and P_2, and the investment amounts by I_1 and I_2. The entrepreneur originally owns S_0 shares.

First-round investors own $S_1 = I_1/P_1$ shares. Suppose now that in the second round the company issues shares at a price $P_2 < P_1$. The number of new shares issued to the new investors is given by $S_2 = I_2/P_2$. In the absence of anti-dilution, nothing else happens; that is, the three parties (entrepreneur, old investors, and new investors), respectively, hold S_0, S_1, and S_2 shares.

The anti-dilution provision protects earlier-round investors against later-round price declines. This is done by repricing the earlier-round based on the lower later-round price. There are several ways of doing this. The simplest method is the "full ratchet" clause. This specifies that whenever P_2 is lower than P_1, the original price P_1 is to be retroactively changed into P_2. That is, instead of receiving $S_1 = I_1 / P_1$. shares, the first-round investor now receives a total of $S_1^{FR} = I_1 / P_2$. shares, where the superscript FR stands for full ratchet. Since $P_2 < P_1$, we know that $S_1^{FR} > S_1$. The company therefore issues an additional number of shares $\left(S_1^{FR} - S_1\right)$ to the first-round investors in order to compensate them for the loss of value due to the lower second-round price.

Anti-dilution provisions also specify some situations where repricing does not occur. These include situations where the number of shares issued is small (e.g., share issues triggered by the exercise of employee stock options), where the issue derives from the conversion of preferred stock, or the issue occurs to finance the acquisition of strategic business partners.

To illustrate how anti-dilution works, we go back to Table 9.1 and focus on the case of two rounds, the first for a $5M investment and the second for a $10M investment. Suppose again that the first round occurs at $1 per share but suppose now that the second round is a down round at a price of $0.75 per share. Table 9.4 shows the calculation for different types of anti-dilution clauses.

Panel A shows the case of no anti-dilution clause, using the standard formulas from Section 4.1. The last column shows the entrepreneur's ownership after two rounds at 35.3%. Panel B shows a full ratchet anti-dilution clause. In this case, the first round gets repriced at $0.75, that is, at the price of the second round. This gives first-round investors 6.67M shares, instead of the original 5M, increasing their ownership from 17.6 to 22.2%. The entrepreneur, however, is now diluted down to 33.3%.

The full ratchet clause adjusts the original share price all the way down to the new lower price. This is particularly punishing for the entrepreneur and may reduce her incentives to keep working hard for the success of the venture. To mitigate this negative effect, the investors can use the alternative repricing "weighted-average" formula that results in a more moderate price adjustment. The adjusted price lies between the original conversion price (P_1) and the new price paid by new investors (P_2). We write:

$$P_1^{WA} = P_1 * AR \tag{9.1}$$

where P_1^{WA} is the adjusted first-round price. The superscript WA stands for weighted average, and AR for adjustment ratio, whose value lies between 0 and 1. S_{Base} denotes

Table 9.4 Examples of Alternative Anti-dilution Clauses.

	Investment ($M)	Share Price ($)	Shares (M)	Ownership after first round	Ownership after second round
A) No anti-dilution clause					
Entrepreneur			10.00	66.7%	35.3%
Round 1	5.0	1.00	5.00	33.3%	17.6%
Round 2	10.0	0.75	13.33		47.1%
B) Full ratchet protection					
Entrepreneur			10.00	57.1%	33.3%
Round 1	5.0	0.75	6.67	42.9%	22.2%
Round 2	10.0	0.75	13.33		44.4%
C) Broad-based protection					
Entrepreneur			10.00	57.1%	34.5%
Round 1	5.0	0.88	5.67	42.9%	19.5%
Round 2	10.0	0.75	13.33		46.0%
D) Narrow-based protection					
Entrepreneur			10.00	57.1%	34.0%
Round 1	5.0	0.82	6.11	42.9%	20.8%
Round 2	10.0	0.75	13.33		45.3%

the number of "base shares," which represent the share to be included for computing dilution (see the next two paragraphs). Then AR is given by:

$$AR = \frac{\left(S_{Base} + \dfrac{I_2}{P_1}\right)}{\left(S_{Base} + \dfrac{I_2}{P_2}\right)}. \tag{9.2}$$

The adjustment ratio AR depends on three elements. First, it depends on the new price P_2. Standard mathematical manipulations show that AR is an increasing function of P_2, so that a higher lower second-round price implies a lower AR. Intuitively, the adjusted ratio moves in the same direction as P_2, so that a lower P_2 leads to a lower AR, and therefore to a lower P_1^{WA}. Second, AR depends on the size of the new investment I_2. Standard mathematical manipulations show that AR is decreasing in I_2. This means that the price drops further for larger rounds. Intuitively, first-round investors need a larger compensation when the new round is large, as the lower share price induces a larger dilution when more new shares are issued. Third, AR depends on the S_{Base}. Standard mathematical manipulations show that AR is increasing in S_{Base}, implying that a larger S_{Base} results in a smaller price adjustment.

There are two types of share base S_{Base}. The broad-based share base is given by $S_{Base} = S_0 + S_1$, and the narrow-based share base is given by $S_{Base} = S_1$. Depending on which is used, the weighted average anti-dilution formula is called broad-based or narrow-based. Given that AR is increasing in S_{Base}, a broad-based anti-dilution clause is more favorable to the entrepreneur. It results in smaller price adjustments and therefore requires that the company issue fewer additional shares to old investors.

Panel C of Table 9.4 shows the effect of a broad-based weighted average anti-dilution clause. The adjustment ratio is obtained using equation (9.2). Using $S_{Base} = S_0 + S_1 = 10M + 5M = 15M$, we obtain:

$$AR = \frac{\left(15M + \dfrac{\$10M}{\$1}\right)}{\left(15M + \dfrac{\$10M}{\$0.75}\right)} = 0.88$$

Using equation (9.1), we see that the adjusted price is given by:

$$P_1^{WA} = P_1 * AR = \$1 * 0.88 = \$0.88.$$

Panel C shows that first-round investors now receive 5.67M shares. Their ownership is now given by 19.5%, which is higher than the 17.6% in the no anti-dilution case of Panel A, but lower than the 22.2% in the full ratchet case of Panel B. Thus, the weighted average formula is a compromise between these two extremes.

Panel D performs similar calculations for the narrow-based weighted average anti-dilution clause. The only difference is that the base is now given by $S_{Base} = S_1 = 5M$. Using similar calculations, we find an adjusted price of $0.82. Panel D shows that relative to the broad-based formula, the narrow-based formula is more favorable to old first-round investors who now get 20.8%.

The anti-dilution clauses of Panels B, C, and D improve the ownership fraction of first-round investors, relative to the no anti-dilution case of Panel A. As expected, they also reduce the entrepreneur's ownership fraction. Another effect is that all three reduce the ownership of the second-round investors. Are the new investors willing to accept the additional dilution? The answer is no because the $0.75 price was based on getting the 47.1% stake shown in Panel A. This brings up an interesting negotiation problem. Second-round investors may ask for further price reductions, to account for the dilution of their stake. This complicates the negotiation. WorkHorse Box 9.4 looks at this in greater detail.

WorkHorse Box 9.4   Anti-dilution in the B Round

As the discussions about the B round accelerated through December, Astrid began to wonder whether there would be any repeat of the previous year where the A round dramatically closed hours before the New Year. However, on Thursday, December 23, she received an out-of-office reply from Dr. Franz Fröhliche, her contact at GestütenTechnik's corporate VC division. It noted that all their offices were closed until the New Year. Apparently, it was time to go to the Düsseldorf Weihnachtsmarkt and enjoy Glühwein. A week after new year, WorkHorse received an informal draft from JetLuck that outlined what a term sheet might look like. As expected, it featured the lower price of $8 per share. The founders were curious to find out what else it might contain. Victoria quickly identified the first issue. In the previous A round, the investors had accepted a broad-based anti-dilution clause. This B round term sheet, however, included a full-ratchet anti-dilution clause that Victoria considered alarming.

To properly understand the issues, Victoria gave an example of what an anti-dilution clause would do: "Suppose that one year from now you run out of money before the development of the 'What-shall-we-call-it' is finished. In that case you will have to raise more money without having hit your milestone, so you should expect a down round. For concreteness sake, suppose you needed to raise another $2M at a post-money valuation of $19.5M, corresponding to a price per share of $6. What would that mean?" She pulled up her laptop and produced the following table:

Anti-dilution		Scenario 1	Scenario 2	Scenario 3	Scenario 4
Variable	Notation	No anti-dilution	Full ratchet	Broad-based weighted average	Narrow-based weighted average
B round					
Existing shares	S_0	1,666,667	1,666,667	1,666,667	1,666,667
Investment ($)	I_1	10,000,000	10,000,000	10,000,000	10,000,000
Price per share (revised, $)	P_1	8.0	6.0	7.8	7.6
B round shares (revised)	S_1	1,250,000	1,666,667	1,282,895	1,319,444
Total shares (revised)	$S_0 + S_1$	2,916,667	3,333,333	2,949,561	2,986,111
Pre-money valuation ($)	V_{PRE}	13,333,333	10,000,000	12,991,453	12,631,579
Post-money valuation ($)	V_{POST}	23,333,333	20,000,000	22,991,453	22,631,579

Base shares	S_{BASE}			2,916,667	1,250,000
Adjustment Ratio	AR			97.4%	94.7%
		C round			
Investment ($)	I_2	2,000,000	2,000,000	2,000,000	2,000,000
Price per share ($)	I_2	6.0	6.0	6.0	6.0
C round shares	S_2	333,333	333,333	333,333	333,333
Total shares	$S_0 + S_2$	3,250,000	3,666,667	3,282,895	3,319,444
Pre-money valuation ($)	V_{PRE}	17,500,000	20,000,000	17,697,368	17,916,667
Post-money valuation ($)	V_{POST}	19,500,000	22,000,000	19,697,368	19,916,667
% ownership: existing shareholders	F_0	51.3%	45.5%	50.8%	50.2%
% ownership: B round investors	F_1	38.5%	45.5%	39.1%	39.7%
% ownership: C round investors	F_2	10.3%	9.1%	10.2%	10.0%

The first scenario showed what would happen in the absence of any anti-dilution. The post-money valuation of the C round of $19.5M would be below the $23.3M from the B round. The existing shareholders (which included the founders, all other common shareholders, and the A round investors) would still own 51.28% of the company. Victoria compared this to the full-ratchet clause. The price of the B round would be readjusted to $6 per share, thereby increasing B round shares from 1.25M to 1.67M. That is, the anti-dilution clause would trigger an issuance of 0.42M shares to the B round investors. The post-money valuation of the B round would effectively be readjusted down to $20M. After the C round, the existing shareholders would be down to 45.45%. By contrast, the B round investors were at 38.46% without anti-dilution, but at 45.45% with the full ratchet (the fact that this was the exact same number as the existing shareholders is a coincidence).

Victoria proceeded to show what a less alarming weighted average formula would do. Scenario 3 showed the case of a broad-based weighted average anti-dilution clause. It used the broadest definition of base shares (S_{Base}) that included the Series B investors as well as all existing shareholders, amounting to just over 2.92M shares. With this information she used equation (9.2) to calculate the adjustment ratio (AR), which amounted to 97.4%. Using equation (1), this meant that the revised price would amount to 97.4% of the original $8 price, which came to $7.8. Based on this price, she found that the post-money valuation in the B round would be adjusted to just under $23M, and the ownership of the existing shareholders after the C round would amount to 50.8%. "The broad-based weighted average formula is much less alarming, isn't it?" Scenario 4 reflected the case of narrow-based weighted average formula. Its base (S_{Base}) consisted of the Series B 1.25M share, which resulted in an adjustment ratio of 94.21%. The valuations and ownership shares were very similar, suggesting that the difference between a broad or narrow base made little difference here.

Brandon took a critical look. While agreeing with the numbers, he disagreed with the underlying economics. He noted that the C round investors had different ownership stakes across the four scenarios. He argued that they would be unlikely to accept different valuations just because of different anti-dilution clauses. He therefore redid Victoria's number on the assumption that the C round price would have to adjust in a way that the valuation of the C round remained constant at $19.5M. He produced the following table.

Anti-dilution with constant C round valuation		Scenario 1	Scenario 2	Scenario 3	Scenario 4
Variable	Notation	No anti-dilution	Full ratchet	Broad-based weighted average	Narrow-based weighted average
B round					
Existing shares	S_0	1,666,667	1,666,667	1,666,667	1,666,667
Investment ($)	I_1	10,000,000	10,000,000	10,000,000	10,000,000
Price per share (revised, $)	P_1	8.00	4.50	7.79	7.54
B round shares (revised, $)	S_1	1,250,000	2,222,222	1,284,449	1,326,754
Total shares (revised, $)	S_0+S_1	2,916,667	3,888,889	2,951,115	2,993,421
Pre-money valuation ($)	V_{PRE}	13,333,333	7,500,000	12,975,734	12,561,983
Post-money valuation ($)	V_{POST}	23,333,333	17,500,000	22,975,734	22,561,983
Base shares	S_{Base}			2,916,667	1,250,000
Adjustment ratio	AR			97.3%	94.2%
C round					
Investment	I_2	2,000,000	2,000,000	2,000,000	2,000,000
Price per share ($)	P_2	6.00	4.50	5.93	5.85
C round shares	S_2	333,333	444,444	337,270	342,105
Total shares	$S_0+S_1+S_2$	3,250,000	4,333,333	3,288,386	3,335,526
Pre-money valuation ($)	V_{PRE}	17,500,000	17,500,000	17,500,000	17,500,000
Post-money valuation ($)	V_{POST}	19,500,000	19,500,000	19,500,000	19,500,000
% ownership: existing shareholders	F_0	51.3%	38.5%	50.7%	50.0%
% ownership: B round investors	F_1	38.5%	51.3%	39.1%	39.8%
% ownership: C round investors	F_2	10.3%	10.3%	10.3%	10.3%

For scenario 2, Brandon found the exact price that would generate a post-money valuation of $19.5M, namely, $4.50. He noted that when the C round investors took anti-dilution into account, something of a downward spiral was at work: a lower price for the C round triggered additional share issuance from the anti-dilution clause, which in turn triggered further declines in the C round price. Thankfully, this spiral converged but at a very low price of $4.50. Brandon considered that price not just alarming but appalling. It would bring existing shareholders down to 38.5%.

In passing, Bharat noted that at $4.50, the anti-dilution from the A round would also kick in and that this would trigger the issuance of even more shares. This, however, was too much for Brandon's spreadsheet skills, so he threw up his hands, exclaiming that by then the A round investors would have forgotten about their anti-dilution rights. Bharat doubted it but let Brandon proceed with his simplifying assumption.

For scenarios 3 and 4, Brandon was out of his mathematical depth. Therefore Bharat derived a mathematical formula that solved what price would give investors their desired valuation of $19.5M. The formula is explained in the accompanying spreadsheet on the book's website (www.entrepreneurialfinance. net). The price adjustments for the C round were much smaller, resulting in a price per share of $5.93 ($5.85) for the broad-based (narrow-based) scenario.

Overall these calculations helped the founders to make up their mind, which Victoria summarized by saying: "That full-ratchet anti-dilution clause is simply unacceptable, it will have to go."

9.3.3 Additional Rights

Inside investors typically obtain some contractual rights that allow them to protect their ownership stake in the company. Preemption rights give existing shareholders the right to purchase a certain percentage of any new share issuance. The standard formula gives an existing investor the right to buy up to his *pro rata* amount (see also Section 9.2.4). Put differently, the company is required to offer an existing shareholder as many shares as needed to maintain his current ownership stake. The remaining shares can be offered to anyone, be their existing or new shareholders.

If one existing shareholder chooses not to purchase his entire *pro rata* share, other existing shareholders can also purchase those shares. Preemption rights do not apply when shares are issued as part of a conversion of convertible stock or to create or replenish an employee stock options pool. Sometimes these rights are only given to shareholders who hold a certain minimum number of shares. This means that the company does not have to contact all small shareholders every time it wants to raise another round.

Closely related to the preemption rights is the right of first refusal. Whereas preemption rights concern the sale of newly issued shares, the right of first refusal concerns the sale of existing shares. To begin with, the company typically reserves for itself a right of first refusal that prevents existing shareholders from selling their shares to third parties. Investors often ask for additional rights of first refusal that allow them, instead of the company, to buy the shares that others want to sell. The goal of the right of first refusal is to prevent a loss of control over who owns company shares; that is, it keeps the ownership in the hands of insiders.

Pay-to-play clauses require old investors to continue investing ("pay") to preserve their preferred privileges ("play"). Paying usually means investing a minimum amount in the new round, typically, the *pro rata* amount, possibly less. The consequences of not investing vary. For example, the investor's preferred stock converts into common. Less dramatic, the investor may lose not only anti-dilution protection but also other preferred privileges, such as liquidation, preemption, or control rights.

The main purpose of the pay-to-play clause is to encourage old investors to continue investing in the company. Doing so affords them ongoing protection (the carrot); not doing so is associated with negative consequences (the stick). Pay-to-play clauses thus address conflicts between different inside investors, where some are keen to participate in a new round and others prefer to sit it out.[22] A slightly different agreement is a pull-up, which provides the carrot without the stick. Specifically, old investors who invest in the new round are offered a conversion of their existing preferred stock into a new class of preferred stock with higher privileges, such as better liquidation preference or stronger anti-dilution rights.

Finally, new funding rounds often require revisiting the stock options pool (Section 4.1.3). Frequently, this pool has been depleted over time and requires some restocking. The new and old investors therefore have to agree who would pay for it.

WorkHorse Box 9.5 illustrates these issues by looking at the closing of the B round.

WorkHorse Box 9.5 Closing the Series B Round

In mid-January, a conference call was convened for all parties to sort out the remaining issues to close the B round: (1) the price per share ($8 or $10), (2) the anti-dilution clause (full ratchet or weighted average), (3) the liquidation stack (subordination or at par), (4) the pay-to-play clause, (5) a new stock option pool, and (6) the composition of the board of directors.

Umija Ulimwengu, the senior partner in charge of the deal at JetLuck, led the deal, and hence the conference call. The negotiations went surprisingly fast once the company agreed to the lower price of $8. In return, Umija agreed to alter the anti-dilution clause from full ratchet to a broad-based weighted average formula. To get Ali and Wolf on board, she dropped the subordination of the Series A shares, instead agreeing that all preferred shares would be at par.

A more complicated discussion ensued concerning a new option pool. The issue arose mainly because of Malcolm, who had joined the company as an interim COO. He enjoyed the work immensely ("beats nuts and bolts" as he would say), and it quickly became apparent that he was the perfect COO. He said he would join the company full-time for an option package involving 100,000 shares. This was half of what each of the owners had, and everyone agreed this would be a fair arrangement. Furthermore, it was agreed that the company should increase its general stock option pool by 100,000. All this required an authorization of 200,000 additional shares overall.

The question was who would effectively pay for that. The founders had prepared a capitalization table which assumed that these additional 200,000 shares would be issued at the same price of $8 (see the first and second case in the following table). Umija Ulimwengu, however, objected to the fact that the post-money valuation rose from $23.33M to $24.93M. She argued that the existing shareholders should bear the cost of dilution and that the post-money valuation should be $23.33M, with the new stock options already taken into account. This would require some price below $8. Bharat readily derived the exact mathematical formula (explained in the accompanying spreadsheet) and produced the third case shown in the table.

The table shows three scenarios: the first is the benchmark case without any new option pool; the second case adds the option pool using a constant share price of $8; and the third case adds an option pool, keeping the post-money valuation constant at $23.33M. The table shows who would effectively pay for the new stock options. Comparing the second model with the first reveals that at constant share prices the option pool diluted all parties proportionately. However, in the third case, the new investors did not experience any dilution, whereas the founders experienced higher dilution than in the second case. The effect on the old investors depended on how much they invested in the B round. Michael Archie, who invested below *pro rata*, experienced greater dilution in the third case. By contrast, Coyo-T Capital, which invested above *pro rata*, experienced less dilution in the third case.

	Before B Round		No option pool				Option pool at constant price				Option pool at constant valuation			
Price per share ($)	4.80		8.00				8.00				7.14			
Pre-money valuation (without pool)			13,333,333				13,333,333				11,904,762			
Post-money valuation (without pool)			23,333,333				23,333,333				21,904,762			
Post-money valuation (with pool)	8,000,000		23,332,936				249,333,333				23,333,333			
	Shares	Ownership	Investment	New shares	Total shares	Ownership	Investment	New shares	Total shares	Ownership	Investment	New shares	Total shares	Ownership
Common:														
Founders	800,000	48.0%	0	0	800,000	27.4%	0	0	800,000	25.7%	$0	0	800,000	24.5%
Michael Archie*	125,000	7.5%	0	0	125,000	4.3%	0	0	125,000	4.0%	$0	0	125,000	3.8%
Other common	325,000	19.5%	0	0	325,000	11.1%	0	0	325,000	10.4%	$0	0	325,000	9.9%
New stock options:					0	0.00%		200,000	200,000	6.4%		200,000	200,000	6.1%
Series A:														
Michael Archie*	41,667	2.5%	100,000	12,500	54,167	1.9%	100,000	12,500	54,167	1.7%	100,000	14,000	55,667	1.7%
Eagle-I Ventures	208,333	12.5%	1,250,000	156,250	364,583	12.5%	1,250,000	156,250	364,583	11.7%	1,250,000	175,000	383,333	11.7%
Coyo-T Capital	166,667	10.0%	2,500,000	312,500	479,167	16.4%	2,500,000	312,500	479,167	15.4%	2,500,000	350,000	516,667	15.8%
Series B:														
JetLuck	0	0.0%	4,000,000	500,000	500,000	17.1%	4,000,000	500,000	500,000	16.0%	4,000,000	560,000	560,000	17.1%
GestütenTechnik	0	0.0%	2,150,000	268,750	268,750	9.2%	2,150,000	268,750	268,750	8.6%	2,150,000	301,000	301,000	9.2%
Total	1,666,667	100%	10,000,000	1,250,000	2,916,617	100%	10,000,000	1,250,000	3,116,667	100%	10,000,000	1,250,000	3,266,667	100%

* Michael Archie held some common stock from the seed round and some preferred stock from the Series A round.

The final issue concerned the board of directors. The expectation was to increase the size of the board to seven, to make room for the additional investors. Umija Ulimwengu quickly agreed to join the board ("Finally another woman!" Astrid thought to herself). Dr. Franz Fröhliche noted that as a corporate investor he only wanted board observer rights, but not a formal board seat. A more delicate issue concerned Malcolm Force's role. Initially, he had been hired as an independent director, but now he had become part of the management team. It was therefore agreed that the seventh director should be a new independent director.

Unfortunately, this is where things got stuck. The company had already earmarked René Réseau, one of Ali's most successful entrepreneurs who had an impressive global network. However, Umija was adamant that the external director should be Stanley Goldmorgan, an investment banker friend of hers who had successfully listed several tech companies on Nasdaq. Sensing that this was Umija's top priority, Astrid seized the opportunity. She offered to horse-trade Stanley for a stock option pool at $8. Umija agreed, the deal was unstuck again, and soon everyone was fine with the deal . . . except for Michael: "I don't want to be petty, but you all have big funds, and I am just a small-town angel. You can easily just ignore me, I have no power here, but I find the pay-to-play clause a little unfair." The term sheet included a retroactive pay-to-play clause that specified that any Series A investor who did not invest his *pro rata* share would have to convert to common shares. Eagle-I Ventures was investing at *pro rata* and Coyo-T Capital above *pro rata*, so neither of them was affected. Michael Archie, however, was affected. He owned 2.5% of the company but could only contribute 1% of the new round. Technically, he invested 40% of his *pro rata* amount, which meant that 60% of his 25,000 out of his 41,667 preferred Series A shares would convert to common. "I thought the pay-to-play clause is to punish investors who are not stepping up to the plate. I realize this is small change for you, but I am investing $100K of my own money. Why should I still get punished?" Umija graciously agreed to waive the play-to-play clause, and the deal was sealed.

Just before hanging up, Umija asked: "What about the 'What-shall-we-call-it', does anybody have a better name for it?" Bharat sounded annoyed, insisting it was called "Micro-voltaic Algorithmically Granularized Infrared Capturization." There was an awkward silence. Suddenly Ali burst out: "I got it! Let's just turn it into an acronym, and it becomes MAGIC!"

9.4 Managing Financial Difficulties

While entrepreneurs and investors always hope for spectacular growth, reality can be more sobering. Even if a new venture is eventually successful, the entrepreneurial path is often tortuous and invariably includes hiccups. In this section, we look at the fundraising implications of such business difficulties. What happens when a company is only able to attract new investors at a lower valuation than before? What if it can only raise funding at terms that effectively wipe out all existing shareholder claims? And what if the company gets cut off from funding altogether?

9.4.1 Down Rounds

Our discussion of anti-dilution clauses in Section 9.3.2 already examined how term sheets deal with down rounds. We now take a deeper look at the broader challenges posed by down rounds. A down round occurs when the price per share is lower than that in the previous round (excluding any stock splits).[23] This is equivalent to having a pre-money valuation that is lower than the post-money valuation of the previous round. Fenwick and West, a leading legal firm, reports data on VC deals in Silicon Valley. For the first quarter of 2018, they found that 15% of rounds were down rounds, 10% were flat, and 75% were up rounds. The share of down rounds is naturally cyclical; in the first quarter of 2009, for instance, 46% of the financings were down rounds, 29% were flat, and only 25% were up.[24]

Structuring a down round can be challenging because it requires the consent of existing investors who are experiencing emotional disappointment with the lack of company progress, as well as financial disappointment stemming from ownership dilution. The extent of financial dilution depends on the type of anti-dilution protection and may be aggravated if new investors ask for onerous terms (Section 9.3), possibly even a renegotiation of prior terms.[25]

Not only are the old investors affected by down rounds, so are the founders. In Section 9.3.3, we show that anti-dilution clauses often hurt common stockholders the most. This can severely hurt the motivation and incentives of founders and executives and may require the issuance of (new) stock options or common stock. Similarly, a down round can be a blow to employee confidence. Employees may regard it as public confirmation that the company is faltering, so that some of them leave. Moreover, a down round affects the value of employee stock options. After a down round, the strike price of existing employee stock options is above the current price per share. The options are therefore considered "under water" (Section 6.3.2) and lose their role of incentives for employees. To retain and reincentivize employees, the company may want to reprice these options, attaching a lower strike price. However, tax and regulatory constraints have to be taken into consideration to avoid windfall tax obligations for the owners of options that are underwater.

A down round also involves legal considerations. Issuing shares at a price lower than in the previous round exposes directors and investors to litigation risks. Investors who are also company directors and approve a down round run the risk of breaching their fiduciary duties toward minority investors. They may be well advised to obtain approval from independent directors, and they may want to exercise extra caution to remain fair. None of this is easy, so down rounds put considerable stress on boards of directors. Box 9.3 discusses some relevant research about this issue.

Box 9.3 Board Conflicts in Down Rounds

The year 2002 marked the middle of the dot.com crash. If start-ups received any funding at all, it was through down rounds. How did boards of directors manage these challenging times? One study examines survey responses from 161 CEOs of VC-backed start-ups at that time.[26] The main finding is that down rounds are associated with substantially higher levels of both task conflicts and relationship conflicts. Task conflicts concern disagreement about the best plans of actions that companies should take. Relationship conflicts concern the interpersonal disaffect and negative emotions that board members have for one another. The first type of conflict could be constructive under circumstances where diversity of opinion leads to novel solutions but could be destructive when it leads to confusion or inaction. The second type of conflict is widely believed to harm company performance.

A surprising finding of the study concerns the distinction between companies with founder versus nonfounder CEOs. One might have thought that the presence of a founder CEO increases conflict. After all, founders famously have strong opinions and strong attachments to their companies. Yet the study finds that in down rounds the levels of conflict are very similar for boards with founder versus nonfounder CEOs. Put simply, in times of down rounds, conflicts are everywhere, no matter who is in charge.

9.4.2 Turnarounds

In a down round, the company may be struggling, but it remains able to raise further funding to continue operations. This means that investors have confidence in the company eventually succeeding. What about companies that seriously struggle to raise any additional financing? There are two possible outcomes: either the company raises funding in what is known as a turnaround, which we will discuss below, or it doesn't raise any funding at all.

Let us first briefly consider the alternative where the company gets cut off from all funding altogether. It either shuts down or tries to continue without new funding (Section 11.5). In the latter case, the struggling company needs to drastically reduce the scope of its economic activities. While hoping for some lucky breakthrough, such a company can only survive by laying off most employees and/or selling off most of its assets. The few remaining managers might seek alternative employment while maintaining a part-time role in the company. A company in this state of affairs is commonly referred to as "walking dead" or "zombie."

Turnaround financing is meant to avoid these problems. It applies to those companies that still have some valuable assets (mainly technology or people) that can be used in a different market, possibly in combinations with different technologies or with a new management team. Turning a start-up around is largely a strategic and managerial challenge. This requires additional capital and is therefore also a financial challenge.[27]

In a turnaround, the company is worth a fraction of its earlier value. The new investors therefore get the vast majority of shares, severely diluting existing shareholders—the old investors, founders, and employees. This is sometimes called a "washout" or "cram-down" round. It may also be necessary to renegotiate any debt in the company, with lenders taking substantial losses. A delicate issue is preserving incentives for any remaining founders and employees. This may require setting aside fresh equity or a new stock option pool.

Turnarounds can create substantial friction between the new and old investors, especially if the old investors are in denial. Turnarounds can end up in legal challenges, with parties on the losing side suing the new investors, either at the time of the turnaround or later when the turnaround turns out to be successful.

Washout rounds also bear reputational risks for investors. Consequently, they are sometimes made by specialized investors, who only invest in troubled companies that need such turnaround capital. These investors have specialized expertise in handling turnaround situations and do not even try to establish an affable reputation with the broader entrepreneurial community.

The opposite case whereby a turnaround is executed by inside investors may pose additional concerns. Inside investors may attempt to exploit information about the real prospect of a company that is unable to attract outside investors. This means they are taking advantage of their power position to impose a very low valuation, knowing that the company is worth considerably more. In this case, the washout round dilutes the founders and other stakeholders, but not the inside investors who are on both sides of the transaction. Forcing a company to accept highly dilutive terms in this manner can be a violation of the fiduciary duties of the inside investors and might result in lawsuits. Box 9.4 looks at an example of how different parties can have different interpretations of what is appropriate and legal.

Box 9.4 Tales from the Venture Archives: Can You Wash Your Hands in Innocence in a Washout Round?

The facts of the case were clear, the question was whether the accused were innocent or guilty. The time was January 1997, and the place was the County Court of Santa Clara, in the heart of Silicon Valley. The case was known as *Kalashian vs. Advent*.[28] It involved the two founders of Alantec Inc., called Michael Kalashian and Jagdish Vij. They faced three VCs: Michael Child (TA Associates), John Dougery (Dougery & Wilder), and Dixon Doll (Accel Partners). The accusation was breach of fiduciary duties. Yet the defendants saw themselves as having saved a company from the brink of failure. A jury would have to decide.

The case facts were as follows. Alantec, builder of novel telecommunication products, had been founded by Michael and Jagdish in 1987. The company had raised several rounds of funding from investors including TA Associates, Dougery & Wilder, and Accel Partners. By the end of 1989, the two founders had become minority shareholders, and the VCs had a majority on the board of directors. In 1990, both founders were fired, and a new management team was installed. The two founders owned approximately 8% of the company by the end of 1990. In 1991, the company raised two additional washout rounds of financing. The investments came from the existing investors, the insiders, who created a new class of stocks that essentially wiped out all common shares. The two founders' ownership was reduced to less than 0.01% of the company. To implement these transactions, the company needed the approval of common shareholders. While the two founders had owned the vast majority of common shares, the company issued a large number of new common stock in 1991. These new common shareholders attained a majority of the common stock, and promptly voted in favor of the washout transactions. After 1991, the company became commercially successful. It went public in February 1994 and was acquired in December 1995 for approximately $770M. If the founder had maintained its 8% ownership, it would have been worth over $40M.[29] Instead, the final value of their shares was around $600K.

The disagreement centered on the interpretation of the facts. The entrepreneurs' view was that the investors took advantage of their power, squeezing them out when they were no longer needed at the company. For them, this is a classic case of the majority imposing its will on a minority.[30] The fact that the common shareholders approved the transaction would argue against this interpretation, but the founders claimed that the additional shareholders were effectively representatives of the investors, who were given their shares in return for a promise to approve the transaction. The core of the legal argument concerns fiduciary duties. Even though investors had a self-interest in proposing the washout transactions, their duty as directors of the company was to look after the best interest of all shareholders. Note that the founders did not question the validity of the firing decision. Their argument was that even after being fired, they remained shareholders in the company, so the board had a duty to protect their economic interests.

The investors' view focused on the (lack of) contributions made by the founders. The investors argued that the vast majority of resources had been provided by the investors and that the founders had consistently underperformed. The investors' money saved a company that was otherwise destined to fail. The washout had occurred at a point in time when the company was facing bankruptcy. The terms of the transaction reflected the precarious state of the business at the time. As to the fact that all the money came from the insiders, they argued that outside investors were simply unwilling to invest in such a troubled company.

What happened in the end? As with most legal cases, there was no verdict. The parties settled out of court for an undisclosed amount. The underlying arguments, however, continue to matter. Cases involving conflicts of interests and breach of fiduciary are rarely clean-cut. They heavily depend on the specifics of the case, as well as the legal rules and traditions of the court in which they are heard. Down rounds can be downright nasty. Redress is difficult to obtain in court, so it's best to avoid them in the first place.

9.5 Dynamic Strategies

The process of staged financing is inherently uncertain, reflecting the fundamental uncertainties of the entrepreneurial process. Entrepreneurs and investors approach this uncertainty with a variety of strategies to manage the process. We focus first on how investors approach the staging process and then on how entrepreneurs manage valuations across stages.

9.5.1 Dynamic Investment Strategies

The entry point of an investor is determined by his stage preferences, which are related to three main aspects. First, different stages require different funding amounts, so investors select those stages that suit their funding resources. Angel investors and government agencies, for example, tend to focus on pre-seed and seed investments, where the required funding amounts fit their limited budgets. VC firms, however, tend to avoid those stages and focus instead on Series A and higher. These rounds require substantial investment amounts, which allows them to invest enough to make it worth their time and effort. Second, investors chose their stage strategy based on their expertise and their ability to add value to the companies. Corporate investors, for example, often avoid earlier stages because start-ups are not yet ready to benefit from the strategic benefits that they offer. In contrast, the mentoring and networking resources of angel investors are most valuable at early stages. Third, investors are attracted to different ends of the risk spectrum. Investment risk changes across stages, being highest at the earliest stages and gradually decreasing as companies move to later stages.

The next strategic decision concerns the reinvestment strategy. There is a spectrum of shallow-pocketed to deep-pocketed investors. Shallow-pocketed investors do not have much choice: they simply do not have the financial resources to continue investing. Deep-pocketed investors like larger VC funds or corporate investors, however, make deliberate choices about how much to invest. Their choices are largely driven by three main factors. First, there is the investor's confidence in the potential of the company. The second factor concerns the portfolio strategy of the investor. How much does he want to increase his exposure to the type of technology, market, and geography risk represented by the company? The third factor involves how much an investor wants to share a deal with co-investors. There is a selfish financial aspect about whether to keep better deals to oneself and share lower quality deals. There is also a network aspect to this, about how much an investor emphasizes syndication and relationships with other investors.

Let us distinguish between three broad reinvestment philosophies: no reinvestment, predictable reinvestment, and opportunity-driven reinvestment philosophies. The first philosophy says that the company should not expect any additional funding from an investor. This is typically because of limited financial resources (e.g., small-town angels) or because of regulatory constraints (e.g., government-funded investor), but it could also be because of an investor's attitude. The second philosophy is based on the notion that, despite the uncertainty, the investor intends to continue to fund the company in a fairly predictable manner. One simple approach is that the investor expects to invest *pro rata* in every round. The third philosophy is opportunity-driven. That is, the investor remains noncommittal about reinvesting. If the company performance is strong and the terms of the new round are attractive, then the investor participates; otherwise he may be out.

There is no saying whether one strategy is better than the other. Companies that performed well in the past may not do so in the future, or they may become overpriced, whereas companies that had setbacks may outperform in the future or may become attractive because they are willing to accept a lower valuation. An academic study by Li and Chi finds that VC firms that pursue a broad diversification strategy are more likely to be opportunistic, whereas VC firms that pursue an industry specialization strategy (Section 12.5.2) more reliably continue funding a company across rounds.[31]

These three approaches have different implications for entrepreneurs. The "no reinvestment" approach forces the entrepreneur to make the company attractive for new investors by the time the initial funding has been used up. The predictable reinvestment strategy has the benefit of giving the entrepreneur greater certainty. It also avoids a signaling problem where other investors get alarmed when insides pass up on a new round. The opportunity-driven strategy is the exact opposite. It allows investors to double down on those companies they consider attractive. Investors want to back their winners and avoid throwing good money after bad with their losers. At the same time, such a selective approach does create a signaling problem where companies not supported by the insiders struggle to raise funding from outsiders.

One important aspect of the reinvesting decision is whether to refinance a struggling company or cut off its funding. In practice, there are a wide range of approaches. On the lenient end of the spectrum, some investors are committed to their companies and support them through their struggles as long as it can be rationalized. Naturally, there is ambiguity here because rarely do we have hard evidence clearly showing whether or not a company is beyond hope. In fact, many successful start-up companies once stood on the brink of failure. On the other end of the spectrum, some investors apply stringent financial discipline on their companies. This is particularly the case with opportunity-driven reinvestment strategies.

The spectrum of lenient to disciplined refinancing decisions is closely related to the trade-off between soft and hard budget constraints discussed in Boxes 9.1 and 9.2. With a soft budget constraint, the project is allowed to continue even if it is slow in delivering. This can give rise to inefficiencies because entrepreneurs know that it is difficult to terminate their projects. Pure insider rounds can be the results of soft budget constraints. Some empirical evidence suggests that they result in systematically lower returns.[32] Instead, with a hard budget constraint the investor has a clear rule for cutting off companies. This provides strong performance incentives for entrepreneurs: if the milestones are achieved, more funding is forthcoming; if not, the money runs dry. However, a hard budget may discourage experimentation as companies worry more about achieving short-term results. In WorkHorse Box 9.1, the company was expected to develop the NokotaStar, a predictable milestone involving limited innovation. Instead, Bharat pursued a much riskier development path that led to the MAGIC (Micro-voltaic Algorithmically Granularized Infrared Capturization) discovery in WorkHorse Box 9.5. Wolf C. Flow surprised everyone by proving to be a much more flexible and lenient investor than originally anticipated.

9.5.2 Dynamic Valuation Profiles

As a final step, we look at how entrepreneurs manage the staging process, focusing specifically on what kind of a valuation profile the company wants to establish across stages. All else equal, entrepreneurs prefer higher over lower valuations. In Box 4.3 we identified an important reason why entrepreneurs sometimes prefer lower valuations, namely, when they come from higher quality investors. We now examine another reason why entrepreneurs sometimes prefer a lower valuation, namely, to manage their company's dynamic valuation profile.

Companies benefit from featuring a rising valuation profile, where in each round the price per share and the post-money valuation keeps going up. This may require accepting slightly lower early-stage valuations to leave room for improvement later on. There are perceptual as well as economic reasons for this, although the argument also has limitations.

Let us start with perceptions. A profile of increasing valuations projects strength, whereas a profile of flat or declining valuations looks disappointing. Some of this perception is based on sound economic fundamentals. A company that hits its milestones and eliminates one risk after another should fetch increasing valuations. However, there can also be some manipulation of naïve beliefs. The example in Box 6.6 implies that an increasing valuations profile could just be hiding increasingly stronger preferred terms. Whether sound or naïve, many investors associate a rising valuation profile with high expected returns. Creating such a belief is useful for the company. It creates an aura of being a rising star. This helps not only with investors, but also with customers, suppliers, and employees.

Another purely economic rationale for managing an upward valuation profile is to avoid down rounds. As we note in Section 9.3.3, anti-dilution clauses can be punishing for founders. Moreover, they undermine the company's stock option plans and may lead to the departure of key employees. Thus, it may be better to avoid high valuations early on if there is a risk that they are likely to come down in the next round.

Let us also note the limitations of these arguments. First, perceptions can be fickle and depend on many factors that are beyond the entrepreneur's control. For example, if an entrepreneur's broader market faces a downturn, then even the most attractive valuation profile will not help to raise additional funding. Second, the argument of keeping valuations low to leave room for higher valuations down the road can easily be invoked to pressure entrepreneurs into accepting lower valuations, when in truth investors are merely trying to get a better deal. Put differently, while managing a valuation profile may prove beneficial, it seems difficult to use as an argument for accepting a significantly lower valuation and thereby giving up a significant ownership stake in the company.

Summary

This chapter examines the process of raising equity in stages. Staging gives investors the option to abandon weaker projects. This increases the attractiveness of investing in the first place. However, staging creates refinancing risk for entrepreneurs. It also requires issuing different securities at different times, which can result in conflicts among new and old investors. We examine the roles of insider investors in later rounds and the economic incentives they have with respect to setting valuations. We also examine the challenges related to structuring term sheets, looking at the stacking of preferred shares across rounds, as well as at the mechanics and rationales for anti-dilution clauses. Other challenges with staging pertain to down rounds and turnarounds where entrepreneurs and investors often find themselves in conflictual situations. The chapter ends with explaining how investors and entrepreneurs adopt dynamic strategies of managing the staged financing process.

In terms of the FIRE framework (Chapter 1), this chapter focuses on the third step, RIDE. Figure 1.8 portrays the staged financing process as a journey from one fuel stop to another. This imagery emphasizes the vital importance of raising additional funding along the way of reaching the final destination. In other words, staged financing is essential for taking a company through the entire entrepreneurial process from start to exit.

Review Questions

1. What are the pros and cons for investors to stage their financial commitments?
2. What is the option value of abandonment? How can one estimate it?
3. When might investors use tranched as opposed to staged financing?
4. When do inside investors prefer higher over lower valuations?
5. What determines the seniority of the preferred terms across different financing rounds?
6. What is the intent behind anti-dilution clauses? Who benefits most from the full-ratchet clause?
7. What does "pay-to-play" mean?
8. What financial, managerial, and legal challenges are commonplace in down rounds?
9. What aspects enter into the formulation of an investor's dynamic investment strategy?
10. How should entrepreneurs manage their valuation profile across stages?

Notes

1. Kerr, Nanda, and Rhodes-Kropf (2014).
2. CB Insights (2018). Quintero (2017) provides a similar analysis.
3. The work of Bergemann and Hege (2005), Cestone (2014), Cornelli and Yosha (2003), Neher (1999), and Repullo and Suarez (2004) provides the economic foundations of staged financing.
4. https://www.nobelprize.org/prizes/economic-sciences/1994/press-release.
5. https://www.nobelprize.org/prizes/economic-sciences/2004/press-release.
6. https://www.nobelprize.org/prizes/economic-sciences/2007/press-release.
7. Maskin (1996) and Kornai, Maskin, and Roland (2003).
8. Gompers (1995).
9. Tian (2011).

10. Copeland and Antikarov (2003), and Metrick and Yasuda (2010b).
11. Maine and Thomas (2017).
12. Manso (2011, 2017).
13. Azoulay, Graff Zivin, and Manso (2011).
14. Nanda and Rhodes-Kropf (2013).
15. Tian and Wang (2014) provide additional evidence.
16. Ewens, Nanda, and Rhodes-Kropf (2018).
17. https://500.co.
18. Bienz and Hirsch (2012).
19. Hellmann and Thiele (2018).
20. Levin and Rocap (2015) provide a comprehensive legal analysis with a U.S. focus.
21. Bengtsson and Sensoy (2015).
22. Nanda and Rhodes-Kropf (2016).
23. Gibson, Margaret, Jack Levin, and Mariano Martinez Navigating Down Round Financings. Available at: https://www.kirkland.com/siteFiles/kirkexp/publications/2472/Document1/Navigating%20Down%20Round%20Financings.pdf.
24. Fenwick and West, Silicon Valley Venture Capital Survey, quarterly issues available at: https://www.fenwick.com/topics/pages/topicsdetail.aspx?topicname=vc%20survey.
25. Bengtsson and Sensoy (2015).
26. Forbes, Korsgaard, and Sapienza (2010).
27. Kirkham and Taylor (2009).
28. The Santa Clara Court case number was CV739278, filed January 21, 1997. Padilla (2001) provides a legal discussion, and Goldberg and Carr (2017) a business perspective.
29. This estimate accounts for dilution at the IPO.
30. La Porta et al. (2000).
31. Li and Chi (2013).
32. Broughman and Fried (2012) and Ewens, Rhodes-Kropf, and Strebulaev (2016).

10

Debt Financing

Learning Goals

In this chapter students will learn:

1. how debt contracts work.
2. why most banks don't lend to start-ups.
3. which types of debt financing are available to entrepreneurial companies.
4. to apply valuation methods for start-ups financed with both debt and equity.

This chapter examines the role of debt in start-up companies. We first examine the structure of debt contracts and compare debt to equity. We expose the fallacy that debt is a cheaper source of financing and discuss the different incentives that debt and equity provide to entrepreneurs and investors. We explain why banks typically don't extend standard loans to start-ups. We also review other forms of debt available to start-ups, considering personal loans, trade credit, discounting and factoring, venture leasing, and venture debt. The chapter also explains how to perform company valuation when a venture is financed by a mix of debt and equity, distinguishing between a company's enterprise value (which includes debt), from a company's equity value (which excludes debt).

10.1 Fundamentals of Debt

10.1.1 What Is Debt?

In this chapter we look at the role of debt financing in entrepreneurial companies. We start by defining debt and explaining how it is structured.

With debt, the investor is called a lender or creditor. He provides the investment amount, called the "principal," to a borrower, who in our context is the entrepreneur. The borrower promises to repay the principal plus interest at predefined points in time. We use the terms *loan* and *debt* as substitutes. The term *credit* signifies the same but is often used more broadly to also encompass borrowing from nonfinancial lenders such as customers or suppliers.

Consider the simplest form of debt, where there is a single repayment at the end of the loan period. The value of a debt obligation (D) as a function of the investment amount (I), the interest rate (r), and the time to repayment (t) is given by:

$$D = I^*(1+r)^t \qquad (10.1)$$

Figure 10.1 graphically represents equation (10.1). The horizontal axis represents the company value at the time of repaying the loan. The vertical axis represents the cash flow to the investor which is determined by the full debt obligation (D).

When the company value exceeds D, the company can repay its debt obligation in full, assuming that the company is liquid and can be sold for its full value (Section 11.1.1). This corresponds to the horizontal line in Figure 10.1. However, when the company value falls short of D, the debtor is in default and the lender has a claim on all the remaining value of the company. This corresponds to the solid segment on the dotted 45° line in Figure 10.1. The cash flow to the entrepreneur is given by the difference between the dotted 45° line and the solid line.

We establish three crucial distinctions upfront. The first distinction is between installment credit and revolving credit. With installment credit, the borrower obtains a fixed amount of money from the lender for a specified period of time. The repayment schedule of interest and principal is fixed. When the loan matures, the principal needs to be paid back in its entirety. The most common form of installment loans are term loans. Commercial paper and bonds, which are only available for

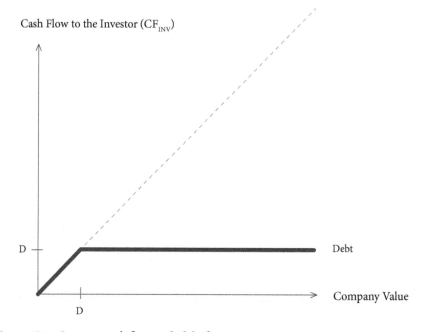

Figure 10.1. Investor cash flow with debt financing.

established corporations are also installment credit. With revolving credit, the borrower gets the option to choose how much credit to draw up to an agreed amount of money over a certain period of time. There is no fixed repayment schedule, and interest is paid only on the amount drawn. Credit lines, credit cards, and overdraft facilities are common forms of revolving credit.

The second distinction is between secured and unsecured credit. A credit is secured when the borrower pledges an asset as security (or "collateral") to reassure the lender. He gets the right ("lien") to possess the asset in case the credit is not paid back. An unsecured credit, on the other hand, is granted on the basis of the venture's ability to produce enough cash flow to repay the credit. Installment and revolving credit can be either secured or unsecured, giving rise to a variety of possible credit structures.

The third distinction is particularly relevant in the entrepreneurial context and concerns personal versus corporate credit. With the former, the entrepreneur takes on credit as a private individual and therefore faces personal risk. With the latter, the credit is taken on by the entrepreneurial company, which is protected by limited liability. Unless otherwise stated, we focus in this chapter on corporate credit. Section 10.4.1, however, takes a look at personal credit.

10.1.2 The Structure of Debt Contracts

In this section, we briefly describe how debt contracts can be structured.[1] We focus on four contractual dimensions: maturity, cost, collateral, and covenants.

10.1.2.(a) Maturity
The maturity of a loan is the date of its final repayment. The time between the loan start and its maturity date is referred to as the loan maturity (e.g., a two-year loan). In an installment loan, the borrower commits to a payback schedule that might have several interim payments and always has a final repayment of the principal. The interim payments may include only interest, as is common in commercial loans, or also a part of the repayment of principal, as is common in mortgages. Interim payments can occur at different intervals, usually monthly, quarterly, or yearly. Loans that have a single final payment are called "bullet" or "balloon" loans. Loans with a maturity within one year are conventionally considered short term, whereas those with a longer maturity are considered long term. Revolving credit typically has a set maturity of up to one year but is renewed ("rolled over") as long as the borrower's credit conditions have not deteriorated.

10.1.2.(b) Cost
The cost of a loan typically has two components: interest rate and fees. The interest rate can be structured in different ways. The most important distinction is between fixed and variable. In the fixed case, the interest rate is set in nominal terms

(e.g., 4%). In the variable case, the interest rate is expressed in terms of a variable base rate, which reflects market conditions, and a fixed premium (e.g., the LIBOR rate plus 1%).[2] In addition, there are several types of fees, which reduce the actual amount of the loan available to the borrower, sometimes materially so. The application fee covers the cost of the loan approval process; it is often a fixed fee that does not depend on the loan amount. With revolving credit, lenders often also charge a commitment fee that compensates them for keeping some capital at the disposal of the borrower. Such a fee is proportional to the amount of capital made available. Other fees depend on either loan characteristics or borrower behavior. For example, an installment loan may have an early repayment fee that compensates the lender for receiving the principal before maturity. Also, borrowers who fail to keep up with their due payments may face a late payment fee, which is often proportional to the delay and the amount due.

10.1.2.(c) Collateral

Collateral is an important part of secured debt contracts. In general, the lender seeks to secure the loan with assets that can be easily seized in case of default. Most collateralized assets, like property, equipment, or inventory, are tangible. Lenders also prefer assets that can be easily resold: some inventory is generic and easy to sell (e.g., fabric), and other inventory is more specific and difficult to sell (e.g., fashion clothes). In some cases, lenders also accept intangible assets such as patents and other intellectual property for collateral (Box 10.5).

A distinction between recourse and nonresource loans matters for recovering defaulted loans. With a nonrecourse loan, the lender has the right to collect the collateral in case of default, but nothing more. With a recourse loan, however, the lender has the right to collect the collateral, but in case the value of the collateral does not cover the full loan repayment, the lender can go further and ask for other forms of repayment.

10.1.2.(d) Covenants

Lenders impose a variety of conditions, called covenants, to protect the value of the money they have committed and to facilitate repossession in case of default. Legally speaking, covenants are conditions that the borrower agrees to observe. As long as the covenants are not broken, lenders cannot take certain actions like calling in the loan.

There are many types of covenants, and riskier loans tend to have more covenants.[3] A first set of covenants concerns the liquidity and solvency of the company. A minimum interest coverage ratio, for example, measures the ability of companies to service their interest payments. Other related measures include the debt to equity ratio, which limits the borrower's ability to issue further debt, and the loan life coverage ratio, which is an interest coverage ratio targeted to a specific loan. A second set of covenants concerns the profitability of the company. Common minimum ratios include return on assets, return on equity, return on capital, or the

EBITDA margin. Covenants can also be based on a wide variety of business-specific indicators. An e-commerce business, for example, could have a covenant based on its customer conversion rate. For these covenants to be effective, they must be reliable indicators of firm performance. As such, they are more suitable for mature and predictable business than for start-ups that have uncertain business prospects and lack reliable performance metrics.

The covenants discussed so far are affirmative covenants that allow the lender to intervene if the covenant is broken. There are also negative covenants, which restrict borrowers from taking certain actions. Examples include restrictions on paying out dividends or changing the corporate structure, such as merging the company with another. Note that such a negative covenant does not prevent a company from merging with another; it simply gives the lender the right to call in the loan when the covenant has been breached.

In case of default, lenders have two choices. First, they can initiate formal bankruptcy proceedings. We discuss this in Section 11.5. Alternatively, lenders can renegotiate the loan. This choice is often less costly and preserves the future lending relationship. Instead of waiting for default, lenders can use covenants to force a loan renegotiation at an earlier date. This leads to a loan restructuring that may preserve the viability of the venture and the value of the collateral, and spare the need for costly formal bankruptcy. In a loan restructuring, the maturity of the loan might be extended and the interest rate increased.

Box 10.1 considers a few examples of loan contracts so that we better can understand their structure.

Box 10.1 Examples of Loan Contracts

Consider first a short-term bullet loan with a one-year maturity. Denote the loan amount by I = $10,000. Suppose that there is no fee and that the annualized interest rate is r = 10%. The repayment at maturity consists of the repayment of principal, plus the payment of interest. Using equation (10.1), this is:

$$D = I^* (1 + r)^t = 10{,}000^*1.1 = 11{,}000$$

where the interest payment is I*r = $10,000 * 10% = $1,000. The net cash flows between borrower and lender are as follows. At loan origination (t = 0), there is a transfer of I = $10,000 from the lender to the borrower. At loan maturity (t = 1), there is a net payment of I*(1 + r) = $11,000 from the borrower to the lender. The total cost of the loan (in nominal terms) is $1,000. If the bank charges a closing fee, say $500, then the borrower only receives I = $9,5000 = $10,000 – $500 and the total cost, inclusive of interest and fee, becomes $1,500. In percentage terms, this becomes $1,500/9,500 = 1.158, or 15.79% in percentage terms—quite an increase.

Consider next a long-term bullet loan with a duration of two years for the same amount of I = \$10,000, which is transferred from the lender to the borrower at loan origination (t = 0). At maturity (end of year 2), the lender repays $I^*(1 + r)^2 = \$10,000^*(1.1)^2 = \$12,100$ from the borrower to the lender. If instead the loan specifies interest-only payments every year, then there is an interim interest payment of $I^*r = \$1,000$ from borrower to lender at the end of year 1, and a final payment of interest and principal of $I^*(1 +r) = \$11,000$ at the end of year 2. Note that in this case the borrower ends up repaying a total of \$12,000, which is \$100 less than before. This is because the interest is no longer compounded.

Finally, consider a revolving credit line, with an upfront commitment fee of \$800 and yearly interest repayments. Suppose the borrower draws the whole \$10,000 during the first year but repays \$5,000 at the end of the year and keeps that balance until maturity. In this case, the cost to the borrower in the first year would be \$1,800 = \$800 + \$1,000 (fee and interest). In the second year, the cost would be $I^*(1 + r) = \$5,000^*10\% = \$500$. The total cost is therefore \$2,300 = \$1,800 + \$800.

10.2 Debt versus Equity

10.2.1 The Fallacy That Debt Is Cheaper Than Equity

One reason why entrepreneurs are often attracted to debt is that it is nondilutive (Section 4.1.5). The idea is that raising finance through debt is cheaper because it allows the entrepreneur to preserve her equity in the venture. This argument may sound compelling, yet it can be misleading. In Box 10.2 we introduce the seminal contribution of three Nobel laureates, who laid the foundations for understanding the cost of debt and equity.

Box 10.2 Nobel Insights on Debt versus Equity

The 1985 Nobel Prize in Economics went to Franco Modigliani "for his pioneering analyses of saving and of financial markets."[4] In 1990, Merton Miller won the prize (together with Harry Markowitz and William Sharpe, whose work we discuss in Box 5.1) "for their pioneering work in the theory of financial economics."[5] Finally, the 2001 Nobel Prize in Economics was awarded to Joseph Stiglitz (together with George Akerlof and Michael Spence, whose work we discuss in Box 2.6) "for their analyses of markets with asymmetric information."[6]

While Modigliani and Miller both produced many important scientific contributions, they are particularly well known for the Modigliani–Miller theorem.[7] This principle states that the value of a firm does not depend on the mix of debt and equity it uses to finance itself. Put differently, the cost of raising debt and equity is always the same, implying that a firm cannot increase its value by replacing one unit of debt with one unit of equity, or vice versa.

The Modigliani–Miller theorem is based on the standard economic logic of valuing a company by discounting its future cash flows. In a world without financial friction, the future cash flows of a company do not depend on who owns them. They are generated by the company's asset side of the balance sheet and do not depend on who owns those assets on the liabilities side. Both debt and equity investors ultimately look at the discounted value of their part of future cash flows. If a company takes on more debt, it gives more of its future cash flows to debt holders and less to equity holders, but the total company value remains the same.

The key assumption of the Modigliani–Miller theorem is that there are no financial frictions. This means that all economic agents have the same information and that the cost of capital is determined purely by market forces. While we know that often this is not the case, the Modigliani–Miller theorem has been influential precisely because it provides a powerful benchmark for assessing the relative costs and benefits of debt versus equity once financial frictions arise.

Some of the most powerful arguments about the effective cost of debt financing have come out of Stiglitz's work. While his contributions to economics are vast, here we will focus on his seminal work about the "moral hazard" and "adverse selections" problems.[8] This concerns situations where one party that has some information advantage uses it to take self-interested actions that negatively affect the other party ("moral hazard"), or conceal negative information to obtain better deals ("adverse selection"). In our context, for example, an entrepreneur might divert investors' money into pet projects that are not profitable. Or the entrepreneur might take bets where the costs are borne by the investor, while the payoffs are shared by entrepreneur and investor. Similarly, the entrepreneur who knows more about the value of her project may conceal unfavorable information to the investor and obtain a higher valuation.

In general, the uninformed party (the investor) cannot directly prevent the informed party (the entrepreneur) from taking these actions, but it can structure a contract that provides good incentives for maximizing the investment's payoff. Stiglitz showed how debt contracts often lead to poor incentives, while equity can provide better (but not perfect) incentives. Stiglitz's work suggests that the true cost of debt is typically invisible to accountants. This is because debt shapes entrepreneurial incentives, which indirectly affect company performance. We return to this point in Section 10.2.2.

Box 10.3 provides a numerical example that illustrates the implications of the Modigliani–Miller theorem.

Box 10.3 The True Cost of Risky Debt

Mario Mozzarella was a Sicilian-born immigrant who settled in San Carlos di Bariloche, a small Patagonian town in the foothills of the Andes. With his Argentinian wife Mercedes Mendocinas, they opened an empañadas restaurant that quickly acquired fame as the best empañadas south of the Panama Canal. They were inundated with requests for home delivery but had to turn down many customers who lived in remote mountain villages. That is, until they invented the "Drone da Forno" (which means Oven Drone in Italian). Their invention allowed empañadas to be baked in mid-flight by a drone, thus allowing for fresh delivery anywhere within 200 miles of Bariloche. Truth be told, Mario and Mercedes had gotten as far as building a working prototype, but they needed money to launch the business.

The company required an investment of one million Argentinian pesos (whose symbol is $). They reckoned that their venture had a 50% chance of being a spectacular success, in which case the company would be worth $7.5M within a year. Otherwise it would fail with a residual asset value of $0.5M. For simplicity, we assume that all parties are risk-neutral and that the safe rate of return in the economy is 10%. This means that all investors require an expected rate of return of 10% on risk-free investments.

Mario and Mercedes debated whether to finance their business with debt or equity. The following table shows the combinations of debt and equity they considered (amounts are in Argentinian pesos). First, they approached Mercedes's friend Andrés Acciones, an empañadas-loving local angel investor. He was willing to invest $1M in the venture in return for an equity stake of 27.5% ("Pure equity" column). This implies a post-money valuation of $3.64M and a pre-money valuation of $2.64M (using equations (4.2) and (4.3)). All amounts reported in the table are in dollars.

Mario also considered debt in order to avoid diluting their ownership. He therefore approached his (steak-loving) friend Paco Prestador, the director of a local bank. Paco said his bank would be willing to lend him $0.4M at a rate of 10%. Mario considered taking it and asked Andres to provide the remaining $0.6M in equity at the same valuation as before, implying a 16.5% stake for him ("Naïve equity and safe debt" column).

Mercedes immediately realized that Andres would never accept this deal. Since equity is junior to debt, his equity would now be "levered" and less valuable than before. Mario and Mercedes would have to first pay Paco $0.44M (principal plus 10% interest) before Andrés and themselves could split any capital gain. The equity would now be worth $7.06M in case of success but only $0.06M in case of failure. The expected equity value of $3.34M would then require an equity stake of 18.5% for Andrés ("Equity and safe debt" column).

	All equity	Naïve equity and safe debt	Equity and safe debt	Equity and naïve risky debt	Equity and risky debt	All risky debt
Debt amount (Paco)	0	400,000	400,000	600,000	600,000	1,000,000
Equity amount (Andrés)	1,000,000	600,000	600,000	400,000	400,000	0
Required debt value at maturity (Paco)	0	440,000	440,000	660,000	660,000	1,100,000
Required exit equity value (Andrés)	1,100,000	660,000	660,000	440,000	440,000	0
Interest rate	10%	10%	10%	10%	37%	70%
Debt value (Paco)	0	440,000	440,000	660,000	820,000	1,700,000
Equity fraction (Andrés)	27.5%	16.5%	18.5%	12.9%	13.2%	0.0%
Expected equity value, net of debt	4,000,000	3,560,000	3,560,000	3,420,000	3,340,000	2,900,000
Equity value, net of debt (if success)	7,500,000	7,060,000	7,060,000	6,840,000	6,680,000	5,800,000
Equity value, net of debt (if failure)	500,000	60,000	60,000	0	0	0
Post-money valuation (net of debt)	3,636,364	3,636,364	3,236,364	3,109,091	3,036,364	n.a
Post-money valuation (gross of debt)	3,636,364	4,036,364	3,636,364	3,709,091	3,636,364	3,636,364
Pre-money valuation	2,636,364	3,036,364	2,636,364	2,709,091	2,636,364	2,636,364

Note that compared to the first column ("Pure equity") the second column ("Naïve equity and safe debt") has the same post-money valuation *net of* debt, whereas the third column ("Equity and safe debt") has the same post-money valuation *gross of* debt. This reflects the difference between the naïve approach (second column), which assumes that the equity investors do not respond to an increase in leverage, versus the logical approach (third column), where equity investors take leverage into account. In the latter case, the total company value remains the same, regardless of how much leverage there is. In Section 10.5, we explain that the post-money valuation excluding debt corresponds to the company's equity value, whereas the post-money valuation including debt corresponds to the company's enterprise value.

Mario and Mercedes also explored what would happen if they asked for more debt from Paco, say $0.6M. Would that be a better solution, given that debt is less dilutive? They expected that the company would reach a higher valuation as shown in the "Equity and naïve risky debt" column. This assumed that Andres required the competitive return rate of 10%, implying an equity share of 12.9%. It also assumed that Paco would continue charging 10% interest. This time it was Mario who realized that Paco could not accept that deal. The loan obligation of $660M (principal plus interest) was larger than the $500M the venture would be worth in case of failure. This meant that Paco was making a risky loan, which would require him to charge a risk premium. The calculations in the "Equity and risky debt" column reveal that Paco would need to charge an interest rate of 37% to achieve an expected return of 10%. This higher interest rate further required adjusting Andres's equity share up to 13.2%. With this, the post-money valuation including debt in the fifth column was again the same as in the first and third columns. That is, once all investors received their expected return of 10%, the enterprise value remained the same, regardless of the mix of debt and equity.

Mario briefly considered using only debt ("Pure risky debt" column). He found out that this would require an interest rate of 70%. Because there was no external equity, the standard formula for calculating post-money valuation (investment divided by investor share; see equation (4.2)) does not apply. Mario obtained the equivalent of the post-money valuation (including debt) by using a 10% discount rate and calculating the NPV of the expected returns to the company. This yielded $3.64M (= 50%*$7.5M + 50%*$0.5M)/(1.1). The pre-money valuation could be obtained as the NPV of the expected returns to the entrepreneur's equity after debt: $2.64M = (50%*$5.8M+50%*$0)/(1.1).

The main insight that Mario and Mercedes took from all these calculations was that as soon a company takes on some debt, this changes the cost of capital of the equity investors, because they have a more leveraged position. Moreover, if the debt component becomes sufficiently large, debt itself becomes risky and requires a higher interest rate. Once the debt and equity are priced correctly, so as to generate the required rate of return to their investors, the cost of capital to the company is the same. They concluded that it was simply not true that debt is cheaper than equity. In the end, Mario and Mercedes decided to take Andres's money: why settle for steak-loving money, when you can get empañadas-loving money!

The key insight from Box 10.3 is that if investors require the same risk-adjusted return on debt and equity, in a world without financial friction the cost of debt and the cost of equity are the same. We now introduce financial frictions into the picture.

10.2.2 Comparing Debt and Equity

Several arguments can be made about whether and when debt is better or worse than equity. Corporate finance books discuss these issues in detail, typically from the perspective of established companies.[9] Here we discuss two forces that are most pertinent to entrepreneurial companies: transaction costs and incentive costs.

We first analyze transaction costs (see also Box 13.2). With debt contracts, transaction costs arise: (1) at the time of investment, (2) during the investment period, and (3) at the time of repayment. At the time of investment, there are due diligence costs for the investor to investigate whether or not the entrepreneur is suitable, and costs of negotiating and legally structuring the investment. Debt contracts are faster and less costly than equity. Second, we analyze taxation matters during the investment period. Corporations have to pay taxes on their profits but can deduct interest payments from taxable profits.[10] There is no equivalent tax shield for equity. While the tax argument is very important for established companies, entrepreneurial ventures are often slow to generate profits. Therefore, the tax argument has relatively little sway in the context of early-stage ventures.[11] Third, when it comes to repayment, debt and equity are very different. The transaction costs of repaying equity are the direct and indirect costs of structuring an exit. We discuss those costs in Chapter 12. For debt, the main problem is the cost of bankruptcy. Without default, the transaction costs of repaying debt are minimal. With default, however, the costs are substantial, as discussed in Section 11.5. Overall, we can say that debt has lower transaction costs for safer companies with low default risk, but higher transaction costs for riskier companies with high default risk. Since the probability of default is highest in the earlier stages, debt is less attractive for early-stage entrepreneurial companies but becomes increasingly viable at later stages.

In discussing the incentive costs of debt and equity, it is useful to start with a graphical representation of their respective cash flows. Figure 10.2, using the same graph, shows the returns to investors holding pure debt and pure equity. The

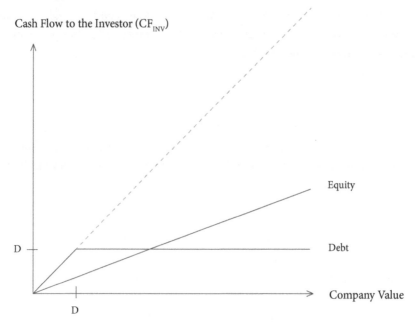

Figure 10.2. Investor cash flow with debt and equity financing.

horizontal axis represents the company value, the vertical axis the cash flows to investors.

Figure 10.2 helps to explain why debt and equity generate different investor incentives. The way to think about incentives is to ask how much the investor benefits from a higher company value. This is reflected in the *slope* of the return curves of Figure 10.2. With debt, lenders have no incentives for improving the company's performance beyond D, which is the point where the company becomes able to repay its obligation. They cannot gain from better performance because their upside is capped. On the downside, however, the lender has a strong incentive to preserve any remaining company value. Put differently, lenders have little to gain from entrepreneurs making it big, as they do not to participate in the upside, but they have a lot to lose from the company becoming insolvent, since they bear the full costs on the downside. Compare this with the incentives of an equity investor. The equity slope is always positive, suggesting that the equity investor always has the incentive to create more value. The strength of this incentive increases with the slope of the investor's equity share. Therefore, the equity investor wants the entrepreneur to make it big, as he participates in the upside returns. The incentive cost of debt thus consists of making the investor's goals differ from those of the entrepreneur.

Consider now the entrepreneur's incentives. With debt the entrepreneur retains all of the upside returns, whereas with equity she shares them with the investor. Still, as long as the entrepreneur's ownership stake remains large enough, she has an incentive to foster the success of her company. With debt, however, a problem can occur on the downside. Once the company value falls deep into the default region (i.e., well below D in Figure 10.2), the entrepreneur loses the incentive to increase the value of the company, since all the gain in value goes to the lender. In fact, the entrepreneur may even try to escape default by "gambling on resurrection": spend all the remaining cash balances on a bold strategic bet, even if the net present value of that bet was negative. This is because with debt she has nothing more to lose (the company is bankrupt if there is no bet or if the bet fails) but has a small chance of getting out of bankruptcy if the bet succeeds. This is exactly the moral hazard problem studied by Stiglitz (see Box 10.2).

One cannot derive general conclusions about whether debt or equity have higher incentives costs. However, whenever investors play an important value-adding role, which we discuss in Chapter 8, the key message is that equity gives the investor an incentive to contribute to the process of entrepreneurial value creation.

10.3 Why Banks Don't Lend to Start-ups

Why does a book on entrepreneurial finance wait until Chapter 10 to discuss bank debt? Aren't bank loans the most common way of financing small businesses? They are, but entrepreneurial companies are not your typical small business (Section 1.1). Established small businesses with predictable positive cash flows are routinely financed by banks, entrepreneurial ventures are not. Let's find out why.

Consider a commercial loan application by a limited liability company. A bank loan officer cares about two criteria: (1) the probability of default and (2) the recovery rate in case of default. The probability of default depends on the expected level and stability of earnings. To assess this probability, the loan officer is likely to look for a track record of steady revenues, stable costs, and an experienced and competent management team. None of these apply to entrepreneurial ventures, as can be seen from the Venture Evaluation Matrix introduced in Chapter 2. Entrepreneurial ventures are in the process of establishing revenue models, have numerous business model uncertainties that affect their costs, and might be led by an inexperienced founder team. Revenues and costs remain unpredictable for several years, and profits may take years to materialize. Second, in case of default, a lender wants to recover as much of the debt obligation as possible. Concretely, the lender asks for collateral that can be claimed in case of default. However, collateral is useful to the bank only if it can be sold easily and quickly. Entrepreneurial ventures, however, typically have intangible assets or specialized inventory that is hard to sell. So they can provide little collateral to a bank.

In principle, the bank could charge a higher interest rate to compensate for the higher risk posed by entrepreneurial ventures. Riskier borrowers always pay higher interest, so why should start-ups be different? Indeed, this is what happens in the example of Box 10.3. In practice, however, several problems prevent banks from simply raising their interest rates. In several countries, usury laws prevent lenders from charging rates above a certain legal threshold. Stiglitz's work on adverse selection and moral hazard, discussed in Box 10.2, shows that charging high interest rates may backfire for lenders. The adverse selection version of the argument is that the only borrowers willing to accept high rates are high-risk borrowers who are unlikely to ever repay the loan. The moral hazard version is the "gambling on resurrection" strategy we discuss at the end of Section 10.2.2: if the gamble works out, they win, but if it fails, it is the bank that loses.

Banks are rarely well equipped to deal with the high risks of start-ups. They therefore prefer to lend to established small businesses rather than start-ups. Small businesses have a reasonably low probability of default since they follow proven business models. They also tend to have tangible assets such as property, machinery (e.g. trucks), or inventory (e.g., clothing) that can easily be sold. To get an idea of the difference between established small businesses versus entrepreneurial ventures, consider data from the 2016 Report on Startup Firms from the Small Business Credit Survey, published by the Federal Reserve Bank of New York. This survey contains data on small private companies under the age of two, as well as those over the age of five. It reports that 64% of companies under the age of two considered availability of credit or funds for expansion as a financial challenge. The corresponding number for companies over 5 years old was 39%. Of the companies under the age of 2 that applied for credit, 26% didn't receive any at all and 40% received some but not all that they applied for. For companies older than five years, 22% didn't receive any at all and 33% received some but not all that they applied for.[12] The most common reason for credit denial was "insufficient credit history" for companies under two years, but "weak business performance" for companies over five years old.[13]

To further understand the perspective of banks, WorkHorse Box 10.1 takes a brief nostalgic look at Brandon's first encounter with a bank.

WorkHorse Box 10.1 Debt at the Dawn of Company Time

Back in the summer of 2019, in the very early days of WorkHorse, Brandon Potro faced some personal financial troubles. The first sign of trouble came the day he was supposed to set up the incorporation papers. The lawyer's assistant called to say that Brandon's credit card had been denied and asked whether he could provide an alternative means of payment. Unfortunately, Brandon knew that his other credit card was also at the limit, so he postponed the meeting by a week to sort out this little financial snafu.

Brandon had two credit cards with a limit of $10K each, both of which were maxed out. He had minimum monthly interest payments of over $200 on each card, so on an annual basis he would pay over $4,800 in interest alone. This was too much, so he decided to go to his local bank, the FSBF Bank of South Eastern

Michigan. Its loan officer, a certain Mr. Blake Blank, greeted Brandon with a big smile.

Mr. Blank: "Great pleasure to meet you, Mr. Brad Potter. Please take a seat. Do you know what FSBF stands for?"

Brandon: "Actually, I am Brandon Potro, and sorry I don't know what FSBF stands for. Maybe something like "Federally Secured Banking Foundation?"

Mr. Blank laughed: "No Sir, no Feds in my bank. FSBF Bank stands for "First Small Business Friendly" Bank. We understand small business better than any other bank because we understand the true needs of the real entrepreneurs. How can I help you today, Mr. Potter?"

Brandon: "It's Potro. I am an entrepreneur, and I would like to apply for a $50K loan."

Mr. Blank: "No problem, you have come to the right place, we understand the true needs of the real entrepreneurs. Were you thinking of a personal or corporate loan?"

Brandon: "I am not sure, what is the difference?"

Mr. Blank: "Well, let's start with you, Mr. Potter. Do you have any personal assets that we can put as collateral? Now, that is a fancy way of asking if you own any house, farm, cattle, gold, or jewelry?"

Brandon: "Sorry, no. If I did I probably wouldn't have come here . . ."

Mr. Blank: "No problem, I didn't think you would, Mr. Potter! Not to worry, here at FSBF we understand the true needs of the real entrepreneurs. Tell me about your business. How old is your company, what does it sell, and what are your revenues?"

Brandon: "Well, here is the problem. We want to incorporate to start a new business. At present we have neither business nor revenues, which is why I am here."

There was a moment of silence before Mr. Blank replied "Sorry . . . I was drawing a blank: ha-ha, pardon the pun! Let me just make sure I understand this correctly. You don't have any revenues and you want a loan? And what exactly would be the purpose of such a loan?

Brandon: "Well, to be honest, the first thing I need to do is pay down my credit card, and after that we have some investments."

Mr. Blank looked horrified: "Sorry, but our corporate loans can never be used to pay down personal credit cards. Not to worry, though, at FSBF we understand the true needs of the real entrepreneurs, so please tell me about these investments. We do all sorts of investment loans. Right now, we have a special loan offering for buying cars, trucks, or farm vehicles. Would that happen to suit you, Mr. Potter?"

Brandon: "Well, not really. We need to buy equipment for photovoltaic solar panels."

Mr. Blank: "Oh, I understand, unfortunately we don't have any special offer for those—what did you call them—those photosynthetic solar panels. Not to worry though, we also have general purpose investment loans. Let me ask you a few questions for that . . . where is that paper again? Oh, here it is: What fixed assets or inventory do you have to secure the loan? What recurring cash flows do you have that we can lend against? What personal guarantees can you provide?

Brandon started to get frustrated: "I already told you, I have no fixed assets, no inventory, no revenues, and no cash flows. I am an entrepreneur who is trying to start a new business. I don't even have a company yet!"

Mr. Blank: "What do you mean, Mr. Brad Potter, you don't even have a company? What on earth are you doing in our bank then? At FSBF we understand the true needs of the real entrepreneurs, but we are not here to give money to kids that want to play with. . . , with those photogenic solar panels."

Brandon tried to keep his calm, speaking slowly: "I am Brandon Potro, I am an entrepreneur. I need to buy equipment for photovoltaic solar panels. Can you help me with that?"

Mr. Blank drew another blank. Finally, he said: "I am sorry, Mr. Potter, but I don't think we can help you. Please come again when you have a real business."

Brandon didn't know whether to laugh or cry, but he knew he had to go elsewhere to solve his financial troubles. Astrid mentioned that when money got tight for her, she always turned to family. Brandon didn't want to ask his parents but instead approached his uncle JP Potro. He asked him for an informal loan, but JP wouldn't hear any of that. Instead he paid off Brandon's credit balances and told him never to use those cards again for business investments. Next, he suggested investing in the company with a convertible note—see WorkHorse Box 5.1. To set up the incorporation papers, JP also paid for the lawyer, and thus WorkHorse was officially born. Brandon never went back to the First Small Business Friendly Bank of South Eastern Michigan.

Although the key message from this section is that early-stage high-risk entrepreneurs can expect relatively little from banks, it is important to note that there are some exceptions. In Section 10.4, we will see that banks provide personal loans and corporate loans with personal guarantees. In addition, banks sometimes lend to entrepreneurs under specific government guarantee programs. In addition, there is a lot of debt outside of the banking system, which we will examine further in Section 10.4. Before we go there, Box 10.4 takes a brief look at economic history, asking whether banks always behaved the way they do today.

Box 10.4 Tales from the Venture Archives: Belgian Banks and the Industrial Revolution

The United Kingdom was the first country to undergo the industrial revolution, starting approximately in the 1760s. Textiles, small machinery, and dyes were among the main industries. Companies financed themselves with a mix of bank loans, commercial paper (i.e., corporate bonds), and trade credit. Most of the financing came from relatively small merchant banks, which relied on an active national commercial paper market for their liquidity needs. The situation on the European Continent was very different. There the industrial revolution required large investments in coal and steel, as well as infrastructure investments such as railways and water canals. Large banks played a key role in financing these new capital-intensive ventures.[14]

The first Continental European country to have a successful industrial revolution was Belgium, starting around the 1830s.[15] Its Société Générale pour favoriser l'industrie nationale was the world's first joint-stock investment bank, raising its money from relatively patient equity investors. It coordinated investments across industries to orchestrate the country's industrial development. For example, it would invest in a steel mill at the same time that it invested in railway companies that depended on a reliable source of steel. Between 1835 and 1838 alone, it organized the formation of 31 industrial joint-stock companies ("société anonymes"). One historian notes that "banks did not respond passively to demand for credit, but actively sought new firms, underwrote their stock issues, financed potential stockholders, held stock in their own names, placed their officers on the boards of directors of the companies they promoted, and ministered to the companies' needs for both working capital and new capital for expansion."[16] This description sounds surprisingly similar to what modern venture capitalists do. Overall, the investments of the Société Générale (and a few other contemporary banks) were highly successful. They helped Belgium emerge as a leading industrial nation by the 1850s. Similar developments subsequently occurred in other European countries, most notably Germany, France, and Northern Italy.

What made these banks different from modern banks? First, there were only a small number of large banks that financed the new industries. These banks not only had the financial resources to undertake large capital investments, they also had sufficient market power to benefit from them.[17] Second, the investments were often secured by fixed assets such as plants and machinery. Third, the banks themselves relied mostly on shareholder equity capital and less on deposits. The banks were therefore less worried about maintaining liquid investments. They were also not subject to the stringent modern banking regulations. Fourth, banks could invest in companies using both debt and equity. Having equity stakes allowed them to benefit from the value created by the companies they financed. Fifth, there were direct personal ties between bankers and industrial entrepreneurs. Interestingly, modern empirical evidence suggests that banks' willingness to lend to smaller entrepreneurial companies declined significantly as computer technology automated banking services, discouraging personal relationships between bankers and companies.[18]

10.4 Alternative Types of Debt

In this section, we discuss the many different types of debt and debt-like instruments entrepreneurs use in a variety of circumstances. We start with personal debt, and then we move on to a variety of corporate debt instruments.

10.4.1 Personal Loans and Credit Cards

To understand the role of personal debt in start-ups, we begin with some data from the Kaufman Firm Survey, which gathered data on over 3,500 U.S. newly founded companies for the period 2004–2007.[19] This survey did not focus solely on high-growth companies, but on all new companies, including sole partnerships and other types of ventures with no growth ambitions. Table 10.1 shows the different types of financial capital used. The first column reports the average amount across the entire sample, counting an amount of $0 for companies that did not use that type of capital. The second column reports the average amount for those companies that actually used that type of capital. The third reports the fraction of companies that used that type of financing.

Table 10.1 Debt and Equity Financing in U.S. Start-up Companies.

Type of financial capital	Average amount, entire sample ($)	Average amount, when actually used ($)	Percentage of companies using this type of financing
Owner equity	31,734	40,536	87%
Owner debt	5,037	15,765	35%
Insider equity	2,102	44,956	5%
Insider debt	6,362	47,873	14%
Outsider equity	15,935	354,540	6%
Outsider debt	47,847	128,706	41%
Total financial capital	109,016	121,981	100%
Trade credit	21,793	93,536	24%

Source: Authors' elaborations on data from Robb and Robinson (2014).

Table 10.2 Outside Debt in U.S. Start-up Companies.

Type of outside debt	Average amount, entire sample ($)	Average amount, when actually used ($)	Percentage of companies using this type of outside debt
Personal bank loans by founders	15,859	92,433	45%
Business bank loans	17,075	261,358	17%
Credit lines	5,057	95,058	15%
Personally-backed business credit cards	1,009	7,107	38%
Business credit cards	812	6,976	31%
Total outside debt	47,847	128,706	100%

Source: Authors' elaborations on data from Robb and Robinson (2014).

Owner equity/debt is the capital provided by the founders themselves, insider equity/debt the capital provided by owner's family, and outside equity/debt the capital provided by all outside parties. Table 10.1 shows that debt is an important source of funding. The largest component of the debt is provided by outside parties, but founders and other insiders also provide some debt. We further note that the last line of Table 10.1 shows the importance of trade credit, which we discuss in Section 10.4.2. Based on the same data source, Table 10.2 takes a deeper look at outside debt by providing a more detailed breakdown.

The two most frequent sources of outside debt are personal bank loans and personally backed business credit cards. While the funding comes from outsiders, the risk is entirely borne by the founders. Even with business bank loans, lenders often ask the owners to personally guarantee the company loan. Table 10.2 therefore shows that founders still bear a substantial amount of risk when taking on outside debt.

Table 10.2 speaks to the use of credit cards. From an entrepreneur's perspective, it is tempting to use credit cards for funding a start-up, as it is relatively easy to get the credit. However, credit cards are an expensive form of financing. After the initial grace period, interest payments accumulate rapidly, with real interest rates that can easily exceed 20%.[20] In addition, defaulting on credit card debt can have severe personal consequences. One study by Lawless and Warren estimates that in 2003 approximately 280K self-employed entrepreneurs in the U.S. filed for personal bankruptcy, representing 17% of all personal bankruptcies.[21] Credit cards can be a good tool for managing short-term cash flow problems, where payments are due ahead of reasonably predictable revenues. However, they are unsuitable for any longer-term investments, where revenues are risky and occur far out into the future.

Credit cards also appeal differently to different entrepreneurs. One academic study by Chatterji and Seamans looks at credit cards and entrepreneurship among

African Americans.[22] A 1978 U.S. Supreme Court decision struck down state-level regulations that limited the interest rate lenders could charge on credit card debt. This deregulation unleashed a boom in credit cards that gave many Americans better access to credit outside of formal banking channels. In turns out that credit cards were disproportionately important to African American entrepreneurs who were more excluded from traditional funding sources. The study finds that the self-employment rate of African Americans increased when states deregulated credit cards. Interestingly, the increase was biggest in those states that had a history of more radical discrimination.

Finally, lending platforms, commonly referred to as peer-to-peer crowdfunding (P2P), are a relatively recent source of personal and business loans. However, for entrepreneurs they play only a limited role because most entrepreneurs either fail to meet specific lending criteria (such as having a minimum amount of sales), or their businesses are considered too risky and too unconventional. Lending platforms are used mainly by more established small and medium-sized enterprises, and only rarely by early-stage start-ups.[23] We discuss these platforms further in Section 13.4, within the broader context of crowdfunding.

10.4.2 Trade Credit

Recall from Section 3.6.2 that working capital consists of current assets minus current liabilities. Because working capital imposes a heavy financial burden on cash-strapped start-ups, founders look for ways to keep it low by decreasing current assets and/or increasing current liabilities. In this subsection, we look at trade credit as a way of increasing current liabilities; in the next subsection, we consider discounting and factoring as a way of decreasing current assets.[24]

Trade credit is a form of supplier credit that is embedded in the payment processes. An invoice gives the buyer a certain period of time to make the payment. In case of an early payment, there may be a discount, and in case of late payments there may be a penalty. At the time of purchase, the buyer therefore has a choice: pay now to get the discount, pay on time at the full price, or pay late with a penalty. Choosing to forego the discount can be thought of as taking a loan from a supplier. This is because the company can keep its cash far longer but pays a higher price for it.

To see how this system works, consider the following simple example. Take an invoice of $100 that requires payment in 60 days, but with a 5% discount for immediate payment. The company can pay $95 now or $100 in 60 days. Not taking the discount can be thought of as a loan of $95, with an interest payment of $5. What is the implicit interest rate for this loan? For this we note that 60 days corresponds approximately to 0.164 years, so that the interest rate is implicitly given by the standard formula for computing interest due: $\$95*(1 + r)^{0.164} = \$100$. The implied interest rate is 36.6%, which is very high. Depending on terms, trade credit can be an expensive way of financing working capital needs. Table 10.3 shows how

Table 10.3 Implied Interest Rates in Trade Credit

Discount:	1%	2%	3%	5%	10%
Extra days:					
15	27.7%	63.5%	109.8%	248.4%	1198.5%
30	13.0%	27.9%	44.9%	86.7%	260.3%
45	8.5%	17.8%	28.0%	51.6%	135.0%
60	6.3%	13.1%	20.4%	36.6%	89.8%
90	4.2%	8.5%	13.1%	23.1%	53.3%
120	3.1%	6.3%	9.7%	16.9%	37.8%

different combinations of (early payment) discount rates and extra days (to payment) generate different implied interest rates.

What about delaying payment beyond the due date? In our example, this means failing to pay the $100 bill even after 60 days. Delaying by a few more days may fall in a grace period, but beyond that, two types of costs arise. In the first type, the terms of the invoice specify a penalty rate, which is often higher than the corresponding discount rate for early payment. In the second, late payments can sour supplier relationships, the worst-case scenario being that the supplier refuses to provide any further supplies.

10.4.3 Discounting and Factoring

Discounting and factoring are methods of obtaining financing that involve borrowing against current assets, effectively reducing account receivables. This is the flipside of trade credit, which reduces working capital by increasing current liabilities.

Discounting, also known as invoice discounting, is a financial transaction in which a company uses its unpaid invoices as collateral to obtain a loan from a lending institution. The value of the invoices receives a discount on the order of 15 to 25%, depending on the credit risk of the account debtor (i.e., the client who has to pay the invoice). The discount reflects the cost of credit but also the risk that the invoice will not be paid on time. With discounting, the start-up retains the responsibility and risk of collecting the invoice.[25]

Factoring involves selling the invoice outright to a specialized intermediary called the "factor." The factor takes ownership of the invoice and thereby the right to receive the associated payment and the responsibility of collecting the payment. There are two main arrangements concerning the risk that customers may fail to pay the invoice. Under recourse factoring the factor gets compensated by the venture if a client fails to pay the invoice; with nonrecourse factoring, the factor assumes the risk of the customer failing to pay.

Factoring is technically not debt because the company receives a payment in return for selling its invoices (account receivables). However, the arrangement closely resembles debt, in the sense that the venture receives money from the factor, and in return the factor receives a larger payment at a later point in time. A study by Dorfleitner, Rad, and Weber about MarketInvoice, an online factoring platform, found that the "gross yield" (i.e., the effective interest rate) was 12.27%, at a time when interest rates were close to zero.[26] The exact discount depends on type of contract, but it will be lower for invoice discounting, higher for recourse factoring, and highest for nonrecourse factoring. A nonmonetary cost of factoring is that the company loses control over the payment process. A factor may aggressively target customers, which may thus sour their relationship with the company.

In this context, we also mention a related source of working capital finance: customer prepayments. In this arrangement, the company collects a payment from the customer in advance of the future delivery of a good or service. While a prepayment is clearly not debt, it usually involves a discounted price, which reflects the financial benefit of obtaining the cash in advance. Customer prepayments are more common in business-to-business transactions. An advantage of prepayments for new products is that they often allow a start-up to involve the customer in testing and improving product quality, such as identifying software bugs or improving product design.

WorkHorse Box 10.2 features several of the working capital tools discussed so far.

WorkHorse Box 10.2 Financing Unexpected Growth

Back in early 2021, WorkHorse faced its first serious working capital problem. WorkHorse's main retailer, PortageLake, had asked WorkHorse to deliver 3,025 units per month, which was much more than what the company had initially planned for. Though happy to receive the order, the founders realized that it also created new financial challenges.

The company's financial projections (see WorkHorse Box 3.3) estimated net revenues of $330.60 per unit sold. The 3,025 units per month therefore implied exactly $1M in revenues per month. Brandon initially felt giddy about this, but soon realized that this could actually bankrupt the company. At a unit cost of goods sold of $127 (see WorkHorse Box 3.5), the company needed $384K a month to produce the orders. These expenses had to be paid well before the revenues came in. In other words, WorkHorse had a massive working capital problem.

The first column of the table below illustrates this. The company experienced an average delay of 90 days between shipping the goods to the retailer and getting paid for them. This reflected the fact that retailers held the goods in store while being sold, and the fact that they never seemed to be in a hurry to pay their bills. It implied that WorkHorse would have account receivables of three times its monthly revenues, a whopping $3M. The average time WorkHorse held inventory was 60 days, reflecting the fact that it still had an inefficient distribution system. This implied inventory of two times the cost of goods sold, which amounted to $768K per month. WorkHorse's average time to pay its own suppliers was 15 days, implying account payables of half a month's cost of goods sold, or $192K. The net working capital requirement thus came out at just over $3.5M. This is why Brandon panicked.

	Working capital	Factoring	Trade credit	Line of credit
Units sold	3,025	3,025	3,025	3,025
Revenues per unit ($)	330.6	330.6	330.6	330.6
Revenues ($)	1,000,000	920,000	1,000,000	1,000,000
COGS per unit ($)	127.0	127.0	129.6	127.0
COGS ($)	384,150	384,150	391,990	384,150
Revenue collection (days)	90	90 or 0	90	90
Inventories (days)	60	60	60	60
Supplier collection (days)	15	15	60	15
Account receivables ($)	3,000,000	600,000	3,000,000	3,000,000
Inventories ($)	768,300	768,300	783,980	768,300
Account payables ($)	192,075	192,075	783,980	192,075
Net working capital ($)	3,576,225	1,176,225	3,000,000	3,576,225

Brandon contacted several factor companies. Within a few days he received an offer from "FunFactor," to take 80% of WorkHorse's bills and pay 90 cents on the dollar, with full recourse in case of customer defaults. The 'Factoring' column shows how this would affect Workhorse's working capital. Of the $1M in monthly revenues, WorkHorse would sell $800K worth of invoices to the factor company, and get $720K right away. The remaining $200K would still be cashed in after 90 days. Monthly revenues would thus be $920K,reflecting the cost of factoring. Account receivables would plummet from $3M to $600K— three months' worth of the $200K that would not be factored. Net working capital would go down to $1.17M. Brandon thought he saw the light at the end of the tunnel.

Annie failed to see the fun in the FunFactor offer and strongly resented giving up $80K a month. Using Table 10.3, she noted that getting 90 extra days by giving up a 10% discount implied a cost of capital of 53.3%. She suggested instead that WorkHorse stretch its average supplier payment to 60 days, by giving up average discounts of 2%. The :Trade credit' column of the table above shows the implications of this solution. Cost of goods sold increase to $129.59 (= $127/0.98), reflecting the loss of 2% discounts. Account payables would rise to 783K, the same level of inventories (both of which take 60 days). The company would now have a net working capital of $3M. Using Table 10.3, Anne's trade credit proposal would give the company 45 additional days, at a price of giving up a 2% discount, implying a cost of capital of 17.8%.

Astrid thought they could do even better. She called Wolf C. Flow, who had many connections in the financial sector. Although he couldn't find any bank to offer the company a line of credit, he pulled a favor with one of his other investments, a firm that specialized in credit products for privately held companies. They offered a $2M line of credit at an annual interest rate of 15%. This implied a monthly interest rate of 1.17%, which would result in monthly interest payments of $23.430 if fully drawn. The credit line was thus the cheapest source of working capital finance for WorkHorse. Michael consider it lucky the company got the offer in the first place: "Without connections like Wolf's, no one would even look at a fledgling start-up like ours."

Annie agreed but questioned whether a $2M line of credit would be enough, given that the working capital requirement was over $3.5M. In response, Bharat produced the table below. It modeled the payments to suppliers and the receipts from customers over the coming months (all sums in dollars). He noted that after one month the company would have to pay half a month's supplier bills, and thereafter it would pay a full month of supplier bills every month (for bills that were always 15 days old on average). On the revenue side, because of 60 days in inventory and 90 days of waiting for invoices, the first revenues of $1M would only materialize after five months. After that, however, there would be $1M in revenues every month (always pertaining to goods originally added to inventory five months ago). The third column reflected the net balance of these two cash flows. Note that this differs from the company's cash flow because it excluded all other expenses. All numbers in the table are in dollars.

Month	Supplier payments	Customer receipts	Balance
1	192,075	0	0
2	384,150	0	−384,150
3	384,150	0	−768,300
4	384,150	0	−1,152,450
5	384,150	1,000,000	−536,600
6	384,150	1,000,000	79,250

Month	Supplier payments	Customer receipts	Balance
7	384,150	1,000,000	695,100
8	384,150	1,000,000	1,310,950
9	384,150	1,000,000	1,926,800
10	384,150	1,000,000	2,542,650

Bharat's main point was that, once the company became profitable, it would be able to bear its working capital requirements. Indeed, after five months the company would regularly receive $1M in revenues, which was considerably higher than the cost of goods sold. However, in the first four months the company needed over $1.15M just to pay its suppliers. This argument convinced Annie that a credit line of $2M would give the company enough room to cope with its working capital needs. The four founders therefore accepted the credit line. It felt like they had come out of the tunnel and were back in the bright daylight.

10.4.4 Venture Leasing

Venture leasing is a form of credit where the lender ("lessor") buys one or more assets and provides the borrower ("lessee") with the right to use them. Leasing is effectively a form of asset-based credit that provides the lender with strong protection through asset ownership. The lender grants use of the asset to the company, in return for predefined lease payments. Typically, the company also has the right to purchase the asset after a certain time. Contracts mostly range from 24 to 48 months, depending on the nature of the asset.

The lease payment is typically monthly, and each installment includes amortization of the loan, that is, repayment of a fraction of the principal. A final balloon repayment covers the remaining value of the principal, usually about 20 to 25% of the principal. The lower the monthly lease, the higher the final payment. At maturity, the lessee typically has the option of purchasing the asset at its residual value. Depending on the nature of the lease and on market conditions, the interest charged is typically 8 to 12% above prime.

Unlike the case with traditional leasing, with venture leasing the lessor typically gets some warrants to buy preferred stock of the lessee. The number of warrants is expressed as the warrant coverage, a percentage of the lease value. For example, a typical contract may specify an 8% coverage. For a lease of $1M this means that the lessor can purchase $80K of preferred stock at the price of the previous round, with the warrant expiring only after five years or so. The warrant coverage tends to fall in the 5 to 10% range.

Lessors are typically either banks or specialized corporate leasing companies. There are also some venture lending funds, run by partners with financial industry experience and strong ties to the venture capital (VC) community. Venture leasing requires assessing the quality of entrepreneurial ventures itself, as well as their backing from investors. This is why venture leasing requires more specialized skills than traditional leasing.

The main difference between an asset-based loan and a lease arrangement concerns the ownership of the asset. In the former case, the company owns the asset but pledges it as collateral, in the latter, the lender owns the asset until it is bought out with a final payment. From the lender's perspective, owning the asset might be safer than recovering the asset as collateral in case of default. From a company perspective, the fixed cost of purchasing an asset is replaced by a variable cost of making lease payments. Even if the terms of the lease might be unattractive for more established companies, venture leasing may be attractive for cash-poor start-ups.

10.4.5 Venture Debt

Venture debt (henceforth VD) is a form of secured lending to start-ups that was pioneered in the 1980s by Silicon Valley Bank and other innovative financial companies such as Equitec and Western Technology Investments. They developed a set of practices to lend to technology start-ups, initially in the semiconductor industry. Over time VD has been used by numerous entrepreneurial ventures, including household names like Facebook, Uber, Google, and Spotify.[27]

VD is typically not available to companies at the start-up stage, but it becomes relevant when companies enter the scale-up phase, once they have a proven business model and their core challenge is to grow market share.[28] In practice, VD is only offered to companies after a Series A, and more often in conjuncture with a later equity round (Series B and later).

Three key factors make VD viable.[29] First, the lender's key risk is not the venture's business risk but rather the risk that there will be another round of venture funding that will keep the company going. Second, venture lenders charge relatively high interest rates, which rewards them for the risk taken. On top of these, lenders obtain some warrants that generate additional returns if and when the company has a successful exit. Third, the lender obtains strong contractual rights, including strong loan covenants.

What are the typical conditions associated with venture debt? The lender recovers the loan partly from periodical payments of interest and principal, and partly from a final payment that can be financed by the venture's subsequent round of VC. The maturity of VD is typically set after the expected date of the next funding round. A typical loan facility lasts anywhere from one to four years. Interest rates depend on market conditions but are often in a range of 10 to 15% above prime. If the loan is repaid early, a two-week notice is required, and a pre-payment premium between 3 and 5% is not uncommon. In case of a default, the interest rate also increases by 3 to 5%. In addition, VD typically gives the lender some warrants, that is, the right to buy company shares. The warrant "coverage" is often above 10% of the loan value. It gives the lender the right to buy preferred stock for the corresponding amount at the last equity round's price. The warrant expiration may be at seven years or more.

Typically, all the assets of the company are used for collateral. The lender may also impose negative pledges on intellectual property, barring the company from selling or licensing it without the lender's permission. The VD contract sometimes includes performance covenants through which the lender has the right to call in the loan if certain business milestones are not met. There may also be financial covenants that require the company to maintain certain financial ratios. An example would be an "interest coverage ratio," which measures the company's ability to continue meeting its interest payments. Such financial covenants, however, are somewhat less common in earlier-stage ventures where financials remain highly unpredictable. Typically, VD contracts also contain several clauses that allow the lender to call in the loan, that is, treat the loan as if it was in default. "Material Adverse Change" clauses tend to be broad, even vague, but they allow the lender to call in the loan whenever the company's business environment undergoes significant changes. Along similar lines, there can be clauses that allow the lender to call in the loan, such as if the equity investors are abandoning the company, or if there has been a change in the management team. Lenders routinely ask the company to be the bank that handles their day-to-day business transactions. Finally, there can be clauses that specify whether or not the lender can reassign the loan to other lenders.

With this understanding of the basic structure of VD contracts, Table 10.4 compares the structure of VD with that of venture leasing and with standard lines of credit.

Venture lenders can be specialized banks like Silicon Valley Bank or mainstream banks like Barclays in the UK. Alternatively, they can be specialized VD funds, like Columbia Lake Partners or Kreos. VD funds operate with a partnership model similar to that of VC firms (see Chapter 12). By and large, banks tend to offer relatively cheaper loans, but with tighter covenants than VD funds. The due diligence on VD lenders has two components. First, they evaluate the strength of the company. For this they may free ride on the certification provided by the equity investors. In practice, most VD lenders work closely with a limited number of top-notch VC firms. Second, VD lenders carefully evaluate the behavior of the equity investors. Particular attention is paid not only to the overall performance record

Table 10.4 Comparing Debt Structures for Entrepreneurial Companies

	Venture debt	Venture leasing	Credit line
Dilution	Small, arising from warrants	Small, arising from warrants	None
Warrants	10–15% of venture debt value	5–10% of lease value	None
Amount	20–60% of last venture round	Based on leased equipment value	Varies
Maturity	12–48 months	12–24 months	Varies, commonly extended
Interest rate (real)	10–15%	8–12%	5–10%
Repayment	Monthly amortized installments and final payment	Monthly amortized installments, option to buy out asset at end of lease	Amortized installments, at maturity either extended or balloon payment
Covenants	Mostly performance related	Mostly performance related	Mostly financial
Collateral	Blanket lien on all assets	Owned by lessor	Varies

of the VC firm, but more specifically to its dynamic strategy of supporting companies over time, as discussed in Section 9.5.1. A key concern of the VD lenders is how much equity investors are willing to support struggling companies through difficult times.

VD is a relatively new phenomenon that has rarely been studied systematically. Box 10.5 reports some first findings from two recent academic studies.

Box 10.5 Show Me the Patent!

One academic study by Tykvova uses a large database on VC-backed companies and looks at the likelihood that these companies raise VD.[30] It estimates that over the period 1995–2013, 16% of companies' funding came from venture debt as opposed to equity from VCs. The time trend is increasing, with fractions over 20% since 2009. The study finds that older and less risky companies are significantly more likely to raise VD. In addition, companies with VD tend to have backing from VCs with higher reputations. The paper argues that VD is a way for good companies to signal their maturity and strength.

A second study, by Hochberg, Serrano, and Ziedonis, looks at a subsegment of the VD market using the specific lens of patents.[31] If a venture debt contract puts a blanket lien on a U.S. company's assets, the lender has an interest in registering any patent-related liens with the U.S. Patent Office. Patent data are therefore a backdoor to studying venture debt. Among U.S. start-ups with patents, an impressive 36% secured a venture loan at some point. VD deals are more likely in sectors where their patents are traded more regularly.

Patents alone are not enough to attract VD; companies also need equity investors, typically VCs. They can start raising VD after their first VC round (Series A). The probability of raising VD financing increases over time, increasing every time a company raises another VC round. Having committed VC investors is crucial. For example, the study finds that start-ups were more likely to obtain a venture loan when they were backed by VC firms that had recently raised a fund. The reason is that at the beginning of their fund cycle, VCs are more likely to keep funding companies' future rounds, something that becomes increasingly difficult toward the end of the fund cycle. The study suggests that instead of thinking of venture debt as an alternative to equity financing, it should really be regarded as a complement. That is, VD is mainly used to augment the funding received from VC investors.[32]

In Section 10.2, we explain the Modigliani–Miller theorem and emphasize the importance of carefully comparing the true cost of debt and equity. VD looks attractive in terms of being largely nondilutive (except for warrants), but one needs to properly understand all the cost involved. In practice, VD is often used as a way of delaying future equity rounds. This is called "extending the cash runway" to achieve the next milestone. Box 10.6 provides an example of how to evaluate the full financial costs of VD.

Box 10.6 Evaluating Venture Debt

KorPho was a (fictional) Korean start-up that had discovered a new ingredient which sped up the fermentation of kimchi, a popular local food item. Its two founders, Seo-yun Park and Min-yun Hong, had met during their studies at KAIST. They founded the company two weeks after graduation and one week after getting married to each other. Their company grew rapidly and raised two rounds of VC financing. After a B round with a $2 share price (all values are expressed in U.S. dollars), the company had 20M outstanding shares and was thus valued at $40M post-money. The company had $4M in cash, with a monthly burn rate (i.e., negative cash flow) of $0.3M. They thus had 13⅓ months before running out of cash. They were keen to extend their runway (i.e., the time before running out of cash) before raising the next round. They thought that, with a bit more time, they could hit another business milestone that would further lift their valuation. Consequently, they decided to look for VD.

After being rejected by all local banks, they were introduced to Din Khatar (or DK in short), the manager of a (fictional) Middle Eastern investment fund who offered a $4M loan with a duration of 48 months from the date of closing. However, the loan would only be drawn down six months after closing. The interest rate was 10% per year, paid by monthly installments. Interest payments would be starting six months after the drawdown date and would last 36 months until the loan maturity date. While there were no fees, DK asked for a warranty coverage of 10% at the price of the B round. This meant that DK could buy up to $0.4M (= 0.1*$4M) worth of shares at $2 per share, or up to 0.2M shares.

Min-yun excitedly said that they should accept the offer. With a .3M monthly burn rate, the $4M loan would give the company an additional 13⅓ months of runway. Seo-yun pulled out her laptop to work it out properly. Her spreadsheet can be found on the books' website (www.entrepreneurialfinance.net). She noted that after drawing down the loan, KorPho would need to repay the principal at a constant rate of $4M/36 = $0.11M per month. In addition, it would need to pay interest on the remaining principal. The interest payment would initially be $33K (= $4M*0.1/12), and would decrease over time. Taking the repayments of principal and interest into account, her spreadsheet showed that DK's offer would give the company an additional six months of runway. Min-yun was surprised and looked more carefully at the numbers. After 20 months, the company would already have repaid over half (i.e., over $2M) of the loan. Over the entire life of the loan, the company would have to pay $0.62M in interest and thus pay back a total $4.62M, which amounted to 115% of the loan amount. Disenchanted with the terms of the VD, they considered making a counter-offer.

Seo-yun proposed delaying the drawdown date to 12 months after the closing, noting that the company didn't really need to borrow for the first year. Her proposal would keep the overall interest payments at $0.62M. To her surprise, the spreadsheet showed that this would only add two months to the company's runway. Min-yun suggested delaying the repayment of principal to the end, that is, making one final balloon payment of $4M at the end of the loan period. This implied that the interest payment would stay at $33K for the entire loan period. The spreadsheet showed that this would extend the runway by five months. A disadvantage, however, was that total interest payments would now amount to $1.2M. Total repayments would thus amount to $5.2M, or 130% of the loan amount. Unfortunately, DK wouldn't hear any of it, saying that its offer was final and asking the company to make a decision.

The two founders therefore asked themselves whether or not the deal was worth it. They turned their attention to what the true cost of the warrants might be. Clearly, they would only be valuable in case of a successful exit. A friend of theirs knew a lot of advanced finance and argued that (using standard assumptions and the Black–Scholes option pricing formula, explained in the spreadsheet), the warrants would be worth approximately $0.3M. As an approximation of the total cost of VD (and ignoring any time discounting), the founders added \$0.3M of warrant costs to \$0.62M of total interest payments, suggesting a total cost of \$0.92M. The founders began to wonder whether taking the VD was really worth it. It all depended on what it would do for the company?

The company wanted to buy time for hitting the additional milestone before raising its next equity round. The founder thought of raising \$20M in the next round. In the absence of hitting the additional milestone, they expected the next round to reach a post-money valuation of \$80M, but with the milestone it would reach \$100M. At the lower valuation, the current shareholders would be diluted by 25% (i.e., \$20M/\$80M); at the higher valuation they would be diluted by 20% (i.e., \$20M/\$100M). The founders thus approximated the benefits of the higher valuation as 5% less dilution. At a valuation of \$100M, this was worth \$5M (= 0.05*\$100M). They knew that without the VD they would not be able to hit the additional milestone. If the VD allowed them to hit it for sure, their rough calculations suggested that it would generate a gain of \$5M, at a cost of \$0.92M. Even if it only increased their chances of hitting the milestone by 20%, it would still be worth it. Thus, they accepted DK's offer. They hit their milestone in time, raised their next round at a valuation \$100M, and threw a party involving copious amounts of kimchi.

10.5 Valuation with Debt

10.5.1 Enterprise versus Equity Value

The valuation models we discuss in Chapter 6 consider equity-only financing for companies that do not have any debt. In this section, we discuss how they can be modified to take debt into account. The question of how to value leveraged companies is central to corporate finance. Much of the debate focuses on how to account for taxes and risk. However, we have already noted that the debt tax shield is of secondary importance to most entrepreneurial ventures. As for risk, in Chapter 6 we argue that finding suitable risk discount factors for start-ups is difficult and somewhat arbitrary. Combining this with the fact that most start-ups have relatively little debt means that typically valuations simply ignore debt. Still, debt may become important for later-stage, larger ventures. Sophisticated investors therefore might want to check how its inclusion might impact valuation models.

In this section, we explain how the valuation methods for entrepreneurial companies discussed in Chapter 6 can be extended to account for debt. For leveraged established companies, there are several standard corporate finance valuation models. These include the use of the WACC (weighted average cost of capital) in the

DCF (Discounted Cash Flow) model, the APV (adjusted present value) model, and the leveraged Capital Asset Pricing Model (Box 5.1).[33]

Central to the valuation models with debt is the distinction between enterprise value and equity value. Enterprise value is the sum of the equity and debt value, that is:

$$\text{Enterprise value} = \text{Equity value} + \text{Debt value}$$

In the example of Box 10.3, for example, we encountered a post-money valuation that excluded debt, which we can think of as the equity value, and a post-money valuation that included debt, which we can think of as the enterprise value. According to the Modigliani–Miller theorem (Box 10.2), in a frictionless world, once debt and equity are priced correctly, the enterprise value remains constant, whereas the equity value varies depending on the relative share of debt and equity.

10.5.2 Adjusting Valuation Methods for Debt

A valuation method that estimates enterprise values is based on the assumption that debt and equity investors ultimately get the same risk-adjusted return. There are three ways to achieve this. One is to modify the VC method (VCM), which we examine in Section 5. The other two are approaches from standard corporate finance.

The VCM starts with an estimate of the exit value. This requires the use of exit comparables based on the values from comparable IPOs or acquisitions (Section 5.4). These can be used for estimating either enterprise or equity values, depending on which comparable metric is being used. If a metric characterizes properties of the enterprise as a whole, then it should be used for enterprise valuation; if it characterizes an equity-based multiple, then it should be used for equity valuation. To see how this works, consider three common comparison metrics: sales, EBIT, and net earnings. The first two measures focus on enterprise performance and should therefore be used to estimate enterprise value. The volume of sales depends on the enterprise as a whole and should be largely independent of the amount of debt. EBIT, and EBITDA for that matter, excludes interest and taxes. This allows us to consider the enterprise value without any leverage effects. Instead, net earnings are directly linked to the compensation of the equity holders and therefore are better suited for estimating equity values. For the VCM, the exit value is thus calculated by using either the enterprise or exit value of the comparable companies, employing the appropriate multiplier (sales or EBIT, or net earnings), and applying it to the company's financial projections. This generates an estimate of the exit value, expressed either as an enterprise or as an equity value. The use of comparable companies with similar levels of debt makes the comparison more convincing.

The two standard corporate finance ways to account for debt are the APV and the WACC. With APV one first estimates the enterprise value for an unlevered version of the company, assuming that the company is all equity financed, and then estimates the value of the tax shield. These estimations are usually done with a DCF approach. The tax shield is often negligible for start-ups but may become material for later-stage companies. The second way to include debt in valuation consists of discounting cash flows in the DFC model using a discount rate that reflects the mix of debt and equity and weighting their respective costs of capital. This is the WACC approach.

The discount rates used for these calculations should reflect relevant risks: the enterprise-level cash flow risk when estimating enterprise value, and the equity-level cash flow risk when estimating equity value. The latter should be higher than the former, reflecting the additional risk from leverage. Corporate finance books explain in detail how to adjust betas and discount rates to account for leverage.[34] In our context, this is probably less important, since there are no precise ways to determine what the discount rates should be in the first place, as discussed in Section 5.2.3.

Overall, we refrain from advocating one method over the other. We believe that the enterprise model works better under some circumstances and the equity value model works better under others. For moderate amounts of debt, it might be practically easier to use simple assumptions about debt and then focus on estimating the equity value. However, once a company raises a substantial amount of debt, it might be more challenging to find appropriate assumptions about the cost of debt. In this case it might be better to estimate enterprise values, where the cost of debt is automatically generated within the model.

WorkHorse Box 10.3 illustrates how our valuation models can be augmented with debt.

WorkHorse Box 10.3 Valuation with Debt

Nothing relaxed Brandon more on a Friday evening than sitting in his favorite armchair and reading a good entrepreneurial finance book. While reading a fascinating chapter about debt financing, he realized that back in 2021, his valuation methods for the A round had not accounted for debt. He became curious to see how debt would change his valuations models. Not that it mattered anymore, but this was his way of relaxing and having fun. So, Brandon pulled up his laptop and made the following additional calculations, extending those from WorkHorse Box 5.5.

	BieBie	FergieTech	Noodles	UniCorNio	Zellie	Median	WH enterprise value at exit ($M)	WH debt value ($M)	WH equity value at exit ($M)
Equity value at exit ($M)	40	15	150	15	12	15.0			
Enterprise value at exit ($M)	55	15	180	18	14	18.0			
Revenues at exit ($M)	30	12	12	10	15	12.0			
Revenue multiple using enterprise value	1.8	1.3	15.0	1.8	0.9	1.8	38.0	6.3	31.7
Debt-equity ratio at exit	38%	0%	20%	20%	17%	20%			

Starting to feel nicely relaxed, Brandon looked up enterprise values for comparable companies and added them to the table. He then added revenue multiples using enterprise values. The median multiple was 1.8. Brandon also computed the debt to equity ratio for comparable companies. The median was 20%, so he used that assumption. Assuming revenues of $21.1M at the time of exit (see WorkHorse Box 3.3), he calculated enterprise, debt, and equity values, as shown in the last three columns of the table above.

Brandon was particularly eager to find out what pre- and post-money valuations these comparables implied. Specifically, he used the (single-period) VCM with enterprise versus equity exit values. His results are shown in the following table.

VC Model with debt	Equity value	Enterprise value	Enterprise value
Equity investment ($)	2,500,000	2,500,000	2,500,000
Debt investment ($)		1,000,000	1,000,000
Total investment ($)	2,500,000	3,500,000	3,500,000
Time to next round/exit (years)	5	5	5
Discount rate	50%	50%	45%
Estimated exit value at exit ($)	31,700,000	38,000,000	38,000,000
Post-money valuation (incl. debt, $)		5,004,115	5,928,483
Pre-money valuation (incl. debt, $)		1,504,115	2,428,483
Post-money valuation (excl. debt, $)	4,174,486	4,004,115	4,928,483
Pre-money valuation (excl. debt, $)	1,674,486	504,115	1,428,483
Founders' ownership	32.1%	13.4%	29.1%
Stock option pool's ownership	8.0%	3.4%	7.3%
First round investors' ownership	59.9%	83.2%	63.6%

The first row shows a valuation based on the equity value, the second on enterprise value. He used the two different exit values derived above from the analysis of exit comparables. In addition, he used different investment amounts. In the first column, only the equity investments were used, Brandon assumed the usual $2.5M. In the second column he added debt investments, where he assumed that the company would raise $1M of debt.

The VCM model with debt generated two different types of pre- and post-money valuations, one including and one excluding debt. Brandon noted with great satisfaction that his original equity-based method yielded a higher valuation than the enterprise-based method. Intuitively, the new enterprise-based valuation came out lower because the debt needed to be priced at a high discount rate. Indeed, the model suggested that debt would be very expensive and would thus bring down the equity valuation.

Brandon realized that using the same discount rate for equity and enterprise values was not entirely correct. In the third column, he used a lower discount rate of 45% (instead of 50%), to reflect the idea that enterprise values should be less risky than equity values. This brought ownership shares, and the pre-money valuation without debt, back to similar levels as in column 1. This reassured him that adding debt to the model did not entirely upend his prior estimates. What a great Friday evening, doing all these calculations was so much fun and so relaxing!

Summary

This chapter studies how entrepreneurial ventures can make use of debt financing. We explain the fundamental features of debt contracts. We debunk the common fallacy that debt is cheaper than equity, and we provide a framework for assessing the relative strengths of these two forms of finance. The chapter explains why banks rarely lend to entrepreneurs. It then proceeds to explore numerous other forms of debt, including personal credit, trade credit, discounting, factoring, venture leasing, venture debt, and peer-to-peer lending. For each type, we explain who the lenders are and how entrepreneurs go about raising debt. The chapter finally examines how debt affects valuation models, introducing the distinction between equity values and enterprise values.

In terms of the FIRE framework (Chapter 1), debt takes place at the second step, INVESTMENT. We note that debt can play different roles at different stages of the company development cycle. In the early days of a venture, personal loans and some nonbank forms of debt, such as trade credit or factoring, can be useful sources of funding. In the later stages, venture leasing and venture debt become more important.

Review Questions

1. What are the main components of a debt contract? What alternative structures exist?
2. What is collateral? What assets are suitable for collateral?
3. The Modigliani–Miller theorem claims that debt and equity are equally costly. Is this true in reality?
4. Why do most banks hesitate to lend to start-ups?
5. How can one infer the true cost of trade credit?

6. What is the difference between discounting and factoring?
7. How does venture leasing differ from traditional leasing?
8. Does venture debt substitute or complement equity capital?
9. What is the difference between enterprise and equity value?
10. How can one adjust the venture capital valuation method to account for debt?

Notes

1. Stewart (2015) is an accessible practical guide to bank loans.
2. What matters for borrowers is the real interest rate, that is, the nominal interest rate net of the inflation rate.
3. Bradley and Roberts (2015) examine loan covenants.
4. https://www.nobelprize.org/prizes/economic-sciences/1985/press-release.
5. https://www.nobelprize.org/prizes/economic-sciences/1990/press-release.
6. https://www.nobelprize.org/prizes/economic-sciences/2001/press-release.
7. Modigliani and Miller (1958).
8. Stiglitz and Weiss (1981), Berger and Udell (1992), and Petersen and Rajan (1994).
9. Fabozzi and Drake (2008), and Myers (2001). The interested reader is referred to corporate finance textbooks, such as Berk and DeMarzo (2016), Brealey, Myers, and Allen (2016), or Welch (2017).
10. Auerbach (2002) and Graham (2008).
11. Exceptions worth noting are "loss carry forward" provisions that preserve tax deductions for several years in the future. They make the debt tax shield more relevant for later-stage ventures that experience large losses before approaching profitability.
12. Federal Reserve Bank of New York (2017).
13. Also Bruno, D'Onfrio, and Marino (2017).
14. Cameron (1967) and Gerschenkron (1962).
15. Chlepner (1943).
16. Cameron (1967, p. 145).
17. Da Rin and Hellmann (2002).
18. Berger (2014).
19. Robb and Robinson (2014).
20. The real interest rate is the difference from the nominal interest rate and the inflation rate.
21. Lawless and Warren (2005).
22. Chatterji and Seamans (2012).
23. Milne and Parboteeah (2016).
24. Cuñat and García-Appendini (2012).
25. The company can also discount its inventory, but in this case the discount may be as large as 50%, reflecting the risk that the goods will not be sold.
26. Dorfleitner, Rad, and Weber (2017).
27. For a practical introduction to venture debt, see the following blog post by Derek Ridgley, available at: https://www.svb.com/blogs/derek-ridgley/extend-your-startups-runway-how-venture-debt-works, accessed April 15, 2019. See also Feinstein and Netterfield (2015).
28. Tykvova (2017).
29. Ibrahim (2010).

30. Tykvova (2017).
31. Hochberg, Serrano, and Ziedonis (2018).
32. de Rassenfosse and Fischer (2016) is a closely related study.
33. Berk and DeMarzo (2016), Brealey, Myers and Allen (2016), or Welch (2017).
34. Chapter 9 in Damodaran (2018) and Chapter 23 in Koller, Goedhart, and Wessels (2015).

11
Exit

Learning Goals

In this chapter students will learn:

1. Why and when investors exit their companies.
2. How to structure the process of taking a company public, selling it to a corporate or financial buyer, or closing it down.
3. To analyze how exiting affects the founders and the development of the company.
4. About the company characteristics, market forces, and investor preferences that affect the type and timing of exit.

This chapter examines how investors exit their companies, obtain liquidity, and realize a return. We start by examining why investors seek an exit in the first place. We then discuss the four most common types of exit: (1) listing the company on a stock market through an Initial Public Offering (IPO); (2) selling the company to another operating company through an acquisition; (3) selling the company to a financial buyer; or (4) closing the company down. For each exit type, we describe the necessary preparations, the structuring and execution, and the consequences for the founders, the investors, and the company itself. We end the chapter by proposing a framework for understanding which type of exit is most suitable for which company, and when.

11.1 The Importance of Exiting Investments

Every investment eventually comes to a conclusion, successful or not. Exiting constitutes the final step of the investment cycle, which allows investors to obtain liquidity. This provides the investors with the returns that motivate the investment in the first place.[1] The company continues to operate under new owners or is closed down.

11.1.1 Reasons for Exit

The main reason for exit is that investors want to realize a return on the funds they invested in the company. This should dispel a common misconception that exit is driven by the company's need to raise money for investment. When investors sell their shares to another party, the money flows to the investors, not to the company. If a company needs further capital, it can look for additional funding in ways we describe in Chapter 9. Admittedly, companies do also raise some money in an Initial Public Offering (IPO), so in this particular case there can be a concurrence of two rationales: the company wants to raise money, and the investors want to sell their shares, either at or after the IPO.

An important feature of entrepreneurial companies is that their shares are illiquid assets. This means that it is difficult for a shareholder to find, in a short period of time, a buyer willing to pay a price that is close to what may be considered a fair market price.[2] In liquid markets, such as commodity or stock exchanges, there are plenty of sellers and buyers who provide liquidity. For privately held companies, however, this is not the case, in large part because of the lack of reliable information to compute a company's fair value.[3] Therefore, investors cannot expect to quickly sell their shares at a fair price. Instead, they actively work with the company to find a buyer in what is called an "exit event" or "liquidity event."

Investors want liquidity for a variety of reasons. Venture capitalists (VCs) need to liquidate portfolio companies at some point because they invest through fund vehicles. After 10 years, they need to return money to their institutional investors (Section 12.1). VCs often hold the contractual power to press a company to list on the stock market or find a buyer so that they can dispose of their investment (Section 6.4.3). Angel investors also want to get back their funds in order to make new investments, especially since their comparative advantage for adding value is at the earlier stages (Section 13.2). They may also want to exit to lock in capital gains before they get diluted by pay-to-play clauses (Section 6.4). Family and friends experience foreseeable liquidity needs (e.g., a child's college tuition), or unforeseeable liquidity "shocks" (e.g., a medical emergency). Accelerators and other early-stage investors, which often have small stakes in the company, may also be eager to cash in, to fund their ongoing activities. Therefore, even though these investors have long horizons, they all reach a point where they want returns from their investment.

As long as investors are actively engaged with the company to provide support, there is a clear rationale for holding equity (Section 8.3). The investors' involvement increases company value, and holding equity gives the investors an incentive to do so. However, the ability to add value to the company tends to diminish over time. For example, an angel investor may have expertise at the start-up stage, but once the company has moved beyond that stage, he may no longer add value, merely biding his time for a chance to sell his shares. At this stage, it would be economically more efficient to sell his equity to some other investor who can add value, for example, by helping to commercialize the company's product.

Another important reason for seeking an exit arises when the current ownership limits a company's business expansion, thus requiring a change in ownership structure. As a start-up grows, it may need access to additional strategic assets that it can only get from specific new owners, be they corporate or financial buyers. For example, a company may need access to customers, distribution channels, production facilities, intellectual property, talent, or other key resources that it can obtain easily by being acquired by another company, typically a large established industry incumbent. Or the company may need investors with different value-adding capabilities than the current ones (Section 8.3), which can be achieved through a sale to a financial buyer. In both cases, the investors can sell their shares and obtain a higher return than if they hold on to them.

Market appetite for entrepreneurial companies fluctuates, and smart investors manage to maximize their returns by properly timing the exit. This is most evident in the case of IPOs, where savvy investors may be able to time the market and take the company public when market valuations peak.[4] Market timing can be equally valuable with acquisitions, striking a deal at a time when the buyers' appetite is greatest. There is also a dark side to the timing of exits: some investors exploit unfavorable insider information about the company's prospects. If they decide to sell their shares, it might just be that the company is overvalued. This can undermine the exit process if buyers get concerned that sellers have such unfavorable information about the company. This is the classical "lemons" problem that we first encountered in Box 2.6. This kind of adverse selection problem can further contribute to the illiquidity of the shares of entrepreneurial companies.

11.1.2 The Four Main Types of Exit

We consider four main types of exit: IPO, acquisition, sale to a financial buyer, and failure. We begin by defining them in this section, and in Sections 11.2–11.5 we analyze their structure and how each exit type affects the investors, the entrepreneurs, and the company itself.

The first type of exit, going public, is often considered the most prestigious and profitable. It means listing company shares on a stock exchange, allowing investors to get a return on their investments by selling their shares to the public. The management team often remains in place. Founders and managers can also obtain liquidity by selling part of their shares. The company remains an independent organization, although becoming a public company has important managerial and financial implications.[5]

The second type of exit is getting acquired by a corporation. In this case, the startup ceases to be an independent company and becomes a unit of the acquiring company. Investors get a return by selling their shares to the acquirer, in exchange for either cash or shares. The management team typically stays the time necessary to ensure a smooth transition but may well disperse thereafter.

The third type of exit is a sale to a financial buyer. The sale can be partial, consisting of the holding of only one or several investors, or full, consisting of the holdings of all shareholders. When the exit is partial, it is called a secondary sale, when it is full it is called a buyout. In both cases, the company remains an independent and privately held organization. Investors get a return on their investments by selling their shares to the financial buyer. The management team typically stays in place, except in the case of a management buy-in where a new management team takes over.

The fourth type of exit is failure, which means closing down the business. If the company has any outstanding debt, it may have to declare bankruptcy. Otherwise it merely sells its remaining assets and ceases operations.

Table 11.1 reports data on exits of VC-backed companies and their value in the U.S. and Europe.

By far, acquisitions are the most common exit route, accounting for over three quarters of all exits. IPOs, by contrast, account for less than 10% and are also less common than financial sales. The data on exit values show that, in the U.S., the total value of IPOs is approximately the same as that of acquisitions. Given that there are much fewer IPOs than acquisitions, this means that the average exit value is significantly higher for IPOs than for acquisitions. IPO values in Europe, however, are considerably smaller. The value of financial sales is the smallest of the three, in both the U.S. and Europe; this also reflects the fact that they occur at an earlier stage of company development than IPOs or acquisitions.

This data does not include closures. Closures are difficult to obtain because they are rarely announced. A study by the National Venture Capital Association (NVCA) found that up to 53% of all U.S. venture-backed companies result in failure.[6] Academic research on U.S. VC investments by Hall and Woodward for the period 1987–2008 suggests that companies exited in the following proportions: 13% did an IPO, 37% were acquired, and 50% failed.[7]

Table 11.1 Exits of Venture Capital-Backed Companies.

	US		Europe	
	Annual exit count	(%)	Annual exit count	(%)
IPOs	56	7%	39	10%
Acquisitions	652	81%	284	76%
Financial sales	94	12%	53	14%
	Annual exit value ($B)	(%)	Annual exit value (€B)	(%)
IPOs	33.0	48%	1.2	15%
Acquisitions	33.8	49%	6.4	78%
Financial sales	2.6	4%	0.5	7%

Data Source: National Venture Capital Association (NVCA) and Invest Europe, 2008–2017.
Financial Sales are called buyouts by the NVCA.

A survey of VCs by Gompers, Gornall, Kaplan, and Stebulaev asked investors about the drivers of success and of failure.[8] Probably the most important insight from the data is how similar the drivers of success and failure are: investors consider the team the key driver in 96% of successes and in 92% of failures. Similarly, investors considered the business model a key driver of 60% of successes and 57% of failures.

Why is failure a hallmark of entrepreneurial ventures? Box 11.1 provides a view from the perspective of experimental psychology.

Box 11.1 Why Do Start-Ups Fail?

There are two views about whether entrepreneurial attitudes matter for success or failure. The "rational" view is that entrepreneurs make good decisions but still fail often because of the many inherent risks of experimentation (Box 1.1). The "behavioral" view is that failure is instead driven by overconfident entrepreneurs who overestimate their chances of success: too many entrepreneurs enter new markets, and consequently many fail.

Experimental psychologists use lab settings and typically invite university students to play carefully constructed experimental games that replicate the real-world setting. A study by Artinger and Powell focuses on the entrepreneurial failure puzzle.[9] They ask whether entrepreneurial opportunities are particularly prone to overconfidence. This would help to explain the high failure rates of start-ups.

The researchers constructed experimental games that emulate market-entry decisions. To distinguish rational from behavioral action, the authors note that rational action should result in a symmetric pattern of either too many or too few companies entering a new market, depending on the market situation. Overconfidence, however, should always lead to excess entry—that is, too many companies entering compared to how many could survive in a competitive market. Next, the researchers characterize markets by two attributes, size and uncertainty, and define entrepreneurial markets as small markets with high uncertainty. The core finding is that entrepreneurial markets have more excess entry than other markets. Excess capacity reaches 250% in entrepreneurial markets and averages 36% in other markets. Moreover, while the experimental subjects made profits in the majority of market settings, they experienced significant losses in entrepreneurial markets.

The researchers also find that more confident and less risk-averse individuals are more likely to enter new markets. They conclude that entrepreneurial overconfidence can at least partly explain the high failure rates of entrepreneurial ventures.

11.1.3 The Exit Decision

Exit is a decision, not an automatic event. We can think of the exit decision as a series of choices that the company faces at various stages of development. Figures 11.1 and 11.2 provide a graphical framework for analyzing the exit choice. We distinguish two types of exit decisions, which occur at different points in time and for different company situations. Figure 11.1 shows the exit decision in the "downside" scenario, where the question is whether to continue operating the company or closing it down. As the data above show, this is the most common exit decision.

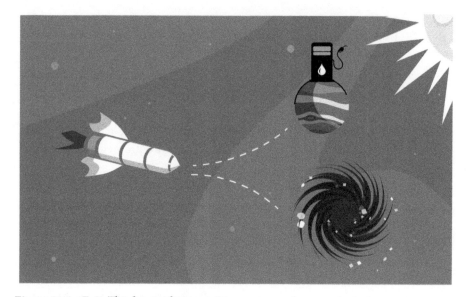

Figure 11.1. Exit: The downside scenario.

Figure 11.2 shows the exit decision in the "upside" scenario, where the question is whether to continue holding shares or to initiate the sale of shares through one of the three main mechanisms: an IPO, an acquisition, or a financial sale.

Both the upside and the downside scenarios always present the choice of continuing. From a financial perspective, this means either doing nothing, which is typical of downside scenarios, or providing additional financing, which hopefully allows the company to reach new milestones and increase its value. This decision is based on the real options reasoning that we discuss in the context of staged financing (Section 9.2.2). Thus, we can think of the exit decision as a trade-off between exit as a certain payoff in the present ("a bird in the hand") and refinancing as an uncertain payoff in the future ("two in the bush").

Closing down the company is necessary when the company runs out of cash (Section 3.7.2) and the investors are unwilling to risk additional money. At the time of closing down, investors may still recover whatever assets are left, but typically this is less than their initial investment. The downward-sloping path indicates the negative company outcome associated with the downside scenario.

Figure 11.2. Exit: The upside scenario.

In the upside scenario, the upward paths represent the positive nature of the exit outcomes. The exit decision for the upside scenario is whether to continue funding it to reach a higher valuation or to sell its shares through an IPO, acquisition, or financial sale. Investors choose to exit when the exit will yield a higher return (or lower loss) than continuing to finance the venture.

11.1.4 The Timing of Exit

What determines the timing of exit? We identify three main forces. First, as noted in Section 11.1.1, investors have liquidity needs that lead them to push for an exit. Second, the business situation of the company evolves over time, requiring owner-ship changes to be made at certain critical junctions. Third, there is opportunistic market timing. We now consider how company conditions affect exit timing in the context of different exit routes.

In the case of an IPO, the company must first be sufficiently mature to satisfy the regulatory requirements and to attract the interest of institutional investors. This typically requires several years of growth and a stable and profitable business model. In addition, IPO market conditions are very important, as investors' appe-tite for IPOs is highly cyclical.[10]

For the case of acquisitions, consider a start-up that, after successfully prototyping its first product, needs to build out its production and a sales organization in prepa-ration to scaling-up its operations. The right time to sell to a strategic buyer is often at that scale-up stage, when the value of the start-up for the buyer is highest. Before the scale-up stage, the strategic buyer has no particular interest in the company

because the product remains untested. After the start-up has developed a full production and distribution network, the strategic buyer can add little more value and
will therefore not make an attractive offer. An alternative situation is when the acquirer is keen to obtain control of the technology early on, before it is tested, either
because it could prove useful or because it could be harmful to the incumbent. For
acquisitions, external market-timing factors have two facets. First, industry cycles,
innovation cycles, and the arrival of competitors affect the demand of acquisitions
by established companies or competing start-ups. Second, company-specific factors
also influence acquirers' interest in the company. Instagram, for example, was acquired by Facebook only 16 months after it was founded, and YouTube was acquired
by Google just 18 months after incorporation. External factors are beyond the control of the company and its investors, but they matter for timing the exit.

An interesting question is whether it is possible to delay exit indefinitely? In
this case, the company would remain a privately held corporation forever. This
is the case of "family firms," whose shareholders receive them largely through
dividends.[11] For entrepreneurial ventures, such an investment model without exit
remains largely unheard of. Dividends only happen after a company generates
stable profits. The time horizon between a start-up investment and a regular flow
of dividend payments is longer than most investors would be willing to accept.
Hence, exit remains a necessary part of the model for financing entrepreneurial
companies.

While exit is essential to the entrepreneurial finance process, there is a recent
trend to delay exit for long periods of time This trend emerged mainly in the aftermath of the 2008 Great Recession.[12] It brought an addition to the business
vocabulary of a very mystical animal, none less than the unicorn. We discuss it in
Box 11.2.[13]

Box 11.2 The Rise of Unicorns

Unicorns are defined as young fast-growing companies that are still privately
held and achieve a valuation of over $1B. In recent years their numbered
mushroomed.[14] At the beginning of 2019, there were 232 unicorns, valued over
$1,100B.[15] The latest vocabulary addition is actually the "dedacorn," defined as a
unicorn that reaches a valuation over $10B. The CB Insight report identified 17
of them as of early 2018. The highest valued ones at the time were Uber ($68B),
Didi Chuxing ($50B), Meituan Dianping ($30B), Airbnb ($29.3B), and SpaceX
($21.5B). 47% of unicorns were based in the U.S., 30% in China, 6% in the UK,
4% in India, and 2% in Germany and Israel. There are also African unicorns: e-
commerce company Jumia became such in 2016 and went on to its IPO on the
New York Stock Exchange (NYSE) in April 2019.[16]

The largest categories were internet software and services companies (15%), E-commerce (14%), and Fintech (12%).

Several factors explain the rise of unicorns.[17] On the investor side, the main driver is the ongoing lack of IPOs. Institutional investors who want to diversify their portfolio with smaller high-growth companies find insufficient investment opportunities on public markets and therefore extend their reach into private markets.[18] They have a strong appetite for high-yield investments and are willing to accept higher risk and lower liquidity. On the company side, there is the need for large financing rounds in order to exploit growth opportunities. This is particularly true for tech companies with ambitions to conquer global markets, especially the U.S., China, India, and the European Union. While starting up new ventures has become cheaper over time and has therefore led to an increase in the number of angel- and venture-backed start-ups, scaling-up remains expensive.[19] Companies growing to a global scale often raise rounds above $100M. In 2017, for instance, Elon Musk's SpaceX raised a round of $351M. That same year Meituan-Dianping, a Chinese group-buying service company, raised a round of $4B—about the same amount it raised at its IPO on the the Hong Kong stock exchange in September 2018.

Becoming a unicorn provides great publicity with potential investors, employees, customers, and suppliers. The ambition to reach this visible milestone therefore puts pressure on companies to reach the one-billion-dollar valuation threshold. This can lead to deceptive manipulations. In Section 6.5, we show how better downside protection can be traded against higher valuations, and Box 6.6 provides an example. In the case of unicorns, a way to do so is through the use of IPO ratchets in later rounds. These are a form of anti-dilution protection that increases the conversion rate of convertible shares in case the IPO price falls below a certain target. They ensure better returns to later-round investors but also inflate valuations.[20] It should therefore not come as a surprise that becoming a unicorn does not guarantee exiting as one. Shazam, a UK music recognition software company was acquired by Apple for about $400M in December 2017. Souq.com, a Dubai-based e-commerce platform company was acquired by Amazon for $580M in March 2017. Both companies had previously reached valuations over $1B.

11.2 Initial Public Offerings

Listing on a stock exchange ("going public") is often the most prestigious exit for entrepreneurs and investors alike. This is because an IPO often offers substantial financial returns. It also provides high visibility and a halo of success to all parties involved. Going public implies a transformation of a private company into a publicly listed one.

11.2.1 Benefits and Costs

The decision to go public involves both benefits and costs.[21] Going public has several benefits for the company and its shareholders. First of all, it provides liquidity to investors and to entrepreneurs, who can cash in their returns and diversify their wealth.[22] Savvy investors time the market to achieve higher returns.[23] Public companies can use their shares to make acquisitions.[24] Furthermore, having a stock price provides valuable feedback to the company about its perceived performance.[25]

An IPO also provides the company with increased visibility, which allows it to reach out to a wider set of lenders, employees, and strategic partners.[26] Liquidity and visibility then allow companies to obtain financial and nonfinancial resources to scale up. Access to investors and more transparency reduce the company's cost of capital, reflected by higher valuation at the IPO, by lower cost of subsequent secondary offerings, and by better access to the corporate bond and loan markets.

The process of going public has both large direct costs (Section 11.2.4) and indirect costs. One indirect cost is the need to disclose information about the company, its products and technology, its future plans, and, more generally, the costs of regulatory compliance. While the information is needed by investors, its disclosure benefits the company's competitors. The process of going public also constitutes a major distraction for the entire top management team. Being a public company exposes the company to hostile takeovers, which may limit entrepreneurial initiative.[27] A related concern is that a public company is under pressure from investors and analysts to meet its quarterly earnings targets. Doing so may constrain its ability to engage in riskier long-term projects. Box 11.3 examines evidence on whether publicly listed companies find it difficult to make risky long-term investments.

Box 11.3 Do IPOs Kill Innovation?

It has long been argued that stock markets encourage short-term decision making.[28] Many CEOs carp about the pressures to meet their quarterly financial targets, which they say prevents them from making longer-term investments. This issue is particularly relevant for technology start-ups that rely on long cycles of innovation. Stock market reaction to information about the company's innovations could discourage exploratory projects and encourage less ambitious ones.[29] The question is thus whether going public harms corporate innovation.

Answering this question is challenging because it requires a counterfactual: what would these companies have done if they hadn't gone public? We clearly cannot observe such a counterfactual. We could compare a sample of companies that went public with another sample that didn't. However, the comparison may be tenuous because those that go public are likely to be different. They may be better performers, and they may be in the process of changing their business model. A study by Bernstein solves this problem by comparing companies that went public with companies that "almost" went public.[30] Specifically, the study looks at all companies that file for an IPO and compares those that managed to complete the IPO to those that didn't. The study identifies those companies that were "unlucky" because the stock market became suddenly "cold" in the two months after they filed, forcing them to withdraw the IPO. Arguably, those companies are structurally very similar to those that completed the IPO, except for the crucial difference that had their IPO thwarted by a market downturn. They can therefore be considered a good approximation of the counterfactual.

The study measures innovation activities through patents. It finds that in the aftermath of an IPO, the number of patents remains stable, but their quality goes down. Moreover, innovative inventors leave their companies after an IPO, and the remaining inventors produce lower quality patents. All of this suggests that going public makes companies less innovative. However, there is an interesting twist. After the IPO, public companies start acquiring private start-ups. The study finds that five years after an IPO, one-third of the patent portfolio of public companies comes from such acquisitions. This suggests that, after going public, companies shift their innovation strategy. They put less emphasis on generating innovations by themselves; instead they acquire innovations from the next generation of inventive start-ups.

11.2.2 Preparing for an IPO

When a company decides to go public, it has to prepare itself in two main respects. One is to mature into a fully fledged independent company able to satisfy the demands of institutional investors. The other is to become ready to comply with the many regulations that apply to listed companies. Getting ready to go public therefore takes considerable time and effort.

Preparing to face the pressure from institutional investors requires the company to develop a well-organized management team and a complete corporate structure. A key step in this preparation is recruiting an experienced chief financial officer (CFO) to deal with the listing process and with the pressure from analysts and investors once the company is public. Another important person is the company counsel, who oversees the legal aspects of the going public process. The board of directors may need to be restructured to include enough independent directors and establish proper audit and compensation committees. Professional venture investors can play an important role in the professionalization process.

Complying with regulatory demands also requires time and money. In order to be listed, a company has to satisfy a stringent set of listing requirements. It typically has to show several years of audited financial statements. As a public company, it becomes subject to several legal, accounting, and other compliance rules, which require proper legal and accounting systems. The company must therefore adopt systematic reporting practices to generate the required information.

Once a decision has been made to go public, the company needs to make two key choices. The first is *where* to take the company public. Most companies list in their home country, but some companies prefer to go abroad. In the U.S., the majority of entrepreneurial companies list on Nasdaq, although some prefer the New York Stock Exchange (NYSE). Listing abroad is costly and cumbersome but may allow a company to reach a wider investor base, gain greater international visibility, obtain a higher valuation (i.e., get a lower cost of capital), and have greater liquidity for its stock.[31]

In some countries, stock exchanges have lower market tiers targeted at young, fast-growing companies. They have less stringent listing requirements that aim to attract more specialized investors. Examples include the Alternative Investment Market (AIM) of the London Stock Exchange, EnterNext of Euronext, and the TSX–Venture of the Toronto Stock Exchange.

The second important choice is about *when* to take the company public (Section 11.1.4).[32] The appetite of public markets for IPOs is highly cyclical. Markets are referred to as "hot," when investors' appetite for new issues is high, and "cold" when it is low (Section 11.6.1).[33] Most IPO activity is clustered in hot markets, and a company may need to wait years before a cold market turns hot again. As a consequence, investors sometimes rush a company to market when markets are hot, at the cost of not waiting for full development of the company.[34] In cold markets, investors often have to steer their company toward a different exit route. Moreover, companies themselves tend to strategically time IPOs in periods where they can show strong accounting performance and before slumps in profits.[35]

The IPO process has five main steps that we summarize in Figure 11.3.[36] The whole process lasts several months, although the exact length varies, depending on the speed of approval of the regulatory filings and on how the company reacts to market conditions.

The first step consists of selecting the investment bankers that will manage the whole process. These are regulated financial institutions that intermediate between the company and the stock market investors. They provide underwriting services and deal with regulators during the IPO. The choice of investment bankers is

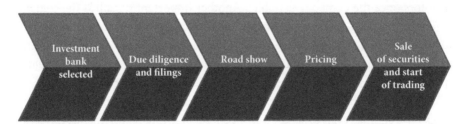

Figure 11.3. The IPO process.

important because of their role in eliciting market interest for the offering, deter-mining the issue price, and stabilizing the stock price in the after-IPO market.[37] Investment bankers usually work as an underwriting syndicate of multiple banks that help to place shares with their own networks of investors. Investment bankers compete for the mandate to become lead underwriter, mostly on the basis of their reputation, industry expertise, and placement capacity.

The second step consists of the investment bankers doing "due diligence" on the company. Due diligence is the process of gathering information on the business, its financial situation, and its business prospects. The information is used to write the IPO prospectus, which is the main document circulated to the public for attracting investors' attention. The IPO prospectus, along with the audited financial accounts, is filed with the relevant regulator. In the U.S., this is the Securities and Exchange Commission (SEC). Due diligence and regulatory filings may take several months. Once the filing is approved, the company has some months to execute the public offering.

The third step is the so-called road show, a period of two or three weeks when company managers meet institutional investors in financial centers such as New York, San Francisco, London, Hong Kong, or Tokyo to stimulate demand for the IPO. The fourth step consists of pricing the IPO (Section 11.2.3) and deter-mining various other aspects of the offering (Section 11.2.4). The final step is to ex-ecute the sale of securities and become a publicly traded company (Section 11.2.5). Box 11.4 examines how in 2012 the U.S. reformed the IPO process to make the stock market more accessible to young high-growth companies.

Box 11.4 The JOBS Act

U.S. securities regulation has strict provisions for companies that want to issue securities. The goal is to preserve investor confidence and maintain trans-parent financial markets. These rules have been developed for large, established corporations.[38] The 2012 Jumpstart Our Business Start-ups (JOBS) Act simpli-fied several rules, adapting them to the needs of fast-growing start-ups. The Act's goal was to help job creation by facilitating access to capital markets for fast-growing start-ups.[39]

The cornerstone of the Act is the concept of an "IPO on-ramp," which reduces the disclosure and compliance costs of the IPO process for start-ups with less than $1B of gross revenues. It reduces the financial information issuers' need to provide to investors. While the principle of full disclosure of all relevant infor-mation remains intact, issuers can provide two instead of three years of financial history. They can submit a simpler analysis of financials and managerial com-pensation, and post-IPO disclosures are streamlined. Corporate governance provisions are less onerous, and some provisions of the Sarbanes-Oxley and Dodd-Frank Acts are waived.

One novel aspect of the Act is that it allows start-ups to file a security registration confidentially, so that competitors cannot see any disclosure before issuance. This lowers the risk of disclosing information before accessing securities markets.[40] Issuers are also allowed to communicate with qualified investors before filing, in order to verify their appetite for a securities offering. Specifically, investors are allowed to communicate during the "quiet period" between the registration of a security and its issuance.

Five years after the introduction of the JOBS Act, the results have been largely positive, albeit possibly underwhelming. The empirical evidence suggests that more companies go public making use of the on-ramp. However, there is a concern that these issuers are of lower quality.[41]

11.2.3 Pricing the IPO

Pricing an IPO is done by the investment bankers, together with the company's management and board of directors. The two main questions involved in pricing are how many shares to issue and at what price. A company will have a target amount of capital it wants to raise. This is relatively low if the company lists mainly to allow existing investors to sell their shares, but high when the company needs money for investments. The total number of shares to be offered, called "free float," is determined first. It should be large enough to ensure liquidity in the aftermarket. Stock markets typically require companies to float a minimum percentage of their shares. Given the number of shares offered, the amount of money actually raised depends on the offer price, which is set at a later stage.

To set the price, the investment banker provides an initial estimate of the market's appetite for the company's shares, typically using the method of exit comparables (Section 5.4.2). This is expressed as a range within which the final price is expected to fall, and it gets updated as information comes in along the process. The final offer price is set the day before the IPO. While the company formally makes the decision, in practice it is the investment bankers who set the price.

There are three main mechanisms for setting the offer price: auctions, fixed price, and book-building.[42] With auctions, the price is set to clear the market, giving the investment bank no discretion regarding the allocation of shares.[43] With fixed price, investors know the price before the IPO is executed. Therefore, there is a risk of deteriorating market conditions, which may lead to a failed issue; consequently, the price is typically set cautiously low. With book-building, the underwriters choose a price based on information they elicit from institutional investors. This can be a somewhat opaque process, since the underwriters have considerable discretion as to which investors get shares.[44] Nonetheless, book-building remains commonly used as investment banks resist switching to auction-based allocations.[45] To date, the only major auction-based IPO remains that of Google.[46]

Most IPOs are underpriced. This means that the offer price is lower than the market price on the first day of trading. In the popular press, underpricing is often portrayed as a success because there are positive returns on the first day of trading. Investors who buy shares at the offer price clearly appreciate this practice, but for the company, it is effectively a cost. If the shares were priced closer to their market price, then the company would raise more money for the same number of shares. Underpricing effectively means the company is "leaving money on the table."[47]

Numerous explanations have been found for the underpricing puzzle.[48] Some leading explanations are based on asymmetric information: investors fear paying too much for a company they know little about. A low offer price is needed to entice them. This is a variant of the lemons problem (Box 2.6) or the winner's curse problem (Box 11.4). This issue is particularly acute when insiders sell large blocks of shares.

11.2.4 Structuring the IPO

Beyond setting the number of prices of shares, an IPO requires several other decisions. One concerns the fraction of primary versus secondary shares. Primary shares are shares newly issued by the company to raise new capital. Secondary shares are existing shares sold by the pre-IPO investors. Large secondary offerings by insiders are viewed with suspicion by new investors, who fear that they reflect unfavorable insider information. This is yet another instance of the lemons problem.

Companies must also decide whether the shares issued in the IPO have the same voting rights as those already held by the founders and investors. If different shares have different voting rights, this is called a "dual" share structure.[49] Some of the most successful entrepreneurial companies that went public (including Baidu, Facebook, Google, Groupon, Lyft, Pinterest, Snap, TripAdvisor, and Zynga) have chosen to issue dual-class shares, giving founders a way to control the company by holding shares with multiple voting rights (Section 8.2.1). Dual-class shares are common in the U.S., Switzerland, Scandinavia, and Benelux, but not in most other countries.[50]

Technology companies claim that dual-class shares give freedom to their visionary founders. Mark Zuckerberg, who controlled 60% of the voting rights of Facebook in 2018, noted: "One of the things that I feel really lucky we have is this company structure where, at the end of the day, it's a controlled company. We are not at the whims of short-term shareholders. We can really design these products and decisions with what is going to be in the best interest of the community over time."[51] But this argument is debatable. Even if visionary founders are crucial to a company at the time of the IPO, this may change over time. Many founders relinquish leadership to professional managers, even if the company proves successful and keeps growing.[52] Those who don't often get in trouble. For example, when in 2018 Facebook faced some scrutiny over privacy issues, critics pointed to Mark Zuckerberg's dual role as CEO and chairman of the board. They argued that lack of oversight had contributed to the company's troubles.[53] More generally, dual-class shares encourage entrenchment, insulating management from the discipline of the market for corporate control. The wedge between ownership and voting rights can weaken incentives for shareholder wealth maximization. The empirical evidence suggests that the larger the wedge, the more likely are wasteful acquisitions and investments. Companies with dual-class shares also do not invest more in R&D or in intangible assets.[54] A recent study finds that firms with dual-class shares achieve higher IPO valuations that a comparable set of companies with single-class shares. However, this advantage fades over time.[55] Such evidence would support allowing 'sunset' provisions that force multiple-vote shares to convert into standard ones over time.

Box 11.5 looks at the fascinating history of Alibaba listing shares on different stock markets, some with and some without dual share structures.

Box 11.5 Tales from the Venture Archives: Alibaba's IPOs

With its name inspired by the children's tale from *One Thousand and One Nights*, Alibaba Group Holding Limited is arguably the most successful Chinese technology start-up to date. Founded in 1999 by Jack Ma, Alibaba established itself as China's leader in e-commerce and related areas, such as electronic payments, cloud computing, and artificial intelligence. After several rounds of venture capital, the company listed its shares on the Hong Kong Stock Exchange (HKSE) in November 2007. The offer price was HK$13.50 (US$1.75), and the company raised HK$13.1B (US$1.7B).

Alibaba's stock rose from HK$13.50 to HK$30 on the first day of trading; that is, it was underpriced by more than 50%. The stock price reached a peak at HK$39.50, then slid to a low of HK$5 in 2008. In February 2012, while its stock price was lingering around $10, Alibaba surprised financial markets by announcing it would delist its shares from the Hong Kong Stock Exchange (HKSE), repurchasing all shares at the original share price of $13.50. At the time, the company was undergoing strategic changes that were expected to have a negative impact on its short-term financial performance. Jack Ma explained: "Taking Alibaba.com private will allow our company to make long-term decisions that are in the best interest of our customers and that are also free from the pressures that come from having a publicly listed company."[56]

In September 2014, less than a thousand and one nights after delisting its shares from HKSE, Alibaba listed its shares again, but this time on the NYSE.

The offer price was set at $68 and rose to almost $94 on the first day of trading. The valuation at IPO exceeded $230B and the amount raised was $25B, making it the largest IPO to date. Why did the company move from HKSE to NYSE? Alibaba wanted a dual-class share structure where 30 key members controlled the company's board of directors. This structure was permissible under NYSE rules but not under the "one-share-one-vote" rule that HKSE had adopted after Alibaba's 2007 listing. By early 2019, the stock price had performed well, rising above $150.

The tale does not end here. Licking its wounds from the loss of Alibaba, the HKSE chose to change its listing regulations in December 2017, to allow dual-class share listings. In June 2019 Alibaba filed a confidential listing with HKSE that would allow it to raise up to $20B.[57]

Another aspect of structuring IPOs concerns overallotment options, often referred to as "Greenshoe" options. These options allow the underwriters to buy additional shares, typically up to 15%, at the offer price and to resell them in the days after the IPO in order to stabilize market prices. The option can be very lucrative for the underwriter if the offering is underpriced.

At the time of structuring the IPO, the underwriters secure lock-up agreements with all major shareholders. These prevent pre-IPO shareholders from selling their stock for a given period after the IPO, usually six months. The goal is to ensure orderly trading in the aftermath of the IPO, avoiding wide stock price fluctuations. To see the importance of lock-ups, consider that Lyft's post-IPO stock performance was negatively influenced by massive short sales and generated debate on the design of its lock-up agreements.[58]

From a company perspective, going public is not cheap. There are several monetary costs. First, there are the listing fees to be paid to the stock exchange. These are typically expressed as a function of the amount raised in the IPO. Each year after the IPO, the company will also need to pay annual listing fees. Second, there are the fees paid to the underwriter. In the U.S., investment banks almost always charge 7% of the total amount raised in the IPO. In European and Asian stock markets, these fees range between 3 and 5%.[59] A third cost is underpricing (Section 11.2.3), which means that the company raises less money in the IPO than its market valuation should allow.

A "direct listing" is an alternative, cheaper and quieter, way of going public. In this case, the company lists its shares on the stock exchange but does not sell any new shares, and so it does not raise any new capital. The company does not need to hire an underwriter and go on a road show. From the day of listing investors, founders and employees can sell their shares to the public. Direct listings have traditionally been associated with smaller companies. This changed in 2018 when Swedish music streaming company Spotify (Box 1.7) decided to list its shares directly on the NYSE. The listing was considered a success, valuing the company $26.5B.[60]

11.2.5 After the IPO

After the expiration of any lock-up period, investors have a choice to sell their shares on the market or to keep their stakes for some time longer. This decision is largely based on their expectations about the company's success going forward. Selling large volumes at the end of the lock-up period can harm the share price, as the market sees it as a negative signal. Sophisticated investors therefore sell their shares gradually over time.

Investors with board seats have to decide when to resign. Some VCs resign before the IPO, whereas others wait until after the IPO in order to ensure a smooth transition to a larger board with members nominated by institutional investors. Some never seem to want to go—Arthur Rock, the early investor in Apple Computers stayed on the board for over a decade after the IPO.

The transition to a public company also matters for founders and managers. Like investors, they can now get some liquidity too. However, their sales of stock are closely watched by the market. Their share sales have to be disclosed, and selling large stakes, especially unexpectedly, can create negative price reactions. Many founders choose to retain large holdings and remain active in the company. Several also retain their CEO or other executive role, sometimes for a long time. In fact, the opportunity to remain at the helm is one reason why founders often prefer an IPO over an acquisition. Others retire to a comfortable life, including exotic pursuits like hen-raising.[61] Many instead become serial entrepreneurs, board members, or angel investors, remaining involved with the entrepreneurial process.

The IPO has important consequences for the company itself. It allows the company to develop as an independent entity with the visibility offered by being listed. Over time, however, many companies still get acquired, often by larger listed companies.[62]

To conclude this section, WorkHorse Box 11.1 looks at the company's IPO prospects.

WorkHorse Box 11.1 The IPO Option

The MAGIC worked! MAGIC was the acronym for Micro-voltaic Algorithmically Granularized Infrared Capturization (WorkHorse Box 9.5), Bharat Marwari's breakthrough solar technology that turned WorkHorse from a B2C company selling solar generators into a B2B technology provider of solar energy products to manufacturing companies. WorkHorse's technology proved successful, and company revenues grew from $10M in 2022 to $35M in 2023, with a projected $80M for 2024.

In early 2024, the company raised a large Series C round, led by Umija Ulimwengu from JetLuck. The existing investors mostly invested pro rata. Stanley Goldmorgan's investment bank, the reputable ShoeHorn Bank, also joined the investment round. The Series C round fetched a share price of $20, resulting in a stunning $80M post-money valuation. The following table shows WorkHorse's capitalization table after the C round.

	Series B		Series C		
Price per share ($)	8.0		20.0		
Investment ($)	10,000,000		17,666,667		
Post-money valuation ($)	24,933,333		80,000,000		
	Shares held	Ownership fraction	Shares bought	Shares held	Ownership fraction
Founders	800,000	25.7%	0	800,000	20.0%
Other common	525,000	16.8%	0	525,000	13.1%
Michael Archie	179,167	5.7%	0	179,167	4.5%
Eagle-I Ventures	364,583	11.7%	103,331	467,914	11.7%
Coyo-T Capital	479,167	15.4%	135,807	614,974	15.4%
JetLuck	500,000	16.0%	300,000	800,000	20.0%
GestütenTechnik	268,750	8.6%	76,170	344,920	8.6%
ShoeHorn Bank			268,026	268,026	6.7%
Total shares:	3,116,667	100%	883,333	4,000,000	100%

Throughout 2024, markets became increasingly bullish on cleantech, and the topic of exit came up in investor conversations. Umija and Stanley advocated that the company should prepare itself for an IPO in early 2025. They argued that ShoeHorn Bank should be the lead underwriter. "Isn't there a conflict of interest?" Annie blurted out, receiving a stern look from Stanley. Umija swiftly asked Stanley to give them an idea of what such an IPO might look like. He offered the following sketch.

Stanley thought that WorkHorse should be listed on Nasdaq. He ran some exit comparables and was confident the company could fetch an offer price between $25 and $30. He suggested that the company should issue 2M new shares, thus raising up to $60M, at a (post-money) valuation of up to $180M. Wolf had heard many similar pitches before and asked with a bored voice: "Let me guess: 7% fees, Greenshoe of 15%, and a 6-month lock-up?"... "Of course!" Stanley replied. Back in their office, Malcolm explained to the founders what it all meant, using the following table.

	High price	Low price
Offer price ($)	30	25
Valuation at IPO ($)	189,000,000	157,500,000
Pre-money valuation at offer price ($)	120,000,000	100,000,000
Funds raised ($)	69,000,000	57,500,000
Proceedings from shares sold ($)	69,000,000	57,500,000
Underwriters' fees (7%)	4,830,000	4,025,000
Funds available for investment ($)	64,170,000	53,475,000
Shares issued at IPO ("primary shares")	2,000,000	2,000,000
Shares issued for the Greenshoe option	300,000	300,000
Shares sold by shareholders ("secondary shares")	0	0
Total shares offered	2,300,000	2,300,000
Shares outstanding after the IPO	6,300,000	6,300,000

The first column described the structure that Stanley had described, with the price at the high end of the proposed range. The underwriter, ShoeHorn Bank, would charge a standard fee of 7% of the amount raised, suggesting a total fee of $4.8M. The IPO would thus net the company new funds for $64.2M, with a valuation of $189M. "It just sounds too good to be true, what's the hook?" Bharat questioned.

Malcolm smiled knowingly, "Don't believe that $30 price! At the time of fixing the price, underwriters often choose a price well below the top of the proposed range, claiming that this will help make the issue sell out." In the second column, Malcolm recalculated the offering with a lower share price of $25. The pre-money valuation fell from $120M to $100M, and the net amount raised increased from $64.2M to $53.5M. "These are such big numbers," Annie exclaimed. "You almost forget that this is a difference of over $10M—more than our entire B round!"

Brandon challenged Malcolm's assumption that the investment bank would want to lower the offer price: "Look, their fees are going from $4.83M to $4.03M. They would be losing $800K in fees by dropping the price. Surely they wouldn't want to do that!" Malcolm smirked, "Look at the Greenshoe. By dropping the price, each share is $5 cheaper, so that is worth $1.5M (= $5*300,000) alone, clearly more than the $800K in lost fees." Wolf had joined the conversation and added: "And just think of how much money ShoeHorn will have made for its clients. If they lower the offer price by $5, then their clients get saved a total of $10M (= $5*2,000,000) to buy the shares. That's basically the $10M that the company didn't raise." Brandon blinked: "Wow: that is a motivation to lower the offer price!"

Ali had also joined the discussion and raised another issue: "I think we are forgetting about secondary shares. Right now, Eagle-I Ventures is under intense pressure to show liquid returns. I can't afford waiting for the lockup period before selling my shares, I need to sell them all in the IPO itself." Astrid raised her eyebrows: "How should we deal with it?"

Malcolm quickly produced the following table to see what options were available.

	Without secondary shares	With secondary shares	With secondary shares and lower offer price
Offer price ($)	25	25	23
Valuation at IPO ($)	157,500,000	157,500,000	144,900,000
Pre-money valuation at offer price ($)	100,000,000	100,000,000	92,000,000
Funds raised ($)	57,500,000	57,500,000	52,900,000
Proceedings from shares sold ($)	57,500,000	69,197,850	63,662,022
Underwriters' fees (7%)	4,025,000	4,025,000	3,703,000
Funds available for investment ($)	53,475,000	53,475,000	49,197,000
Shares issued at IPO ("primary shares")	2,000,000	2,000,000	2,000,000
Shares issued for the Greenshoe option	300,000	300,000	300,000
Shares sold by shareholders ("secondary shares")	0	467,914	467,914
Total shares offered	2,300,000	2,767,914	2,767,914
Shares after the IPO	6,300,000	6,300,000	6,300,000

The first column reported the baseline offering with the $25 offer price. The second column added to the offering Ali's 467,914 secondary shares. Nothing changed in the numbers, as Ali would simply sell Eagle-I's shares to some investors at the offer price. The only difference, highlighted in the "Proceedings from shares sold" row, was that the public would now put nearly $22M to buy Eagle-I's shares. That money would go directly into the VC's pockets and not into WorkHorses'.

"Then let's sell also some of our shares!" cheeringly whispered Annie. "I knew you would ask this," dryly replied Malcom. "So have a look at the third column." The column reported the calculations with an offer price of $20, the bottom of the pricing range. "Investors watch you. When they see pre-IPO shareholders sell their shares, they get nervous. They fear you know something bad about the company, and will only buy with a price discount." "I see," said the four founders with one voice. "Should investors see the founders themselves selling shares, the price drop would be even larger." The one voice was now a disappointed "Oooh."

Astrid frowned. "So when an investment banker says the company will raise over $60M, in reality they mean less than $50M. . . ." Ali replied kindly but firmly: "Astrid, this is about our exit, not your investment! But don't worry, exit is a game, and we will definitely consider all options."

11.3   Acquisitions

Getting acquired is the most common exit route for entrepreneurial ventures (Table 11.1). It is also an important channel through which established companies obtain innovations to develop and commercialize. A study by Arora, Cohen, and Walsh shows that nearly half of U.S. manufacturing companies that introduced an innovative product between 2007 and 2009 obtained the invention externally, largely through acquisition of start-ups [63] Thus, acquisitions are financial transactions with a strategic motive. Figure 11.2 shows that acquisitions are one of the three main upside exit routes. Acquisitions have less pronounced cycles than IPOs, so that exit is also a possibility in market downturns.[64] They are also less expensive, the main fees being to investment bankers that act as financial advisors and perform due diligence. Acquisitions require fewer public information disclosures than going public, which is important for companies with substantial proprietary knowledge. At the same time, potential acquirers expect to have access to more detailed and confidential information than what gets disclosed to stock market regulators. Acquisitions involve a loss of independence and control for the founders. As their company is absorbed by the acquirer, they either become employees of a larger company, or they quit.

11.3.1 Strategic Motives

An entrepreneurial venture that is a potential target for an acquisition faces a trade-off between "build or sell." Building requires going alone and raising additional funding with the aim of eventually going public. For example, the start-up may have to develop a fully fledged sales and marketing organization, attract a complete management team, or negotiate international distribution deals. An established company may already have all these things in place. In the strategic management literature, these are referred to as complementary assets.[65] The Venture

Evaluation Matrix provides a useful framework for understanding the range of complementary assets. Let us focus on the last row, which specifically identifies the three strategic challenges of sales, operations, and organization. On the sales side, incumbents can offer an established sales team, market access, marketing know-how, and brand. On the production side, established companies already have many established supply relations, some of which the start-up may be able to use right away. On the organization side, entrepreneurial companies may be able to fill key positions in the management team. Partnering with an acquirer that possesses complementary assets therefore leads to smoother and potentially more profitable integrations.[66]

An established company similarly faces a "build or buy" trade-off. It can decide to enter the market by itself, replicating the investments of the entrepreneurial company by developing similar products and services. There are three problems with the "build" option. First, it may not be easy to replicate what the entrepreneurial venture is offering, let alone improve on it. This is not merely a technical challenge, but also an organizational challenge of getting employees within the established company to adopt the new ideas and approaches that were developed by the entre-preneurial company. Second, building takes times. Time to market can be of great importance in a competitive environment, and the established company risks being late to market. Third, the decision to build or buy affects the competitive landscape. From an acquirer's perspective, a benefit of buying is to eliminate the target company as a competitor. In this context, it is worth noting that most acquisitions of entrepreneurial companies do not come within the radar of antitrust authorities. Typically, the acquired companies are too small, or the markets too young, to attract their attention.

Acquisitions are not without risks for the buyers either. First, there may be a fear of overpaying. Second, there is a risk of picking the wrong start-up. Moreover, it can be difficult to integrate the start-up into the established company without ruining its entrepreneurial spirit.[67] Integration requires what management scholars call "absorptive capacity," that is, the ability to evaluate the technology, assimilate it into the buyer's organization, and develop it profitably (Section 11.3.4).[68]

For some acquisitions the main rationale is to hire the team of founders, engin-eers, or scientists. Such acquisitions are sometimes called "acqui-hires." The first acqui-hire was reportedly Dodgeball, a New York-based social location service ac-quired by Google in May 2005, hiring founders Alex Reinert and Doug Jaeger.[69] Active acqui-hirers include Facebook and Yahoo!, and unicorns like Dropbox, Pinterest, and Airbnb. Most targets are young, small start-ups that face difficulties in gaining traction but have talented founders and employees. For example, in 2009 Facebook acquired FriendFeed, which had been founded less than two years before, to offer a platform for social networking updates. The stated goal of this $50M ac-quisition was to hire founder Bret Taylor and his engineering team.[70] Acqui-hires are not announced as such and are therefore difficult to identify, but observers esti-mate that in Silicon Valley alone there are between 50 and 100 per year.

Acqui-hires have clear benefits. First, the acqui-hires gets a large number of talented individuals in one go. As such, acqui-hires are viewed as a tool in the competition for talent.[71] Second, they allow a team that works well to stay together. Third, they appeal to the recruits as they transform income into capital gains, which have lighter tax rates. Critics of acqui-hires point to their cost. First, the new hires may remain only through their lock-up period—typically, 12 to 24 months. Second, transplanting a new team that enjoys high pay and star status may prove destabilizing. Third, acqui-hires often entail costly sign-up bonuses.

11.3.2 Preparing for an Acquisition

Seasoned practitioners often say that "companies are bought, not sold." Getting an acquisition offer is far from trivial and requires preparation. Thus, getting acquired is rarely a coincidence; instead it is the outcome of a strategic plan to generate interest among potential acquirers. The objective here is subtle. On the one hand, the start-up wants to configure itself so that it can easily be bought and integrated into the acquiring company. For example, a software start-up can specialize its product to a particular platform of a potential acquirer. On the other hand, too much specialization makes the start-up overly dependent on one potential acquirer and reduces its bargaining power. The start-up must therefore craft its strategy so as to remain an attractive target, without becoming beholden to any one acquirer.

Some acquirers have prior strategic relationships with the companies they acquire. These could be supplier/buyer relationships, licensing arrangements, or strategic alliances. In some cases, the strategic relationship is accompanied by an investment by the established corporation (Section 13.3). An equity stake gives the potential acquirer a "toehold" in the start-up company and ensures privileged access to company information.

In the end, the start-up only needs one acquirer, but having multiple potential bidders greatly increases its negotiation power. At the same time, there is a danger that by courting a second potential buyer, the start-up risks losing the interest of the first one. In some cases, the entrepreneurial venture openly engages with multiple potential buyers, and in other cases it prefers to keep negotiations confidential. Investment bankers can also play an important role in discreetly approaching different potential buyers.

Buyers also need to prepare to make acquisitions by developing what is called "absorptive capacity."[72] This means having in place the financial and human resources as well as the organizational practices to find targets, make deals, and integrate smoothly. Indeed, for large technology companies like Alibaba, Cisco, or Google, acquisitions are central to their R&D strategy.[73] They maintain teams of specialists who continuously search for acquisition targets and then have the expertise and resources to quickly strike a deal at any time.

11.3.3 Structuring an Acquisition

Valuation is of central importance to any acquisition deal. Shareholders want to fetch the highest possible price. The price paid by the acquirer reflects not only the beliefs about the underlying value of the target company, but also the competitive environment. The term *auctions* is not only used for the sale of antique objects but also describes more broadly a wide array of competitive selling procedures. "Auction theory" studies how the choice of procedures affects prices. Box 11.6 examines some key insights worthy of a Nobel Prize.

Box 11.6 Nobel Insights on Auction Theory

The 1996 Nobel Prize in Economics went to William Vickrey, who is considered the father of auction theory.[74] He showed how prices are formed as the outcome of competitive bidding processes. This analysis directly applies to the determination of exit values. Auction theory provides insights into how to manage the process of selling a venture to potential acquirers. It also provides insights into the structuring of IPOs, buyouts, and secondary sales.

There are several types of auctions. English auction houses such as Christie's or Sotheby's use "ascending-bid" auctions where the price goes up until only one willing buyer is left. Most acquisitions are effectively conducted in this manner. Dutch auction houses use another system: the offer price gradually comes down from an initial value, and the first buyer to bid wins the object. This was the method used for Google's IPO. Most IPOs use a variation of the "sealed-bid" auction method, in which potential buyers submit private bids. After the deadline, the highest bid is revealed, but the price paid by the winning bidder is only the second-highest price. Vickrey showed that second-price sealed bid auctions create surprisingly simple bidding strategies. In a second-price auction, the winning bidder doesn't actually pay his or her own bid, but the price of the next-highest bidder. As a result, bidders always bid exactly what the object is actually worth to them, without the need to think strategically how their own bid stacks up against the others.

Auction theory makes a distinction between "private" and "common" values. In the private case, every individual has an independent valuation for the object on sale. For example, the value of a fine bottle of wine to the buyer does not depend on its value to other buyers. Things become more complicated with common values, as it is with company shares. The value of a share depends on its resale value and, therefore, on the value other potential buyers place on it. The share has a "common" value that is not known by the investors who bid. This generates a "winner's curse" problem. Whenever a bidder wins a common value auction, it must be true that other bidders estimated the asset to be of a lower value than the winning bidder. Sophisticated bidders are aware of this thinking and rationally decide to bid below their perceived value. Less sophisticated bidders may naively bid their perceived value. If they win, they may end up paying more than everybody else thought fair. The winner's curse problem helps to explain why sophisticated acquirers might be cautious in bidding for companies and why IPO prices often increase on the first day of trading.

To understand the valuation of acquisitions, consider the following simple bargaining approach, which is based on Nash bargaining (Box 7.4). The lower bound of the price range is given by the value of the start-up to its owners as a stand-alone unit. Below that price they are unwilling to sell. The upper bound of the range is given by the value of the start-up to the acquirer, including all the synergies created by asset complementarity. Above that price, the acquirer is unwilling to buy. In the absence of competition, the buyer can offer prices near the lower bound of that range, knowing that remaining a stand-alone company is the only alternative to the seller. However, when several strategic buyers compete, they will get close to the upper bound of the range. This is essentially an auction where the winning bidder is the buyer with the highest synergies. In practice, start-ups typically negotiate with a preferred buyer, while maintaining some threat of switching to alternative ones. For these reasons, both parties try to generate competition on the other side. Start-ups try to elicit interest from multiple potential buyers, and incumbents try to reach out to competing entrepreneurial companies.

If the valuation falls somewhere in the middle of this range, the acquisition can be thought of as a win–win outcome, where buyer and seller split the surplus generated by the synergistic acquisition. An implication is that the value of the acquirer should increase upon the announcement of an acquisition. Indeed, there is empirical evidence that stock market valuations increase when companies announce private acquisitions. Interestingly, the same is not true for large acquisitions of publicly listed companies.[75]

An important aspect of the deal is the method of payment. Buyers can pay either with cash or by issuing company shares. The latter only happens when the buyer is a publicly listed company because sellers rarely accept illiquid shares from a privately held company. For the acquirers, the benefit of using shares over cash is that they do not need to raise additional capital. However, this is only a benefit if the cost of raising outside capital is higher than the dilution cost of issuing shares. Evidence for U.S. listed companies supports the view that acquirers tend to use stock when their own equity is overvalued.[76] From the seller's perspective, accepting shares is riskier, so they want to rebalance their stock portfolio by selling their shares over time.

In order to mitigate concerns that they are overpaying, acquirers sometimes include an earn-out clause.[77] This clause stipulates that a fraction of the acquisition price is paid outright and the rest is "earned out" by the seller if the acquired venture achieves some performance targets. Earn-out agreements risk misaligning incentives after the acquisition. The acquiring company may even deliberately miss the performance targets in order to reduce earn-out payments.

The situation gets difficult when the acquisition value falls short of the investors' preferred terms (Section 6.2). In this case, the entrepreneur (and other common equity holders) receive nothing and may thus try to prevent the acquisition from happening. To avoid this possibility, investors sometimes "carve out" part of their ownership and give it to the common equity holders. A study by Broughman and Fried shows that this type of renegotiation is more common when investors have insufficient control rights to force an acquisition.[78]

The acquirer often offers the founder and managers an employment contract. This serves two purposes. First, it may be necessary to get reluctant founders to agree to the sale of their company. Second, it helps ensure a smooth transition and integration of the start-up. The acquirer often asks these managers and employees to stay for some lock-up period, typically anywhere from three months to two years.

11.3.4 After the Acquisition

The main challenge for the acquirer is to integrate the acquired unit along strategic, marketing, operational, and human resource dimensions. Larger acquisitions pose larger challenges to the buyer. While the acquired company itself gets absorbed by the acquirer, in some cases it retains its own independent brand. This was, for example, the case in Google's acquisition of YouTube. In many other cases, however, the product and brand get fully integrated with the acquirer. This was, for example, the case of Like.com, which after Google's acquisition became integrated with Google's shopping search engine.

The extent to which the acquirer can benefit from the acquired start-up depends on its ability to motivate and retain its talent. When the technical capabilities are deeply embedded in the acquired team, then the transplant into a larger organization is risky. The acquired team may lack independence and the incentives to continue innovating. From the acquirer's perspective, there is a trade-off between integration and autonomy.[79] There is a concern that bright engineers dislike becoming "small fish in a bigger pond" and lose their creative drive.[80]

The problem of talent retention is particularly salient for the founders and senior managers of the acquired company. After the initial transition phase, there is considerable uncertainty about the role of the entrepreneurs. In some cases, they like to stay with the acquirers. They may have a strong commitment to their product or team, so they make it their next career goal to look after the continued growth and success of their venture. Some acquirers may let them realize this goal, but often there are clashes between the entrepreneurs and the managers of the acquiring company, especially as the venture gets integrated into the acquirer and loses its identity. Many founders also find it difficult to think of themselves as corporate managers. Consequently, many entrepreneurs do not stay with the acquirer for a long time.[81]

Thus, over time many entrepreneurs and employees leave. They may take a pause to enjoy the fruits of their labor from the acquisition. After that, they perhaps start another company or become an angel investor in other start-up companies or become a VC partner. This "recycling" of entrepreneurial talent is an important building block of an entrepreneurial ecosystem because the experiences of seasoned entrepreneurs are valuable for the next generation of new entrepreneurs. We discuss this issue in greater detail in Chapter 14.

WorkHorse Box 11.2 looks at the company's acquisition option.

WorkHorse Box 11.2 The Acquisition Option

When Ali said that the investors would consider all exit options, he meant it. In fact, as a VC, he considered it an important part of his job to constantly talk to potential acquirers. Ali had high hopes that Golden Gate Inc., a large public-listed technology company, would be interested in acquiring WorkHorse. Golden Gate had a diversified portfolio of technology products and services, mostly targeted toward industrial clients. Ali had previously negotiated a strategic alliance for one of his other portfolio companies. He knew that Golden Gate was keen to expand its solar energy offering, so acquiring WorkHorse would seem a natural step.

From the perspective of WorkHorse, being acquired by Golden Gate would offer several strategic advantages. WorkHorse needed to aggressively expand its sales force to support its market expansion, yet often found it difficult to hire seasoned commercial managers. Golden Gate already had a large and technically savvy sales force in place. Industrial clients were also reluctant to source mission-critical technologies from start-ups, instead preferring to work with large "blue-chip," established corporations like Golden Gate. On the operations side, Golden Gate also had a vast network of suppliers that could provide greater supply chain reliability. In short, an acquisition could create significant synergies, though it was difficult to quantify them.

Ali was initially rebuffed by Goldie TomKat, Golden Gate's senior vice-president of Corporate Development. She dismissed WorkHorse as an acquisition target because of GestütenTechnik, which was Golden Gate's competitor in several of its markets: "Let's be honest. Once you see a corporate investor in a start-up, it is game over for us," she commented. "Why should we work hard on structuring a deal when our competitor can always exercise an option to acquire?" Ali explained that GestütenTechnik had no such legal option and had no intention whatsoever of acquiring WorkHorse. Reluctantly, she agreed to meet the founders and take a closer look at WorkHorse.

Astrid and Brandon met Goldie TomKat on a foggy November day at Golden Gate's headquarters in San Francisco. Goldie TomKat surprised the founders by announcing that Golden Gate was open to acquiring the company. "Let's be honest, you are a good strategic fit for us, so we want to propose you a deal." Astrid gasped, but Goldie went straight ahead. "We will not offer you cash, but our own stock. That is better for you, as I am sure you will agree that we are grossly undervalued by the market." Brandon tried to keep a straight face. "Currently, our stock price is hovering around $10 per share, so we propose to offer two Golden Gate shares for every WorkHorse share, or 8M Golden Gate shares in total. This makes it an $80M acquisition on paper, but since we are grossly undervalued, it's really worth a lot more."

The idea of getting acquired provoked mixed feelings in Astrid. Numerous thoughts raced through her head: "Selling WorkHorse = Yuck; Working for Golden Gate = Yum; Leaving Ann Arbor = Double Yuck; Moving to San Francisco = Double Yum." Putting aside these complicated feelings, she surprised herself by how calmly she responded: "So what other conditions did you have in mind?"

Goldie TomKat explained: "Let's be honest, we want your management team to integrate your products into our production, so we require a one-year employment contract and a two year noncompete. Your shares will vest linearly with a one-year cliff and will be subject to a simple earn-out clause. You see, you said this morning that you will make $120M in revenues next year. If that's true, then you deserve all our shares, but we want to make sure that you actually hit that target. For every $1M missed, we would reduce the share conversion rate of the management team by 2%. Suppose revenues were only $110M instead of the promised $120M, then we would have to withhold 20% of your stakes." "But will we even be in charge of sales, to have some control over the milestone?" Astrid let slip. Goldie TomKat looked surprised: "Oh no, we have a great VP of marketing and sales to take care of that." Astrid regained clarity of mind: Earn-out clause = Triple Yuck!!!

The next day Astrid met Ali in his Palo Alto office, fuming over the terms of the offer. "How can I accept a revenue-based earn-out when we are not even in control of revenues? They could just fiddle the numbers for one year, and we end up with nothing. Sorry, I simply cannot accept this offer." Ali remained poised: "Let me be direct, it is not up to you to decide. It is up to the board to decide, and you don't control that. If the investors want to do this deal, they can." Astrid felt a cold shudder going through her bones, but Ali smiled: "But please don't worry, we won't do that to you. Exit is a game. We have an underwriter who wants to take us public, we now have an offer to get acquired by Golden Gate, but let's not rush it. Let's make sure we consider all exit options."

11.4 Sale to Financial Buyers

Investors can also achieve liquidity by selling the company to a financial buyer. This sale can take two different forms: (1) If the sale involves the transfer of all shares, we call it a buyout. (2) If the share sale is only partial, we call it a "secondary sale" or "secondary." We examine them in turn.

11.4.1 Buyouts

A buyout is a financial transaction in which a new set of financial investors buys all of a company's equity. Often, the investors are institutions, especially private equity funds (also called buyout funds).[82] Unlike acquirers, these buyers are financially motivated and do not integrate the venture into a larger corporate structure. Instead, the buyout preserves the company as an independent entity. Buyouts typically occur in the later stages of company development. While acquisitions and IPOs fundamentally transform the venture, buyouts are not meant to rattle the corporate organization.

The structure of a buyout transaction is simple: the buyer becomes the new owner of the company and gets all of the equity. The buyer also assumes all the liabilities, including debt obligations. If a large amount of debt is raised to finance the purchase of shares, the transaction is called a leveraged buyout (LBO). If the transaction is initiated by the incumbent management team that wants to increase its hold over the company, it is called a management buyout (MBO). A variation of an MBO is a buyback, where the founders repurchase shares from the investors. This usually happen when the company is slow to develop, and the original investors want liquidity by exercising redemption rights (Section 6.4.3). In such cases, it is common to have a private equity fund provide financing to the founders. Finally, if the buyout is initiated by an investor with the goal of taking over the company and installing an outside management team, the transaction is called a management buy-in (MBI).

The complexity of the deal structure typically depends on the size of the transaction. Smaller ventures with simple operations can be bought out without using any complex financial instruments. The buyers simply acquire all of the sellers' equity and become the new owners. Buying out larger and more established companies, however, involves more complex deal structures with several layers of debt, each with its covenants and maturity structures.

The process through which a company is sold to a financial buyer is either by negotiation or by an auction. Smaller entrepreneurial companies can only find a limited number of potential buyers, so the process is typically by negotiation. Larger and more established companies, however, may be able to attract multiple interested parties. Therefore, they often organize an auction through an investment banker, or else they structure the negotiation in a competitive manner that resembles an auction.

11.4.2 Secondary Sales

"Secondaries" is the term used to describe the secondary sale of shares in the context of private market transactions. Secondaries are similar to buyouts in that they preserve the structure of the company as an independent privately held entity. As in buyouts, the buyers are typically financial firms, but they only buy the stake of one or few investors. Secondaries have become increasingly important in recent years. The underlying trend is that companies tend to achieve IPO status and acquisition exits at ever later stages of development (Box 11.2).

One word of caution. The term *secondaries* is used for the sale of company shares that we discuss in this section, but it is also used for the sale of VC partnership shares, which are financial claims on an entire VC portfolio. We discuss the latter in Section 12.6.2.

There are three types of secondary share sellers, each with their own motives: (1) investors who want liquidity for their investments (Section 11.1.1); (2) employees who want to cash in the common stock they have obtained by exercising stock options; and (3) the founders or senior managers themselves. These sellers have two reasons to sell. First, they typically earn a modest salary (Section 6.3.2) and therefore have a demand for liquidity. Second, they hold an undiversified portfolio; with their entire wealth tied up with the company, they may want to reduce their personal risk by selling some of their shares. The pressure to obtain liquidity from founders and employees can be strong and create some friction with investors, as was the case with data-mining unicorn Palantir.[83]

Secondaries have three types of buyers. First, there are existing investors who buy secondary shares from their peers. They may do so by exercising a right of first refusal, which gives investors the right to purchase shares offered by other investors (Section 9.3.3). Second, there are investors who are new to the company, who purchase secondary shares from existing investors. The third type of buyer is the company itself, which may repurchase some of its own shares. This last type of transaction is relatively rare and typically applies in special circumstances such as the removal of undesirable shareholders—for example, departed founders and employees who choose to become a nuisance to the company.

Shareholders can sell their shares in three types of secondary transactions: (1) as part of a funding round, (2) in a stand-alone transaction, or (3) on a specialized market. First, in a funding round, later-stage investors may buy shares from existing shareholders. Since a funding round is done to raise funds for the company, new investors buy secondary shares when they want to invest more in the company than it needs to raise.

Second, in a stand-alone purchase of secondary shares, a financial buyer agrees to buy a block of shares from a specific set of shareholders. Financial buyers are typically other VC firms. There are also VC secondary funds who specialize in such deals. For example, Delta-v Capital and Harvest Growth Capital are specialized Silicon Valley firms, founded by veteran VCs who specialize in secondaries.

Stand-alone purchases require the approval of the company's board of directors and possibly other shareholders who hold rights of first refusal. Since the transaction risks the disclosure of valuation information, there can be resistance, especially when the valuation is lower than in the previous funding round. Structuring such secondaries may thus involve difficult negotiations among the buyers, existing shareholders, and the company.

The third way of buying and selling secondary shares is through a dedicated marketplace that allows for trading of privately held company stock. In recent years, several attempts have been made to create markets that cater to the liquidity needs of private company shareholders, especially for large private technology companies ("pre-IPOs"). These attempts are motivated by both demand and supply forces. The supply of shares comes largely from founders and employees who seek liquidity for their common shares or stock options. On the demand side, there are investors keen to put money into successful companies that are believed to be heading for an IPO. Box 11.7 considers the history of platforms for secondaries.

Box 11.7   A Primer on Secondary Platforms

Secondary sales have long been an opaque niche business. In the last decade, however, several pioneers have tried to create online marketplaces for them. In 2009, SecondMarket, set up five years earlier to trade illiquid assets, introduced a platform for exchanging restricted stock of private companies. It catered to Facebook employees trying to sell some of their shares. SecondMarket's transaction volume peaked in the 2012 run-up to the Facebook IPO. However, Facebook itself disliked the fact that its shares were trading ahead of the IPO and tried to stop it. More generally, SecondMarket found it difficult to get support from companies whose shares were being traded on its platform.

Also in 2009, SharesPost created a competing platform to match individual buyers and sellers and assist in executing transactions. SharesPost teamed up with Nasdaq in 2013 to create an intermediated secondary market. Again, the model was met with hostility by private companies who wanted to keep control of their shareholders. It also exposed the difficulty of running a marketplace with little information and high regulatory hurdles. In 2015, SharesPost and Nasdaq parted ways, and Nasdaq acquired SecondMarket, with the goal of gathering support from the private companies. SecondMarket became Nasdaq Private Market, providing companies with proprietary software solutions and help in executing company-sponsored "structured liquidity programs." As for SharesPost, it became a broker–dealer specializing in matching individual sellers and buyers of pre-IPO company shares.

Around 2013, secondaries became a fertile ground for Fintech companies. Of particular note are EquityZen and ForgeGlobal (formerly Equidate), both of which aim at servicing pre-IPO shareholders seeking liquidity, and accredited investors seeking investments. EquityZen introduced the use of a fund structure that minimizes the impact of transactions on the company's Cap Table. The fund acquires the shares of several sellers and becomes the shareholder of the company. Buyers purchase fractional ownership of the fund. ForgeGlobal created a proprietary derivative structure that does not impact the company's Cap Table. Instead of trying to transfer restricted stock itself, the company creates derivative shares that transfer the financial gains but not the legal ownership and voting rights. The seller obtains a payment that corresponds to the agreed value of the shares, but retains legal ownership of the shares. The buyer makes the payment and receives a derivative that promises to pay the value of the shares at the future exit date.

Considerable experimentation is still ongoing, and no winning model has yet emerged. For instance, crowdfunding platforms like MicroVentures, founded in 2009, and UK-based SEEDRS have also expanded into secondary trading. An increasingly important element in shaping future developments is the behavior of the relevant regulators. Since 2016, the U.S. Securities and Exchange Commission (SEC) has stepped up its oversight of secondary market trading, as part of a wider policy of securing equal treatment for all investors across private and public markets.[84]

Secondaries pricing is always delicate for two main reasons. First, sellers typically have an informational advantage. A willingness to sell may always be motivated by unfavorable insider information. This is once again the lemons problem of Box 2.6. Second, common stock has a lower price than preferred stock, especially at earlier rounds (Section 6.5). Because pricing this difference in a small transaction can be challenging, secondaries are mostly for common stock held by founders and employees

WorkHorse Box 11.3 The Secondaries Option

Ali promised to consider all exit options, so after meeting with Astrid he contacted Wolf C. Flow to discuss what further options they could pursue. Wolf thought that a full financial buyout would be difficult to organize, but that maybe there was a chance of raising a D round and using that occasion for some secondary sales. "At Eagle-I you are under liquidity pressure, but we at Coyo-T Capital are not in a hurry," Wolf noted. "In fact, we would be open to double down on WorkHorse. Besides, putting a round offer on the table might put some pressure on the other exit options." He summarized his proposed offer in a table.

Wolf suggested a step-up price of $25, for a $120M post-money ($100M pre-money) valuation. He envisioned that JetLuck and GestütenTechnik would each invest $10M of primary shares and that Coyo-T Capital would buy all of Eagle-I shares in a secondary transaction amounting to almost $12M. "Let's see if JetLuck and GestütenTechnik come along with this plan" Wolf noted. "If not, we could even do a pure secondary transaction on our own."

	Series C		Proposed Series D		
Price per share ($)	20.0		25.0		
Investment ($)	17,666,667		20,000,000		
Post-money valuation ($)	80,000,000		120,000,000		
Pre-money valuation ($)	62,333,333		100,000,000		
Value of secondary sale ($)			11,697,850		
	Shares held	Ownership fraction	Shares bought	Shares held	Ownership fraction
Founders	800,000	20.0%	0	800,000	16.7%
Other common	525,000	13.1%	0	525,000	10.9%
Michael Archie	179,167	4.5%	0	179,167	3.7%
Eagle-I Ventures	467,914	11.7%	-467,914	0	0.0%
Coyo-T Capital	614,974	15.4%	467,914	1,082,888	22.6%
JetLuck	800,000	20.0%	400,000	1,200,000	25.0%
GestütenTechnik	344,920	8.6%	400,000	744,920	15.5%
Stanley Goldmorgan	268,026	6.7%	0	268,026	5.6%
Total shares	4,000,000	100%	800,000	4,800,000	100%

Ali greatly appreciated Wolf's offer but still felt compelled to ask: "We have three good exit options, I wonder if there is anything else that we could do?" Wolf replied: "Well, according to that authoritative entrepreneurial finance book by Da Hell, or whatever they were called, there is only one other exit option left. That is closing down the company. We are clearly not going to do that, so why don't we get serious and make a decision soon." Ali hesitated "Agreed, but what I miss is that sense of competition, of anxiety, of urgency! Maybe this exit game needs a few more phone calls."

WorkHorse Box 11.3 examines the possibility of doing a secondary sale.

11.5 Closing Down the Company

Our discussion so far has focused on the upside exit scenario illustrated in Figure 11.2. We now return to Figure 11.1, which looks at the downside exit decisions. In this case, the company is likely to be underperforming, showing symptoms such as lagging sales or excessive costs, failing to deliver breakthroughs, missing milestones, or suffering from the rise of competitive threats. In Section 9.4, we discuss how investors make the decision about whether or not to refinance the company. If they don't, companies decide whether to attempt continuing without funding (the "walking dead" scenario) or closing down operations. It is important to notice that investors often decide to close down companies in which they invested millions. Such was the case of Jibo, a social robot invented in 2014 by robotics engineer Cynthia Breazeal. The homonymous company had raised over $70M in venture funding, but sales sagged as the machine failed to provide the expected user experience.[85] We now follow the final steps when a company actually closes down.

In many cases, the process of closure is straightforward: the venture experiences a quiet death. When the money runs out, employees leave, economic activities cease, and the shareholders liquidate any remaining proceeds. An alternative way to closing down the company can be to have it acquired for a price that reflects the value of the remaining assets. This saves the costs of closure and may mask the negative outcome. For instance, in October 2016, Groupon Inc., the e-commerce platform, acquired LivingSocial for a "nonmaterial" amount. LivingSocial had previously raised about $900M and was valued over $4B, but it was outcompeted by Groupon. After the acquisition, Groupon retained the LivingSocial brand to hold on to its customer base.[86]

If a company owes debt that it cannot repay, then it has to enter some form of court-administered bankruptcy procedure, with the goal of restructuring assets to repay the debt. When the company is experiencing temporary financial distress but remains economically viable, the court will allow the company to maintain its operation, restructure its debt, and return to normal operations. Restructuring debt becomes the core task of such bankruptcy proceedings. This requires negotiations between the company and the lenders, as well as among the lenders themselves. Typical outcomes include extensions of loan maturity, higher interest rates or fees, new lending facilities, and possibly some loan forgiveness. In the U.S., the procedures for restructuring companies are governed under Chapter 11 of the bankruptcy code.[87] When the company is considered no longer economically viable, then the role of bankruptcy procedures is to ensure its orderly dissolution. In this case, the bankruptcy court oversees the transfer of collateral, the sale of all remaining assets, and the distribution of all final proceeds according to credit seniority. In the U.S., the procedures for closing down companies are governed under Chapter 7 of the bankruptcy code.

Bankruptcy imposes direct and indirect costs on the parties involved.[88] There are direct administrative costs of bankruptcy, such as paying lawyers, accountants, and other experts. Some of these costs are borne by the company directly, others by the lenders. There are also indirect losses associated with business disruption. In case of Chapter 11, there may be some loss of revenue (customers may avoid purchasing from companies on the brink of bankruptcy), higher costs (suppliers may be less inclined to offer concessions to companies on the brink of bankruptcy), as well as a significant burden on management time. In case of Chapter 7 business closure, the fire sale value of assets is often below their true value.[89]

If the founders provided personal funding to their start-up, there can be personal bankruptcy.[90] In case of actual personal bankruptcy, the private consequences can be severe. Beyond personal stress, there can be consequences for future access to credit. Entrepreneurs may even experience a stigma of failure that taints their reputation and affects their subsequent career opportunities.[91] The legal rules governing personal bankruptcy may also impact the decision to become an entrepreneur in the first place, the extent to which entrepreneurs want to borrow, and how much lenders are willing to lend.[92]

Finally, it should be noted that every country has its own bankruptcy laws and procedures. In some countries, such as Canada or Germany, bankruptcy laws mainly protect creditors. These countries strictly enforce seniority rules; that is, senior creditors get paid before junior creditors. However, in other countries such as the U.S. or France, bankruptcy laws are more lenient toward debtors (i.e., companies). Their rules allow breaking seniority rules.[93] Arguments can be made for both approaches: favoring creditors can lead to too many closures, favoring debtors can lead to too many inefficient continuations. Moreover, different bankruptcy regimes give different incentives. Regimes that favor creditors (debtors) increase (reduce) the willingness of lenders to make loans. At the same time, they may discourage (encourage) firms from making risky investments.[94]

11.6 Determinants of the Exit Decision

We are now in a position to discuss how investors and companies actually make exit decisions. We identify three sets of forces that affect this decision. First, there are market forces that at different times favor certain exit types over others. Second, each company has its own economic fundamentals and development path. Third, company-level dynamics between entrepreneurs and investors affect the timing and choice of exit.

11.6.1 Market Forces

To understand the market forces underlying the exit decision, it is useful to distinguish between institutional factors, which are stable over time but vary across countries, and cyclical market factors, which change over time. Consider first institutional factors. Different countries have different legal and regulatory environments, as well as different business practices and cultural norms. Stock markets are a clear case in point. In some countries, such as the U.S., favorable legislation supports stock exchanges. Markets in these countries are accessible to young and small, providing funding and liquidity for the investors (Box 11.4). In other countries such as Germany or Japan, however, stock markets play a much more limited role. In these countries entrepreneurial companies find it more difficult to access stock markets. Taxation also matters. For example, the type of exit can affect the capital gains tax owed by different shareholders. Finally, there are cultural factors. The prestige of different exit channels varies across cultures.

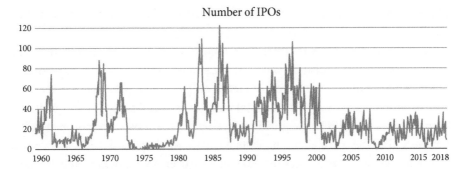

Figure 11.4. IPO waves.

This figure shows the monthly number of IPOs on U.S. exchanges for the period 1960–2018.

Source: Jay Ritter's website: https://site.warrington.ufl.edu/ritter/ipo-data.

In addition to these institutional factors, exit options are affected by cyclical market dynamics. The variability in the IPO market is particularly important (Section 11.2.2) and may sometimes lead to withdrawing the IPO.[95] Figure 11.4 shows the wide fluctuations in the number of IPOs on U.S. exchanges. By and large,

---

Box 11.8 If You Buy One, I'll Buy One Too!

Competitors imitate each other at every step, always anxious not to miss out on the latest trick. If one established company acquires a start-up in a new techno-logical subfield, its competitors may rush to make a similar acquisition. A recent study by Ozmel, Reuer, and Wu looks at acquisitions in the biotechnology industry, where established pharmaceutical companies rely on the acquisition of innovative biotech start-ups to maintain their competitive edge.[97] The study examines the probability of getting acquired in a sample of 1,369 venture capital-backed biotech start-ups. It finds that the larger the number of recent acquisitions in a company's industry segment, the greater the likelihood that the company gets acquired. This effect is stronger when acquisitions are made by more prominent acquirers. These findings are consistent with the notion that established competitors respond to each other's acquisitions, thereby causing acquisition waves within specific industry segments.

An additional finding is that acquisition waves are more pronounced in areas of biotechnology that appear to be riskier. This may come as a surprise, for one might think that established companies tread more carefully in riskier environments. The researchers point out that established companies rely on two types of information when assessing the attractiveness of new industry segments: their own internal assessment and the signals they can glean from competitors. They rely more on their own internal assessment in less risky segments, but more on their competitors' cues in more uncertain segments. Put differently, if you buy one, I'd better buy one too, especially if I am not really sure what is going on.

there were many more IPOs in the last two decades of last century than in the first two decades of the new century.

Acquisitions also come in waves that tend to be industry specific.[96] Box 11.8 looks at research on acquisition waves from a strategic management perspective.

Figure 11.5 provides interesting evidence on global exit patterns over the 2005 to 2018 period. Panel A reports the total number of exits divided into acquisitions, financial sales, and IPOs. Acquisitions are by far the most common exit route. For every IPO there are about six exits over the whole period. IPOs show some cyclicality, while financial sales increase slightly over time. Looking at exit values (Panel B) gives us a different picture: collectively, IPOs are worth much more than acquisitions. This happens in almost all years.

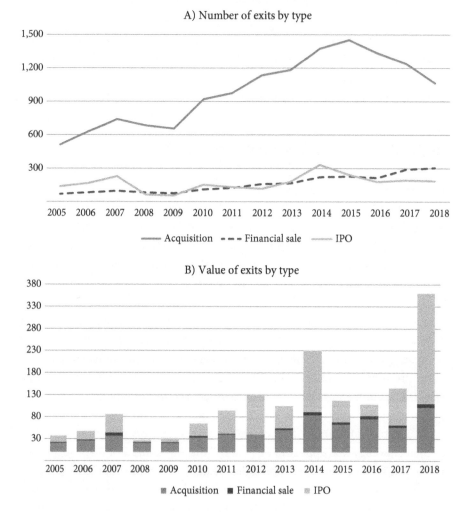

Figure 11.5. Exit patterns.

Data in U.S. dollar billions. Source: PitchBook Data.

Moreover, the underlying data show that the average IPO company has a valuation of $358M, while the average acquisition is only $48M. There is also a stable difference across regions. The average IPO in the U.S. achieves a valuation of $512M versus $154M in Europe. The corresponding valuations for acquisitions are $55M and $27M, respectively. The rest of the world shows intermediate values.

11.6.2 Economic Fundamentals

A company's business situation, competitive environment, and strategic prospects—its "economic fundamentals"—clearly influence its exit choice. Recall that even though exit concerns the sale of investor shares, the choice of exit also affects the underlying business. In this section, we therefore examine how economic fundamentals guide exit choices. Figure 11.6 shows a simple decision tree that models this choice.

Looking at exit from the perspective of the company's shareholders leads us to ask two questions. The first is whether the company should remain an independent entity or become integrated into a larger organization? The latter option implies getting acquired. If the company chooses to remain independent, it faces a second question: should it remain private or go public? If the shareholders are better off with a privately held company, then investors can achieve an exit through a financial sale, or they may simply continue funding the company with an additional round of financing (see Chapter 9). We now examine these two strategic questions more closely.

As we see in Section 13.3.3, the company should get acquired whenever the acquisition price exceeds its value as an independent entity. What predicts whether and when attractive acquisition offers are likely to be forthcoming? To answer this question, we need to ask whether there are enough synergies from integrating the start-up with an acquirer (see also Section 13.3.1).

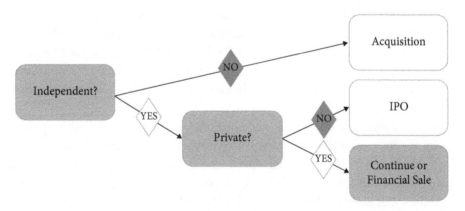

Figure 11.6. Economic fundamentals of the exit decision.

The benefits of integration can be thought of as the things that the start-up can only do after being acquired. Often, this means getting access to distribution channels and supply chains. For example, a software company that develops a business application may find it difficult to market its product as a stand-alone. An established provider of a software suite may be able to integrate the new application and bring it to success, while also enhancing its own customer value. An example is the acquisition of Trello, a project management app developer, which was acquired in January 2017 for $425M by Atlassian, a developer of software collaboration tools.[98] Other examples of complementary assets include access to intellectual property, production technology, or specialized expertise. One caveat is that access to key assets can alternatively be achieved through a strategic partnership. However, integrating through an acquisition is a more comprehensive arrangement that is usually preferable when substantial synergies can be captured.

Remaining independent has two principal benefits. One is maintaining entrepreneurial incentives. In a stand-alone company, founders and managers are held accountable for their own performance. This becomes more difficult in a larger organization when the acquired unit no longer has its own profit and loss statement. Add to that the administrative complexity of any larger organization, and it quickly becomes difficult to identify who is accountable for what.

The second benefit of remaining an independent entity is the option value of waiting. The decision to get acquired or stay independent is a dynamic one: Staying independent doesn't necessarily mean doing so forever; it may simply mean holding out long enough to create better exit options. A start-up may refuse an acquisition offer in the hope of generating more and better offers at a future time. For instance, Snapchat refused a $3B acquisition offer by Facebook in 2013, and went public in 2017, achieving a market capitalization of $33B (Box 3.2).[99] In other words, the benefits of being a stand-alone entity may be temporary. It buys the company time to resolve some uncertainties before eventually accepting an attractive offer from the right buyer.

If a company decides to remain independent, the second question in Figure 11.6 is whether the company should be publicly listed or privately held. In the former case, the investors obtain liquidity at or after the IPO. In the latter case, the investors obtain liquidity through a sale to financial buyers. Section 11.2.1 discusses the pros and cons from a company perspective. Whether or not a company can go public depends on regulations (Section 11.2.2) and market factors (Section 11.6.1).

Here we note that the benefits and costs of staying private need not be permanent; they can actually be temporary. The question is not whether to go public or stay private forever; rather, it is whether to go public now or stay private for a while longer and reconsider the decision at a later point. If the company remains private, investors may continue funding it or choose to obtain liquidity through a private sale, whether a buyout or a secondary sale (Section 11.4).

11.6.3 Internal Company Dynamics

The third element affecting the exit decision is the internal company dynamics and the managerial process of how the exit decision is actually made. Ultimately, it is the board of directors that decides on exit. Although there are many idiosyncratic factors that differ across companies, we focus here on some common issues. In general, the biggest conflicts are between the entrepreneurs and the investors. There can also be further disagreements among the investors themselves, who may have different opinions and objectives.

The core driver of the exit decision is the desire for liquidity. Both founders and incumbent investors like liquidity, but founders also favor control over the way the company is managed, and venture capital investors may need liquidity to send money back to their own funders (Section 12.3). Founders may cherish the idea of remaining at the helm of their company after an IPO. They may also have feelings about losing control after an acquisition, objecting to restrictive employment contracts or onerous earn-out clauses.

We noted in the context of Figure 11.2 that an exit decision is a recurring choice between a certain return in the present versus a risky return in the future. Exit decisions are therefore affected by beliefs about the company's future. Founders are often more optimistic than investors about their business, constantly seeing new opportunities on the horizon.[100] They might therefore favor keeping the company private and independent. By contrast, more level-headed investors often prefer exiting the company when an occasion arrives. Different financial incentives also affect the exit decision. We noted in Section 5.2 that preferred shares usually have an automatic conversion clause in case of an IPO. This may give investors an incentive to push for an acquisition where the preferred terms apply, rather than an IPO where they are automatically lost.[101]

If entrepreneurs and investors disagree on the exit decision, how does this get resolved? In Chapter 6 we saw how term sheets determine control over the exit decision. All control levers can be activated to influence an exit decision. Term sheets may give investors veto rights over exit, and/or specify explicit rights to initiate the sale of their shares, with registration and drag-along rights (Section 6.4.3).[102] Exit decisions are made by the board of directors but may also need the approval of a majority of shareholders, thereby involving voting rights. Finally, in addition to formal control rights, there is informal control, especially the power of persuasion and the power of individuals. It is difficult for investors to get a company public or acquired if the founders and senior managers don't support it. Their opposition can easily derail the entire IPO process. For example, Applied Medical Corp.'s VC investors filed for IPO registration in November 2011 and engaged in a bitter dispute with the company, which ended in the withdrawal of the registration in June 2013.[103]

Overall, we note that whereas market conditions and economic fundamentals determine the set of exit choices from which entrepreneurs and investors can choose

FUNDAMENTALS OF ENTREPRENEURIAL FINANCE

WorkHorse Box 11.4 The Final Decision

On a bitter cold day in late November, the four founders huddled together at "Het Trappe," their favorite Ann Arbor Dutch trappist beer joint, to discuss the future of WorkHorse. They had toiled on their start-up for over five years, experiencing unexpected highs and numerous lows. In a few weeks, their board of directors would meet and discuss three potential exit options: an IPO led by ShoeHorn Bank, an acquisition by Golden Gate, or another round of financing with a secondary sale. The founders felt that this was the end of the road for their adventure. They wanted it to finish in style.

Annie opened the conversation: "JetLuck and Shoehorn will definitely try to shoehorn us into an IPO, that's for sure." Brandon continued: "GestütenTechnik won't interfere with the exit decision, and Wolf C. Flow prefers a D-round." Astrid noted: "I am worried about Ali. Eagle-I really needs some liquidity. He even considered that awful earn-out offer from Golden Gate. Thankfully, he now prefers Wolf's D-round with a secondary sale for him. What would we do without Wolf?" Bharat reminded her that she had not always felt so warmly about Wolf. He went on: "I hope you all realize that we are heading straight for a major confrontation at our next board meeting: JetLuck and ShoeHorn will fight for an IPO, Eagle-I and Coyo-T Capital for a D-round, and no one will listen to us."

Astrid sighed: "If we could only get a better offer out of Golden Gate." Suddenly Annie exclaimed: "How about we get an offer from Gou Taiyang Jilie?" "Gou Who?" bellowed the other three in unison. Annie looked exasperated: "Gou Taiyang Jilie, or GTJ if you prefer. It is one of the biggest Chinese technology companies." Bharat objected: "We know that, but they don't do solar!" Annie persisted: "That's the point. They are Golden Gate's arch enemy. The last thing Golden Gate wants is GTJ to acquire us and thereby enter solar." Astrid lightened up: "Even if Golden Gate just hears rumors about GTJ getting interested, they will be all over us. Ali must know someone at GTJ. Let's ask him to make one more call."

A few days later Ali called back. GTJ had had WorkHorse on its radar since its B round and was considering making an offer, subject to due diligence and a clarification of several legal issues. The process was relatively quick, and a week later GTJ called back with a proposal to buy WorkHorse for $110M in cash, subject to legal due diligence. "Amazing! What's next?" Astrid replied. "Easy," Ali responded. "We continue to play the great exit game. Let me send this offer over to our friends at Golden Gate. I am curious to hear what Goldie has to say." Two days later Ali called again: "I am just off the line with Goldie TomKat. Golden Gate is happy to increase their offer to three Golden Gate shares for every WorkHorse share. At a share price of $10 that would amount to a $120M acquisition. Should I call GTJ once more?" Astrid replied: "Call them until Golden Gate drops the earn-out clause." Three days later Ali had further updates. "GTJ is willing to pay $115M in cash. Golden Gate is sticking to $120M but is willing to drop the earn-out clause. Whom should I call next?" Without hesitation Astrid replied: "Let's call a board meeting!"

In a conference call the next day, the board unanimously approved Golden Gate's acquisition offer. When the acquisition was announced in early 2025, analysts praised it enthusiastically. On that day Golden Gate's stock price jumped 10%, to $11 per share.

WorkHorse Box 11.5   Epilogue

After two years of working at Golden Gate, the four founders decided to go their separate ways. Astrid accepted Ali Ad-Lehr's invitation to join at Eagle-I Ventures. Brandon returned to Ann Arbor where he became the CEO of one of Michael Archie's latest companies. Bharat accepted a position at Stanford University that entailed scientific research and teaching entrepreneurship, both of which he loved and excelled at. Annie traveled the world for a year before settling in Shanghai where she married Bjorn, a Swedish artist with a passion for good food. They started a new company where she could practice her newfound passion, a Nordic bakery.

The evening before parting ways, the four founders gathered for a beer at "Het Trappe." "Was it really worth all the effort?" Astrid asked rhetorically. To everyone's surprise, Brandon pulled out yet another spreadsheet: "I was wondering about that myself last night, so I ran the numbers." He produced the following tables that showed the ownership, investments, and (gross of tax) returns of all the parties ever involved with WorkHorse. He computed cash-on-cash (CCR), internal rate of return (IRR), and net present value (NPV) figures (Section 4.2.2).

"We obviously did pretty well ourselves, but do you know which investors made the highest percentage returns? Well, it depends on whether you look at CCR or IRR metrics, but my uncle JP Potro, Michael Archie, and the Ang brothers did the best. Also, using a 20% discount rate, everyone made a positive NPV. Interestingly, our NPV is really high, but it assumes no investment." The three others stared at Brandon. "No investment?" growled Astrid. "We put our savings and sleepless nights in it!" "And the risk of coming out empty-handed!" added Bahrat. "Yes, I know" Brandon replied, "these numbers alone cannot tell our whole story." A heated debate ensued, but they eventually concluded that all these years together had been about a lot more than just making a financial return. As they prepared to leave, Brandon concluded: "Obviously, there is all that financial stuff, but as for the experience and the friendships . . . well for me, that has an infinite post-money valuation."

WorkHorse's capitalization table.

Round	Pre-seed	Seed	A Round	B Round	C Round	Exit	Ownership
Date	2019	2020	2021	2022	2024	2025	
Share price ($)		2.00	4.80	8.00	20.00	28.50	
Round investment ($)	80,000	500,000	2,000,000	10,000,000	17,666,667		
Pre-money valuation ($)		2,000,000	6,000,000	14,933,333	62,333,333	114,000,000	
Post-money valuation ($)		2,500,000	8,000,000	24,933,333	80,000,000	114,000,000	
New shares issued	1,000,000	250,000	416,667	1,450,000	883,333		
Shares outstanding	1,000,000	1,250,000	1,666,667	3,116,667	4,000,000		
Individual shareholdings:							
Astrid Dala	210,604					210,604	5.3%
Annie Ma	198,442					198,442	5.0%
Bharat Marwari	144,264					144,264	3.6%
Brandon Potro	246,690					246,690	6.2%
University of Michigan	50,000					50,000	1.3%
Stock option pool	100,000			200,000		300,000	7.5%
JP Potro	50,000					50,000	1.3%
Michael Archie		125,000	41,667	12,500		179,167	4.5%
Ang brothers		125,000				125,000	3.1%
Eagle-I Ventures			208,333	156,250	103,331	467,914	11.7%
Coyo-T Capital			166,667	312,500	135,807	614,973	15.4%
JetLuck				500,000	300,000	800,000	20.0%
GestütenTechnik				268,750	76,170	344,920	8.6%
Stanley Goldmorgan					268,026	268,026	6.7%
Total new shares	1,000,000	250,000	416,667	1,450,000	883,333	4,000,000	
Total shares	1,000,000	1,250,000	1,666,667	3,116,667	4,000,000	4,000,000	100%

WorkHorse's investments and returns.

	Investments							Returns		
	Pre-seed	Seed round	A Round	B Round	C Round	Value at exit ($)	Total invested ($)	Cash-on-cash returns (CCR)	Internal rate of return (IRR)	Net present value (NPV)
Year:	2019	2020	2021	2022	2024					
Astrid Dala						6,002,212				2,010,129
Annie Ma						5,655,585				1,894,044
Bharat Marwari						4,111,533				1,376,944
Brandon Potro						7,030,670				2,354,557
University of Michigan						1,425,000				477,230
Stock Option Pool						8,550,000				2,863,378
JP Potro	80,000					1,425,000	80,000	17.8	61.6%	397,230
Michael Archie		250,000	200,000	100,000		5,106,250	550,000	9.3	65.8%	1,537,625
Ang brothers		250,000				3,562,500	250,000	14.3	70.1%	1,181,689
Eagle-I Ventures			1,000,000	1,250,000	2,066,620	13,335,559	4,316,620	3.1	53.9%	2,742,069
Coyo-T Capital			800,000	2,500,000	2,716,134	17,526,741	6,016,134	2.9	53.1%	3,338,791
JetLuck				4,000,000	6,000,000	22,800,000	10,000,000	2.3	50.9%	4,235,767
GestütenTechnik				2,150,000	1,523,396	9,830,214	3,673,396	2.7	51.8%	2,279,776
Stanley Goldmorgan					5,360,517	7,638,737	5,360,517	1.4	42.5%	1,005,097
Total	80,000	500,000	2,000,000	10,000,000	17,666,667	114,000,000	30,246,667	3.8	54.6%	
Cumulative Investment	80,000	580,000	2,580,000	12,580,000	30,246,667					

from, company dynamics, and especially the relative preferences of entrepreneurs and investors, determine the actual choices made. The process by which these choices are made is shaped by the company's corporate governance structure.

WorkHorse Box 11.4 looks at the final exit decision.

WorkHorse Box 11.5 contains the epilogue to the story.

Summary

This chapter examines the process through which investors exit entrepreneurial ventures. We look at the motivations for exit, as well as the consequences for the entrepreneur, the investor, and the company. We analyze why different types of investors eventually need to realize a return on the companies they finance, and we discuss the timing of the exit decision. We examine in detail the process of exiting the company, considering four exit routes: listing the company on a stock exchange (IPO), selling it to an industrial incumbent (acquisition), selling it to a financial buyer (buyout or secondary sale), or closing it down. We distinguish three levels of exit determinants: market forces, business forces that affect the development of the specific company, and company-internal dynamics around the exit decision.

With this chapter we reach the end of the FIRE framework (Chapter 1). The final step, EXIT, brings to conclusion the investment cycle, hopefully allowing both parties to generate some financial returns. Exit, however, is not imposed from outside. Instead it is the outcome of a complex decision process that is influenced by multiple parties: the entrepreneurs, the investors, the potential acquirers, stock market investors, underwriters, regulators, and others. Understanding their objectives and constraints is the key to understanding the exit process.

Review Questions

1. Why do investors and entrepreneurs want an exit?
2. What affects the optimal timing of exit?
3. Why are IPOs often underpriced?
4. What are the advantages and disadvantages of dual-class share listings?
5. What are the most common strategic motives for acquiring start-ups?
6. How do financial buyers differ from strategic buyers?
7. What are the main challenges of structuring secondary markets for private shares?
8. Why are there several bankruptcy regimes? What are their respective objectives?
9. How are exit decisions affected by market forces?
10. What are the most common sources of internal conflict around exit decisions?

Notes

1. Michelacci and Suarez (2004).
2. Amihud, Mendelson, and Pedersen (2006) discuss of the concept and measures of liquidity of financial assets.
3. Koeplin, Sarin, and Shapiro (2000).
4. Gompers et al. (2008).
5. Lowry, Michaely and Volkova (2017).
6. This estimate is for companies first funded between 1991 and 2000 (NVCA 2013 Yearbook, page 8).
7. Hall and Woodward (2010).
8. Gompers et al. (2019).
9. Artinger and Powell (2016).
10. Ljungqvist, Nanda, and Singh (2006).
11. Bertrand and Schoar (2006).
12. Gao, Ritter, and Zhu (2013).
13. The term *unicorn* was coined by venture capitalist Aileen Lee in 2013, with the idea of identifying the rare, fast-growing, and transformative companies any venture investor aims to fund. It has since become a very common term in the jargon (Lee, 2013).
14. Brown and Wiles (2015). The Wall Street Journal's Billion Dollar Start-up Club is an interactive database of unicorns on a global scale: https://www.wsj.com/graphics/billion-dollar-club. Other data repositories are Crunchbase's Unicorn Leader Board:" https://www.crunchbase.com/lists/unicorn-leaderboard-privately-held/488c2557-4d5a-4c25-8bd3-61c519f07508, and CB Insights' Global Unicorn Club: https://www.cbinsights.com/research-unicorn-companies. All websites accessed on April 15, 2019.
15. https://www.cbinsights.com/research-unicorn-companies. Accessed April 15, 2019.
16. Bright (2019).
17. Bender, Evans, and Kupor (2015) and Ramadan et al. (2015).
18. Chernenko, Lerner, and Zeng (2017) and Ewens and Farre-Mensa (2018).
19. Ewens, Nanda, and Rhodes-Kropf (2018)
20. Gornall and Strebulaev (2019) provide a detailed analysis and several examples, and Bhashyam (2015) analyzes the use of ratchets in Square's IPO.
21. Brau and Fawcett (2006) and Levis and Vismara (2013).
22. Boot, Gopalan, and Thakor (2008).
23. Gompers et al. (2008).
24. Celikyurt, Sevilir, and Shivdasani (2010) show that newly public firms make acquisition at a higher rate than mature firms in the same industry.
25. Maksimovic and Pichler (2001).
26. Pagano, Panetta, and Zingales (1998), and Pollock and Gulati (2007).
27. Boot, Gopalan, and Thakor (2006).
28. Stein (1989).
29. Ferreira, Manso, and Silva (2014).
30. Bernstein (2015). The work of Aggarwal and Hsu (2013) is also closely related.
31. Karolyi (2006).
32. Chemmanur, He, and Nandy (2010).
33. Helwege and Liang (2004).
34. Ball, Chiu, and Smith (2011).
35. Pagano, Panetta and Zingales (1998).

36. Bochner, Avina, and Cheng (2016) provide a detailed description of the IPO process from a legal perspective.
37. Fang (2005).
38. Seligman (2003).
39. The full text of the JOBS Act can be found on the SEC website: https://www.sec.gov/spotlight/jobs-act.shtml, accessed April 15, 2019.
40. Chaplinsky, Hanley, and Moon (2017) and Dambra, Field, and Gustafson (2015).
41. Barth, Landsman, and Taylor (2017) and Krishna (2018).
42. Ritter (2003).
43. Wilhelm (2005).
44. Cornelli and Goldreich (2001).
45. Jenkinson, Jones, and Suntheim (2018).
46. Choo (2005).
47. Loughran and Ritter (2002).
48. Ljungqvist (2008) for a survey.
49. Grossman and Hart (1988), and Adams and Ferreira (2008).
50. The Council of Institutional Investors maintains a list of companies listed in the U.S. with dual-class shares: https://www.cii.org/dualclass_stock.
51. Klein (2018).
52. Adams, Almeida, and Ferreira (2009) document that only a small fraction of Fortune 500 companies is still led by their founders.
53. Kuchler (2018).
54. Arugaslan, Cook, and Kieschnick (2010), Atanassov (2013), Bebchuk and Kastiel (2017), Gompers, Ishii, and Metrick (2010) and Masulis, Wang, and Xie (2009).
55. Cremers, Lauterbach, and Pajuste (2018).
56. See the press release by Alibaba Group on February 21, 2012, available at: https://www.alibabagroup.com/en/news/press_pdf/p120221a.pdf.
57. Zhu (2019).
58. Levine (2019).
59. Chen and Ritter (2000).
60. Aitken (2018), Constine (2018), and Mikolajczak and Nellis (2018).
61. Holley (2018).
62. Anderson, Huang, and Torna (2017).
63. Arora, Cohen, and Walsh (2016).
64. See Faulkner, Teerikangas, and Joseph (2014) for an overview of acquisition activity.
65. Teece (1986).
66. Åstebro and Serrano (2015).
67. Graebner, Eisenhardt, and Roundy (2010).
68. Cohen and Levinthal (1989).
69. Geron (2016).
70. Helft (2011).
71. Coyle and Polsky (2013).
72. Cohen and Levinthal (1990).
73. See the Tech Start-up M&As 2018 Report, available at: https://mindthebridge.com/mtbcrunchbase-techstart-up-mas-2018.
74. In addition to the documents released for the Nobel Prize itself (available at https://www.nobelprize.org/nobel_prizes/economic-sciences). The most important reference is Vickrey (1961).
75. Capron and Shen (2007), and Eckbo (2009).
76. Fu, Li, and Officer (2013).

77. Fried, Frank, Harris, Shriver, and Jacobson LLP (2018).
78. Brougman and Fried (2010).
79. Puranam and Srikanth (2007).
80. Paruchuri, Nerkar, and Hambrick (2006).
81. Hellmann, Blackburn. Kozinski, and Murphy (1996).
82. Demaria (2010) provides an introduction to buyouts in an entrepreneurial context.
83. Dwoskin, Winkler, and Pulliam (2015).
84. See the speech of SEC Chair Mary Jo White at Stanford University in March 2016, available at: https://www.sec.gov/news/speech/chair-white-silicon-valley-initiative-3-31-16.html.
85. Mitchell (2018).
86. Lunden (2017).
87. For a practical guide to corporate bankruptcy in the U.S., see Newton (2003).
88. Bris, Welch, and Zhu (2006).
89. LoPucki and Doherty (2007).
90. Fan and White (2003).
91. Simmons, Wiklund, and Levie (2014).
92. Cerqueiro and Penas (2017) and Cerqueiro et al. (2016).
93. Claessens and Klapper (2005).
94. Acharya and Subramanian (2009), Lee et al. (2011), and Senbet and Wang (2012) provide an academic perspective, and O'Neill (2017) presents a practical introduction to bankruptcy.
95. Bernstein (2015).
96. Maksimovic, Phillips, and Yang (2013) and Ahern and Harford (2014).
97. Ozmel, Reuer, and Wu (2017).
98. https://techcrunch.com/2017/01/09/atlassian-acquires-trello.
99. Wells and Farrell (2018).
100. Åstebro et al. (2014).
101. Cumming (2008) and Hellmann (2006).
102. Bienz and Walz (2010).
103. Primack (2013) and Gormley (2013).

12

Venture Capital

Learning Goals

In this chapter students will learn:

1. The nature of venture capital investors as financial intermediaries.
2. How venture capital funds are structured, compensated, and incentivized.
3. Which trade-offs affect building a VC investment portfolio strategy.
4. How to calculate the gross and net returns to a venture capital fund.

This chapter examines the structure of venture capital (VC). We first explain that VC firms (or General Partners, GPs) are financial intermediaries that raise funds from institutional investors (or Limited Partners, LPs). We describe how institutional investors choose to allocate part of their portfolio to VC funds and how a Limited Partnership Agreement (LPA) specifies the rights, obligations, and compensation of the GP. We then examine the organization of VC firms, including their internal structure, fundraising activities, relationships with other venture capitalists (VCs), and the way they attract and select talented professionals. We discuss the structure of VC firms' investment strategies, and conclude by reviewing evidence on the gross and net returns of VC funds.

12.1 The Venture Capital Model

Chapters 2 to 11 explore the investment cycle from the perspective of the entrepreneurial venture. We now switch perspective and examine the investors. We make use of the FUEL framework described in Chapter 1 to examine investors' structure, motivation, resources, and investment style. In Chapter 12 we focus on VC, which constitutes the benchmark model for providers of entrepreneurial finance, and has a complex structure that is worth studying in its own right. In Chapter 13 we examine the other investor types and how they differ from VC. Finally, Chapter 14 looks at the entrepreneurial ecosystem in its entirety.

Figure 12.1 illustrates the VC model through the set of contractual relations and financial flows. The three main parties are the institutional investor, the VC firm with its fund vehicle, and the entrepreneurial company. At the top is the

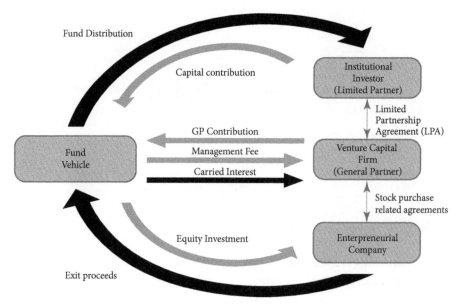

Figure 12.1. The VC model.

institutional investor, also called the Limited Partner (LP), which manages investment funds and provides the money to VC firms. At the middle level we find the VC firm, also called the General Partner (GP), and its fund vehicle. While the VC firm manages the investment process, the fund is the legal vehicle that receives the money from the investors and channels it to the companies. At the bottom level is the entrepreneurial company that receives funding to invest and grow, with the hope of achieving a successful exit.

The relationship between an institutional investor and a VC firm is governed by a Limited Partnership Agreement (LPA). This is a contract that sets out the rules concerning the creation of the fund vehicle, the financial flows, and the duties and rights of both parties. We examine the LPA in Section 12.3. The fund vehicle is legally structured as a limited liability partnership. The VC firm assumes the role of general partner by managing the fund and does not enjoy limited liability. This arrangement shields the LPs from lawsuits or other liabilities toward third parties. By remaining at arm's length, they cannot be held liable for the actions of the GP and its portfolio companies. Finally, the relationship between the VC firm and the entrepreneurial company is governed by the stock purchase agreements and other related legal documents that provide final legal form to the term sheets agreements we examine in Chapter 6.

Figure 12.1 shows that financial flows are structured into two phases, which form a full cycle. The first is the "investment phase," where money moves from the LP to the fund and down to the entrepreneurial company. The second is the "return phase," where the company generates a return that is passed back up to the LP. The gray arrows in Figure 12.1 pertain to the investment phase, the black arrows to the return phase.

Consider first the investment phase. When the LP commits money to a fund, it agrees to invest a certain amount ("capital contribution"). While the vast majority of funding comes from LPs, the VC also provides some funding ("GP contribution") to ensure commitment toward creating value through the fund. GP contributions typically amount to 1 to 2% of the fund size. Figure 12.1 also shows that the VC firm receives a management fee for managing the VC fund, which is fixed and independent of the fund's eventual return. This payment compensates the VC firm for its management services. The final arrow in the investment phase concerns the equity investment in the company.

Consider next the return phase. Once a company achieves a successful exit (Chapter 11), the VC fund obtains some proceeds ("exit proceeds"), either as cash or stock. These are divided between the LP and the VC firm. The share of the VC firm is called a "carried interest" (or just "carry"). The remainder of the proceeds is given back to the LPs ("distribution").

An important message of Figure 12.1 is that VC is a form of financial intermediation. VC firms raise funds from institutional investors and deploy them into entrepreneurial companies. In this chapter we show the consequences of investing other's money for the investment process.

Figure 12.1 simplifies by looking at a single LP, which invests in a single fund managed by a GP, which in turn is investing in a single company. In reality, there are multiple players at each level. Specifically, multiple LPs invest in a single fund; successful GPs manage several funds at the same time; and a fund invests in multiple companies. Throughout the chapter, we discuss the implications of this rich web of interactions.

We conclude this section by taking a look at fundraising activity around the world. Figure 12.2 reports the amount of funds raised (Panel A) and the number of VC funds raised (Panel B). For the period 2005–2018, an average of 213 new VC funds per year succeeded in closing their fundraising campaigns in the U.S. In Europe the average was 105, and in the rest of the world (RoW) 96. The average yearly amount raised was $30B in the U.S., $8B in Europe, and $12B in the RoW. Figure 12.2 also shows the cyclicality of fundraising. It further documents the increasing number of funds raised in the U.S. in the post-crisis period, which contrast with a stable, even slightly decreasing, trend in other countries.

12.2 Institutional Investors (LPs)

Institutional investors are financial firms that manage large amounts of financial assets.[1] There are several types of institutional investors. Pension funds, private or public, invest the pension contributions of employees. Insurance companies invest insurance premiums in order to draw on them when claims arise. Banks, beyond collecting deposits and lending, also manage the assets of wealthy clients. Sovereign wealth funds invest on behalf of governments for the benefit of their citizens, primarily by contributing to public finances. Established corporations provide

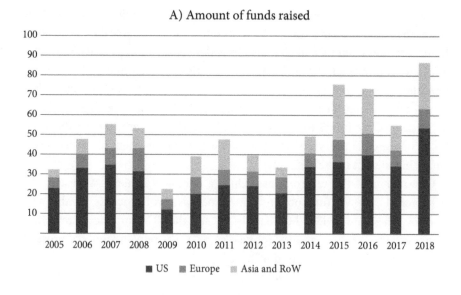

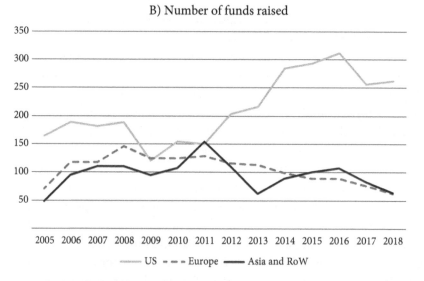

Figure 12.2. Fundraising by VC funds, by region.
Amount data in U.S. billion dollars. Source: PitchBook Data.

funding to start-ups directly (Section 13.3) but sometimes also invest in VC firms. The endowments of universities and foundations invest to generate resources to be deployed for institutional goals. Finally, high net worth individuals invest through so-called family offices.

A study by Da Rin and Phalippou measures the number of limited partners in VC and buyout funds: 23% are banks and finance companies, 21% are public pension funds, 21% are corporate pension funds, 21% are endowments, 8% are insurance companies, and 6% other.[2] Another industry report provides a break-down of amounts invested in European VC funds in the 2013–2017 period: 25.2% of funding came from government agencies, 16.0% from asset managers (including funds-of-funds), 15.2% from corporate investors, 13.8% from private individuals, 6.7% from pension funds, 6.2% from family offices, 5.1% from banks, 4.6% from endowments and foundations, 3.7% from insurance companies, 2% from capital markets, 1.1% from sovereign wealth funds, and 0.7% from academic institutions.[3]

12.2.1 Portfolio Allocation Choices

Institutional investors need to allocate their funds into an investment portfolio composed of several assets.[4] How do they make such choices? Portfolio allocation largely follows a top-down logic where funds are allocated first to asset classes and then within these asset classes. At a high level, institutional investors distribute their assets across four main asset classes: bonds, stocks, commodities, and alternative assets. Bonds include fixed-income securities like government bonds, corporate bonds, mortgage-based securities, and other interest-bearing assets, which are often exchange-traded. This asset class is widely believed to be the safest of the four, the main risks concerning default and inflation. Stocks, also called equities, include publicly traded company shares and derivative securities (options and futures) that have stocks as their underlying asset. Commodities include mainly agricultural products, oil and gas, metals, and currencies. They are often exchange-traded and therefore liquid, though possibly quite volatile. Alternative assets are a residual category that includes all other assets, mainly hedge funds, real assets (real estate and woodlands), private equity (buyouts and growth funds), and VC funds. What they have in common is that they are illiquid. This means that they cannot be quickly bought and sold on an exchange; instead they require a more patient investment approach. Institutional investors occasionally make these investments by themselves but mostly delegate them to specialized funds, including VC funds.

Institutional investors choose their asset portfolio based on their expectations about the risk and return of different assets and about the degree of their correlation. This is true also of VC funds. In Section 12.6, we examine the risk and return to these investments. The VC industry often claims that its investments have a low correlation with the stock market and are therefore attractive from a diversification standpoint. Our discussion in Section 12.6, however, casts some doubt on this argument. It also shows that the returns record of VC funds has often been disappointing. Many institutional investors have therefore decided to shun this asset class altogether. However, a substantial number of investors remain committed to VC. Their allocations to VC are typically in the range of about 3 to 5% of the total portfolio.

To better understand the portfolio investment challenges LPs face, it is useful to understand some key concepts from modern portfolio analysis. In Box 5.1 we introduced the Capital Asset Pricing Model (CAPM), which provides the foundations for modern portfolio allocation. In Box 12.1 we discuss subsequent findings of modern finance that also generated several Nobel Prizes in Economics.

Box 12.1 Nobel Insights on Financial Portfolio Analysis

The 2013 Nobel Prize in Economics was awarded jointly to Eugene Fama, Lars Peter Hansen, and Robert Shiller "for their empirical analysis of asset prices."[5] The 1997 Prize went to Robert Merton and Myron Scholes "for a new method to determine the value of derivatives."[6]

Fama developed the three-factor asset pricing model with Kenneth French, which has become known as the Fama–French model.[7] The purpose of asset pricing models is to explain excess returns, that is, individual stock returns over and above the returns to the market. The benchmark model, which we examine in Box 5.1, is the CAPM, a one-factor model based on the correlation of an asset with the market return. When researchers tested the CAPM, they found a variety of anomalies (i.e., other factors that consistently predicted asset prices). Some of these anomalies disappeared once they were discovered. For example, calendar time effects, such as a Monday, end-of-month, or January effects, all disappeared once investors developed trading strategies to profit from them. Two important anomalies, however, persist across time and markets. The Fama–French model includes them in an elegant extension of the CAPM. First, there is a size effect, where size is measured by market capitalization: Smaller stocks have higher excess returns than larger stocks. Second, there is a value effect: stocks with a higher book-to-market ratio ("value stocks") have higher excess returns than stocks with a lower book-to-market ratio ("growth stocks"), where the book-to-market ratio is the ratio of the book value of the firm's assets over its market capitalization.

The Fama–French model has implications for the valuation of VC-backed companies going public (Section 11.2). VCs invest in companies with a lower book-to-market ratio ("growth stocks"). The Fama–French model predicts lower returns and therefore higher valuations. However, the relatively smaller size of their companies implies larger returns and lower valuations. The net of these two effects can go either way.

Fama argued that once the three factors are taken into account, there is no predictability left in the stock market. He takes this as proof that markets are efficient. Shiller found himself on the opposite side of this debate, arguing that there are market inefficiencies.[8] As such, he became one of the pioneers of behavioral finance, alongside Kahneman and Thaler, whose work we discuss in

Box 3.3. Shiller focused his attention on stock market bubbles. To his credit, he correctly foretold the dot-com crash of 2000, as well as the U.S. housing market crash of 2008. His empirical work suggests that there is excess volatility in stock prices, that is, more volatility than even the Fama–French model would predict.[9] Shiller emphasizes the importance of investor sentiment in generating volatility. Even though Shiller never studied VC itself, his work on bubbles and volatility is relevant for understanding the interest of institutional investors in VC. For one, the VC market is highly cyclical and subject to sudden swings in investor sentiment. Moreover, as an asset class, VC competes for attention with volatile stock markets. Shiller argues that long-term investors would be better served investing their money in illiquid assets, such as VC, instead of chasing illusive short-run returns in the stock market.

The work of Merton and Scholes helps explain the prices of derivatives, such as stock options.[10] Institutional investors routinely purchase such derivatives, sometimes for hedging specific risks, sometimes for speculative investments. The value of an option is entirely driven by the value and volatility of the underlying stock. The Black–Scholes formula provides an elegant mathematical solution to this problem, and it has since been widely adopted by investors.[11] Merton further extended this line of research by showing how to value options in continuous time.

One important insight from option pricing is that holding an option increases the appetite for risk. Suppose you have a choice between two assets: Asset A has a certain value of $10, and Asset B gets a value of either $15 or $5 with equal probabilities (50%). Any risk-averse individual would prefer Asset A over B, because it has the same expected value but no risk. Consider next an option that gives its holder the right, but not the obligation, to buy the asset for $10.[12] The option on asset A is worthless because the holder can only buy an asset worth $10 for exactly $10, leaving no profits. The option on asset B, however, is valuable. With probability 50%, the holder can purchase an asset worth $15 at a price of $10. When the asset value is $5, the holder does not exercise the option, as this would lead to a loss. Even risk-averse individuals prefer an option on asset B over an option on asset A. In this sense, options engender greater risk-taking. In our context, we show in Section 12.3 that the compensation structure of VC funds has an option-like structure. This encourages VCs to take large risks and helps us understand their sometimes bold approach to managing their investments.

12.2.2 Building a VC Portfolio

Investing in alternative assets, such as VC, involves venturing into illiquid, opaque, long-term markets. How should LPs proceed? Their portfolio allocation choice consists of three decisions. The first decision concerns allocating money across asset classes; the second is about allocating money to VC within the alternative assets class; and the third is about building a VC portfolio by selecting which GPs to invest in. We consider the first two choices in Section 12.2.1. We now look at the GP selection process and argue that picking the right GPs is particularly challenging.

VC markets are opaque, illiquid, and segmented. LPs that understand and are able to access good opportunities in such inefficient markets can make considerable investment returns, but those that don't stand to lose. In a typical bond portfolio, the top and bottom performers are not very far apart, but the top performers in an alternative asset class are likely to outperform the bottom by a considerable margin (Section 12.6.3). This suggests that there are important differences in the LPs skill sets and their market access opportunities.

Some LPs use gatekeepers, which are paid consultants that help LPs through the fund selection process. On the other side of the transaction, small VC firms that want to raise funds sometimes use placement agents. These agents help those small VC firms to make contact with LPs or their gatekeepers.[13]

Building a portfolio of VC funds is different from building a portfolio of bonds or stocks. With the latter, an investor can quickly reach any desired allocation by buying or selling securities in the market. With VC funds, the challenge is that at any moment there is a limited number of funds that correspond to an LP's criteria. Investment opportunities in GP funds only arrive sporadically and are often only available to select LPs, mostly those that invested in the GP in the past. Build-up of a portfolio can therefore take several years.

An alternative approach for LPs is to invest through funds-of-funds, that is, a fund that invests in several VC funds. This approach allows institutional investors to reach funds that might not accept new investors. The main disadvantage is that there are now two layers of fund managers. The money first goes from the institutional investors to the fund-of-funds and then to the VC fund before finally reaching the entrepreneurial company. LPs end up paying two sets of management fees and carried interest, and have little control over the investments made.

LP investment allocations are strongly influenced by prudential regulation. Alternative assets are risky, and VC funds are among the riskier within that class, because of both the nature of returns and the low liquidity. Many pension funds shy away from investing in VC, unless given clear regulatory clearance. The 1979 relaxation of the Employee Retirement Income Security Act (ERISA) rules for pension funds is widely credited as a key impetus for the development of the U.S.' VC industry. Sometimes the effect of financial regulation is more indirect. For example, a cornerstone of current European financial regulation is the Markets in Financial Instruments Directive (MiFID). It protects investors and provides greater market transparency, but there is a concern that MiFID regulation impedes LPs from outside of Europe to invest in EU VC funds.

12.3 Limited Partnership Agreements

The institutional investors and the VC firm form a limited partnership that is governed by a Limited Partnership Agreement (LPA). This contract is designed to overcome several challenges. The GP has better knowledge of the state and prospects of their portfolio companies. It also has investment expertise that LPs lack. All this gives it ample room for opportunistic behavior. Moreover, institutional investors maintain their limited liability status by not intervening in the management of the fund. To address these issues, the LPA sets out the structure of the fund and regulates the duties and rights of the two parties.[14] The most important elements concern the fund structure, the fund rules, and the compensation of GPs. We will discuss each of these elements in turn.[15] Before doing so, however, it is useful to ask who has the power. Box 12.2 reviews some recent academic research about that issue.

Box 12.2 The Power of Large LPs

In many economic contexts, size improves one's bargaining power vis-à-vis competitors, suppliers, or customers. Research by Da Rin and Phalippou finds that LPs are no exception.[16] LPs with larger absolute dollar exposure to VC and private equity systematically obtain more favorable terms in their LPAs. Part of the reason may be that larger investors are more likely to have a team dedicated to private equity investment that develops valuable expertise in this asset subclass. Larger LPs are also less likely to invest in fund-of-funds or to delegate due diligence to gatekeepers. They play a more active role in the selection and monitoring of GPs, spending more time on performing due diligence, recalculating GPs' performance reports, and benchmarking them against other GPs.[17] This contrasts with the passive attitude of smaller LPs, which rarely negotiate LPA terms or visit portfolio companies to talk to their executives. Smaller LPs also rarely take a seat on their GPs' advisory board.

The most surprising finding from the study is that LP size is the only characteristic that is systematically associated with LP activities. Other characteristics, such as LP experience with private equity, the LP's organizational type, location, or compensation structure, all turn out not to affect the level of LP activism.

These results complement those of another academic study, by Dyck and Pomorski, which looks at the net returns to LP for investing in VC funds.[18] The study confirms the importance of LP size. In the two decades running up to 2009, LPs with a significant investment in private equity received higher net returns (Section 12.6.2): Investors in the largest size quintile enjoy 7.4% higher yearly net returns than investors in the smallest size quintile.

12.3.1 Fund Structure

VC funds can range from as small as $10M to over $1B. Compensation structures give GPs strong incentives to raise larger funds (Section 12.3.3). On the other hand, several factors constrain fund size. Probably the most important is the track record of the VC firm. VCs that raise their first fund do not have a track record, so LPs are reluctant to risk committing large amounts. At the other extreme, VC firms with a strong track record are able to attract large LP commitments. Fund size also depends on stage and sector focus. Earlier-stage ventures require less capital than later-stage ones. Capital-intensive sectors, like clean tech, require larger funding than sectors that rely more on human capital, such as software.

Figure 12.3 reports data on the size distribution of VC funds raised from 2005 to 2017. Panel A compares the median fund size in the U.S., Europe, and Asia and the rest of the world. There is some cyclical variation, but the figures are relatively stable and similar across regions. The median fund is quite small, around $50M in the U.S. and slightly larger in Europe and Asia. Panel B focuses on fundraising by U.S. GPs and reports averages for the 2005–2017 period. In the average year, 213 new funds raised about $30B. The average fund size was $140M, almost three times as large as the median. Only four funds raised over $1B, for a total of about $7B; 10 funds raised between $500M and $1B, for a total of $6.3B; and 24 funds raised between $250M and $500M, for a total of $8B. On the opposite end of the spectrum we find 93 funds that raised under $50M, for a total just below $1.5B. Therefore, a few GPs raise very large funds, while most raise small funds. There is also a constant inflow of new VC firms entering the industry. In 2018, 52 of the 257 funds raised were first-time funds, raising collectively $5.3B.

While LPs commit a certain investment amount upfront, not all the money is transferred at the beginning of the fund's life. Instead, the LPs provide funding through a series of capital contributions (see Figure 12.1). The GPs give periodic notices, called "capital calls," to their LPs about how much money they need for the period. Capital calls are usually quarterly and cover management fees and investments expected to be made that quarter. Periodic capital calls have the advantage of maximizing the financial return of the fund, as any capital not invested has a negative impact on the calculation of fund returns (Section 4.2.2). In the rare case that an LP fails to live up to its capital commitment, the LPA foresees drastic consequences, possibly losing its entire stake in the partnership. Delinquent LPs also lose their reputation with GPs and might be excluded from future fund investment opportunities.

A typical VC fund has a 10-year horizon. This means that the LPs have a right to receive back their investment with its capital gains within 10 years. The first five years or so are considered the "investment" period, when companies are selected and receive funding. The remaining years are called the "harvesting" period, when companies are exited. The LPA often states that, after the investment period, the

A) Median amount of funds raised

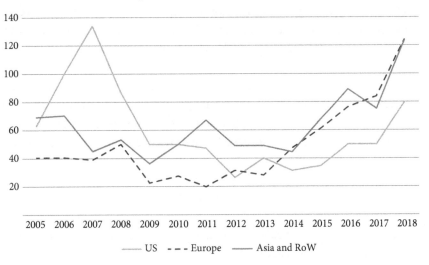

B) Number and size of US VC funds raised, 2005-2018

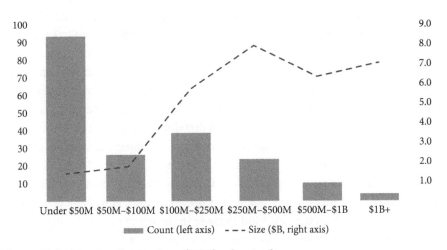

Figure 12.3. The size distribution of VC funds raised.
Amount in U.S. dollar billions. Source: PitchBook Data.

fund can no longer invest in new companies, but can continue to provide funding to its existing portfolio companies.

Why do funds last 10 years? The 10-year fund cycle is the accepted norm not only for VC but also for other types of funds, such as buyout funds. The rationale is to give GPs sufficient time to make long-term investments, while at the same time forcing them to generate returns within a deadline. LPs have less information than the GPs and limited powers to ask for liquidity. With a 10-year horizon, GPs can allocate their initial investments over several years without being rushed to make lower quality investments. It also gives companies enough time to grow and achieve successful exit outcomes.

There is some debate about the benefits of imposing a 10-year limit on VC funds. Some academic studies find that investors become more short-term-oriented in the later stages of the fund cycle.[19] In practice, LPs also leave some room for flexibility, giving GPs extensions to wrap up the remaining investments. Such extensions need approval by a qualified majority of the LPs. From an LP perspective, there is a trade-off between granting the extension, which locks in their capital for longer, and forcing a liquidation of the remaining portfolio, which might result in lower returns. In Section 12.4.4, we discuss an alternative "evergreen" model where funds have no fixed horizon, and exit proceeds can be recycled into new investments.

12.3.2 Fund Rules

We focus on three types of rules: investment restrictions, fund management rules, and restrictions on partner activities.

A fund promises its LPs to invest according to an investment strategy that is defined in terms of size, stage, industry, geography, and other characteristics (Section 12.5). The LPA delimits some boundaries around that promise, defining what investments are within or off limits. Such boundaries are important to LPs, which often invest in a fund to cover a specific business space. At the same time, in a fast-changing environment, it may be difficult to define and enforce sectoral definitions. There are further restrictions on how investments are made. For example, exposure limits specify that no single company can receive more than a certain percentage of the fund, or an investment larger than a certain amount. Another common restriction is that a fund is not allowed to invest in a company already invested by a previous fund. Since different funds of the same VC firm are likely to have different LPs, this restriction prevents the VC firm from using the new fund to bail out some troubled investments made by a previous fund, effectively transferring returns from the LPs in the new fund to those in the previous one. It also prevents LPs in a previous fund from suing in the case of success, claiming that the previous fund had, or should have had, follow-on investment rights that were instead given to the new fund.

The LPA also includes rules concerning the management of the fund. First and foremost, once an exit has occurred, the proceeds have to be distributed back to the LPs. However, there is some leeway about what is returned and when. Concerning what is returned, the fund can distribute either cash or stock of listed companies. However, LPs would not accept (illiquid) private company stock. GPs have some discretion over the timing of distributions, which they can exploit strategically. The GP's profit share in an investment (the carried interest) is based not on the date that the exit occurred, but on the date that the cash or stock proceedings are distributed to the LP. Consequently, bullish GPs may take a gamble on the stock of their companies that went public, holding their stock for some time before distributing it to the LPs. With well-established GPs, the LPA may allow some "recycling" of exit proceeds. This is usually limited to early exits whose proceeds can be reinvested within the investment period, and up to a certain amount. Recycling gives experienced GPs an opportunity to increase the returns of their fund by using the same capital twice.

Finally, the LPA places some restrictions on the activities of individual VC partners. It may specify the circumstances under which a partner can or cannot make personal investments in the funds' companies. The agreement also defines the obligations of the individual partners, curtail competing outside activities, and specify what happens if they leave the VC firm. The typical LPA also contains a so-called key man rule. This protects LPs from the departure of a managing partner who is considered of key importance to the fund. If such a key partner leaves, the LP is relieved from its future commitments to the VC fund.

12.3.3 GP Compensation

GP compensation is a crucial part of the LPA. Performance-based compensation gives GPs an incentive to create value for their LPs. The traditional "2–20" VC compensation model consists of a 2% management fee and 20% carried interest. Both payments are made by the fund to the VC firm.

The management fee is a fixed yearly payment that does not depend on performance. It is meant to pay for the expenses incurred by the VC fund during the investment process, as well as for the salaries of partners and employees of the VC firm. It consists of two elements: a fee level and a fee basis. Consider first a baseline arrangement that specifies a 2% fee level with a fee basis equal to the capital committed to the fund. In the case of a $100M fund, this means an annual fee of $2M, paid in quarterly installments, amounting to a total of $20M over 10 years.

There are three common variations on this arrangement that reduce the fee volume. First, it is common for the fee level to decrease in the harvest period, usually to 1% (or even less). Second, the fee basis is often equal to the amount invested, that is, the part of the committed capital already invested in portfolio companies, net of those investments that have been exited or written off. Invested capital has an inverted V shape: it starts at a low level, increases as investments are made, and then decreases as the fund distributes exit proceeds to investors. Third, the fee basis often decreases over time. Basing the fee on invested capital gives the VC firm an inefficient incentive to rush the deployment of funds. This is why committed capital is the more common fee basis during the investment period. In the harvest period, however, invested capital is the more common fee basis. This is because it is hard to justify charging a management fee on investments that have already completed the entire cycle. A typical arrangement, therefore, might be to have a 2% fee in the investment period, based on committed capital, and a 1% fee in the harvest period, based on invested capital. For a $100M fund, this would amount to $2M in management fees per year for the first five years. After that, the management fee would shrink to less than $1M per year for the remaining years. Box 12.9 provides an example of how to calculate management fees. We also note that management fees vary across VC firms, where VC firms with stellar track records can charge higher fees (say up to 3%).

The fixed nature of management fees gives VCs the incentive to target larger fund sizes. A 2% management fee with committed capital as the basis on a $0.5B fund gives the VC firm an annual budget of $10M for its operations, or $100M over its lifetime, arguably a generous arrangement. However, a $10M fund would merely receive an annual budget of $0.2M, which would hamper operations. Even if the carry earned on a larger fund is slightly lower, from the perspective of the VC firm the increase in fees may well make the larger fund more appealing.

While the management fee is given to the VC firm regardless of performance, carried interest is a share of the fund's profit paid to the GP to incentivize good performance. The carry also consists of a level and a basis. Moreover, it includes timing rules that regulate when the fund pays the GP for the achieved profits. Consider the common case of a 20% carried interest, meaning that the GP receives 20% of the carry basis, given by the fund's profits. A standard approach to define profits is to take the total proceeds of the fund and subtract the amount invested and the management fee (i.e., the total LP contributions).

Consider again the example of a $100M fund with a 2% management fee on committed capital and a 20% carried interest. Suppose the fund paid the management fee of $20M to the VC firm and invested $80M in companies that generated exit proceeds worth $350M. The fund's profit would be $250M (= $350M – $100M), so the carry would amount to $50M. The distributions to the LPs amount to $300M (= $350M – $50M), and their profit to $200M (= $300M – $100M).

There are also some variations on the standard 20% carried interest formula. First, it is possible to vary the carry level. Successful VC firms manage to negotiate rates of 25%, sometimes even 30%, whereas others manage to negotiate only 10 or 15%. However, there seems to be strong concentration around the 20% level. Second, it is possible to use an alternative definition of the carry base that does not subtract the management fees. This leads to a higher fund profit level, which favors the GP. In the above example, this would mean a profit of $270M (= $350M – $80M) and a carry of $54M. This would yield the LPs $196M (= $350M – $54M – $100M). Third, in order to protect the financial interests of the LPs, it is possible to specify a hurdle rate that LPs have to receive before the GP can get any carried interest. The level of the hurdle depends on the relative bargaining power of the LPs over the GP. A common hurdle rate is 8%, with some variation over time and across markets. Once the LPs have achieved their hurdle rate, there may be a variety of catch-up provisions that allow the GP to recoup part of all of their carry. For sufficiently large profits, the catch-up provisions ensure that the GP is in fact paid all of its carry, as if the hurdle never existed.[20] Box 12.3 reviews some research results on GP compensation.

Box 12.3 GP Compensation Unveiled

Despite the dearth of publicly available data on GP compensation, some academic studies have managed to gain access to proprietary data and have found interesting results. A first surprise is that management fees constitute a large part of GP compensation. Simulations based on a sample of 94 VC funds, by Metrick and Yasuda, suggest that a typical $100M fund would earn $8.2M of carry and $14.6M of management fees, in net present value terms.[21] This supports the view that fee structures encourage GPs to raise larger funds. The study also finds that this effect is stronger for buyout funds, which can be scaled up to a much larger extent than VC funds.

The next question is whether these fees are well earned: do they reflect high net returns for LPs (Section 12.6.2), or are they a transfer from LPs to GPs unrelated to performance? A study by Robinson and Sensoy supports the former view.[22] It looks at the statistical association between fees charged by private equity funds with net returns to LPs. Relative to lower-fee funds, higher-fee funds typically earn sufficiently higher gross returns to offset their higher fees. This suggests that fees are well earned. The study also finds that the level of GP compensation increases during fundraising booms, and shifts toward management fees, which do not depend on performance. This supports the view that GP compensation depends on market conditions.

Finally, research by Chung, Sensoy, Stern, and Weisbach, looks into the dynamics of GP compensation across several funds.[23] It finds that VC partners' lifetime income is affected by their current fund's performance in two ways: directly through current fees and carry, and indirectly through its reputational effect that matters for future fund raising. The study suggests that on average the indirect effect is smaller than the direct effect. This is largely due to the fact that VC is not a scalable business, and future fund sizes can only grow to a limited extent. However, it also finds substantial variation in these effects across VC firms. The indirect compensation effect is much more important for those few VC firms that manage to achieve global scale (Section 12.5.1).

The payment of carried interest is governed by rules about its timing and structure, which reflect the timing of the fund's investments and exits. Investments occur in the early years of the fund, at irregular intervals. Some achieve faster exits than others, and not necessarily in the order in which they were made. This complicates the computation of carried interest; two approaches are common. First, the GP can claim its carry only after the entire amount of contributed capital has been distributed back to LPs, including any hurdle rate. This is referred to as the "European Waterfall" rule. This rule encourages GPs to rush the exits of portfolio companies, possibly at the cost of a lower return. Second, the "American waterfall" rule instead allows the GP to take some early carried interest by calculating profits on a deal-by-deal basis. At each distribution to LPs, payment of the associated carried interest to the GP also takes place. This approach is attractive from the GP perspective, since it accelerates payment of the carry. However, early payment of carry exposes LPs to the risk of overpaying. Consider a fund whose first exit yields a $300M profit, which generates a carry of $60M. If all other investments generate a loss of $100M, the fund's overall profit would be $200M, and the carry finally due to the GP only $40M. In cases like this, the LPs can exercise so-called clawback rights and force the GPs to pay back the $20M "excess" carried interest. In practice, exercising these clawback rights can be difficult if the partners of the VC firm have already spent the carry, making it more difficult to recoup.[24]

Considerable controversy surrounds the taxation of carried interest.[25] Historically, U.S. tax rules treat carried interest as a capital gain, so that the (relatively low) capital gains tax rate applies. However, it can be argued that carried interest is a form of labor compensation, and therefore income. This means it should be taxed at the marginal income tax rate (which tends to be higher). Similar debates also exist outside of the U.S..[26]

12.3.4 GP Incentives

LPAs address difficulties created by uncertainty, asymmetric information, and diverging goals of LPs and GPs. What do these difficulties imply for the behavior of GPs toward LPs and portfolio companies?

First and foremost, VC firms have an incentive to raise larger funds. This is simply because management fees are roughly proportional to fund size. Yet investing a $500M fund requires a different strategy than investing a $100M fund. The partners of a VC firm could in principle grow their operations by a factor of five, but that would require sharing the management fees with additional partners. Investing in more companies with the same number of partners is also challenging, as it would require more work for each partner. Most VC firms choose instead to invest more money without materially increasing the number of portfolio companies. This requires looking for larger deals, which in turn means moving into later-stage investing. A common phenomenon therefore is that VC firms that have excelled at early-stage investments with moderately-sized funds manage to increase the size of their next fund. This leads them to become later-stage investors, which may or may not be where their true expertise lies.

LPAs also affect incentives for risk-taking. LPs pursue a diversification strategy by investing across asset classes that provide exposure to different types of risk. Within the VC asset subclass, LPs pursue diversification by picking GPs that operate in well-defined investment spaces in terms of size, stage, geography, industry, and so on. LPs therefore want GPs to stick to the promised focused investment strategy

(Section 12.5). GPs, however, would like to have the freedom to pursue appealing opportunities that may arise outside of their core sectors of competency. This can cause some tension with the LPs because they have already invested in other GPs that have specific expertise for investing in those industry segments or geographies. LPs discourage transitioning from one strategy to another, called "style drift," because they want GPs to stick to the promised strategy. In practice, it is difficult to deter style drift because it is difficult to define it exactly. This leaves GPs with some leeway to explore promising opportunities outside of the original strategy mentioned in the LPA. (We discuss fund-level risk management in Section 12.5.3.)

Consider next the performance incentives provided by the carried interest. A GP that manages a fund that is failing to generate successful exits, and so to generate carried interest has no incentives to generate additional returns, since these would go to the LPs. Reputational concerns are, however, a powerful countervailing incentive, as failing to generate good returns makes it difficult for the GP to raise additional funds. Finally, consider a GP managing a fund whose profitability is still uncertain. The GP has incentives to make some large bets. If the bet pays off, the GP wins and earns a carried interest, but if the bets fail, then it is the LP, not the GP, that bears the cost. Put in technical terms, the payoff function of the GP is convex and therefore encourages risk-taking behavior.

The LPA also has consequences for VC portfolio companies. The 10-year fund structure, for instance, constrains the type of companies that are investable. Companies that require a longer development period are not suitable, since investors need to achieve exit within half a dozen years or so. A notable example is that of biotech, where a long drug development and approval period make strategic alliances with large pharmaceutical companies a common source of funding for startups.[27] The limited timeframe also explains contractual terms such as registration rights, which allow the investor to push for an exit when the fund comes close to its maturity. LPA terms that restrict the size of any single investment also imply that capital-intensive companies may find it harder to find venture backing. The need to generate returns and the scarcity of capital and time may also bring VC firms to adopt a strategy of focusing resources on their best performing companies, leaving aside slower performing ones.[28]

12.4 VC Firms (GPs)

12.4.1 Internal Structure

VC firms tend to have a relatively simple structure, typically a three-layered hierarchy. Partners are at the top, associates in the middle, and support staff at the bottom. In addition, there can be "venture partners" who are involved with bringing in and managing some investments, without being permanent members of the partnership.[29]

Unlike consulting or law firms, VC partnerships do not scale up much. A recent survey of U.S. VCs finds that early-stage VC firms have on average 3.9 partners, 1.2 venture partners, 2 associates, and 3.2 other employees. The comparable figures for later-stage VC firms are 6.3 partners, 1.4 venture partners, 4.7 associates, and 5.3 other employees. These numbers are similar to those of other studies for the U.S. and Europe.[30]

The partners lead the firm investment and fundraising strategies. They make all of the major investment decisions, typically by some consensual decision process; negotiate deals (Chapters 6, 7, and 9); interact with portfolio companies (Chapter 8); and manage the exit process (Chapter 11). All partners share in the profits of the VC firm, although different partners may receive different shares, reflecting their seniority and status within the firm. Junior partners are sometimes called principals, but terminology varies across firms and geographies.

According to a survey of VCs by Gompers, Gornall, Kaplan, and Strebulaev, the average partner works 55 hours per week. Approximately 15 hours are spent on sourcing deals, 18 on assisting portfolio companies, 7 on hours on networking, 9 on managing the firm, 3 on meeting LPs, and another 3 on miscellaneous other tasks.[31]

Associates are salaried early-career professionals hoping to become partners. Similar to consulting and law firms, many VC firms use an "up-or-out" promotion scheme, where an associate either gets promoted to become a partner, or else leaves the firm. Some firms may have additional layers of employees (such as senior professionals who are not on a partner track), or different levels of seniority (such as junior vs. senior partner). Partners and associates are supported by analysts, who perform research tasks but are not client-facing.

Associates often have degrees in relevant areas of science and engineering. They tend to have several years of industry experience working for entrepreneurial or established business, and they frequently hold an MBA degree. Analysts are recruited straight out of college. Partners mainly come from two types of backgrounds: through promotion from the ranks of associates, either at their own firm or another VC firm; and through a successful entrepreneurial or corporate career.

In terms of decision making, most VC firms use some group decision rule. A survey of VC firms finds that 48% of all respondent firms use unanimity, 22% use simple majority, and 20% a consensus model. Only 4% reported using decentralized decision making by individual partners.[32]

Succession is a major challenge to the partnership model. Senior partners have few incentives to retire from their lucrative position and may fail to prepare the next generation of partners. Talented junior partners may then leave the firm, often to set up their own. Some reputable VC firms eventually declined or disintegrated, in part because their senior partners failed to develop an appropriate succession strategy. Examples might include the American Research and Development, the first VC firm of modern times; Burr, Egan, Deleage & Co., which was founded in 1979 but was dissolved in 1996; and Technology Venture Investors, the VC firm that originally invested in Microsoft.[33]

It is often argued that the VC industry lacks diversity. There is a high concentration of partners with MBA degrees from a very small set of elite schools. An industry report found that 80% of all professionals in the top 200 U.S. VC firms came from the business schools at Harvard, Wharton, or Stanford.[34] There is also a predominance of white partners, and the percentage of female partners at VC firms remains very low.

Lack of diversity extends to other dimensions. One study by Gompers and Wang quantifies the gender and ethnicity of entrepreneurs and VCs in the U.S. from 2010 to 2015.[35] Females accounted for 47% of the U.S. labor force, with similar percentages for consultants (44%), physicians (50%), and lawyers (51%), and somewhat lower percentages in banking (34%). Yet only 11% of VC-backed entrepreneurs and 9% of all VC partners were female. The situation in Europe is similar: 93% of capital invested and 85% of all deals in 2018 went to all-male teams.[36]

In terms of ethnic composition, African Americans accounted for 12% of the U.S. labor force; 6% were investment bankers, 9% consultants, and less than 1% were entrepreneurs or VC partners. Hispanics accounted for 16% of the labor force; 6% in investment banking, 5% in consulting, 5% entrepreneurs, and 4% VCs. Asians accounted for 5% of the labor force, 17% of consulting, 25% of investment banking, 18% of entrepreneurs, and 15% of VCs. [37] Box 12.4 takes a look at some research on gender issues in VC firms.

Box 12.4 Gender and Performance in VC

The lack of diversity in VC is typically perceived as a problem in terms of equity. It could also be seen as a missed opportunity for VC firms. Would more inclusion lead to higher returns? It is often argued that team diversity results in better decision making, though the psychological bases for this regularity are not yet fully understood. If the VC industry is an "old boys' club," then including more women, more racial minorities, or more partners with an unconventional background should result in better investments.

A recent study by Gompers and Wang provides some intriguing evidence on this topic.[38] The study first asks what kind of VC firms hire senior female partners. It finds that VC firms are more likely to hire women when their senior partners have a daughter, specifically increasing the probability of hiring a senior female partner from 8 to nearly 10%. The study cannot fully explain how having a daughter changes VC partners' preferences and actions, but conjectures that parenting triggers some psychological shifts. The second finding of the study is that adding a female partner to a VC firm improves fund performance, in terms of both exit rates and returns. Having a daughter increases a fund's return by 3.2%, compared to that of similar funds. The study provides evidence that increasing diversity can be good for business too.

12.4.2   Fundraising

VC firms go through their own fundraising process to raise a fund. This process requires identifying suitable LPs and convincing them to invest. First-time GP teams that are new to the market face a particular challenge convincing LPs, since they cannot point to any track record. To overcome this hurdle, they need to find a cornerstone LP that validates the GP team. Sometimes this cornerstone LP gets preferential terms or lower fees.[39] First funds tend to be small, and their LPAs have more LP-friendly terms.

Seasoned GPs that already have a track record face a lower hurdle for convincing LPs. If their track record is particularly good, they can simply rely on their current LPs, although often they prefer to add new LPs to expand their network. GPs thus establish numerous relationships with LPs over time. Successful GPs usually raise a new fund well before the end of their current fund's investment period in order to continue making investments without interruption. They may thus raise a new fund every two to three years, typically increasing the size of their funds over time. Note, however, that the need to regularly go back to LPs imposes some market discipline on these GPs.

Market conditions matter for the fundraising process. When the LP's appetite for venture funds is high, it is easier to raise funds, funds are larger, and LPAs become more GP friendly. To test market conditions, a VC firm typically sets an initial range for what it hopes to raise, specifying a minimum fund size and possibly a maximum. LPs consider the proposal and make initial commitments. If the commitments never reach the minimum goal, the fund fails to close, and all of the commitments are void. This is often the case with aspiring first-fund venture teams. When commitments exceed the minimum, then the VC firm can close the fund. Sometimes the VC firm creates two closings: a first closing to secure the commitments already made and a second closing to bring in any further commitments from institutional investors that may have been on the fence for the first closing. Typically, all the LPs receive the exact same types of partnership shares, in proportion to the amounts they commit, although there are exceptions.[40]

12.4.3   Networks

VC firms do not work in isolation; rather, they maintain networks of contacts with a variety of parties that provide relevant complementary skills and services. First, there is the deal flow network that links the VC firm to entrepreneurs (Section 7.3.2). Founders of previous portfolio companies, lawyers, and accountants are important members of this network. Next, there is the network of investors, mostly other VC firms, but also angels and corporate investors. They may invite a VC firm to co-invest or be invited to join a deal (Section 7.4). Finally, there is the funding network, consisting of the LPs that provide funding to the VC firm's funds.

VCs also maintain networks with a variety of professionals: lawyers and accountants evaluate and structure deals; and strategic and technical consultants provide insights into market trends or into specific technical issues. There are also working relationships with organizations. Established corporations can engage in strategic alliances and acquire portfolio companies. Similarly, preparing for an IPO requires establishing relationships with investment bankers. The networks of VCs may sometimes even extend to politicians and policymakers, especially when they invest in regulated industries.

12.4.4 Alternatives to the Partnership Model

Most VC firms use a limited partnership model, but our discussion indicates that this is not without problems. Of particular concern are situations where LP and GP interests become misaligned, including the artificial 10-year time horizon, constraints to investments, or compartmentalization across different funds.

Three main alternatives to the limited partnership model have been developed. The first alternative is the evergreen model—a fund structure where the VC can reinvest the exit proceeds into new portfolio companies without limitations. This means that the fund is not forced to provide liquidity to LPs within a specific horizon. In effect, this model turns the fund into a standard investment company, where investors receive returns through dividends or by selling their shares. Sutter Hill Ventures in Silicon Valley and Oxford Science Innovation, a private VC fund dedicated to financing spin-offs from the University of Oxford, are examples of this structure.[41] To date, this structure has been used only rarely, probably because its unlimited life does not provide investors much reassurance about exploitation by the GP.

The second alternative is a publicly listed VC fund. In this case, the VC firm raises money on the stock exchange by offering shares to the general public. This subjects the VC to listing and disclosure requirements. The illiquid and opaque nature of entrepreneurial companies makes it difficult to continuously value the portfolio of these vehicles. This is at odds with the nature of stock markets. Historic examples include ARDC and CMGI, both of which were considered failures.[42] Investors have shown little interest in public VC funds in recent times, resulting in low stock prices and an inability of these vehicles to raise funds consistently.

The third alternative, "captive" funds, are wholly owned by a parent organization and have been the most successful alternative to the partnership model. The parent is typically a corporation, but it could also be a bank, a foundation, or a branch of government. Examples include Intel Capital, BPI France, or Temasek Holdings.[43] In the case of a corporate parent, the captive VC fund is usually structured as a division or a wholly owned subsidiary (Section 13.3). It is accountable to the board and the senior managers of its parent, and the managing partners are employees of the VC subsidiary. The parent operates the VC division to pursue some strategic goals and therefore wants some control over the direction of the captive fund. Decision making in captive funds is therefore more constrained than in VC partnerships. Similar observations also apply when the parent is the government.

12.5 Investment Strategies

12.5.1 The Investment Strategy

An investment strategy defines the investment approach of a VC fund and helps it to differentiate itself from its competitors.[44] LPs scrutinize the strategy before investing in a fund. Key aspects of the strategy are included in the LPA and therefore constitute a commitment. GPs design a new strategy of each fund they raise. It has to be credible, reflect current investment opportunities, and be consistent with the GP's expertise and experience. Since strategy is defined at the fund level, a VC may raise several funds with different strategies, for instance, some that are focused on early, and others on late-stage deals, or some only pursuing specific industries or geographies. An investment strategy has three main dimensions: industry, geography, and stage.

First, at each point in time, VCs only invest in a relatively small number of industries. These industries meet three important criteria. First, they are dynamic industries where new companies have a chance to create new markets or new business models that allow them to challenge incumbents. Such opportunities arise from a combination of technological progress (e.g., artificial intelligence), changes in regulation (e.g., financial services), or changes in consumer preferences (e.g., health and fitness). Second, they require intermediate levels of capital for starting a company: not too small to require venture funding (e.g., no one-person consultancies), but not so large as to exceed fund capacity (e.g., no nuclear power stations). Third, they must allow for scalable new companies, able to reach very large levels of sales and profits within a relatively short time (e.g., no Mars colonies).

At the VC fund level, the relevant decision is whether to focus on a small number of industries or to span a variety of industries. At one end of the spectrum are "specialist" VC firms that define their investment strategy very narrowly. Their aim is to generate high returns by being an expert in a specific domain. At the other end of the spectrum are "generalist" VC firms which have a broader investment strategy, investing in a defined set of industries that may or may not be related. This may allow them to capture opportunities from a broader pool and to generate high returns by achieving flexibility in managing the development path of their companies. Available evidence points to a positive effect of specialization on the probability of achieving a successful exit. This effect is driven by the industry specialization of

individual partners. Generalist VCs seem to suffer from a difficulty in allocating investment across industries..[45]

Second, VC investment strategies are also delimited by geography. VC firms
often prefer investing in locations close to their offices.[46] The most important
reasons for this preference are proximity to the entrepreneur and familiarity with
the business environment, including the legal system, regulation, and business
culture. Active hands-on investors (see Chapter 8), for example, expect to spend
considerable time with their companies and therefore care about the travel distance to the company.[47]

Over time, the VC industry has become relatively more open to distant investments, and a significant number of VC firms have developed various approaches to non-local investing.[48] Consider a U.S.-based VC fund
thinking about investing in India. A first approach would be to make individual
investments there. These deals would typically be syndicated with, and sourced
by, a local Indian VC. Some VC firms establish stable links with co-investors in
distant regions or countries.[49] Oak Investment Partners, an East Coast VC, for
example, used this approach. An alternative might be to hire one or more partners with a strong network in India, maybe an Indian national with good knowledge of U.S. venture practices. Menlo Ventures adopted this strategy. A third step
might then be to open an office in India, initially with a partner seconded from
the U.S. headquarters, and local partners hired once the deal flow proves steady.
Lightspeed Venture Partners, for instance, established offices over time in Delhi
and Bangalore. A final alternative might be to raise an India-focused fund from
LPs interested in exposure to that region. The fund could be run by a local office
or by the U.S. headquarters; an example of this approach is Sequoia Capital, a
leading Silicon Valley firm (Box 12.5).

Third, an investment strategy specifies the preferred investment stage. Investing
in early- versus late-stage deals requires different setups. Early-stage investors take
high risks that the technology or business model are not successful and manage
them by having significant domain expertise, by staying actively involved in their
companies, and by staging investments (Section 9.2.2). However, early-stage
funding itself does not require as much financial resources. Late-stage investors
face a different set of risks about successfully scaling companies. They often require
greater financial expertise, as well as more commercialization-oriented networks.
They also need large funds to meet the high capital demands of fast-growing
companies. Stage preferences broadly fall into three categories: early-stage, late-
dstage, and all stages. Investing across all stages is the most demanding strategy,
as it requires large funds and an integration of two distinct investment methods.
Therefore, it is adopted by relatively few VCs.

To understand VC fund strategy, it is useful to examine how these three
dimensions can be combined. Consider the two-by-two combination of industry
and geography. We distinguish between a specialist versus generalist industry

strategy, and a local versus global geographic strategy (where global does not mean investing across the entire globe, but rather in some distant regions or countries). This results in four prototype strategies: local specialists, global specialists, local generalists, and global generalists. Each of these combinations then has a further specification in the choice between an early- or late-stage focus, creating a "cube" of eight possible combinations.

Local specialists are typically smaller funds that compete on their significant domain expertise and knowledge of local markets and of industries clustered in those markets. Pantera Capital in San Francisco and Fenbushi Capital in Shanghai are two such examples, investing in only Blockchain-related companies. New VC firms often start as local specialists and, if successful, move into a broader strategy. One common option is to become a global specialist. This means exploiting existing domain expertise and reaching out to a progressively broader set of entrepreneurs (and syndication partners) that are operating in other parts of the country or of the world. Focus is useful to attract deal flow, leveraging reputation with entrepreneurs in one domain, and to market the fund to LPs, which look for specialization. Focus can be achieved around one industry; around thematic investing (investing in a theme that may cut across industries, like social media or urban mobility); or around thesis investing (investing in a macro-level vision of future change, like "software is eating the world").[50] For example, Paris-based Sofinnova has been focusing on global life-science investments for many years. Chrysalix is a Vancouver-based VC firm investing globally in science-based ventures with selected themes, such as robotics and energy. New York-based Union Square Ventures is famous for its thesis-based investment approach, which led them to successful investments such as Twitter, Tumblr, Etsy, and Foursquare. Berlin-based Point Nine Capital similarly invested in software platforms such as Clio, Humanity, and Zendesk.

The other way to move out of local specialization is to become a local generalist. This can be achieved by hiring partners with expertise in areas outside of those where its current partners built their success. Often, these strategy changes are accompanied by a move into later stages. Octopus Ventures in London and Industrifonden in Stockholm are VCs that invest in a select array of industries in their country and region.

Finally, some of the most successful VC firms tend to take one of these two paths and further expand to become global generalists. These firms manage to develop brand name and global networks that they deploy to source deals across a wide range of industries. Their brand and networks need to be particularly powerful to outweigh the appeal of global specialists toward entrepreneurs. Global generalists invest their very large funds across a company's life cycle. Examples include Sequoia, Benchmark, and New Enterprise Associates in the U.S., Index Ventures in Europe, Tencent Holdings in China, and the Softbank Vision Fund in Japan. To delve deeper into the evolution of a venture giant, Box 12.5 takes a look at one of the titans of the industry.

Box 12.5 Tales from the Venture Archives: How Sequoia Capital Grew from Seedling to Giant

The largest trees in the world are the giant Sequoia trees found in California's Sequoia National Park, a four-hour drive from Silicon Valley. Doubtless inspired by these majestic trees, Don Valentine founded Sequoia Capital in the early 1970s, at a time when there was very little VC in California.[51] The investment firm grew as one would hope a healthy Sequoia tree would do: In 1974, Sequoia Capital I raised just under $3M. In September 2018, the firm raised its Sequoia Global Growth Fund III at the $8B mark, the largest venture fund ever raised at that time.[52]

Don Valentine is considered one of the founding fathers of the VC industry. His first investment was in Atari, the iconic start-up that invented Pong, the first video game in history. Steve Jobs worked for Atari, so Sequoia became an early investor in Apple. Two other early successes were Oracle and Cisco. More recent successes include Airbnb, Dropbox, Google, Instagram, LinkedIn, PayPal, WhatsApp, and YouTube. It is estimated that Sequoia-backed start-ups account for 22% of Nasdaq's stock market value. Sequoia also made some big bets that failed spectacularly, such as eToys and Webvan.[53]

Don Valentine's investment philosophy is based on market size. In a speech delivered in 2010 at Stanford University, he noted that "[w]e have always focused on market size . . . because our objective was always to build big companies. If you don't attack a very big market, it's highly unlikely you're ever going to build a big company. So, we don't spend a lot of time wondering about where people went to school, how smart they are, and all the rest of that."[54] One might say that Don Valentine was a firm believer in the importance of the first column of the Venture Evaluation Matrix (see Chapter 2).

Sequoia's focus on large markets led the firm to spread its seeds further afield. While most Silicon Valley VCs prefer to invest locally, Sequoia was one of the first firms to venture abroad. Starting in the early 2000s, it specifically focused on three countries: India and China, because of their domestic market sizes, and Israel for its technology and teams that want to grow global businesses. Sequoia opened multiple offices across these three countries, building a new investment team in each country and giving each team considerable autonomy. Another novel approach was to raise separate funds for each of the three country operations. Some of the notable investments that came out of this include Alibaba (Box 11.5) and Didi in China, Ola and Zomato in India, and CloudShare and Snaptu in Israel.

Based on these successes, Sequoia seized the opportunity to create growth capital funds that invest in later-stage deals on a global basis. The first of these funds raised $700M in 2012, followed by a $2B fund in 2017 and by the $8B fund in 2018.

12.5.2 Investment Strategy Styles

Industry, geography, and stage define the core traits of an investment strategy. GPs can further define their fund's strategy through additional elements that define their investment style. We focus on three important ones here.

First, VCs have different approaches to sourcing deals. Ideally, every VC wants "proprietary deal flow," that is, investment opportunities where they have a relational edge over competitors. Hoping to close a deal before others see it may be wishful thinking, given that most entrepreneurs talk to several investors. However, proprietary deal flow is based on relationships. A VC that has already built a positive relationship with an entrepreneur, usually through past business interactions, can leverage this into becoming preferred investor. This may mean that the VC sees the deal first, leads the deal, or gets a guaranteed slot within the funding syndicate. VCs use a variety of strategies to generate such proprietary deal flows. They spend time talking to early-stage entrepreneurs well before they are ready to seek VC; they support accelerator programs; they attend pitch events and trade events; and they generally are active in local entrepreneurial communities. VCs also build relationships with angels and other early-stage investors, who bring their own deals to them. This is another reason why networks are so important for VCs. People in their network will know about their investment preferences and therefore only introduce those entrepreneurs that have a legitimate chance of getting an investment. Part of the VCs deal sourcing strategy is therefore to signal to their network what kind of deals they will consider.

A second style aspect concerns a VC's preferences for syndication and the approach to managing relations with co-investors (Section 7.4). These preferences contribute to shaping investor networks and further show the importance of building and managing relational capital. For a young VC firm, being able to build good relationships with established incumbents is important to access good deals. Being able to generate valuable local deal flow and use it to invite established VCs to syndicate can be a step toward being invited by them to future good deals. More established firms use syndication to define their sphere of influence and to restrict access to good deals to friendly VCs.[55] VCs may also differ in how they structure their syndicates (size and composition). For instance, they may not participate in very large syndicates in which they have little say.

A third style aspect reflects the interactions with entrepreneurs. This begins with a VC's preferences for how term sheets are negotiated and structured (see Chapter 6). Most VCs have a preferred term sheet style that reflects how they intend to deal with the company during the investment period. Some VCs have a preference for simple standard term sheets; others like more complex terms tailored to each specific deal. Some VCs aim for strong control rights, whereas others prefer stronger cash flow rights.

Different VCs also work differently with their companies after the investment has been made, in terms of how active they get engaged with the company (Chapter 8). Investors vary profoundly in their ability and willingness regarding involvement.[56] A closely related issue is how founder-friendly a VC firm is. Some VCs are ready to bring in professional managers from their own network, including the CEO, at the first difficulties. This would relegate the founders to more technical or functional roles. Other VCs are more supportive and mentor founders toward developing the required leadership skills. A key aspect of effective investment is to match the entrepreneur's and investor's desires and expectations about involvement.

12.5.3   Implementing the Investment Strategy

With regard to implementation of the investment strategy, we consider several closely related choices: the size of the investments, its timing, and the risk management of the portfolio. Let us start with some simple portfolio math. Consider again the $100M fund example, which pays out $20M in fees and invests $80M (Section 12.3.3). How many investments should it make? If it made 32 investments, it could invest an average of $2.5M per company. For a fund with four partners, this would mean that each partner looked after eight companies over the fund's lifetime. A very different investment strategy would be to make 80 investments of $1M on average, with each partner looking after 20 companies. Or how about only making 16 investments? Each company receives $5M on average, and each partner looks only after four companies.

While the LPA may put some limits on the portfolio structure, these three alternative structures have different implications for how a fund is run. The first might be considered a balanced strategy, where each partner looks after a manageable number of companies, and the fund has enough money to support each company. The second structure is sometimes labeled "spray-and-pray."[57] The fund tries to be in as many ventures as possible, expecting several of them not to survive. In this case, fund managers do have not have much time to spend with any one company. For example, if each company had quarterly board meetings, a partner would have to attend 80 board meetings a year. This would clearly be unmanageable, so the fund may adopt a policy of not sitting on a board. The third structure would be highly focused but also very risky. While each company gets plenty of partner time, and there is plenty of money for each company, the fund has relatively few shots on goal. That is, the fund relies on being lucky with a few companies but faces a significant risk that none of the companies in the portfolio performs well. These three examples reveal some of the basic trade-offs for managing a VC fund portfolio, which we now examine.

One trade-off concerns how many companies to fund versus how many resources to invest in them. Deciding on the number of portfolio companies implies deciding on a strategy for the use of partner time, and on how much a single company can make use of resources from the investor's network. Although investing in more companies provides an exposure to a broader set of opportunities, it also restricts the extent to which they can be nurtured. Moreover, investing in fewer companies provides stronger incentives for active involvement, which benefits their development.[58]

Should all companies receive similar amounts, or should the fund make larger bets on a few select companies? LPAs often put an upper limit on how much a fund can invest in any one company. Within these limits, however, the VC fund can decide to concentrate funding on a few companies Another aspect is that, with staged financing the investors provide additional money to those companies that perform well, but stop funding those that show insufficient progress (Section 9.1). Therefore, VCs also have to decide how much to set aside for future funding rounds. This is called the "dry-powder" of the VC fund. It matters for the fund's ability to keep funding companies that have traction.

A popular advice is to double down on winners. Though intuitive, this strategy is not without danger. The relevant metric is not how the company has fared to date, but how it will perform in the future, which is difficult to predict.

Another trade-off concerns the timing of portfolio investments. This affects the drawdown pattern of funds from the LPs' money. VCs have incentives to deploy funds rapidly. Investing quickly gives companies longer time horizons to experiment and respond to market feedback. Moreover, most VC firms try to raise another fund within two to four years. Being able to show a good deal flow and progress with early investments within the current fund helps with securing the next. However, there are also reasons to spread out the investments over time. One is that the selection of deals and the accompanying due diligence are labor intensive. In addition, there is the simple fact that not all good deals show up at the very beginning of a fund's life. Indeed, the option value of waiting applies also to initial investment decisions.

Another element of the portfolio strategy concerns the management of risk. The LPA constrains the fund's investment strategy within the limits of a VC's area(s) of expertise, thus limiting risk diversification at the fund level (Section 12.3.4). This still leaves the VC firm some ways to reduce the investment risk of its fund. Investing in a large set of companies reduces the risk that none of the investments pan out. At the same time, focusing on few companies where the VC partners have a strong domain expertise may help reduce the risk by actively managing it. On another level, the VC can invest in companies that are exposed to different sources of risk. Geographic diversification is one possibility; another is diversification by stage, by industry segment, or by business model. Staggering investments over the fund's investment period also helps to manage risk, as they are exposed to different economic cycles. Finally, risk can also be managed by selecting a mix of long-shot early-stage deals that require little money upfront but will require significant financial resources if they gain traction, and some lower-risk later-stage deals that might create more predictable exits.

Our analysis of VC portfolio strategies focuses on VC funds. VC firms with multiple funds may pursue some broader firm-level strategy that overlies individual fund-level strategies. Such a firm-level strategy relates to the issues discussed in Section 12.4 about how a VC firm manages its internal structure and external networks. In addition, it relates to what kind of expertise and reputation the VC firms want to cultivate.

12.5.4 An Example

The exposition of this chapter follows the FUEL framework (Chapter 1). Box 12.6 applies the framework to a fictional VC firm called Rocketfueler Partners to illustrate some core principles from the framework. It also sets up a numerical example that illustrates the structure of VC returns, which is the topic of the next section.

Box 12.6 Rocketfueler Partners

The three founders of Rocketfueler Partners, Julienne Jupiter, Neal Neptune, and Sotaro Saturn, proudly looked back at their work in the 20s. Not their own twenties (they were definitely past that) but the decade of the 2020s, during which they managed their first VC fund, called Rocketfueler I, which closed its fundraising in December 2019. They were preparing a final report to their LPs, and used the opportunity to reflect back on its achievement. They liked structured approaches, so it came natural to them to use the FUEL framework to describe their fund.

In terms of the fundamental structure (the F in FUEL), they stayed with the partnership structure. Their LPs had committed $100M to a 10-year fund. The GPs received the standard 2% annual management fee and 20% carry, with an 8% hurdle rate. Their LPA was fairly standard and can be found on the book's website (www.entrepreneurialfinance.net).

In terms of the underlying motivation (the U in FUEL), they considered themselves purely financial investors, but with a long-term perspective and high-risk tolerance. The fund itself was highly undiversified since it focused exclusively on the commercial air and space industry. The fund had several sovereign wealth funds among its LPs. These had a very long investment horizon and were keen to explore the long-term return potential of commercial space exploration. They encouraged the partners to take some "moonshots"—this was also the inspiration for the name Rocketfueler.

In terms of expertise and networks (the E in FUEL), the three partners had an engineering and science background, with early careers in the transportation, air, and space sectors. They became friends during their MBA studies at a prestigious business school. Given their shared interest in space exploration, they vowed to stay in touch. After graduation, Sotaro went back to Japan. He worked for a large conglomerate and was soon put in charge of corporate development. Neal joined a large California VC firm as an associate. He was asked to focus on transportation and space, but sometimes found it difficult to get the full attention of his senior partners, who were mostly focused on whatever was currently hot. Julienne co-founded a Swiss-based commercial space start-up that was successfully acquired by Sotaro's conglomerate. When the three decided to start their own space-focused fund, they were confident that they had built the right combination of entrepreneurial, investment, and corporate experiences. Their networks were global and focused on their core expertise. However, they also recognized the need to bring in additional expertise. After the closing of the fund, they hired three associates and created two venture partner positions. For those positions they recruited an entrepreneur, who recently sold his company, and an executive from Airbus. They joined for a three-year term, to help with deal flow and portfolio company support. They got involved in some of the deals, with their venture partners ending up as CEOs of portfolio companies.

In terms of the logic and style (the L in FUEL), Rocketfueler I was a global specialist. They only considered investments in air and space, scouring for opportunities in far-off places to find the best ideas and entrepreneurs worldwide. Julienne decided to base herself in Paris, Neal in California, and Sotaro in Tokyo, with a small satellite office in Shanghai. Their investment philosophy was to be the first professional investor, that is, the first VC round. When possible, they participated in follow-up rounds, provided the company performed well. All their investments were syndicated. In a first round, they usually invested between $1M and $2M themselves. Given the limited size of their fund, they never invested more than $5M in any round or more than $10M in any company. They were active investors and insisted on having board representation in all their companies.

The following table summarizes the fund-level cash flow from investments and gross proceeds from exit for all their companies, conveniently labeled C01 to C16. All amounts are expressed in $M.

Rocketfueler I: Investments and company-level gross returns.
Amounts in $M. All transactions assumed to take place on December 31 of the respective year.

Company	2020	2021	2022	2023	2024	2025	2026	2027	2028	2029	2030	Total Investments	Total Exit Proceeds	Gross profits	NPV	CCR	IRR
C01	-1											-1	0	-1	-0.87	0.00	-100%
C02	-1	0	-1									-2	0	-2	-1.53	0.00	-100%
C03	-1	-2	0	-4	0	6						-7	6	-1	-2.07	0.86	-5%
C04	-1	0	0	2								-1	2	1	0.27	2.00	26%
C05		-1	0	-5	0	2						-6	2	-4	-3.16	0.33	-39%
C06		-1	0	-2	0	-1	0	0	-4	0	60	-8	60	52	10.84	7.50	42%
C07		-2	-2	0	5							-4	5	1	-0.39	1.25	9%
C08		-2	0	-2	0	-4	0	0	10			-8	10	2	-1.77	1.25	5%
C09			-1	-1	0	0	-2	0	0	50		-4	50	46	13.73	12.50	59%
C10			-2	0	-2	0	0	0	35			-4	35	31	10.10	8.75	52%
C11			-2	0	0	1						-2	1	-1	-1.17	0.50	-21%
C12				-1	-1	-2	0	-5	150			-9	150	141	59.42	16.67	139%
C13				-1	-1	0	-2	15				-4	15	11	4.69	3.75	64%
C14				-2	0	-2	-3	-3	0			-10	0	-10	-6.26	0.00	-100%
C15				-1	0	-4	0	6				-5	6	1	-0.52	1.20	8%
C16				-1	-3	0	0	0	-1	0	8	-5	8	3	-0.96	1.60	9%

Rocketfueler I financed 16 companies, investing a total of $80M and generating $350M in gross proceeds from exit. The average investment per company was thus $5M. Investments were spread over 40 investment rounds, resulting in an average round contribution of $2M. Three companies received a single investment, five received two rounds of investment, five others three rounds, and three, four rounds. The average investment size was $1.3M for the first, $2.2M for the second, $2.4M for the third, and $4.0M for the fourth investment (the accompanying spreadsheet contains all calculations).

Rocketfueler I's largest investment was the ill-fated C14. Julienne explained: "If you think big, you may also fail big. Mistakes like C14 hurt, but in the end, you make money on your winners, not your losers. Rocketfueler I made its day by being the first VC investor in C12. We only invested $9M in the company, which got acquired for over $1B, generating exit proceeds of $150M for us. Without a doubt, C12 is what saved us."

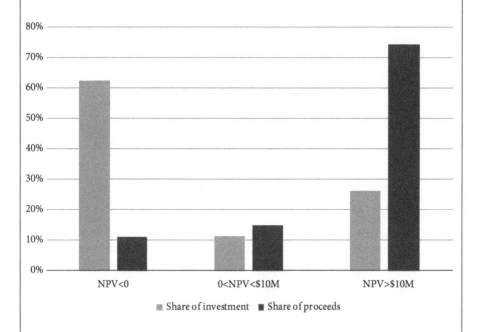

Neal elaborated that this was common in the VC industry. Most funds made the majority of their returns on a small number of winners, while spending the majority of their money on companies that generated modest returns or losses. He created the graph below which showed that Rocketfueler I spent 62% of its funds on 10 companies, which ultimately resulted in a negative NPV. These companies accounted for a mere 10% of all exit proceeds. About 11% had been spent on companies that generated modest returns (i.e., M < NPV < \$10M), accounting for 15% of the exit proceeds. Most of these investments consisted of a first round only, as the company quickly faded out. By contrast, Only 26% of Rocketfueler I was spent on its three real winners (i.e., NPV > \$10M), which accounted for 74% of all the proceeds. "This is what taking moonshots is all about," Peter concluded.[59] These three moonshots, however, required considerable investment across several rounds, as the fund kept investing pro rata to avoid dilution (Section 9.2.4). By comparison, the three companies that yielded a positive but moderate NPV absorbed less than half the funds of the big winners and returned only about a fifth of the proceeds.

12.6 Risk and Return in VC

We close this chapter by looking at how LPs and GPs share risks and returns. Our discussion starts with company-level returns, discusses how to aggregate them up to the VC fund level, and finally examines how fees affect the returns to LPs.

12.6.1 Gross Returns to the VC Fund

The return to a VC fund is computed by aggregating company-level returns (Section 4.2). Company-level returns are right skewed, that is, largely driven by a small number of high realizations on the upside. Their distribution has a fat left tail and a thin right tail, meaning that a few very high returns have a disproportionate effect on average returns. Therefore, average returns are higher than median returns (Figure 4.1).[60] Aggregating these company-level returns to the fund level generates what is called a fund's gross returns.

There are two measurement problems with these types of returns. One is data availability. VCs are not required to disclose their returns to any regulator. Some data providers, such as Cambridge Associates, Pitchbook, Preqin, and Thomson One, obtain some data from GPs and LPs on a voluntary basis. This creates a concern that their data may be biased, since VCs have an incentive not to disclose their poorly performing investments.

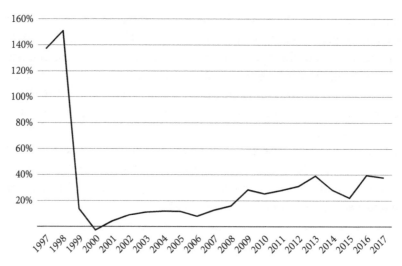

Figure 12.4. Company-level VC returns, U.S.
Source: Cambridge Associates (2018).

A second difficulty concerns unrealized exits. The 10-year horizon of VC funds implies that realized fund returns can be computed only for cohorts that are over 10 years old. Estimating unrealized returns for companies that have not yet been exited requires assuming their current value. A common approach is to use the latest valuation. However, this has several shortcomings. Valuations based on preferred shares that will convert into common shares at exit could be biased upward (Section 6.6). The same could occur if the valuation was driven by a strategic investor willingness to pay for strategic benefits (Section 13.3). On the other hand, the last round's valuation could be biased downward if the company had performed above expectations since then. Unrealized returns are therefore an inaccurate predictor of realized returns. Reporting and valuation of unrealized assets are important to LPs, to the point that that the Institutional Limited Partner Association (ILPA) has issued best practice guidelines.[61]

Figure 12.4 shows company-level returns for the U.S. since 1997, based on the year of first investment. We observe a dramatic time pattern, reflecting the cyclicality of exit markets (see Chapter 11), including the most pronounced cycle of all, the dotcom bubble and its burst. Average returns were 137% in 1997 and 151% in 1998, then fell sharply with the burst of the bubble to a low of –3% in 2000. Returns then gradually recovered to around 30% after 2009. The average yearly return is 32% over the entire period.

To get an idea of how fund-level gross returns work in practice, Box 12.7 returns to the fictional Rocketfueler example.

Box 12.7 Rocketfueler's Fund-level Gross Returns

Fund level cash flows	2020	2021	2022	2023	2024	2025	2026	2027	2028	2029	2030
Investment ($M)	−4	−8	−8	−20	−7	−13	−7	−8	−5	0	0
Exit proceeds ($M)	0	0	0	2	5	9	0	21	195	50	68
Fund net cash flow ($M)	−4	−8	−8	−18	−2	−4	−7	13	190	50	68

Rocketfueler's investment levels varied across years, with a peak of $20M in 2023 and decreasing thereafter. Exit proceeds started appearing in 2023 and peaked in 2028, which is when company C12 has its exit. As noted before, Rocketfueler I generated $350M in exit proceeds, based on $80M in investments, implying a gross profit of $270M. The cash-on-cash return was 4.4 (= $350M/ $80M). Using a 15% discount rate, the net present value was $55M. The IRR at the fund level was 36%. It is interesting to note how different this is from the average IRR across companies, which was 3% (as shown in the accompanying spreadsheet). This confirms the importance of aggregating cash flows to the fund level.

12.6.2 Net Returns to Limited Partners

Net returns are the returns actually received by the LPs. They differ from gross returns in two respects. First, they take out the GP's compensation, that is, the management fees and the carried interest received by the GP. Second, they are based on a different timing of cash flows than gross returns. For gross returns, the cash outflows are measured at the time that the investment is made into a company and the cash inflows at the time that the exit proceeds flow into the fund. For net returns, instead, the cash outflows occur at the time of the LP's capital contributions into the fund, and the cash inflows are measured at the time of the distributions from the fund back to the LP. In Figure 12.1, the lower half shows company equity investments and exit proceeds, on which gross returns are built, and the upper half shows LP capital contributions and distributions, on which net returns are built.

Net returns are an important statistic for the VC industry. The most common way of presenting the data is to report the aggregate fund-level net returns by fund vintage year, defined as the year in which a fund is raised. After the entire fund cycle has been completed, the IRRs represent realized returns. Before that, they also

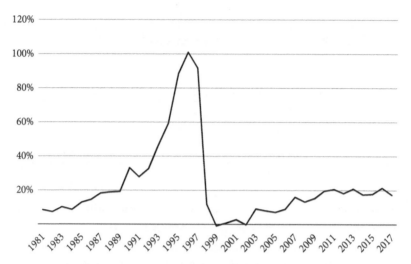

Figure 12.5. Net IRR for U.S. VC funds, by vintage year.
Source: Cambridge Associates (2018).

include some unrealized returns that are calculated on the basis of the net asset value of the unexited investment portfolio. Figure 12.5 shows the vintage year net IRR to U.S. VC funds for the period 1981–2017.

We note a spike for the vintage years 1995–1997. These correspond to funds that deployed most of their capital during the dot-com bubble and managed to achieve extraordinary returns in the period 1998–2000. The worst performing vintage years are 1999–2002, whose funds were deployed either at the peak of the of the dot-com bubble at dramatically overvalued prices or after its burst, in a period of low exit valuations. Interestingly, we note that the Great Recession of 2008 hardly left a mark on these returns. The average (median) IRR, unweighted for the period 1981–2017, is 22.8% (17.5%).

In addition to vintage IRRs, two other measures are commonly reported in the industry. One is the cash-on-cash returns for vintage funds. The average (median) cash-on-cash return for the period 1981–2017 was 2.34 (1.96). The other is an index measure of annual net returns, which captures the increase in the value of VC portfolios over a set horizon. For the period 1981–2017, for example, the Cambridge Associates US Venture Capital Index was 30.7% for 25 years, 18.8% for 10 years, and 9.5% for three years.

From an asset allocation perspective, LPs need to compare returns from investing into VC funds to the returns from other asset classes. In principle, LPs should consider the returns to other asset classes, their risks, and also the illiquid nature of investing in VC. Although there are methods for estimating these (Section 12.6.2), in practice LPs often employ more rudimentary benchmark comparisons. Usually, the comparison is to some investment benchmarks such as the S&P 500 stock index. A popular measure for this is the public market equivalent (or PME). This compares investor returns against a hypothetical investment that has the same cash

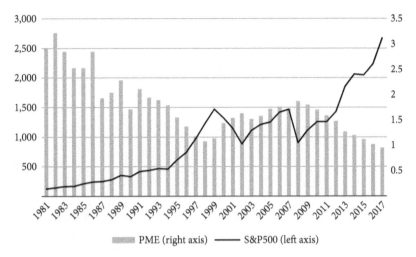

Figure 12.6. PME for U.S. VC funds, by vintage year.
Data: Cambridge Associates (2018).

outlays as the actual investment, but it looks at what returns these outlays would have generated if they had been invested in a benchmark market index, such as the S&P 500. A PME greater (smaller) than one means that the investment in the VC fund generated higher (lower) returns than a comparable investment in the index.[62] Figure 12.6 reports this measure for U.S. data.

In Figure 12.6, PMEs are calculated by vintage year. While the S&P rose over this period, PMEs declined until 1999, to rebound until 2009. Notice the difference with the previous figures, where the dot-com bubble corresponded to a spike in absolute returns. The difference is explained by the relative nature of the PME, which compares absolute returns to the benchmark index. As the S&P 500 also spiked in the dot-com bubble, this kept the PME from ballooning. Still, it is remarkable that even at its lowest point in 1999, the PME stayed above 1, suggesting that VC fund returned more than a comparable investment in the S&P500. However, one needs to consider that the PME abstracts from correcting returns for the risk level, which is higher in VC than in listed equity (Section 4.3.6).[63]

Historical data on fund performance outside the U.S. is less complete and less reliable, though the gap is narrowing as VC activity worldwide grows. Figure 12.7 provides return data for funds outside the U.S., pooling together private equity and VC.

Figure 12.7 shows vintage returns of private equity and VC funds for the period 1995–2016. The solid area represents IRRs, which range from a high of 32% in 1995 to a low of 4% in 2005. The average (median) for the period was 15.1% (14.5%). The bar represents cash-on-cash returns, which range from 2% in 1995 to 1% in 2015 The average (median) for the period was 2% (2%). The IRR is more variable, largely because of varying time horizons. In particular, returns often materialize faster (slower) in up (down) markets, thus accentuating variation in returns.

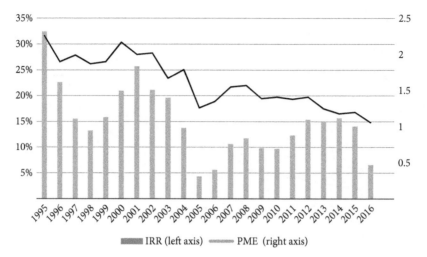

Figure 12.7. Returns to private equity and VC funds outside of the U.S., by vintage year.
Source: Cambridge Associates (2018).

Our discussion so far assumes that LPs hold their partnership shares in VC funds until payback occurs. Over the last decade, a secondary market has emerged where LPs can trade partnership shares. This market should not be confused with the secondary market for company shares that we discuss in Section 11.4.2. The secondary market for partnership shares allows LPs to sell their shares in case they want earlier liquidity. The buyers are either other LPs or some specialized secondary funds. Partnership shares typically trade at a significant discount relative to the estimated net asset value of the underlying portfolio, suggesting that sellers sell under pressure.[64]

12.6.3 Assessing VC Fund Performance

We now discuss the performance of VC funds and its implication for LPs. We start by asking whether past performance can predict future performance. Box 12.8 looks into some academic research on the persistence of VC returns.

Box 12.8 How Persistent Are VC Returns?

Institutional investors looking at investing in VC funds put a lot of emphasis on past performance. This may seem surprising since, in many situations, past financial performance is no indicator of future performance.[65] For example, the mutual funds with the highest returns in one year do not achieve higher returns the next year, and so on.[66] Is VC any different in this respect? Several academics have looked at the available evidence, and the consensus is that VC returns tend to be persistent.[67]

An early study by Kaplan and Schoar found that a VC whose previous fund had 10% higher performance than the benchmark can expect to achieve a 6% higher performance in the current fund.[68] This is considered very strong persistence. The study further found that superior performance increases the probability of raising a subsequent fund, as well as its size.

Given the limits to which fund size can grow, early access to successful GPs generates future higher returns.[69] Later studies confirmed these findings, although there is a debate about the exact magnitude of the persistence effect.[70] Despite the dramatic cycles in the industry, persistence of VC returns also does not seem to have changed much since the 1990s.

Why is there persistence? One view is that more successful VCs have better skills. Do certain VC firms consistently obtain better returns because of their organization capability and brand name or because of the quality of the individual partners? One academic study by Ewens and Rhodes-Kropf decomposes the relative importance of the VC firm versus VC partners.[71] It shows that individual partners are largely responsible for generating consistent gross returns. Specifically, it finds that partners who achieved profitable exits early in their careers continue to have a constant flow of exits in their VC firms, even if they moved from one to another VC firm, or founded their own VC firm. LPs should thus not only look at the track record of the VC firm, but also the individuals who are behind it.

The next question is why those better VCs do not capture the full value of their skills by charging higher fees? One explanation is that the market for funds is not fully competitive because incumbent LPs have inside information about the true skills of different GPs, which makes it more difficult for other LPs to compete.[72] Similarly, it appears that brand name matters for attracting deal flow and that good VC firms want to maintain a reputation for superior performance to ensure LP support in good and in bad times. The illiquid nature of partnership shares might also contribute to persistence: LPs cannot move in or out of a fund during its 10-year life, which stands in stark contrast with mutual funds. Since GPs raise funds only every few years, this severely limits the ability of LPs to shift money out of worse performing GPs and into better performing ones. The fact that a fund's realized returns become known only when it is liquidated limits the information available to LPs and further reinforces persistence.[73]

What is the risk of investing in VC funds? At the company level, we saw a skewed distribution of returns, with a large number of failures, reflecting the well-known fact that the outcome of entrepreneurial experimentation is very difficult to predict (Section 12.6.1). However, at the VC fund level we are not interested in total risk but in undiversifiable risk, that is, the risk that cannot be diversified away in a large portfolio (Section 4.2.1). The Capital Asset Pricing Model (Box 5.1) suggests using beta as the measure of undiversifiable risk. In addition, investors might require a premium to account for the lack of liquidity of the asset class.

To estimate the beta of an LP's VC portfolio, one needs to look at the correlation of fund-level net returns with the returns from a diversified market portfolio. Using a variety of empirical approaches, academic studies have estimated betas for VC fund investments to be consistently higher than 1, in fact ranging between 1.1 and 2.8.[74] This evidence sits uncomfortably with the claims made by the VC industry that it provides diversification. Instead, the data suggests that VC investments are pro-cyclical and therefore provide limited diversification.[75]

To see how net returns are calculated in practice, we go back to the Rocketfueler example in Box 12.9.

Box 12.9 Rocketfueler's LP Returns

The three partners were proud to present their LPs with the following table. The first part concerns the capital calls and use of funds. Rocketfueler I drew $10M of capital in each of the first two years, and then $20M for the next four years.[76] This was according to plan and ensured that the fund was always ready to invest. The 2% management fee totaled $20M.

The second part of the table computes profits and hurdle rates. Rocketfueler I returned the exit proceeds to the LPs immediately. It also had a European waterfall rule, so it only received its carried interest after paying off all of the capital investments and the hurdle rate. The "Capital plus hurdle" row identifies the amount owed to LPs with the hurdle. The next two rows identify the net profits (which are net of management fees), once with and once without hurdle. The final two rows calculate the division of profits without hurdle, for those years where the hurdle was cleared. This part of the table shows that Rocketfueler I did not have positive net profits (with or without hurdle) until 2028.

The third part of table shows the distributions of the fund to its LPs. Up to the end of 2027, all of the exit proceeds went straight to the LPs. Starting in 2028, however, LPs received back distributions covering their capital and the hurdle rate ($161M), so Rocketfueler I finally started receiving carried interest. From that point, the division of exit proceeds moved to the 20–80 of net profits, without any more hurdle rate. The total carry thus amounted to $50M by the end of the fund, corresponding to 20% of the $250M net profits.

The LPs were reasonably satisfied with Rocketfueler I. They had invested $100M, and a total of $300M had been returned to them, implying a net CCR of 3. Their net profits were $200M, which implied an NPV of $24M (using a 15% discount rate). The net IRR was 22%, naturally lower than the gross IRR of 36% (Box 12.7). Similarly, the net CCR of 3 was smaller than the gross CCR of 4.4.

LP level analysis ($M)	2020	2021	2022	2023	2024	2025	2026	2027	2028	2029	2030	Total
Capital calls and use of funds												
Capital calls	10	10	20	20	20	20	0	0	0	0	0	100
Investments	-4	-8	-8	-20	-7	-13	-7	-8	-5	0	0	-80
Management fee	-2	-2	-2	-2	-2	-2	-2	-2	-2	-2	0	-20
Fund net balance	4	4	14	12	23	28	19	9	2	0	0	
Profits and hurdle rates												
Exit proceeds	0	0	0	2	5	9	0	21	195	50	68	350
Cumulative exit proceeds	0	0	0	2	7	16	16	37	232	282	350	
Capital plus hurdle	11	22	46	71	98	128	138	149	161	174	188	
Net profits above hurdle rate	-11	-20	-46	-69	-91	-112	-122	-112	71	108	162	
Net profits without hurdle rate	-100	-110	-100	-98	-93	-84	-84	-63	132	182	250	
Carried Interest (20% of net profits)									26	36	50	
Capital plus 80% of net profits									206	246	300	
Distributions												
Carried interest	0	0	0	0	0	0	0	0	26	10	14	50
Distributions to LPs	0	0	0	2	5	9	0	21	169	40	54	300
Cumulative distributions to LPs	0	0	0	2	7	16	16	37	206	246	300	
LPs net cash flow	-10	-10	-20	-18	-15	-11	0	21	169	40	54	54

Summary

This chapter sets out to understand the structure of VC firms. We begin by asking how institutional investors provide funding to VC firms in order to diversify their investment portfolios and achieve satisfactory returns. We examine the structure of these investments and show that funds are typically structured as limited partnerships with a 10-year horizon. The limited partnership agreement compensates VC firms with management fees and performance-related fees called carried interest. We examine how fees affect VC firms' incentives, and further we look at the internal structure of VC firms and at how the partners define portfolio strategies and investment styles. We finally review the returns record of VC investors. We distinguish between the gross returns that come from the funds' investments in companies and the net returns that are earned by the institutional investors after deducting fees.

In Chapter 1 we introduced the FUEL framework for understanding the structure of investor organizations. In this chapter we apply this framework to VC firms. For the fundamental structure (the F in FUEL), Section 12.2 focuses on funding sources, examining how LPs allocate funds to VCs. For the underlying motivation (the U in FUEL), Section 12.3 looks at how the limited partnership agreement shapes VC firms' objectives. For expertise and networks (the E in FUEL), Section 12.4 examines how VC firms are structured and how they forge relationships externally. For logic and style (the L in FUEL), Section 12.5 examines VC firms' investment strategies.

Review Questions

1. From the perspective of institutional investors, what are the pros and cons of investing in VC funds?
2. What are the main components of a limited partnership agreement (LPA)? Why is it needed?
3. Why do most VC funds have a 10-year horizon? What are the alternatives?
4. What is the difference between management fees and carried interest? What incentives do they give to the general partners (GPs)?
5. Who are the people working at VC firms?
6. What affects the success of raising a VC fund?
7. What are the main dimensions of a VC investment strategy?
8. What are the possible growth strategies for a successful VC firm?
9. What is the difference between gross and net returns in VC?
10. What does it mean that returns in VC persist? Why is it surprising? Which factors could be behind this fact?

Notes

1. Davis and Steil (2004).
2. Da Rin and Phalippou (2017).
3. See the State of European Tech 2018 Report by Atomico, a venture firm, available at: https://2018.stateofeuropeantech.com.
4. Bodie, Kane, and Marcus (2017) provide a comprehensive treatment of this topic.
5. https://www.nobelprize.org/prizes/economic-sciences/2013/press-release.
6. https://www.nobelprize.org/prizes/economic-sciences/1997/press-release.
7. Fama and French (1993, 1995).
8. Shiller (2016).
9. Shiller (1981).
10. Black and Scholes (1973), Merton (1973).
11. Fisher Black died in 1995, and in 1997 the Nobel Committee announcement gave him credit for his contribution to the option pricing formula.
12. Section 4.1.3 examines stock options.
13. Ebrahim (2014).
14. Gompers and Lerner (1996, 1999), Litvak (2009), and Metrick and Yasuda (2010a) discuss evidence on the structure of LPAs, including GP compensation.
15. Levin and Rocap (2015) provide a detailed legal analysis of venture capital transactions, including LPAs.
16. Da Rin and Phalippou (2017).
17. For a practical example of how this is done by one VC firm, see Mead (2016).
18. Dyck and Pomorski (2016).
19. Barrot (2016) and Kandel, Leshchinskii, and Yuklea (2011).
20. Sussman (2014).
21. Metrick and Yasuda (2010a).
22. Robinson and Sensoy (2013).
23. Chung et al. (2012).
24. Sussman (2014).
25. Fleischer (2008), Herzig (2009), Viard (2008), and Weisbach (2008).
26. See Lee and MacFarlane (2016) for a global perspective.
27. Robinson and Stuart (2007) and Rothaermel and Deeds (2004).
28. Ozmel and Guler (2015).
29. See Fred Wilson's post in his AVC blog: https://avc.com/2010/08/what-is-a-venture-partner-and-does-it-matter-to-you, accessed April 15, 2019.
30. Metrick and Yasuda (2010a) provide evidence for the U.S., and Bottazzi, Da Rin, and Hellmann (2008) for Europe.
31. Gompers et al. (2019).
32. Gompers et al. (2019).
33. Hower (2012).
34. White (2013).
35. Gompers and Wang (2017a) and Hegde and Tumlinson (2014).
36. See the State of European Tech 2018 Report, available at: https://2018.stateofeuropeantech.com.
37. Fairlie, Robb, and Robinson (2016) discuss evidence on access to finance by entrepreneurs from a racial minority.
38. Gompers and Wang (2017b).

39. Da Rin and Phalippou (2017).

40. Wong (2005) and Kollmann, Kuckertz, and Nils (2014) discuss the fundraising process.

41. Whyte (2017) and https://www.oxfordsciencesinnovation.com.

42. Hsu and Kenney (2005) and Cline (2016).

43. See their respective websites: http://www.intelcapital.com, http://www.bpifrance.com, and https://www.temasek.com.sg.

44. Hochberg, Mazzeo, and McDevitt (2015).

45. Gompers, Kovner, and Lerner (2009) and Matusik, and Fitza (2012).

46. This preference was first documented by Lerner (1995).

47. Bernstein, Giroud, and Townsend (2016).

48. Aizenman and Kendall (2012), Bottazzi, Da Rin, and Hellmann (2016), and Nahata, Hazarika, and Tandon (2014).

49. Chemmanur, Hull, and Krishnan (2016) and Liu and Maula (2015).

50. Cash (2017). About thesis investment, see the website of Union Square Ventures: https://www.usv.com/blog/usv-thesis-30, Martinez (2015), and Evans (2015).

51. On Sequoia Capital, see https://www.sequoiacap.com, https://www.crunchbase.com/organization/sequoia-capital, accessed April 15, 2019.

52. Pitchbook, "2018 in Review," available at: https://pitchbook.com/news/articles/2018-in-review-top-5-global-vc-deals-exits-funds. .

53. Anders (2014).

54. https://www.youtube.com/watch?v=nKN-abRJMEw, accessed April 15 and summarized in Hardymon, Nicholas, and Kind (2014).

55. Hochberg, Ljungqvist, and Lu (2010)

56. Bottazzi, Da Rin, and Hellmann (2008, 2009).

57. Ewens, Nanda, and Rhodes-Kropf (2018).

58. Fulghieri and Sevilir (2009).

59. A similar conclusion is reached using CCR or IRR as return metrics.

60. Korteweg and Sørensen (2010).

61. Uupdated documents can be found at: www.ilpa.org.

62. There are also variants of the PME measure that further account for risk. Sørensen and Jagannathan (2015) and Korteweg and Nagel (2016) provide additional discussion and implementations based on sophisticated statistical tools.

63. For additional discussion, see Harris, Jenkinson, and Kaplan (2014, 2016) and Kaplan and Schoar (2005).

64. Arcot et al. (2015), Degeorge, Martin, and Phalippou (2016), Ibrahim (2012), and Lerner and Schoar (2004).

65. Wermers (2011).

66. Berk and van Binsbergen (2015), Berk and Green (2004).

67. Harris, Jenkinson, and Kaplan (2014), Hochberg, Ljungqvist, and Vissing-Jørgensen (2014), Kaplan and Schoar (2005), and Korteweg and Sørensen (2010). Nanda, Samila, and Sorenson (2018) further show that early success translates to improved access to quality deal flow.

68. Kaplan and Schoar (2005).

69. Sensoy, Wang, and Weisbach (2014) document this in a rare study with data at the LP portfolio level.

70. Phalippou (2010) and Phalippou and Gottschalk (2009). Harris, Jenkinson, and Kaplan (2014, 2016) provide a review of these results accessible to a nontechnical audience.

71. Ewens and Rhodes-Kropf (2015).

72. Hochberg, Ljungqvist, and Vissing-Jørgensen (2014).

73. Korteweg and Sørensen (2017).

74. Ang et al. (2018), Driessen, Lin, and Phalippou (2012), Ljungqvist and Richardson (2003), and Korteweg and Sørensen (2010).

75. Robinson and Sensoy (2016).

76. In practice, most VC funds make quarterly capital calls. We use annual capital calls to simplify calculations.

13

Early-Stage Investors

Learning Goals

In this chapter students will learn:

1. About a range of alternative funding sources for early-stage start-ups.
2. To understand the investment approaches and constraints of early-stage investors.
3. How innovations such as crowdfunding and Initial Coin Offerings are changing the financing landscape.
4. To relate the funding needs of entrepreneurs with the available choices of investor types.

This chapter examines alternative sources of capital that entrepreneurs use to finance the early stages of their venture's development. We start with informal funding sources from family and friends, which may be particularly important at the time of new venture creation. We then examine the role of angel investors, including angel groups. Next, we analyze corporate investors, which in addition to financial goals pursue a variety of strategic goals. We examine different types of crowdfunding models based on donations, loans, or equity. Initial Coin Offerings (ICOs), based on Blockchain technology, are a related and very recent phenomenon. We also discuss additional funding options such as accelerators, incubators, technology transfer funds (TTFs), and social impact funds. The chapter provides a framework for comparing and contrasting different early-stage investor types.

13.1 Founders, Family, and Friends

13.1.1 Reasons for Investing

The very first investment in a start-up typically is from the founders themselves.[1] This comes from private savings or personal debt, such as second mortgages, credit cards, or personal loans (Section 10.4.1). Within founder teams, different founders may contribute different amounts of funding (Section 4.4).

Many entrepreneurs, especially younger ones, don't have much savings. This is where personal debt comes in. Banks typically offer a variety of personal loan facilities. For example, home owners can top up their primary mortgage, which is used to finance the real estate, with a second mortgage, which can be used for any other purpose. Recent research shows that home ownership helps to overcome credit constraints precisely when home owners can take a second mortgage to fund their venture. Moreover, the relatively large amounts that come from a second mortgage allow entrepreneurs to create larger companies that outgrow smaller ones.[2]

A source of personal debt that requires no personal guarantees are credit cards. While it is often easy to get credit this way, the costs may be high as soon as balances are not paid off at the end of the month. Credit cards are convenient for transactions and for smoothing out short-term cash fluctuations but are an expensive form of finance. Still, in practice, credit cards remain an important source of early-stage funding for many entrepreneurs.

Why do founders use their own money to fund their venture? From a portfolio perspective, investing in one's own venture leads to poor diversification, since the financial returns are highly correlated with personal income. The main reason why founders invest in their own company is sheer necessity. In the very early stages of venture development, founders typically have too little to show to outsiders to convince anyone to invest. So, they use their own savings to explore the viability of their idea. Even when the company obtains outside funding, founders might be asked to invest some of their own money. This is because outside investors want to see "skin in the game."[3] From an economics perspective, investors are concerned about "adverse selection" (they expect founders to invest as a signal of their confidence in the venture) and "moral hazard" (they want founders to maintain a sufficient stake to continue being focused on financial value creation—see Box 2.2). Some wealthy founders also prefer to invest in their own venture to retain more control.

A founder's family and friends also often provide funding very early on, either directly into the venture, or indirectly through a loan or gift. Ann Winblad founded the Open System software company in 1976 and later became one of the first women in Silicon Valley to found a VC firm called Hummer Winblad Venture Partners. She recalls: "I exhausted all of my savings on the incorporation fees and was about $500 short, which I had to borrow from my brother, who was in high school. But he had a job. He was the only one who had $500 to borrow from that I knew."[4] Other successful entrepreneurs like Jeff Bezos or Sir Richard Branson initially relied on funding from their family to get started.

A company that is getting all its initial funding from founders, family, and friends is said to be bootstrapping.[5] These investors are sometimes (half) jokingly referred to as the 3Fs, which stands for family, friends, and fools. This is meant to reflect a presumed lack of business sophistication. Many founders are cautious about asking family and friends for money because of the deep personal connections. For those who do, it motivates them not to disappoint. John Gabbert, the founder of

Pitchbook, a venture capital data provider eventually acquired by Morningstar in 2016, put it this way: "For me, when you have friends and family that write checks—people you see at Christmas—if you lose their money, it changes Christmas. I don't want to wreck Christmas."[6] However, personal connections may also limit the risk that entrepreneurs are willing to take.[7] Most founders, families, and friends only have modest savings. As a rough estimate, most start-ups would not expect to raise more than $100K from these investors, although in some cases the funding can be larger.

Informal funding plays an especially large role in emerging economies. One academic study by Wu, Si, and Wu gathers data on the use of informal debt by Chinese entrepreneurs.[8] It finds that better access to informal funding helps innovative entrepreneurs achieve higher sales from new products. The effect, however, weakens when informal funding becomes abundant. The presence of formal financing options, such as official bank financing, reduces the effect of informal financing. Interestingly, the authors find that a higher level of institutional development, such as a better legal system, strengthens the innovative effect of informal financing.

Even though they may hope to reap a financial return, family members' main rationale for investing is based on personal relationships. There may also be a sense of social obligation. With friends, investments are mostly motivated by a desire to help out. Relative to family, friends presumably find it easier to decline investing.

13.1.2 How Family and Friends Invest

Founder financing deal structures tend to be very simple, with an informal approach to the negotiations and contracting. Investments made by a sole founder go directly into the company. Founder teams need to keep track of who invested what because at some later date they have to discuss how they get compensated for it. Founder investments are typically structured as equity or as loans (Sections 4.4 and 10.1).

In the case of family and friends, three investment structures are common. First, some family members simply donate money without wanting anything back. Second, some families and friends structure their investments as a loan, either as a "pay back when you can" interest-free loan with no fixed maturity, or as an interest-paying loan, usually at better terms than a bank loan. Third, in some cases, family and friends want equity in return for their investment. They either agree on a valuation upfront or else defer valuing the venture until it raises some equity from professional investors. Whether formalized or not, this last structure corresponds to a convertible note or a SAFE, which we discuss in Section 6.6.

Informal investors typically invest on a social basis. While there are exceptions, they mostly have limited expertise. Their relevant networks tend to be small and often overlap with those of the founders. In most cases, family and friends also remain passive investors. Entrepreneurs typically do not expect to receive substantial help, except maybe a shoulder to cry on. Informal investors rarely have deep pockets. Entrepreneurs may thus need to set appropriate expectations, explaining that in the absence of further investments, their ownership stakes will get diluted over time (Section 9.2.1).

13.2 Angel Investors

13.2.1 Different Types of Angel Investors

Angel investors ("Angels") are private individuals who invest their own money in start-ups. Unlike family and friends, they have no prior social relationships with the founders. They range from middle-class wage earners (e.g., teachers) and professionals (e.g., doctors and lawyers) to successful entrepreneurs, all the way up to billionaires. Angels can invest as individuals or through a variety of structures that bring them together. We distinguish between "angel networks" and "angel funds" and collectively refer to them as "angel groups." Such arrangements are becoming increasingly popular.[9]

Many angel networks are a loose affiliation of angel investors that meet at regular intervals to listen to entrepreneurs' pitches. They then leave it up to the individual angels to decide whether and how much to invest in each venture. Some networks are more structured, so that angels collectively organize due diligence and negotiate deals. Individual angels then decide on a deal-by-deal basis whether they want to invest or not.

Angel funds are instead investment vehicles where participants pool their money to jointly make investments. There is a core of active investors who manage the fund on behalf of the remaining passive angels. When they invest alongside the active angels, such funds are sometimes called "sidecar funds." Most angel funds are smaller than VC funds, typically below $10M. The fees and carried interest are sometimes used to fund the angel group's activities. Examples of angel funds include the $5M Acorn Fund raised in 2009 by the San Francisco-based group Band of Angels, or the AUD$10M sidecar funds raised in 2016 by the Sydney Angels group.

The vast majority of individual angel investments cluster in the $10K–$50K range and rarely go beyond above $100K. Given the relatively small amounts of money available, they often co-invest with each other. Wealthy angels, such as successful entrepreneurs, may write larger checks of $100K and upwards. Angel networks are often able to invest up to $1M. Angel funds can invest even more, and syndicate with VC firms with which they establish long-term co-investment relationships. Figure 13.1 reports data about the volume of angel investments in different regions over time. As for VC investments, this form of funding is cyclical. It is also more common and more resilient in the U.S. than elsewhere. One

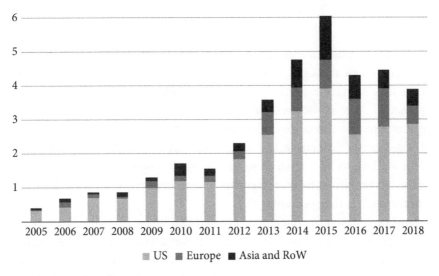

Figure 13.1. Angel investments, by region.
Data in U.S. dollar billions. Source: Pitchbook Data.

should be aware that the vast majority of angel investments go unrecorded, given that they are informal and decentralized. Observers often consider the visible deals that are captured in statistics to account for 20% of the whole market, or even less. So any reported numbers are likely to substantially underestimate this source of funding.

A special case of angel investing is that of family offices, which are investment funds owned by a wealthy individual or family. Some family offices are set up to invest largely in entrepreneurial companies sometimes referred to as "super angels." Other family offices are run by a staff of professionals who invest across a broad spectrum of financial assets, including start-ups. Some family offices even become institutional investors and contribute as LPs to VC funds (Section 12.2).

In terms of motivation, angels invest their own money and can do so in any way they please. Beyond financial returns, they are motivated by a range of other goals. Some angels invest because they like the idea, care about the product, or appreciate the social contribution of the new venture. Other angels invest because they like working with ambitious entrepreneurs and enjoy the process of contributing to a venture without having to run it. Yet others use angel investing as a way to learn about promising areas of opportunity, testing the waters as to which venture they want to pursue next. By and large, angels have a high degree of risk tolerance and a long-term investment horizon. However, in some angel funds there is pressure to exit, to satisfy some angels with shorter exit horizons.

A fundamental difference between angels and VC firms is that angels are only accountable to themselves, whereas VC firms are accountable to institutional investors (Section 12.1). This explains why we find considerably more variety of structures and motivations among angel investors than VC firms.

13.2.2 How Angels Invest

Angel investors can have a wide variety of expertise and networks. Angels who acquired their wealth through professional income, investments, or inheritances, may have little relevant expertise, and their networks may not be very useful to entrepreneurs. Angels who have been successful entrepreneurs bring not only money, but also a wealth of experience and contacts. Mentoring from an experienced angel can be invaluable to entrepreneurs. Any one angel's expertise and networks is likely to be limited to some specific industry and geographic area. Therefore, it is important for entrepreneurs to contact angels who can make a relevant contribution to their venture.

In terms of investment preferences, angels often invest in their proximity, especially when they plan to stay involved with the development of the venture. Similarly, they tend to focus on industries that match their expertise. Angels naturally focus on the early investment stages, where investment amounts are moderate.

Finding individual angel investors can be challenging. Some angels keep a low profile, quietly scouting for opportunities without advertising their presence.[10] Angel groups are more readily identifiable than individual angels. They have a public presence, such as a public website, and openly advertise their presence. Indeed, the main reason for forming an angel group is to create a vehicle for attracting potential entrepreneurs and organizing the process of evaluating them.

Selection of business proposals is very different when the entrepreneur deals with individual angels or with networks. Each individual investor behaves differently, with varying degrees of due diligence. By contrast, angel networks hold structured meetings where entrepreneurs are invited to pitch. Investors may then coordinate their due diligence and investment decisions. With angel funds, the investment decision is made by the individuals managing the fund. Box 13.1 looks at research on how angels choose which companies to invest in.

Box 13.1 How Angel Investors Select Which Companies to Invest in

---

Selecting which ventures to fund is one of the most difficult investment tasks. Investors first narrow down a large set of applicants to a short list, and then they select among those that have been short-listed. A recent study by Maxwell, Jeffrey, and Lévesque considers short-listing applicants for the Canadian version of the Dragon Den's (Box 4.1).[11] It turns out that experienced angels use a simple way to drop applicants: a single major flaw in their plan eliminates the venture. Another study, by Carpentier and Suret, found that, among Canadian angel investors, market risk is a prominent rejection reason (Section 2.5).[12]

Research by Kerr, Lerner, and Schoar looks at the investment decision of two well-established U.S. angel groups.[13] The study examines how angel groups make decisions by aggregating scores from individual angels. Reaching a minimum score is necessary to be considered for investment, but scores alone do not determine the final investment decision; due diligence provides further information that leads to the final decision. The study documents that angel funding leads to better performance in terms of employment growth and patenting activity. One of the angel groups achieved financial returns comparable to those of venture firms, suggesting that they select deals as well as their VC counterparts.

Individual angels range from being passive to very active. Their involvement depends on their industry expertise and on their willingness to support the company. In some cases, angel investors, especially those with an entrepreneurial background, become deeply involved, joining the board or taking on management responsibilities.[14] Angel networks often include a group of passive angels and a smaller group of active angels who look after the investments. In angel funds, the angels managing the fund are expected to remain involved with the company.

When it comes to structuring the deal, angels mostly use common equity due to its simplicity. At the seed stage, convertible notes and SAFEs are also increasingly popular (Section 6.6). Larger angel groups sometimes ask for preferred shares, although this request can prove futile if subsequent venture investors use their bargaining power to undo the preferred terms (Section 9.1).[15] Angel term sheets are typically light on control rights, although experienced angels and larger angel groups ask for board representation and other control rights.[16]

13.3 Corporate Investors

Corporations constitute a large and diverse class of investors. Corporate VC is not a side show in entrepreneurial finance. Figure 13.2 shows the volume of global investment volume since 2011. Both the total volume and the number of deals have increased considerably over time, reaching $53B invested in 2,740 deals in 2018. This accounts for about 20% of all VC deals (Figure 1.2).[17] The 2018 CB Insight Corporate Venture Capital Report finds that 41% of the deals were made in North America, 38% in Asia, and 17% in Europe. The report identifies 773 active corporate VC arms, the five most active ones being Google Ventures, Intel Capital, Salesforce Ventures, Baidu Ventures, and Legend Capital (a subsidiary of the Legend Group, best known for its Lenovo Brand). There were four non-U.S. players among the 10 most active: SBI Investment (part of a Japanese financial conglomerate), Kakao Ventures (a subsidiary of a South Korean telecom group), Fosun RZ Capital (a subsidiary of Fosun International, a diversified conglomerate), and Mitsubishi Capital (a subsidiary of the Mitsubishi conglomerate from Japan).

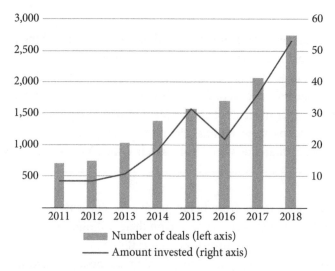

Figure 13.2. Global Corporate Venture Capital investments.
Amount data in U.S. dollar billions. Source: CB Insights CVC Reports,
various years.

13.3.1 The Motivation of Corporate Investors

In order to understand corporate investors, we begin by asking a seemingly simple, but actually deep, question: Which activities happen within the corporate boundary and which ones outside? This issue has preoccupied many eminent economists, generating several Economics Nobel Prizes. Box 13.2 looks at how transactions within firms differ from transactions across firms.

Box 13.2 Nobel Insights on Firms versus Markets

The 1974 Nobel Prize in Economics went to Friedrich von Hayek "for [his] penetrating analysis of the interdependence of economic, social and institutional phenomena."[18] The 1991 Prize went to Ronald H. Coase "for his discovery and clarification of the significance of transaction costs and property rights for the institutional structure and functioning of the economy."[19] The 2009 Prize went to Oliver Williamson "for his analysis of economic governance, especially the boundaries of the firm."[20]

In 1937, Coase wrote a paper, modestly called "The Nature of the Firm," in which he asked which economic activities should be performed inside firms and which in markets.[21] While markets and prices are good for balancing demand and supply, there are also costs associated with using the market mechanism. Coase called these "transaction costs." They include the costs of bargaining and writing and enforcing contracts. The alternative to transacting in markets is to organize activities inside firms, where resources are allocated by managers on the basis of authority, not market prices. Coase's main insight is that transactions should take place within firms when transaction costs are high. For example, it is more efficient to hire workers and let their boss decide each day what they should do rather than continuously contract in the market for each single task they have to perform.

While Coase identified the transaction costs of using markets, Hayek identified the benefits of markets[22] Hayek emphasizes the importance of prices to convey information to economic agents. He argues that prices allow economic agents to make efficient decisions because they incorporate localized knowledge. For example, observing higher prices for artisanal ice cream, an entrepreneur may decide to open another ice cream parlor to profit from high demand. Hayek also exposed the difficulty of coordinating decisions within organizations that disregard localized knowledge.

Williamson's work further explored the costs and benefits of market transactions identified by Coase and Hayek.[23] He developed Coase's concept of transaction costs into a broader theory of the benefits and costs of market transactions. One central insight he brought up concerns the importance of asset specialization. When two assets are specialized to each other, and therefore become complementary (i.e., interdependent), the owner of one asset can be held up by the owner of the other asset, who may threaten to withdraw his own asset or invest too little in the relationship. Williamson called this the "hold-up problem." The argument is that complementary assets should be managed within a single firm to avoid the hold-up problem altogether. Many other great economists have since contributed further to what has come to be known as the "theory of the firm."[24]

What does this theory teach us about strategic venture investors? Consider a biotechnology start-up that needs the production and marketing capabilities of an established pharmaceutical company. A recent example is the investment of Novartis, one of the largest pharmaceutical companies, in Vor Biopharma, an immuno-oncology start-up.[25]

Let us think of these as two assets, "Bio" and "Pharma," and apply Coase's fundamental trade-off between firm and market. Under the firm solution, Pharma acquires Bio, so that they integrate into one company (Section 11.3). A single management team oversees the activities of the two divisions. Under the market solution, the two companies would remain independent, so that Bio contracts out production and marketing to Pharma. Each firm's management allocates resources within its company. A contract specifies the marketing services provided by Pharma for Bio, as well as the associated payments. Because their assets are interdependent, there is a potential for hold-up. For example, after signing the initial contract, Pharma may threaten to discontinue its services, or it may provide minimal effort, unless Bio offers to pay higher prices for its services.

Strategic investments come into the picture as an intermediate solution, where Pharma makes an equity investment into Bio.[26] Both companies retain independent management teams, but as an investor, Pharma has some say on Bio's major decisions. Bio and Pharma still need a contractual agreement, but Pharma's ownership stake in Bio better aligns their objectives. Moreover, the chances of hold-up are reduced since Pharma would be holding up its own investment.

The promise of a strategic investment is therefore to get the "best of both worlds." Ownership is used to reduce transaction costs (as emphasized by Coase) and to help alleviate the hold-up problem (as emphasized by Williamson). This arrangement retains the benefits of independent managers using decentralized knowledge (as emphasized by Hayek). From the established company's perspective, having an equity stake in a related start-up gives it cash flow rights that allow it to participate in the venture's financial success, as well as control rights that allow it to influence its strategic direction.

While strategic investments can be an effective solution while the start-up develops its technology, these benefits tend to decrease as the start-up becomes a more mature company. This is why strategic investments are often temporary arrangements, leading either to full integration (e.g., Pharma acquires Bio) or a dissolution of the investment relationship (e.g., Pharma sells its stake in Bio).

These Nobel insights into the nature of the firm show that, in addition to financial returns, the main motivation of corporate investments in entrepreneurial ventures is strategic.[27] In a large corporation, a high return on a venture portfolio barely changes the overall profits of the corporation, while positive strategic benefits can have a profound effect on corporate profits.[28] The strategic motive of a corporate investor can also be beneficial to the entrepreneur when there is strategic alignment. However, it can also be a double-edged sword. It can give rise to conflicts of interest and raise questions about the true intent of the corporation. This brings us to further examine the interplay between corporate motives and the needs of entrepreneurs.

A first strategic benefit of corporate venture investing is that it gives the company a window on new developments in technology. By engaging in corporate venturing, the organization is exposed to some of the latest technologies and ideas that affect its industry and that they could miss out on if they were to remain focused on their own operations. It can also reach out to talented entrepreneurs and recruit them.[29] The strategic interest of the corporate investor is highly stage-dependent. The sweet spot of corporate venture capital (CVC) is around those technologies that are likely to become commercially relevant in the near future. Earlier technologies are too speculative for the established company to seriously consider. Fully developed technologies require more drastic actions, such as acquiring other companies or building internal capabilities.

A study by Chemmanur, Loutskina, and Tian finds that CVCs invest in younger companies with riskier projects than VC firms. Over time these start-ups obtain more patents than those backed by VC firms. This is consistent with the notion that CVCs have stronger industry domain knowledge than VC firms, which helps them to select and support more innovative start-ups. It may also be that they are more risk tolerant, and thus willing to invest in more innovative projects that create more patents.[30]

A second strategic benefit for corporate investors is to establish valuable vertical relationships with innovators. Corporations can develop business relationships where the entrepreneurial company becomes an upstream supplier, helping the corporation to lower its costs or improve its offering. In other cases, the venture becomes a downstream buyer, helping the corporation to sell in existing or new markets. Strategic benefits can also be more indirect. Companies that provide technology platforms, such as Facebook, Amazon, or Tencent, have a strategic interest to encourage new services and products that make use of their platform.

Third, established corporations sometimes use strategic investments to influence competitive dynamics. One way to do this is to invest in potential competitors and buy them out to neutralize the threat they pose. Less drastically, a corporate investor can stir the start-up away from direct competition and redirect it toward a more complementary business model.

We now turn to the question of how corporate investors can find ways of cooperating with entrepreneurial ventures. A survey of leading European corporations inquired about the ways these established companies interacted with start-ups and internal ventures: 84% of all respondents procured products or services from start-ups, 71% had invested in entrepreneurial companies, 52% ran an accelerator program, 50% invested via a dedicated corporate VC program, and 36% acquired at least one start-up.[31]

In order to understand how corporate investors choose among these different approaches, Table 13.1 provides a classification that builds on the contributions of Coase, Hayek, and Williamson examined in Box 13.2.[32] The columns represent the extent to which the assets of the corporation and the start-up are complementary, whereas the rows indicate the complexity of the business transactions between the two companies.

The upper left quadrant of the table describes the simple business transactions involved in establishing customer/supplier relationships. These mainly concern the exchange of goods and services, but there may also be some financial aspects. For example, if the corporation is a supplier to a start-up, financial support can be provided in the form of trade credit (Section 10.4.2). As a customer, the corporation

Table 13.1 Cooperation Models Between Corporations and Start-Ups.

Asset Complementarity:	Low	High
Business Transactions:		
Simple	Customer / supplier relationship	Strategic investment
Complex	Strategic alliance	Joint venture / acquisition

may also provide some prepayments that alleviate a start-up's cash flow problems. Customer financing is nondilutive in the sense that the start-up doesn't have to give up any equity (Section 9.3.3). The customer might therefore ask for a price discount for providing upfront payments. This type of customer financing is limited to business-to-business transactions and is particularly useful when the start-up builds a customized product or service, such as custom design or custom research.

The lower left quadrant of the table shows the role of the strategic alliance, a contractual agreement of how two companies plan to cooperate. For example, the start-up and the corporation may undertake some joint research or share some marketing and sales resources without directly selling products or services to each other. A typical alliance specifies the resources each company makes available to the other. In the case of a research alliance, for example, these resources may include agreements on cross-licensing or access to specialized equipment or human resources. A strategic alliance tends to be accompanied by a set of payments, typically from the corporation to the start-up. These may include upfront payments, as well as payments that are based on the completion of previously agreed milestones. As part of the overall agreement, the established company might also take some equity in the start-up. This ties the start-up closer to the corporation and helps align their interests.

The upper-right quadrant of Table 13.1 looks at cooperation when asset complementarity is high. An example might be an established hardware provider and a start-up software developer that provides software to improve hardware usability. In such situations, strategic investments are particularly effective because they allow the corporation to align itself with the start-up and the start-up to remain a flexible independent organization. While in principle most corporations could make strategic investments in start-ups, in practice few do so on a regular basis. Such investments absorb financial resources and require specialized expertise and a long-term commitment. The strategic benefits are difficult to measure and happen in a more distant future. Many corporations therefore do not have any explicit arrangements for making strategic investment. Still, when a compelling opportunity comes along, they may strike a once-off deal.

The bottom-right quadrant of Table 13.1 describes a situation where complex business transactions involve highly complementary assets. One possibility is to set up a joint venture where the two companies create a jointly owned subsidiary and make specific commitments about how they share resources. Such arrangements are more common when both parties are large corporations. In the case of a corporation dealing with a start-up, it is often easier for the corporation to simply make an acquisition (Section 11.3).

One special case worth mentioning briefly is franchising. In this case, the corporation (franchisor) provides licenses, supplies, and know-how that allow the start-up (franchisee) to operate. In addition to receiving basic fees and royalties, the franchisor sometimes also gets equity in return for making a financial investment.[33]

13.3.2 The Structure of Corporate Investors

There are numerous ways to organize corporate venturing efforts.[34] They can be thought of along a spectrum from more to less autonomy. A tightly controlled approach has the corporate development team closely working with business line managers. Senior managers help to identify the strategic priorities of the venture team, control its budgets, and approve final investment decisions. At the other end of the spectrum, senior managers delegate authority to a professional venture team, which manages its own venture fund and has the freedom to make investment decisions. In a corporate venture capital (CVC) fund, operations resemble those of independent VC firms, and the role of the corporate parent is similar to that of a limited partner. Most corporate venturing efforts fall somewhere between these two extremes. Intel Capital, for example, has a large fund that has its own management team but still remains closely integrated within the parent corporation.[35]

Once a company establishes a CVC fund or a strategic investment division, it needs to hire a team of corporate venture managers. In many respects, their job is comparable to that of private VCs, except that corporate managers don't have to worry about raising funds from limited partners (Section 12.4.4). Instead, they have to ensure that, besides their financial targets, they deliver strategic value to the corporation. Corporate venture capitalists (CVCs) spend considerable time within the corporation understanding its strategic needs and forging relationships with key corporate managers, who can help screen start-ups and provide them with support and advice.

Strategic investment initiatives face two major difficulties. One concerns the compensation of corporate venture managers, which does not match the generous compensation packages common in VC. Issues of internal fairness constrain the compensation of CVCs. For example, a Silicon Valley-based venture manager for SAP, the German software company, found himself on the same pay scale as all other 22,000 SAP employees, while his Silicon Valley peers made considerably more.[36] The compromise typically involves compensation packages that contain some of the incentive elements used by independent VC funds, but less high-powered. This makes it challenging for corporations to attract top talent from the VC industry to run their corporate venture programs.

The second difficulty concerns the support of the corporate divisions to the strategic investment unit. Even if a strategic investment benefits the company overall, there are often parts of the organization that lose. They invariably cry foul fastest and loudest. Even if there are no identifiable losers, a problem of inertia remains: "Not invented here" is a well-known corporate syndrome in which managers do not take seriously any innovations that come from outside their organization.[37] Preexisting reporting lines and tightly delimited corporate budgets can further impede the collaboration of corporate divisions with the venture development teams and their investment companies.

Given all these difficulties, how do corporate venture programs perform? Box 13.3 discusses some empirical evidence.

Box 13.3 The Performance of Corporate Venture Capital

Studying the performance of CVC programs is challenging because it is difficult to assemble comprehensive datasets. One study by Dushnitsky and Shapira compares the performance of CVC funds against that of independent VC firms in the 1990s.[38] This study considers over 13,000 investments made by 2,830 VCs, 300 of which were CVCs. The finding is that CVCs are more focused on late-stage investments, with 62% of late-stage deals versus 52% for independent VCs. More than half of all CVC investments were in information technology. CVCs also frequently invest alongside independent VCs, typically joining larger syndicates. The average syndicate size for deals involving CVCs was 4.5, compared to 2.6 for deals without CVCs.

The rate of successful exits in this sample is 30%. However, CVCs achieve a significantly higher rate of 47%.[39] This can be partly explained by the different types of investments made by CVCs, such as the greater emphasis on late-stage deals, which are less risky than early-stage deals. However, after controlling for numerous factors, the study still finds that the exit rate of CVCs is almost 7% higher than that for independent VCs. The study also looks at how CVCs are compensated. It finds that those CVCs that receive high-powered incentive compensation enjoy a higher success rate. After controlling for other factors, high-incentive CVCs have a rate of successful exits 19% higher than independent VCs.

While the structure of independent VC funds is stable for 10 years, corporate venture programs are less consistent over time. Strategic motives are inherently dynamic and therefore change frequently; so do corporate CEOs and their senior management teams, who decide on the continuation of previous strategic investment initiatives. Internal resistance further contributes to the instability of strategic investment programs. Overall, corporations have a reputation for being somewhat fickle investment partners: they can enthusiastically engage with start-ups one moment but can quickly lose interest in the next.

Strategic investing concerns start-ups that originated from outside the organization. A related phenomenon concerns corporations that finance internal projects as part of a broader strategy of stimulating "intrapreneurial" behavior, where employees of the organization generate and implement new venture ideas.[40] These internally focused venturing efforts seek to promote intrapreneurship among employees. In some cases, the new venture ideas are adopted within the existing divisions; in others, the corporation creates a new division within the organization; and in yet other cases the venture is spun into a separate company. In the last case, the parent company typically takes an ownership stake in the newly created spin-off company. Being "intrapreneurial" is, however, easier said than done. Many companies struggle with efficiently managing their core businesses on the one hand, and flexibly experimenting with a variety of intrapreneurial ideas on the other hand.

The history of corporate venturing at Xerox is an interesting example of this difficult balancing act. We explore it in Box 13.4.

Box 13.4 Tales from the Venture Archives: How Xerox Lost the Mouse

In the early 1980s, the Xerox PARC Research Center, located in the heart of Silicon Valley, attracted considerable engineering talent and developed numerous new technologies.[41] Xerox PARC guided its inventors toward projects relevant to Xerox's core business. For this purpose, it determined whether a project was internally relevant or not. The latter were spin-offs, and Xerox had a policy of not investing in them. 3COM was one such spin-off. It licensed from Xerox the Ethernet technology, a key building block of the Internet, and it became a large publicly listed company.

One of the projects that failed to get internal traction was the computer mouse. Xerox wanted to make an investment in a promising new start-up called Apple Computers, and invited Steve Jobs to its PARC facilities. This is where Jobs first saw the mouse, along with its Graphical User Interface (GUI). The rest is history: XEROX will always be remembered for having "lost the mouse."

PARC also illustrates the instability of corporate venturing programs. In 1989, after the publication of a book exposing Xerox's blunders, the company reversed its approach to internal venturing.[42] It launched Xerox Technology Ventures, a $30M corporate VC fund, to invest in its own spin-off companies. This reversed the prior "no investment" policy and encouraged employees to aim for spin-offs. Some successful investments came out of this fund; the fund was financially successful, generating an IRR of 56%. However, the attractiveness of starting spin-off companies meant that employees had fewer incentives to develop technologies relevant to Xerox's core businesses. Indeed, few internally relevant technologies emerged in that period.

As a consequence, Xerox refocused its internal venturing approach once more in the mid-1990s. The new program focused on the strategic needs of Xerox's internal divisions. It encouraged internal adoption. It gave internal divisions nine months to make a decision on whether or not they wanted to adopt a technology. This created a slow and bureaucratic environment that was not well suited to the fast pace of Silicon Valley. In the early 2000s, Xerox distanced itself from PARC, first spinning it off into a subsidiary and then gradually adding external partners to make it an independent research center, free of the expectations of delivering strategic value to its parent.

The history of Xerox PARC contains some useful lessons for corporate venturing. Corporations not only struggle with the trade-off between internal adoption and external commercialization, but also face the difficult challenge of motivating and managing entrepreneurial employees. It is important to realize that Xerox was not a poorly managed company. In fact, it was a very efficient and highly profitable organization. What its example suggests is that tightly managed efficient organizations are rarely well positioned to foster innovation and intrapreneurship.

13.3.3 How Corporates Invest

While the overall investment processes of corporate VCs are broadly similar to those of independent VCs, an important difference concerns their access to corporate resources. Corporate investors may have less expertise and weaker networks in entrepreneurial circles, but they often have more expertise and stronger networks when it comes to technology and business development. For example, at the due diligence stage, corporate investors can get expert technical opinions from inside the corporation. Corporations can also provide access to distribution channels, which can help start-ups to grow quickly.[43]

Deal flow and selection of business opportunities are driven by strategic considerations. Captive investors are sought by entrepreneurs who seek technical validation of their technology or a commercial partner. This may lead to a natural self-selection of the applicants toward the right target. VC firms also often involve CVCs as co-investors in deals where they need an expert second opinion.

The term sheets used by strategic investors are similar to those we discuss in Chapter 6, except for a few aspects. Many corporate investors prefer minority ownership stakes especially if majority stakes require consolidating financial accounts (which decreases reported earnings). They also shy away from holding formal board seats to avoid liabilities to the corporation. Instead, they may get board observer rights, which allow them to participate in the board discussion without bearing legal responsibilities.

One sensitive issue concerns the protection of intellectual property (IP). Some entrepreneurs shun corporate investors because they fear that they will steal their ideas. Box 13.5 looks into what conditions lead entrepreneurs to accept strategic investing.

Box 13.5 Which Conditions Favor Strategic Investing?

Entrepreneurs are often nervous about approaching corporate investors because they fear having their ideas stolen. A famous example was Robert Kearns, who in the 1960s invented the intermittent windshield wipers and soon found that the Ford Motor Company stole his idea.[44] This suggests that strategic investing should be more common when start-ups can protect their ideas with patents.

A study of U.S. corporate venture deals by Dushnitsky and Shaver shows that in industries where patents are more defensible (e.g., pharmaceuticals and medical equipment), strategic investments are more common.[45] Research by Colombo and Shafi shows that entrepreneurs often postpone a deal with a CVC to later stages, until IP protection has been more firmly established.[46] Alternatively, start-ups seek funding from reputable VC firms before approaching CVCs in order to better protect their venture.

A related study by Katila, Rosenberger, and Eisenhardt notes that start-ups are more willing to accept the risk of IP expropriation when the corporation has unique assets, such as a strong commercial network.[47] They also accept such risk when it is difficult to find other investors or partners. Strategic investments therefore involve a trade-off between maintaining defense mechanisms versus accessing valuable corporate resources.

Corporate venture investors are often expected to pay a higher valuation, given that they benefit both financially and strategically. While they might disagree with this view, and stress the strategic benefits they bring to start-ups, competitive pressure frequently leads corporations to offer higher valuations, especially when competing against top-tier private VCs or against other corporations.[48]

Some corporate investors ask for an option to acquire the entrepreneurial company from its shareholders. This goes well beyond the standard preemption rights that allow an investor to maintain ownership (Section 9.3.3). It is a powerful right that can later prove problematic for the start-up. Once a corporate investor has such an option, it becomes virtually impossible to generate acquisition offers from other companies. In fact, even without the contractual option to acquire, taking on a corporate investor creates expectations that the venture is likely to be acquired by the corporate investor. One study by Benson and Ziedonis examines acquisitions by large corporations with active corporate VC programs. It finds that 17% of the start-ups acquired had prior strategic investments from the acquirer.[49]

13.4   Crowdfunding

13.4.1 The Structure of Crowdfunding Platforms

Crowdfunding is not an investor type per se; instead it is a method of funding entrepreneurial ventures by connecting them to distant investors through an online platform. Crowdfunding is still a young phenomenon, evolving rapidly as new approaches are being tried out in response to technological and regulatory changes.[50] It is best understood as a two-sided matching market where buyers and seller meet according to some protocol. In traditional markets, such as commodities or stock markets, buyers and sellers anonymously trade standardized products. In matching markets, it is all about finding a fit: is a particular candidate suitable for a specific job, rental apartment, romantic partner, and so on?[51]

At the center of crowdfunding is a platform provider that offers intermediary services to investors and entrepreneurs. The main challenge of platform intermediaries is to create a "thick" marketplace that simultaneously attracts many buyers and sellers. This requires simple processes that allow buyers and many sellers to easily find good matches.

Crowdfunding leverages the technological possibilities of the Internet, including advances in cloud-based computing and electronic commerce, as well as the increased social acceptance of transacting online. On one side of the platform are the entrepreneurs, who ask for money, and on the other are the investors, who provide money.

We distinguish three types of crowdfunding platforms relevant to entrepreneurs: (1) reward and donation, (2) lending, and (3) equity. Table 13.2 provides a summary overview of these platforms.[52]

Reward and donation crowdfunding requires no financial contract, and the entrepreneur is not expected to pay anything back. Funders only expect some non-monetary reward, such as an acknowledgment (in case of donations), a symbolic token of appreciation (e.g., a T-shirt), or some kind of preferential treatment (e.g., a backstage pass to meet the musicians). Donations have achieved some success in funding targeted medical research, especially for rare diseases.[53] A more substantial reward that is particularly relevant for start-ups is that the entrepreneur raises money in exchange for the future delivery of a new product that is under development. In this case, crowdfunding is a form of customer prepayment. The crowdfunding campaign provides information about the level of customer demand and about which product attributes or characteristics are most sought by customers.[54]

Lending platforms allow borrowers to raise debt from lenders through peer-to-peer (P2P) lending.[55] The name suggests that it is private individuals who lend

Table 13.2 Crowdfunding Platform Types.

Platform: Features:	Reward and donation	Lending	Equity
Entrepreneurs	Individuals (e.g., musicians), organizations (e.g., charity ball), or start-ups (e.g., new gadget)	Individuals (e.g., home improvement loan) or corporations (e.g., purchase equipment)	Start-ups (e.g., home brewery software app)
Funders	Individuals (small amounts)	Individuals (small amounts) and financial institutions (banks, hedge funds; large amounts)	Individuals (small amounts), also some angel investors providing larger amounts
Types of rewards	Pre-sold products small gifts, acknowledgments (for donations)	Principal and interest	Equity
Examples	Kickstarter (US), Indeigogo (US), RocketHub (US), ThundaFund (South Aftrica), Ulule (France), KissKissBankBank (France), Boomerang (Denmark), Pozible (Australia)	Lending Club (US), Prosper (US), Kiva (US), Lending Circle (UK), Zopa (UK), Younited Credit (France), AuxMoney (Germany), Faircent (India), Fairplace (Brazil), Afluenta (Latin America), Harmoney (New zealand)	OurCrowd (Israel), Crowdcube (UK), SEEDRS (UK), AngelList (US) CircleUp (US), Companisto (Germany), Symbid (Netherlands), Fundnel (Singapore)

money to other individuals. This is in fact how lending platforms started, but over time the set of lenders has expanded significantly. In addition to individuals, the main lenders on these platforms are banks, hedge funds, or specialized lenders. On the borrower side there are three main categories: (1) private individuals seeking consumer loans; (2) a growing market for home mortgages; and (3) businesses borrowing on P2P lending platforms.

The novelty of P2P lending is not the product, which is a simple term loan, but the fact that intermediation happens in an online marketplace. This is a cost-effective and competitive environment, often resulting in attractive interest rates for borrowers.[56] The vast majority of business borrowers on lending platforms are established small businesses, not start-ups. This is because P2P lenders face the same difficulties of providing debt to entrepreneurs that we discuss in Section 10.3, namely, that entrepreneurial start-ups are risky, lack track records, and are difficult to understand. Some entrepreneurs use P2P platforms not for business loans but for personal loans.

Equity crowdfunding allows investors to take equity stakes in the companies they invest in. This type of crowdfunding has developed more slowly. In most countries, regulators have been cautious in allowing these kinds of investments. There is a perception that this type of crowdfunding is particularly prone to fraud. The first country to take a more liberal regulatory approach was the UK, which has developed a vibrant equity crowdfunding market.[57] Over time, other countries, most notably the U.S., have introduced legislation allowing some forms of equity crowdfunding.[58]

Regulators also distinguish between "sophisticated" and "unsophisticated" investors. Sophisticated investors are wealthy individuals with enough financial knowledge to fully understand the investment risks. Legally, they have the status of "accredited" investor. The latter are less wealthy individuals, legally "unaccredited" investors. Some crowdfunding platforms, such as AngelList, mainly target accredited investors, whereas others, such as Crowdcube and SEEDRS, are open to all investors.

The relative amounts of funding obtained on different platform varies considerably. Rewards-based platform tend to be used for relatively small amounts. The average campaign amount of Indiegogo is about $1.5K, and it is about $23K for Kickstarter. P2P lending sites typically provide similar amounts. U,S.-based Lending Club has an average loan size of around $15K, while UK-based Funding Circle's average loan is around £100K. Equity-based crowdfunding platform allow entrepreneurs to raise larger amounts. U.S.-based AngelList's average amount is around $350K, UK-based SEEDR's around £500K.[59] Note, however, that these averages hide considerable variation. The most successful Kickstarter campaign to date, for example, is Star Citizen, a video game company that raised over $200M.[60]

13.4.2 Motivations in Crowdfunding

From the investor's perspective, using crowdfunding has two main benefits: (1) the ability to reach to a much wider deal flow, and therefore to find opportunities that match one's target deals more closely, and (2) the ease with which transactions can be closed. It should also be noted that online and offline investment processes are not mutually exclusive. For instance, AngelList facilitates a mix of online and offline interactions. Platforms typically screen entrepreneurs and sometimes investors, too. They help entrepreneurs to find interested investors and may also process the transaction.[61]

From the entrepreneur's perspective, crowdfunding has the immediate appeal of being able to reach a large number and variety of investors. Crowdfunding appeals to a much broader set of start-ups across a wide variety of sectors, not just high-tech. Crowdfunding also appeals to entrepreneurs who traditionally find it challenging to obtain funding. Box 13.6 examines whether crowdfunding effectively democratizes access to capital for entrepreneurs.

When evaluating the attractiveness of crowdfunding, entrepreneurs face two important trade-offs. The first concerns information disclosure. Listing an

Box 13.6 Does Crowdfunding Democratize Access to Capital?

Does crowdfunding improve access to capital for underrepresented groups of entrepreneurs? One academic study by Marom, Robb, and Sade looks at gender effects on Kickstarter.[62] It finds that 34.5% of all projects are led by a female entrepreneur, compared to 9% in VC (Box 12.3). The ratio of female entrepreneurs is highest in Dance (77.1%) and Fashion (58.2%), and lowest in Games (7.7%) and Comics (13.7%). The study also finds that 44% of investors are female and that they are significantly more likely to invest in female-led projects. Female-led campaigns asked for considerably less money and were more likely to succeed than male-led campaigns. Moreover, successful male-led campaigns end up raising more than five times what they asked for, compared to less than one and a half times for female-led campaigns.

Traditionally, investors tend to focus on companies that are located close to them and therefore mostly in larger urban clusters. Crowdfunding, however, is accessible to companies located anywhere in the investor's country and often also beyond. Research by Agrawal, Catalini, and Goldfarb looks at data from Sellaband, a crowdfunding platform for music bands.[63] It finds that crowdfunding allows entrepreneurs to reach more distant investors. A prevailing pattern is that early in the campaign investors tend to be local and close to the entrepreneur. However, as the campaign gathers momentum, there is increasing interest from more distant investors that have no prior linkages to the entrepreneur.

Further research by Catalini and Hui finds that crowdfunding has increased equity flows to U.S. regions with low-intensity VC activity. This effect can get as large as 33% of pre-crowdfunding flows into those regions. These changes reflect the increased ability of venture investors in VC hubs to use their screening ability to select promising ventures that would otherwise not be noticed.[64]

Overall, it appears that crowdfunding gives entrepreneurs access to capital that would have been more difficult to unlock in a traditional offline environment.

---

entrepreneurial project on a crowdfunding platform makes it visible not only to a large set of potential investors, but also to competitors, which is a potential risk for the entrepreneur. The second trade-off concerns timing. A unique feature of crowdfunding is the potential of learning from the crowd. In the case of lending or equity-based crowdfunding, a campaign reveals something about investors' interest. Moreover, a product-based crowdfunding campaign reveals information about consumer demand. Offline investors may wait for the results of a crowdfunding campaign before making any investment decision. Consequently, entrepreneurs have to be strategic about the appropriate timing of a crowdfunding campaign. If they launch the campaign prematurely, a poor outcome can create a negative stigma that is difficult to reverse.

Turning to the perspective of the crowdfunding platforms, we note that most of them are for-profit businesses that generate revenues through a variety of fees. The fee structure determines their financial rewards, but also guides their behavior in learning how to succeed in the online environment. There are four main revenue sources for platform operators. First, they can charge entrepreneurs for listing their companies (quite common), and investors for accessing them (less uncommon). Second, companies pay a percentage of the amount of funds raised. Third, in the case of equity crowdfunding, the platform may take an equity stake in the company or receive a carried interest. This is similar to what VCs receive (Section 12.3.3). Fourth, the platform may offer ancillary services to entrepreneurs (e.g., help with preparing a listing) or investors (e.g., data analytics). Different fee structures create different incentives for how to structure the platform. Company listing fees and ancillary services create incentives for the platform to list as many companies as possible. Taking equity or carried interest encourages platforms to be more selective because returns only come from those companies that have a successful exit.

A key choice is how to set prices or fees on the platform. Providers have to determine which side of the market pays fees and how much. To understand this choice, we need to consider two different types of externality, First, on each side of the market, competition creates negative externalities: sellers want fewer other competing sellers and buyers want fewer competing buyers. Second, there are positive externalities coming from the other side of the platform: buyers benefit from having more sellers on the platform, and sellers benefit from more buyers on the platform. This second type of externality is responsible for the "winner takes all" property frequently associated with two-sided markets, where there is only one platform that attracts the majority of buyers and sellers.[65] Examples of winner takes all markets are Alibaba, Amazon, eBay, or Uber.

This "winner takes all" property explains why competing platforms are often willing to incur short-term losses in order to attract a critical mass of buyers and sellers. Platform providers often waive all fees to whichever side of the market is harder to attract. For example, many investment platforms charge listing fees to entrepreneurs, knowing that they are eager to list their investment proposals. However, they refrain from charging fees to investors, who tend to be less convinced that they actually need these platforms.

13.4.3 Crowdfunding Campaigns

The process begins with entrepreneurs preparing an information package that explains the nature of the business. Visual information, especially video, are particularly important for communicating an entrepreneur's message. The platform operator then performs some legal and business due diligence on the venture. It has to ensure that the entrepreneur does not engage in any illegal activities and that the information is not misleading or false. Moreover, the platform ensures that the proposed venture fits the desired profile.

Prior to campaign launch, the entrepreneur has to define exactly what it is that she is offering in return for the investment. In the case of rewards, she needs to define what the reward will be, and when the customers can expect to receive it. In the case of lending and equity platforms, she needs to specify the price, the fundraising goal, and the investment terms. Let us look at each of these.

The price of the financing is the interest rate in case of lending and the price per share in case of equity. Given the number of preexisting shares, the price per share determines the pre-money valuation of the company (Section 4.1). The post-money valuation depends on the number of shares actually issued at the end of the campaign. In most cases, the entrepreneur fixes the price, and investors decide whether or not to invest. Some platforms allow for some price discovery during the campaign, for example through an auction mechanism where investors specify the price at which they are willing to invest.

The entrepreneur specifies a fundraising goal. If the campaign does not reach the goal within a specified timeframe, the campaign is considered failed and the investors are relieved from their commitment. Failure is common. As of early 2019, Kickstarter, one of the largest platforms, reported a success rate of about 36%.[66]

When the campaign hits its goal, then the entrepreneur is typically allowed to raise more than the original goal. In this case, the entrepreneur's choice of when to close the campaign determines the amount of funding raised. In some cases, there is also a maximum amount that a company can raise through crowdfunding. For U.S. equity crowdfunding, for example, current securities regulation imposes an upper limit of $1.07M per company over any 12-month period. Platforms typically also impose some upper limits on how much any one investor can invest. Kickstarter, for example, has a maximum pledge amount of $10K per investor.[67]

Crowdfunding platforms require the entrepreneurs to offer highly standardized financial terms. A platform generally requires the use of a standard template that defines the terms of the loan or equity offering. Most lending platforms require simple term loans, most equity platforms common equity.

A unique feature of crowdfunding is that information about investors' interests are revealed in real time. This has two implications for the dynamics of the campaign.[68] First, investors can react to the investments made by other investors. Second, the entrepreneur needs to promote the venture during the campaign, to encourage investments.

While investors may have an opinion on the quality of a given campaign, they often pay close attention to the decisions of other investors. There are two diametrically opposed views about this. The positive view is that crowdfunding facilitates information aggregation, where the opinions of different investors are brought together to reveal the demand for the product or the interest for the investment opportunity. Under this view, the individuals in the crowd contribute valuable information that gets aggregated into a broader picture. This is called "wisdom of the crowd." The negative view is that the blind leads the blind. Individuals simply follow each other because they believe others have relevant information, or because they want to "join the rising tide."[69]

This behavior can turn into a self-fulfilling prophecy, where the belief that a campaign with early momentum will be successful leads others to also invest in the campaign, and thereby ensures that the campaign actually is successful. This type of herd behavior, rational or irrational, can lead to poor investment choices. In particular, some early signals may sway the crowd in the wrong direction, especially if the early signals contain relatively little information about the true merits of the venture.[70]

While the verdict on these two views is still out, it is reasonable to think that both forces operate at the same time and that their relative importance varies across different campaigns. The information of one investor is more pertinent to all others in equity crowdfunding than in reward crowdfunding. The wisdom of the crowd may also depend on the underlying type of business. For example, we might expect the crowd to have more relevant information on consumer-facing businesses, rather than business-to-business opportunities that require more specialized industry knowledge.

Given the fragile nature of these campaign dynamics, entrepreneurs are eager to influence investor behavior during the campaign in order to sway the crowd in the right direction. Most platforms allow entrepreneurs to communicate with the crowd throughout the campaign. Experience shows that the performance in the first few days of a campaign strongly predicts its eventual chances of success. Entrepreneurs can influence early performance by arranging early investments from family and friends. Naturally, the crowd comes to expect this, as all entrepreneurs try to do the same things. Not pre-arranging any early investment thus becomes a recipe for failure. Moreover, the most credible early signals come from investments that are unusually large and/or from investors that are well known.[71]

13.4.4 Returns from Crowdfunding

The most important issue after the campaign is to ensure that the investors get their promised return. In the case of rewards, this is mostly a question of whether and when the promised token of appreciation is delivered. Some projects never deliver, whereas others struggle to deliver what they actually promised or to deliver on time. In one famous example, the producer of the "Pebble" watch, a pioneer in wearable computing, raised more than $10M on Kickstarter but then faced severe supply chain challenges and delivered the watches with considerable delay.[72] A study estimates that 9% of campaigns fail to deliver on their promises.[73]

In the case of lending platforms, investors expect timely interest payments and the repayment of principle. The average interest was around 13% for Lending Club and 10% for Funding Circle, although the actual rate depends on the lender's risk characteristics.[74] Data from Lending Club suggests that 77% of loans are paid back on time, 3% are paid back in full but with some late payments, and 20% involve some default.[75]

In equity crowdfunding, investors hold onto their shares until the company gets acquired or goes public. This involves three challenges. The first concerns ownership dilution in subsequent financing rounds. Future rounds of funding lead to the dilution of the existing owners, unless they continue to invest in the company pro rata (Section 9.3). Individual investors in crowdfunding platforms do not have financial resources to keep investing in a successful venture. Even if they had them, they may not be able to invest if the company turns to professional investors. Crowd investors typically do not obtain preemptive rights, that is, the right to participate in future rounds.

The second challenge concerns control rights. A standard crowdfunding term sheet gives investors fewer rights than an angel or VC term sheets (Sections 6.4 and 9.3). This has two reasons. First, offering equity to the crowd calls for simplicity. Second, adding these rights would hamper certain corporate decisions, such as future fundraising or exit as the company would legally have to contact and obtain permissions from each of a large number of investors.[76]

The third challenge is exit itself. If the company is successful, and the entrepreneur is willing to have an exit for the investors, then all is well. However, some entrepreneurs may never want to sell the company, or wait for a long time. If the company is profitable, investors could in principle get paid through dividends, but crowd investors rarely have the control rights to force the entrepreneur to pay out dividends.

This brings us to a broader governance challenge with equity crowdfunding. Investors tend to be dispersed, unsophisticated, and uninformed, creating a governance vacuum. While some entrepreneurs are attracted to equity crowdfunding precisely because of the lack of governance control, this could lead to adverse selection problems where investors face a pool of entrepreneurs that value their independence a little too much. Different crowdfunding platforms offer different solutions. Some channel the investments into a special purpose vehicle (SPV). While the cash flow rights associated with the company shares are passed through the SPV to the crowd investors, the control rights remain with the platform operator, or another trustee, which can vote for the crowd.

Another potential solution is to combine crowdfunding with a syndicate leader. The lead investor commits to providing a significant portion of the investment rounds. He may also assume certain responsibilities, such as sitting on the company's board of directors. In return, the lead investors may be entitled to extra compensation, which can be structured in ways similar to the carried interest compensation of VC firms (Section 12.3.3). For example, the syndicate leaders in AngelList receive some carried interest compensation for organizing investment syndicates.[77]

13.5 Initial Coin Offerings

13.5.1 The Blockchain and Cryptocurrencies

Blockchain and its applications are a very novel phenomenon that is currently developing very rapidly. While we can describe the current situation as of early 2019, we expect this phenomenon to change significantly in the near future. Thus, some of the content of this section may become out of date before long.

To understand the Blockchain, we first need a broader background. Recordkeeping is central to economic activity. To be effective, it requires trust in the truthfulness of public records. Such trust is provided by an organization that all participants consider trustworthy. When purchasing a good or service with cash, the trust resides in the banknotes issued by a central bank. The seller does not need to trust the buyer, just the central bank whose banknotes she receives. With electronic payments, parties trust the financial intermediaries (banks or credit card companies) that manage the transfer of funds in exchange for a fee.

The Blockchain is an online technology that changes this architecture by substituting a central trustworthy organization with a decentralized network of recordkeepers that provide independent verification services. The Blockchain is a distributed ledger technology (DLT) that allows the storage and circulation of digital records of information (often transactions). It keeps track of records as they occur over time, organized in blocks for efficient processing, thus generating a chain of blocks that are ordered chronologically. The resulting distributed ledger is a database containing all past transactions that are stored on the computers of all network members. This technology allows for digital recordkeeping that is safe from tampering, thus dispensing with the need for a central authority to validate transactions.[78] Box 13.7 provides a brief primer on how the technology works.

Box 13.7 What Is the Blockchain?

The Blockchain is a potentially disruptive technology that promises to shrink the cost of recordkeeping of financial transactions. We identify five major steps:

1. Block formation. Nodes in the Blockchain network receive requests to include users' transactions into a new "block." Upon verifying the transactions, the nodes assemble them into a block and propose its validation to the network. This involves the use of cryptography.
2. Mining. Nodes compete to add the block to the distributed ledger, which is a database containing all past transactions that are stored on the computers of all network members. Competition is based on solving a difficult mathematical puzzle that requires increasingly large computational power as the chain develops. Nodes competing for adding blocks are called miners, and the process is called mining.
3. Verification. The first node to solve the puzzle wins the competition. A majority of the other nodes must agree that the solution is correct, which they can easily verify within the system.

4. Logging. The transactions block is logged into the distributed ledger and becomes part of the Blockchain. As the chain expands, forging a block becomes more difficult as all subsequent blocks must be forged as well to reconstruct a valid chain. This is computationally challenging and thus provides a powerful safeguard of the chain's integrity.

5. Reward. The winning miner is awarded a compensation by the network. The compensation comes from two sources. One is the transaction fees that participants may offer to miners to speed up the inclusion of their transactions into a block. The other is the reward that the network bestows on successful mining, in the form of a number of cryptocurrency tokens.

The first Blockchain application was Bitcoin. It was invented by the mysterious Satoshi Nakamoto, a pseudonym whose true identity remains a matter of debate. In 2009, Nakamoto proposed the creation of Bitcoin, which became the first and still the most successful cryptocurrency.[79] Its success spawned additional cryptocurrencies that differentiate themselves by targeting different user needs. Cryptocurrencies are open systems that are regulated by a protocol, which determines the supply of currency tokens, their ownership, and circulation, as well as any admissible transactions.[80] Through online exchanges, cryptocurrencies can be converted into each other and into traditional currencies, like the U.S. dollar. By late 2018, the total market capitalization of the 100 main cryptocurrencies was hovering around $200B.[81]

Ethereum is one of the pioneering platforms, with Ether as its native token. Its differentiation is the use of smart contracts. These are computer programs that implement a series of preset contractual agreements and allow verification by the network without the need for a central party. Several applications have been developed. For instance, the German company Slock.it developed a Blockchain for automating sharing contracts of cars and motorbikes, using a private encryption key stored on one's smartphone. Litecoin targets users who need faster execution for smaller transactions. Ripple aims to help financial institutions manage high-volume low-value cross-border transactions.

The benefits and risks of the Blockchain and cryptocurrencies remain hotly debated. At the core of the debate is the idea that trust in a central authority is replaced by trust in an underlying computer protocol. While a central authority might be able to use its position of power to extract some fees or other economic rents, the protocol does not. Moreover, the use of digital data and cryptography reduces the costs of verification and ensures privacy. However, all this can also have some unintended consequences. A key element of the Bitcoin Blockchain, for example, is mining, which is clearly wasteful, as it requires vast amounts of energy to solve the mathematical puzzles that are inherently useless. As the chain grows and the puzzle difficulty increases, increasingly large investments in computing power and electricity are required. In fact, a significant challenge for the viability of Blockchain projects is to maintain the interest of miners, who are facing increasing costs of solving crypto puzzles. The time to complete transactions on the Blockchain remains slow. As the supply of tokens is limited, rewarding miners also becomes increasingly expensive. A solution that is currently emerging is the use of transaction fees for completing transactions. However, this makes transaction more expensive, effectively reintroducing the economic rents that the Blockchain aimed to eliminate.

13.5.2 The Structure of Initial Coin Offerings

Initial Coin Offerings (ICOs) are Blockchain applications that involve the use of coins, or tokens, that can be exchanged into mainstream cryptocurrencies like Bitcoins or Ethers. [82] ICOs involve the initial sale of these tokens to the public, allowing the issuer to raise money for a new project. An example is Filecoin, whose ICO raised over $250M in 2017 to fund a Blockchain for data storage services.

To explain how ICOs work, let us use the analogy of a children's fun fair. In order to participate in all the wonderful rides, you first get your wallet and take some money to buy tokens that can then be used for the rides. Digital tokens operate on these basic principles and promise users access to certain services. The key difference to a traditional token is that everything happens on a digital platform, with a distributed ledger operating on an underlying Blockchain.

Consider now a fair with a peculiar owner whose token booth is only open in the early morning hours, well before the fair opens. Anybody arriving at the fair after its opening would not be able to buy tokens from the booth. The only way to take a fun ride would be to buy a token from one of the early risers who purchased the token in the morning. The price of the token during the day will thus not be the same as the morning price at the boot. If lots of people show up later in the day, tokens will be in short supply and the price of tokens will go up. However, there is also a risk that few people show up and the price of the token will take a dive. Speculators who believe the fair will become popular will arrive before the opening of the fair and will buy many tokens, hoping to resell them at a profit.

ICOs closely resemble our peculiar fair owner. They involve the initial sale of coins or tokens that are meant to be used on an electronic Blockchain-based platform. The platform promises some future services that can only be purchased with those tokens. Moreover, while a traditional children's fair might have predictable services (the usual fun rides), ICOs offer new and unproved services. It is like speculators buying tokens before the owner even assembled the fairground in the first place.

According to Coinschedule, a leading listing site and data aggregator, the four largest categories in 2018 were Infrastructure, Finance, Communications, and Trading and Investing; together they accounted for 60.5% of the total fundraising. They report 456 ICOs for 2017, raising about $6.5B, and 927 ICOs in 2018, raising about $21.5B.[83] An academic study by Lyandres, Palazzo, and Rabetti reports $7.1B and $22.7B for these two years.[84] To date, the two largest ICOs by far have been those of the EOS Blockchain, which raised \$4.2B, and that of Telegram, which raised \$1.7B. Both took place in the first half of 2018.

Consider now the process of launching an ICO.[85] Prior to issuing tokens, issuers produce a so-called white paper to inform potential buyers of the token sale. In principle, this could be compared to an IPO prospectus, but in practice it is nothing like it. The white paper, which is currently unregulated, is typically a short document that describes the intent of the company and covers technical aspects of the platform architecture. Sometimes it also describes the business model and mentions the founders and their background.[86] More informative papers include a development roadmap that explains how the platform will be built over time.

The founders need to choose how many tokens to issue, which fraction of token supply will be sold, and how many will be kept for the founders and pre-ICO investors, both of whom may already have shares in the underlying company. Creating some scarcity of tokens is the key to creating the potential for financial returns and therefore will attract speculation. The Bitcoin protocol creates scarcity on the basis of the mining process (Box 13.7). Different ICOs adopt different rules about how many tokens will be issued and under what circumstances.

Issuers often choose an upper limit on the proceeds they will raise in an ICO. It is important to raise enough funds to make the project viable and to involve a large enough community. Raising more than what is needed, however, may encourage founders to invest in wasteful activities. Thus, many ICOs have a preset fundraising cap. Note also that ICO sales can sometimes be extremely rapid, with several ICOs selling out within less than an hour. The current record is held by Brave, which raised \$24M in less than 30 seconds.[87]

The issuer needs to choose a pricing mechanism. A popular method is to simply fix the issue price. Some ventures, however, choose mechanisms that allow for price discovery and adjust the token supply on the basis of buyer demand. Purchases are typically paid in cryptocurrencies, the most popular being Bitcoin, Ethereum, and Litecoin. After the ICO, the company also needs to choose whether to list its tokens on an online exchange.

An important goal for issuers is to ensure distributed ownership of tokens, avoiding concentration of power among large stakeholders. Since buyers can shield their true identify, this can be tricky. The anonymity of buyers raises concerns about price manipulation. For example, it is alleged that some large Bitcoin owners (called Bitcoin whales) regularly manipulate prices in their favor.[88]

In some cases, the ICO may be preceded by a pre-sale that helps the issuer fund the ICO marketing, signal the participation of well-regarded investors, and gauge market demand. Pre-sale investors receive a price discount, as in the case of convertible notes (Section 6.6). In March 2018, for example, Telegram planned an ICO with a pre-sale of \$500M and a subsequent public sale of \$700M. However, the pre-sale alone raised \$1.7B. Telegram even canceled its public sale to avoid the regulatory risk.[89]

An interesting question is who are the buyers in an ICO? There is no direct evidence for this issue because buyers can easily disguise their identity by using anonymous digital wallets. Moreover, individuals can further mask their identities by owning multiple digital wallets or employing specialized services that pool the orders of several customers into a single trade. Indirect evidence suggests that buyers fall into four categories. First, there are miners who own cryptocurrencies due to their mining activities. Second, there are the founders and investors of successful crypto ventures who might seek new investments in the crypto space. Third, there are financial investors with speculative motives. This group includes VCs, private equity investors, hedge funds, investment banks, as well as wealthy individuals. For example, a group of top VC firms, including Sequoia, Andreessen Horowitz, and Union Square Ventures, have invested in Polychain Capital, a fund with more than \$1B to invest in ICOs.[90] The final, fourth category is made up by the actual users of tokens.

While the term ICO resembles that of IPO (Section 11.2), they are different in many respects. ICOs are done by very early-stage ventures, whereas IPOs are done by more mature companies. With ICOs no company shares are issued and sold. Instead, what is sold are tokens that generally give no ownership in the company. ICOs also typically try to stay outside of securities regulation, whereas IPOs are heavily regulated. ICOs are instead closer to crowdfunding. ICOs are sold to a large anonymous crowd via an electronic platform. Tokens may also be considered another type of crowdfunding.

13.5.3 The Current Debate About Initial Coin Offerings

ICOs have attracted considerable controversy. Advocates hail them as an innovative breakthrough that gives power to entrepreneurs and allows more democratic economic relationships. Detractors worry about the lack of clear business models, speculative bubbles, and outright fraud. The role of ICOs remains unclear at present. More time is needed to clarify the benefits and challenges of this form of funding. Here we provide a preliminary assessment.

From an entrepreneur's perspective, ICOs allow nondilutive and inexpensive fundraising. There is no exercise of corporate governance in ICOs, as token buyers typically do not get any control rights. ICO companies are often domiciled in countries with lax regulations. ICOs are mostly governed by rules, not discretion. They have smart contracts with algorithmic rules for key activities, such as the release of new tokens. Moreover, their network-based business models are typically based on decentralized decision making.

From the buyer's perspective, there are two main reasons for buying tokens: as a user of the services and as a speculator hoping for the price of tokens to appreciate. Given that many platforms are not yet operational at the time of the ICO, speculators are typically the main buyers. The lack of a transparent market, the uncertainty about what value is created by cryptocurrencies and smart contracts, and the lack of institutions that can ascertain quality, all create a conducive environment for speculation. Consequently, there is a concern about asset price bubbles. Nobel

Laureate Robert Schiller (Box 12.1), a pioneer of behavioral finance, publicly voiced concerns about Bitcoin being a bubble.[91]

Regulators' concerns focus on three areas: protection of investors from outright scams, compliance with securities regulation, and taxes. In our children's fair example, why should the owner ever bother to open the fair, after having sold the tokens in the morning? There is a clear incentive to take the money and run. This seems to have happened with several of the ICOs, where founders disappeared after receiving the money. One way of preventing such fraud is to give the founders incentives to stay. For example, one can put the ICO proceeds into an escrow account that only releases them over time as the venture achieves verifiable milestones, or the community may vote to release tokens based on a progress report. It is also difficult to distinguish between failure and fraud. A murky set of unwanted outcomes can follow ICOs, ranging from entrepreneurial failure to inaction to outright fraud where issuers take the money and run.[92]

A second concern of regulators is whether or not ICO tokens should be considered financial securities. The answer is far from obvious and depends on the nature of the token. An attempt is being made to distinguish between utility and security tokens. Utility tokens are based on a service delivery logic and therefore are treated as (tradable) prepayments. Security tokens are based on a financial return logic and therefore qualify as securities. However, this is not an exact classification, and in practice most tokens have both functional and speculative characteristics. Note that tokens used purely as a means of exchange, like Bitcoin, are not considered financial securities but cryptocurrencies.

In the U.S., the Howey Test defines what a security is.[93] The test has four parts, three of which clearly apply to ICO tokens, namely, that a financial investment is made, that the investment is toward a company, and that the company's success depends on third-party promoters (i.e., the founders). The fourth criterion concerns whether or not the investor has an expectation of financial gain. To make that call, the Securities and Exchange Commission has indicated that it would review ICOs on a case-by-case basis.[94] At present, regulatory ambiguity continues to be pervasive.[95] Some ICO issuers simply avoid the U.S., while others carefully try to structure their tokens as utility token and yet others accept regulatory oversight and design their venture in accordance with regulation. In fact, a recent development has been the rise of Security Token Offerings (STOs), which are fully compliant with U.S. securities regulation.

Outside the U.S., different countries have taken different regulatory approaches. Some countries have put few constraints on ICOs. Switzerland is probably the most permissive country, with the canton of Zug being dubbed Crypto-valley. Singapore and Japan are also considered friendly jurisdictions for cryptocurrencies. On the other end of the spectrum is China, which has outlawed all cryptocurrencies and therefore ICOs. Other countries that restrict them include Russia and Saudi Arabia.

A third aspect relevant for regulators is the taxation of token sales and returns. Taxation can lead issuers to domicile in countries with low sales tax rates. Investors, however, may only be able to avoid taxation in their home country by placing their investments in offshore accounts. As long as transactions are conducted online and the money is only held in cryptocurrencies, it remains unclear which tax authority is in charge. Moreover, given the ease of disguising identities, the online environment is conducive for tax evasion.

Overall, regulators face a difficult trade-off between innovation and experimentation on the one side, and consumer protection and financial stability on the other. Nearly 30 regulators have formed the Global Financial Innovation Network (GFIN) to share experiences in encouraging some experimentation within so-called regulatory sandboxes. The idea is that innovative companies can apply for regulatory exemption in order to test novel financial products. These trials are carefully monitored by the regulatory authorities, which seek to learn and to contain any potential damage.[96]

It cannot be overstated how young the Blockchain and ICOs are. To show how fresh and unsettled the entire phenomenon still is, Box 13.8 examines a fascinating instance of how an ICO for a truly innovative idea encountered some unexpected challenges.

Box 13.8 The Rise and Fork of the DAO

In Chapter 1, we asked whether the first venture capitalist was a man or a woman (Box 1.8). We forgot to ask who the first gender-free decentralized autonomous venture capitalist was. Well, that would be the DAO or Decentralized Autonomous Organization.[97] It was a Blockchain application based on the Ethereum platform. The idea was to create a computer program that would allocate Ethers to promising new crypto ventures. As a radical departure from the VC model, the DAO proposed to use smart contracts to automate the investment process. Ventures could submit applications. Investment proposals would be put on a "white list" by a set of decentralized curators. The community of DAO token holders could then vote on a proposal. If a proposal received more than 20% of the votes, the required amount of Ethers would be automatically disbursed. The DAO's objective was to be fully transparent; its code was a fully open source. It was a stateless organization with no employees and no corporate infrastructure.

In March 2016, the DAO launched an ICO that became the most successful offering at the time, raising 12.7M Ethers, worth approximately $150M. The DAO was about to move into implementation when on June 17/18, 2016, a hacker exploited a weakness in the program. The hacker extracted 3.6M Ethers, placing them in an account that could be withdrawn 28 days later. Even though the Blockchain was fully transparent, its rapid development and complexity had opened up vulnerabilities to such opportunistic behavior. When the DAO community identified the hack, it faced a difficult decision as to what to do about it. Some, including the anonymous hacker, argued that the hack was within the rules of the DAO and that the rules of the Blockchain constituted its own law.

Others, however, argued that this was clearly theft and that the DAO was still too young to anticipate all possible misuses. At times, the debate became deeply philosophical: in a stateless online environment, should the law be laid down by humans or by computer programs?

In the end, the DAO community voted for a "hard fork." This meant that the entire Ethereum Blockchain was split into two. The new Ethereum (labeled ETH) returned the 3.6M Ethers into the DAO's account, whereas the old Ethereum (renamed Ethereum Classic and labeled ETC) did not. Effectively, this meant that there were now two distinct Ethereum Blockchains. There was a clear stir that the community should adopt the new ETH and abandon the old ETC. The majority of the community did indeed adopt the new ETH, but a minority stuck to the old ETC, thus creating two separate Blockchains. The DAO itself imploded. In the end, the first decentralized autonomous venture capitalist ended up not only without humans, but also without investments.

13.6 Further Investor Types

13.6.1 Accelerators and Incubators

Accelerators are essentially training programs for entrepreneurs, where funding is not the central concern.[98] They typically bring together a cohort of entrepreneurs who are in the early stages of starting their companies and who are given some guidance by mentors. Accelerators have a standardized selection process that is based on companies submitting applications. A small committee typically makes the admission decisions. Programs are typically short (three months) and require the entrepreneurs to demonstrate progress. They usually culminate in a "demo day" attended by the local investment community. As such, accelerators are less of a funding vehicle, and more of a facilitator for entrepreneurs to reach out to angel or VC investors. A central part of accelerators' value proposition is adding value through mentoring and organized activities such as master classes.[99] Still, some accelerator programs have a funding component that pays a modest stipend to support the entrepreneur for the duration of the program. They may also provide limited funding for specific tasks, such as prototyping or market research. However, accelerators do not fund later rounds. Their business model is to take a stake at the very beginning and then passively wait until exit occurs.

Most accelerators offer standardized investment terms on a take-it-or-leave-it basis. They usually take an equity stake in their companies. The San Francisco-based Y-Combinator, started in 2007, is widely regarded as the first modern accelerator. It invests $150K for a 7% stake in the company, implying a standard post-money valuation of $2.1M. Similarly, Seedcamp in the UK charges 7.5% for £100K, implying a post-money valuation of £1.3M. Other programs, such as StartX, based at Stanford

University, or the Creative Destruction Lab, a university-based network of seed-stage programs, make no investments and take no equity.

One interesting special case are corporate accelerators. They are run by large established organizations, with a strategic objective of forging relationships with entrepreneurs who might provide useful solutions to the company. They are therefore closely related to other corporate investment initiatives (Section 13.3).[100] TechStars, for example, operates numerous programs for a wide variety of corporations, such as Barclays' Rise accelerators, which focuses on Fintech.

Similar to accelerators, incubators are primarily a service provider rather than an investor. Their core proposition is to provide a conducive work environment for entrepreneurs. Some incubators merely provide office space, while others create a community of like-minded entrepreneurs and even provide business mentors. Some only provide serviced office space, and others also provide specialized facilities, such as maker spaces or wet labs. In recent years, the concept has also been extended to co-working spaces, where instead of renting their own office, entrepreneurs have access to "hot desks," and a variety of associated services. Many of these incubators and co-working spaces are also networking hubs that help entrepreneurs meet investors. An example is WeWork's Lab accelerator.[101] In return for their space and services, incubators either charge entrepreneurs rent or fees, or sometimes take equity or convertible notes. Most incubators do not make any investments at all. If they do, they are small, for example, investing less than $10K per company, with overall investments below $1M.

13.6.2 Technology Transfer Funds

Universities are an important source of entrepreneurial ideas. In the last few decades, universities around the world have established processes for technology commercialization.[102] This begins with academic research that leads to new scientific discoveries. The ensuing commercialization leverages these scientific discoveries to create entrepreneurial ventures. The early stages of this commercialization process require applied research that looks into what markets a technology might be applied to. Another priority at this stage is to protect the intellectual property (IP) through patents, copyrights, or other measures. For research-based innovations the IP belongs to the university.

To administer the IP and promote commercialization, many universities have a technology transfer office.[103] This office decides either to license the IP to an established company or to create a new company on the basis of the IP. The latter case is typically labeled as a "university spin-off." A delicate question is who owns the equity of these spin-offs.[104] Different universities have different approaches to dividing the equity between the university, the inventors (i.e., the professors and/or students), and the spin-off's management team.

Technology transfer funds specifically focus on the funding problems of university spin-offs. Universities receive a lot of the research funding that is provided through grants from government and private foundations. Some of these grants are for academic research, others for early commercialization efforts. These grants involve no dilution of equity. However, most spin-offs need more funding than what is available through grants. This is where technology transfer funds come in. The management of such funds may be provided by an internal team or may be delegated to external venture managers who work closely with the university technology transfer office. Investments in university spin-offs are usually structured either as convertible notes or common equity. In addition, there can be licensing agreements that specify the terms under which the spin-offs receive the required IP. Beyond financial returns, technology transfer funds aim at disseminating university inventions and positively impacting the local economy.

13.6.3 Social Impact Venture Investors

Social impact investing is a large and growing segment of the financial sector. As such, it encompasses a vast array of investments, ranging from stock market investments, social bond issues, and infrastructure investments, all the way to start-up financing. For our purposes, we will only focus on the financing of entrepreneurial ventures. We collectively call their investors "social impact venture investors," which we conveniently abbreviate as SIVIs. They are generally associated with charitable foundations or other socially minded organizations.

There are a large variety of SIVIs, with no clear definition. Some people consider SIVI a distinct type of investor, and others classify them as one of the usual types of investor (such as VC or corporate) but with a different motivation. Among the SIVIs, some consider social impact as their prime or even sole objective, but others include social impact into a mix of objectives. In the absence of a precise definition, we pragmatically consider SIVIs as those start-up investors who pursue some kind of social objective in an explicitly and meaningful way.[105]

SIVIs invest in companies across a broad spectrum of commercial to social ventures. Traditionally, social and commercial entrepreneurs were considered to be two distinct and diametrically opposed types, the former seeking to create a better world and the latter seeking to maximize financial returns. However, there is a growing consensus that they can also be viewed as forming a spectrum, where most entrepreneurial ventures fall somewhere in between the two polar extremes. Indeed, most entrepreneurs have dual objectives of making money and having some impact. Naturally, these objectives can matter to different degrees for different entrepreneurs, and there are many subtle nuances to this trade-off. The point, however, is that many socially minded entrepreneurs have come to appreciate the methods and discipline of commercial entrepreneurs. At the same time, many commercially minded entrepreneurs also espouse pursuing social goals to some extent.

An important debate is how financial and social investment objectives interact. Some argue that there is a fundamental trade-off: higher social impact comes at a cost of lower financial returns. This logic is typically based on a trade-off between profit and costs. For example, if a company provides better health services to its workers, then it increases its costs and reduces its profit. Others, however, reject this trade-off perspective. They emphasize how social objectives can enhance financial returns. This logic is usually based on an efficiency argument. For example, if a company provides better health services to its workers, then it may have healthier and better motivated employees. This improves productivity by more than the costs of providing health care. Needless to say, these arguments often take on political and ideological overtones.

An important difference between purely financially motivated investors and SIVIs lies in the metrics they use for evaluating company performance. Financial investors use standard financial reporting metrics (see Chapter 3) for tracking the progress of their investments. SIVIs track an additional set of impact measures. They vary depending on the activity but may include the number of people affected by the program/product, as well as indicators of how their lives improve, such as better health outcomes, job creation, and crime reduction. Overall, SIVIs are a fairly recent addition to the entrepreneurial funding landscape. One can expect their role to further evolve over time.

13.7 Comparing Early-Stage Investors

To conclude this chapter, we provide a comparison of the investor types that we examined in this chapter. To be comprehensive, we further include banks (Chapter 10), venture capitalists (Chapter 12), and two types of government funding: government funding programs (Section 14.3.2) and government grants and tax credits (Section 14.3.3).

The following four tables summarize these investors' characteristics using the FUEL framework that we introduced in Chapter 1. Each table corresponds to one of the four dimensions of the FUEL framework. Each row represents an investor type, each column a specific aspect of investor activities. While our focus so far has been on a systematic explanation of each investor type row by row, we now turn to comparisons along the columns. This approach highlights key differences across investor types. Each cell in these tables contains a highly simplified summary of our previous discussion.

Table 13.3 looks at investors' fundamental structure. The first column focuses on the organizational structure of the investment entity, and the second on the financial resources that investors can provide to start-up companies.

We notice at least three distinct types of organizational structures. First, there are informal investors—private individuals investing on their own behalf. This category consists of founders, family and friends, angel investors, and angel groups. By and large, their financial resources are limited ("shallow pockets"). Second, there are professional investors which invest on behalf of others, be it

Table 13.3 Investors' Fundamental Structure.

Investor type	Organizational structure	Financial resources
Venture capital	Limited partnership model, funds invested on behalf of institutional investors	"Deep pockets" allow funding over multiple rounds
Founders, family, and friends	Private individuals connected to founders	Own money, typically limited funding ("shallow pockets")
Angel investors	Private individuals not connected to founders	Wide range, but typically limited funding ("shallow pocket")
Angel groups	Angels organized in networks or managing funds with other investors' money	Pooling of resources allows larger deals, but often unable to continue funding in later rounds
Corporate investors	Funded and managed internally, through a division or a dedicated corporate venture capital arm	Corporate financing allows funding over multiple rounds ("deep pockets")
Crowdfunding	Online platforms matching entrepreneurs to individual investors (the crowd)	Enough for early-stage funding, but no follow-on funding ("shallow pockets")
Initial Coin Offerings (ICOs)	Anonymous online investors using cryptocurrencies	Individual and institutional investors, wide range of resources
Accelerators and incubators	Independent, corporate, or government-led programs and facilities	Minimal financing ("shallow pockets")
Technology Transfer Funds (TTFs)	Funds provided by universities, science parks, or government agencies	Limited funding ("shallow pockets")
Social Impact Venture Investors (SIVIs)	Various fund structures, backed by individuals, foundations, government agencies, or NGOs	Mostly limited funding, follow-on funding rare ("shallow pockets")
Banks	Financial intermediaries	Most banks have limited to no interest in start-ups, focus on scale-ups ("deep pockets")
Government funding programs	Government-owned programs working with or through private investors	May match private funding. Programs can be large but individual investments often small ("shallow pockets")
Government grants and tax credits	Central or local government agencies	Programs can be large, but with limits on individual grants/credit

their limited partners or their shareholders. This category includes VC, corporate investors, TTFs, SIVIs, banks, or governments. They tend to have larger amounts of funding available, though they may face limits to how much they can invest in a single venture. Some of them are able to support companies across multiple rounds. Finally, there are intermediaries that focus on linking investors to start-ups. This category includes crowdfunding, ICOs, and accelerators and incubators. The amount of financial resources they can intermediate is typically smaller and structured as a single round transaction. Their fundamental structure limits what different types of investors can do and therefore what entrepreneurs can expect from them.

Table 13.4 examines investors' underlying motivation. The first column focuses on their investment objectives, and the second on their level of risk tolerance and patience.

Almost all investors have financial returns as their main motivation. The exceptions are family and friends, SIVIs, and government. There are two important messages here. First, financial returns matter for understanding the behavior of almost all investor types. Second, what distinguishes alternative early-stage investor types is not their focus on financial returns, but the other objectives that they may also have. These other objectives can be very diverse. Angel investors care about their personal passion, corporate investors about strategic returns, SIVIs about social impact, TTFs about innovation impact, and governments about job creation and local ecosystem development.

Table 13.4 Investors' Underlying Motivation.

Investor type	Objectives	Risk tolerance and patience
Venture capital	Financial returns	High risk tolerance, investment horizon up to 10 years
Founders, family, and friends	"Love" money	Blind to risk and very patient
Angel investors	Financial returns and personal passion	High risk tolerance and often considerable patience
Angel groups	Mainly financial returns, also personal passion	High risk tolerance and often considerable patience
Corporate investors	Strategic and financial returns	High risk tolerance, patience depends on (changing) strategic interests
Crowdfunding	Financial returns, sometimes personal passion	High risk tolerance, varying time horizons
Initial Coin Offerings (ICOs)	Financial returns	High risk tolerance, does not require patient investors because token can be resold
Accelerators and incubators	Own profits, stimulate local ecosystem, generate financial returns	High risk tolerance. Accelerators have tight deadlines. Incubators are more patient
Technology Transfer Funds (TTFs)	Commercialization of research, demonstrate innovation, impact, and financial returns	High risk tolerance with varying time horizon
Social Impact Venture Investors (SIVIs)	Social impact, sufficient financial returns to sustain organization	High risk tolerance and considerable patience
Banks	Financial returns	Low risk tolerance, limited patience due to liquidity concerns
Government funding programs	Development of local and national ecosystems, innovation, job creation, financial returns	Mostly high risk tolerance and high patience
Government grants and tax credits	Development of local and national ecosystems, support of innovation	Varying risk tolerance, very patient funding since there are no return expectations

Most venture investors may be described as having high risk tolerance and patience; this is essentially a prerequisite for investing in start-ups. However, there are some differences, too. Banks, for example, have much lower risk tolerance than other venture investors (Section 10.3). Or ICO investors do not require much patience, as they can quickly flip their investments by reselling their tokens on online exchanges.

In Table 13.5, the first column considers the expertise that different investors bring to the table, and the second the networks they have access to.

Table 13.5 Investors' Expertise and Networks.

Investor type	Expertise	Networks
Venture capital	Substantial financial, industry, and entrepreneurial expertise	Strong financial and industry networks
Founders, family, and friends	Limited, rarely strong	Highly overlapping with founder networks
Angel investors	Limited, occasionally strong	Networks based on prior professional experience, often also know other angels and VCs
Angel groups	Pooling of individuals' expertise, lead investor contributes most	Wide network based on many individuals' networks
Corporate investors	Technical validation, industry expertise, and strategic advice	Access to internal and external corporate networks
Crowdfunding	"Wisdom of the crowd"	No networking benefits for entrepreneurs, only campaign marketing effects
Initial Coin Offerings (ICOs)	Anonymous relationship makes investor expertise irrelevant	No networks to benefit company development; however, ventures try to create user networks
Accelerators and incubators	Often specialize in specific industries, thus attracting relevant expertise	Provide access to networks of experienced entrepreneurs, mentors and investors. Quality varies across organizations
Technology Transfer Funds (TTFs)	Expertise mostly in science and technology, occasional industry specialization	Access to science and technology networks, and to local ecosystems
Social Impact Venture Investors (SIVIs)	Understand social issues and program management, sometimes have relevant expertise	Mostly access to donor and support networks
Banks	Expertise in lending and loan monitoring, limited understanding of new technologies and industries	Generic business networks, mostly local, some investment banks have large global networks
Government funding programs	Reliance on private-sector investors to implement government initiatives	May have access to networks of local and foreign investors
Government grants and tax credits	Grants may be based on peer reviews, tax credits purely based on eligibility criteria	None

This table reveals numerous ways in which investors can support the entrepreneurs they finance. There are vast differences in the relevant expertise and networks of different investor types, ranging from an almost complete absence of expertise and networks with government and also most family and friends to highly specialized investors, such as VCs, corporate investors, and some angel investors. In between is a diverse landscape of expertise and networks. Crowdfunding may not involve expert investors but may generate a wisdom of the crowd; accelerators may not have the expertise in house but can connect entrepreneurs to relevant mentors and investors; SIVIs may not be the best at building businesses but they can strongly support the social cause of a venture.

Table 13.6 finally looks at investors' logic and style. The first column examines the deal sourcing process, that is, the way that entrepreneurs and investors are matched to each other. The second column looks at the financial securities used, and the third at the corporate governance regime.

Table 13.6 Investors' Logic and Style.

Investor type	Deal generation	Investment securities	Corporate governance
Venture capital	Active deal sourcing	Preferred equity, strong control rights	Frequent contact and active governance
Founders, family, and friends	Personal networks	Donations, debt, convertible notes, common equity	Informal and supportive
Angel investors	Informal networks, often difficult to find for entrepreneurs	Convertible notes, common equity	Active involvement but largely passive governance
Angel groups	Pitch events	Convertible notes, common equity, or preferred equity	Active involvement with light governance control, delegated to lead investor
Corporate investors	Highly visible, active in early-stage ecosystems	Common or preferred equity, but also licensing and alliances	Often passive, aimed at providing technical contributions and generating strategic benefits
Crowdfunding	Entrepreneurs apply for listing; platforms do some screening	Donations, rewards, debt, or common equity	Minimal interaction, except for entrepreneurs providing required updates
Initial Coin Offerings (ICOs)	ICOs are launched by companies and marketed through online platforms	Tokens	Governance through smart contracts
Accelerators and incubators	Application-based selection, programs actively market themselves	Common equity or rental payments	Provide space, support, and venture acceleration, passive governance

Table 13.6 *Continued*

Investor type	Deal generation	Investment securities	Corporate governance
Technology Transfer Funds (TTFs)	Deals come from within the institution	Grants, IP support, convertible notes, common equity	Focus on helping scientists structure commercial ventures, and structure IP
Social Impact Venture Investors (SIVIs)	Often based on applications, some funds syndicate with commercial investors	Grants, debt, convertible notes, and common equity	Sometimes managerial services and training
Banks	Sourcing from traditional relationships, use standard loan approvals	Lending based on personal guarantees and company collateral, sometimes take warrants or equity	Traditional lending approach, based on loan repayments and covenants
Government funding programs	Deal sourced by private co-investors, otherwise by government fund managers	Mostly rule-based implementation of the program, resulting in (often subsidized) funding through grants, loans, or common equity	Governance mostly delegated to private investors; some programs provide support services
Government grants and tax credits	Application-based or tax code rules	Non-dilutive financing	Rule-based compliance controls

This table identifies a wide variety of investment logics and styles. Some investor types have highly formalized matching processes where entrepreneurs apply and get selected on the basis of various eligibility criteria. Such are angel groups, crowdfunding platforms, accelerators and incubators, and government grants, Other investor types, most notably VCs and corporate investors, work with much more customized processes. However, this does not mean that they are less rigorous than the more formal processes. Indeed, VC is often considered one of the most difficult sources of funding to obtain.

The majority of investors seek equity investment, although there are variations. Many early-stage investors use convertible notes (or SAFEs), and a few investors also accept debt. Moreover, the use of preferred equity also differs by investor types, with VC typically being the most insistent on obtaining investment preferences. Finally, there is a wide variety of governance styles. On the more passive end of the spectrum one would find the family and friends, crowdfunding, ICOs, accelerators, TTFs, and government grants and tax credits. On the more active end of the spectrum are professional investors: VCs, and corporate investors.

Finally, let us briefly comment on the relationship between the analysis in this section and the MATCH tool developed in Section 7.3.3 and available on the book's website (www.entrepreneurialfinance.net). Tables 13.3–13.6 provide a detailed comparison of the properties of different early-stage investor types. They help us to understand how different investors are structured, have different motives, expertise, and networks, and which different investment behaviors result from that. This information provides an overview of what types of investors are suitable in different situations. Once an appropriate investor type has been identified, the MATCH tool helps entrepreneurs to evaluate specific investors, both within and across investor types. Tables 13.3–13.6 thus provide a broader overview of the financing landscape, whereas the MATCH tool provides a more detailed evaluation of specific investor–company matches.

Summary

This chapter examines a variety of early-stage investors, including family and friends, individual angels and angel groups, corporate investors, crowdfunding, Initial Coin Offerings, accelerators and incubators, technology transfer funds, and social impact venture investors. We examine them through the FUEL framework (Chapter 1). Each investor type has a different fundamental structure and a different underlying investment motivation. In addition to generating financial returns, each investor type places different emphasis on additional investment aspects, such as strategic benefits, innovativeness, or social impact. Different investors also have different expertise and networks, and adopt different investment logics when dealing with entrepreneurs. We examine some of the recent Fintech developments, where investors leverage modern online approaches. Crowdfunding platforms offer novel ways of matching entrepreneurs with investors. Initial Coin Offerings provide an entirely new and controversial model of investing in tokens instead of equity. Overall, the chapter provides an overview of the rich and changing landscape of funding options available to entrepreneurs. We also explain what types of entrepreneurs fit with what types of investors.

Review Questions

1. Why do founders often invest in their own venture?
2. What are the investment motives of family and friends? How can they help?
3. Why do angel investors coordinate through networks or groups?
4. How do angel funds differ from VC funds?
5. Why do corporations fund start-ups? How should an entrepreneur view them?
6. What alternative approaches can corporate investors use for cooperating with start-ups?
7. What alternative crowdfunding options are available to entrepreneurs? Which options are most suitable for which entrepreneurs?
8. How does an ICO differ from an IPO?
9. How do accelerators, incubators, and technology transfer funds prepare companies for fundraising?

10. How do social impact venture investors differ from purely financially moti-
    vated venture investors?

Notes

1. Kotha and George (2012) and Robb and Robinson (2014).
2. Corradin and Popov (2015) and Schmalz, Sraer, and Thesmar (2017).
3. Frid, Wyman, and Gartner (2015).
4. Chapter 22 in Livingston (2009).
5. Grichnik et al. (2014).
6. Bort (2016) and https://www.prnewswire.com/news-releases/morningstar-to-acquire-pitchbook-data-agreement-will-combine-leading-providers-of-public-and-private-company-research-300345025.html.
7. Lee and Persson (2016).
8. Wu, Si, and Wu (2016).
9. Lerner et al. (2018).
10. Engineer, Schure, and Vo (2019).
11. Maxwell, Jeffrey, and Lévesque (2011).
12. Carpentier and Suret (2015).
13. Kerr, Lerner, and Schoar (2014).
14. Dutta and Folta (2016).
15. Hellmann and Thiele (2015).
16. Ibrahim (2008).
17. CB Insights Global CVC Report 2018, available at: https://www.cbinsights.com/research/report/corporate-venture-capital-trends-2018, accessed April 15, 2019.
18. https://www.nobelprize.org/prizes/economic-sciences/1974/press-release.
19. https://www.nobelprize.org/prizes/economic-sciences/1991/press-release.
20. https://www.nobelprize.org/prizes/economic-sciences/2009/press-release.
21. Coase (1937).
22. Hayek (1944, 1945).
23. Williamson (1975).
24. Holmström and Roberts (1998), and Williamson (2002).
25. The press release is available on https://www.businesswire.com/news/home/20190213005927/en, accessed April 15, 2019.
26. Arora and Gambardella (1990).
27. Maula, Keil, and Zahra (2012).
28. Hellmann (2002).
29. de Bettignies and Chemla (2007) and Fulghieri and Sevilir (2009).
30. Chemmanur, Loutskina, and Tian (2014) and Park and Steensma (2012).
31. Bielli et al. (2017).
32. Teece (1986) applies the notion of resource complementarity to strategic alliances.
33. Blair and Lafontaine (2005).
34. Ireland and Webb (2007) and Mason, Arrington, and Mawson (2019).
35. Chesbrough (2002b) and http://www.intelcapital.com.
36. Dushnitsky and Shapira (2010).
37. Lichtenthaler and Ernst (2006).
38. Dushnitsky and Shapira (2010).

39. Other studies found lower success rates. Gompers and Lerner (1998), for example, find an exit rate of 34%.
40. Zahra (1993), Desouza (2017), and Parker (2011).
41. Chesbrough (2002a).
42. Smith and Alexander (1988).
43. Åstebro and Serrano (2015) and Dushnitsky and Lenox (2005).
44. Gans and Stern (2003).
45. Dushnitsky and Shaver (2009).
46. Colombo and Shafi (2000). Conti, Thursby, and Thursby (2013) provide a rationalization and additional evidence for Israel.
47. Katila, Rosenberger, and Eisenhardt (2008).
48. Gompers and Lerner (1998) and Hellmann (2002).
49. Benson and Ziedonis (2010).
50. Dushnitsky and Fitza (2018).
51. Roth and Sotomayor (1992) and Rysman (2009).
52. Belleflamme, Lambert, and Shwienbacher (2014).
53. Rodríguez Fernández (2019) and Young and Scheinberg (2017).
54. Ting (2017).
55. Freedman and Jin (2017) and Wales (2017).
56. Wei and Lin (2016).
57. Vulkan, Åstebro, and Fernandez Sierra (2016).
58. Armour and Enriques (2018) examine the regulatory issues surrounding equity crowdfunding.
59. Takahashi (2018), https://www.kickstarter.com/help/stats?ref=global-footer, https://www.lendingclub.com/info/demand-and-credit-profile.action, https://www.fundingcircle.com/uk/statistics/, https://angel.co/done-deals, and https://www.seedrs.com/learn/blog/beauhurst-confirms-seedrs-as-the-uks-top-funder. All accessed on April 15, 2019.
60. Takahashi (2018).
61. https://www.ourcrowd.com is an equity platform that has stringent selection criteria on both sides.
62. Marom, Robb, and Sade (2016).
63. Agrawal, Catalini, and Goldfarb (2015).
64. Catalini and Hui (2018).
65. Rochet and Tirole (2003, 2006).
66. https://www.kickstarter.com/help/stats.
67. https://www.kickstarter.com/help/faq/creator+questions?ref=faq_livesearch#faq_62961, accessed on April 15, 2019.
68. Mollick (2014).
69. Zhang and Liu (2012).
70. Kuppuswamy and Bayus (2017).
71. Åstebro et al. (2017).
72. Matthews (2018).
73. Mollick (2015).
74. https://www.lendingclub.com/info/demand-and-credit-profile.action, and https://www.fundingcircle.com/uk/statistics, accessed on April 15, 2019.
75. https://www.lendingclub.com/info/demand-and-credit-profile.action. The calculations are based on 736,589 loans in the period 2007 to 2016.
76. Wroldsen (2017).
77. https://angel.co/economics-syndicates, accessed April 15, 2019.

78. For an introduction to the blockchain technology see, among others: Abadi and Brunnermeier (2018), Andolfatto (2018), Catalini (2017), Catalini and Gans (2017), Coindesk (https://www.coindesk.com/information/what-is-blockchain-technology), Narayanan et al. (2016), and Witte (2016).

79. Nakamoto (2009).

80. For an introduction to cryptocurrencies, see Berentsen and Schär (2018), Böhme et al. (2015), Lee and Chuen (2015), and Velde (2013).

81. https://coinmarketcap.com.

82. For an introduction to ICOs see Dowlat (2018a), Hao (2018), and Lewis (2017).

83. Coinschedule (https://www.coinschedule.com). Another data aggregator, Coindesk, reports similar but slightly smaller figures: 343 ICOs in 2017 raising about $5.5B, and 460 ICOs in 2018 raising about $14.3B, https://www.coindesk.com.

84. Lyandres, Palazzo, and Rabetti (2019).

85. Howell, Niessner, and Yermack (2018) and Fisch (2019).

86. Zetzsche et al. (2019).

87. Russel (2017).

88. Kharif (2017).

89. Russell and Butcher (2018).

90. Roberts (2018).

91. Detrixhe (2018).

92. Dowlat (2018b) estimates that 80% of ICOs are in some way scams, though they account for less than 10% of the raised amounts. Jenkinson (2018) reports several specific examples.

93. Viola (2018).

94. In the U.S., the SEC issued provisional rules in September 2017: https://www.sec.gov/news/press-release/2017-176. See also SEC chair Jay Clayton's testimony to Congress in February 2018, available at: https://www.sec.gov/news/testimony/testimony-virtual-currencies-oversight-role-us-securities-and-exchange-commission, accessed April 15, 2019. The SEC maintains a page on ICO regulations: https://www.sec.gov/ICO.

95. Robinson (2019) and Rohr and Wright (2018).

96. https://www.fca.org.uk/firms/global-financial-innovation-network.

97. Falkon (2017), https://www.sec.gov/litigation/investreport/34-81207.pdf, and Madeira (2019).

98. Wright and Drori (2018).

99. Fehder and Hochberg (2018).

100. Shankar and Shepherd (2019).

101. https://www.wework.com/labs and Ha (2019).

102. Colyvas et al. (2002).

103. Markman et al.(2005).

104. Lockett and Wright (2005).

105. Azevedo (2018).

14

Ecosystems

Learning Goals

In this chapter students will learn:

1. The structure and geography of entrepreneurial ecosystems.
2. How entrepreneurs, investors, and supporting parties interact within an ecosystem.
3. What policies governments use to foster the entrepreneurial environment.
4. The importance of capital and talent mobility across ecosystems.

This chapter examines entrepreneurial ecosystems. Silicon Valley is the most famous example of an entrepreneurial ecosystem, but there are other successful ecosystems across the world. To explain the structure of ecosystems, we emphasize the interactions between entrepreneurs, investors, and supporting parties. We examine the role of governments, why and when they might intervene, and what the challenges are. We specifically look at government funding of entrepreneurial ventures, tax credits for investors and companies, regulation of capital markets, and design of the institutional infrastructure of the economy. The chapter ends with a discussion of how different ecosystems across the globe depend on the cross-border movement of capital and talent.

14.1 Entrepreneurial Ecosystems

In this final chapter we look at entrepreneurial finance from an ecosystem perspective. This means that, instead of looking at specific actions or actors of the financing process, we look at the system as a whole. We examine how entrepreneurs and investors interact with each other and how together they form an environment that can either help or hinder the creation and growth of entrepreneurial ventures.

There are vast differences in how successful different locations across the globe have been in fostering entrepreneurship. The aim of this chapter is thus to understand how entrepreneurial ecosystems are structured, why some become more successful than others, and what can be done to foster their development.[1]

14.1.1 Ecosystem Structure

There is no single definition of what an entrepreneurial ecosystem is, and it is often difficult to draw precise boundaries, both conceptually and geographically. Typically, an ecosystem is defined as a cluster of entrepreneurial activities by high-growth-oriented ventures (Section 1.1) supported by investors and specialized service providers. Ecosystems are defined at the regional level, often centering on a major city.[2] Entrepreneurial ecosystems further focus on a subset of industries (e.g., cybersecurity, artificial intelligence, biotech, new materials).

In order to analyze entrepreneurial ecosystems, we first identify the three key parties and then examine their interactions. The three parties are entrepreneurial talent, investors, and relevant third parties such as governments (Section 14.3), universities, and service providers (lawyers, accountants, consultants, etc.).

The first party is a talent pool that provides the human capital necessary to build new ventures. The talent pool includes the entrepreneurs themselves, but also employees and managers in established companies and entrepreneurial ventures. These people provide entrepreneurs with the technical and managerial talent necessary for building and growing companies. The talent pool also includes former and aspiring entrepreneurs.

The second party is the investors, who are of central interest to our analysis (Chapters 12 and 13). Investors are attracted by locations with a high concentration of talented individuals who pursue entrepreneurial ambitions. Most investors prefer to invest locally, although many also participate in investment syndicates in locations farther away. A deep pool of diverse investors is useful for giving start-ups access to capital and expertise at all stages of development. It also results in competition and thus better deals for the entrepreneurs.

The third parties of an entrepreneurial ecosystem consist of the many supporters whose activities and services matter for entrepreneurs and investors. This heterogeneous group of actors includes universities, research facilities, established corporations, lawyers, accountants, recruiters, consultants, and various layers of government. These actors support entrepreneurial activities in different ways. Universities provide highly educated workers, ideas and scientific advances, and expert consulting on technical matters. Some academics also become entrepreneurs.[3] Public and private research labs play a similar role, as do science parks.[4] Large established companies, some of which initially were start-ups, can be customers or suppliers. They can help new ventures figure out how to structure and market their products and services. Employees at incumbents can sometimes be lured into joining a start-up, possibly even as founders. Lawyers, accountants, and technical consultants provide their specialized services. Finally, the government has an important role in creating conditions suitable for entrepreneurial activity to flourish (Section 14.3).

Before we delve into analysis of the ecosystems, we introduce some economic concepts useful for understanding them. Once again, this is a field with many Nobel minds, as discussed in Box 14.1.

Box 14.1 Nobel Insights into General Equilibrium and Ecosystem Agglomeration

The 1972 Nobel Prize for Economics was awarded to John R. Hicks and Kenneth J. Arrow "for their pioneering contributions to general economic equilibrium theory and welfare theory."[5] The 2008 Prize was awarded to Paul Krugman, "for his analysis of trade patterns and location of economic activity."[6] The 2009 Prize went to Elinor Ostrom "for her analysis of economic governance, especially the commons."[7]

"Ecosystem" is a relatively new addition to the business vocabulary, describing the interplay among many connected economic agents. Economists have been studying ecosystems for a long time under the name of general equilibrium, analyzing how prices and quantities interact with each other across multiple markets: product markets, labor markets, financial markets, and others. General equilibrium effects allow policymakers to perform social welfare analysis, examining how economic policies affect the entire economic system, through direct and indirect effects.[8]

Arrow is considered the father of several branches of economics, including general equilibrium theory, welfare theory, social choice theory, and information economics. His first welfare theorem states that any competitive equilibrium is Pareto-efficient, meaning that it is impossible to make any agent better off without making at least one other agent worse off. The theorem is based on a stylized model of a competitive economy, one that is unencumbered by market imperfections. In such a competitive economy, there is neither asymmetric information nor market power, prices are competitive, and there are no other frictions. Arrow's result suggests that in such an economy there are no easy win–win moves for policymakers. Subsequent work by others (including Joseph Stiglitz, whose work we discuss in Box 10.2), showed that this welfare theorem breaks down whenever there are market imperfections. Still, Arrow's first welfare theorem therefore sets a powerful benchmark: any policy move needs first to be justified in terms of some market imperfection.

Hicks is another pioneer of general equilibrium analysis because of his work on substitution effects between labor and capital. If there is a shortage in the labor supply, we would expect real wages to rise to restore equilibrium with labor demand. Hicks argues that things don't stop there. Faced with higher labor costs, firms will substitute capital for labor by investing in new technologies that require less labor. Over time, the demand for labor will therefore shrink, and the cost of labor (i.e., wages) fall. At the same time, the cost of capital will increase to reflect the fact that it is in higher demand. Such substitution between capital and labor helps us understand ecosystem dynamics. For example, policymakers worry that artificial intelligence (AI) will reduce the demand for skilled labor. They ask themselves what kind of substitution effects this will engender, and how it will affect wages, interest rates, and the overall economy. A general equilibrium perspective can help identify which people are likely to be affected, and how.

Krugman is credited with advancing our understanding of economic geography.[9] One of the central questions he addressed concerns agglomeration: why are some economic activities geographically clustered? Why did the industrial revolution cluster in the north of England, the automobile industry around Detroit, and the Indian IT industry around Bangalore? Using a general equilibrium approach, Krugman breaks away from the assumption of no economies of scale in production technology. Instead he points to the frequent existence of lumpy fixed cost investments, such as the location decision of a company's new plant. Such investments cause agglomeration effects that have large ramifications for local labor markets and supply chains. His analysis shows how small regional advantages in costs or quality can help one economic region to attract investments, grow, and thus create larger advantages over time. The benefit of locating an automotive company in Detroit over Cleveland may have been small at the beginning of the 1910s but grew large by the 1950s.[10] Similarly, the difference between Bangalore and other Indian cities was small at the beginning of the 1980s but became substantial three decades later.[11]

Krugman identifies several drivers of agglomeration that square well with entrepreneurial ecosystems.[12] First, the above argument about fixed investments shows why specialized suppliers want to locate next to their customers. Proximity to specialized suppliers encourages experimentation and improves production process. This was the case with the automotive sector around Detroit, where co-location of suppliers also reduced transportation costs. In modern entrepreneurial ecosystems, it is investors and service providers who need to be nearby. Networking, informal knowledge gathering, and in-person communication are the main benefits of proximity to entrepreneurs. Second, there are knowledge spillovers, where new ideas circulate informally across personal contacts within local areas. In all ecosystems, certain bars and cafés are known to be hotbeds of new ideas (alongside plenty of gossip, of course). Third, labor market pools matter. Talented individuals locate where their skills are in demand. Once settled, they typically prefer to move across employers within the region, instead of uprooting to another region. In Silicon Valley, it is famously possible to change employer without changing your parking spot. As a consequence, entrepreneurs locate in places where they can find the required talent.

Krugman (and the ensuing research he inspired) shows that these agglomeration forces are counterbalanced by other general equilibrium forces, most notably substitution effects of the type Hicks had studied for capital and labor. As labor and housing costs rise in a successful ecosystem, numerous substitution effects kick in, such as companies relocating labor-intensive activities to outlying areas (e.g., Intel moving production to Portland, Oregon, in the 1990s), or entrepreneurs developing less labor-intensive business models (e.g., replacing people with robots). The general equilibrium models of Arrow, Hicks, and Krugman thus provide the foundations for understanding how geographic clusters hold the balance between agglomeration forces and substitution effects.

Ostrom approaches ecosystem interactions from an economic sociology perspective. Her work looks at how the interactions between economic agents are affected by cultural and social norms. Her analysis recognizes that in addition to purely economic trade-offs, there are behavioral biases that can favor or hinder cooperation within ecosystems. One of the central themes of her analysis is the role of communication for building trust.[13] This accords well with our discussion in Section 7.6.1 about the importance of communication and trust for enabling investments in start-ups.[14] Ostrom's work implies that trust is a glue that holds entrepreneurial ecosystems together.

She then proposed another concept useful in our context: polycentric governance. Studying a large variety of contexts, ranging from police departments in Indianapolis to irrigation systems in Nepal, her work consistently finds that complex economic systems function best when control is distributed across multiple interacting decision makers, rather than centered in a single point of control.[15] Entrepreneurial ecosystems thrive from having multiple decision makers, such as entrepreneurs, large corporations, venture capitalists, universities, or policymakers, which find ways of competing and collaborating at the same time.

Interestingly, Ostrom already introduced the concept of public entrepreneurs in her doctoral dissertation in 1965. She noted that solving important public problems requires an entrepreneurial approach, which can be useful to "secure appropriate forms of community action in providing common goods and services."[16]

14.1.2 Overview of Leading Ecosystems

There are vast disparities in how different locations succeed in attracting entrepreneurs and investors: San Francisco is considered hot, Saskatoon not. According to the Start-Up Genome project, the top 10 regions in 2017 were Silicon Valley, New York, London, Beijing, Boston, Tel Aviv, Berlin, Shanghai, Los Angeles, and Seattle.[17] This ranking is based on several indicators that measure different aspects of the ecosystem. Singapore, for example, ranked 12th overall, ranked 16th in terms of performance and funding, but 1st in terms of talent. Toronto ranked 20th in terms of talent but 5th in terms of market reach. Rankings also change over time. Bangalore was ranked 15th in 2016 but fell to 20th in 2017.

Different ecosystems specialize in different technology sectors. London attracts strong Fintech start-ups, Tel Aviv is strong in cybersecurity, the research triangle in North Carolina in life sciences, and so on. Moreover, some ecosystems are better for early-stage financing than for later-stage financing. Israel, for example, is a strong eco-system for starting companies, but most companies either get acquired early or else scale their operations in the U.S. This is also the case for many parts of Canada and Europe.[18]

How do entrepreneurial ecosystems emerge and grow? A good case to illustrate this is Silicon Valley which became the epicenter of high-tech entrepreneurship only after World War II. Before that, it was a valley of fruits and nuts—not to mention the epicenter of earthquakes. The origins of Silicon Valley's success have been attributed to numerous factors: the U.S. government support for developing the West after World War II, the predominance of immigrants and migrants from the midwestern U.S., the involvement of Stanford University, and a pragmatic nonhierarchical culture.[19] There may even have been a little dose of luck. According to some historians, Silicon Valley owes a lot to the ill health of one man's grandmother[20] In 1956, William Shockley founded Shockley Semiconductor Laboratory not on the East Coast, where he lived, but in Palo Alto, now the heart of Silicon Valley, mainly to be close to his ailing grandmother. His company was the first commercial semiconductor start-up and is mostly remembered for the eight engineers who left the firm to create Fairchild Semiconductors. This move was assisted by Arthur Rock, who became a legendary VC (Section 2.2.3). The founding team included Gordon Moore, who moved on to found Intel, and Eugene Kleiner, who later founded Kleiner, Perkins, Caufield and Byers (KPCB). It remains one of the most successful VC firms of all times, having invested in Amazon.com, Compaq, Genentech, Google, Sun Microsystems, and more recently in Airbnb, Spotify, and Uber. Many companies were spun out of Fairchild, and even more were created out of these spin-offs, creating an impressive family tree of companies that shaped the evolution of Silicon Valley's entrepreneurial ecosystem.

While Silicon Valley is the most famous ecosystem, several other ecosystems have done well in recent years. Box 14.2 looks at a few select cases from around the world.

Box 14.2 Tales from the Venture Archives: Alternative Routes to Building Ecosystems

---

Israel only came together as a nation in 1948. It is a small state of only 8 million people, as large as Vermont or Slovenia. Its population has a tradition of migration and strong links to many countries. Jewish culture played an important role in the creation of a national ecosystem.[21] First, it rewards knowledge and achievement, leading to strong educational institutions and a large number of science graduates. In the 1990s, a wave of highly educated Russian Jew immigrants further increased this number. Second, Jewish culture encourages risk-taking and individual responsibility. Another pillar of the Israeli ecosystem is the large amount of public R&D, often for military purposes. While these factors created conditions favorable to creating innovative high-tech companies, the small size of the domestic economy initially hindered the development of specialized financial intermediaries. To overcome this problem, the government created Yozma in 1993.[22] Yozma was a funds-of-funds (Section 14.3.2) that invested $80M in 10 newly created private VC funds and another $20M directly into companies. The 10 Israeli VC funds also attracted foreign capital and experienced investors to kick start the Israeli VC industry. Yozma was structured so as to reduce the risk of investing without appropriating any profit, thus providing a strong incentive to foreign VCs. It was a bold government strategy that resulted in a large number of high-quality ventures. By 2000 Israeli companies had attracted over $3B investments. The Israeli ecosystem took nearly two decades to build but has proven to be resilient since.

A different case is Chile, which also relied on attracting resources from abroad, focusing in particular on entrepreneurial talent. Start-up Chile (SUP) was set up in 2010 as a public accelerator that would offer $40K of nondilutive capital to early-stage start-ups that would relocate in Chile for at least six months (the duration of the program).[23] Entrepreneurs have to spend some time mentoring local peers and engaging in local initiatives to show the potential impact of entrepreneurial ventures. SUP has also been working to attract VC for its companies. Several venture investors set up an office in Santiago, attracted also by business-friendly public policies. By 2018, nearly 1,500 start-ups had graduated from SUP, raising over $400M of outside equity funding from private investors and reaching a combined valuation above $1.3B.[24] To bolster its impact, in 2015 SUP started the Scale Initiative, which provides $100K in capital for some start-ups that graduate from the entry program.[25] SUP has managed to create a large community of entrepreneurs, though one issue remains: many return to their home countries. The area around Santiago has been dubbed Chilecon Valley. It is considered strong in Fintech, one of the few successful hubs in Latin America. However, the Chilean ecosystem remains fragile and much smaller than Israel's.

Shenzhen is one of China's most important entrepreneurship hubs.[26] The region developed in the 1980s and 1990s as China's low-cost hardware production area, specializing in low-tech labor-intensive production. With the turn of the century, Shenzhen has gradually become one of China's innovative centers. One important element has been a policy favoring immigration, especially the talented and the entrepreneurial, with about half of the 16 million citizens coming from outside the region. While the region initially lacked strong research universities, both Tsinghua and Beijing universities opened large campuses in Shenzhen in 2000. The government has pursued increasing education levels, and about one-third of the population currently holds a university degree. Public R&D is among the highest in China; combined with private R&D, total R&D reaches about 4% of GDP. The impressive success of four companies has contributed to generating further opportunities for start-ups: BYD (rechargeable batteries), DJI (drones), Huawei (electronics), and Tencent (internet content). All were founded around the turn of the century and quickly achieved great success. The region has also attracted considerable private VC flows.

These examples show that there may be different routes to the rise of an ecosystem, but attracting talent and capital seems to be a common thread across all.

What are the world's leading ecosystems? Beyond Silicon Valley, the U.S. is home to several hotbeds of innovation. New York, traditionally a financial hub, has become the second largest U.S. ecosystem, home to a large number of unicorns (Box 11.2).[27] It covers several industries, with a prominent role for cybersecurity, which is of great interest to the financial industry. Other big cities that host important ecosystems are Boston, with a strong biotech sector; Chicago, which specializes in Fintech, AI, and Big Data; and Los Angeles, home to many innovative media ventures.[28] Smaller cities also manage to attract talent and investors. For instance, Seattle, home to Amazon and Microsoft, is strong in AI and Big Data. Phoenix is home to a thriving EdTech ecosystem that is powered by the pioneering activity of the Arizona State University.[29] In Canada, Toronto and Montreal have become important hubs for AI, attracting foreign talent and capital. In Latin America, the main entrepreneurial hub is its most populous city, São Paulo, which has attracted some of the world's most successful VC firms.[30]

In Europe, some capital cities have developed a strong start-up culture. London, Berlin, and Paris are the three largest. London is Europe's main center for Fintech and Blockchain. Berlin has strong Fintech activity and a Biotech hub propelled by its universities. Paris has a broad range of entrepreneurial activities, particularly in HealthTech. Among smaller cities, Amsterdam has developed an AgriTech hub centered around the country's successful high-tech intensive agriculture, a business worth more than $1.5B. Helsinki has developed a strong gaming and AI focus, which exploits the strong Baltic programmers' community. Switzerland and Malta currently lead in cryptocurrencies and Initial Coin Offerings (Section 13.5).

Asia is growing fast and is creating ecosystems that are often larger than those in Europe or America. In China, Beijing, Shanghai, and Shenzhen are considered the three biggest entrepreneurial hotspots. Beijing is an important hub for AI and Big Data, and Shanghai has strong Fintech expertise, also because of its proximity to financial institutions. Both Beijing and Shanghai benefit from the presence of strong universities. India's main ecosystem remains Bangalore, which has a talented community of entrepreneurs and employees with IT training, recently boasting competence in the Internet-of-Things and in AI. Other important Asian ecosystems are in Singapore, Hong Kong, and Manila.

This overview strongly suggests that it is impossible to trace the development of an ecosystem to any one single factor. Multiple factors interact in complex and sometimes random ways to create entrepreneurial ecosystems. Consequently, there also cannot be a single recipe of success for developing an ecosystem. In order to understand the necessary conditions for a well-functioning ecosystem, we next examine the various ingredients and how they interact.

14.2 How Do Entrepreneurial Ecosystems Work?

We now explain how the three key parties of an entrepreneurial ecosystem interact with each other. Economic theory makes a useful distinction between two types of interactions: transactions and externalities. Transactions concern two or more parties getting together to strike a business deal. The parties voluntarily agree on some transaction structure where they exchange money for goods or services. Externalities, by contrast, are interactions in which the parties do not necessarily transact with each other but affect each other indirectly. Externalities can be either positive or negative. Scientific knowledge is a positive externality (everyone benefits from a better understanding of thermodynamics), and physical congestion is a negative externality (no one likes getting stuck in traffic). To understand ecosystems, we need to go beyond an analysis of business transactions and examine externalities, such as the agglomeration effects discussed in Box 14.1. We now examine three broad categories of externalities, concerning talent pools, investor interactions, and the role of supporting parties.

14.2.1 Interactions Within the Talent Pool

We begin by looking at the core actors in the ecosystem, namely, the entrepreneurial talent pool. The majority of entrepreneurial ventures are composed of founder teams, so finding a good match for a co-founder is an important first step in the entrepreneurial process.[31] Founder teams often require diverse skill sets, combining technical talent with business know-how and industry experience. Ecosystems with a larger number and greater diversity of individuals along dimensions such as education, professional experience, and seniority, but also gender, ethnicity, and personality traits, offer greater chances of building a strong founder team.

One salient dimension is experience. Young, inexperienced founders may bring greater energy and a fresh approach to a venture, but on their own may falter because each problem is a new challenge to them. Older, more experienced founders, mentors, and investors, may fill that gap, thereby creating stronger companies. A case in point is that of Eric Schmidt, a seasoned software executive, who joined Sergey Brin and Larry Page in the early days of Google.[32] More generally, there is a dynamic cycle where younger generations of entrepreneurs benefit from the presence of older generations who have "seen it all before." Ecosystems improve their resilience over time due to the greater cumulative experience. By the same token, nascent ecosystems face greater challenges due to a shortage of experienced founders, mentors, and investors. Talent pools can improve their depth and their diversity when they are open to immigration from different regions or countries.[33]

The benefits of a large and diverse talent pool extend beyond founders to managers and employees of start-up companies. In Silicon Valley or New York, it is relatively easy to find a CEO who has successfully grown a start-up into a larger company, yet such talent is rare in many other places. The same holds for many functional roles: in Boston you can find a deep pool of specialized managers and engineers (e.g., marketing, software, hardware). In Europe, London, Paris, Madrid, and Berlin are good locations for finding highly skilled software developers.[34] Outside of these hotspots, however, it is much more difficult to hire experienced software engineers.

There is also the question of how easy it is for start-ups to actually hire talent. This depends on how flexible the job market is. Legal rules concerning job mobility matter. In some states and countries, there are noncompete clauses that prohibit an employee from working at another company (Section 6.3.1). Since most employees want to exercise their industry expertise, and stay in their current location, such noncompetes can pose a formidable barrier to changing jobs. Different jurisdictions have different rules about the enforcement of such noncompete clauses. For instance, the State of California does not enforce the vast majority of employee noncompete agreements. It has been argued that this lies at the origins of the high job mobility in Silicon Valley.[35] There are also cultural norms that affect the mobility of employees. Japan, for example, has a tradition of lifetime employment, so changing one's employer is inherently a risky proposal. Box 14.3 looks at the consequences of noncompete clauses.

Box 14.3 Do Noncompete Clauses Matter?

Are noncompete clauses a legal detail or a more serious impediment for entrepreneurial ecosystems?[36] A study of a legislative change in Michigan by Marx, Strumsky, and Fleming finds that noncompetes reduce worker mobility. The effect is concentrated among inventors with firm-specific skills and among those with high technological specialization.[37] A second study of U.S. technical professionals by Marx shows that about a quarter of technology workers who sign a noncompetes experience career difficulty in case they leave their company.[38] These career detours are motivated by the need to avoid a lawsuit and have long-term consequences in terms of career development and earnings growth.

Noncompetes also affect also relationships between companies. Younge, Tong, and Fleming look at the Michigan legislative change and find that enforcing noncompetes is associated with more acquisitions, as acquirers find it easier to retain the target's talented workers.[39] Moreover, the effect is more pronounced in industries that rely more on human capital and that are more competitive, which is where restricting mobility is more important to acquirers.

At an even broader level, noncompetes affect the way talent migrates across regions. An academic study by Samila and Sorenson looks at differences in noncompete enforcement across U.S. metropolitan areas. It finds that in low-enforcement metropolitan areas, an increase in VC investment leads to more start-ups, more innovations as measured by patents, and more employment.[40] Yet these positive effects are weaker in areas with high enforcement of noncompete clauses. Taking a legal research perspective, Aran further points out that stock options reinforce the restrictive nature of noncompete clauses.[41] Talented employees at successful companies have an incentive to remain until a liquidity event makes their shares tradeable. In the U.S., delaying exit is becoming increasingly common (Box 11.2), making it harder for employees to leave the company.

So far, we have examined ecosystem interactions between individuals. The argument is very similar for companies. Start-ups can benefit from the presence of other start-ups for various types of cooperation, such as sharing resources and learning from each other. Yet there are also some important countervailing forces at play. Some start-ups will likely become competitors. They may also compete for scarce resources, such as employees and office space. The rapidly increasing salaries and property prices in Silicon Valley or Shenzhen are clear testimony to that. There is also a concern about how to protect ideas and trade secrets when a company's employees are in regular contact with their professional peers who work for competing start-ups. These countervailing forces may convince some entrepreneurs to locate their start-ups in smaller emerging ecosystems. For example, the rise of Portland, Oregon, not far north from Silicon Valley, may be partly explained by Silicon Valley entrepreneurs seeking a cheaper location and less direct competition.

14.2.2 Interactions with Investors

Our next interests are the interactions between entrepreneurs and investors. Recall our discussion of two-sided markets in Section 13.4. In these markets, the buyers benefit from facing a large and diverse set of sellers, and equivalently, the sellers benefit from facing a large and diverse set of buyers. Many e-commerce models function in this way; examples include products (eBay), recruitment (Monster.com), or accommodation (Airbnb). Such platforms bring buyers and seller together.[42] A similar logic applies to the financing of start-ups. Entrepreneurs want a large and diverse choice of investors, and investors want a large and diverse choice of investable companies. A fundamental insight from the economics of two-sided markets is that only a limited number of platforms can flourish. This is because they are governed by agglomeration forces that make it beneficial for buyers and sellers to look for each other in a common location. In e-commerce, we see a limited number of winner-take-all companies, such as Tinder or Grindr in the dating market. For the financing of start-ups, we can similarly think of local ecosystems as platforms where entrepreneurs and investors look for each other.

Let us take a closer look at how investors benefit from being in a large and diverse ecosystem. Investing in start-ups requires a close fit between the interests and expertise of the investor and what the entrepreneur can offer. This is the basis of the MATCH tool discussed in Section 7.3.3. Having a larger and more diverse offering clearly increases the probability that an investor finds a good match. Moreover, investors think in terms of portfolios and therefore seek portfolio risk diversification. Facing a larger and more diverse set of start-ups increases an investor's ability to diversify across industries, stages, and business models. Being in a larger ecosystem also facilitates benchmarking and comparison across portfolio companies, which is particularly useful for refinancing decisions.

From the perspective of the entrepreneurs, there are also substantial benefits of facing a larger and more diverse set of investors. To begin with, a larger market is likely to be more competitive, which means that entrepreneurs are less beholden to the power of any one investor. Next, the evaluation of entrepreneurial ideas is inherently subjective (Section 2.5). For any pitch by an entrepreneur, different investors come to different conclusions. Most investors find most pitches to be hopeless; only rarely is there a glimmer of hope for a potential match. Moreover, the more unconventional the idea, the lower the probability of finding a believer among the investors. Hence the need for entrepreneurs to get as many opportunities to pitch as possible (Section 7.2). Investor diversity also helps with many other aspects of the investment process. For example, some start-ups need limited capital and rely mainly on angel financing; others need the larger financial resources controlled by VCs. Some entrepreneurs are very control-oriented and therefore mainly seek passive investors, whereas others are more open to receiving guidance from more active investors. Having a variety of investor types within the ecosystem gives entrepreneurs a better chance of finding a suitable match.

In small ecosystems, investors tend to be broad generalists with relatively superficial knowledge about many industries, thus getting interested in a broad range of opportunities (Section 12.5.1). In larger ecosystems, however, investors tend to become more specialized along two main dimensions: industry and stage. Such investors tend to focus on few industries (e.g., medical diagnostics), where they become experts (e.g., they have medical or engineering education and follow diagnostics innovations) and develop specialized networks (e.g., they know all relevant experts and leading companies). Similarly, investors who specialize by stage can better understand the specific challenges of their companies. For example, a late-stage specialist may have considerable expertise and networks for growing a management team, scaling sales and operations, or taking a company global. Entrepreneurs value such industry or stage specialization, as it increases the value of having an active investor (Section 8.3.2).

Interactions among investors themselves are also important. Clearly, there is an element of competition, as different investors pursue the limited pool of investment opportunities. However, there is also a significant amount of cooperation and positive externalities. Investors often syndicate deals to pool their risk and share their expertise and networks (Section 7.4). Even if they do not syndicate a deal, investors often share information about entrepreneurs and market developments, creating positive network effects. For example, investors often refer deals to each other. VCs refer to business angel deals that are too small or early for them, and angels refer to VC deals that are too large for them. In addition to these direct interactions, there can be more indirect effects. As the number of investors in entrepreneurial companies grows, an ecosystem improves its reputation, thus attracting more entrepreneurs. Having more investors also helps with developing and sharing best practices around venture investing.

14.2.3 Interactions with Supporting Parties

Next we consider interactions involving third parties.[43] First, universities can be important anchors for entrepreneurial ecosystems. It is hard to imagine Boston without MIT and Harvard, or Tel Aviv without Technion. Universities provide two critical inputs to the ecosystem: people and ideas. People are the pivotal force driving entrepreneurship, and universities produce students and faculty. Highly educated students are a major component of successful ecosystems and are important to staff both start-ups and established companies. A relatively small number of students starts ventures right after graduation, but many more do so at later stages of their careers. Faculty members sometimes become entrepreneurs, but otherwise play important roles as scientific advisers or expert consultants. Prior to becoming president of Stanford University, for example, John Hennessy had been a professor of electrical engineering who not only contributed to the development of the RISC technology, but in 1984 also became a co-founder of MIPS Computer Systems.[44]

Second, universities provide entrepreneurs with ideas, through both formal and informal processes. The formal process is led by technology transfer offices (TTOs), which administer the intellectual property owned by the university. In most countries, universities take ownership of inventions that were generated from research activities in the form of patents, copyrights, and equity in spin-off companies.[45] Many universities also maintain close relationships with the local investment community and in some cases even manage their own investment vehicles (Section 13.6.2). Universities thus become a source of the innovative ideas that fuel the supply of entrepreneurial ventures.[46]

A second group of relevant players are established corporations who are also an important source of entrepreneurial ideas and ventures. In some cases, they deliberately create corporate spin-off companies to pursue new ideas outside their main line of business. Other times it is their employees who leave to start their own ventures, provided noncompete clauses don't block them (Box 14.3).[47] The presence of large corporations can benefit start-ups in various ways. They may become customers or strategic partners for the start-ups in the ecosystem. They often harbor the technical and managerial talent pool from which start-ups do their hiring. Sometimes they also employ the spouses of founders, thus providing financial stability to entrepreneurs' households.

A third group of players are specialized professionals whose services entrepreneurs depend on. Start-ups need lawyers and accountants who are familiar with their challenges. A traditional law firm would not be very experienced negotiating a VC term sheet or setting up an employee stock option pool. Other important service providers include specialized head hunters who focus on the recruiting needs of start-ups and scale-ups; technology consultants who specialize in managing intellectual property or structuring research alliances; or marketing consultants who help start-ups reach customers using the latest techniques.

Strong ecosystems also have bankers who specialize in working with entrepreneurial companies. On the commercial banking side, most banks do not lend to innovative start-ups (Section 10.3), but there are some banks that specialize in venture debt. Silicon Valley Bank is a pioneer for this type of lending, Boost&Co is very active in Europe, and Innoven and Alteria are active in Asia. On the investment banking side, not all large investment houses are comfortable working with innovative start-ups. However, in advanced ecosystems such as Silicon Valley, New York, or London, later-stage companies (especially unicorns that remain private for a long time) can find specialized investment bankers who understand their specific needs. They can help them raise funding through private placements or Initial Public Offerings. For example, in late 2018 Uber raised about $2B in a private bond sale, advised by Morgan Stanley.[48] Other unicorns, such as Alibaba, Didi Chuxing, Sea Ltd, and Spotify, have also raised private debt with the help of investment bankers.

Service providers strengthen the ecosystem, but at the same time, they are interested in offering their specialized services only if there are enough high-quality entrepreneurs and investors. To take the example of a law firm, it only makes sense to specialize in start-ups if there is a critical mass of transactions to keep the law firm busy. This is the case in a Berlin, New York, or Tel Aviv, but it would not be possible in cities with smaller ecosystems.

14.3 The Role of Government

One key stakeholder that deserves further discussion is the government. Politicians and administrators have influence over government policies that sometimes help and sometimes hinder the development of entrepreneurial ecosystems. Government policies affect all aspects of economic activities and are particularly important for the development and well functioning of entrepreneurial ecosystems. We therefore now examine how government actions influence entrepreneurial activities, with a focus on finance. A thorough analysis of these topics would require a book of its own, so we limit ourselves to an overview of the main issues.

14.3.1 Should the Government Support Entrepreneurial Ecosystems?

To answer this question we need to distinguish between the normative and the positive roles of government. The normative concerns what the government should do to maximize social welfare, and the positive, what governments actually do. The two can differ in material ways. We first explore some of the normative reasons why governments should or shouldn't support entrepreneurial ecosystems, and then turn to what governments actually do.[49]

Any discussion of what governments should do is colored by political and ideological convictions. Indeed, there is a wide spectrum of views. On one end, the argument is that governments should stay as far away from entrepreneurs as possible. On the other end, there is the view that governments should actively manage the entire ecosystem. To provide some logical basis for this debate, it is useful to start with some fundamental economics. A commonly shared objective is economic growth. As discussed in Section 1.3, there is strong evidence that entrepreneurs are an important driver of economic growth, and that a lack of financing can hamper entrepreneurial success. Still the question remains as to whether any government action is needed. We can think of this as a trade-off between market failures and government failures.

Four main types of market failure might justify government support for entrepreneurship: imperfect information, innovation externalities, market power, and framework conditions. Competitive markets are known to work well when there is good information, but a substantial body of research shows that imperfect information can lead to important market distortions (Box 14.1). At the source are often adverse selection and moral hazard problems (Box 2.6). In our context, adverse selection occurs when investors worry that the only companies that want their money are those that are worse than they look. Moral hazard occurs when entrepreneurs can get away with taking self-interested actions that benefit themselves but harm the investors. More generally, imperfect information can lead to market failures where there is too little (or no) funding for entrepreneurs, relative to what would be the economically efficient level. The natural reaction to these kinds of problems is for investors to simply withdraw from investing. However, this deprives deserving entrepreneurs of perhaps realizing gains from transacting with the investors. While a government would not be able to solve the underlying information imperfections, it may compensate for the lack of private capital.

Innovation externalities arise when the value of an innovation to society is larger than the private value captured by the innovator. Knowledge is a public good that can be used and reused by multiple people.[50] Innovations can improve the lives of many, often in unexpected ways. Yet the entrepreneurs and investors generating innovations only take into account those uses that they can charge for. For example, the societal benefits of Thomas Edison's invention of the light bulb far exceeded the revenues from General Electric's sales of light bulbs. This is similarly the case for

Skype, the internet telecom company founded by Niklas Zennström and Janus Friis in 2003 and acquired by Microsoft in 2005. More generally, the argument is that whenever the societal value of innovations exceeds the innovators' private returns, then there is bound to be an undersupply of innovation. This calls for government support of innovative activities. An example is long-term R&D whose uncertainty makes it unappealing to private investments.

When some incumbent companies become large enough to exert market power, they can distort competition.[51] This may be a powerful way to keep challengers at bay and discourage entrepreneurial entry in the first place. Research by Acemoglu, Akcigit, Alp, Bloom, and Kerr finds that the beneficial impact of policies that remove protection of inefficient monopolistic incumbents is by far larger than the impact of other entrepreneurship policies.[52]

Finally, market transactions require conducive framework conditions, that is, a supportive environment. These conditions refer to institutions that are more effectively run by a government than by a private company, like the judiciary system and regulatory bodies. Some framework conditions apply to all business: a stable macroeconomy, low inflation, the quality of accounting standards, the enforcement of contracts, and the rule of law. Some institutions are vital for finance providers, such as a payment system and a stable banking system. Other framework conditions are more specific to innovation and entrepreneurship, such as well-defined intellectual property rules, laws that preserve contractual freedom, and limited red tape for starting new companies. If these frameworks are missing, this will hamper or even prevent the financing of start-ups. This is because entrepreneurs and investors cannot find a way of successfully structuring a deal or building a successful company.

Naturally, the benefit of any government action has to be traded off against two elements. One is the cost of providing those actions, and the other involves likely government failures. The cost of providing framework conditions is generally low compared to their benefits. A more serious concern is whether the government can solve market failures.[53] There are numerous reasons why government actions turn out to be flawed, related to wrong incentives, organizational rigidity, incompetence, corruption, and so on. In our context, there is an additional concern that government action is inherently too slow to match the rapidly changing needs of entrepreneurs and technology markets. The debate about the relative importance of market failures versus government failures is difficult to resolve conclusively. Still, any government initiative should be conceptually evaluated in light of both market failures and government failures.

With this understanding about the reasons for and against government support, we now turn to examining government policy from a positive perspective, asking how the government actually supports the financing of entrepreneurs. We divide government policies for stimulating entrepreneurial ecosystems into supply side and demand side policies.[54]

Governments can use public supply policies to stimulate the supply of capital, fostering investments in entrepreneurial companies. This may involve funding initiatives that support the financing of entrepreneurs (Section 14.3.2), tax credits for investors and entrepreneurs (Section 14.3.3), and regulation of capital markets (Section 14.3.4). At a higher level, the government sets the regulatory framework that defines broad parameters of economic activity: rule of law, macroeconomic stability, financial regulation, accounting standards, and taxation (Section 14.3.5). In addition, governments can use demand side policies to stimulate the demand for capital, promoting entrepreneurship and encouraging innovation (discussed in Section 14.3.6). This may involve infrastructure investments in science and technology and human capital, and competition regulation.

14.3.2 Government Funding

We focus here on government policies directed at increasing access to equity, ignoring policies directed at debt. Within equity there are multiple ways that policymakers can support the funding of entrepreneurs, such as directly funding start-ups, co-investing in VC funds, or setting up funds-of-funds to invest in multiple VCs. Figure 14.1 provides an overview of these three approaches. It is based on Figure 12.1, which shows the three-tiered structure of the venture capital industry, with limited partners, general partners, and companies. The new aspect of Figure 14.1 is the role of government as a potential funder at these three levels.

The first approach is for the government to directly fund companies. This can be down through a government-owned VC fund, as shown with arrow 1. Such investment funds are typically managed by a government-owned development bank. Examples include the Business Development Bank of Canada, Zero2IPO in China, or BPI France. Government VC funds sometimes join syndicates of private VC funds. A study by Brander, Du, and Hellmann suggests that companies funded solely by government VCs have lower exit rates, but that those co-investing with

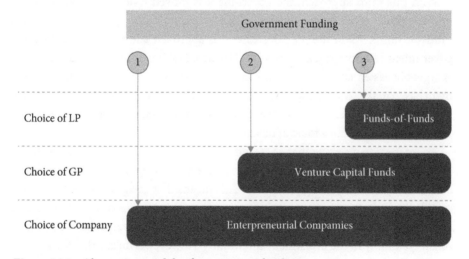

Figure 14.1. Alternative models of government funding.

private VCs have the same or even higher exit rates.[55] Government co-investment funds are an interesting variation on this approach. Some countries constrain their VC funds syndicate with private VCs. The Scottish Co-Investment Fund and the Ontario Capital Growth Corporation are examples of this approach.

The second approach is for the government to act as a limited partner. In this case, the government does not pick companies but VC firms, which in turn pick companies. Arrow 2 in Figure 14.1 indicates a government investing in private VC funds. There are numerous examples of this type of approach, including programs managed by the European Investment Fund and national promotional banks such as the British Business Banks, BPI France, or KfW in Germany. In the U.S., the SBIC program, administered by the Small Business Administration, pursues a similar approach of supporting the formation of VC funds, although it relies on financial instruments that are closer to debt than partnership shares.

By investing as an LP, governments try to increase the size of their national VC market. Removing the government from picking portfolio companies addresses concerns that it lacks the expertise and appropriate incentives for making good investment decisions. Moreover, the government is just one of several LPs, further limiting its influence over the VC firms. On the other hand, the cost of delegating investment decision is that the government has to pay management fees and carried interest. From the perspective of private VC firms, the benefit of additional funding has to be weighed against the fact that government money comes with additional restrictions and reporting requirements that may limit the flexibility of the fund.

The third approach is for the government to invest through funds-of-funds that then invest in VC firms. As with the previous approach, private investors co-invest alongside with the government into the funds-of-funds. Examples include the Canadian Federal VCAP and VCCI programs, Quebec's Teralys Capital, as well as the Venture EU fund of the European Union and the European Investment Bank.

With this third approach, the government is moved away from companies by one additional level: it doesn't even pick VC teams; it only picks one or several funds-of-funds. As in the previous case, this approach addresses concerns about government's ability to pick successful VC teams. Picking funds-of-funds managers is arguably easier, and it reduces the number of investment decisions the government has to make. The biggest cost of this approach is a second layer of management fees and carried interest. The relative advantages and disadvantages of government funds-of-funds remain a topic of debate.

An interesting question that arises with all three approaches concerns the terms at which the government invests. Many government programs use a very simple benchmark called investing *pari passu*. This means that the government invests at exactly the same terms as any private co-investor. This approach is not only simple and transparent, but being "in the same boat" also helps government investors to retain credibility in the investment community. However, it means that the government isn't really providing any subsidies.

If the government wants to provide subsidies to attract private investors, it can use two main approaches. First, some programs lure private investors by giving them more upside potential. For this, the government caps its upside returns, thereby leaving private investors with more returns in case of success. The structure of the SBIC program in the U.S. is based on this approach. Second, some programs lure private investors by giving them better downside protection, thereby capping their risk. The government agrees to take its returns only after private investors have achieved certain hurdle returns.

While government financing may address market failures, it gives rise to the opposite concern that government funding might "crowd out" private funding. The argument is that public money would displace private money by offering investment at subsidized rates, or at softer conditions. The counter to that thinking would be that the public money goes into underserved market where there little or no private money. Ultimately, these are empirical questions. The limited evidence to date remains inconclusive but suggests that crowding-in or crowding-out effects are not particularly strong.[56]

14.3.3 Tax Credits

Taxes are an important instrument of public policies, as they directly affect financial returns to all parties.[57] Numerous tax credits or tax reliefs directly or indirectly encourage entrepreneurship. Tax credits can be given to investors, in which case we think of them as supply side policies. They can also be given directly to companies, in which case we think of them as demand side policies. Moreover, tax credits may apply to either investments (i.e., inputs) or returns (i.e., outputs). With these two dimensions, we categorize tax policies using the simple two-by-two matrix shown in Table 14.1.

In the top left quadrant are R&D tax credits or other forms of credits to corporate investments. Most countries give such tax credits, such as the U.S. research and experimentation tax credit under IRS code 41 or the Canadian Scientific Research and Experimental Development (SR&ED) tax credit.

In the top right quadrant, we find investor-based tax credits, where eligible investors receive a credit on their equity investments. Examples are the EIS/SEIS tax credit program in the UK or the French FCPI program, which requires investing in a designated tax-advantaged fund. Investment tax credits are mainly used for investments in early-stage start-ups, partly because the costs of offering them to later-stage companies would be too large.

Table 14.1 Alternative Tax Credit Policies

	For companies	For investors
Credit on investments	R&D tax credits	Investment tax credits
Credit on returns	Corporate income tax relief	Capital gains relief

The left bottom quadrant concerns corporate income tax relief, that is, a reduction of the taxes paid on company income. Such programs make starting a company more attractive. While most start-ups are loss-making, and therefore do not pay corporate taxes in the first place, many countries allow the possibility to "carry forward" losses for several years, making the relief still attractive to start-ups.

The right bottom quadrant concerns capital gains relief. This is only valuable to successful companies that generate capital gains. This policy should be relevant to both entrepreneurs and investors. Since most returns to investments in entrepreneurial companies are generated by relatively few highly successful exits, the gains to the "winners" can potentially be quite large. At the same time, these tax breaks only occur at the time of exit, which at the time of investment may seem far into the future.

We can compare tax benefits for investors in the right column of Table 14.1.Tax credits reward investors for just making investments, regardless of their eventual success. Capital gains relief, by contrast, is only valuable in case of success. We can think of this as a trade-off between risk and return. With investment tax credit, the government shares some risk; with capital gains relief the government increases investors' return on the upside but not the downside. The relative effectiveness of these two policies depends on the degree of investor risk-aversion and on the investor's response to upside incentives. For example, large VCs are used to risk and strongly focus on upside returns. By contrast, individual angel investors might be more risk-averse and less focused on returns. Consequently, we might expect VCs to be more responsive to capital gains relief, whereas angels might be more responsive to investment tax credits.

It is also interesting to compare tax policies to the funding policies discussed in Section 14.3.2. An important difference is that tax benefits are entirely driven by rules, while funding policies require some degree of discretion. Tax benefits therefore may help to eliminate political favoritism, but also limit the government's ability to target what it considers the most deserving investments. In practice, tax benefits are also difficult to reverse, as they typically require political consensus for legislative changes. By contrast, funding policies give the government discretion in choosing which companies (arrow 1 in Figure 14.1) or investors (arrows 2 and 3 in Figure 14.1) to fund. Another important difference is that, with funding policies, the government takes ownership in companies and therefore has the potential of generating returns. From a budgetary perspective, this is attractive because it holds the promise that programs will become (partly) self-sustaining in the long run. By contrast, tax policies always have a negative impact on the government budget, in terms of payments made or taxes forgone. Obviously, what is attractive from the government's budget perspective is unattractive from the companies' (or investors') perspectives, and vice versa. Specifically, funding policies require the company to give up equity, whereas tax credits are entirely nondilutive subsidies.

14.3.4 Capital Markets

Some government policies affect how companies raise money on capital markets. Stock markets play a vital role in the venture investment cycle, ensuring that investors realize liquid returns. In the U.S., the key markets are the New York Stock Exchange and Nasdaq. In Europe, the London and Frankfurt Stock Exchanges focus mostly on larger, more established companies. The same can be said about the Hong Kong Stock Exchange or the Tokyo Stock Exchange. Stock market regulation involves trade-offs. On the one hand, there is a benefit of relaxing listings and disclosure requirements in order to attract more companies to list. On the other hand, lower requirements deter investors. Stock markets themselves are small ecosystems that require the complementary services of many specialized parties, including investment bankers, brokers, analysts, and many others. Various government policies and initiatives affect the liveliness of a stock market environment.

Some specialized stock exchanges focus on smaller and younger companies. Examples include the Toronto-based TSX Venture Exchange, the London-based Alternative Investment Market, and the Shenzhen Stock Exchange in China (Section 11.2.2). These lower-tier alternative markets enjoy a different set of rules than the main exchanges. In particular, they have less demanding listing and disclosure requirements. The main exchanges typically require companies to demonstrate a long history of positive earnings, whereas the alternative markets only require shorter histories or even none at all. Similarly, disclosure requirements tend to be lower on the alternative markets, requiring less detailed disclosures. Governments take different stances. China's Shenzhen stock market was an explicit attempt to create an alternative to the main Shanghai Stock Exchange. By contrast, the U.S. doesn't have a proper alternative market; instead, Title I of the JOBS Act (Box 11.4) tried to increase access to the main U.S. stock exchanges.

14.3.5 Framework Conditions

Policies to improve framework conditions concern the entire corporate sector, not just start-ups. A basic requirement is the need for a legal system that supports economic transactions and is consistently enforced. Economic growth requires the enforcement of contracts. Of particular importance is the protection of minority shareholders. This is because investors cannot generate adequate returns if company owners can easily take away their rights.[58] A widespread idea is that common law (such as in the U.S. or the United Kingdom) is friendlier to investors than civil law (such as in Japan or France). The argument is that common law is inherently more flexible because it relies on precedent and its evolving interpretations. By contrast, civil law is based on explicit rules that may ensure greater clarity but are less flexible over time.

Corruption is clearly detrimental to the development of entrepreneurial ecosystems.[59] Regulatory barriers to entering industries and bureaucratic red tape can also be detrimental to the formation of new ventures.[60] The World Bank publishes the annual Doing Business Index on how easy it is to start a business across different countries. In 2018, New Zealand was 1st, Singapore 2nd, and Denmark 3rd. The U.S. came in 6th, China 78th, India 100th, and Brazil 125th.

Labor legislation matters greatly for the development of entrepreneurial ecosystems. Rigid labor regulations hinder the creation and growth of entrepreneurial ventures. For example, if it is difficult to fire employees, risky start-ups become reluctant to hire employees in the first place. At the same time, employee protection has been found to foster innovative behavior, as it protects innovative employees from being unjustly dismissed.[61] Yet, not all labor market regulations deter entrepreneurship. Unemployment insurance, for example, has been shown to increase entrepreneurs' willingness to start ventures. Fear of failure inhibits the development of a vibrant entrepreneurial ecosystem. Having a safety net from unemployment insurance alleviates these concerns and encourages more risk-taking.[62]

Governments sometimes set sector-specific priorities with the hope of developing expertise in certain technologies or industries. In the U.S., for example, San Diego's local government implemented a broad development strategy over decades in order to foster a local life-sciences cluster. In Canada, Communitech developed an innovation hub around the Waterloo area. The Taiwanese government implemented a nationwide development program to promote its entry into the semiconductor business. In London, Tech City was a government-led initiative to promote entrepreneurship, especially around Fintech. It started with a focus on the Silicon Roundabout, a tech-focused urban revival project in East London. It was subsequently renamed Tech Nation with a UK-wide remit. Start-up Nation Central in Israel aims to promote the growth of start-ups and scale-ups, with a focus on making Israel a place not only to start but also to grow companies.

Throughout Section 14.2 we noted that ecosystems thrive on interactions. As a consequence, governments have a potential role in ensuring better interconnectivity. Governments can provide efficient transportation networks and up-to-date telecommunications infrastructure. In addition, there can be initiatives around social connectivity. For example, governments support business networks among entrepreneurs, business angels, and other supporting parties. It has even been argued that fostering entertainment and cultural institutions is important for attracting creative talent, which in turn attracts knowledge workers and entrepreneurs.[63]

14.3.6 Demand Side Policies

Several policies directly or indirectly stimulate the demand side, meaning they promote the creation and growth of entrepreneurial companies that subsequently demand capital. Broadly speaking, these policies focus on three critical inputs: ideas, people, and real estate.

Governments can promote the development of entrepreneurial ideas by boosting research and facilitating its commercialization. Most developed countries have agencies that award grants to researchers in universities, corporations, and other research facilities. In the U.S., the National Science Foundation (NSF) and the National Institute of Health (NIH) are examples of such agencies. Some grants go into fundamental research, others are called translational grants that help to translate fundamental research into more applied knowledge, and still others are specifically targeted at the commercialization of that applied knowledge. Typically, such agencies also have core programs that are very broad, as well as special initiatives that focus on specific needs (e.g., solar energy, AI). Granting agencies do not focus primarily on the creation of new companies, but their money nonetheless provides a critical input into entrepreneurial ecosystems, both directly in terms of giving grants to start-ups and indirectly in terms of pushing scientific advances.[64] Mike Lazaridis, co-founder of Research in Motion (RIM), which became Blackberry, which at one point was Canada's most successful start-up, recalls funding the company in its early days: "We heard about these government programs, and we started applying for them. It was a lot of work to actually apply. . . . They were rather small . . . but it was very helpful when we needed it."[65]

Central to the process of developing scientific discoveries into commercial applications is the creation of intellectual property. Research universities have technology transfer offices that administer the university's intellectual property (Section 14.2.3). Governments influence their activities by setting ownership rules. In the U.S., the 1980 Bayh-Dole Act allocated to universities the ownership of intellectual property that came out of federally funded research. This regulation is widely credited for the creation of technology transfer offices.[66] In Taiwan, government support for research and technology transfer in the 1970s and 1980s was vital. More recently, the governments' influence relates to its stance on open innovation. The key idea here is to create pools of knowledge that are deliberately free of intellectual property protection. An important example is the Human Genome Project, in which the government organized large-scale collaboration among researchers to create an open-access database for sequencing the entire human genome.[67] Such open innovation initiatives can become the basis for new entrepreneurial ventures.

In addition to fostering ideas, governments may play a role in fostering the quality of the talent pool. Governments have a large sway over the education system and can therefore influence the types of skills available in the economy. Start-ups often care about the availability of technical skills. In most places, there are complaints about shortages for science, technology, engineering, and mathematics (STEM) graduates, especially software programmers. Governments have multiple points of leverage to address such shortages. They can offer student bursaries, and there are numerous training programs. Some focus on advanced skills (e.g., AI, coding), and others on basic skills (e.g., essential IT skills). More broadly, the success of the technology sector relies heavily on the quality of the education system. All these programs help to form a pool of employees ready to work in the technology sector. There are also some government programs to encourage entrepreneurial skills more directly. Many initiatives offer training courses and mentoring services to people at various stages of forming a company.[68] More recently, governments have also started to run or support accelerator programs (Section 13.6.1).

As noted earlier, ecosystems thrive on interaction and therefore require physical proximity.[69] Finding affordable real estate matters to cash-strapped start-ups and their employees. Consequently, urban planning policies matter. Governments can sometime convert underutilized real estate into space for entrepreneurial activities. Parts of London's East side and Paris's Station F are examples of that. Governments can also give zoning permissions for establishing new business parks where entrepreneurs can work close to each other, and ideally also close to research universities or other relevant institutions. Beijing's Haidian Park is an example of that. Finally, in some cases, governments try to create entirely new ecosystems by designing entire new cities that are focused on innovation. France's Sophia Antipolis is a science and technology park that was created with such a greenfield approach.

So far we have noted that government support can increase the pool of ideas, the talent base, and access to real estate. It should be remembered, however, that government intervention can always go awry. Malaysia's attempt at creating a Multimedia Super Corridor and BioValley are widely believed to have been such a failure.[70]

14.4 Global Ecosystems

Our discussion has to this point focused on understanding the internal dynamics of entrepreneurial ecosystems. Beyond that, there are important interactions across ecosystems. Ecosystems tend to be tightly knit local clusters, but they do not operate in isolation. On the contrary, capital and talent can flow from one ecosystem to the other. We thus consider the global movement of capital and talent.

14.4.1 The Global Movement of Capital

There are multiple reasons for making cross-border investments. From the investors' perspective, investing abroad is purely driven by opportunity; they simply want to invest in the best deals. However, not all investors are comfortable with long-distance investing, as there are monitoring benefits to being close to the company (Section 8.3.1).[71]

Consider data from Europe, where U.S. investors have become an important source of funding. In 2016, approximately 23% of the amount of investments in

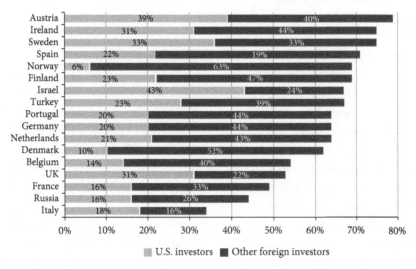

Figure 14.2. Sources of financing amounts for European VC-backed companies.
Source: Dealroom (2018).

European VC-backed companies came from U.S. investors, and another 29% from foreign sources other than the U.S. Interestingly, however, only 13% of deals involved U.S. investors. This is because U.S. investors tend to invest in larger rounds, typically in later-stage companies. Figure 14.2 presents further details on European countries.

What makes a country attractive to foreign venture investors? Investing at a distance takes more time and makes communication difficult, especially in a cross-border context. Numerous academic studies have documented that greater physical distance (or longer travel times) between investor and company decreases the likelihood of an investment. The pool of high-quality investable companies and the risk diversification opportunities they provide are very important. The quality of the legal system in the companies' country also matters. Other factors include relative macroeconomic conditions in the two countries, common language, colonial ties, and the level of trust between people from different nation pairs.[72]

From the entrepreneurs' perspective, there are also costs and benefits. Foreign investors might be less available, and cultural differences might make it more difficult to deal with them. On the other hand, seeking out foreign investors increases the pool of available funding sources. Taking foreign money can be a purely opportunistic choice. However, in many cases it is a strategic choice, meant to increase the company's access to foreign business networks. Foreign investors can help a company access new customers and markets, as well as suppliers or other strategic partners. They may also pave the way to exit. Indeed, a common reason for taking on U.S. investors is to prepare for a listing on a U.S. stock exchange or for a sale to a U.S. acquirer. Box 14.4 examines some research findings about cross-border venture investments.

Box 14.4 Venturing Across Borders

Cross-border investing is costly, so it should have clear benefits. An academic study by Chemmanur, Hull, and Krishnan looks at companies in emerging economies.[73] It finds that exit and operating performance is highest when these countries raise money from syndicates of both foreign and domestic investors. It is the combination of local and foreign that is beneficial; raising funding only from a foreign investor or only from a domestic one leads to lower performance. Why? The authors argue that foreign investors contribute superior expertise, while domestic investors have better local knowledge. It is the combination of these two elements that brings success.

If partnering with local investors leads to more success, why doesn't everyone do it? Research by Liu and Maula argues that two distinct types of uncertainty are relevant.[74] There is venture uncertainty that partnering with local investors helps to overcome. In addition, there is country uncertainty, which local partners cannot change. Over time, foreign investors learn to better judge these uncertainties, but the two types of learning point in different directions. Learning about local ventures and funders increases the likelihood of syndicating with local investors. However, learning about country risk makes foreign investors less dependent on local investors.

Foreign investors also tend to behave differently than local investors. Devigne, Manigart, and Wright find that cross-border investors terminate poorly performing investments faster than purely domestic investors.[75] Domestic investors are embedded in their national business environment, so that termination decisions are affected by social pressures. Foreign investors find it easier to eschew these social constraints.

Individual investors and entrepreneurs clearly benefit from cross-country investments, but the question that remains is what effect such investments have on a company's local ecosystem. The answer depends to a large extent on whether the company remains in its local ecosystem or relocates to the foreign investor's country. In the next section, we look at the case where companies relocate; for now let us focus on the case where companies stay.

In most accounts, foreign investments benefit the local ecosystem, not only in terms of direct benefits to the investee company, but also in terms of indirect benefits to other ecosystem participants. Foreign investors are likely to learn about the local ecosystem, so that one investment can lead to another. Foreign VC firms might hire local scouting agents and, if they like what they see, proceed to open a satellite office. Foreign investors are also likely to interact with the local investment community, thereby increasing access to international expertise and networks. Foreign investors are also likely to spur the interest of other foreign investors, which may further add to this process.

One sensitive issue with foreign investors is the question of ownership. When military technologies or cybersecurity are involved, foreign investments may be curtailed by national security rules. The question of foreign ownership also matters at the exit stage, so that a start-up in a sensitive area may have fewer options of getting acquired.

14.4.2 The Global Movement of Talent

In addition to the movement of capital across ecosystems, there is movement of talent, that is, companies and people. This movement is sometimes referred to as brain drain and concerns not only start-ups, but also knowledge workers and innovative companies more broadly.[76] The movement of talent is driven by the ambition of talented workers in weaker ecosystems to pursue opportunities in stronger ecosystems. Entrepreneurial talent flows from all parts of the world to the U.S., especially to Silicon Valley;[77] it flows from eastern Europe to western Europe; and so on. There are not only international moves, but also domestic moves. Talent flows from all over India to Bangalore. For example, Flipkart's founders Sachin Bansal and Binny Bansal moved there in 2007 after finishing their studies at the Indian Institute of Technology in Delhi. In China, talent flows to Beijing, Shanghai, and Shenzhen. For example, Frank Wang, moved from Hong Kong to Shenzhen in 2006 to found drone manufacturer DJI. In the U.S., Mark Zuckerberg famously moved his company from Boston to Silicon Valley.

Talent can move at different stages of the entrepreneurial cycle. Some entrepreneurs move prior to founding their company, believing they have better chances in the stronger ecosystem. Some move their start-up at the time of their first fundraising, looking for better suited investors and possibly higher valuations. Some move after obtaining one or several rounds of financing. In many cases, they do so with the help of a foreign investor from the stronger ecosystem. Some companies move before exit in order to prepare for a foreign listing or to attract offers from potential acquirers. Finally, some companies relocate after exit, typically at the behest of an acquirer.

The decision to relocate is not necessarily binary. In many cases, companies retain some activity in their home country, while growing the rest of their business abroad. For example, it might be advantageous to keep an engineering team at home because of lower wages, but grow a sales organization in the foreign country, especially if that is where the key customers are.

Reasons to relocate are driven by the comparative advantages of the two ecosystems. All of the factors we discuss in Section 14.2 matter, such as the density of entrepreneurs, investors, and supporting parties. Greater ease of finding investors and getting better valuations are certainly part of it, as is the belief that being in a stronger ecosystem increases chances of success. Potential reasons for not moving include lack of familiarity with the foreign ecosystem, lower labor costs at home, quality of life considerations, and relocation costs, not to mention the personal circumstances of individual founders. Relocation is also affected by government regulations and immigration policies that can encourage or discourage it (Section 14.3).

When entrepreneurs relocate, they presumably do so because it is to their advantage. The question remains: what effect do such relocations have on the domestic ecosystem? A main concern is "brain drain," that is, the loss of talent and the related loss of economic activity.[78] While people in the home country sometimes begrudge the success of their most talented entrepreneurs abroad, it is questionable whether any of that success could have happened at home. Would Sergey Brin have created a Google back in Russia?

Relocations also create an indirect loss of ecosystem externalities. In Section 14.2, we describe various positive interaction effects where the presence of one start-up generates positive externalities for other start-ups, investors, and supporting parties. When a start-up leaves, these forces work in reverse. Of particular concern is the fact that often it is the best entrepreneurs and start-ups that move, thus depriving the local ecosystems of their most talented members.

What is a loss to the home country is naturally a gain to the ecosystems that attract the talent. This can be seen by looking at the role of immigrant entrepreneurs. In the U.S., over 20% of entrepreneurs are immigrants, and over 30% of new firms have at least one immigrant entrepreneur.[79] The strength of Silicon Valley, in particular, depends on being a global hub for entrepreneurial talent. Foreign entrepreneurs not only have a direct effect on creating new economic activity, but they also generate ecosystem externalities in their new home.[80]

Although the short-term loss to the home country is apparent, there can also be some longer-term benefits that are less visible. Of particular note is the possibility that departed entrepreneurs subsequently give back to their ecosystems at home. This can happen in several ways. Some entrepreneurs achieve success abroad, and then return to their home country to establish their next venture. Others use their acquired wealth to invest in start-ups in their home country. They combine their familiarity of their old home with their newly acquired expertise and networks abroad. Finally, in addition to making investments, there are many informal ways by which successful entrepreneurs give back to their ecosystems back home, such as being a mentor or role model. Box 14.5 looks at Chinese returnee entrepreneurs.

Box 14.5 Sea Turtles

Some entrepreneurs return to their home country or city after being successful elsewhere. In China, they are dubbed "sea turtles." While they are generally welcome and bring many benefits with them, three recent studies provide interesting additional insights about the role of these returnees.[81]

First, research by Li, Zhang, Li, Zhou, and Zhang finds that while returnees bring back strong experience, they often lose touch with their original ecosystem.[82] Like foreign investors, they therefore have some advantages but also need to regain their contextual embeddedness in their home base. The extent to which they manage to do so determines their eventual success. Second, in a detailed study of the information and communication technology (ICT) industry in China, India, and Taiwan over the past few decades, Kenney, Breznitz, and Murphree find that sea turtles are not pathbreakers within their home ecosystem. Rather, they consolidate the progress spearheaded by local entrepreneurs.[83] Third, Qin, Wright, and Gao document the fact that sea turtles are quicker to react to entrepreneurial opportunities in their home ecosystem, especially when they possess technological know-how and access to foreign resources, most notably finance.[84]

An interesting question is to what extent governments can influence the international movement of talent. Apart from policies to strengthen the domestic ecosystem, discussed in Section 14.3, there are some policies that directly affect the movement of people and companies. On the receiving end, immigration policy affects the ease with which people can move. Moreover, governments can ensure that there are no unnecessary barriers to setting up companies or foreign subsidiaries. As for the country at risk of losing talent, there are different ways of preventing brain drain. Drastic measures such as restricting the freedom of movement are rarely effective and ethically questionable. A more enlightened approach is to build networks with the expatriate community in order to encourage the return of people and capital to the domestic ecosystem. Taiwan, for example, built its entrepreneurial ecosystem in part by cultivating networks with its expat community in Silicon Valley.[85]

Summary

This concluding chapter takes a broad perspective, looking at how entrepreneurs, investors, and supporting parties interact with each other in what is called an entrepreneurial ecosystem. The creation and financing of entrepreneurial ventures tend to concentrate in relatively few locations. The most famous is Silicon Valley, but others such as New York, Boston, London, Berlin, Beijing, Shenzhen, São Paulo, or Tel Aviv are increasingly recognized for their entrepreneurial strengths too. We explain that, at their core, ecosystems are defined by the interactions between three sets of key parties: the entrepreneurs and employees who create new ventures; the investors who provide the required financing; and a variety of supporting parties, including universities, established corporations, lawyers, consultants, and others. We distinguish between direct interactions that result in economic transactions from indirect interactions that result in externalities.

We identify numerous positive externalities that explain why entrepreneurial activity often occurs within a relatively confined geographic area. Such externalities also provide a potential reason for government policies to foster the development of entrepreneurial ecosystems. We review some potential policy interventions and discuss their potential benefits and downsides. The chapter ends with an analysis of how different ecosystems around the globe are interconnected with each other. We explain the determinants of cross-border investments and look at the movement of people and companies across ecosystems.

Review Questions

1. Who are the main actors in an entrepreneurial ecosystem?
2. What are the main factors contributing to the agglomeration of economic activity?
3. Within an ecosystem, what are the main externalities among entrepreneurial companies?
4. Why does investor diversity matter for an ecosystem?
5. What is the role of professional service providers within an ecosystem?
6. What are the main arguments for and against government intervention in entrepreneurial finance?
7. What is the difference between supply and demand side policies?
8. What is the relative advantage of governments investing directly in companies, investing in VC funds, or investing in funds-of-funds?
9. Should countries welcome foreign venture investors?
10. Who benefits and loses from brain drain?

Notes

1. Chatterji, Glaeser, and Kerr (2014) survey studies on the links between agglomeration and innovation.
2. Ács, Autio, and Szerb (2014), Florida and Mellander (2016), O'Connor et al. (2018) and Stam and Spigel (2018).
3. Boh, De-Haan, and Strom (2016)
4. Koh, Koh, and Tschanga (2005)
5. https://www.nobelprize.org/prizes/economic-sciences/1972/press-release.
6. https://www.nobelprize.org/prizes/economic-sciences/2008/press-release.
7. https://www.nobelprize.org/prizes/economic-sciences/2009/press-release.
8. For an introduction to general equilibrium theory, see Starr (2011).
9. Krugman (1996) provides a widely accessible introduction to agglomeration economics.
10. Klepper (2010).
11. Lorenzen and Mudambi (2013).
12. Krugman (1998, 2011).

13. Ostrom and Walker (2003)
14. Bottazzi, Da Rin, and Hellmann (2016) and Welter (2012).
15. Agrawal and Ostrom (2001) and Ostrom and Whitaker (1973).
16. Ostrom (1965).
17. Start-Up Genome, Global Startup Ecosystem Report 2017, available at: https://startupgenome.com/all-reports.
18. Duruflé, Hellmann, and Wilson (2017)
19. Saxenian (1994), Kenney and von Burg (1999), Lee et al. (2000), Gilson (1999), and Sturgeon (2000).
20. Lécuyer (2005).
21. On the creation of the Israeli ecosystem and its continued growth, see Senor and Singer (2011) and Bussgang and Stern (2015).
22. Avnimelech and Teubal (2006) and http://www.yozma.com.
23. Egusa and O'Shee (2016), Gonder (2012), Gonzalez-Uribe and Leatherbee (2018), and http://www.startupchile.org.
24. http://www.startupchile.org/impact.
25. http://www.startupchile.org/scale.
26. Chen and Ogan (2017).
27. Crichton (2018).
28. Wilkins (2018).
29. Morse (2018).
30. Lemos (2018).
31. Ruef, Aldrich, and Carter (2003) and Wasserman (2012).
32. Crowley Redding (2018) and Gilbert (2008).
33. Jackson, Joshi, and Erhardt (2003).
34. Atomico, "The State of European Tech, 2017" Available at: https://2017.stateofeuropeantech.com.
35. Gilson (1999) and Marx, Strumsky, and Fleming (2009).
36. Marx and Fleming (2012) provide an overview. Kaplan and Strömberg (2004) document the use of non-compete clauses in venture capital deals.
37. Marx, Strumsky, and Fleming (2009).
38. Marx (2011).
39. Younge, Tong, and Fleming (2015).
40. Samila and Sorenson (2011).
41. Aran (2018).
42. Rochet and Tirole (2003).
43. Delgado, Porter, and Stern (2010).
44. https://hennessy.stanford.edu/biography.
45. Mowery et al. (2004) examine the importance of regulations about patenting of university-based research for entrepreneurial innovation.
46. Shane (2004) and Link, Siegel, and Wright (2015).
47. Agrawal and Cockburn (2003), Gompers, Lerner, and Scharfstein (2005), and Klepper and Sleeper (2005).
48. Bond (2018).
49. For an overview, Lerner (2009) and Mazzucato (2013) provide two alternative perspectives.
50. Laffont (2008) provides an excellent introduction to public goods and to government intervention more generally.
51. Léautier (2019).
52. Acemoglu et al. (2018).
53. Mills (1986) and Stiglitz (1989) analyze government failures.

54. Wilson and Silva (2013) and Wilson (2015).
55. Brander, Du, and Hellmann (2015).
56. Leleux and Surlemont (2003), and Brander, Du, and Hellmann (2015).
57. Hall (2019) is a good introduction.
58. La Porta (1997) and Lerner and Schoar (2005).
59. Anokhin and Schulze (2009).
60. Djankov et al. (2002) and Klapper, Laeven, and Rajan (2006).
61. Acharya, Baghai, and Subramanian (2013).
62. Bozkaya and Kerr (2014), Hombert et al. (2014), Landier (2005), and Simmons, Wiklund, and Levie (2014).
63. Florida (2012).
64. Da Rin, Nicodano, and Sembenelli (2006).
65. Page 146 in Livingston (2009).
66. Jaffe and Lerner (2001).
67. Palladino (2001).
68. Fairlie, Karlan, and Zinman (2015).
69. Samila and Sorenson (2017).
70. Lerner (2009).
71. Bradley et al. (2019).
72. Aizenman and Kendall (2012), Bernstein, Giroud, and Townsend (2016), Bottazzi, Da Rin, and Hellman (2016), Lerner and Schoar (2005), and Schertler and Tykvová (2011).
73. Chemmanur, Hull, and Krishnan (2016), Dai, Jo, and Kassicieh (2012) find similar results for investments into six major Asian economies.
74. Liu and Maula (2015).
75. Devigne, Manigart, and Wright (2016).
76. Kerr (2018) and Pekkala Kerr et al. (2016).
77. Wuebker, Acs, and Florida (2010).
78. Docquier and Rapoport (2012). See also Mayr and Peri (2009) for an overview of the brain drain and its economic consequences.
79. Kerr (2008) and Kerr and Pekkala Kerr (2016).
80. Kapur (2010) and Nanda and Khanna (2010) analyze the case of India, which has been subject to both brain drain and the return of talented emigrants for several generations.
81. Dai and Liu (2009).
82. Li et al. (2012).
83. Kenney, Breznitz, and Murphree (2013).
84. Qin, Wright, and Gao (2017).
85. Saxenian (2002).

Bibliography

Abadi, Joseph, and Markus Brunnermeier. 2018. "Blockchain Economics." Working Paper 25407. NBER.

Abernathy, William, and James Utterback. 1978. "Patterns of Industrial Innovation." *Technology Review* 80 (7): 40–47.

Acemoglu, Daron. 2009. *Introduction to Modern Economic Growth*. Princeton, NJ: Princeton University Press.

Acemoglu, Daron, Ufuk Akcigit, Harun Alp, Nicholas Bloom, and William Kerr. 2018. "Innovation, Reallocation, and Growth." *American Economic Review* 108 (11): 3450–91.

Acharya, Viral, Ramin Baghai, and Krishnamurthy Subramanian. 2013. "Labor Laws and Innovation." *The Journal of Law and Economics* 56 (4): 997–1037.

Acharya, Viral, and Lasse Heje Pedersen. 2005. "Asset Pricing with Liquidity Risk." *Journal of Financial Economics* 77 (2): 375–410.

Acharya, Viral, and Krishnamurthy Subramanian. 2009. "Bankruptcy Codes and Innovation." *The Review of Financial Studies* 22 (12): 4949–88.

Ács, Zoltán, Erkko Autio, and László Szerb. 2014. "National Systems of Entrepreneurship: Measurement Issues and Policy Implications." *Research Policy* 43 (3): 476–94.

Adams, Renée, Heitor Almeida, and Daniel Ferreira. 2009. "Understanding the Relationship between Founder–CEOs and Firm Performance." *Journal of Empirical Finance* 16 (1): 136–50.

Adams, Renée, and Daniel Ferreira. 2008. "One Share-One Vote: The Empirical Evidence." *Review of Finance* 12 (1): 51–91.

Adams, Renée, Benjamin Hermalin, and Michael Weisbach. 2010. "The Role of Boards of Directors in Corporate Governance: A Conceptual Framework and Survey." *Journal of Economic Literature* 48 (1): 58–107.

Aggarwal, Vikas, and David Hsu. 2013. "Entrepreneurial Exits and Innovation." *Management Science* 60 (4): 867–87.

Aggarwal, Vikas, David Hsu, and Andy Wu. 2015. "Across-Team Diversity Compared to Within-Team Diversity as Drivers of Innovative Output." Mimeo. INSEAD.

Aghion, Philippe, and Richard Holden. 2011. "Incomplete Contracts and the Theory of the Firm: What Have We Learned over the Past 25 Years?" *Journal of Economic Perspectives* 25 (2): 181–97.

Aghion, Philippe, and Peter Howitt. 1992. "A Model of Growth through Creative Destruction." *Econometrica* 60 (2): 323–51.

———. 1998. *Endogenous Growth Theory*. Cambridge, MA: MIT Press.

Aghion, Philippe, and Jean Tirole. 1997. "Formal and Real Authority in Organizations." *Journal of Political Economy* 105 (1): 1–29.

Agrawal, Ajay, Christian Catalini, and Avi Goldfarb. 2015. "Crowdfunding: Geography, Social Networks, and the Timing of Investment Decisions." *Journal of Economics and Management Strategy* 24 (2): 253–74.

Agrawal, Ajay, and Iain Cockburn. 2003. "The Anchor Tenant Hypothesis: Exploring the Role of Large, Local, R&D-Intensive Firms in Regional Innovation Systems." *International Journal of Industrial Organization* 21 (9): 1227–53.

Agrawal, Ajay, Joshua Gans, and Avi Goldfarb. 2018. *Prediction Machines: The Simple Economics of Artificial Intelligence*. Cambridge, MA: Harvard Business Press.

Agrawal, Arun, and Elinor Ostrom. 2001. "Collective Action, Property Rights, and Decentralization in Resource Use in India and Nepal." *Politics and Society* 29 (4): 485–514.

Ahern, Kenneth, and Jarrad Harford. 2014. "The Importance of Industry Links in Merger Waves." *The Journal of Finance* 69 (2): 527–76.

Aitken, Roger. 2018. "Will Spotify's $30B NYSE 'Non-IPO' Direct Listing Hit The Spot?" Forbes. April 3rd. https://www.forbes.com/sites/rogeraitken/2018/04/03/will-spotifys-30b-nyse-non-ipo-direct-listing-hit-the-spot.

Aizenman, Joshua, and Jake Kendall. 2012. "The Internationalization of Venture Capital." *Journal of Economic Studies* 39 (5): 488–511.

Akcigit, Ufuk, and William Kerr. 2018. "Growth through Heterogeneous Innovations." *Journal of Political Economy* 126 (4): 1374–1443.

Amihud, Yakov, Haim Mendelson, and Lasse Pedersen. 2006. "Liquidity and Asset Prices." *Foundations and Trends in Finance* 1 (4): 269–364.

Amit, Raphael, James Brander, and Christoph Zott. 1998. "Why Do Venture Capital Firms Exist? Theory and Canadian Evidence." *Journal of Business Venturing* 13 (6): 441–66.

Anagnostopoulou, Seraina. 2008. "R&D Expenses and Firm Valuation: A Literature Review." *International Journal of Accounting and Information Management* 16 (1): 5–24.

Anders, George. 2014. "Inside Sequoia Capital: Silicon Valley's Innovation Factory." *Forbes*, April 14th.

Anderson, Christopher, Jian Huang, and Gökhan Torna. 2017. "Can Investors Anticipate Post-IPO Mergers and Acquisitions?" *Journal of Corporate Finance* 45 (August): 496–521.

Andolfatto, David. 2018. "Blockchain: What It Is, What It Does, and Why You Probably Don't Need One." *Federal Reserve Bank of St. Louis Review, Second Quarter 2018* 100 (2): 87–95.

Ang, Andrew, Bingxu Chen, William Goetzmann, and Ludovic Phalippou. 2018. "Estimating Private Equity Returns from Limited Partner Cash Flows." *The Journal of Finance* 73 (4): 1751–83.

Anokhin, Sergey, and William Schulze. 2009. "Entrepreneurship, Innovation, and Corruption." *Journal of Business Venturing*, Special Issue Ethics and Entrepreneurship, 24 (5): 465–76.

Anshuman, V. Ravi, John Martin, and Sheridan Titman. 2012. "An Entrepreneur's Guide to Understanding the Cost of Venture Capital." *Journal of Applied Corporate Finance* 24 (3): 75–83.

Ante, Spencer. 2008. *Creative Capital: Georges Doriot and the Birth of Venture Capital*. Cambridge, MA: Harvard Business Press.

Anthony, Scott, Patrick Viguerie, Evan Schwartz, and John Van Landerghem. 2018. "Corporate Longevity Forecast: Creative Destruction Is Accelerating." *Innosight* (blog). February. https://www.innosight.com/insight/creative-destruction.

Aran, Yifat. 2018. "Beyond Covenants Not to Compete: Equilibrium in High-Tech Startup Labor Markets." *Stanford Law Review* 70 (4): 1235–94.

Arcot, Sridhar, Zsuzsanna Fluck, José-Miguel Gaspar, and Ulrich Hege. 2015. "Fund Managers under Pressure: Rationale and Determinants of Secondary Buyouts." *Journal of Financial Economics* 115 (1): 102–35.

Armour, John, and Luca Enriques. 2018. "The Promise and Perils of Crowdfunding: Between Corporate Finance and Consumer Contracts." *The Modern Law Review* 81 (1): 51–84.

Armstrong, Chris, Antonio Davila, and George Foster. 2006. "Venture-Backed Private Equity Valuation and Financial Statement Information." *Review of Accounting Studies* 11 (1): 119–54.

Arora, Ashish, Wesley Cohen, and John Walsh. 2016. "The Acquisition and Commercialization of Invention in American Manufacturing: Incidence and Impact." *Research Policy* 45 (6): 1113–28.

Arora, Ashish, and Alfonso Gambardella. 1990. "Complementarity and External Linkages: The Strategies of the Large Firms in Biotechnology." *The Journal of Industrial Economics* 38 (4): 361–79.

Arrow, Kenneth. 1962. "Economic Welfare and the Allocation of Resources for Invention." In *The Rate and Direction of Inventive Activity: Economic and Social Factors*, edited by Richard Nelson, 629–626. Princeton, NJ: Princeton University Press.

Artinger, Sabrina, and Thomas Powell. 2016. "Entrepreneurial Failure: Statistical and Psychological Explanations." *Strategic Management Journal* 37 (6): 1047–64.

Arugaslan, Onur, Douglas Cook, and Robert Kieschnick. 2010. "On the Decision to Go Public with Dual Class Stock." *Journal of Corporate Finance* 16 (2): 170–81.

Åstebro, Thomas, and Samir Elhedhli. 2006. "The Effectiveness of Simple Decision Heuristics: Forecasting Commercial Success for Early-Stage Ventures." *Management Science* 52 (3): 395–409.

Åstebro, Thomas, Manuel Fernández Sierra, Stefano Lovo, and Nir Vulkan. 2018. "Herding in Equity Crowdfunding." Mimeo. University of Oxford, Saïd Business School.

Åstebro, Thomas, Holger Herz, Ramana Nanda, and Roberto Weber. 2014. "Seeking the Roots of Entrepreneurship: Insights from Behavioral Economics." *Journal of Economic Perspectives* 28 (3): 49–70.

Åstebro, Thomas, and Carlos Serrano. 2015. "Business Partners: Complementary Assets, Financing, and Invention Commercialization." *Journal of Economics and Management Strategy* 24 (2): 228–52.

Atanasov, Vladimir, Vladimir Ivanov, and Kate Litvak. 2012. "Does Reputation Limit Opportunistic Behavior in the VC Industry? Evidence from Litigation against VCs." *The Journal of Finance* 67 (6): 2215–46.

Atanassov, Julian. 2013. "Do Hostile Takeovers Stifle Innovation? Evidence from Antitakeover Legislation and Corporate Patenting." *The Journal of Finance* 68 (3): 1097–1131.

Atomico. 2018. "The State of European Tech."

Auerbach, Alan. 2002. "Chapter 19 - Taxation and Corporate Financial Policy." In *Handbook of Public Economics*, edited by Alan Auerbach and Martin Feldstein, 3:1251–92. Amsterdam, North Holland: Elsevier.

Avnimelech, Gil, and Morris Teubal. 2006. "Creating Venture Capital Industries That Co-Evolve with High Tech: Insights from an Extended Industry Life Cycle Perspective of the Israeli Experience." *Research Policy* 35 (10): 1477–98.

Azevedo, Mary Ann. 2018. "Growth With An Impact: The Rise Of VCs Looking To Fund A (Profitable) Cause." Crunchbase News. February 2nd. https://news.crunchbase.com/news/growth-impact-rise-vcs-looking-fund-profitable-cause.

Azoulay, Pierre, Joshua Graff Zivin, and Gustavo Manso. 2011. "Incentives and Creativity: Evidence from the Academic Life Sciences." *The RAND Journal of Economics* 42 (3): 527–54.

Bahler, Kristen. 2018. "Meet the 34-Year-Old Founder of Spotify, Who Could Be Worth Billions This Year." Business Insider. January 8th. http://uk.businessinsider.com/meet-the-34-year-old-millionaire-founder-of-spotify-2018-1.

Baker, Malcolm, and Paul Gompers. 2003. "The Determinants of Board Structure at the Initial Public Offering." *The Journal of Law and Economics* 46 (2): 569–98.

Balderton. 2017. "The Balderton Essential Guide to Employee Equity." November 24th. https://www.balderton.com/news/the-balderton-essential-guide-to-employee-equity.

Ball, Eric, Hsin Hui Chiu, and Richard Smith. 2011. "Can VCs Time the Market? An Analysis of Exit Choice for Venture-Backed Firms." *The Review of Financial Studies* 24 (9): 3105–38.

Barker, Richard. 2011. *Short Introduction to Accounting*. Cambridge, UK: Cambridge University Press.

Barnett, William, and Arar Han. 2012. "Facebook 2012." Case Study E468. Stanford University, Stanford Graduate School of Business.

Baron, James, M. Diane Burton, and Michael Hannan. 1996. "The Road Taken: Origins and Evolution of Employment Systems in Emerging Companies." *Industrial and Corporate Change* 5 (2): 239–75.

Barreto, Humberto, and Frank Howland. 2005. *Introductory Econometrics: Using Monte Carlo Simulation with Microsoft Excel*. Cambridge, UK: Cambridge University Press.

Barringer, Bruce, and Duane Ireland. 2015. *Entrepreneurship: Successfully Launching New Ventures*. Fifth Edition. Boston: Pearson.

Barrot, Jean-Noël. 2016. "Investor Horizon and the Life Cycle of Innovative Firms: Evidence from Venture Capital." *Management Science* 63 (9): 3021–43.

Barth, Mary, Wayne Landsman, and Daniel Taylor. 2017. "The JOBS Act and Information Uncertainty in IPO Firms." *The Accounting Review* 92 (6): 25–47.

Bartlett, Joseph. 1999. *Fundamentals of Venture Capital*. Madison Books.

Bates, Timothy. 2005. "Analysis of Young, Small Firms That Have Closed: Delineating Successful from Unsuccessful Closures." *Journal of Business Venturing* 20 (3): 343–58.

Baum, Joel, and Brian Silverman. 2004. "Picking Winners or Building Them? Alliance, Intellectual, and Human Capital as Selection Criteria in Venture Financing and Performance of Biotechnology Startups." *Journal of Business Venturing* 19 (3): 411–36.

Bazley, John, Cynthia Schweer Rayner, and Aunnie Patton Power. 2015. "Zoona Mobile Money: Investing for Impact (Cases A and B)." Case Study. Graduate School of Business, University of Cape Town.

Bebchuk, Lucian, and Kobi Kastiel. 2017. "The Untenable Case for Perpetual Dual-Class Stock." *Virginia Law Review* 103: 585.

Belenzon, Sharon, Aaron Chatterji, and Brendan Daley. 2019. "Choosing between Growth and Glory." *Management Science*, Forthcoming.

Belleflamme, Paul, Thomas Lambert, and Armin Schwienbacher. 2014. "Crowdfunding: Tapping the Right Crowd." *Journal of Business Venturing* 29 (5): 585–609.

Bender, Morgan, Benedict Evans, and Scott Kupor. 2015. "U.S. Tech Funding — What's Going On?" Working Paper. Andreessen Horowitz.

Bengtsson, Ola. 2013. "Relational Venture Capital Financing of Serial Founders." *Journal of Financial Intermediation* 22 (3): 308–34.

Bengtsson, Ola, and John Hand. 2011. "CEO Compensation in Venture-Backed Firms." *Journal of Business Venturing* 26 (4): 391–411.

Bengtsson, Ola, and Berk Sensoy. 2015. "Changing the Nexus: The Evolution and Renegotiation of Venture Capital Contracts." *Journal of Financial and Quantitative Analysis* 50 (3): 349–75.

Benson, David, and Rosemarie Ziedonis. 2010. "Corporate Venture Capital and the Returns to Acquiring Portfolio Companies." *Journal of Financial Economics* 98 (3): 478–99.

Berentsen, Aleksander, and Fabian Schär. 2018. "A Short Introduction to the World of Cryptocurrencies." *Federal Reserve Bank of St. Louis Review, First Quarter 2018* 100 (1): 1–16.

Bergemann, Dirk, and Ulrich Hege. 2005. "The Financing of Innovation: Learning and Stopping." *The RAND Journal of Economics* 36 (4): 719–52.

Berger, Allen. 2014. "Small Business Lending by Banks: Lending Technologies and the Effects of Banking Industry Consolidation and Technological Change." In *The Oxford Handbook of Banking, Second Edition*, edited by Allen Berger, Philip Molyneux, and John Wilson, 292–311. Oxford, UK: Oxford University Press.

Berger, Allen, and Gregory Udell. 1992. "Some Evidence on the Empirical Significance of Credit Rationing." *Journal of Political Economy* 100 (5): 1047–77.

Berk, Jonathan, and Jules van Binsbergen. 2015. "Measuring Skill in the Mutual Fund Industry." *Journal of Financial Economics* 118 (1): 1–20.

Berk, Jonathan, and Peter DeMarzo. 2016. *Corporate Finance*. Fourth Edition. Boston: Pearson.

Berk, Jonathan, and Richard Green. 2004. "Mutual Fund Flows and Performance in Rational Markets." *Journal of Political Economy* 112 (6): 1269–95.

Bernstein, Shai. 2015. "Does Going Public Affect Innovation?" *The Journal of Finance* 70 (4): 1365–1403.

Bernstein, Shai, Xavier Giroud, and Richard Townsend. 2016. "The Impact of Venture Capital Monitoring." *The Journal of Finance* 71 (4): 1591–1622.

Bernstein, Shai, Arthur Korteweg, and Kevin Laws. 2017. "Attracting Early-Stage Investors: Evidence from a Randomized Field Experiment." *The Journal of Finance* 72 (2): 509–38.

Beroutsos, Andrea, Andrew Freeman, and Conor Kehoe. 2007. "What Public Companies Can Learn from Private Equity." *McKinsey Quarterly* 1: 1–12.

Bertrand, Marianne, and Antoinette Schoar. 2006. "The Role of Family in Family Firms." *Journal of Economic Perspectives* 20 (2): 73–96.

Bettignies, Jean-Etienne de, and Gilles Chemla. 2007. "Corporate Venturing, Allocation of Talent, and Competition for Star Managers." *Management Science* 54 (3): 505–21.

Bhashyam, Shriram. 2015. "Square's S-1: Of Ratchets And Unicorn Valuations." TechCrunch. November 11th. http://social.techcrunch.com/2015/11/10/squares-s-1-of-ratchets-and-unicorn-valuations.

Bhimani, Alnoor. 2017. *Financial Management for Technology Start-Ups: A Handbook for Growth.* London: Kogan Page.

Bhuiyan, Johana. 2018. "Stitch Fix CEO Katrina Lake Says Her One Regret with the IPO Is That They Let Expectations Get Really High." Recode. May 30th. https://www.recode.net/2018/5/30/17385382/katrina-lake-stitch-fix-code-conference-interview-ipo.

Bielli, Simona, Augustina Sol Eskenazi, Christopher Haley, and Johnathan Bone. 2017. "Open Innovation in Europe - a Snapshot of the SEP Europe's Corporate Startup Stars 2017." *Nesta* (blog). December 17th. https://www.nesta.org.uk/blog/open-innovation-in-europe-a-snapshot-of-the-sep-europes-corporate-startup-stars-2017.

Bienz, Carsten, and Julia Hirsch. 2012. "The Dynamics of Venture Capital Contracts." *Review of Finance* 16 (1): 157–95.

Bienz, Carsten, and Uwe Walz. 2010. "Venture Capital Exit Rights." *Journal of Economics and Management Strategy* 19 (4): 1071–1116.

Binkley, Christina. 2010. "Charity Gives Shoe Brand Extra Shine." *Wall Street Journal*, April 1st. https://www.wsj.com/articles/SB10001424052702304252704575155903198032336.

Black, Fischer, and Myron Scholes. 1973. "The Pricing of Options and Corporate Liabilities." *Journal of Political Economy* 81 (3): 637–54.

Blair, Roger, and Francine Lafontaine. 2005. *The Economics of Franchising.* Cambridge, UK: Cambridge University Press.

Blank, Steve. 2010. "No Plan Survives First Contact With Customers – Business Plans versus Business Models." *Steve Blank* (blog). April 8th. https://steveblank.com/2010/04/08/no-plan-survives-first-contact-with-customers-%e2%80%93-business-plans-versus-business-models.

———. 2013. *The Four Steps to the Epiphany: Successful Strategies for Products That Win.* Fifth Edition. San Mateo, CA: K&S Ranch.

Blank, Steve, and Bob Dorf. 2012. *The Startup Owner's Manual: The Step-by-Step Guide for Building a Great Company.* First Edition. Pescadero, CA: K&S Ranch.

Blevins, Dane, and Roberto Ragozzino. 2018. "An Examination of the Effects of Venture Capitalists on the Alliance Formation Activity of Entrepreneurial Firms." *Strategic Management Journal* 39 (7): 2075–91.

Bochner, Steven, Jon Avina, and Calise Cheng. 2016. *Guide to the Initial Public Offering.* Eighth Edition. Merill Corporation.

Bodie, Zvi, Alex Kane, and Alan Marcus. 2017. *Investments.* Eleventh Edition. New York: McGraw-Hill Education.

Boh, Wai Fong, Uzi De-Haan, and Robert Strom. 2016. "University Technology Transfer through Entrepreneurship: Faculty and Students in Spinoffs." *The Journal of Technology Transfer* 41 (4): 661–69.

Böhme, Rainer, Nicolas Christin, Benjamin Edelman, and Tyler Moore. 2015. "Bitcoin: Economics, Technology, and Governance." *Journal of Economic Perspectives* 29 (2): 213–38.

Bond, Shannon. 2018. "Uber Raises $2bn in Debut Bond Sale after Strong Investor Demand." *Financial Times*, October 18th.

Boorstin, Daniel. 1983. "The American Surprise." In *The Discoverers*, 203–54. New York: Random House.

Boot, Arnoud, Radhakrishnan Gopalan, and Anjan Thakor. 2006. "The Entrepreneur's Choice between Private and Public Ownership." *The Journal of Finance* 61 (2): 803–36.

———. 2008. "Market Liquidity, Investor Participation, and Managerial Autonomy: Why Do Firms Go Private?" *The Journal of Finance* 63 (4): 2013–59.

Booth, Richard. 2006. "Give Me Equity or Give Me Death - The Role of Competition and Compensation in Silicon Valley." *Entrepreneurial Business Law Journal* 1 (2): 265–82.

Bort, Julie. 2016. "How a Cold Call to a Billionaire Led This Founder to Sell His Company for $225 Million." Business Insider. December 19th. https://www.businessinsider.com.au/a-cold-call-to-a-billionaire-led-pitchbook-to-a-225-million-sale-2016-12.

Bottazzi, Laura, Marco Da Rin, and Thomas Hellmann. 2008. "Who Are the Active Investors?: Evidence from Venture Capital." *Journal of Financial Economics* 89 (3): 488–512.

———. 2009. "What Is the Role of Legal Systems in Financial Intermediation? Theory and Evidence." *Journal of Financial Intermediation* 18 (4): 559–98.

———. 2016. "The Importance of Trust for Investment: Evidence from Venture Capital." *The Review of Financial Studies* 29 (9): 2283–2318.

Bower, Joseph, and Clayton Christensen. 1995. "Disruptive Technologies: Catching the Wave." *Harvard Business Review* 73 (1): 43–53.

Bozkaya, Ant, and William Kerr. 2014. "Labor Regulations and European Venture Capital." *Journal of Economics and Management Strategy* 23 (4): 776–810.

Bradley, Michael, and Michael Roberts. 2015. "The Structure and Pricing of Corporate Debt Covenants." *Quarterly Journal of Finance* 5 (2).

Bradley, Wendy, Gilles Duruflé, Thomas Hellmann, and Karen Wilson. 2019. "Cross-Border Venture Capital Investments: What Is the Role of Public Policy?" *Journal of Risk and Financial Management* 12 (112): 1–22.

Brander, James, Raphael Amit, and Werner Antweiler. 2002. "Venture-Capital Syndication: Improved Venture Selection vs. The Value-Added Hypothesis." *Journal of Economics and Management Strategy* 11 (3): 423–52.

Brander, James, Qianqian Du, and Thomas Hellmann. 2015. "The Effects of Government-Sponsored Venture Capital: International Evidence." *Review of Finance* 19 (2): 571–618.

Brau, James, and Stanley Fawcett. 2006. "Initial Public Offerings: An Analysis of Theory and Practice." *The Journal of Finance* 61 (1): 399–436.

Brav, Alon, and Paul Gompers. 1997. "Myth or Reality? The Long-Run Underperformance of Initial Public Offerings: Evidence from Venture and Nonventure Capital-Backed Companies." *The Journal of Finance* 52 (5): 1791–1821.

Brealey, Richard, Stewart Myers, and Franklin Allen. 2016. *Principles of Corporate Finance.* Twelfth Edition. New York: McGraw-Hill Education.

Bright, Jake. 2019. "African E-Commerce Startup Jumia's Shares Open at $14.50 in NYSE IPO." *TechCrunch* (blog). April 12th. http://social.techcrunch.com/2019/04/12/african-e-commerce-startup-jumias-shares-open-at-14-50-in-nyse-ipo.

Bris, Arturo, Ivo Welch, and Ning Zhu. 2006. "The Costs of Bankruptcy: Chapter 7 Liquidation versus Chapter 11 Reorganization." *The Journal of Finance* 61 (3): 1253–1303.

Broughman, Brian. 2013. "Independent Directors and Shared Board Control in Venture Finance." *Review of Law and Economics* 9 (1): 41–72.

Broughman, Brian, and Jesse Fried. 2010. "Renegotiation of Cash Flow Rights in the Sale of VC-Backed Firms." *Journal of Financial Economics* 95 (3): 384–99.

———. 2012. "Do VCs Use inside Rounds to Dilute Founders? Some Evidence from Silicon Valley." *Journal of Corporate Finance* 18 (5): 1104–20.

Brown, Eliot. 2019. "WeWork's CEO Makes Millions as Landlord to WeWork." *Wall Street Journal*, January 17th. https://www.wsj.com/articles/weworks-ceo-makes-millions-as-landlord-to-wework-11547640000.

Brown, Keith, and Kenneth Wiles. 2015. "In Search of Unicorns: Private IPOs and the Changing Markets for Private Equity Investments and Corporate Control." *Journal of Applied Corporate Finance* 27 (3): 34–48.

———. 2016. "Opaque Financial Contracting and Toxic Term Sheets in Venture Capital." *Journal of Applied Corporate Finance* 28 (1): 72–85.

Brown, Tim. 2008. "Design Thinking." *Harvard Business Review* 86 (6): 84–92.

———. 2009. *Change by Design: How Design Thinking Transforms Organizations and Inspires Innovation.* New York: HarperCollins.

Bruno, Brunella, Alexandra D'Onfrio, and Immacolata Marino. 2017. "Determinants of Bank Lending in Europe and the United States: Evidence from Crisis and Post-Crisis Years." In *Finance and Investment: The European Case*, edited by Colin Mayer, Stefano Micossi, Marco Onado, Andrea Polo, and Marco Pagano, 95–136. Oxford, UK: Oxford University Press.

Burt, Ronald. 2004. "Structural Holes and Good Ideas." *American Journal of Sociology* 110 (2): 349–99.

———. 2005. *Brokerage and Closure: An Introduction to Social Capital*. Oxford, UK: Oxford University Press.

Bussgang, Jeffrey, and Omri Stern. 2015. "How Israeli Startups Can Scale." *Harvard Business Review* 93 (9) 2–9.

Bygrave, William, and Andrew Zacharakis. 2014. *Entrepreneurship*. Third Edition. Hoboken, NJ: John Wiley & Sons.

Cabral, Luis, and David Backus. 2002. "Betamax and VHS." Mini Case. New York University, Stern School of Business.

Cambridge Associates. 2018. *US Venture Capital Index and Selected Benchmark Statistics*. Cambridge, MA: Cambridge Associates.

Cameron, Rondo. 1967. *Banking in the Early Stages of Industrialization: A Study in Comparative Economic History*. Oxford, UK: Oxford University Press.

Capron, Laurence, and Will Mitchell. 2012. *Build, Borrow, or Buy: Solving the Growth Dilemma*. Cambridge, MA: Harvard Business Press.

Capron, Laurence, and Jung-Chin Shen. 2007. "Acquisitions of Private vs. Public Firms: Private Information, Target Selection, and Acquirer Returns." *Strategic Management Journal* 28 (9): 891–911.

Cardon, Melissa, Corinne Post, and William Forster. 2017. "Team Entrepreneurial Passion: Its Emergence and Influence in New Venture Teams." *Academy of Management Review* 42 (2): 283–305.

Carland, James, Frank Hoy, William Boulton, and Jo Ann Carland. 1984. "Differentiating Entrepreneurs from Small Business Owners: A Conceptualization." *The Academy of Management Review* 9 (2): 354–59.

Carpentier, Cécile, and Jean-Marc Suret. 2015. "Angel Group Members' Decision Process and Rejection Criteria: A Longitudinal Analysis." *Journal of Business Venturing* 30 (6): 808–21.

Carreyrou, John. 2018a. "SEC Charges Theranos CEO Elizabeth Holmes With Fraud." *Wall Street Journal*, March 14th. https://www.wsj.com/articles/sec-charges-theranos-and-founder-elizabeth-holmes-with-fraud-1521045648.

———. 2018b. *Bad Blood: Secrets and Lies in a Silicon Valley Startup*. New York: Knopf.

Casamatta, Catherine. 2003. "Financing and Advising: Optimal Financial Contracts with Venture Capitalists." *The Journal of Finance* 58 (5): 2059–85.

Casamatta, Catherine, and Carole Haritchabalet. 2014. "Dealing with Venture Capitalists: Shopping Around or Exclusive Negotiation." *Review of Finance* 18 (5): 1743–73.

Cash, Sam. 2017. "Get Ready to See More Sector-Specific Venture Firms." VentureBeat. August 7th. https://venturebeat.com/2017/08/07/get-ready-to-see-more-sector-specific-venture-firms.

Cassar, Gavin. 2009. "Financial Statement and Projection Preparation in Start-Up Ventures." *The Accounting Review* 84 (1): 27–51.

———. 2014. "Industry and Startup Experience on Entrepreneur Forecast Performance in New Firms." *Journal of Business Venturing* 29 (1): 137–51.

Catalini, Christian. 2017. "How Blockchain Technology Will Impact the Digital Economy." *MIT IDE Research Brief* 2017.5.

Catalini, Christian, Chris Foster, and Ramana Nanda. 2018. "Soft Information Versus Bias in New Venture Finance: Machine Intelligence Versus Human Judgement." Mimeo. Harvard University, Harvard Business School.

Catalini, Christian, and Joshua Gans. 2017. "Some Simple Economics of the Blockchain." Mimeo. MIT.

Catalini, Christian, and Xiang Hui. 2018. "Online Syndicates and Startup Investment." Working Paper 24777. NBER.

CB Insights. 2018. "Venture Capital Funnel Shows Odds of Becoming a Unicorn Are About 1%." CB Insights Research. September 6th. https://www.cbinsights.com/research/venture-capital-funnel-2.

Celikyurt, Ugur, Merih Sevilir, and Anil Shivdasani. 2010. "Going Public to Acquire? The Acquisition Motive in IPOs." *Journal of Financial Economics* 96 (3): 345–63.

Cerqueiro, Geraldo, Deepak Hegde, María Fabiana Penas, and Robert Seamans. 2016. "Debtor Rights, Credit Supply, and Innovation." *Management Science* 63 (10): 3311–27.

Cerqueiro, Geraldo, and María Fabiana Penas. 2017. "How Does Personal Bankruptcy Law Affect Startups?" *The Review of Financial Studies* 30 (7): 2523–54.

Cestone, Giacinta. 2014. "Venture Capital Meets Contract Theory: Risky Claims or Formal Control?" *Review of Finance* 18 (3): 1097–1137.

Chaplinsky, Susan, Kathleen Weiss Hanley, and Katie Moon. 2017. "The JOBS Act and the Costs of Going Public." *Journal of Accounting Research* 55 (4): 795–836.

Chatterji, Aaron, Edward Glaeser, and William Kerr. 2014. "Clusters of Entrepreneurship and Innovation." *Innovation Policy and the Economy* 14 (1): 129–66.

Chatterji, Aaron, and Robert Seamans. 2012. "Entrepreneurial Finance, Credit Cards, and Race." *Journal of Financial Economics* 106 (1): 182–95.

Chemmanur, Thomas, Shan He, and Debarshi Nandy. 2010. "The Going-Public Decision and the Product Market." *The Review of Financial Studies* 23 (5): 1855–1908.

Chemmanur, Thomas, Tyler Hull, and Karthik Krishnan. 2016. "Do Local and International Venture Capitalists Play Well Together? The Complementarity of Local and International Venture Capitalists." *Journal of Business Venturing* 31 (5): 573–94.

Chemmanur, Thomas, Karthik Krishnan, and Debarshi Nandy. 2011. "How Does Venture Capital Financing Improve Efficiency in Private Firms? A Look Beneath the Surface." *The Review of Financial Studies* 24 (12): 4037–90.

Chemmanur, Thomas, Elena Loutskina, and Xuan Tian. 2014. "Corporate Venture Capital, Value Creation, and Innovation." *The Review of Financial Studies* 27 (8): 2434–73.

Chen, Hsuan-Chi, and Jay Ritter. 2000. "The Seven Percent Solution." *The Journal of Finance* 55 (3): 1105–31.

Chen, Jing. 2013. "Selection and Serial Entrepreneurs." *Journal of Economics and Management Strategy* 22 (2): 281–311.

Chen, Xiangming, and Taylor Ogan. 2017. "China's Emerging Silicon Valley: How and Why Has Shenzhen Become a Global Innovation Centre." *European Financial Review*, January, 55–62.

Chernenko, Sergey, Josh Lerner, and Yao Zeng. 2017. "Mutual Funds as Venture Capitalists? Evidence from Unicorns." Working Paper 23981. NBER.

Chesbrough, Henry. 2002a. "Graceful Exits and Missed Opportunities: Xerox's Management of Its Technology Spin-off Organizations." *Business History Review* 76 (4): 803–37.

———. 2002b. "Making Sense of Corporate Venture Capital." *Harvard Business Review* 3: 4–11.

Chlepner, Ben-Surge. 1943. *Belgian Banking and Banking Theory*. Washington, DC: The Brookings Institution.

Choo, Eugene. 2005. "Going Dutch: The Google IPO." *Berkeley Technology Law Journal* 20: 405.

Christensen, Clayton. 1997. *The Innovator's Dilemma: When New Technologies Cause Great Firms to Fail*. Cambridge, MA: Harvard Business Press.

Chung, Ji-Woong, Berk Sensoy, Léa Stern, and Michael Weisbach. 2012. "Pay for Performance from Future Fund Flows: The Case of Private Equity." *The Review of Financial Studies* 25 (11): 3259–3304.

Claessens, Stijn, and Leora Klapper. 2005. "Bankruptcy around the World: Explanations of Its Relative Use." *American Law and Economics Review* 7 (1): 253–83.

Clifford, Stephanie. 2007. "Pandora's Long Strange Trip." Inc.Com. October 1st. https://www.inc.com/magazine/20071001/pandoras-long-strange-trip.html.

Cline, Kieth. 2016. "Could CMGi Have Been the Google of Boston?" VentureFizz. October 7th. https://venturefizz.com/stories/boston/could-cmgi-have-been-google-boston.

Coase, Ronald. 1937. "The Nature of the Firm." *Economica* 4 (16): 386–405.

Cochrane, John. 2005. "The Risk and Return of Venture Capital." *Journal of Financial Economics* 75 (1): 3–52.

Cohen, Wesley, and Daniel Levinthal. 1989. "Innovation and Learning: The Two Faces of R & D." *The Economic Journal* 99 (397): 569–96.

———. 1990. "Absorptive Capacity: A New Perspective on Learning and Innovation." *Administrative Science Quarterly* 35 (1): 128–52.

Collins, James, and Jerry Porras. 1994. *Built to Last: Successful Habits of Visionary Companies*. First Edition. New York: HarperBusiness.

Colombo, Massimo, and Kourosh Shafi. 2016. "Swimming with Sharks in Europe: When are They Dangerous and What Can New Ventures Do to Defend Themselves?" *Strategic Management Journal*, 37 (11): 2307–322.

Colyvas, Jeannette, Michael Crow, Annetine Gelijns, Roberto Mazzoleni, Richard Nelson, Nathan Rosenberg, and Bhaven Sampat. 2002. "How Do University Inventions Get Into Practice?" *Management Science* 48 (1): 61–72.

Constine, Josh. 2018. "Here's Why Spotify Will Go Public via Direct Listing on April 3rd." TechCrunch. March 15th. http://social.techcrunch.com/2018/03/15/spotify-direct-listing-date.

Conti Annamaria, Jerry Thursby, and Marie Thursby, 2013. "Patents as Signals for Startup Financing." *Journal of Industrial Economics* 61 (3): 592–622.

Copeland, Tom, and Vladimir Antikarov. 2003. *Real Options: A Practitioner's Guide*. New York: Texere Publishing.

Cornelli, Francesca, and David Goldreich. 2001. "Bookbuilding and Strategic Allocation." *The Journal of Finance* 56 (6): 2337–69.

Cornelli, Francesca, and Oved Yosha. 2003. "Stage Financing and the Role of Convertible Securities." *The Review of Economic Studies* 70 (1): 1–32.

Corradin, Stefano, and Alexander Popov. 2015. "House Prices, Home Equity Borrowing, and Entrepreneurship." *The Review of Financial Studies* 28 (8): 2399–2428.

Cosh, Andy, Douglas Cumming, and Alan Hughes. 2009. "Outside Enterpreneurial Capital." *The Economic Journal* 119 (540): 1494–1533.

Cowgill, Bo, and Eric Zitzewitz. 2015. "Corporate Prediction Markets: Evidence from Google, Ford, and Firm X." *The Review of Economic Studies* 82 (4): 1309–41.

Coyle, John, and Gregg Polsky. 2013. "Acqui-Hiring." *Duke Law Journal* 63 (2): 281.

Cremers, Martijn, Beni Lauterbach, and Anete Pajuste. 2018. "The Life-Cycle of Dual Class Firm Valuation." Finance Working Paper No. 550. European Corporate Governance Institute.

Crichton, Danny. 2018. "Special Report: New York's Enterprise Infrastructure Ecosystem." TechCrunch. April 21st. http://social.techcrunch.com/2018/04/21/new-yorks-enterprise-infrastructure-ecosystem.

Croce, Annalisa, José Martí, and Samuele Murtinu. 2013. "The Impact of Venture Capital on the Productivity Growth of European Entrepreneurial Firms: 'Screening' or 'Value Added' Effect?" *Journal of Business Venturing* 28 (4): 489–510.

Crowley Redding, Anna. 2018. *Google It: A History of Google*. New York: Feiwel & Friends.

Cumming, Douglas. 2008. "Contracts and Exits in Venture Capital Finance." *The Review of Financial Studies* 21 (5): 1947–82.

Cuñat, Vicente, and Emilia García-Appendini. 2012. "Trade Credit and Its Role in Entrepreneurial Finance." In *The Oxford Handbook of Entrepreneurial Finance*, edited by Douglas Cumming, 526–57. New York: Oxford University Press.

Da Rin, Marco, and Thomas Hellmann. 2002. "Banks as Catalysts for Industrialization." *Journal of Financial Intermediation* 11 (4): 366–97.

Da Rin, Marco, Thomas Hellmann, and Manju Puri. 2013. "A Survey of Venture Capital Research." In *Handbook of the Economics of Finance*, edited by George Constantinides, Milton Harris, and René Stulz, 2: 573–648. Amsterdam, North Holland: Elsevier.

Da Rin, Marco, Giovanna Nicodano, and Alessandro Sembenelli. 2006. "Public Policy and the Creation of Active Venture Capital Markets." *Journal of Public Economics* 90 (8): 1699–1723.

Da Rin, Marco, and Ludovic Phalippou. 2017. "The Importance of Size in Private Equity: Evidence from a Survey of Limited Partners." *Journal of Financial Intermediation* 31 (July): 64–76.

Dai, Na, Hoje Jo, and Sul Kassicieh. 2012. "Cross-Border Venture Capital Investments in Asia: Selection and Exit Performance." *Journal of Business Venturing* 27 (6): 666–84.

Dai, Ou, and Xiaohui Liu. 2009. "Returnee Entrepreneurs and Firm Performance in Chinese High-Technology Industries." *International Business Review* 18 (4): 373–86.

Dambra, Michael, Laura Casares Field, and Matthew Gustafson. 2015. "The JOBS Act and IPO Volume: Evidence That Disclosure Costs Affect the IPO Decision." *Journal of Financial Economics* 116 (1): 121–43.

Damodaran, Aswath. 2012. *Investment Valuation: Tools and Techniques for Determining the Value of Any Asset*. Third Edition. New York: John Wiley & Sons.

———. 2018. *The Dark Side of Valuation: Valuing Young, Distressed, and Complex Businesses*. Third Edition. Upper Saddle River, NJ: FT Prentice-Hall.

Davidsson, Per. 2015. "Entrepreneurial Opportunities and the Entrepreneurship Nexus: A Re-Conceptualization." *Journal of Business Venturing* 30 (5): 674–95.

Davila, Antonio, and George Foster. 2005. "Management Accounting Systems Adoption Decisions: Evidence and Performance Implications from Early-Stage/Startup Companies." *The Accounting Review* 80 (4): 1039–68.

———. 2009. "The Adoption and Evolution of Management Control Systems in Entrepreneurial Companies: Evidence and a Promising Future." In *Handbooks of Management Accounting Research*, edited by Christopher Chapman, Anthony Hopwood, and Michael Shields, 3:1323–36. Elsevier.

Davis, E. Philip, and Benn Steil. 2004. *Institutional Investors*. Cambridge, MA: MIT Press.

Davis, Morton. 1997. *Game Theory: A Nontechnical Introduction*. Mineola, NY: Dover Publications.

Dawson, Christopher, David de Meza, Andrew Henley, and Reza Arabsheibani. 2014. "Entrepreneurship: Cause and Consequence of Financial Optimism." *Journal of Economics and Management Strategy* 23 (4): 717–42.

Dealroom. 2018. "Annual European Venture Capital Report." https://blog.dealroom.co/wp-content/uploads/2018/02/Dealroom-2017-vFINAL.pdf.

Decker, Ryan, John Haltiwanger, Ron Jarmin, and Javier Miranda. 2014. "The Role of Entrepreneurship in US Job Creation and Economic Dynamism." *Journal of Economic Perspectives* 28 (3): 3–24.

Degeorge, Francois, Jens Martin, and Ludovic Phalippou. 2016. "On Secondary Buyouts." *Journal of Financial Economics* 120 (1): 124–45.

Delgado, Mercedes, Michael Porter, and Scott Stern. 2010. "Clusters and Entrepreneurship." *Journal of Economic Geography* 10 (4): 495–518.

Demaria, Cyril. 2010. *Introduction to Private Equity*. First Edition. Hoboken, NJ: John Wiley & Sons.

Denison, Daniel. 1990. *Corporate Culture and Organizational Effectiveness*. Corporate Culture and Organizational Effectiveness. Oxford, UK: John Wiley & Sons.

Desouza, Kevin. 2017. *Intrapreneurship: Managing Ideas Within Your Organization*. Rotman-utp Publishing.

Detrixhe, John. 2018. "Robert Shiller Wrote the Book on Bubbles and Still Thinks That's What Bitcoin Is." Quartz. January 25th. https://qz.com/1189516/robert-shiller-said-at-the-wef-in-davos-that-bitcoin-is-characterized-by-speculation.

Devigne, David, Sophie Manigart, and Mike Wright. 2016. "Escalation of Commitment in Venture Capital Decision Making: Differentiating between Domestic and International Investors." *Journal of Business Venturing* 31 (3): 253–71.

Dimov, Dimo, and Hana Milanov. 2010. "The Interplay of Need and Opportunity in Venture Capital Investment Syndication." *Journal of Business Venturing* 25 (4): 331–48.

Dimov, Dimo, and Dean Shepherd. 2005. "Human Capital Theory and Venture Capital Firms: Exploring 'Home Runs' and 'Strike Outs.'" *Journal of Business Venturing* 20 (1): 1–21.

Dixit, Avinash, and Robert Pindyck. 1994. *Investment under Uncertainty*. Princeton, NJ: Princeton University Press.

Djankov, Simeon, Rafael La Porta, Florencio Lopez-de-Silanes, and Andrei Shleifer. 2002. "The Regulation of Entry." *The Quarterly Journal of Economics* 117 (1): 1–37.

Docquier, Frédéric, and Hillel Rapoport. 2012. "Globalization, Brain Drain, and Development." *Journal of Economic Literature* 50 (3): 681–730.

Dorfleitner, Gregor, Jacqueline Rad, and Martina Weber. 2017. "Pricing in the Online Invoice Trading Market: First Empirical Evidence." *Economics Letters* 161 (December): 56–61.

Dowlat, Sherwin. 2018a. "Cryptoasset Market Coverage Initiation: Technical Underpinnings." SATIS Group.

———. 2018b. "Cryptoasset Market Coverage Initiation: Network Creation." SATIS Group.

Driessen, Joost, Tse-Chun Lin, and Ludovic Phalippou. 2012. "A New Method to Estimate Risk and Return of Nontraded Assets from Cash Flows: The Case of Private Equity Funds." *Journal of Financial and Quantitative Analysis* 47 (3): 511–35.

Dunbar, Craig, Stephen Foerster, and Ken Mark. 2018. "Spotify's Direct-Listing IPO." Mimeo, University of Western Ontario.

Durlauf, Steven, and Marcel Fafchamps. 2006. "Chapter 26 - Social Capital." In *Handbook of Economic Growth*, edited by Philippe Aghion and Steven Durlauf, 1639–99. Amsterdam, North Holland: Elsevier.

Duruflé, Gilles, Thomas Hellmann, and Karen Wilson. 2017. "From Start-Up to Scale-Up: Examining Public Policies for the Financing of High-Growth Ventures." In *Finance and Investment: The European Case*, edited by Colin Mayer, Stefano Micossi, Marco Onado, Andrea Polo, and Marco Pagano, 179–219. Oxford, UK: Oxford University Press.

Dushnitsky, Gary, and Markus Fitza. 2018. "Are We Missing the Platforms for the Crowd? Comparing Investment Drivers Across Multiple Crowdfunding Platforms." *Journal of Business Venturing Insights* 10 (November).

Dushnitsky, Gary, and Michael Lenox. 2005. "When Do Firms Undertake R&D by Investing in New Ventures?" *Strategic Management Journal* 26 (10): 947–65.

Dushnitsky, Gary, and Zur Shapira. 2010. "Entrepreneurial Finance Meets Organizational Reality: Comparing Investment Practices and Performance of Corporate and Independent Venture Capitalists." *Strategic Management Journal* 31 (9): 990–1017.

Dushnitsky, Gary, and Myles Shaver. 2009. "Limitations to Interorganizational Knowledge Acquisition: The Paradox of Corporate Venture Capital." *Strategic Management Journal* 30 (10): 1045–64.

Dutta, Supradeep, and Timothy Folta. 2016. "A Comparison of the Effect of Angels and Venture Capitalists on Innovation and Value Creation." *Journal of Business Venturing* 31 (1): 39–54.

Dwoskin, Elizabeth, Rolfe Winkler, and Susan Pulliam. 2015. "Palantir and Investors Spar Over How to Cash In." *Wall Street Journal*, December 29th. https://www.wsj.com/articles/palantir-and-investors-spar-over-how-to-cash-in-1451439352.

Dyck, Alexander, and Lukasz Pomorski. 2016. "Investor Scale and Performance in Private Equity Investments." *Review of Finance* 20 (3): 1081–1106.

Ebrahim, Yasin. 2014. " 'What I Wish I Knew'—Hiring My First Placement Agent." *The Journal of Private Equity* 17 (4): 20–23.

Eckbo, Espen. 2009. "Bidding Strategies and Takeover Premiums: A Review." *Journal of Corporate Finance*, Special Issue on Corporate Control, Mergers, and Acquisitions, 15 (1): 149–78.

Edwards, Jim. 2017. "The Alleged Betrayal Described in These Photos, Texts, and Emails Cost Snapchat $158 Million." Business Insider. February 3rd. https://www.businessinsider.com.au/snapchat-founders-lawsuit-internal-photos-texts-emails-2017-2.

Eesley, Charles, and Edward Roberts. 2012. "Are You Experienced or Are You Talented?: When Does Innate Talent versus Experience Explain Entrepreneurial Performance?" *Strategic Entrepreneurship Journal* 6 (3): 207–19.

Egusa, Conrad, and Veronica O'Shee. 2016. "A Look into Chile's Innovative Startup Government." *TechCrunch* (blog). October 16th. http://social.techcrunch.com/2016/10/16/a-look-into-chiles-innovative-startup-government.

Engineer, Merwan, Paul Schure, and Dan Vo. 2018. "Hide and Seek Search: Why Angels Hide and Entrepreneurs Seek." *Journal of Economic Behavior and Organization* 157 (December): 523–40.

Epure, Mircea, and Martí Guasch. 2019. "Debt Signaling and Outside Investors in Early Stage Firms." *Journal of Business Venturing*, Forthcoming.

Evans, Benedict. 2015. "16 Mobile Theses." Benedict Evans. December 18th. https://www.ben-evans.com/benedictevans/2015/12/15/16-mobile-theses.

Ewens, Michael, and Joan Farre-Mensa. 2018. "The Deregulation of the Private Equity Markets and the Decline in IPOs." Mimeo, California Institute of Technology.

Ewens, Michael, and Matt Marx. 2018. "Founder Replacement and Startup Performance." *The Review of Financial Studies* 31 (4): 1532–65.

Ewens, Michael, Ramana Nanda, and Matthew Rhodes-Kropf. 2018. "Cost of Experimentation and the Evolution of Venture Capital." *Journal of Financial Economics* 128 (3): 422–42.

Ewens, Michael, and Matthew Rhodes-Kropf. 2015. "Is a VC Partnership Greater Than the Sum of Its Partners?" *The Journal of Finance* 70 (3): 1081–1113.

Ewens, Michael, Matthew Rhodes-Kropf, and Ilya Strebulaev. 2016. "Insider Financing and Venture Capital Returns." Mimeo. California Institue of Technology.

Fabozzi, Frank, and Pamela Drake. 2008. "Capital Structure: Lessons from Modigliani and Miller." In *Handbook of Finance*, edited by Frank Fabozzi, 617–22. Hoboken, NJ: John Wiley & Sons.

Fairlie, Robert, Dean Karlan, and Jonathan Zinman. 2015. "Behind the GATE Experiment: Evidence on Effects of and Rationales for Subsidized Entrepreneurship Training." *American Economic Journal: Economic Policy* 7 (2): 125–61.

Fairlie, Robert, Alicia Robb, and David Robinson. 2016. "Black and White: Acess to Capital among Minority-Owned Startups." Mimeo. IZA Institute of Labor Economics.

Falkon, Samuel. 2017. "The Story of the DAO — Its History and Consequences." *Medium* (blog). December 24th. https://medium.com/swlh/the-story-of-the-dao-its-history-and-consequences-71e6a8a551ee.

Fama, Eugene, and Kenneth French. 1993. "Common Risk Factors in the Returns on Stocks and Bonds." *Journal of Financial Economics* 33 (1): 3–56.

———. 1995. "Size and Book-to-Market Factors in Earnings and Returns." *The Journal of Finance* 50 (1): 131–55.

Fan, Wei, and Michelle White. 2003. "Personal Bankruptcy and the Level of Entrepreneurial Activity." *The Journal of Law and Economics* 46 (2): 543–67.

Fang, Lily. 2005. "Investment Bank Reputation and the Price and Quality of Underwriting Services." *The Journal of Finance* 60 (6): 2729–61.

Faulkner, David, Satu Teerikangas, and Richard Joseph. 2014. *The Handbook of Mergers and Acquisitions*. First Edition. Oxford, UK: Oxford University Press.

Federal Reserve Bank of New York. 2017. "Small Business Credit Survey: Report on Startup Firms." https://www.newyorkfed.org/medialibrary/media/smallbusiness/2016/SBCS-Report-StartupFirms-2016.pdf.

Fehder, Daniel, and Yael Hochberg. 2018. "Can Accelerators Accelerate Local High-Growth Entrepreneurship? Evidence from Venture-Backed Startup Activity." Mimeo. Rice University, Jones Graduate School of Business.

Feinstein, Brian, and Craig Netterfield. 2015. "Ten Questions Every Founder Should Ask Before Raising Venture Debt." *TechCrunch* (blog). August 7th. http://social.techcrunch.com/2015/08/07/ten-questions-every-founder-should-ask-before-raising-venture-debt.

Feld, Brad, and Mahendra Ramsinghani. 2014. *Startup Boards: Getting the Most Out of Your Board of Directors*. New York: John Wiley & Sons.

Felser, Josh. 2017. "Founders, Don't Trust Your Venture Capitalists. . . or Should You?" *TechCrunch* (blog). January 19th. http://social.techcrunch.com/2017/01/19/founders-dont-trust-your-venture-capitalists-or-should-you.

Ferreira, Daniel, Gustavo Manso, and André Silva. 2014. "Incentives to Innovate and the Decision to Go Public or Private." *The Review of Financial Studies* 27 (1): 256–300.

Fisch, Christian. 2019. "Initial Coin Offerings (ICOs) to Finance New Ventures." *Journal of Business Venturing* 34 (1): 1–22.

Fitzpatrick, Rob. 2013. *The Mom Test: How to Talk to Customers and Learn If Your Business Is a Good Idea When Everyone Is Lying to You*. First Edition. Leipzig, Germany: CreateSpace Independent Publishing Platform.

Fleischer, Victor. 2008. "Two and Twenty: Taxing Partnership Profits in Private Equity Funds." *New York University Law Review* 83 (1): 1–59.

———. 2011. "Taxing Founders' Stock." *UCLA Law Review* 59: 60.

Florida, Richard. 2012. *The Rise of the Creative Class--Revisited: Revised and Expanded.* Philadelphia: Basic Books.

Florida, Richard, and Charlotta Mellander. 2016. "Rise of the Startup City: The Changing Geography of the Venture Capital Financed Innovation." *California Management Review* 59 (1): 14–38.

Forbes, Daniel, Audrey Korsgaard, and Harry Sapienza. 2010. "Financing Decisions as a Source of Conflict in Venture Boards." *Journal of Business Venturing* 25 (6): 579–92.

Forlani, David, and John Mullins. 2000. "Perceived Risks and Choices in Entrepreneurs' New Venture Decisions." *Journal of Business Venturing* 15 (4): 305–22.

Foster, Richard, and Sarah Kaplan. 2003. *Creative Destruction: Why Companies That Are Built to Last Underperform the Market–And How to Successfully Transform Them.* New York: Crown Business.

Franzoni, Francesco, Eric Nowak, and Ludovic Phalippou. 2012. "Private Equity Performance and Liquidity Risk." *The Journal of Finance* 67 (6): 2341–73.

Freedman, Seth, and Ginger Zhe Jin. 2017. "The Information Value of Online Social Networks: Lessons from Peer-to-Peer Lending." *International Journal of Industrial Organization* 51 (March): 185–222.

Frid, Casey, David Wyman, and William Gartner. 2015. "The Influence of Financial 'Skin in the Game' on New Venture Creation." *Academy of Entrepreneurship Journal* 21 (2): 1–14.

Fried, Frank, Harris, Shriver, and Jacobson LLP. 2018. "The Enduring Allure and Perennial Pitfalls of Earnouts," January. https://www.lexology.com/library/detail.aspx?g= dae677ba-a34c-45f6-ad16-fce8b5791a16.

Fulghieri, Paolo, and Merih Sevilir. 2009. "Organization and Financing of Innovation, and the Choice between Corporate and Independent Venture Capital." *Journal of Financial and Quantitative Analysis* 44 (6): 1291–1321.

Gans, Joshua, David Hsu, and Scott Stern. 2002. "When Does Start-Up Innovation Spur the Gale of Creative Destruction?" *RAND Journal of Economics* 33 (4): 571–86.

Gans, Joshua, Erin Scott, and Scott Stern. 2020. *Entrepreneurial Strategy.* New York: Norton.

Gans, Joshua, and Scott Stern. 2003. "The Product Market and the Market for 'Ideas': Commercialization Strategies for Technology Entrepreneurs." *Research Policy* 32 (2): 333–50.

Gao, Xiaohui, Jay Ritter, and Zhongyan Zhu. 2013. "Where Have All the IPOs Gone?" *Journal of Financial and Quantitative Analysis* 48 (6): 1663–92.

Garg, Sam. 2013a. "Venture Boards: Distinctive Monitoring and Implications for Firm Performance." *Academy of Management Review* 38 (1): 90–108.

———. 2013b. "Microfoundations of Board Monitoring: The Case of Entrepreneurial Firms." *Academy of Management Review* 39 (1): 114–17.

Garg, Sam, and Kathleen Eisenhardt. 2016. "Unpacking the CEO–Board Relationship: How Strategy Making Happens in Entrepreneurial Firms." *Academy of Management Journal* 60 (5): 1828–58.

Geron, Tomio. 2016. "Acquihires from 2005 to Today: From Hype to Pragmatism." Exitround. January 19th. https://exitround.com/acquihires-from-2005-to-today-from-hype-to-pragmatism.

Gerschenkron, Alexander. 1962. *Economic Backwardness in Historical Perspective.* Cambridge, MA: Harvard University Press.

Gilbert, Sara. 2008. *The Story of Google.* Mankato, MN: Creative Education.

Gilson, Ronald. 1999. "The Legal Infrastructure of High Technology Industrial Districts: Silicon Valley, Route 128, and Covenants Not to Compete." *New York University Law Review* 74 (3): 575–627.

Goldberg, Lena, and Chad Carr. 2017. "Washout: The Founders' Tale and the Investors' Tale." Case Study 311–078. Harvard Business School.

Gompers, Paul. 1995. "Optimal Investment, Monitoring, and the Staging of Venture Capital." *The Journal of Finance* 50 (5): 1461–89.

———. 1996. "Grandstanding in the Venture Capital Industry." *Journal of Financial Economics,* 43(1), 133–56.

Gompers, Paul, William Gornall, Steven Kaplan, and Ilya Strebulaev. 2019. "How Do Venture Capitalists Make Decisions?" *Journal of Financial Economics*, Forthcoming.

Gompers, Paul, Joy Ishii, and Andrew Metrick. 2010. "Extreme Governance: An Analysis of Dual-Class Firms in the United States." *The Review of Financial Studies* 23 (3): 1051–88.

Gompers, Paul, Steven Kaplan, and Vladimir Mukharlyamov. 2016. "What Do Private Equity Firms Say They Do?" *Journal of Financial Economics* 121 (3): 449–76.

Gompers, Paul, Anna Kovner, and Josh Lerner. 2009. "Specialization and Success: Evidence from Venture Capital." *Journal of Economics and Management Strategy* 18 (3): 817–44.

Gompers, Paul, Anna Kovner, Josh Lerner, and David Scharfstein. 2008. "Venture Capital Investment Cycles: The Impact of Public Markets." *Journal of Financial Economics* 87 (1): 1–23.

———. 2010. "Performance Persistence in Entrepreneurship." *Journal of Financial Economics* 96 (1): 18–32.

Gompers, Paul, and Josh Lerner. 1996. "The Use of Covenants: An Empirical Analysis of Venture Partnership Agreements." *The Journal of Law and Economics* 39 (2): 463–98.

———. 1998. "The Determinants of Corporate Venture Capital Successes: Organizational Structure, Incentives, and Complementarities." Working Paper 6725. NBER.

———. 1999a. "An Analysis of Compensation in the U.S. Venture Capital Partnership." *Journal of Financial Economics* 51 (1): 3–44.

———. 1999b. "Conflict of Interest in the Issuance of Public Securities: Evidence from Venture Capital." *The Journal of Law and Economics* 42 (1): 1–28.

———. 2000. "Money Chasing Deals? The Impact of Fund Inflows on Private Equity Valuation." *Journal of Financial Economics* 55 (2): 281–325.

Gompers, Paul, Josh Lerner, and David Scharfstein. 2005. "Entrepreneurial Spawning: Public Corporations and the Genesis of New Ventures, 1986 to 1999." *The Journal of Finance* 60 (2): 577–614.

Gompers, Paul, Vladimir Mukharlyamov, and Yuhai Xuan. 2016. "The Cost of Friendship." *Journal of Financial Economics* 119 (3): 626–44.

Gompers, Paul, and Sophie Wang. 2017a. "Diversity in Innovation." Working Paper 23082. NBER.

———. 2017b. "And the Children Shall Lead: Gender Diversity and Performance in Venture Capital." Working Paper 23454. NBER.

Gonder, Ted. 2012. "An Early Assessment of Start-Up Chile (Innovations Case Commentary: Start-Up Chile)." *Innovations: Technology, Governance, Globalization* 7 (2): 29–32.

Gonzalez-Uribe, Juanita, and Michael Leatherbee. 2018. "The Effects of Business Accelerators on Venture Performance: Evidence from Start-Up Chile." *The Review of Financial Studies* 31 (4): 1566–1603.

Gorman, Michael, and William Sahlman. 1989. "What Do Venture Capitalists Do?" *Journal of Business Venturing* 4 (4): 231–48.

Gormley, Brian. 2013. "Surgical-Device Maker Applied Medical Pulls IPO Registration." *Wall Street Journal*, June 5th. https://www.wsj.com/articles/DJFVW00020130605e965smhe7.

Gornall, Will, and Ilya Strebulaev. 2015. "The Economic Impact of Venture Capital: Evidence from Public Companies." Research Paper No 15-55. Stanford University, Stanford Graduate School of Business.

———. 2019. "Squaring Venture Capital Valuations with Reality." *Journal of Financial Economics*, Forthcoming

Graebner, Melissa, Kathleen Eisenhardt, and Philip Roundy. 2010. "Success and Failure in Technology Acquisitions: Lessons for Buyers and Sellers." *Academy of Management Perspectives* 24 (3): 73–92.

Graham, John. 2008. "Taxes and Corporate Finance." In *Handbook of Empirical Corporate Finance*, edited by Espen Eckbo, 59–133. Amsterdam, North Holland: Elsevier.

Graham, John, and Campbell Harvey. 2001. "The Theory and Practice of Corporate Finance: Evidence from the Field." *Journal of Financial Economics* 60 (2): 187–243.

Granovetter, Mark. 1973. "The Strength of Weak Ties." *American Journal of Sociology* 78 (6): 1360–80.

Green, Joseph, and John Coyle. 2016. "Crowdfunding and the Not-So-Safe Safe." *Virginia Law Review Online* 102 (December): 168.

———. 2018. "The SAFE, the KISS, and the Note: A Survey of Startup Seed Financing Contracts." UNC Legal Studies Research Paper.

Grégoire, Denis, and Dean Shepherd. 2012. "Technology-Market Combinations and the Identification of Entrepreneurial Opportunities: An Investigation of the Opportunity-Individual Nexus." *Academy of Management Journal* 55 (4): 753–85.

Grichnik, Dietmar, Jan Brinckmann, Luv Singh, and Sophie Manigart. 2014. "Beyond Environmental Scarcity: Human and Social Capital as Driving Forces of Bootstrapping Activities." *Journal of Business Venturing* 29 (2): 310–26.

Grossman, Sanford, and Oliver Hart. 1986. "The Costs and Benefits of Ownership: A Theory of Vertical and Lateral Integration." *Journal of Political Economy* 94 (4): 691–719.

———. 1988. "One Share-One Vote and the Market for Corporate Control." *Journal of Financial Economics* 20 (1): 175–202.

Guiso, Luigi, Paola Sapienza, and Luigi Zingales. 2009. "Cultural Biases in Economic Exchange?" *The Quarterly Journal of Economics* 124 (3): 1095–1131.

Ha, Anthony. 2019. "Rebooted Startup Program WeWork Labs Celebrates Its One-Year Anniversary." *TechCrunch* (blog). January 30th. http://social.techcrunch.com/2019/01/30/wework-labs-anniversary.

Hall, Bronwyn. 2009. "The Use and Value of IP Rights." Prepared for the UK IP Ministerial Forum on the Economic Value of Intellectual Property.

———. 2016. *Economics of Research and Development*. Edward Elgar, Camberley.

———. 2019. "Tax Policy for Innovation." Mimeo. University of California, Berkely.

Hall, Robert, and Susan Woodward. 2010. "The Burden of the Nondiversifiable Risk of Entrepreneurship." *American Economic Review* 100 (3): 1163–94.

Haltiwanger, John, Ron Jarmin, and Javier Miranda. 2013. "Who Creates Jobs? Small versus Large versus Young." *The Review of Economics and Statistics* 95 (2): 347–61.

Hamm, John. 2002. "Why Entrepreneurs Don't Scale." *Harvard Business Review* 80 (12): 110–15, 134.

Hand, John. 2005. "The Value Relevance of Financial Statements in the Venture Capital Market." *The Accounting Review* 80 (2): 613–48.

———. 2008. "Give Everyone a Prize? Employee Stock Options in Private Venture-Backed Firms." *Journal of Business Venturing* 23 (4): 385–404.

Hao, David. 2018. "The Rise of ICOs: A Comprehensive Primer of Initial Coin Offerings." Medium. January 28th. https://medium.com/the-ledger-group/the-rise-of-icos-a-comprehensive-primer-of-initial-coin-offerings-96050529257.

Hardymon, Felda, Tom Nicholas, and Liz Kind. 2014. "Don Valentine and Sequoia Capital." Case Study 814-096. Harvard Business School.

Harris, Robert, Tim Jenkinson, and Steven Kaplan. 2014. "Private Equity Performance: What Do We Know?" *The Journal of Finance* 69 (5): 1851–82.

———. 2016. "How Do Private Equity Investments Perform Compared to Public Equity?" *Journal of Investment Management* 14 (3): 1–24.

Harrison, David, and Katherine Klein. 2007. "What's the Difference? Diversity Constructs as Separation, Variety, or Disparity in Organizations." *Academy of Management Review* 32 (4): 1199–1228.

Hart, Oliver. 1995. *Firms, Contracts, and Financial Structure*. Oxford, UK: Clarendon Press.

Hart, Oliver, and John Moore. 1990. "Property Rights and the Nature of the Firm." *Journal of Political Economy* 98 (6): 1119–58.

Hayek, Friedrich. 1944. *The Road to Serfdom*. Routledge, Abingdon.

———. 1945. "The Use of Knowledge in Society." *The American Economic Review* 35 (4): 519–30.

Hegde, Deepak, and Justin Tumlinson. 2014. "Does Social Proximity Enhance Business Partnerships? Theory and Evidence from Ethnicity's Role in U.S. Venture Capital." *Management Science* 60 (9): 2355–80.

Helft, Miguel. 2011. "For Buyers of Web Start-Ups, Quest to Corral Young Talent." *The New York Times*, May 17th.

Hellmann, Thomas. 2002. "A Theory of Strategic Venture Investing." *Journal of Financial Economics* 64 (2): 285–314.

———. 2006. "IPOs, Acquisitions, and the Use of Convertible Securities in Venture Capital." *Journal of Financial Economics* 81 (3): 649–79.

———. 2007. "Entrepreneurs and the Process of Obtaining Resources." *Journal of Economics and Management Strategy* 16 (1): 81–109.

———. 2010. "The PROFEX Valuation Model." Mimeo. University of British Columbia, Sauder School of Business.

Hellmann, Thomas, Jeff Blackburn, Stephanie Kozinski, and Matt Murphy. 1996. "Symantec Corporation: Acquiring Entrepreneurial Companies." Case Study SM-27. Stanford University, Stanford Graduate School of Business.

Hellmann, Thomas, and Manju Puri. 2000. "The Interaction between Product Market and Financing Strategy: The Role of Venture Capital." *The Review of Financial Studies* 13 (4): 959–84.

———. 2002. "Venture Capital and the Professionalization of Start-Up Firms: Empirical Evidence." *The Journal of Finance* 57 (1): 169–97.

Hellmann, Thomas, and Veikko Thiele. 2015a. "Friends or Foes? The Interrelationship between Angel and Venture Capital Markets." *Journal of Financial Economics* 115 (3): 639–53.

———. 2015b. "Contracting among Founders." *The Journal of Law, Economics, and Organization* 31 (3): 629–61.

———. 2018. "May the Force Be with You: Investor Power and Company Valuations." Mimeo. University of Oxford, Saïd Business School.

Hellmann, Thomas, and Noam Wasserman. 2016. "The First Deal: The Division of Founder Equity in New Ventures." *Management Science* 63 (8): 2647–66.

Helwege, Jean, and Nellie Liang. 2004. "Initial Public Offerings in Hot and Cold Markets." *Journal of Financial and Quantitative Analysis* 39 (3): 541–69.

Henderson, Rebecca, and Kim Clark. 1990. "Architectural Innovation: The Reconfiguration of Existing Product Technologies and the Failure of Established Firms." *Administrative Science Quarterly* 35 (1): 9–30.

Henrekson, Magnus, and Tino Sanandaji. 2018. "Stock Option Taxation: A Missing Piece in European Innovation Policy?" *Small Business Economics* 51 (2): 411–24.

Herzig, David. 2009. "Carried Interest: Can They Effectively Be Taxed." *Entrepreneurial Business Law Journal* 4 (1): 21.

Hess, Cynthia, Mark Leahy, and Khang Tran. 2018. "Silicon Valley Venture Capital Survey – Second Quarter 2018." September 10th. https://www.fenwick.com/publications/Pages/Silicon-Valley-Venture-Capital-Survey-Second-Quarter-2018.aspx.

Hisrich, Robert, Michael Peters, and Dean Shepherd. 2016. *Entrepreneurship*. Tenth Edition. New York: McGraw-Hill.

Hochberg, Yael. 2012. "Venture Capital and Corporate Governance in the Newly Public Firm." *Review of Finance* 16 (2): 429–80.

Hochberg, Yael, Laura Lindsey, and Mark Westerfield. 2015. "Resource Accumulation through Economic Ties: Evidence from Venture Capital." *Journal of Financial Economics* 118 (2): 245–67.

Hochberg, Yael, Alexander Ljungqvist, and Yang Lu. 2007. "Whom You Know Matters: Venture Capital Networks and Investment Performance." *The Journal of Finance* 62 (1): 251–301.

———. 2010. "Networking as a Barrier to Entry and the Competitive Supply of Venture Capital." *The Journal of Finance* 65 (3): 829–59.

Hochberg, Yael, Alexander Ljungqvist, and Annette Vissing-Jørgensen. 2014. "Informational Holdup and Performance Persistence in Venture Capital." *The Review of Financial Studies* 27 (1): 102–52.

Hochberg, Yael, Michael Mazzeo, and Ryan McDevitt. 2015. "Market Structure and Competition in the Venture Capital Industry." *Review of Industrial Organisation* 46 (4): 323–47.

Hochberg, Yael, Carlos Serrano, and Rosemarie Ziedonis. 2018. "Patent Collateral, Investor Commitment, and the Market for Venture Lending." *Journal of Financial Economics* 130 (1): 74–94.

Holley, Peter. 2018. "The Silicon Valley Elite's Latest Status Symbol: Chickens." Washington Post. March 2nd. https://www.washingtonpost.com/news/business/wp/2018/03/02/feature/the-silicon-valley-elites-latest-status-symbol-chickens.

Holmström, Bengt. 1982. "Moral Hazard in Teams." *The Bell Journal of Economics* 13 (2): 324–40.

Holmström, Bengt, and John Roberts. 1998. "The Boundaries of the Firm Revisited." *Journal of Economic Perspectives* 12 (4): 73–94.

Hombert, Johan, Antoinette Schoar, David Sraer, and David Thesmar. 2014. "Can Unemployment Insurance Spur Entrepreneurial Activity?" Working Paper 20717. NBER.

Horn, John, John Dan Lovallo, and Patrick Viguerie. 2006. "Learning to Let Go: Making Better Exit Decisions." *McKinsey Quarterly,* 2: 64–75.

Horowitz, Ben. 2014. *The Hard Thing About Hard Things: Building a Business When There Are No Easy Answers.* New York: HarperCollins.

Howell, Sabrina, Marina Niessner, and David Yermack. 2018. "Initial Coin Offerings: Financing Growth with Cryptocurrency Token Sales." Working Paper 24774. NBER.

Hower, Lee. 2012. "The Rise and Fall of Great Venture Firms." AgileVC. July 11th. https://agilevc.com/blog/2012/07/11/the-rise-fall-of-great-venture-firms-part-1.

———. 2013. "Angel Investing: Know (What Motivates) Thyself." AgileVC. December 19th. https://agilevc.com/blog/2013/12/19/angel-investing-know-what-motivates-thyself.

Hsu, David. 2004. "What Do Entrepreneurs Pay for Venture Capital Affiliation?" *The Journal of Finance* 59 (4): 1805–44.

———. 2006. "Venture Capitalists and Cooperative Start-up Commercialization Strategy." *Management Science* 52 (2): 204–19.

———. 2007. "Experienced Entrepreneurial Founders, Organizational Capital, and Venture Capital Funding." *Research Policy* 36 (5): 722–41.

Hsu, David, and Martin Kenney. 2005. "Organizing Venture Capital: The Rise and Demise of American Research and Development Corporation, 1946–1973." *Industrial and Corporate Change* 14 (4): 579–616.

Huang, Laura, and Jone Pearce. 2015. "Managing the Unknowable: The Effectiveness of Early-Stage Investor Gut Feel in Entrepreneurial Investment Decisions." *Administrative Science Quarterly* 60 (4): 634–70.

Huet, Ellen, and Olivia Zaleski. 2017. "Silicon Valley's $400 Juicer May Be Feeling the Squeeze." *Bloomberg,* April 19th. https://www.bloomberg.com/news/features/2017-04-19/silicon-valley-s-400-juicer-may-be-feeling-the-squeeze.

Hurst, Erik, and Benjamin Pugsley. 2011. "What Do Small Businesses Do?" *Brookings Papers on Economic Activity* 43 (2): 73–142.

Hvide, Hans, and Georgios Panos. 2014. "Risk Tolerance and Entrepreneurship." *Journal of Financial Economics* 111 (1): 200–23.

Ibrahim, Darian. 2008. "The (Not So) Puzzling Behavior of Angel Investors." *Vanderbilt Law Review* 61: 1405.

———. 2010. "Debt as Venture Capital." *University of Illinois Law Review,* no. 4: 1169–1210.

———. 2012. "The New Exit in Venture Capital." *Vanderbilt Law Review* 65: 1.

Inderst, Roman, and Holger Müller. 2004. "The Effect of Capital Market Characteristics on the Value of Start-up Firms." *Journal of Financial Economics* 72 (2): 319–56.

Ireland, Duane, and Justin Webb. 2007. "Strategic Entrepreneurship: Creating Competitive Advantage through Streams of Innovation." *Business Horizons* 50 (1): 49–59.

Jackson, Susan, Aparna Joshi, and Niclas Erhardt. 2003. "Recent Research on Team and Organizational Diversity: SWOT Analysis and Implications." *Journal of Management* 29 (6): 801–30.

Jaffe, Adam, and Josh Lerner. 2001. "Reinventing Public R&D: Patent Policy and the Commercialization of National Laboratory Technologies." *The RAND Journal of Economics* 32 (1): 167–98.

Jenkinson, Gareth. 2018. "Unpacking the 5 Biggest Cryptocurrency Scams." Cointelegraph. April 18th. https://cointelegraph.com/news/unpacking-the-5-biggest-cryptocurrency-scams.

Jenkinson, Tim, Howard Jones, and Felix Suntheim. 2018. "Quid Pro Quo? What Factors Influence IPO Allocations to Investors?" *The Journal of Finance* 73 (5): 2303–41.

Jorion, Philippe. 2010. *Financial Risk Manager Handbook.* Sixth Edition. Hoboken, NJ: John Wiley & Sons.

Kahneman, Daniel. 2011. *Thinking, Fast and Slow.* New York: Farrar, Straus, and Giroux.

Kandel, Eugene, Dima Leshchinskii, and Harry Yuklea. 2011. "VC Funds: Aging Brings Myopia." *Journal of Financial and Quantitative Analysis* 46 (2): 431–57.

Kaplan, Steven, and Antoinette Schoar. 2005. "Private Equity Performance: Returns, Persistence, and Capital Flows." *The Journal of Finance* 60 (4): 1791–1823.

Kaplan, Steven, Berk Sensoy, and Per Strömberg. 2009. "Should Investors Bet on the Jockey or the Horse? Evidence from the Evolution of Firms from Early Business Plans to Public Companies." *The Journal of Finance* 64 (1): 75–115.

Kaplan, Steven, and Per Strömberg. 2003. "Finincial Contracting Theory Meets the Real World: An Empirical Analysis of Venture Capital Contacts." *The Review of Economic Studies* 70 (2): 281–315.

———. 2004. "Characteristics, Contracts, and Actions: Evidence from Venture Capitalist Analyses." *The Journal of Finance* 59 (5): 2177–2210.

Kapur, Devesh. 2010. *Diaspora, Development, and Democracy: The Domestic Impact of International Migration from India.* Princeton, NJ: Princeton University Press.

Karolyi, Andrew. 2006. "The World of Cross-Listings and Cross-Listings of the World: Challenging Conventional Wisdom." *Review of Finance* 10 (1): 99–152.

Katila, Riitta, Jeff Rosenberger, and Kathleen Eisenhardt. 2008. "Swimming with Sharks: Technology Ventures, Defense Mechanisms and Corporate Relationships." *Administrative Science Quarterly* 53 (2): 295–332.

Kennedy, Gavin. 2008. *Everything Is Negotiable.* Fourth Edition. London: Random House Business.

Kenney, Martin, Dan Breznitz, and Michael Murphree. 2013. "Coming Back Home after the Sun Rises: Returnee Entrepreneurs and Growth of High Tech Industries." *Research Policy* 42 (2): 391–407.

Kenney, Martin, and Urs von Burg. 1999. "Technology, Entrepreneurship and Path Dependence: Industrial Clustering in Silicon Valley and Route 128." *Industrial and Corporate Change* 8 (1): 67–103.

Kerr, Sari, William Kerr, and Tina Xu. 2018. "Personality Traits of Entrepreneurs: A Review of Recent Literature." *Foundations and Trends in Entrepreneurship* 14 (3): 279–356.

Kerr, William. 2008. "Ethnic Scientific Communities and International Technology Diffusion." *The Review of Economics and Statistics* 90 (3): 518–37.

———. 2018. *The Gift of Global Talent: How Migration Shapes Business, Economy and Society.* Stanford, CA: Stanford Business Books.

Kerr, William, Josh Lerner, and Antoinette Schoar. 2014. "The Consequences of Entrepreneurial Finance: Evidence from Angel Financings." *The Review of Financial Studies* 27 (1): 20–55.

Kerr, William, and Ramana Nanda. 2015. "Financing Innovation." *Annual Review of Financial Economics* 7 (1): 445–62.

Kerr, William, Ramana Nanda, and Matthew Rhodes-Kropf. 2014. "Entrepreneurship as Experimentation." *Journal of Economic Perspectives* 28 (3): 25–48.

Kerr, William, and Sari Pekkala Kerr. 2016. "Immigrants Play a Disproportionate Role in American Entrepreneurship." *Harvard Business Review* 95 (5) 2–6.

Kharif, Olga. 2017. "1,000 People Own 40% of the Bitcoin Market." *Bloomberg*, December 8th. https://www.bloomberg.com/news/articles/2017-12-08/the-bitcoin-whales-1-000-people-who-own-40-percent-of-the-market.

Kihlstrom, Richard, and Jean-Jacques Laffont. 1979. "A General Equilibrium Entrepreneurial Theory of Firm Formation Based on Risk Aversion." *Journal of Political Economy* 87 (4): 719–48.

Kirkham, Christopher, and Jennifer Taylor. 2009. "Working through a Workout: A Practitioner's Guide from the Perspective of Private Equity Sponsors, Venture Capital Funds and Other Significant Equity Investors." *Hastings Business Law Journal* 5: 355.

Kirsch, David, Brent Goldfarb, and Azi Gera. 2009. "Form or Substance: The Role of Business Plans in Venture Capital Decision Making." *Strategic Management Journal* 30 (5): 487–515.

Klapper, Leora, Luc Laeven, and Raghuram Rajan. 2006. "Entry Regulation as a Barrier to Entrepreneurship." *Journal of Financial Economics* 82 (3): 591–629.

Klein, Ezra. 2018. "Mark Zuckerberg on Facebook's Hardest Year, and What Comes Next." Vox. April 2nd. http://social.techcrunch.com/2013/11/02/welcome-to-the-unicorn-club.

Klemperer, Paul. 2008. "Network Goods (Theory)." In *The New Palgrave Dictionary of Economics*, edited by Steven Durlauf and Lawrence Blume, Second Edition, 915–17. Basingstoke, UK: Palgrave Macmillan.

Klepper, Steven. 2010. "The Origin and Growth of Industry Clusters: The Making of Silicon Valley and Detroit." *Journal of Urban Economics*, Special Issue: Cities and Entrepreneurship, 67 (1): 15–32.

Klepper, Steven, and Sally Sleeper. 2005. "Entry by Spinoffs." *Management Science* 51 (8): 1291–1306.

Klotz, Anthony, Keith Hmieleski, Bret Bradley, and Lowell Busenitz. 2014. "New Venture Teams: A Review of the Literature and Roadmap for Future Research." *Journal of Management* 40 (1): 226–55.

Knight, Frank. 1921. *Risk, Uncertainty and Profit*. Boston: Houghton Mifflin Company.

Koellinger, Philipp, and Roy Thurik. 2012. "Entrepreneurship and the Business Cycle." *The Review of Economics and Statistics* 94 (4): 1143–56.

Koeplin, John, Atulya Sarin, and Alan Shapiro. 2000. "The Private Company Discount." *Journal of Applied Corporate Finance* 12 (4): 94–101.

Koh, Francis, Winston Koh, and Feichin Tschang. 2005. "An Analytical Framework for Science Parks and Technology Districts with an Application to Singapore." *Journal of Business Venturing*, Special Issue on Science Parks and Incubators, 20 (2): 217–39.

Kolhatkar, Sheelah. 2018. "At Uber, a New C.E.O. Shifts Gears," April 9th. https://www.newyorker.com/magazine/2018/04/09/at-uber-a-new-ceo-shifts-gears.

Koller, Tim, Marc Goedhart, and David Wessels. 2015. *Valuation: Measuring and Managing the Value of Companies*. Sixth Edition. Hoboken, NJ: John Wiley & Sons.

Kollmann, Tobias, Andreas Kuckertz, and Nils Middelberg. 2014. "Trust and Controllability in Venture Capital Fundraising." *Journal of Business Research* 67 (11): 2411–18.

Kornai, János, Eric Maskin, and Géard Roland. 2003. "Understanding the Soft Budget Constraint." *Journal of Economic Literature* 41 (4): 1095–1136.

Korteweg, Arthur, and Stefan Nagel. 2016. "Risk-Adjusting the Returns to Venture Capital." *The Journal of Finance* 71 (3): 1437–70.

Korteweg, Arthur, and Morten Sørensen. 2010. "Risk and Return Characteristics of Venture Capital-Backed Entrepreneurial Companies." *The Review of Financial Studies* 23 (10): 3738–72.

———. 2017. "Skill and Luck in Private Equity Performance." *Journal of Financial Economics* 124 (3): 535–62.

Kortum, Samuel, and Josh Lerner. 2000. "Assessing the Contribution of Venture Capital to Innovation." *The RAND Journal of Economics* 31 (4): 674–92.

Kotha, Reddi, and Gerard George. 2012. "Friends, Family, or Fools: Entrepreneur Experience and Its Implications for Equity Distribution and Resource Mobilization." *Journal of Business Venturing* 27 (5): 525–43.

Krause, Ryan, and Garry Bruton. 2013. "Agency and Monitoring Clarity on Venture Boards of Directors." *Academy of Management Review* 39 (1): 111–14.

Krishna, Anantha. 2018. "Raising Equity across Public and Private Markets: Evidence from the JOBS Act." Mimeo. University of Oxford, Saïd Business School.

Krueger, Norris. 2003. "The Cognitive Psychology of Entrepreneurship." In *Handbook of Entrepreneurship Research: An Interdisciplinary Survey and Introduction*, edited by Zoltan Acs and David Audretsch, 105–40. London: Springer.

Krugman, Paul. 1996. *The Self Organizing Economy*. Malden, MA: Blackwell Publishers.

———. 1998. "What's New about the New Economic Geography?" *Oxford Review of Economic Policy* 14 (2): 7–17.

———. 2011. "The New Economic Geography, Now Middle-Aged." *Regional Studies* 45 (1): 1–7.

Kuchler, Hannah. 2018. "Zuckerberg's Dual Role at Facebook Helm Draws Fresh Fire." *Financial Times*, April 15th.

Kuppuswamy, Venkat, and Barry Bayus. 2017. "Does My Contribution to Your Crowdfunding Project Matter?" *Journal of Business Venturing* 32 (1): 72–89.

Kuratko, Donald. 2016. *Entrepreneurship: Theory, Process, Practice*. Ninth Edition. Mason, OH: Cengage Learning.

La Porta, Rafael, Florencio Lopez-De-Silanes, Andrei Shleifer, and Robert Vishny. 1997. "Legal Determinants of External Finance." *The Journal of Finance* 52 (3): 1131–50.

La Porta, Rafael, Florencio Lopez-de-Silanes, Andrei Shleifer, and Robert Vishny. 2000. "Investor Protection and Corporate Governance." *Journal of Financial Economics* 58 (1): 3–27.

Laffont, Jean-Jacques. 2008. *Fundamentals of Public Economics*. Cambridge, MA: The MIT Press.

Lake, Katrina. 2018. "How Stitch Fix Turned Personal Style into a Data Science Problem." *Harvard Business Review* 96 (3): 35–40.

Landier, Augustin. 2005. "Entrepreneurship and the Stigma of Failure." Mimeo, Available on SSRN.

Lawless, Robert, and Elizabeth Warren. 2005. "The Myth of the Disappearing Business Bankruptcy." *California Law Review* 93 (3): 743–95.

Lazear, Edward. 2005. "Entrepreneurship." *Journal of Labor Economics* 23 (4): 649–80.

Léautier, Thomas-Olivier. 2019. *Imperfect Markets and Imperfect Regulation: An Introduction to the Microeconomics and Political Economy of Power Markets*. MIT Press.

Lécuyer, Christophe. 2005. *Making Silicon Valley: Innovation and the Growth of High Tech, 1930-1970*. Cambridge, MA: MIT Press.

Lee, Aileen. 2013. "Welcome to the Unicorn Club: Learning from Billion-Dollar Startups." TechCrunch. November 2nd. http://social.techcrunch.com/2013/11/02/welcome-to-the-unicorn-club.

Lee, Chong-Moon, William Miller, Marguerite Hancock, and Henry Rowen. 2000. *The Silicon Valley Edge: A Habitat for Innovation and Entrepreneurship*. Stanford, CA: Stanford Business Books.

Lee, David, and Kuo Chuen. 2015. *Handbook of Digital Currency: Bitcoin, Innovation, Financial Instruments, and Big Data*. Amsterdam, North Holland: Academic Press.

Lee, Guo Sun, and Mark McFarlane. 2016. "Taxation of Carried Interest – a Global View." King & Wood Mallesons. July 22nd. https://www.kwm.com/en/uk/knowledge/insights/taxation-of-carried-interest-a-global-view-20160715.

Lee, Matthew, and Julie Battilana. 2013. "How the Zebra Got Its Stripes: Imprinting of Individuals and Hybrid Social Ventures." Working Paper 14–005. Harvard Business School.

Lee, Samuel, and Petra Persson. 2016. "Financing from Family and Friends." *The Review of Financial Studies* 29 (9): 2341–86.

Lee, Seung-Hyun, Yasuhiro Yamakawa, Mike Peng, and Jay Barney. 2011. "How Do Bankruptcy Laws Affect Entrepreneurship Development around the World?" *Journal of Business Venturing* 26 (5): 505–20.

Leleux, Benoît, and Bernard Surlemont. 2003. "Public versus Private Venture Capital: Seeding or Crowding out? A Pan-European Analysis." *Journal of Business Venturing* 18 (1): 81–104.

Lemos, Manoel. 2018. "Brazil's Tech Startups Begin to Expand Globally." TechCrunch. May 8th. http://social.techcrunch.com/2018/05/08/brazils-tech-startups-begin-to-expand-globally.

Leonard-Barton, Dorothy. 1992. "Core Capabilities and Core Rigidities: A Paradox in Managing New Product Development." *Strategic Management Journal* 13 (S1): 111–25.

Lerner, Josh. 1994a. "The Syndication of Venture Capital Investments." *Financial Management* 23 (3): 16–27.

———. 1994b. "Venture Capitalists and the Decision to Go Public." *Journal of Financial Economics* 35 (3): 293–316.

———. 1995. "Venture Capitalists and the Oversight of Private Firms." *The Journal of Finance* 50 (1): 301–18.

———. 2009. *Boulevard of Broken Dreams: Why Public Efforts to Boost Entrepreneurship and Venture Capital Have Failed–and What to Do About It.* Princeton, N.J.: Princeton University Press.

Lerner, Josh, and Antoinette Schoar. 2004. "The Illiquidity Puzzle: Theory and Evidence from Private Equity." *Journal of Financial Economics* 72 (1): 3–40.

———. 2005. "Does Legal Enforcement Affect Financial Transactions? The Contractual Channel in Private Equity." *The Quarterly Journal of Economics* 120 (1): 223–46.

Lerner, Josh, Antoinette Schoar, Stanislav Sokolinski, and Karen Wilson. 2018. "The Globalization of Angel Investments: Evidence across Countries." *Journal of Financial Economics* 127 (1): 1–20.

Lev, Baruch. 2000. *Intangibles: Management, Measurement, and Reporting.* Brookings Institution Press.

Levin, Jack, and Donald Rocap. 2015. *Structuring Venture Capital, Private Equity and Entrepreneurial Transactions.* Wolters Kluwer Law & Business.

Levine, Matt. 2019. "Lyft Is Angry About Lockups." *Bloomberg*, April 8th. https://www.bloomberg.com/opinion/articles/2019-04-08/lyft-is-angry-about-lockups.

Levis, Mario, and Silvio Vismara. 2013. *Handbook of Research on IPOs.* Cheltenham, UK: Edward Elgar.

Lewis, Antony. 2017. "A Gentle Introduction to Initial Coin Offerings (ICOs)." Bits on Blocks. April 25th. https://bitsonblocks.net/2017/04/25/a-gentle-introduction-to-initial-coin-offerings-icos.

Lewis, Michael. 2014. *The New New Thing: A Silicon Valley Story: How Some Man You've Never Heard of Just Changed Your Life.* W. W. Norton & Company.

Li, Feng, and Suraj Srinivasan. 2011. "Corporate Governance When Founders Are Directors." *Journal of Financial Economics* 102 (2): 454–69.

Li, Haiyang, Yan Zhang, Yu Li, Li-An Zhou, and Weiying Zhang. 2012. "Returnees Versus Locals: Who Perform Better in China's Technology Entrepreneurship?" *Strategic Entrepreneurship Journal* 6 (3): 257–72.

Li, Yong, and Tailan Chi. 2013. "Venture Capitalists' Decision to Withdraw: The Role of Portfolio Configuration from a Real Options Lens." *Strategic Management Journal* 34 (11): 1351–66.

Lichtenthaler, Ulrich, and Holger Ernst. 2006. "Attitudes to Externally Organising Knowledge Management Tasks: A Review, Reconsideration and Extension of the NIH Syndrome." *R&D Management* 36 (4): 367–86.

Lindsey, Laura. 2008. "Blurring Firm Boundaries: The Role of Venture Capital in Strategic Alliances." *The Journal of Finance* 63 (3): 1137–68.

Link, Albert, Donald Siegel, and Mike Wright. 2015. *The Chicago Handbook of University Technology Transfer and Academic Entrepreneurship.* Chicago: University of Chicago Press.

Litvak, Kate. 2009. "Venture Capital Limited Partnership Agreements: Understanding Compensation Arrangements." *The University of Chicago Law Review* 76 (1): 161–218.

Liu, Jing, Doron Nissim, and Jacob Thomas. 2002. "Equity Valuation Using Multiples." *Journal of Accounting Research* 40 (1): 135–72.

Liu, Yu, and Markku Maula. 2015. "Local Partnering in Foreign Ventures: Uncertainty, Experiential Learning, and Syndication in Cross-Border Venture Capital Investments." *Academy of Management Journal* 59 (4): 1407–29.

Livingston, Jessica. 2009. *Founders at Work: Stories of Startups' Early Days.* Fourth Edition. Berkeley, CA: Apress.

Ljungqvist, Alexander. 2008. "IPO Underpricing." In *Handbook of Empirical Corporate Finance*, edited by Espen Eckbo, 375–425. Amsterdam, North Holland: Elsevier.

Ljungqvist, Alexander, Vikram Nanda, and Rajdeep Singh. 2006. "Hot Markets, Investor Sentiment, and IPO Pricing." *The Journal of Business* 79 (4): 1667–1702.

Ljungqvist, Alexander, and Matthew Richardson. 2003. "The Cash Flow, Return and Risk Characteristics of Private Equity." Working Paper 9454. NBER.

Lo Pucki, Lynn, and Joseph Doherty. 2007. "Bankruptcy Fire Sales." *Michigan Law Review* 106 (1): 1–59.

Lockett, Andy, and Mike Wright. 2005. "Resources, Capabilities, Risk Capital and the Creation of University Spin-out Companies." *Research Policy*, The Creation of Spin-off Firms at Public Research Institutions: Managerial and Policy Implcations, 34 (7): 1043–57.

Lorenzen, Mark, and Ram Mudambi. 2013. "Clusters, Connectivity and Catch-up: Bollywood and Bangalore in the Global Economy." *Journal of Economic Geography* 13 (3): 501–34.

Loughran, Tim, and Jay Ritter. 2002. "Why Don't Issuers Get Upset About Leaving Money on the Table in IPOs?" *The Review of Financial Studies* 15 (2): 413–44.

Lowry, Michelle, Roni Michaely, and Ekaterina Volkova. 2017. "Initial Public Offerings: A Synthesis of the Literature and Directions for Future Research." *Foundations and Trends in Finance* 11 (3–4): 154–320.

Lucas, Robert. 1988. "On the Mechanics of Economic Development." *Journal of Monetary Economics* 22 (1): 3–42.

Lundun, Ingrid. 2017. "Groupon Closes up 23% after Q4 Report, Says It Paid Nothing for LivingSocial." *TechCrunch* (blog). February 15th. http://social.techcrunch.com/2017/02/15/groupon-q4-livingsocial.

Lyandres, Evgeny, Berardino Palazzo, and Daniel Rabetti. 2019. "Do Tokens Behave Like Securities? An Anatomy of Initial Coin Offerings." Mimeo. Boston University, Questrom School of Business.

Madeira, Antonio. 2019. "The DAO, The Hack, The Soft Fork and The Hard Fork." CryptoCompare. March 12th. https://www.cryptocompare.com/coins/guides/the-dao-the-hack-the-soft-fork-and-the-hard-fork.

Maine, Elicia, and Jon Thomas. 2017. "Raising Financing through Strategic Timing." *Nature Nanotechnology* 12 (2): 93–98.

Maksimovic, Vojislav, Gordon Phillips, and Liu Yang. 2013. "Private and Public Merger Waves." *The Journal of Finance* 68 (5): 2177–2217.

Maksimovic, Vojislav, and Pegaret Pichler. 2001. "Technological Innovation and Initial Public Offerings." *The Review of Financial Studies* 14 (2): 459–94.

Malhotra, Deepak. 2013. "How to Negotiate with VCs." *Harvard Business Review* 91 (5): 84–90.

Malhotra, Deepak, and Keith Murnighan. 2002. "The Effects of Contracts on Interpersonal Trust." *Administrative Science Quarterly* 47 (3): 534–59.

Manso, Gustavo. 2011. "Motivating Innovation." *The Journal of Finance* 66 (5): 1823–60.

———. 2017. "Creating Incentives for Innovation." *California Management Review* 60 (1): 18–32.

March, James. 1991. "Exploration and Exploitation in Organizational Learning." *Organization Science* 2 (1): 71–87.

———. 2008. *Explorations in Organizations.* Stanford, CA: Stanford University Press.

Markman, Gideon, Phillip Phan, David Balkin, and Peter Gianiodis. 2005. "Entrepreneurship and University-Based Technology Transfer." *Journal of Business Venturing*, Special Issue on Science Parks and Incubators, 20 (2): 241–63.

Marom, Dan, Alicia Robb, and Orly Sade. 2016. "Gender Dynamics in Crowdfunding (Kickstarter): Evidence on Entrepreneurs, Investors, Deals and Taste-Based Discrimination." Mimeo.

Martinez, Rodrigo. 2015. "HaaS - An Investment Thesis for Hardware Startups." *Point Nine Land* (blog). June 10th. https://medium.com/point-nine-news/haas-an-investment-thesis-for-hardware-startups-e3500c8d7007.

Marx, Matt. 2011. "The Firm Strikes Back: Non-Compete Agreements and the Mobility of Technical Professionals." *American Sociological Review* 76 (5): 695–712.

Marx, Matt, and Lee Fleming. 2012. "Non-Compete Agreements: Barriers to Entry . . . and Exit?" *Innovation Policy and the Economy* 12 (1): 39–64.

Marx, Matt, and David Hsu. 2015. "Strategic Switchbacks: Dynamic Commercialization Strategies for Technology Entrepreneurs." *Research Policy* 44 (10): 1815–26.

Marx, Matt, Deborah Strumsky, and Lee Fleming. 2009. "Mobility, Skills, and the Michigan Non-Compete Experiment." *Management Science* 55 (6): 875–89.

Maskin, Eric. 1996. "Theories of the Soft Budget-Constraint." *Japan and the World Economy* 8 (2): 125–33.

Maslow, Abraham. 1943. "A Theory of Human Motivation." *Psychological Review* 50 (4): 370–96.

Mason, Heidi, Elizabeth Arrington, and James Mawson. 2019. *Corporate Venturing: A Survival Guide.* Global Corporate Venturing.

Masulis, Ronald, Cong Wang, and Fei Xie. 2009. "Agency Problems at Dual-Class Companies." *The Journal of Finance* 64 (4): 1697–1727.

Matthews, Kayla. 2018. "The Sad Story of Pebble." SmartWatches. February 6th. https://smartwatches.org/learn/sad-story-pebble.

Matusik, Sharon, and Markus Fitza. 2012. "Diversification in the Venture Capital Industry: Leveraging Knowledge under Uncertainty." *Strategic Management Journal* 33 (4): 407–26.

Maula, Markku, Thomas Keil, and Shaker Zahra. 2012. "Top Management's Attention to Discontinuous Technological Change: Corporate Venture Capital as an Alert Mechanism." *Organization Science* 24 (3): 926–47.

Maxwell, Andrew, Scott Jeffrey, and Moren Lévesque. 2011. "Business Angel Early Stage Decision Making." *Journal of Business Venturing* 26 (2): 212–25.

Mayr, Karin, and Giovanni Peri. 2009. "Brain Drain and Brain Return: Theory and Application to Eastern-Western Europe." *The B.E. Journal of Economic Analysis and Policy* 9 (1).

Mazzucato, Mariana. 2013. The Entrepreneurial State: Debunking Public vs. Private Sector Myths. First Edition. London: Anthem Press.

Mead, Winter. 2016. "Why Your Investor Might Pass On Your Next Fund." *Medium* (blog). April   20th.   https://medium.com/sapphire-ventures-perspectives/why-your-investor-might-pass-on-your-next-fund-884dfc34f8d0.

Merton, Robert. 1973. "Theory of Rational Option Pricing." *The Bell Journal of Economics and Management Science* 4 (1): 141–83.

Metrick, Andrew, and Ayako Yasuda. 2010a. "The Economics of Private Equity Funds." *The Review of Financial Studies* 23 (6): 2303–41.

———. 2010b. *Venture Capital and the Finance of Innovation.* Second Edition. Hoboken, N.J: John Wiley & Sons.

Meuleman, Miguel, Mikko Jääskeläinen, Markku Maula, and Mike Wright. 2017. "Venturing into the Unknown with Strangers: Substitutes of Relational Embeddedness in Cross-Border Partner Selection in Venture Capital Syndicates." *Journal of Business Venturing* 32 (2): 131–44.

Michelacci, Claudio, and Javier Suarez. 2004. "Business Creation and the Stock Market." *The Review of Economic Studies* 71 (2): 459–81.

Mikolajczak, Chuck, and Stephen Nellis. 2018. "Spotify Shares Jump in Record-Setting Direct Listing." *Reuters*, April 4th. https://uk.reuters.com/article/uk-spotify-ipo-idUKKCN1HA13X.

Miller-Nobles, Tracie, Brenda Mattison, and Ella Mae Matsumura. 2015. *Horngren's Financial and Managerial Accounting.* Fifth Edition. Boston: Pearson.

Mills, Edwin. 1986. *The Burden of Government.* First Edition. Stanford, CA: Hoover Institution Press.

Milne, Alistair, and Paul Parboteeah. 2016. "The Business Models and Economics of Peer-to-Peer Lending." *European Credit Research Institute Research Report*, no. 17.

Mitchell, Oliver. 2018. "Jibo Social Robot: Where Things Went Wrong." The Robot Report. June 28th. https://www.therobotreport.com/jibo-social-robot-analyzing-what-went-wrong.

Modigliani, Franco, and Merton Miller. 1958. "The Cost of Capital, Corporation Finance and the Theory of Investment." *The American Economic Review* 48 (3): 261–97.

Molla, Rani, and Theodore Schleifer. 2018. "Here's Who Controls Uber After Its Megadeal with   SoftBank."   Recode.   January   8th.   https://www.recode.net/2018/1/8/16865598/uber-softbank-control-board-power-stocks-benchmark-travis-kalanick-dara-khosrowshahi.

Mollick, Ethan. 2014. "The Dynamics of Crowdfunding: An Exploratory Study." *Journal of Business Venturing* 29 (1): 1–16.

———. 2015. "Delivery Rates on Kickstarter." Mimeo, Wharton School, University of Pennsylvania.

Mollick, Ethan, and Ramana Nanda. 2015. "Wisdom or Madness? Comparing Crowds with Expert Evaluation in Funding the Arts." *Management Science* 62 (6): 1533–53.

Moore, Geoffrey. 1991. *Crossing the Chasm: Marketing and Selling High-Tech Products to Mainstream Customers*. New York: HarperBusiness.

Morgenstern, Oskar, and John von Neumann. 1944. *Theory of Games and Economic Behavior*. Princeton, NJ: Princeton University Press.

Morse, Stephanie. 2018. "How Did Phoenix Become the Silicon Valley of EdTech?" AZ Bigmedia. March 12th. https://azbigmedia.com/phoenix-become-silicon-valley-edtech.

Mort, Marshall, and Ariel Gaknoki. 2018. "409A Guidance on Nonqualified Deferred Compensation Plans for Beginners." June 1st. https://www.fenwick.com/publications/pages/409a-guidance-on-nonqualified-deferred-compensation-plans-for-beginners.aspx.

Mowery, David, Richard Nelson, Bhaven Sampat, and Arvids Ziedonis. 2004. *Ivory Tower and Industrial Innovation: University-Industry Technology Transfer Before and After the Bayh-Dole Act*. Stanford, CA: Stanford University Press.

Mullins, John. 2010. *The New Business Road Test: What Entrepreneurs and Executives Should Do before Writing a Business Plan*. Fifth Edition. London: FT Publishing International.

Murnieks, Charles, Melissa Cardon, Richard Sudek, Daniel White, and Wade Brooks. 2016. "Drawn to the Fire: The Role of Passion, Tenacity and Inspirational Leadership in Angel Investing." *Journal of Business Venturing* 31 (4): 468–84.

Myers, Stewart. 2001. "Capital Structure." *The Journal of Economic Perspectives* 15 (2): 81–102.

Nahata, Rajarishi, Sonali Hazarika, and Kishore Tandon. 2014. "Success in Global Venture Capital Investing: Do Institutional and Cultural Differences Matter?" *Journal of Financial and Quantitative Analysis* 49 (4): 1039–70.

Nakamoto, Satoshi. 2009. "Bitcoin: A Peer-to-Peer Electronic Cash System." Mimeo, Available at: https://bitcoin.org/bitcoin.pdf.

Nanda, Ramana, and Tarun Khanna. 2010. "Diasporas and Domestic Entrepreneurs: Evidence from the Indian Software Industry." *Journal of Economics and Management Strategy* 19 (4): 991–1012.

Nanda, Ramana, and Matthew Rhodes-Kropf. 2013. "Investment Cycles and Startup Innovation." *Journal of Financial Economics* 110 (2): 403–18.

———. 2016. "Financing Risk and Innovation." *Management Science* 63 (4): 901–18.

Nanda, Ramana, Sampsa Samila, and Olav Sorenson. 2018. "The Persistent Effect of Initial Success: Evidence from Venture Capital." Working Paper 24887. NBER.

Narayanan, Arvind, Joseph Bonneau, Edward Felten, Andrew Miller, and Steven Goldfeder. 2016. *Bitcoin and Cryptocurrency Technologies: A Comprehensive Introduction*. Princeton, NJ: Princeton University Press.

Nash, John. 1950. "The Bargaining Problem." *Econometrica* 18 (2): 155–62.

Neher, Darwin. 1999. "Staged Financing: An Agency Perspective." *The Review of Economic Studies* 66 (2): 255–74.

Newton, Grant. 2003. *Corporate Bankruptcy: Tools, Strategies and Alternatives*. Hoboken, NJ: John Wiley & Sons.

Nielsen, Sabina. 2010. "Top Management Team Diversity: A Review of Theories and Methodologies." *International Journal of Management Reviews* 12 (3): 301–16.

Nisen, Max. 2013. "Here's What 'Shark Tank' Looks Like In 9 Different Countries." Business Insider. November 12th. https://www.businessinsider.com/shark-tank-international-versions-2013-11.

O'Connor, Allan, Erik Stam, Fiona Sussan, and David Audretsch. 2018. *Entrepreneurial Ecosystems: Place-Based Transformations and Transitions*. International Studies in Entrepreneurship. Springer International Publishing.

OECD. 2017. *Entrepreneurship at a Glance*. Paris: OECD Publishing.

O'Neill, Cara. 2017. *The New Bankruptcy: Will It Work for You?* Seventh Edition. Berkeley, CA: NOLO.

Osterwalder, Alexander, and Yves Pigneur. 2010. *Business Model Generation: A Handbook for Visionaries, Game Changers, and Challengers*. Hoboken, NJ: John Wiley & Sons.

Osterwalder, Alexander, Yves Pigneur, Gregory Bernarda, Trish Papadakos, and Alan Smith. 2014. *Value Proposition Design: How to Create Products and Services Customers Want*. Hoboken, NJ: John Wiley & Sons.

Ostrom, Elinor. 1965. "Public Entrepreneurship: A Case Study in Ground Water Basin Management." Doctoral Dissertation. University of California, Los Angeles.

Ostrom, Elinor, and James Walker. 2003. *Trust and Reciprocity: Interdisciplinary Lessons for Experimental Research*. New York: Russell Sage Foundation.

Ostrom, Elinor, and Gordon Whitaker. 1973. "Does Local Community Control of Police Make a Difference? Some Preliminary Findings." *American Journal of Political Science* 17 (1): 48–76.

Ozmel, Umit, and Isin Guler. 2015. "Small Fish, Big Fish: The Performance Effects of the Relative Standing in Partners' Affiliate Portfolios." *Strategic Management Journal* 36 (13): 2039–57.

Ozmel, Umit, Jeffrey Reuer, and Cheng-Wei Wu. 2017. "Interorganizational Imitation and Acquisitions of High-Tech Ventures." *Strategic Management Journal* 38 (13): 2647–65.

Ozmel, Umit, David Robinson, and Toby Stuart. 2013. "Strategic Alliances, Venture Capital, and Exit Decisions in Early Stage High-Tech Firms." *Journal of Financial Economics* 107 (3): 655–70.

Padilla, Jose. 2001. "What's Wrong with a Washout: Fiduciary Duties of the Venture Capitalist Investor in a Washout Financing." *Houston Business and Tax Law Journal* 1: 269.

Pagano, Marco, Fabio Panetta, and Luigi Zingales. 1998. "Why Do Companies Go Public? An Empirical Analysis." *The Journal of Finance* 53 (1): 27–64.

Paik, Yongwook. 2014. "Serial Entrepreneurs and Venture Survival: Evidence from U.S. Venture-Capital-Financed Semiconductor Firms." *Strategic Entrepreneurship Journal* 8 (3): 254–68.

Palladino, Michael. 2001. *Understanding The Human Genome Project*. First Edition. New York: Pearson.

Panchadar, Arjun, and Vibhuti Sharma. 2018. "Sirius XM to Buy Pandora in $3.5 Billion Streaming Push." *Reuters*, September 24th. https://uk.reuters.com/article/uk-pandora-m-a-sirius-xm-holdings-idUKKCN1M4190.

Parhankangas, Annaleena, and Michael Ehrlich. 2014. "How Entrepreneurs Seduce Business Angels: An Impression Management Approach." *Journal of Business Venturing* 29 (4): 543–64.

Park, Haemin Dennis, and Kevin Steensma. 2012. "When Does Corporate Venture Capital Add Value for New Ventures?" *Strategic Management Journal* 33 (1): 1–22.

Parker, Simon. 2011. "Intrapreneurship or Entrepreneurship?" *Journal of Business Venturing* 26 (1): 19–34.

———. 2013. "Do Serial Entrepreneurs Run Successively Better-Performing Businesses?" *Journal of Business Venturing* 28 (5): 652–66.

Paruchuri, Srikanth, Atul Nerkar, and Donald Hambrick. 2006. "Acquisition Integration and Productivity Losses in the Technical Core: Disruption of Inventors in Acquired Companies." *Organization Science* 17 (5): 545–62.

Pekkala Kerr, Sari, William Kerr, Ozden Çaglar, and Christopher Parsons. 2016. *Global Talent Flows*. Policy Research Working Papers. The World Bank.

Petersen, Mitchell, and Raghuram Rajan. 1994. "The Benefits of Lending Relationships: Evidence from Small Business Data." *The Journal of Finance* 49 (1): 3–37.

Phalippou, Ludovic. 2010. "Venture Capital Funds: Flow-Performance Relationship and Performance Persistence." *Journal of Banking and Finance* 34 (3): 568–77.

Phalippou, Ludovic, and Oliver Gottschalg. 2009. "The Performance of Private Equity Funds." *The Review of Financial Studies* 22 (4): 1747–76.

Plattner, Hasso, Christoph Meinel, and Larry Leifer. 2010. *Design Thinking: Understand – Improve – Apply*. Berlin, Germany: Springer.

Podolny, Joel. 2001. "Networks as the Pipes and Prisms of the Market." *American Journal of Sociology* 107 (1): 33–60.

Pollock, Timothy, and Ranjay Gulati. 2007. "Standing out from the Crowd: The Visibility-Enhancing Effects of IPO-Related Signals on Alliance Formation by Entrepreneurial Firms." *Strategic Organization* 5 (4): 339–72.

Polsky, Gregg, and Brant Hellwig. 2012. "Examining the Tax Advantage of Founders Stock." *Iowa Law Review* 97: 1085.

Popov, Alexander, and Peter Roosenboom. 2012. "Venture Capital and Patented Innovation: Evidence from Europe." *Economic Policy* 27 (71): 447–82.

Pozen, Robert. 2007. "If Private Equity Sized up Your Business." *Harvard Business Review* 85 (11): 78–87, 152.

Primack, Dan. 2013. "The Kicking and Screaming IPO." Fortune. January 7th. http://fortune.com/2013/01/07/the-kicking-and-screaming-ipo.

Puranam, Phanish, and Kannan Srikanth. 2007. "What They Know vs. What They Do: How Acquirers Leverage Technology Acquisitions." *Strategic Management Journal* 28 (8): 805–25.

Puri, Manju, and David Robinson. 2007. "Optimism and Economic Choice." *Journal of Financial Economics* 86 (1): 71–99.

Puri, Manju, and Rebecca Zarutskie. 2012. "On the Life Cycle Dynamics of Venture-Capital- and Non-Venture-Capital-Financed Firms." *The Journal of Finance* 67 (6): 2247–93.

Qin, Fei, Mike Wright, and Jian Gao. 2017. "Are 'Sea Turtles' Slower? Returnee Entrepreneurs, Venture Resources and Speed of Entrepreneurial Entry." *Journal of Business Venturing* 32 (6): 694–706.

Quintero, Sebastian. 2017. "How Much Runway Should You Target between Financing Rounds?" *Medium* (blog). October 26th. https://medium.com/radicle/how-much-runway-should-you-target-between-financing-rounds-478b1616cfb5.

Ragozzino, Roberto, and Dane Blevins. 2016. "Venture–Backed Firms: How Does Venture Capital Involvement Affect Their Likelihood of Going Public or Being Acquired?" *Entrepreneurship Theory and Practice* 40 (5): 991–1016.

Ram, Sundaresan, and Jagdish Sheth. 1989. "Consumer Resistance to Innovations: The Marketing Problem and Its Solutions." *Journal of Consumer Marketing* 6 (2): 5–14.

Ramadan, Al, Christopher Lockhead, Dave Peterson, and Kevin Maney. 2015. "Time to Market Cap: The New Metric That Matters." *A Category Design Research Report,* Play Bigger Advisors, LLC.

Rao, Leena. 2011. "Pandora Prices IPO At $16 Per Share, Now Valued At $2.6 Billion." TechCrunch. June 14th. http://social.techcrunch.com/2011/06/14/pandora-prices-ipo-at-16-per-share-now-valued-at-2-6-billion.

Rassenfosse, Gaétan de, and Timo Fischer. 2016. "Venture Debt Financing: Determinants of the Lending Decision." *Strategic Entrepreneurship Journal* 10 (3): 235–56.

Reinganum, Jennifer. 1983. "Uncertain Innovation and the Persistence of Monopoly." *The American Economic Review* 73 (4): 741–48.

Repullo, Rafael, and Javier Suarez. 2004. "Venture Capital Finance: A Security Design Approach." *Review of Finance* 8 (1): 75–108.

Reynolds, Garr. 2011. *Presentation Zen: Simple Ideas on Presentation Design and Delivery.* Second Edition. Berkeley, CA: New Riders.

Ries, Eric. 2011. *The Lean Startup: How Today's Entrepreneurs Use Continuous Innovation to Create Radically Successful Businesses.* New York: Crown Business.

Ritter, Jay. 2003. "Chapter 5 - Investment Banking and Securities Issuance." In *Handbook of the Economics of Finance,* edited by George Constantinides, Milton Harris, and René Stulz, 1:255–306. Corporate Finance. Amsterdam, North Holland: Elsevier.

Robb, Alicia, and David Robinson. 2012. "The Capital Structure Decisions of New Firms." *The Review of Financial Studies* 27 (1): 153–79.

———. 2014. "The Capital Structure Decisions of New Firms." *The Review of Financial Studies* 27 (1): 153–79.

Roberts, Jeff. 2018. "Polychain Becomes First $1 Billion Crypto Fund: What Happens Now?" Fortune. June 26th. http://fortune.com/2018/06/26/polychain-capital-bitcoin.

Robinson, David, and Berk Sensoy. 2013. "Do Private Equity Fund Managers Earn Their Fees? Compensation, Ownership, and Cash Flow Performance." *The Review of Financial Studies* 26 (11): 2760–97.

———. 2016. "Cyclicality, Performance Measurement, and Cash Flow Liquidity in Private Equity." *Journal of Financial Economics* 122 (3): 521–43.

Robinson, David, and Toby Stuart. 2007. "Financial Contracting in Biotech Strategic Alliances." *The Journal of Law and Economics* 50 (3): 559–96.

Robinson, Randolph. 2018. "The New Digital Wild West: Regulating the Explosion of Initial Coin Offerings." *Tennessee Law Review*, 85 (4): 897–960.

Rochet, Jean-Charles, and Jean Tirole. 2003. "Platform Competition in Two-Sided Markets." *Journal of the European Economic Association* 1 (4): 990–1029.

———. 2006. "Two-Sided Markets: A Progress Report." *The RAND Journal of Economics* 37 (3): 645–67.

Rock, Arthur. 1987. "Strategy Vs. Tactics from a Venture Capitalist." *Harvard Business Review* 65 (6): 1–5.

Rodríguez Fernández, Clara. 2019. "Equity Crowdfunding for Biotech Startups: Does It Work?" Labiotech. January 30th. https://labiotech.eu/features/equity-crowdfunding-biotech-startups.

Rogers, Everett. 2003. *Diffusion of Innovations*. New York: Free Press.

Rohr, Jonathan, and Aaron Wright. 2018. "Blockchain-Based Token Sales, Initial Coin Offerings, and the Democratization of Public Capital Markets." University of Tennessee Legal Studies Research Paper No. 338.

Romer, Paul. 1986. "Increasing Returns and Long-Run Growth." *Journal of Political Economy* 94 (5): 1002–37.

———. 1990. "Endogenous Technological Change." *Journal of Political Economy* 98 (5): 71–102.

———. 1994. "The Origins of Endogenous Growth." *Journal of Economic Perspectives* 8 (1): 3–22.

Rosen, Alex, and Auren Hoffman. 2018. "An inside Look into a Venture Negotiation." *TechCrunch* (blog). February 6th. http://social.techcrunch.com/2018/02/06/an-inside-look-into-a-venture-negotiation.

Roth, Alvin, and Marilda Sotomayor. 1992. "Two-Sided Matching." In *Handbook of Game Theory with Economic Application, Vol. 1*, edited by Robert Aumann and Sergiu Hart, 485–541. Amsterdam: North-Holland.

Rothaermel, Frank, and David Deeds. 2004. "Exploration and Exploitation Alliances in Biotechnology: A System of New Product Development." *Strategic Management Journal* 25 (3): 201–21.

Ruef, Michael, Howard Aldrich, and Nancy Carter. 2003. "The Structure of Founding Teams: Homophily, Strong Ties, and Isolation among U.S. Entrepreneurs." *American Sociological Review* 68 (2): 195–222.

Russell, Jon. 2017. "Former Mozilla CEO Raises $35M in under 30 Seconds for His Browser Startup Brave." *TechCrunch* (blog). June 1st. http://social.techcrunch.com/2017/06/01/brave-ico-35-million-30-seconds-brendan-eich.

Russell, Jon, and Mike Butcher. 2018. "Telegram's Billion-Dollar ICO Has Become a Mess." TechCrunch. May 3rd. http://social.techcrunch.com/2018/05/03/telegrams-billion-dollar-ico-has-become-a-mess.

Rysman, Marc. 2009. "The Economics of Two-Sided Markets." *Journal of Economic Perspectives* 23 (3): 125–43.

Sahlman, William. 1990. "The Structure and Governance of Venture-Capital Organizations." *Journal of Financial Economics* 27 (2): 473–521.

Samila, Sampsa, and Olav Sorenson. 2011a. "Venture Capital, Entrepreneurship, and Economic Growth." *The Review of Economics and Statistics* 93 (1): 338–49.

———. 2011b. "Noncompete Covenants: Incentives to Innovate or Impediments to Growth." *Management Science* 57 (3): 425–38.

———. 2017. "Community and Capital in Entrepreneurship and Economic Growth." *American Sociological Review* 82 (4): 770–95.

Samonas, Michael. 2015. *Financial Forecasting, Analysis, and Modelling: A Framework for Long-Term Forecasting*. Chichester, UK: John Wiley & Sons.

Sapienza, Harry. 1992. "When Do Venture Capitalists Add Value?" *Journal of Business Venturing* 7 (1): 9–27.

Sapienza, Harry, and Anil Gupta. 1994. "Impact of Agency Risks and Task Uncertainty on Venture Capitalist–CEO Interaction." *Academy of Management Journal* 37 (6): 1618–32.

Sapienza, Harry, Sophie Manigart, and Wim Vermeir. 1996. "Venture Capitalist Governance and Value Added in Four Countries." *Journal of Business Venturing* 11 (6): 439–69.

Saxenian, Annalee. 1994. *Regional Advantage: Culture and Competition in Silicon Valley and Route 128*. Cambridge, MA: Harvard University Press.

———. 2002. "Transnational Communities and the Evolution of Global Production Networks: The Cases of Taiwan, China and India." *Industry and Innovation* 9 (3): 183–202.

Schein, Edgar. 1988. *Organizational Culture and Leadership*. San Francisco, CA: Jossey-Bass.

Schertler, Andrea, and Tereza Tykvová. 2011. "Venture Capital and Internationalization." *International Business Review* 20 (4): 423–39.

Schilling, Melissa. 2016. *Strategic Management of Technological Innovation*. Fifth Edition. New York: McGraw-Hill Education.

Schmalz, Martin, David Sraer, and David Thesmar. 2017. "Housing Collateral and Entrepreneurship." *The Journal of Finance* 72 (1): 99–132.

Schoar, Antoinette. 2010. "The Divide between Subsistence and Transformational Entrepreneurship." *Innovation Policy and the Economy* 10 (1): 57–81.

Schramm, Carl. 2018. *Burn the Business Plan: What Great Entrepreneurs Really Do*. New York: Simon & Schuster.

Schumpeter, Joseph. 1934. *The Theory of Economic Development: An Inquiry into Profits, Capital, Credit, Interest, and the Business Cycle*. New Brunswick, NJ: Transaction Publishers.

———. 1942. *Capitalism, Socialism and Democracy*. London: Routledge.

Sedláček, Petr, and Vincent Sterk. 2017. "The Growth Potential of Startups over the Business Cycle." *American Economic Review* 107 (10): 3182–210.

Seligman, Joel. 2003. *The Transformation of Wall Street: A History of the Securities and Exchange Commission and Modern Corporate Finance*. Third Edition. New York: Aspen Publishers.

Senbet, Lemma, and Tracy Yue Wang. 2012. "Corporate Financial Distress and Bankruptcy: A Survey." *Foundations and Trends in Finance* 5 (4): 243–335.

Senor, Dan, and Saul Singer. 2011. *Start-Up Nation: The Story of Israel's Economic Miracle*. New York: Twelfth Edition.

Sensoy, Berk, Yingdi Wang, and Michael Weisbach. 2014. "Limited Partner Performance and the Maturing of the Private Equity Industry." *Journal of Financial Economics* 112 (3): 320–43.

Shane, Scott. 2003. *A General Theory of Entrepreneurship: The Individual-Opportunity Nexus*. New York: Edward Elgar.

———. 2004. *Academic Entrepreneurship: University Spinoffs and Wealth Creation*. Cheltenham, UK: Elgar Publishing.

———. 2012. "Start Up Failure Rates: The Definitive Numbers." *Small Business Trends* (blog). December 17th. https://smallbiztrends.com/2012/12/start-up-failure-rates-the-definitive-numbers.html.

Shane, Scott, and Daniel Cable. 2002. "Network Ties, Reputation, and the Financing of New Ventures." *Management Science* 48 (3): 364–81.

Shankar, Raj, and Dean Shepherd. 2019. "Accelerating Strategic Fit or Venture Emergence: Different Paths Adopted by Corporate Accelerators." *Journal of Business Venturing*, Forthcoming.

Shapiro, Carl, and Hal Varian. 1998. *Information Rules: A Strategic Guide to the Network Economy*. Cambridge, MA: Harvard Business Press.

Shepherd, Dean, and Holger Patzelt. 2018. *Entrepreneurial Cognition: Exploring the Mindset of Entrepreneurs*. Cham, Switzerland: Palgrave Macmillan.

Shiller, Robert. 1981. "Do Stock Prices Move Too Much to Be Justified by Subsequent Changes in Dividends?" *American Economic Review* 71 (3): 421–36.

———. 2016. *Irrational Exuberance*. Third Edition. Princeton, NJ: Princeton University Press.

Shleifer, Andrei, and Robert Vishny. 1997. "A Survey of Corporate Governance." *The Journal of Finance* 52 (2): 737–83.

Shubber, Kadhim. 2017. "A Look at an Early Deliveroo Investor Deck." Financial Times. December 5th. http://ftalphaville.ft.com/2017/12/05/2196397/a-look-at-an-early-deliveroo-investor-deck.

Simmons, Sharon, Johan Wiklund, and Jonathan Levie. 2014. "Stigma and Business Failure: Implications for Entrepreneurs' Career Choices." *Small Business Economics* 42 (3): 485–505.

Singh, Jasjit, and Ajay Agrawal. 2011. "Recruiting for Ideas: How Firms Exploit the Prior Inventions of New Hires." *Management Science* 57 (1): 129–50.

Smith, Douglas, and Robert Alexander. 1988. *Fumbling the Future: How Xerox Invented, Then Ignored, the First Personal Computer*. New York: William Morrow.

Smith, Gordon. 2005. "The Exit Structure of Venture Capital." *UCLA Law Review* 53: 315.

Soh, Pek-Hooi. 2010. "Network Patterns and Competitive Advantage before the Emergence of a Dominant Design." *Strategic Management Journal* 31 (4): 438–61.

Solow, Robert. 2000. *Growth Theory: An Exposition*. Second Edition. New York: Oxford University Press.

Somerville, Heather. 2017. "Uber Battle Escalates as Investors Try to Intervene in Benchmark." *Reuters*, August 25th. https://www.reuters.com/article/us-uber-benchmark-lawsuit-idUSKCN1B42FP.

Sørensen, Morten. 2007. "How Smart Is Smart Money? A Two-Sided Matching Model of Venture Capital." *The Journal of Finance* 62 (6): 2725–62.

Sørensen, Morten, and Ravi Jagannathan. 2015. "The Public Market Equivalent and Private Equity Performance." *Financial Analysts Journal* 71 (4): 43–50.

Sorenson, Olav, and Toby Stuart. 2001. "Syndication Networks and the Spatial Distribution of Venture Capital Investments." *American Journal of Sociology* 106 (6): 1546–88.

———. 2008. "Bringing the Context Back In: Settings and the Search for Syndicate Partners in Venture Capital Investment Networks." *Administrative Science Quarterly* 53 (2): 266–94.

Spradley, James. 2016. *Participant Observation*. Long Grove, IL: Waveland Press.

Stam, Erik. 2015. "Entrepreneurial Ecosystems and Regional Policy: A Sympathetic Critique." *European Planning Studies* 23 (9): 1759–69.

Stam, Erik, and Ben Spigel. 2018. "Entrepreneurial Ecosystems." In *The SAGE Handbook of Small Business and Entrepreneurship*, edited by Robert Blackburn, Dirk De Clercq, and Jarna Heinonen. London: SAGE Publications.

Starr, Ross. 2011. *General Equilibrium Theory: An Introduction*. Second Edition. Cambridge, UK: Cambridge University Press.

Stein, Jeremy. 1989. "Efficient Capital Markets, Inefficient Firms: A Model of Myopic Corporate Behavior." *The Quarterly Journal of Economics* 104 (4): 655–69.

Stempel, Johnathan. 2011. "Winklevoss Twins End Appeal of Facebook Settlement." *Reuters*, June 23rd. https://www.reuters.com/article/us-facebook-winklevoss/winklevoss-twins-end-appeal-of-facebook-settlement-idUSTRE75L7NS20110623.

Stevenson, Howard, Michael Roberts, and Irving Grousbeck. 1998. *New Business Ventures and the Entrepreneur*. Fourth Edition. Homewood, IL: McGraw-Hill.

Stewart, Alan. 2015. *Approved!: An Insider's Guide to Getting Your Bank Loan Approved*. San Diego, CA: SmallBizTraining, Inc.

Stiglitz, Joseph. 1989. *The Economic Role of the State*. Cambridge, MA: Blackwell.

Stiglitz, Joseph, and Andrew Weiss. 1981. "Credit Rationing in Markets with Imperfect Information." *The American Economic Review* 71 (3): 393–410.

Stuart, Toby, and Olav Sorenson. 2003. "Liquidity Events and the Geographic Distribution of Entrepreneurial Activity." *Administrative Science Quarterly* 48 (2): 175–201.

Sturgeon, Timothy. 2000. "How Silicon Valley Came to Be." In *Understanding the Silicon Valley: Anatomy of an Entrepreneurial Region*, edited by Martin Kenney, 23–47. Stanford, CA: Stanford University Press.

Suarez, Fernando, Stine Grodal, and Aleksios Gotsopoulos. 2015. "Perfect Timing? Dominant Category, Dominant Design, and the Window of Opportunity for Firm Entry." *Strategic Management Journal* 36 (3): 437–48.

Sunstein, Cass, and Richard Thaler. 2008. *Nudge: Improving Decisions About Health, Wealth and Happiness*. New Haven, CT: Yale University Press.

Sussman, Davis. 2014. "Private Equity Funds Clawbacks and Investor Givebacks." *Duane Morris,* August.

Swift, Taylor. 2014. "For Taylor Swift, the Future of Music Is a Love Story." *Wall Street Journal,* July 7th.

Swift, Tim. 2016. "The Perilous Leap between Exploration and Exploitation." *Strategic Management Journal* 37 (8): 1688–98.

Takahashi, Dean. 2018. "Star Citizen Creator Cloud Imperium Games Raised $46 Million to Launch Big Game in 2020." *VentureBeat* (blog). December 20th. https://venturebeat.com/2018/12/20/star-citizen-creator-cloud-imperium-games-raised-46-million-to-launch-big-game-in-2020.

Taylor, Kate. 2017. "A Forgotten Stitch Fix Cofounder Likely Walked Away Empty-Handed after the Startup's $1.6 Billion IPO." Business Insider. November 17th. https://www.businessinsider.com.au/stitch-fix-forgotten-cofounder-2017-11.

Teece, David. 1986. "Profiting from Technological Innovation: Implications for Integration, Collaboration, Licensing and Public Policy." *Research Policy* 15 (6): 285–305.

———. 2007. "Explicating Dynamic Capabilities: The Nature and Microfoundations of (Sustainable) Enterprise Performance." *Strategic Management Journal* 28 (13): 1319–50.

———. 2010. "Business Models, Business Strategy and Innovation." *Long Range Planning,* Business Models, 43 (2): 172–94.

Teece, D.J., Pisano, G. and Shuen, A. 1997. "Dynamic Capabilities and Strategic Management." *Strategic Management Journal,* 18, 509–33.

The Economist. 2018. "How Flixbus Conquered the European Coach Market," May 10th. https://www.economist.com/business/2018/05/10/how-flixbus-conquered-the-european-coach-market.

Thomas, Oliver. 2018. "Two Decades of Cognitive Bias Research in Entrepreneurship: What Do We Know and Where Do We Go from Here?" *Management Review Quarterly* 68 (2): 107–43.

Tian, Xuan. 2011. "The Causes and Consequences of Venture Capital Stage Financing." *Journal of Financial Economics* 101 (1): 132–59.

———. 2012. "The Role of Venture Capital Syndication in Value Creation for Entrepreneurial Firms." *Review of Finance* 16 (1): 245–83.

Tian, Xuan, and Tracy Wang. 2014. "Tolerance for Failure and Corporate Innovation." *The Review of Financial Studies* 27 (1): 211–55.

Timmons, Jeffry, and Stephen Spinelli. 2008. *New Venture Creation: Entrepreneurship for the 21st Century.* Sixth Edition. Boston: McGraw-Hill.

Ting, Xu. 2017. "Learning from the Crowd: The Feedback Value of Crowdfunding." Mimeo. University of Virginia, Darden School of Business.

Tversky, Amos, and Daniel Kahneman. 1981. "The Framing of Decisions and the Psychology of Choice." *Science* 211 (4481): 453–58.

Tykvová, Tereza. 2017. "When and Why Do Venture-Capital-Backed Companies Obtain Venture Lending?" *Journal of Financial and Quantitative Analysis* 52 (3): 1049–80.

Ueda, Masako. 2004. "Banks versus Venture Capital: Project Evaluation, Screening, and Expropriation." *The Journal of Finance* 59 (2): 601–21.

Velde, François. 2013. "Bitcoin: A Primer." Chicago Fed Letter 317. Federal Reserve of Chicago.

Vereshchagina, Galina. 2018. "The Role of Individual Financial Contributions in the Formation of Entrepreneurial Teams." Mimeo. Arizona State University, W.P. Carey School of Business.

Viard, Alan. 2008. "The Taxation of Carried Interest: Understanding the Issues." *National Tax Journal* 61 (3): 445–60.

Vickrey, William. 1961. "Counterspeculation, Auctions, and Competitive Sealed Tenders." *The Journal of Finance* 16 (1): 8–37.

Viola, Daniel. 2018. "Clarity from the SEC—Bitcoin and Ether Likely Fail the Howey Test." *Medium* (blog). June 21st. https://medium.com/xtradeio/clarity-from-the-sec-bitcoin-and-ether-likely-fail-the-howey-test-4d646217ac67.

Vulkan, Nir, Thomas Åstebro, and Manuel Fernández Sierra. 2016. "Equity Crowdfunding: A New Phenomena." *Journal of Business Venturing Insights* 5 (June): 37–49.

Wales, Kim. 2017. *Peer-to-Peer Lending and Equity Crowdfunding: A Guide to the New Capital Markets for Job Creators, Investors, and Entrepreneurs.* Santa Barbara, CA: Praeger.

Wasserman, Noam. 2003. "Founder-CEO Succession and the Paradox of Entrepreneurial Success." *Organization Science* 14 (2): 149–72.

———. 2008. "The Founder's Dilemma." *Harvard Business Review* 86 (2): 103–9.

———. 2012. *The Founder's Dilemmas: Anticipating and Avoiding the Pitfalls That Can Sink a Startup*. Princeton, NJ: Princeton University Press.

———. 2017. "The Throne vs. the Kingdom: Founder Control and Value Creation in Startups." *Strategic Management Journal* 38 (2): 255–77.

Wasserman, Noam, and L. P. Maurice. 2008. "Savage Beast." Case Study 809–069. Cambridge, MA: Harvard University, Harvard Business School.

Wei, Zaiyan, and Mingfeng Lin. 2016. "Market Mechanisms in Online Peer-to-Peer Lending." *Management Science* 63 (12): 4236–57.

Weisbach, David. 2008. "The Taxation of Carried Interests in Private Equity." *Virginia Law Review* 94 (3): 715–64.

Welch, Ivo. 2017. *Corporate Finance*. Fourth Edition. Ivo Welch.

Wells, Georgia, and Maureen Farrell. 2018. "Evan Spiegel's Imperious Style Made Snapchat a Success—Until Users Fled." *Wall Street Journal*, December 23rd. https://www.wsj.com/articles/evan-spiegels-imperious-style-made-snapchat-a-successuntil-users-fled-11545588892.

Welter, Friederike. 2012. "All You Need Is Trust? A Critical Review of the Trust and Entrepreneurship Literature." *International Small Business Journal* 30 (3): 193–212.

Wermers, Russ. 2011. "Performance Measurement of Mutual Funds, Hedge Funds, and Institutional Accounts." *Annual Review of Financial Economics* 3 (1): 537–74.

Wernerfelt, Birger. 1984. "A Resource-Based View of the Firm." *Strategic Management Journal* 5 (2): 171–80.

White, Andy. 2013. "Harvard, 4 Other Schools, Make Up Most MBAs at PE & VC Firms." Pitchbook. September 18th. https://pitchbook.com/news/articles/harvard-4-other-schools-make-up-most-mbas-at-pe-vc-firms.

Whyte, Amy. 2017. "Why Critics Are Slamming an Increasingly Popular Private Equity Format." Institutional Investor. November 8th. https://www.institutionalinvestor.com/article/b15jkqt382wm4r/why-critics-are-slamming-an-increasingly-popular-private-equity-format.

Wilhelm, William. 2005. "Bookbuidling, Auctions, and the Future of the IPO Process." *Journal of Applied Corporate Finance* 17 (1): 55–66.

Wilkins, Peter. 2018. "How Illinois Universities Power The Chicago Startup Ecosystem." *Forbes*, February 20th.

Williamson, Oliver. 1975. *Markets and Hierarchies: Analysis and Antitrust Implications*. New York: Macmillan.

———. 2002. "The Theory of the Firm as Governance Structure: From Choice to Contract." *Journal of Economic Perspectives* 16 (3): 171–95.

Wilson, Karen. 2011. *Financing High-Growth Firms The Role of Angel Investors: The Role of Angel Investors*. Paris: OECD Publishing.

———. 2015. "Policy Lessons from Financing Young Innovative Firms." OECD Science, Technology and Industry Policy Papers No. 24. OECD Publishing.

Wilson, Karen, and Filipe Silva. 2013. "Policies for Seed and Early Stage Finance." OECD Science, Technology and Industry Policy Papers No. 9. OECD Publishing.

Witte, Ian. 2016. "The Blockchain: A Gentle Introduction." Mimeo. Imperial College London, Imperial College Business School.

Wolf, Cam. 2018. "Stitch Fix Thinks It Can Hack Your Style." GQ. May 29th. https://www.gq.com/story/stitch-fix-wants-to-hack-personal-style.

Wong, Lin Hong. 2005. *Venture Capital Fund Management: A Comprehensive Approach to Investment Practices and the Entire Operations of a VC Firm*. Aspatore Books.

Wright, Mike, and Drori Drori. 2018. *Accelerators: Successful Venture Creation and Growth*. Edward Elgar, Camberley.

Wright, Mike, and Andy Lockett. 2003. "The Structure and Management of Alliances: Syndication in the Venture Capital Industry." *Journal of Management Studies* 40 (8): 2073–2102.

Wroldsen, Jack. 2017. "Crowdfunding Investment Contracts." *Virginia Law and Business Review* 11 (3): 543–611.

Wu, Jie, Steven Si, and Xiaobo Wu. 2016. "Entrepreneurial Finance and Innovation: Informal Debt as an Empirical Case." *Strategic Entrepreneurship Journal* 10 (3): 257–73.

Wu, Veronica. 2017. "A Machine-Learning Approach to Venture Capital." McKinsey, June. https://www.mckinsey.com/industries/high-tech/our-insights/a-machine-learning-approach-to-venture-capital.

Wuebker, Robert, Zoltan Acs, and Richard Florida. 2010. "The Globalization of Innovation and Entrepreneurial Talent." In *Handbook of Entrepreneurship Research: An Interdisciplinary Survey and Introduction*, edited by Zoltan Acs and David Audretsch, 457–84. International Handbook Series on Entrepreneurship. New York: Springer.

Yermack, David. 1997. "Good Timing: CEO Stock Option Awards and Company News Announcements." *The Journal of Finance* 52 (2): 449–76.

Young, Michael, and Ethan Scheinberg. 2017. "The Rise of Crowdfunding for Medical Care: Promises and Perils." *JAMA* 317 (16): 1623–24.

Younge, Kenneth, Tony Tong, and Lee Fleming. 2015. "How Anticipated Employee Mobility Affects Acquisition Likelihood: Evidence from a Natural Experiment." *Strategic Management Journal* 36 (5): 686–708.

Zacharakis, Andrew, and Dean Shepherd. 2007. "The Pre-Investment Process: Venture Capitalists' Decision Policies." In *Handbook of Research on Venture Capital*, edited by Hans Landström, 177–92. Cheltenham, UK: Edward Elgar.

Zahra, Shaker. 1993. "Environment, Corporate Entrepreneurship, and Financial Performance: A Taxonomic Approach." *Journal of Business Venturing* 8 (4): 319–40.

———. 2008. "The Virtuous Cycle of Discovery and Creation of Entrepreneurial Opportunities." *Strategic Entrepreneurship Journal* 2 (3): 243–57.

Zetzsche, Dirk, Ross Buckley, Douglas Arner, and Linus Föhr. 2019. "The ICO Gold Rush: It's a Scam, It's a Bubble, It's a Super Challenge for Regulators." *Harvard International Law Journal* 63 (2).

Zhang, Juanjuan, and Peng Liu. 2012. "Rational Herding in Microloan Markets." *Management Science* 58 (5): 892–912.

Zhang, Lei, and Isin Guler. 2015. "Evolution Of Venture Capital Syndicates over Rounds: Who May Be The New Comer?" *Academy of Management Proceedings* 2015 (1): 18059.

Zott, Christoph, Raphael Amit, and Lorenzo Massa. 2011. "The Business Model: Recent Developments and Future Research." *Journal of Management* 37 (4): 1019–42.

Index

Note: 'b' next to a page reference refers to a box; 'f' to a figure; 't' to a table'; whb to a WorkHorse box